ISBN: 9781313544498

Published by:
HardPress Publishing
8345 NW 66TH ST #2561
MIAMI FL 33166-2626

Email: info@hardpress.net
Web: http://www.hardpress.net

CORNELL
UNIVERSITY
LIBRARY

Cornell University Library
BX9815 .C45 1869
v.3-4
Works.

olin   3 1924 029 477 175

BX
9815
C45
1869
v.3-4

THE

WORKS

OF

WILLIAM E. CHANNING, D. D

NINETEENTH COMPLETE EDITION.

WITH

AN INTRODUCTION.

VOL. III.

BOSTON:
AMERICAN UNITARIAN ASSOCIATION.
1869.

Entered according to Act of Congress, in the year 1841, by
GEORGE G. CHANNING,
In the Clerk's Office of the District Court for the District of Massachusetts.

CONTENTS OF VOL. III.

	PAGE
PREACHING CHRIST: DISCOURSE AT THE ORDINATION OF THE REV. JOHN EMERY ABBOT.	7
WAR: DISCOURSE BEFORE THE CONGREGATIONAL MINISTERS OF MASSACHUSETTS.	29
UNITARIAN CHRISTIANITY: DISCOURSE AT THE ORDINATION OF THE REV. JARED SPARKS.	59
THE EVIDENCES OF REVEALED RELIGION: DISCOURSE BEFORE THE UNIVERSITY IN CAMBRIDGE.	105
THE DEMANDS OF THE AGE ON THE MINISTRY: DISCOURSE AT THE ORDINATION OF THE REV. E. S. GANNETT.	137
UNITARIAN CHRISTIANITY MOST FAVORABLE TO PIETY: DISCOURSE AT THE DEDICATION OF THE SECOND CONGREGATIONAL UNITARIAN CHURCH IN NEW YORK.	163
THE GREAT PURPOSE OF CHRISTIANITY: DISCOURSE AT THE INSTALLATION OF THE REV. M. I. MOTTE.	207
LIKENESS TO GOD: DISCOURSE AT THE ORDINATION OF THE REV. F. A. FARLEY.	227
THE CHRISTIAN MINISTRY: DISCOURSE AT THE DEDICATION OF DIVINITY HALL, CAMBRIDGE.	257
THE DUTIES OF CHILDREN.	287
HONOR DUE TO ALL MEN.	299
THE EVIDENCES OF CHRISTIANITY: PART I.	315
PART II.	359

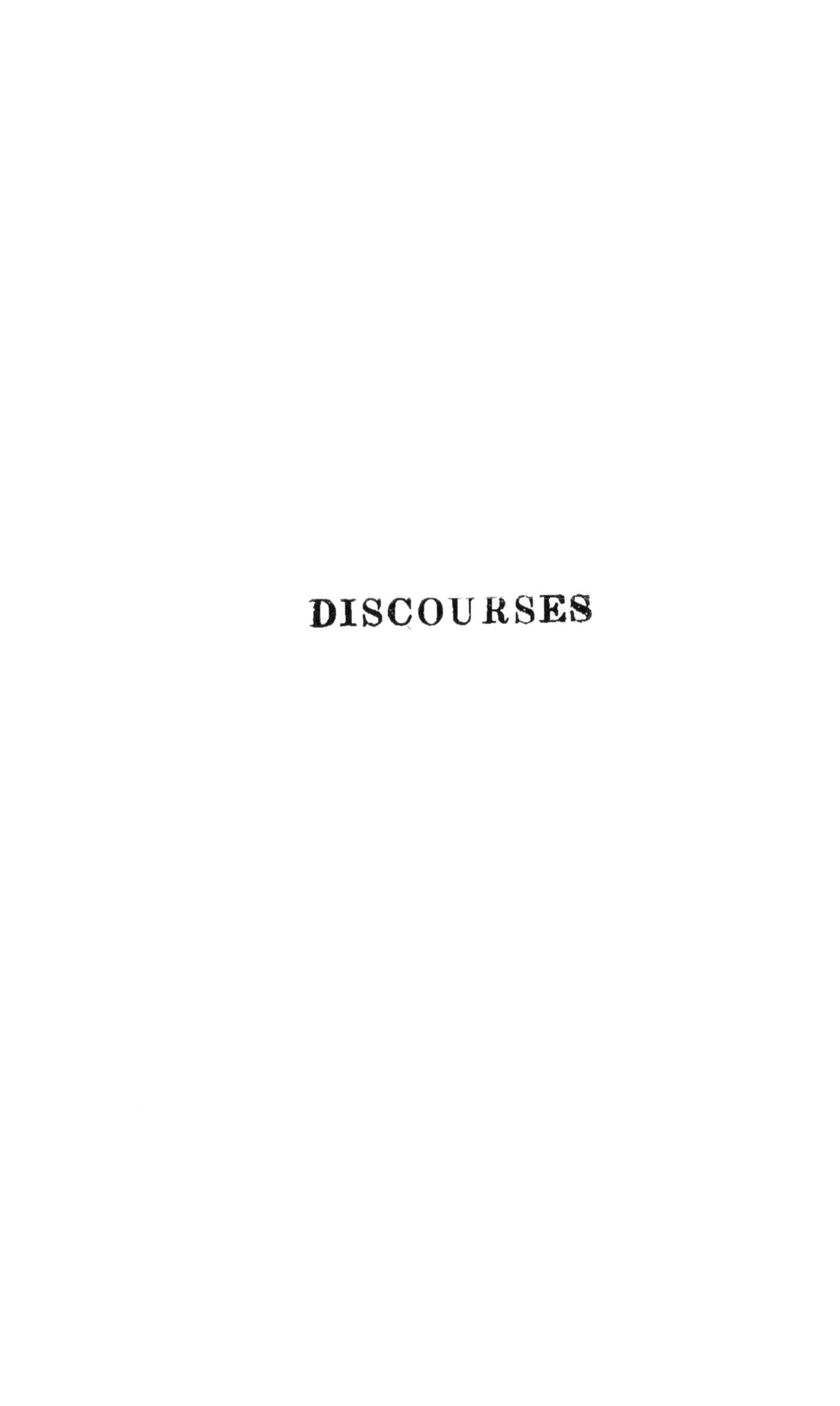

DISCOURSES

PREACHING CHRIST.

DISCOURSE

AT THE

ORDINATION OF THE REV. JOHN EMERY. ABBOT.

SALEM, 1815.

COLOSSIANS i. 28: "Whom we preach, warning every man, and teaching every man in all wisdom, that we may present every man perfect in Christ Jesus."

IN the verses immediately preceding the text, we find the Apostle enlarging with his usual zeal and earnestness on a subject peculiarly dear to him; on the glorious *mystery* of God, or in other words, on the great purpose of God, which had been kept *secret* from ages, to make the Gentile world partakers, through faith, of the blessings of the long-promised Messiah. "Christ, the hope of glory to the Gentiles," was the theme on which Paul, the Apostle of the Gentiles, delighted to expatiate. Having spoken of Jesus in this character, he immediately adds, "Whom we preach, warning every man, and teaching every man in all wisdom, that we may present every man perfect in Christ Jesus."

On the present occasion, which invites us to consider the design and duties of the Christian ministry,

I have thought that these words would guide us to many appropriate and useful reflections. They teach us what the Apostle preached ; "We preach Christ." They teach us the end or object for which he thus preached ; "That we may present every man perfect in Christ Jesus." Following this natural order, I shall first consider what is intended by "preaching Christ." I shall then endeavour to illustrate and recommend the end or object for which Christ is to be preached ; and I shall conclude with some remarks on the methods by which this end is to be accomplished. In discussing these topics, on which a variety of sentiment is known to exist, I shall necessarily dissent from some of the views which are cherished by particular classes of Christians. But the frank expression of opinion ought not to be construed into any want of affection or esteem for those from whom I differ.

I. What are we to understand by "preaching Christ"? This subject is the more interesting and important, because, I fear, it has often been misunderstood. Many persons imagine, that Christ is never preached, unless his name is continually repeated and his character continually kept in view. This is an error, and should be exposed. Preaching Christ, then, does not consist in making Christ perpetually the subject of discourse, but in inculcating, on his authority, *the religion which he taught*. Jesus came to be the light and teacher of the world ; and in this sublime and benevolent character he unfolded many truths relating to the Universal Father, to his own character, to the condition, duties, and prospects of mankind, to the perfection and true happiness of the human soul, to a future state of retribution, to the terms of forgiveness, to the means of virtue, and of everlasting life. Now whenever we teach, on the authority of Jesus, any doctrine or precept included in this extensive system, we "preach Christ." When, for instance, we inculcate on his authority the duties of forgiving enemies, of denying ourselves, of hungering after righteousness, we "preach Christ" as truly as when we describe his passion on the cross, or the purpose and the importance of his sufferings.

By the word "Christ" in the text and in many other places, we are to understand his religion rather than his person. Among the Jews nothing was more common than to give the name of a religious teacher to the system of truth which he taught. We see this continually exemplified in the New Testament. Thus, it is said of the Jews, "They have Moses and the prophets." What is meant by this? that they had Moses residing in person among them? Certainly not; but that they had his law, his religion. Jesus says, "I came not to destroy the prophets." What did he mean? that he had not come to slay or destroy the prophets who had died ages before his birth? Certainly not; he only intended that his doctrines were suited to confirm, not to invalidate, the writings of these holy men. According to the same form of speech, Stephen was accused of blasphemy against Moses, because some of his remarks were construed into a reproach on the law of Moses. These passages are sufficient to show us, that a religion was often called by the name of its teacher; and conformably to this usage, when Paul says, "We preach Christ," we ought to understand him as affirming, that he preached the whole system of doctrines and duties which Christ taught, whether they related to Jesus himself, or to any other subject.

But there is one passage more decisive on this point than any which I have adduced. In the Acts of the Apostles,* James says, "Moses of old time hath in every city them that preach him, being read in the synagogue every Sabbath-day." Here we find the Apostle declaring, that in every city there were men who *preached Moses;* and we are told in what this preaching consisted ; " Moses is *read* in the synagogue every Sabbath-day." No one, acquainted with the ancient services of the synagogue, can suppose, for a moment, that the character and offices of Moses were the themes of the Jewish teachers every Sabbath, and that they preached nothing else. It was their custom to read the books of the law in course, and to offer comments upon obscure or important passages. In many parts of these books the name of Moses is not mentioned. We have whole chapters about the tabernacle, and about the rites of cleansing from the leprosy. But, according to James, when these portions were read and explained, Moses was preached ; not because his character was the subject, but because the instructions contained in these chapters were a part of the religion which he was appointed to communicate to the children of Israel. The name of the teacher was given to his doctrine. This form of speech was not peculiar to the Jews ; all nations have probably adopted it. At the present day, nothing is more common than to hear, that Locke, or Newton, or some other distinguished philosopher, is published, or taught; not that his personal character and history are made public, but his system of doctrines. In the same way, Christ is preached, published, proclaimed when his instructions are delivered, although these instructions

* Acts xv. 21.

may relate to other topics beside his own offices and character.

I hope I shall not be misunderstood in the remarks which I have now made. Do not imagine, that I would exclude from the pulpit, discourses on the excellence of Jesus Christ. The truths which relate to Jesus himself, are among the most important which the Gospel reveals. The relations which Jesus Christ sustains to the world, are so important and so tender; the concern which he has expressed in human salvation, so strong and disinterested; the blessings of pardon and immortal life which he brings, so undeserved and unbounded; his character is such a union of moral beauty and grandeur; his example is at once so pure and so persuasive; the events of his life, his miracles, his sufferings, his resurrection and ascension, and his offices of intercessor and judge, are so strengthening to faith, hope, and charity, that his ministers should dwell on his name with affectionate veneration, and should delight to exhibit him to the gratitude, love, imitation, and confidence of mankind.

But, whilst the Christian minister is often to insist on the life, the character, the offices, and the benefits of Jesus Christ, let him not imagine that he is preaching Christ only when these are his themes. If he confine himself to these, he will not in the full sense of the word preach Christ; for this is to preach the whole religion of Jesus, and this religion is of vast extent. It regards man in his diversified and ever-multiplying relations to his Creator and to his fellow-creatures, to the present state and to all future ages. Its aim is, to instruct and quicken us to cultivate an enlarged virtue to cultivate our whole intellectual and moral nature.

It collects and offers motives to piety from the past and from the future, from heaven and hell, from nature and experience, from human example, and from the imitable excellences of God, from the world without and the world within us. The Gospel of Christ is indeed an inexhaustible treasury of moral and religious truth. Jesus, the first and best of evangelical teachers, did not confine himself to a few topics, but manifested himself to be the wisdom of God by the richness and variety of his instructions. To preach Christ is to unfold, as far as our feeble and narrow powers permit, all the doctrines, duties, and motives, which are recorded in the Gospels and in the writings of his inspired Apostles.

It is not intended by these remarks, that all the instructions of Christ are of equal importance, and that all are to be urged with equal frequency and zeal. Some undoubtedly are of greater moment and of more universal application than others. But a minister of a sound and candid mind, will be very cautious lest he assign so high a rank to a few doctrines, that the rest will sink into comparative insignificance, and almost fade from the minds of his hearers. He will labor to give enlarged and harmonious views of all the principles of Christianity, recollecting that each receives support from the rest, and that no doctrine or precept will exert its proper influence, if swelled into disproportioned importance, or detached from the truths which ought to modify and restrain it.

It has been the object of these remarks, to show, that preaching Christ does not imply that the offices and character of Christ are to be made perpetually the subjects of discourse. Where this idea prevails, it too often happens that the religion of Jesus is very partial-ly preached. A few topics are repeated without end. Many delightful and ennobling views of Christianity are seldom or never exhibited. The duties of the Gospel receive but a cursory attention. Religion is thought to consist in a fervid state of mind, produced by the constant contemplation of a few affecting ideas; whilst the only acceptable religion, which consists in living "soberly, righteously, and godly in the world," seems to be undervalued as quite an inferior attainment. Where this mistake prevails, we too often discover a censorious spirit among hearers, who pronounce with confidence on this and another minister, that they do not preach Christ, because their discourses do not turn on a few topics in relation to the Saviour, which are thought to contain the whole of Christianity. Very often the labors of a pious and upright minister are defeated by this prejudice; nor must he wonder, if he find himself decried, as an enemy to the faith, by those whose want of education or capacity confines them to the narrowest views of the Christian system. — May I be permitted, with deference and respect, to beseech Christian ministers not to encourage by example this spirit of censure among private Christians. There is no lesson which we can teach our hearers more easily, than to think contemptuously and to speak bitterly of other classes of Christians, and especially of their teachers. Let us never forget, that we none of us preach Christ in the full import of that phrase. None of us can hope that we give a complete representation of the religion of our Master; that we exhibit every doctrine without defect or without excess, in its due proportions, and in its just connexions. We of necessity communicate a portion of our own weakness and darkness to the religion which we dispense. The degree of imperfection indeed differs in different teachers; but none are free from the universal frailty, and none are authorized to take the seat of judgment, and, on the ground of imagined errors, to deny to others, whose lives are as spotless as their own, a conscientious purpose to learn and to teach the whole counsel of God.

II. Having thus considered what is intended by preaching Christ, I proceed to consider, secondly, for what end Christ is to be preached. We preach Christ, says the Apostle, "warning every man, and teaching every man, that we may present every man perfect in Christ Jesus;" that is, perfect in the religion of Christ, or a perfect Christian. From the passage we derive a most important sentiment, confirmed by the whole New Testament, that the great design of all the doctrines and precepts of the Gospel, is to exalt the character, to promote eminent purity of heart and life, to make men perfect as their Father in heaven is perfect. For what end then is Christianity to be preached? The answer is plain. We must preach, not to make fiery partisans, and to swell the number of a sect; not to overwhelm the mind with fear, or to heat it with feverish rapture; not to form men to the decencies of life, to a superficial goodness, which will secure the admiration of mankind. All these effects fall infinitely short of the great end of the Christian ministry. We should preach, that we may make men perfect Christians; perfect, not according to the standard of the world, but according to the law of Christ; perfect in heart and in life, in solitude and in society, in the great and in the common concerns of life. Here is the purpose of Christian preaching. In this, as in a common centre, all the truths of the Gospel meet; to this they all conspire; and no doctrine has an influence on salvation, any farther than it is an aid and excitement to the perfecting of our nature.

The Christian minister needs often to be reminded of this great end of his office, the perfection of the human character. He is too apt to rest in low attainments himself, and to be satisfied with low attainments in others. He ought never to forget the great distinction and glory of the Gospel, — that it is designed to perfect human nature. All the precepts of this divine system are marked by a sublime character. It demands that our piety be fervent, our benevolence unbounded, and our thirst for righteousness strong and insatiable. It enjoins a virtue which does not stop at what is positively prescribed, but which is prodigal of service to God and to mankind. The Gospel enjoins inflexible integrity, fearless sincerity, fortitude which despises pain and tramples pleasure under foot in the pursuit of duty, and an independence of spirit which no scorn can deter and no example seduce from asserting truth and adhering to the cause which conscience approves. With this spirit of martyrs, this hardness and intrepidity of soldiers of the cross, the Gospel calls us to unite the mildest and meekest virtues; a sympathy which melts over others' woes; a disinterestedness which finds pleasure in toils, and labors for others' good; a humility which loves to bless unseen, and forgets itself in the performance of the noblest deeds. To this perfection of social duty, the Gospel commands us to join a piety which refers every event to the providence of God, and every action to his will; a love which counts no service hard, and a penitence which esteems no judgment severe; a gratitude which offers praise even in adversity; a holy trust unbroken by protracted suffering, and a hope triumphant over death. In one word, it enjoins, that, loving and confiding in Jesus Christ, we make his spotless character, his heavenly life, the model of our own. Such is the sublimity of character which the Gospel demands, and such the end to which our preaching should ever be directed.

I have dwelt on this end of preaching, because it is too often forgotten, and because a stronger conviction of it will give new force and elevation to our instructions. We need to feel more deeply, that we are intrusted with a religion which is designed to ennoble human nature; which recognises in man the capacities of all that is good, great, and excellent; and which offers every encouragement and aid to the pursuit of perfection. The Christian minister should often recollect, that man, though propense to evil, has yet powers and faculties which may be exalted and refined to angelic glory; that he is called by the Gospel to prepare for the community of angels; that he is formed for unlimited progress in intellectual and moral excellence and felicity. He should often recollect, that in Jesus Christ our nature has been intimately united with the divine, and that in Jesus it is already enthroned in heaven. Familiarized to these generous conceptions, the Christian preacher, whilst he faithfully unfolds to men their guilt and danger, should also unfold their capacities of greatness; should reveal the splendor of that destiny to which they are called by Christ; should labor to awaken within them aspirations after a nobler character and a higher existence, and to inflame them with the love of all the graces and virtues with which Jesus came to enrich and adorn the human soul. In this way he will prove that he understands the true and great design of the Gospel and the ministry, which is nothing less than the perfection of the human character.

May I be permitted to say, that perhaps one of the greatest defects in our preaching, is, that it is not sufficiently directed to ennoble and elevate the minds of men. It does not breathe a sufficiently generous spirit. It appeals too constantly to the lowest principle of human nature; I mean the principle of fear, which under judicious excitement is indeed of great and undoubted use, but which, as every parent knows, when habitually awakened, is always found to debase the mind, to break the spirit, to give tameness to the character, and to chill the best affections. Perhaps one cause of the limited influence of Christianity, is, that, as it is too often exhibited, it seems adapted to form an abject, servile character, rather than to raise its disciples to true greatness and dignity. Perhaps, were Christianity more habitually regarded as a system, whose great design it is to infuse honorable sentiments, magnanimity, energy, an ingenuous love of God, a superiority to the senses, a spirit of self-sacrifice, a virtue akin to that of heaven, its reception would be more cordial, and its influence more extensive, more happy, more accordant with its great end, the perfection of human nature.

III. Having thus considered the end of Christian preaching, I now come to offer, in the third place, a few remarks on the best method of accomplishing it; and here I find myself obliged to omit a great variety of topics, and can only offer one or two of principal importance. That the Gospel may attain its end, may exert the most powerful and ennobling influence on the human character, it must be addressed at once to the understanding and to the heart. It must be so preached as to be firmly believed and deeply felt.— To secure to Christianity this firm belief, I have only time to observe, that it should be preached in a *rational* manner. By this I mean, that a Christian minister should beware of offering interpretations of Scripture, which are repugnant to any clear discoveries of reason or dictates of conscience. This admonition is founded upon the very obvious principle, that a revelation from God must be adapted to the rational and moral nature which he has conferred on man; that God can never contradict in his Word what he has himself written on the human heart, or teaches in his works and providence. Every man who reads the Bible knows, that, like other books, it has many passages which admit a variety of interpretations. Human language does not admit entire precision. It has often been observed by philosophers, that the most familiar sentences owe their perspicuity, not so much to the definiteness of the language, as to an almost incredible activity of the mind, which selects from a variety of meanings that which each word demands, and assigns such limits to every phrase as the intention of the speaker, his character and situation, require. In addition to this source of obscurity, to which all writings are exposed, we must remember that the Scriptures were written in a distant age, in a foreign language, by men who were unaccustomed to the systematic arrangements of modern times, and who, although inspired, were left to communicate their thoughts in the style most natural or habitual. Can we wonder, then, that they admit a variety of interpretations ? Now, we owe it to a book, which records, as we believe, revelations from Heaven, and which is plainly designed for the moral improvement of the race, to favor those explications of obscure passages, which are seen to harmonize with the moral attributes of God, and with the acknowledged teachings of nature and conscience. All those interpretations of the Gospel, which strike the mind at once as inconsistent with a righteous government of the universe, which require of man what is disproportioned to his nature, or which shock any clear conviction which our experience has furnished, cannot be viewed with too jealous an eye by him, who, revering Christianity, desires to secure to it an intelligent belief.

It is in vain to say, that the first and most obvious meaning of Scripture is always to be followed, no matter where it leads. I answer, that the first and most obvious meaning of a passage, written in a foreign language, and in remote antiquity, is very often false, and such as farther inquiry compels us to abandon. I answer, too, that all sects of Christians agree, and are forced to agree, in frequently forsaking the literal sense, on account of its incongruity with acknowledged truth. There is, in fact, no book in the world, which requires us more frequently to restrain unlimited expressions, to qualify the letter by the spirit, and to seek the meaning in the state and customs of the writer and of his age, than the New Testament. No book is written in a more popular, figurative, and animated style, the very style which requires the most constant exercise of judgment in the reader. The Scriptures are not a frigid digest of Christianity, as if this religion were a mere code of civil laws

They give us the Gospel warm from the hearts of its preachers. The language is not that of logicians, not the language of retired and inanimate speculation, but of affection, of zeal, of men who burned to convey deep and vivid impressions of the truth. In understanding such writers, moral feeling is often a better guide than a servile adherence to the literal and most obvious meaning of every word and phrase. It may be said of the New as well as the Old Testament, that sometimes the letter killeth whilst the spirit giveth life. Almost any system may be built on the New Testament by a commentator, who, forgetting the general scope of Christianity and the lessons of nature and experience, shall impose on every passage the literal signification which is first offered to the mind. The Christian minister should avail himself, in his exposition of the Divine Word, of the aids of learning and criticism, and also of the aids of reason and conscience. Those interpretations of difficult passages, which approve themselves to his clear and established conceptions of rectitude, and to his devout and benevolent affections, he should regard with a favorable eye; whilst those of an opposite character should be regarded with great distrust.

I have said, that this rational method of preaching Christianity is important, if we would secure a firm belief to Christianity. Some men may indeed be reconciled to an unreasonable religion; and terror, that passion which more than any other unsettles the intellect, may silence every objection to the most contradictory and degrading principles. But in general the understanding and conscience cannot be entirely subdued. They resist the violence which is done them. A lurking incredulity mingles with the attempt to believe what contradicts the highest principles of our nature. Particularly the most intelligent part of the community, who will ultimately govern public sentiment, will doubt and disbelieve the unreasonable system, which, perhaps, they find it prudent to acknowledge ; and will either convert it into an instrument of policy, or seize a favorable moment for casting off its restraints and levelling its institutions with the dust. Thus important is it that Christianity should be recommended to the understandings of men.

But this is not enough. It is also most important that the Gospel should be recommended to the heart. Christianity should be so preached, as to interest the affections, to awaken contrition and fear, veneration and love, gratitude and hope. Some preachers, from observing the pernicious effects of violent and exclusive appeals to the passions, have fallen into an opposite error, which has rendered the labors of their lives almost wholly unfruitful. They have addressed men as mere creatures of intellect ; they have forgotten, that affection is as essential to our nature as thought, that action requires motive, that the union of reason and sensibility is the health of the soul, and that without moral feeling there can be no strength of moral purpose. They have preached ingeniously, and the hearer has pronounced the teaching true. But the truth, coldly imparted, and coldly received, has been forgotten as fast as heard ; no energy of will has been awakened ; no resistance to habit and passion been called forth ; perhaps not a momentary purpose of self-improvement has glanced through the mind. Preaching, to be effectual, must be as various as our nature. The sun warms, at the same moment that it enlightens ; and, unless religious truth be addressed at once to the reason and the affections, unless it kindles whilst it guides, it is a useless splendor ; it leaves the heart barren ; it produces no fruits of godliness. Let the Christian minister, then, preach the Gospel with earnestness, with affection, with a heart warmed by his subject, not thinking of himself, not seeking applause, but solicitous for the happiness of mankind. tenderly concerned for his people, awake to the solemnities of eternity, and deeply impressed with the worth of the human soul, with the glory and happiness to which it may be exalted, and with the misery and ruin into which it will be plunged by irreligion and vice. Let him preach, not to amuse, but to convince and awaken ; not to excite a momentary interest, but a deep and lasting seriousness ; not to make his hearers think of the preacher, but of themselves, of their own characters and future condition. Let him labor, by delineating with unaffected ardor the happiness of virtue, by setting forth religion in its most attractive forms, by displaying the paternal character of God, and the love of Christ which was stronger than death, by unfolding the purity and blessedness of the heavenly world, by revealing to the soul its own greatness, and by persuasion, by entreaty, by appeals to the best sentiments of human nature, by speaking from a heart convinced of immortality ; let him labor, by these methods, to touch and to soften his hearers, to draw them to God and duty, to awaken gratitude and love, a sublime hope and a generous desire of exalted goodness. And let him also labor, by solemn warning, by teaching men their responsibility, by setting before sinners the aggravations of their guilt, by showing them the ruin and immediate wretchedness wrought by moral evil in the soul, and by pointing them to approaching death, and the retributions of the future world ; let him labor, by these means, to reach the consciences of those whom higher motives will not quicken, to break the slumbers of the worldly, to cut off every false hope, and to persuade the sinner, by a salutary terror, to return to God, and to seek, with a new earnestness, virtue, glory, and eternal life.

NOTE

ON THE FIRST HEAD OF THE PRECEDING DISCOURSE

The error which I have opposed on the subject of "preaching Christ," may be traced in a great measure to what appears to me a wrong interpretation of the two first chapters of the First Epistle to the Corinthians. In these chapters, Paul says, that he "determined to know nothing among the Corinthians, save Jesus Christ and him crucified," and speaks once and again of "preaching Christ crucified," &c. It has been supposed, that the Apostle here intended to select the particular point on which preaching should chiefly turn, and that we have his authority for censuring a discourse which does not relate immediately to the character of Christ, and especially to his sufferings on the cross. But I think that a little attention to the circumstances of the Apostle and of the Corinthians will show us, that Paul referred to the religion of Jesus generally, as the subject of his preaching, and not to a very limited part of it.

Corinth, being the most commercial city of Greece, was inhabited by Jews as well as Greeks. These Jews, as Paul tells us, "wanted a sign," just as the Pharisees in the time of Christ demanded "a sign from heaven." That is, they wanted a Messiah who should be marked out to them by a visible descent from heaven, or by some glorious appearance from heaven, or by some outward majesty which should be a pledge of his breaking the Roman yoke, and raising Judea to the empire of the world. They wanted a splendid and temporal Messiah. The Greeks, on the other hand, who were a speculative people, wanted *wisdom*, or a system of philosophy, and could hear nothing patiently but the subtile disputations and studied harangues with which they were amused by those who pretended to wisdom. Such was the state of Corinth, when Paul entered it. Had he brought with him an account of a triumphant Messiah, or an acute philosopher, he would have been received with eagerness. But none were desirous to hear the simple religion of Jesus of Nazareth, who proved his mission, not by subtilties of eloquence, but by miracles evincing the power of God, and who died at last on the ignominious cross. Paul, however, in opposition to Jew and Greek, determined to know nothing of a worldly Messiah, nothing of any old or new scheme of philosophy; but to know and to preach Jesus Christ, and to exhibit him in a light which Judaism and philosophy would alike abhor, as crucified for the recovery of men from error, sin, and condemnation. In other words, he resolved to preach the religion of Jesus, in its greatest simplicity, without softening its most offensive feature, the cross of its author, or without borrowing any thing from Moses or from any Gentile philosopher, to give currency to his doctrines. This is the amount of what Paul teaches in these chapters.

We must not imagine, when we read these chapters, that Corinth was a city of professing Christians; that among these Christians a difference of opinion had arisen as to the proper subjects of Christian preaching, and that Paul intended to specify the topic on which ministers should chiefly or exclusively insist. This, I fear, is the common impression under which this portion of Scripture is read; but this is altogether erroneous. No controversy of this kind existed; and Paul, in these chapters, had not the most distant idea of recommending one part of the Gospel in preference to others, but intended to recommend the whole Gospel, the whole religion of Jesus Christ, in distinction from Judaism and Gentile philosophy. The dangers of the Corinthian Christians required that he should employ every effort to secure their fidelity to the simple Gospel of Jesus. Having been educated in the Jewish or Heathen religions; living in the midst of Jews and Heathens; hearing perpetually, from one class, that the Messiah was to be a triumphant prince, and that without submission to the law of Moses, no one could partake his blessings; and hearing, from the other, perpetual praises of this and another philosopher, and perpetual derision of the Gospel, because in its doctrines and style it bore no resemblance to the refinements and rhetoric of their most celebrated sages; the Corinthian Christians, in these trying circumstances, were strongly tempted to assimilate the Gospel to the prevalent religions, to blend with it foreign doctrines, to keep the humiliation of its author out of sight, and to teach it as a system of philosophy resting on subtile reasoning rather than on miracles and the authority of God. To save them from this danger, a danger which at present we can hardly estimate, the Apostle reminded them, that when he came to them he came not with "excellency of speech and with enticing words of man's wisdom," but in demonstration of the Spirit and of miraculous powers; that he did not comply with the demands of Greek or Jew; that he preached a crucified Messiah, and no other teacher or deliverer; and that he always insisted, that the religion of Jesus, unaided by Judaism or philosophy, was able to make men wise to salvation. He also reminded them, that this preaching, however branded as foolishness, had proved divinely powerful, and had saved them from that ignorance of God, from which human wisdom had been unable to deliver them. These remarks, I hope, will assist common readers in understanding the chapters under consideration.

We are too apt, in reading the New Testament, and particularly the Epistles, to forget, that the Gospel was a new religion, and that the Apostles were called to preach Jesus to those, who, perhaps, had never before heard his name, and whose prejudices and passions prepared them to contemn and reject his claims. In these circumstances, they had to begin at the very foundation, to prove to the unbelieving world that Jesus was the Messiah, or sent from God to instruct and save mankind. This is often called "preaching Christ," especially in the Acts. — When converts were made, the work of the Apostles was not ended. These converts wished to bring with them a part of their old religion into the church; and some of the Jews even insisted that obedience to Moses was essential to salvation. These errors the Apostles resolutely opposed, and, having previously established the Messiahship of Jesus, they next proceeded to establish the sufficiency and perfection of his religion, to show that faith in him, or reception of his Gospel, was all that was required to salvation. This is sometimes called "preaching Christ." — These difficulties, which called the Apostles to so much anxiety and toil, are now in a great measure removed. Christian ministers, at the present day, are not often called to preach Christ in opposition to the infidel, and never in opposition to the weak convert who would incorporate Judaism or Gentile philosophy with Christianity. The great foundation, on which the Apostles spent so much strength, is now firmly laid. Our hearers generally acknowledge Jesus to be the Messiah, sent by God to be the light of the world, and "able to save to the uttermost all who come to God by him." We are therefore seldom called to preach Christ in the senses which have just been considered, and our preaching must of course differ in a measure from that of the Apostles. But there is another sense of preaching Christ, involved in both the preceding, in which our work precisely accords with theirs. Like them, we are to unfold to those who acknowledge Jesus as their Lord, all the truths, motives, and precepts, which he has left to guide and quicken men to excellence, and to prepare them for a happy immortality.

WAR.

DISCOURSE

BEFORE THE

CONGREGATIONAL MINISTERS OF MASSACHUSETTS

BOSTON, 1816.

[ISAIAH ii. 4: "Nation shall not lift up sword against nation, neither shall they learn war any more."

I HAVE chosen a subject, which may seem at first view not altogether appropriate to the present occasion, the subject of WAR. It may be thought, that an address to an assembly composed chiefly of the ministers of religion, should be confined to the duties, dangers, encouragements of the sacred office. But I have been induced to select this topic, because, after the slumber of ages, Christians seem to be awakening to a sense of the pacific character of their religion, and because I understood, that this Convention were at this anniversary to consider the interesting question, whether no method could be devised for enlightening the public mind on the nature and guilt of war. I was unwilling that this subject should be approached and dismissed as an ordinary affair. I feared, that, in the pressure of business, we might be satisfied with the expression of customary disapprobation; and that, having in this way relieved our consciences, we should relapse into our former indifference, and continue to hear the howlings of this dreadful storm of human passions with as much unconcern as before. I resolved to urge on you the duty, and I hoped to excite in you the purpose, of making some new and persevering efforts for the abolition of this worst vestige of barbarism, this grossest outrage on the principles of Christianity. The day I trust is coming, when Christians will look back with gratitude and affection on those men, who, in ages of conflict and bloodshed, cherished generous hopes of human improvement, withstood the violence of corrupt opinion, held forth, amidst the general darkness, the pure and mild light of Christianity, and thus ushered in a new and peaceful era in the history of mankind. May you, my brethren, be included in the grateful recollection of that day.

The *miseries* and *crimes* of war, its *sources*, its *remedies*, will be the subjects of our present attention.

In detailing its miseries and crimes, there is no temptation to recur to unreal or exaggerated horrors. No depth of coloring can approach reality. It is lamentable, that we need a delineation of the calamities of war, to rouse us to exertion. The mere idea of human beings employing every power and faculty in the work of mutual destruction, ought to send a shuddering through the frame. But on this subject, our sensibilities are dreadfully sluggish and dead. Our ordinary sympathies seem to forsake us, when war is named. The sufferings and death of a single fellow-being often excite a tender and active compassion; but we hear without emotion of thousands enduring every variety of woe in war. A single murder in peace thrills through our frames. The countless murders of war are heard as an amusing tale. The execution of a criminal depresses the mind, and philanthropy is laboring to substitute milder punishments for death. But benevolence has hardly made an effort to snatch from sudden and untimely death, the innumerable victims immolated on the altar of war. This insensibility demands that the miseries and crimes of war should be placed before us with minuteness, with energy, with strong and indignant feeling.

The miseries of war may be easily conceived from its very nature. By war, we understand the resort of nations to force, violence, and the most dreaded methods of destruction and devastation. In war, the strength, skill, courage, energy, and resources of a whole people are concentrated for the infliction of pain and death. The bowels of the earth are explored, the most active elements combined; the resources of art and nature exhausted, to increase the power of man in destroying his fellow-creatures.

Would you learn what destruction man, when thus aided, can spread around him ? Look, then, at that extensive region, desolate and overspread with ruins ; its forests rent, as if blasted by lightning ; its villages prostrated, as by an earthquake ; its fields barren, as if swept by storms. Not long ago, the sun shone on no happier spot. But ravaging armies prowled over it war frowned on it ; and its fruitfulness and happiness are fled. Here thousands and ten thousands were gathered from distant provinces, not to embrace as brethren, but to renounce the tie of brotherhood ; and thousands, in the vigor of life, when least prepared for death, were hewn down and scattered like chaff before the whirlwind.

Repair, my friends, in thought, to a field of recent battle. Here, are heaps of slain, weltering in their own blood, their bodies mangled, their limbs shattered, and almost every vestige of the human form and countenance destroyed. Here, are multitudes trodden under foot, and the war-horse has left the trace of his hoof in many a crushed and mutilated frame. Here, are severer sufferers; they live, but live without hope or consolation. Justice despatches the criminal with a single stroke; but the victims of war, falling by casual, undirected blows, often expire in lingering agony, their deep groans moving no compassion, their limbs writhing on the earth with pain, their lips parched with a burning thirst, their wounds open to the chilling air, the memory of home rushing on their minds, but not a voice of friendship or comfort reaching their ears. Amidst this scene of horrors, you see the bird and beast of prey gorging themselves with the dead or dying, and human plunderers rifling the warm and almost palpitating remains of the slain. If you extend your eye beyond the immediate field of battle, and follow the track of the victorious and pursuing army, you see the roads strewed with the dead; you see scattered flocks, and harvests trampled under foot, the smoking ruins of cottages, and the miserable inhabitants flying in want and despair; and even yet, the horrors of a single battle are not exhausted. Some of the deepest pangs which it inflicts, are silent, retired, enduring, to be read in the widow's countenance, in the unprotected orphan, in the aged parent, in affection cherishing the memory of the slain, and weeping that it could not min-

I have asked you to traverse, in thought, a field of battle. There is another scene often presented in war, perhaps more terrible. I refer to a besieged city. The most horrible pages in histroy are those which record the reduction of strongly fortified places. In a besieged city, are collected all descriptions and ages of mankind, women, children, the old, the infirm. Day and night, the weapons of death and conflagration fly around them. They see the approaches of the foe, the trembling bulwark, and the fainting strength of their defenders. They are worn with famine, and on famine presses pestilence. At length the assault is made, every barrier is broken down, and a lawless soldiery, exasperated by resistance, and burning with lust and cruelty, are scattered through the streets. The domestic retreat is violated ; and even the house of God is no longer a sanctuary. Venerable age is no protection, female purity no defence. Is woman spared amidst the slaughter of father, brother, husband, and son ? She is spared for a fate, which makes death in comparison a merciful doom. With such heart-rending scenes history abounds ; and what better fruits can you expect from war ?

These views are the most obvious and striking which war presents. There are more secret influences, appealing less powerfully to the senses and imagination, but deeply affecting to a reflecting and benevolent mind —Consider, first, the condition of those who are immediately engaged in war ? The sufferings of soldiers from battle we have seen ; but their sufferings are not limited to the period of conflict. The whole of war is a succession of exposures too severe for human nature. Death employs other weapons than the sword. It is computed, that in ordinary wars, greater numbers perish by sickness than in battle. Exhausted by long and rapid marches, by unwholesome food, by exposure to storms, by excessive labor under a burning sky through the day, and by interrupted and restless sleep on the damp ground and in the chilling atmosphere of night, thousands after thousands of the young pine away and die. They anticipated that they should fall, if to fall should be their lot, in what they called the field of honor; but they perish in the inglorious and crowded hospital, surrounded with sights and sounds of woe, far from home and every friend, and denied those tender offices which sickness and expiring nature require.

Consider next the influence of war on the character of those who make it their trade. They let themselves for slaughter, place themselves servile instruments, passive machines, in the hands of rulers, to execute the bloodiest mandates, without a thought on the justice of the cause in which they are engaged. What a school is this for the human character! From men trained in battle to ferocity, accustomed to the perpetration of cruel deeds, accustomed to take human life without sorrow or remorse, habituated to esteem an unthinking courage a substitute for every virtue, encouraged by plunder to prodigality, taught improvidence by perpetual hazard and exposure, restrained only by an iron discipline which is withdrawn in peace, and unfitted by the restless and irregular career of war for the calm and uniform pursuits of ordinary life; from such men, what ought to be expected but contempt of human rights and of the laws of God? From the nature of his calling, the soldier is almost driven to sport with the thought of death, to defy and deride it, and, of course, to banish the thought of that retribution to which it leads; and.

though of all men the most exposed to sudden death, he is too often of all men most unprepared to appear before his Judge.

The influence of war on the community at large, on its prosperity, its morals, and its political institutions, though less striking than on the soldiery, is yet baleful. How often is a community impoverished to sustain a war in which it has no interest? Public burdens are aggravated, whilst the means of sustaining them are reduced. Internal improvements are neglected. The revenue of the state is exhausted in military establishments, or flows through secret channels into the coffers of corrupt men, whom war exalts to power and office. The regular employments of peace are disturbed. Industry in many of its branches is suspended. The laborer, ground with want, and driven to despair by the clamor of his suffering family, becomes a soldier in a cause which he condemns, and thus the country is drained of its most effective population. The people are stripped and reduced, whilst the authors of war retrench not a comfort, and often fatten on the spoils and woes of their country.

The influence of war on the morals of society is also to be deprecated. The suspension of industry multiplies want; and criminal modes of subsistence are the resource of the suffering. Commerce, shackled and endangered, loses its upright and honorable character, and becomes a system of stratagem and collusion. In war, the moral sentiments of a community are perverted by the admiration of military exploits. The milder virtues of Christianity are eclipsed by the baleful lustre thrown round a ferocious courage. The disinterested, the benignant, the merciful, the forgiving, those whom

Jesus has pronounced blessed and honorable, must give place to the hero, whose character is stained not only with blood, but sometimes with the foulest vices, but all whose stains are washed away by victory. War especially injures the moral feelings of a people, by making human nature cheap in their estimation, and human life of as little worth as that of an insect or a brute.

'War diffuses through a community unfriendly and malignant passions. Nations, exasperated by mutual injuries, burn for each others' humiliation and ruin. They delight to hear that famine, pestilence, want, defeat, and the most dreadful scourges which Providence sends on a guilty world, are desolating a hostile community. The slaughter of thousands of fellow-beings, instead of awakening pity, flushes them with delirious joy, illuminates the city, and dissolves the whole country in revelry and riot. Thus the heart of man is hardened. His worst passions are nourished. He renounces the bonds and sympathies of humanity. Were the prayers, or rather the curses of warring nations prevalent in heaven, the whole earth would long since have become a desert. The human race, with all their labors and improvements, would have perished under the sentence of universal extermination.

But war not only assails the prosperity and morals of a community; its influence on the political condition is threatening. It arms government with a dangerous patronage, multiplies dependents and instruments of oppression, and generates a power, which, in the hands of the energetic and aspiring, endangers a free constitution. War organizes a body of men, who lose the feelings of the citizen in the soldier; whose habits detach them from the community; whose ruling passion is devotion to a chief; who are inured in the camp to despotic sway; who are accustomed to accomplish their ends by force, and to sport with the rights and happiness of their fellow-beings; who delight in tumult, adventure, and peril; and turn with disgust and scorn from the quiet labors of peace. Is it wonderful, that such protectors of a state should look with contempt on the weakness of the protected, and should lend themselves base instruments to the subversion of that freedom which they do not themselves enjoy? In a community, in which precedence is given to the military profession, freedom cannot long endure. The encroachments of power at home are expiated by foreign triumphs. The essential interests and rights of the state are sacrificed to a false and fatal glory. Its intelligence and vigor, instead of presenting a bulwark to domestic usurpation, are expended in military achievements. Its most active and aspiring citizens rush to the army, and become subservient to the power which dispenses honor. The nation is victorious, but the recompense of its toils is a yoke as galling as that which it imposes on other communities.

Thus, war is to be ranked among the most dreadful calamities which fall on a guilty world; and, what deserves consideration, it tends to multiply and perpetuate itself without end. It feeds and grows on the blood which it sheds. The passions, from which it springs, gain strength and fury from indulgence. The successful nation, flushed by victory, pants for new laurels; whilst the humbled nation, irritated by defeat, is impatient to redeem its honor and repair its losses. Peace becomes a truce, a feverish repose, a respite to sharpen anew the sword, and to prepare for future struggles.

Under professions of friendship, lurk hatred and distrust; and a spark suffices to renew the mighty conflagration. When from these causes, large military establishments are formed, and a military spirit kindled, war becomes a necessary part of policy. A foreign field must be found for the energies and passions of a martial people. To disband a numerous and veteran soldiery, would be to let loose a dangerous horde on society. The blood-hounds must be sent forth on other communities, lest they rend the bosom of their own country. Thus war extends and multiplies itself. No sooner is one storm scattered, than the sky is darkened with the gathering horrors of another. Accordingly, war has been the mournful legacy of every generation to that which succeeds it. Every age has had its conflicts. Every country has in turn been the seat of devastation and slaughter. The dearest interest and rights of every nation have been again and again committed to the hazards of a game, of all others the most uncertain, and in which, from its very nature, success too often attends on the fiercest courage and the basest fraud.

Such, my friends, is an unexaggerated, and, I will add, a faint delineation of the miseries of war; and to all these miseries and crimes the human race have been continually exposed, for no worthier cause, than to enlarge an empire already tottering under its unwieldy weight, to extend an iron despotism, to support some idle pretension, to repel some unreal or exaggerated injury. For no worthier cause, human blood has been poured out as water, and millions of rational and immortal beings have been driven like sheep to the field of slaughter.

Having considered the crimes and miseries of war, I proceed, as I proposed, to inquire into its sources ; an important branch of our subject, for it is only by a knowledge of the sources, that we can be guided to the remedies of war. And here, I doubt not, many will imagine that the first place ought to be given to malignity and hatred. But justice to human nature requires, that we ascribe to national animosities a more limited operation than is usually assigned to them, in the production of this calamity. It is indeed true, that ambitious men, who have an interest in war, too often accomplish their views by appealing to the malignant feelings of a community, by exaggerating its wrongs, ridiculing its forbearance, and reviving ancient jealousies and resentments. But it is believed, that, were not malignity and revenge aided by the concurrence of higher principles, the false splendor of this barbarous custom might easily be obscured, and its ravages stayed.

One of the great springs of war may be found in a very strong and general propensity of human nature, in the love of excitement, of emotion, of strong interest ; a propensity which gives a charm to those bold and hazardous enterprises which call forth all the energies of our nature. No state of mind, not even positive suffering, is more painful than the want of interesting objects. The vacant soul preys on itself, and often rushes with impatience from the security which demands no effort, to the brink of peril. This part of human nature is seen in the kind of pleasures which have always been preferred. Why has the first rank among sports been given to the chase ? Because its difficulties, hardships, hazards, tumults, awaken the mind, and give to it a new consciousness of existence, and a deep feeling of its powers. What is the charm which attaches the statesman to an office which almost weighs him down with labor and an appalling responsibility ? He finds much of his compensation in the powerful emotion and interest, awakened by the very hardships of his lot, by conflict with vigorous minds, by the opposition of rivals, and by the alternations of success and defeat. What hurries to the gaming table the man of prosperous fortune and ample resource ? The dread of apathy, the love of strong feeling and of mental agitation. A deeper interest is felt in hazarding, than in securing wealth, and the temptation is irresistible. One more example of this propensity may be seen in the attachment of pirates and highwaymen to their dreadful employment. Its excess of peril has given it a terrible interest ; and to a man who has long conversed with its dangers, the ordinary pursuits of life are vapid, tasteless, and disgusting. We have here one spring of war. War is of all games the deepest, awakening most powerfully the soul, and, of course, presenting powerful attraction to those restless and adventurous minds, which pant for scenes of greater experiment and exposure than peace affords. The savage, finding in his uncultivated modes of life few objects of interest, few sources of emotion, burns for war as a field for his restless energy. Civilized men, too, find a pleasure in war, as an excitement of the mind. They follow, with an eager concern, the movements of armies, and wait the issue of battles with a deep suspense, an alternation of hope and fear, inconceivably more interesting than the unvaried uniformity of peaceful pursuits.

Another powerful principle of our nature, which is the spring of war, is the passion for superiority, for triumph, for power. The human mind is aspiring, impatient of inferiority, and eager for preëminence and control. I need not enlarge on the predominance of this passion in rulers, whose love of power is influenced by the possession, and who are ever restless to extend their sway. It is more important to observe, that, were this desire restrained to the breasts of rulers, war would move with a sluggish pace. But the passion for power and superiority is universal; and as every individual, from his intimate union with the community, is accustomed to appropriate its triumphs to himself, there is a general promptness to engage in any contest, by which the community may obtain an ascendency over other nations. The desire, that our country should surpass all others, would not be criminal, did we understand in what respects it is most honorable for a nation to excel ; did we feel, that the glory of a state consists in intellectual and moral superiority, in preëminence of knowledge, freedom, and purity. But to the mass of a people, this form of preëminence is too refined and unsubstantial. There is another kind of triumph, which they better understand, the triumph of physical power, triumph in battle, triumph, not over the minds, but the territory of another state. Here is a palpable, visible superiority; and for this, a people are willing to submit to severe privations. A victory blots out the memory of their sufferings, and in boasting of their extended power, they find a compensation for many woes.

I now proceed to another powerful spring of war; and it is the admiration of the brilliant qualities displayed in war. These qualities, more than all things, have prevented an impression of the crimes and miseries of this savage custom. Many delight in war, not for its carnage and woes, but for its valor and apparent magnanimity, for the self-command of the hero, the fortitude which despises suffering, the resolution which courts danger, the superiority of the mind to the body, to sensation, to fear. Let us be just to human nature even in its errors and excesses. Men seldom delight in war, considered merely as a source of misery. When they hear of battles, the picture which rises to their view is not what it should be, a picture of extreme wretchedness, of the wounded, the mangled, the slain. These horrors are hidden under the splendor of those mighty energies, which break forth amidst the perils of conflict, and which human nature contemplates with an intense and heart-thrilling delight. Attention hurries from the heaps of the slaughtered to the victorious chief, whose single mind pervades and animates a host, and directs with stern composure the storm of battle; and the ruin which he spreads is forgotten in admiration of his power. This admiration has, in all ages, been expressed by the most unequivocal signs. Why that garland woven? that arch erected? that festive board spread? These are tributes to the warrior. Whilst the peaceful sovereign, who scatters blessings with the silence and constancy of Providence, is received with a faint applause, men assemble in crowds to hail the conqueror, perhaps a monster in human form, whose private life is blackened with lust and crime, and whose greatness is built on perfidy and usurpation. Thus, war is the surest and speediest road to renown; and war will never cease, while the field of battle is the field of glory, and the most luxuriant laurels grow from a root nourished with blood.

Another cause of war is a false patriotism. It is a natural and generous impulse of nature to love the country which gave us birth, by whose institutions we have been moulded, by whose laws defended, and with whose soil and scenery innumerable associations of early years, of domestic affection, and of friendship, have been formed. But this sentiment often degenerates into a narrow, partial, exclusive attachment, alienating us from other branches of the human family, and instigating to aggression on other states. In ancient times, this principle was developed with wonderful energy, and sometimes absorbed every other sentiment. To the Roman, Rome was the universe. Other nations were of no value but to grace her triumphs, and illustrate her power; and he, who in private life would have disdained injustice and oppression, exulted in the successful violence by which other nations were bound to the chariot-wheels of this mistress of the world. This spirit still exists. The tie of country is thought to absolve men from the obligations of universal justice and humanity. Statesmen and rulers are expected to build up their own country at the expense of others; and, in the false patriotism of the citizen, they have a security for any outrages, which are sanctioned by success.

Let me mention one other spring of war. I mean the impressions we receive in early life. In our early years, we know war only as it offers itself to us at a review; not arrayed in terror, not stalking over fields of the slain, and desolated regions, its eye flashing with fury, and its sword reeking with blood. War, as we first see it, is decked with gay and splendid trappings, and wears a countenance of joy. It moves with a measured and graceful step to the sound of the heart-stir fife and drum. Its instruments of death wound only the air. Such is war ; the youthful eye is dazzled with its ornaments ; the youthful heart dances to its animated sounds. It seems a pastime full of spirit and activity, the very sport in which youth delights. These false views of war are confirmed by our earliest reading. We are intoxicated with the exploits of the conqueror, as recorded in real history or in glowing fiction. We follow, with a sympathetic ardor, his rapid and triumphant career in battle, and, unused as we are to suffering and death, forget the fallen and miserable who are crushed under his victorious car. Particularly by the study of the ancient poets and historians, the sentiments of early and barbarous ages on the subject of war are kept alive in the mind. The trumpet, which roused the fury of Achilles and of the hordes of Greece, still resounds in our ears ; and, though Christians by profession, some of our earliest and deepest impressions are received in the school of uncivilized antiquity. Even where these impressions in favor of war are not received in youth, we yet learn from our early familiarity with it, to consider it as a necessary evil, an essential part of our condition. We become reconciled to it as to a fixed law of our nature ; and consider the thought of its abolition as extravagant as an attempt to chain the winds or arrest the lightning.

I have thus attempted to unfold the principal causes of war. They are, you perceive, of a moral nature. They may be resolved into wrong views of human glory, and into excesses of passions and desires, which, by right direction, would promote the best interests of humanity. From these causes we learn, that this savage custom is to be repressed by moral means, by salutary influences on the sentiments and principles of mank'nd. And thus we are led to our last topic, the remedies of war. In introducing the observations which I have to offer on this branch of the subject, I feel myself bound to suggest an important caution. Let not the cause of peace be injured by the assertion of extreme and indefensible principles. I particularly refer to the principle, that war is absolutely, and in all possible cases, unlawful, and prohibited by Christianity. This doctrine is considered, by a great majority of the judicious and enlightened, as endangering the best interests of society ; and it ought not therefore to be connected with our efforts for the diffusion of peace, unless it appear to us a clear and indubitable truth. War, as it is commonly waged, is indeed a tremendous evil ; but national subjugation is a greater evil than a war of defence ; and a community seems to me to possess an indisputable right to resort to such a war, when all other means have failed for the security of its existence or freedom. It is universally admitted, that a community may employ force to repress the rapacity and violence of its own citizens, to disarm and restrain its internal foes ; and on what ground can we deny to it the right of repelling the inroads and aggressions of a foreign power ? If a government may not lawfully resist a foreign army, invading its territory to desolate and subdue, on what principles can we justify a resistance of a combination of its own citizens for the same injurious purpose ? Government is instituted for the very purpose of protecting the community from all violence, no matter by what hands it may be offered ; and rulers would be unfaithful to their trust, were they to abandon the rights, interests, and improvements of society to unprincipled rapacity, whether of domestic or foreign foes.

We are indeed told, that the language of Scripture is " resist not evil." But the Scriptures are given to us as reasonable beings. We must remember, that, to the renunciation of reason in the interpretation of Scripture, we owe those absurdities, which have sunk Christianity almost to the level of Heathenism. If the precept to " resist not evil," admit no exception, then civil government is prostrated; then the magistrate must, in no case, resist the injurious ; then the subject must, in no case, employ the aid of the laws to enforce his rights. The very end and office of government is, to *resist* evil men. For this, the civil magistrate bears the sword ; and he should beware of interpretations of the Scriptures which would lead him to bear it in vain. The doctrine of the absolute unlawfulness of war, is thought by its advocates to be necessary to a successful opposition to this barbarous custom. But, were we employed to restore peace to a contentious neighbourhood, we should not consider ourselves as obliged to teach, that self-defence is in every possible case a crime ; and equally useless is this principle, in our labors for the pacification of the world. Without taking this uncertain and dangerous ground, we may, and ought to assail war, by assailing the principles and passions which gave it birth, and by improving and exalting the moral sentiments of mankind.

For example ; important service may be rendered to the cause of peace, by communicating and enforcing just and elevated sentiments in relation to the true honor of rulers. Let us teach, that the prosperity, and not the extent of a state, is the measure of a ruler's glory ; that the brute force and crooked policy which annex a conquest, are infinitely inferior to the wisdom, justice, and beneficence, which make a country happy ; and that the earth holds not a more abandoned monster, than the sovereign, who, intrusted with the dearest interests of a people, commits them to the dreadful hazards of war, that he may extend his prostituted power, and fill the earth with his worthless name. Let us exhibit to the honor and veneration of mankind the character of the Christian ruler, who, disdaining the cheap and vulgar honor of a conqueror, aspires to a new and more enduring glory ; who, casting away the long-tried weapons of intrigue and violence, adheres with a holy and unshaken confidence to justice and philanthropy, as a nation's best defence ; and who considers himself as exalted by God, only that he may shed down blessings, and be as a beneficent deity to the world.

To these instructions in relation to the true glory of rulers, should be added, just sentiments as to the glory of nations. Let us teach, that the honor of a nation consists, not in the forced and reluctant submission of other states, but in equal laws and free institutions, in cultivated fields and prosperous cities ; in the developement of intellectual and moral power, in the diffusion of knowledge, in magnanimity and justice, in the virtues and blessings of peace. Let us never be weary in reprobating that infernal spirit of conquest, by which a nation becomes the terror and abhorrence of the world, and inevitably prepares a tomb, at best a splendid tomb, for its own liberties and prosperity. Nothing has been more common, than for nations to imagine themselves great and glorious on the ground of foreign conquest, when at home they have been loaded with chains

Cannot these gross and monstrous delusions be scattered? Can nothing be done to persuade Christian nations to engage in a new and untried race of glory, in generous competitions, in a noble contest for superiority in wise legislation and internal improvements, in the spirit of liberty and humanity?

Another most important method of promoting the cause of peace is, to turn men's admiration from military courage to qualities of real nobleness and dignity. It is time that the childish admiration of courage should give place to more manly sentiments; and, in proportion as we effect this change, we shall shake the main pillar of war, we shall rob military life of its chief attraction. Courage is a very doubtful quality, springing from very different sources, and possessing a corresponding variety of character. Courage sometimes results from mental weakness. Peril is confronted, because the mind wants comprehension to discern its extent. This is often the courage of youth, the courage of unreflecting ignorance, —a contempt of peril because peril is but dimly seen. Courage still more frequently springs from physical temperament, from a rigid fibre and iron nerves, and deserves as little praise as the proportion of the form or the beauty of the countenance. Again, every passion, which is strong enough to overcome the passion of fear, and to exclude by its vehemence the idea of danger, communicates at least a temporary courage. Thus revenge, when it burns with great fury, gives a terrible energy to the mind, and has sometimes impelled men to meet certain death, that they might inflict the same fate on an enemy. You see the doubtful nature of courage. It is often associated with the worst vices. The most wonderful examples of it may be found in the history of pirates and robbers, whose fearlessness is generally proportioned to the insensibility of their consciences, and to the enormity of their crimes. Courage is also exhibited with astonishing power in barbarous countries, where the child is trained to despise the hardships and pains to which he is exposed by his condition ; where the absence of civil laws obliges every man to be his own defender ; and where, from the imperfection of moral sentiment, corporeal strength and ferocious courage are counted the noblest qualities of human nature. The common courage of armies is equally worthless with that of the pirate and the savage. A considerable part of almost every army, so far from deriving their resolution from love of country and a sense of justice, can hardly be said to have a country, and have been driven into the ranks by necessities, which were generated by vice. These are the brave soldiers, whose praises we hear ; brave from the absence of all reflection ; prodigal of life, because their vices have robbed life of its blessings ; brave from sympathy ; brave from the thirst of plunder ; and especially brave, because the sword of martial law is hanging over their heads. Accordingly, military courage is easily attained by the most debased and unprincipled men. The common drunkard of the streets, who is enlisted in a fit of intoxication, when thrown into the ranks among the unthinking and profane, subjected to the rigor of martial discipline, familiarized by exposure to the idea of danger, and menaced with death if he betray a symptom of fear, becomes as brave as his officer, whose courage may often be traced to the same dread of punishment, and to fear of severer infamy than attends on the cowardice of the common soldier. Let the tribute of honor be freely and liberally given to the soldier of principle, who exposes his life for a cause which his conscience approves, and who mingles clemency and mercy with the joy of triumph. But as for the multitude of military men, who regard war as a trade by which to thrive, who hire themselves to fight and slay in any cause, and who destroy their fellow-beings with as little concern, as the husbandman does the vermin that infest his fields, I know no class of men on whom admiration can more unjustly and more injuriously be bestowed. Let us labor, my brethren, to direct the admiration and love of mankind to another and infinitely higher kind of greatness, to that true magnanimity, which is prodigal of ease and life in the service of God and mankind, and which proves its courage by unshaken adherence, amidst scorn and danger, to truth and virtue. Let the records of past ages be explored, to rescue from oblivion, not the wasteful conqueror, whose path was as the whirlwind, but the benefactors of the human race, martyrs to the interests of freedom and religion, men who have broken the chain of the slave, who have traversed the earth to shed consolation into the cell of the prisoner, or whose sublime faculties have explored and revealed useful and ennobling truths. Can nothing be done to hasten the time, when to such men eloquence and poetry shall offer their glowing homage, — when for these the statue and monument shall be erected, the canvass be animated, and the laurel entwined, — and when to these the admiration of the young shall be directed, as their guides and forerunners to glory and immortality?

I proceed to another method of promoting the cause of peace. Let Christian ministers exhibit with greater clearness and distinctness, than ever they have done, the pacific and benevolent spirit of Christianity. My brethren, this spirit ought to hold the same place in our preaching, which it holds in the Gospel of our Lord. Instead of being crowded and lost among other subjects, it should stand in the front of Christian graces; it should be inculcated as the life and essence of our religion. We should teach men, that charity is greater than faith and hope; that God is love or benevolence; and that love is the brightest communication of divinity to the human soul. We should exhibit Jesus in all the amiableness of his character, now shedding tears over Jerusalem, and now, his blood on Calvary, and in his last hours recommending his own sublime love as the badge and distinction of his followers. We should teach men, that it is the property of the benevolence of Christianity, to diffuse itself like the light and rain of heaven, to disdain the limits of rivers, mountains, or oceans, by which nations are divided, and to embrace every human being as a brother. Let us never forget, that our preaching is evangelical, just in proportion as it inculcates and awakens this disinterested and unbounded charity; and that our hearers are Christians, just as far and no farther than they delight in peace and beneficence.

It is a painful truth, which ought not to be suppressed, that the pacific influence of the Gospel has been greatly obstructed by the disposition, which has prevailed in all ages, and especially among Christian ministers, to give importance to the peculiarities of sects, and to rear walls of partition between different denominations. Shame ought to cover the face of the believer, when he remembers, that under no religion have intolerance and persecution raged more fiercely than under the Gospel of the meek and forbearing Saviour. Christians have made the earth to reek with blood and to resound with denunciation. Can we wonder, that, while the spirit of war has been cherished in the very bosom of the church, it has continued to ravage among the nations? Were the true spirit of Christianity to be inculcated with but half the zeal, which has been wasted on doubtful and disputed doctrines, a sympathy, a coöperation might in a very short time be produced among Christians of every nation, most propitious to the pacification of the world. In consequence of the progress of knowledge and the extension of commerce, Christians of both hemispheres are at this moment brought nearer to one another, than at any former period; and an intercourse, founded on religious sympathies, is gradually connecting the most distant regions. What a powerful weapon is furnished by this new bond of union to the ministers and friends of peace! Should not the auspicious moment be seized to inculcate on all Christians, in all regions, that they owe their first allegiance to their common Lord in heaven, whose first, and last, and great command is, love? Should they not be taught to look with a shuddering abhorrence on war, which continually summons to the field of battle, under opposing standards, the followers of the same Saviour, and commands them to imbrue their hands in each others' blood? Once let Christians of every nation be brought to espouse the cause of peace with one heart and one voice, and their labor will not be in vain in the Lord. Human affairs will rapidly assume a new and milder aspect. The predicted ages of peace will dawn on the world. Public opinion will be purified. The false lustre of the hero will grow dim. A nobler order of character will be admired and diffused. The kingdoms of the world will gradually become the kingdoms of God and of his Christ.

My friends, I did intend, but I have not time, to notice the arguments which are urged in support of war. Let me only say, that the common argument, that war is necessary to awaken the boldness, energy, and noblest qualities of human nature, will, I hope, receive a practical refutation in the friends of philanthropy and peace. Let it appear in your lives, that you need not this spark from hell to kindle a heroic resolution in your breasts. Let it appear, that a pacific spirit has no affinity with a tame and feeble character. Let us prove, that courage, the virtue which has been thought to flourish most in the rough field of war, may be reared to a more generous height, and to a firmer texture, in the bosom of peace. Let it be seen, that it is not fear, but principle, which has made us the enemies of war. In every enterprise of philanthropy which demands daring, and sacrifice, and exposure to hardship and toil, let us embark with serenity and joy. Be it our part, to exhibit an undaunted, unshaken, unwearied resolution, not in spreading ruin, but in serving God and mankind, in alleviating human misery, in diffusing truth and virtue, and especially in opposing war. The doctrines of Christianity have had many martyrs. Let us be willing, if God shall require it, to be martyrs to its spirit, the neglected, insulted spirit of peace and love. In a better service we cannot live; in a nobler cause we cannot die. It is the cause of Jesus Christ, supported by Almighty Goodness, and appointed to triumph over the passions and delusions of men, the customs of ages, and the fallen monuments of the forgotten conqueror.

NOTE.

I have deferred to this place a few remarks on the arguments which are usually adduced in support of war.

War, it is said, kindles patriotism; by fighting for our country, we learn to love it. But the patriotism which is cherished by war, is ordinarily false and spurious, a vice and not a virtue, a scourge to the world, a narrow, unjust passion, which aims to exalt a particular state on the humiliation and destruction of other nations. A genuine, enlightened patriot discerns, that the welfare of his own country is involved in the general progress of society; and, in the character of a patriot, as well as of a Christian, he rejoices in the liberty and prosperity of other communities, and is anxious to maintain with them the relations of peace and amity.

It is said, that a military spirit is the defence of a country. But it more frequently endangers the vital interests of a nation, by embroiling it with other states. This spirit, like every other passion, is impatient for gratification, and often precipitates a country into unnecessary war. A people have no need of a military spirit. Let them be attached to their government and institutions by habit, by early associations, and especially by experimental conviction of their excellence, and they will never want means or spirit to defend them.

War is recommended as a method of redressing national grievances. But unhappily, the weapons of war, from their very nature, are often wielded most successfully by the unprincipled. Justice and force have little congeniality. Should not Christians everywhere strive to promote the reference of national as well as of individual disputes to an impartial umpire? Is a project of this nature more extravagant than the idea of reducing savage hordes to a state of regular society? The last has been accomplished. Is the first to be abandoned in despair?

It is said, that war sweeps off the idle, dissolute, and vicious members of the community. Monstrous argument! If a government may for this end plunge a nation into war, it may with equal justice consign to the executioner any number of its subjects, whom it may deem a burden on the state. The fact is, that war commonly generates as many profligates as it destroys. A disbanded army fills the community with at least as many abandoned members as at first it absorbed. There is another method, not quite so summary as war, of ridding a country of unprofitable and injurious citizens, but vastly more effectual; and a method, which will be applied with spirit and success, just in proportion as war shall yield to the light and spirit of Christianity. I refer to the exertions, which Christians have commenced, for the reformation and improvement of the ignorant and poor, and especially for the instruction and moral culture of indigent children. Christians are entreated to persevere and abound in these godlike efforts. By diffusing moral and religious principles and sober and industrious habits through the laboring classes of society, they will dry up one important source of war. They will destroy in a considerable degree the materials of armies. In proportion as these classes become well principled and industrious, poverty will disappear, the population of a country will be more and more proportioned to its resources, and of course the number will be diminished of those, who have no alternative but beggary or a camp. The moral care, which is at the present day extended to the poor, is one of the most honorable features of our age. Christians! remember that your proper warfare is with ignorance and vice, and exhibit here the same unwearied and inventive energy, which has marked the warriors of the world.

It is sometimes said, that a military spirit favors liberty. But how is it, that nations, after fighting for ages, are so generally enslaved? The truth is, that liberty has no foundation but in private and public virtue; and virtue, as we have seen, is not the common growth of war.

But the great argument remains to be discussed. It is said, that, without war to excite and invigorate the human mind, some of its noblest energies will slumber, and its highest qualities, courage, magnanimity, fortitude, will perish. To this I answer, that if war is to be encouraged among nations, because it nourishes energy and heroism, on the same principle war in our families, and war between neighbourhoods, villages, and cities ought to be encouraged; for such contests would equally tend to promote heroic daring and contempt of death. Why shall not different provinces of the same empire annually meet with the weapons of death, to keep alive their courage? We shrink at this suggestion with horror; but why shall contests of nations, rather than of provinces or families, find shelter under this barbarous argument?

I observe again; if war be a blessing, because it awakens energy and courage, then the savage state is peculiarly privileged; for every savage is a soldier and his whole modes of life tend to form him to invincible resolution. On the same principle, those early periods of society were happy, when men were called to contend, not only with one another but with beasts of prey; for to these excitements we owe the heroism of Hercules and Theseus. On the same principle, the feudal ages were more favored than the present ; for then every baron was a military chief, every castle frowned defiance, and every vassal was trained to arms. And do we really wish, that the earth should again be overrun with monsters, or abandoned to savage or feudal violence in order that heroes may be multiplied ? If not, let us cease to vindicate war as affording excitement to energy and courage.

I repeat, what I have observed in the preceding discourse, we need not war to awaken human energy There is at least equal scope for courage and magnanimity in blessing, as in destroying mankind. The condition of the human race offers inexhaustible objects for enterprise, and fortitude, and magnanimity. In relieving the countless wants and sorrows of the world, in exploring unknown regions, in carrying the arts and virtues of civilization to unimproved communities, in extending the bounds of knowledge, in diffusing the spirit of freedom, and especially in spreading the light and influence of Christianity, how much may be dared, how much endured ! Philanthropy invites us to services, which demand the most intense, and elevated, and resolute, and adventurous activity. Let it not be imagined, that, were nations imbued with the spirit of Christianity, they would slumber in ignoble ease; that, instead of the high-minded murderers, who are formed on the present system of war, we should have effeminate and timid slaves. Christian benevolence is as active as it is forbearing. Let it once form the character of a people, and it will attach them to every important interest of society. It will call forth sympathy in behalf of the suffering in every region under heaven. It will give a new extension to the heart, open a wider sphere to enterprise, inspire a courage of exhaustless resource, and prompt to every sacrifice and exposure for the improvement and happiness of the human race. The energy of this principle has been tried and displayed in the fortitude of the martyr, and in the patient labors of those who have carried the Gospel into the dreary abodes of idolatry. Away then with the argument, that war is needed as a nursery of heroism. The school of the peaceful Redeemer is infinitely more adapted to teach the nobler, as well as the milder virtues, which adorn humanity.

UNITARIAN CHRISTIANITY.

DISCOURSE

AT THE

ORDINATION OF THE REV. JARED SPARKS.

BALTIMORE, 1819.

1 THES. v. 21: "Prove all things; hold fast that which is good."

THE peculiar circumstances of this occasion not only justify, but seem to demand a departure from the course generally followed by preachers at the introduction of a brother into the sacred office. It is usual to speak of the nature, design, duties, and advantages of the Christian ministry; and on these topics I should now be happy to insist, did I not remember that a minister is to be given this day to a religious society, whose peculiarities of opinion have drawn upon them much remark, and may I not add, much reproach. Many good minds, many sincere Christians, I am aware, are apprehensive that the solemnities of this day are to give a degree of influence to principles which they deem false and injurious. The fears and anxieties of such men I respect; and, believing that they are grounded in part on mistake, I have thought it my duty to lay before you, as clearly as I can, some of the distinguishing opinions of that class of Christians in our country, who are known to sympathize with this religious society. I must ask your patience, for such a subject is not to be despatched in a narrow compass. I must also ask you to remember, that it is impossible to exhibit, in a single discourse, our views of every doctrine of Revelation, much less the differences of opinion which are known to subsist among ourselves. I shall confine myself to topics, on which our sentiments have been misrepresented, or which distinguish us most widely from others. May I not hope to be heard with candor? God deliver us all from prejudice and unkindness, and fill us with the love of truth and virtue.

There are two natural divisions under which my thoughts will be arranged. I shall endeavour to unfold, 1st, The principles which we adopt in interpreting the Scriptures. And 2dly, Some of the doctrines, which the Scriptures, so interpreted, seem to us clearly to express.

I. We regard the Scriptures as the records of God's successive revelations to mankind, and particularly of the last and most perfect revelation of his will by Jesus Christ. Whatever doctrines seem to us to be clearly taught in the Scriptures, we receive without reserve or exception. We do not, however, attach equal importance to all the books in this collection. Our religion, we believe, lies chiefly in the New Testament. The dispensation of Moses, compared with that of Jesus, we consider as adapted to the childhood of the human race, a preparation for a nobler system, and chiefly useful now as serving to confirm and illustrate the

Christian Scriptures. Jesus Christ is the only master of Christians, and whatever he taught, either during his personal ministry, or by his inspired Apostles, we regard as of divine authority, and profess to make the rule of our lives.

This authority, which we give to the Scriptures, is a reason, we conceive, for studying them with peculiar care, and for inquiring anxiously into the principles of interpretation, by which their true meaning may be ascertained. The principles adopted by the class of Christians in whose name I speak, need to be explained, because they are often misunderstood. We are particularly accused of making an unwarrantable use of reason in the interpretation of Scripture. We are said to exalt reason above revelation, to prefer our own wisdom to God's. Loose and undefined charges of this kind are circulated so freely, that we think it due to ourselves, and to the cause of truth, to express our views with some particularity.

Our leading principle in interpreting Scripture is this, that the Bible is a book written for men, in the language of men, and that its meaning is to be sought in the same manner as that of other books. We believe that God, when he speaks to the human race, conforms, if we may so say, to the established rules of speaking and writing. How else would the Scriptures avail us more, than if communicated in an unknown tongue?

Now all books, and all conversation, require in the reader or hearer the constant exercise of reason; or their true import is only to be obtained by continual comparison and inference. Human language, you well know, admits various interpretations; and every word and every sentence must be modified and explained according to the subject which is discussed, according to the purposes, feelings, circumstances, and principles of the writer, and according to the genius and idioms of the language which he uses. These are acknowledged principles in the interpretation of human writings; and a man, whose words we should explain without reference to these principles, would reproach us justly with a criminal want of candor, and an intention of obscuring or distorting his meaning.

Were the Bible written in a language and style of its own, did it consist of words, which admit but a single sense, and of sentences wholly detached from each other, there would be no place for the principles now laid down. We could not reason about it, as about other writings. But such a book would be of little worth; and perhaps, of all books, the Scriptures correspond least to this description. The Word of God bears the stamp of the same hand, which we see in his works. It has infinite connexions and dependences. Every proposition is linked with others, and is to be compared with others; that its full and precise import may be understood. Nothing stands alone. The New Testament is built on the Old. The Christian dispensation is a continuation of the Jewish, the completion of a vast scheme of providence, requiring great extent of view in the reader. Still more, the Bible treats of subjects on which we receive ideas from other sources besides itself; such subjects as the nature, passions, relations, and duties of man; and it expects us to restrain and modify its language by the known truths, which observation and experience furnish on these topics.

We profess not to know a book, which demands a

more frequent exercise of reason than the Bible. In addition to the remarks now made on its infinite connexions, we may observe, that its style nowhere affects the precision of science, or the accuracy of definition. Its language is singularly glowing, bold, and figurative, demanding more frequent departures from the literal sense, than that of our own age and country, and consequently demanding more continual exercise of judgment. — We find, too, that the different portions of this book, instead of being confined to general truths, refer perpetually to the times when they were written, to states of society, to modes of thinking, to controversies in the church, to feelings and usages which have passed away, and without the knowledge of which we are constantly in danger of extending to all times, and places, what was of temporary and local application. — We find, too, that some of these books are strongly marked by the genius and character of their respective writers, that the Holy Spirit did not so guide the Apostles as to suspend the peculiarities of their minds, and that a knowledge of their feelings, and of the influences under which they were placed, is one of the preparations for understanding their writings. With these views of the Bible, we feel it our bounden duty to exercise our reason upon it perpetually, to compare, to infer, to look beyond the letter to the spirit, to seek in the nature of the subject, and the aim of the writer, his true meaning ; and, in general, to make use of what is known for explaining what is difficult, and for discovering new truths.

Need I descend to particulars, to prove that the Scriptures demand the exercise of reason ? Take, for example, the style in which they generally speak of

God, and observe how habitually they apply to him human passions and organs. Recollect the declarations of Christ, that he came not to send peace, but a sword; that unless we eat his flesh, and drink his blood, we have no life in us; that we must hate father and mother, and pluck out the right eye; and a vast number of passages equally bold and unlimited. Recollect the unqualified manner in which it is said of Christians, that they possess all things, know all things, and can do all things. Recollect the verbal contradiction between Paul and James, and the apparent clashing of some parts of Paul's writings with the general doctrines and end of Christianity. I might extend the enumeration indefinitely; and who does not see, that we must limit all these passages by the known attributes of God, of Jesus Christ, and of human nature, and by the circumstances under which they were written, so as to give the language a quite different import from what it would require, had it been applied to different beings, or used in different connexions.

Enough has been said to show, in what sense we make use of reason in interpreting Scripture. From a variety of possible interpretations, we select that which accords with the nature of the subject and the state of the writer, with the connexion of the passage, with the general strain of Scripture, with the known character and will of God, and with the obvious and acknowledged laws of nature. In other words, we believe that God never contradicts, in one part of Scripture, what he teaches in another; and never contradicts, in revelation, what he teaches in his works and providence. And we therefore distrust every interpretation, which, after deliberate attention, seems repugnant to any established truth. We reason about the Bible precisely as civilians do about the constitution under which we live; who, you know, are accustomed to limit one provision of that venerable instrument by others, and to fix the precise import of its parts, by inquiring into its general spirit, into the intentions of its authors, and into the prevalent feelings, impressions, and circumstances of the time when it was framed. Without these principles of interpretation, we frankly acknowledge, that we cannot defend the divine authority of the Scriptures. Deny us this latitude, and we must abandon this book to its enemies.

We do not announce these principles as original, or peculiar to ourselves. All Christians occasionally adopt them, not excepting those who most vehemently decry them, when they happen to menace some favorite article of their creed. All Christians are compelled to use them in their controversies with infidels. All sects employ them in their warfare with one another. All willingly avail themselves of reason, when it can be pressed into the service of their own party, and only complain of it, when its weapons wound themselves. None reason more frequently than those from whom we differ. It is astonishing what a fabric they rear from a few slight hints about the fall of our first parents; and how ingeniously they extract, from detached passages, mysterious doctrines about the divine nature. We do not blame them for reasoning so abundantly, but for violating the fundamental rules of reasoning, for sacrificing the plain to the obscure, and the general strain of Scripture to a scanty number of insulated texts.

We object strongly to the contemptuous manner in which human reason is often spoken of by our adversaries, because it leads, we believe, to universal skepticism. If reason be so dreadfully darkened by the fall, that its most decisive judgments on religion are unworthy of trust, then Christianity, and even natural theology, must be abandoned; for the existence and veracity of God, and the divine original of Christianity, are conclusions of reason, and must stand or fall with it. If revelation be at war with this faculty, it subverts itself, for the great question of its truth is left by God to be decided at the bar of reason. It is worthy of remark, how nearly the bigot and the skeptic approach. Both would annihilate our confidence in our faculties, and both throw doubt and confusion over every truth. We honor revelation too highly to make it the antagonist of reason, or to believe that it calls us to renounce our highest powers.

We indeed grant, that the use of reason in religion is accompanied with danger. But we ask any honest man to look back on the history of the church, and say, whether the renunciation of it be not still more dangerous. Besides, it is a plain fact, that men reason as erroneously on all subjects, as on religion. Who does not know the wild and groundless theories, which have been framed in physical and political science? But who ever supposed, that we must cease to exercise reason on nature and society, because men have erred for ages in explaining them? We grant, that the passions continually, and sometimes fatally, disturb the rational faculty in its inquiries into revelation. The ambitious contrive to find doctrines in the Bible, which favor their love of dominion. The timid and dejected discover there a gloomy system, and the mystical and fanatical, a visionary theology. The vicious can find examples or assertions on which to build the hope of a late repentance, or of acceptance on easy terms. The falsely refined contrive to light on doctrines which have not been soiled by vulgar handling. But the passions do not distract the reason in religious, any more than in other inquiries, which excite strong and general interest; and this faculty, of consequence, is not to be renounced in religion, unless we are prepared to discard it universally. The true inference from the almost endless errors, which have darkened theology, is, not that we are to neglect and disparage our powers, but to exert them more patiently, circumspectly, uprightly. The worst errors, after all, having sprung up in that church, which proscribes reason, and demands from its members implicit faith. The most pernicious doctrines have been the growth of the darkest times, when the general credulity encouraged bad men and enthusiasts to broach their dreams and inventions, and to stifle the faint remonstrances of reason, by the menaces of everlasting perdition. Say what we may, God has given us a rational nature, and will call us to account for it. We may let it sleep, but we do so at our peril. Revelation is addressed to us as rational beings. We may wish, in our sloth, that God had given us a system, demanding no labor of comparing, limiting, and inferring. But such a system would be at variance with the whole character of our present existence; and it is the part of wisdom to take revelation as it is given to us, and to interpret it by the help of the faculties, which it everywhere supposes, and on which it is founded.

To the views now given, an objection is commonly urged from the character of God. We are told, that God being infinitely wiser than men, his discoveries wil surpass human reason. In a revelation from such a teacher, we ought to expect propositions, which we cannot reconcile with one another, and which may seem to contradict established truths ; and it becomes us not to question or explain them away, but to believe, and adore, and to submit our weak and carnal reason to the Divine Word. To this objection, we have two short answers. We say, first, that it is impossible that a teacher of infinite wisdom should expose those, whom he would teach, to infinite error. But if once we admit, that propositions, which in their literal sense appear plainly repugnant to one another, or to any known truth, are still to be literally understood and received, what possible limit can we set to the belief of contradictions ? What shelter have we from the wildest fanaticism, which can always quote passages, that, in their literal and obvious sense, give support to its extravagances ? How can the Protestant escape from transubstantiation, a doctrine most clearly taught us, if the submission of reason, now contended for, be a duty ? How can we even hold fast the truth of revelation, for if one apparent contradiction may be true, so may another, and the proposition, that Christianity is false, though involving inconsistency, may still be a verity ?

We answer again, that, if God be infinitely wise, he cannot sport with the understandings of his creatures. A wise teacher discovers his wisdom in adapting himself to the capacities of his pupils, not in perplexing them with what is unintelligible, not in distressing them with apparent contradictions, not in filling them with a skeptical distrust of their own powers. An infinitely wise teacher, who knows the precise extent of our minds, and the best method of enlightening them, will surpass all other instructors in bringing down truth to our apprehension, and in showing its loveliness and harmony. We ought, indeed, to expect occasional obscurity in such a book as the Bible, which was written for past and future ages, as well as for the present. But God's wisdom is a pledge, that whatever is necessary for *us*, and necessary for salvation, is revealed too plainly to be mistaken, and too consistently to be questioned, by a sound and upright mind. It is not the mark of wisdom, to use an unintelligible phraseology, to communicate what is above our capacities, to confuse and unsettle the intellect by appearances of contradiction. We honor our Heavenly Teacher too much to ascribe to him such a revelation. A revelation is a gift of light. It cannot thicken our darkness, and multiply our perplexities.

II. Having thus stated the principles according to which we interpret Scripture, I now proceed to the second great head of this discourse, which is, to state some of the views which we derive from that sacred book, particularly those which distinguish us from other Christians.

1. In the first place, we believe in the doctrine of God's UNITY, or that there is one God, and one only. To this truth we give infinite importance, and we feel ourselves bound to take heed, lest any man spoil us of it by vain philosophy. The proposition, that there is one God, seems to us exceedingly plain. We understand by it, that there is one being, one mind, one person, one intelligent agent, and one only, to whom underived and infinite perfection and dominion belong. We conceive, that these words could have conveyed no

other meaning to the simple and uncultivated people, who were set apart to be the depositaries of this great truth, and who were utterly incapable of understanding those hair-breadth distinctions between being and person, which the sagacity of later ages has discovered. We find no intimation, that this language was to be taken in an unusual sense, or that God's unity was a quite different thing from the oneness of other intelligent beings.

We object to the doctrine of the Trinity, that, whilst acknowledging in words, it subverts in effect, the unity of God. According to this doctrine, there are three infinite and equal persons, possessing supreme divinity, called the Father, Son, and Holy Ghost. Each of these persons, as described by theologians, has his own particular consciousness, will, and perceptions. They love each other, converse with each other, and delight in each other's society. They perform different parts in man's redemption, each having his appropriate office, and neither doing the work of the other. The Son is mediator and not the Father. The Father sends the Son, and is not himself sent; nor is he conscious, like the Son, of taking flesh. Here, then, we have three intelligent agents, possessed of different consciousnesses, different wills, and different perceptions, performing different acts, and sustaining different relations; and if these things do not imply and constitute three minds or beings, we are utterly at a loss to know how three minds or beings are to be formed. It is difference of properties, and acts, and consciousness, which leads us to the belief of different intelligent beings, and, if this mark fails us, our whole knowledge falls; we have no proof, that all the agents and persons in the universe are not one and the same mind. When we attempt to conceive of three Gods, we can do nothing more than represent to ourselves three agents, distinguished from each other by similar marks and peculiarities to those which separate the persons of the Trinity; and when common Christians hear these persons spoken of as conversing with each other, loving each other, and performing different acts, how can they help regarding them as different beings, different minds?

We do, then, with all earnestness, though without reproaching our brethren, protest against the irrational and unscriptural doctrine of the Trinity. "To us," as to the Apostle and the primitive Christians, "there is one God, even the Father." With Jesus, we worship the Father, as the only living and true God. We are astonished, that any man can read the New Testament, and avoid the conviction, that the Father alone is God. We hear our Saviour continually appropriating this character to the Father. We find the Father continually distinguished from Jesus by this title. "God sent his Son." "God anointed Jesus." Now, how singular and inexplicable is this phraseology, which fills the New Testament, if this title belong equally to Jesus, and if a principal object of this book is to reveal him as God, as partaking equally with the Father in supreme divinity! We challenge our opponents to adduce one passage in the New Testament, where the word God means three persons, where it is not limited to one person, and where, unless turned from its usual sense by the connexion, it does not mean the Father. Can stronger proof be given, that the doctrine of three persons in the Godhead is not a fundamental doctrine of Christianity?

This doctrine, were it true, must, from its difficulty, singularity, and importance, have been laid down with great clearness, guarded with great care, and stated with all possible precision. But where does this statement appear? From the many passages which treat of God, we ask for one, one only, in which we are told, that he is a threefold being, or that he is three persons, or that he is Father, Son, and Holy Ghost. On the contrary, in the New Testament, where, at least, we might expect many express assertions of this nature, God is declared to be one, without the least attempt to prevent the acceptation of the words in their common sense; and he is always spoken of and addressed in the singular number, that is, in language which was universally understood to intend a single person, and to which no other idea could have been attached, without an express admonition. So entirely do the Scriptures abstain from stating the Trinity, that when our opponents would insert it into their creeds and doxologies, they are compelled to leave the Bible, and to invent forms of words altogether unsanctioned by Scriptural phraseology. That a doctrine so strange, so liable to misapprehension, so fundamental as this is said to be, and requiring such careful exposition, should be left so undefined and unprotected, to be made out by inference, and to be hunted through distant and detached parts of Scripture, this is a difficulty, which, we think, no ingenuity can explain.

We have another difficulty. Christianity, it must be remembered, was planted and grew up amidst sharp-sighted enemies, who overlooked no objectionable part of the system, and who must have fastened with great earnestness on a doctrine involving such apparent contradictions as the Trinity. We cannot conceive an opinion, against which the Jews, who prided themselves on an adherence to God's unity, would have raised an equal clamor. Now, how happens it, that in the apostolic writings, which relate so much to objections against Christianity, and to the controversies which grew out of this religion, not one word is said, implying that objections were brought against the Gospel from the doctrine of the Trinity, not one word is uttered in its defence and explanation, not a word to rescue it from reproach and mistake? This argument has almost the force of demonstration. We are persuaded, that had three divine persons been announced by the first preachers of Christianity, all equal, and all infinite, one of whom was the very Jesus who had lately died on a cross, this peculiarity of Christianity would have almost absorbed every other, and the great labor of the Apostles would have been to repel the continual assaults, which it would have awakened. But the fact is, that not a whisper of objection to Christianity, on that account, reaches our ears from the apostolic age. In the Epistles we see not a trace of controversy called forth by the Trinity.

We have further objections to this doctrine, drawn from its practical influence. We regard it as unfavorable to devotion, by dividing and distracting the mind in its communion with God. It is a great excellence of the doctrine of God's unity, that it offers to us ONE OBJECT of supreme homage, adoration, and love, One Infinite Father, one Being of beings, one original and fountain, to whom we may refer all good, in whom all our powers and affections may be concentrated, and whose lovely and venerable nature may pervade all our thoughts. True piety, when directed to an undivided

Deity, has a chasteness, a singleness, most favorably to religious awe and love. Now, the Trinity sets before us three distinct objects of supreme adoration, three infinite persons, having equal claims on our hearts; three divine agents, performing different offices, and to be acknowledged and worshipped in different relations. And is it possible, we ask, that the weak and limited mind of man can attach itself to these with the same power and joy, as to One Infinite Father, the only First Cause, in whom all the blessings of nature and redemption meet as their centre and source? Must not devotion be distracted by the equal and rival claims of three equal persons, and must not the worship of the conscientious, consistent Christian, be disturbed by an apprehension, lest he withhold from one or another of these, his due proportion of homage?

We also think, that the doctrine of the Trinity injures devotion, not only by joining to the Father other objects of worship, but by taking from the Father the supreme affection, which is his due, and transferring it to the Son. This is 'a most important view. That Jesus Christ, if exalted into the infinite Divinity, should be more interesting than the Father, is precisely what might be expected from history, and from the principles of human nature. Men want an object of worship like themselves, and the great secret of idolatry lies in this propensity. A God, clothed in our form, and feeling our wants and sorrows, speaks to our weak nature more strongly, than a Father in heaven, a pure spirit, invisible and unapproachable, save by the reflecting and purified mind. — We think, too, that the peculiar offices ascribed to Jesus by the popular theology, make him the most attractive person in the Godhead. The Father is the depositary of the justice, the vindicator of the rights, the avenger of the laws of the Divinity. On the other hand, the Son, the brightness of the divine mercy, stands between the incensed Deity and guilty humanity, exposes his meek head to the storms, and his compassionate breast to the sword of the divine justice, bears our whole load of punishment, and purchases with his blood every blessing which descends from heaven. Need we state the effect of these representations, especially on common minds, for whom Christianity was chiefly designed, and whom it seeks to bring to the Father as the loveliest being? We do believe, that the worship of a bleeding, suffering God, tends strongly to absorb the mind, and to draw it from other objects, just as the human tenderness of the Virgin Mary has given her so conspicuous a place in the devotions of the Church of Rome. We believe, too, that this worship, though attractive, is not most fitted to spiritualize the mind, that it awakens human transport, rather than that deep veneration of the moral perfections of God, which is the essence of piety.

2. Having thus given our views of the unity of God, I proceed in the second place to observe, that we believe in the unity of Jesus Christ. We believe that Jesus is one mind, one soul, one being, as truly one as we are, and equally distinct from the one God. We complain of the doctrine of the Trinity, that, not satisfied with making God three beings, it makes Jesus Christ two beings, and thus introduces infinite confusion into our conceptions of his character. This corruption of Christianity, alike repugnant to common sense and to the general strain of Scripture, is a remarkable proof of the power of a false philosophy in disfiguring the simple truth of Jesus.

According to this doctrine, Jesus Christ, instead of being one mind, one conscious intelligent principle, whom we can understand, consists of two souls, two minds; the one divine, the other human; the one weak, the other almighty; the one ignorant, the other omniscient. Now we maintain, that this is to make Christ two beings. To denominate him one person, one being, and yet to suppose him made up of two minds, infinitely different from each other, is to abuse and confound language, and to throw darkness over all our conceptions of intelligent natures. According to the common doctrine, each of these two minds in Christ has its own consciousness, its own will, its own perceptions. They have, in fact, no common properties. The divine mind feels none of the wants and sorrows of the human, and the human is infinitely removed from the perfection and happiness of the divine. Can you conceive of two beings in the universe more distinct? We have always thought that one person was constituted and distinguished by one consciousness. The doctrine, that one and the same person should have two consciousnesses, two wills, two souls, infinitely different from each other, this we think an enormous tax on human credulity.

We say, that if a doctrine, so strange, so difficult, so remote from all the previous conceptions of men, be indeed a part and an essential part of revelation, it must be taught with great distinctness, and we ask our brethren to point to some plain, direct passage, where Chris is said to be composed of two minds infinitely different, yet constituting one person. We find none. Other Christians, indeed, tell us, that this doctrine is necessary to the harmony of the Scriptures, that some texts ascribe to Jesus Christ human, and others divine properties, and that to reconcile these, we must suppose two minds, to which these properties may be referred. In other words, for the purpose of reconciling certain difficult passages, which a just criticism can in a great degree, if not wholly, explain, we must invent an hypothesis vastly more difficult, and involving gross absurdity. We are to find our way out of a labyrinth, by a clue which conducts us into mazes infinitely more inextricable.

Surely, if Jesus Christ felt that he consisted of two minds, and that this was a leading feature of his religion, his phraseology respecting himself would have been colored by this peculiarity. The universal language of men is framed upon the idea, that one person is one person, is one mind, and one soul; and when the multitude heard this language from the lips of Jesus, they must have taken it in its usual sense, and must have referred to a single soul all which he spoke, unless expressly instructed to interpret it differently. But where do we find this instruction? Where do you meet, in the New Testament, the phraseology which abounds in Trinitarian books, and which necessarily grows from the doctrine of two natures in Jesus? Where does this divine teacher say, " This I speak as God, and this as man; this is true only of my human mind, this only of my divine "? Where do we find in the Epistles a trace of this strange phraseology? Nowhere. It was not needed in that day. It was demanded by the errors of a later age.

We believe, then, that Christ is one mind, one being, and, I add, a being distinct from the one God. That Christ is not the one God, not the same being with the Father, is a necessary inference from our former head, in which we saw that the doctrine of three persons in God is a fiction. But on so important a subject, I would add a few remarks. We wish, that those from whom we differ, would weigh one striking fact. Jesus, in his preaching, continually spoke of God. The word was always in his mouth. We ask, does he, by this word, ever mean himself? We say, never. On the contrary, he most plainly distinguishes between God and himself, and so do his disciples. How this is to be reconciled with the idea, that the manifestation of Christ, as God, was a primary object of Christianity, our adversaries must determine.

If we examine the passages in which Jesus is distinguished from God, we shall see, that they not only speak of him as another being, but seem to labor to express his inferiority. He is continually spoken of as the Son of God, sent of God, receiving all his powers from God, working miracles because God was with him, judging justly because God taught him, having claims on our belief, because he was anointed and sealed by God, and as able of himself to do nothing. The New Testament is filled with this language. Now we ask, what impression this language was fitted and intended to make? Could any, who heard it, have imagined that Jesus was the very God to whom he was so industriously declared to be inferior; the very Being by whom he was sent, and from whom he professed to have received his message and power? Let it here be remembered, that the human birth, and bodily form, and humble circumstances, and mortal sufferings of Jesus, must all have prepared men to interpret, in the most unqualified manner, the language in which his inferiority to God was declared. Why, then, was this language used so continually, and without limitation, if Jesus were the Supreme Deity, and if this truth were an essential part of his religion ? I repeat it, the human condition and sufferings of Christ tended strongly to exclude from men's minds the idea of his proper Godhead ; and, of course, we should expect to find in the New Testament perpetual care and effort to counteract this tendency, to hold him forth as the same being with his Father, if this doctrine were, as is pretended, the soul and centre of his religion. We should expect to find the phraseology of Scripture cast into the mould of this doctrine, to hear familiarly of God the Son, of our Lord God Jesus, and to be told, that to us there is one God, even Jesus. But, instead of this, the inferiority of Christ pervades the New Testament. It is not only implied in the general phraseology, but repeatedly and decidedly expressed, and unaccompanied with any admonition to prevent its application to his whole nature. Could it, then, have been the great design of the sacred writers to exhibit Jesus as the Supreme God ?

I am aware that these remarks will be met by two or three texts, in which Christ is called God, and by a class of passages, not very numerous, in which divine properties are said to be ascribed to him. To these we offer one plain answer. We say, that it is one of the most established and obvious principles of criticism, that language is to be explained according to the known properties of the subject to which it is applied. Every man knows, that the same words convey very different ideas, when used in relation to different beings. Thus, Solomon *built* the temple in a different manner from the architect whom he employed ; and God *repents* differently from man. Now we maintain, that the known properties and circumstances of Christ, his birth, sufferings, and death, his constant habit of speaking of God as a distinct being from himself, his praying to God, his ascribing to God all his power and offices, these acknowledged properties of Christ, we say, oblige us to interpret the comparatively few passages which are thought to make him the Supreme God, in a manner consistent with his distinct and inferior nature. It is our duty to explain such texts by the rule which we apply to other texts, in which human beings are called gods, and are said to be partakers of the divine nature, to know and possess all things, and to be filled with all God's fulness. These latter passages we do not hesitate to modify, and restrain, and turn from the most obvious sense, because this sense is opposed to the known properties of the beings to whom they relate; and we maintain, that we adhere to the same principle, and use no greater latitude, in explaining, as we do, the passages which are thought to support the Godhead of Christ.

Trinitarians profess to derive some important advantages from their mode of viewing Christ. It furnishes them, they tell us, with an infinite atonement, for it shows them an infinite being suffering for their sins. The confidence with which this fallacy is repeated astonishes us. When pressed with the question, whether they really believe, that the infinite and unchangeable God suffered and died on the cross, they acknowledge that this is not true, but that Christ's human mind alone sustained the pains of death. How have we, then, an infinite sufferer? This language seems to us an imposition on common minds, and very derogatory to God's justice, as if this attribute could be satisfied by a sophism and a fiction.

We are also told, that Christ is a more interesting object; that his love and mercy are more felt, when he is viewed as the Supreme God, who left his glory to take humanity and to suffer for men. That Trinitarians are strongly moved by this representation, we do not mean to deny; but we think their emotions altogether founded on a misapprehension of their own doctrines. They talk of the second person of the Trinity's leaving his glory and his Father's bosom, to visit and save the world. But this second person, being the unchangeable and infinite God, was evidently incapable of parting with the least degree of his perfection and felicity. At the moment of his taking flesh, he was as intimately present with his Father as before, and equally with his Father filled heaven, and earth, and immensity. This Trinitarians acknowledge; and still they profess to be touched and overwhelmed by the amazing humiliation of this immutable being! But not only does their doctrine, when fully explained, reduce Christ's humiliation to a fiction, it almost wholly destroys the impressions with which his cross ought to be viewed. According to their doctrine, Christ was comparatively no sufferer at all. It is true, his human mind suffered; but this, they tell us, was an infinitely small part of Jesus, bearing no more proportion to his whole nature, than a single hair of our heads to the whole body, or than a drop to the ocean. The divine mind of Christ, that which was most properly himself, was infinitely happy, at the very moment of the suffering of his humanity. Whilst hanging on the cross, he was the happiest being in the universe, as happy as the infinite Father; so that his pains, compared with his felicity, were nothing This Trinitarians do, and must, acknowledge. It follows necessarily from the immutableness of the divine nature, which they ascribe to Christ ; so that their system, justly viewed, robs his death of interest, weakens our sympathy with his sufferings, and is, of all others, most unfavorable to a love of Christ, founded on a sense of his sacrifices for mankind. We esteem our own views to be vastly more affecting. It is our belief, that Christ's humiliation was real and entire, that the whole Saviour, and not a part of him, suffered, that his crucifixion was a scene of deep and unmixed agony. As we stand round his cross, our minds are not distracted, nor our sensibility weakened, by contemplating him as composed of incongruous and infinitely differing minds, and as having a balance of infinite felicity. We recognise in the dying Jesus but one mind. This, we think, renders his sufferings, and his patience and love in bearing them, incomparably more impressive and affecting than the system we oppose.

3. Having thus given our belief on two great points, namely, that there is one God, and that Jesus Christ is a being distinct from, and inferior to, God, I now proceed to another point, on which we lay still greater stress. We believe in the *moral perfection of God*. We consider no part of theology so important as that which treats of God's moral character ; and we value our views of Christianity chiefly as they assert his amiable and venerable attributes.

It may be said, that, in regard to this subject, all Christians agree, that all ascribe to the Supreme Being infinite justice, goodness, and holiness. We reply, that it is very possible to speak of God magnificently, and to think of him meanly ; to apply to his person high-sounding epithets, and to his government, principles which make him odious. The Heathens called Jupiter the greatest and the best; but his history was black with cruelty and lust. We cannot judge of men's real ideas of God by their general language, for in all ages they have hoped to soothe the Deity by adulation. We must inquire into their particular views of his purposes, of the principles of his administration, and of his disposition towards his creatures.

We conceive that Christians have generally leaned towards a very injurious view of the Supreme Being. They have too often felt, as if he were raised, by his greatness and sovereignty, above the principles of morality, above those eternal laws of equity and rectitude, to which all other beings are subjected. We believe, that in no being is the sense of right so strong, so omnipotent, as in God. We believe that his almighty power is entirely submitted to his perceptions of rectitude; and this is the ground of our piety. It is not because he is our Creator merely, but because he created us for good and holy purposes; it is not because his will is irresistible, but because his will is the perfection of virtue, that we pay him allegiance. We cannot bow before a being, however great and powerful, who governs tyrannically. We respect nothing but excellence, whether on earth or in heaven. We venerate not the loftiness of God's throne, but the equity and goodness in which it is established.

We believe that God is infinitely good, kind, benevolent, in the proper sense of these words; good in disposition, as well as in act; good, not to a few, but to all; good to every individual, as well as to the general system.

We believe, too, that God is just; but we never

forget, that his justice is the justice of a good being, dwelling in the same mind, and acting in harmony, with perfect benevolence. By this attribute, we understand God's infinite regard to virtue or moral worth expressed in a moral government; that is, in giving excellent and equitable laws, and in conferring such rewards, and inflicting such punishments, as are best fitted to secure their observance. God's justice has for its end the highest virtue of the creation, and it punishes for this end alone, and thus it coincides with benevolence; for virtue and happiness, though not the same, are inseparably conjoined.

God's justice thus viewed, appears to us to be in perfect harmony with his mercy. According to the prevalent systems of theology, these attributes are so discordant and jarring, that to reconcile them is the hardest task, and the most wonderful achievement, of infinite wisdom. To us they seem to be intimate friends, always at peace, breathing the same spirit, and seeking the same end. By God's mercy, we understand not a blind instinctive compassion, which forgives without reflection, and without regard to the interests of virtue. This, we acknowledge, would be incompatible with justice, and also with enlightened benevolence. God's mercy, as we understand it, desires strongly the happiness of the guilty, but only through their penitence. It has a regard to character as truly as his justice. It defers punishment, and suffers long, that the sinner may return to his duty, but leaves the impenitent and unyielding, to the fearful retribution threatened in God's Word.

To give our views of God in one word, we believe in his Parental character. We ascribe to him, not only the name, but the dispositions and principles of a father. We believe that he has a father's concern for his creatures, a father's desire for their improvement, a father's equity in proportioning his commands to their powers, a father's joy in their progress, a father's readiness to receive the penitent, and a father's justice for the incorrigible. We look upon this world as a place of education, in which he is training men by prosperity and adversity, by aids and obstructions, by conflicts of reason and passion, by motives to duty and temptations to sin, by a various discipline suited to free and moral beings, for union with himself, and for a sublime and ever-growing virtue in heaven.

Now, we object to the systems of religion, which prevail among us, that they are adverse, in a greater or less degree, to these purifying, comforting, and honorable views of God; that they take from us our Father in heaven, and substitute for him a being, whom we cannot love if we would, and whom we ought not to love if we could. We object, particularly on this ground, to that system, which arrogates to itself the name of Orthodoxy, and which is now industriously propagated through our country. This system indeed takes various shapes, but in all it casts dishonor on the Creator. According to its old and genuine form, it teaches, that God brings us into life wholly depraved, so that under the innocent features of our childhood is hidden a nature averse to all good and propense to all evil, a nature which exposes us to God's displeasure and wrath, even before we have acquired power to understand our duties, or to reflect upon our actions. According to a more modern exposition, it teaches, that we came from the hands of our Maker with such a constitution, and are placed under such influences and circumstances, as to render certain and infallible the total depravity of every human being, from the first moment of his moral agency; and it also teaches, that the offence of the child, who brings into life this ceaseless tendency to unmingled crime, exposes him to the sentence of everlasting damnation. Now, according to the plainest principles of morality, we maintain, that a natural constitution of the mind, unfailingly disposing it to evil and to evil alone, would absolve it from guilt ; that to give existence under this condition would argue unspeakable cruelty; and that to punish the sin of this unhappily constituted child with endless ruin, would be a wrong unparalleled by the most merciless despotism.

This system also teaches, that God selects from this corrupt mass a number to be saved, and plucks them, by a special influence, from the common ruin ; that the rest of mankind, though left without that special grace which their conversion requires, are commanded to repent, under penalty of aggravated woe ; and that forgiveness is promised them, on terms which their very constitution infallibly disposes them to reject, and in rejecting which they awfully enhance the punishments of hell. These proffers of forgiveness and exhortations of amendment, to beings born under a blighting curse, fill our minds with a horror which we want words to express.

That this religious system does not produce all the effects on character, which might be anticipated, we most joyfully admit. It is often, very often, counteracted by nature, conscience, common sense, by the general strain of Scripture, by the mild example and precepts of Christ, and by the many positive declarations of God's universal kindness and perfect equity. But still we think that we see its unhappy influence.\ It tends to discourage the timid, to give excuses to the bad, to feed the vanity of the fanatical, and to offer shelter to the bad feelings of the malignant. By shocking, as it does, the fundamental principles of morality, and by exhibiting a severe and partial Deity, it tends strongly to pervert the moral faculty, to form a gloomy, forbidding, and servile religion, and to lead men to substitute censoriousness, bitterness, and persecution, for a tender and impartial charity. We think, too, that this system, which begins with degrading human nature, may be expected to end in pride; for pride grows out of a consciousness of high distinctions, however obtained, and no distinction is so great as that which is made between the elected and abandoned of God.

The false and dishonorable views of God, which have now been stated, we feel ourselves bound to resist unceasingly. Other errors we can pass over with comparative indifference. But we ask our opponents to leave to us a GOD, worthy of our love and trust, in whom our moral sentiments may delight, in whom our weaknesses and sorrows may find refuge. We cling to the Divine perfections. We meet them everywhere in creation, we read them in the Scriptures, we see a lovely image of them in Jesus Christ; and gratitude, love, and veneration call on us to assert them. Reproached, as we often are, by men, it is our consolation and happiness, that one of our chief offences is the zeal with which we vindicate the dishonored goodness and rectitude of God.

4. Having thus spoken of the unity of God; of the unity of Jesus, and his inferiority to God; and of the

perfections of the Divine character; I now proceed to give our views of the mediation of Christ, and of the purposes of his mission. With regard to the great object which Jesus came to accomplish, there seems to be no possibility of mistake. We believe, that he was sent by the Father to effect a moral, or spiritual deliverance of mankind; that is, to rescue men from sin and its consequences, and to bring them to a state of everlasting purity and happiness. We believe, too, that he accomplishes this sublime purpose by a variety of methods; by his instructions respecting God's unity, parental character, and moral government, which are admirably fitted to reclaim the world from idolatry and impiety, to the knowledge, love, and obedience of the Creator; by his promises of pardon to the penitent, and of divine assistance to those who labor for progress in moral excellence; by the light which he has thrown on the path of duty; by his own spotless example, in which the loveliness and sublimity of virtue shine forth to warm and quicken, as well as guide us to perfection; by his threatenings against incorrigible guilt; by his glorious discoveries of immortality; by his sufferings and death; by that signal event, the resurrection, which powerfully bore witness to his divine mission, and brought down to men's senses a future life; by his continual intercession, which obtains for us spiritual aid and blessings; and by the power with which he is invested of raising the dead, judging the world, and conferring the everlasting rewards promised to the faithful.

We have no desire to conceal the fact, that a difference of opinion exists among us, in regard to an interesting part of Christ's mediation; I mean, in regard to the precise influence of his death on our forgiveness.

Many suppose, that this event contributes to our pardon, as it was a principal means of confirming his religion, and of giving it a power over the mind; in other words, that it procures forgiveness by leading to that repentance and virtue, which is the great and only condition on which forgiveness is bestowed. Many of us are dissatisfied with this explanation, and think that the Scriptures ascribe the remission of sins to Christ's death, with an emphasis so peculiar, that we ought to consider this event as having a special influence in removing punishment, though the Scriptures may not reveal the way in which it contributes to this end.

Whilst, however, we differ in explaining the connexion between Christ's death and human forgiveness, a connexion which we all gratefully acknowledge, we agree in rejecting many sentiments which prevail in regard to his mediation. The idea, which is conveyed to common minds by the popular system, that Christ's death has an influence in making God placable, or merciful, in awakening his kindness towards men, we reject with strong disapprobation. We are happy to find, that this very dishonorable notion is disowned by intelligent Christians of that class from which we differ. We recollect, however, that, not long ago, it was common to hear of Christ, as having died to appease God's wrath, and to pay the debt of sinners to his inflexible justice; and we have a strong persuasion, that the language of popular religious books, and the common mode of stating the doctrine of Christ's mediation, still communicate very degrading views of God's character. They give to multitudes the impression, that the death of Jesus produces a change in the mind of God towards man, and that in this its efficacy chiefly consists.

No error seems to us more pernicious. We can endure no shade over the pure goodness of God. We earnestly maintain, that Jesus, instead of calling forth, in any way or degree, the mercy of the Father, was sent by that mercy, to be our Saviour; that he is nothing to the human race, but what he is by God's appointment; that he communicates nothing but what God empowers him to bestow; that our Father in heaven is originally, essentially, and eternally placable, and disposed to forgive; and that his unborrowed, underived, and unchangeable love is the only fountain of what flows to us through his Son. We conceive, that Jesus is dishonored, not glorified, by ascribing to him an influence, which clouds the splendor of Divine benevolence.

We farther agree in rejecting, as unscriptural and absurd, the explanation given by the popular system, of the manner in which Christ's death procures forgiveness for men. This system used to teach as its fundamental principle, that man, having sinned against an infinite Being, has contracted infinite guilt, and is consequently exposed to an infinite penalty. We believe, however, that this reasoning, if reasoning it may be called, which overlooks the obvious maxim, that the guilt of a being must be proportioned to his nature and powers, has fallen into disuse. Still the system teaches, that sin, of whatever degree, exposes to endless punishment, and that the whole human race, being infallibly involved by their nature in sin, owe this awful penalty to the justice of their Creator. It teaches, that this penalty cannot be remitted, in consistency with the honor of the divine law, unless a substitute be found to endure it or to suffer an equivalent. It also teaches, that, from the nature of the case, no substitute is adequate to this work, save the infinite God himself; and accordingly, God, in his second person, took on him human nature, that he might pay to his own justice the debt of punishment incurred by men, and might thus reconcile forgiveness with the claims and threatenings of his law. Such is the prevalent system. Now, to us, this doctrine seems to carry on its front strong marks of absurdity; and we maintain that Christianity ought not to be encumbered with it, unless it be laid down in the New Testament fully and expressly. We ask our adversaries, then, to point to some plain passages where it is taught. We ask for one text, in which we are told, that God took human nature that he might make an infinite satisfaction to his own justice; for one text, which tells us, that human guilt requires an infinite substitute; that Christ's sufferings owe their efficacy to their being borne by an infinite being; or that his divine nature gives infinite value to the sufferings of the human. Not *one word* of this description can we find in the Scriptures; not a text, which even hints at these strange doctrines. They are altogether, we believe, the fictions of theologians. Christianity is in no degree responsible for them. We are astonished at their prevalence. What can be plainer, than that God cannot, in any sense, be a sufferer, or bear a penalty in the room of his creatures? How dishonorable to him is the supposition, that his justice is now so severe, as to exact infinite punishment for the sins of frail and feeble men, and now so easy and yielding, as to accept the limited pains of Christ's human soul, as a full equivalent for the endless woes due from the world? How plain is it also, according to this doctrine, that God.

instead of being plenteous in forgiveness, never forgives; for it seems absurd to speak of men as forgiven, when their whole punishment, or an equivalent to it, is borne by a substitute? A scheme more fitted to obscure the brightness of Christianity and the mercy of God, or less suited to give comfort to a guilty and troubled mind, could not, we think, be easily framed.

We believe, too, that this system is unfavorable to the character. It naturally leads men to think, that Christ came to change God's mind rather than their own; that the highest object of his mission was to avert punishment, rather than to communicate holiness; and that a large part of religion consists in disparaging good works and human virtue, for the purpose of magnifying the value of Christ's vicarious sufferings. In this way, a sense of the infinite importance and indispensable necessity of personal improvement is weakened, and high-sounding praises of Christ's cross seem often to be substituted for obedience to his precepts. For ourselves, we have not so learned Jesus. Whilst we gratefully acknowledge that he came to rescue us from punishment, we believe, that he was sent on a still nobler errand, namely, to deliver us from sin itself, and to form us to a sublime and heavenly virtue. We regard him as a Saviour, chiefly as he is the light, physician, and guide of the dark, diseased, and wandering mind. No influence in the universe seems to us so glorious, as that over the character; and no redemption so worthy of thankfulness, as the restoration of the soul to purity. Without this, pardon, were it possible, would be of little value. Why pluck the sinner from hell, if a hell be left to burn in his own breast? Why raise him to heaven, if he remain a stranger to its sanctity and love? With these impressions, we are accustomed to value the Gospel chiefly as it abounds in effectual aids, motives, excitements to a generous and divine virtue. In this virtue, as in a common centre, we see all its doctrines, precepts, promises meet; and we believe, that faith in this religion is of no worth, and contributes nothing to salvation, any farther than as it uses these doctrines, precepts, promises, and the whole life, character, sufferings, and triumphs of Jesus, as the means of purifying the mind, of changing it into the likeness of his celestial excellence.

5. Having thus stated our views of the highest object of Christ's mission, that it is the recovery of men to virtue, or holiness, I shall now, in the last place, give our views of the nature of Christian virtue, or true holiness. We believe that all virtue has its foundation in the moral nature of man, that is, in conscience, or his sense of duty, and in the power of forming his temper and life according to conscience. We believe that these moral faculties are the grounds of responsibility, and the highest distinctions of human nature; and that no act is praiseworthy, any farther than it springs from their exertion. We believe, that no dispositions infused into us without our own moral activity, are of the nature of virtue, and therefore, we reject the doctrine of irresistible divine influence on the human mind, moulding it into goodness, as marble is hewn into a statue. Such goodness, if this word may be used, would not be the object of moral approbation, any more than the instinctive affections of inferior animals, or the constitutional amiableness of human beings.

By these remarks, we do not mean to deny the importance of God's aid or Spirit; but by his Spirit. we mean a moral, illuminating, and persuasive influence, not physical, not compulsory, not involving a necessity of virtue. We object, strongly, to the idea of many Christians respecting man's impotence and God's irresistible agency on the heart, believing that they subvert our responsibility and the laws of our moral nature, that they make men machines, that they cast on God the blame of all evil deeds, that they discourage good minds, and inflate the fanatical with wild conceits of immediate and sensible inspiration.

Among the virtues, we give the first place to the love of God. We believe, that this principle is the true end and happiness of our being, that we were made for union with our Creator, that his infinite perfection is the only sufficient object and true resting-place for the insatiable desires and unlimited capacities of the human mind, and that, without him, our noblest sentiments, admiration, veneration, hope, and love, would wither and decay. We believe, too, that the love of God is not only essential to happiness, but to the strength and perfection of all the virtues; that conscience, without the sanction of God's authority and retributive justice, would be a weak director; that benevolence, unless nourished by communion with his goodness, and encouraged by his smile, could not thrive amidst the selfishness and thanklessness of the world; and that self-government, without a sense of the divine inspection, would hardly extend beyond an outward and partial purity. God, as he is essentially goodness, holiness, justice, and virtue, so he is the life, motive, and sustainer of virtue in the human soul.

But, whilst we earnestly inculcate the love of God, we believe that great care is necessary to distinguish it from counterfeits. We think that much which is called piety is worthless. Many have fallen into the error, that there can be no excess in feelings which have God for their object; and, distrusting as coldness that self-possession, without which virtue and devotion lose all their dignity, they have abandoned themselves to extravagances, which have brought contempt on piety. Most certainly, if the love of God be that which often bears its name, the less we have of it the better. If religion be the shipwreck of understanding, we cannot keep too far from it. On this subject, we always speak plainly. We cannot sacrifice our reason to the reputation of zeal. We owe it to truth and religion to maintain, that fanaticism, partial insanity, sudden impressions, and ungovernable transports, are any thing rather than piety.

We conceive, that the true love of God is a moral sentiment, founded on a clear perception, and consisting in a high esteem and veneration, of his moral perfections. Thus, it perfectly coincides, and is in fact the same thing, with the love of virtue, rectitude, and goodness. You will easily judge, then, what we esteem the surest and only decisive signs of piety. We lay no stress on strong excitements. We esteem him, and him only a pious man, who practically conforms to God's moral perfections and government; who shows his delight in God's benevolence, by loving and serving his neighbour; his delight in God's justice, by being resolutely upright; his sense of God's purity, by regulating his thoughts, imagination, and desires; and whose conversation, business, and domestic life are swayed by a regard to God's presence and authority. In all things else men may deceive themselves. Disordered nerves may give them strange sights, and sounds, and impressions. Texts of Scripture may come to them as from Heaven. Their whole souls may be moved, and their confidence in God's favor be undoubting. But in all this there is no religion. The question is, Do they love God's commands, in which his character is fully expressed, and give up to these their habits and passions? Without this, ecstasy is a mockery. One surrender of desire to God's will, is worth a thousand transports. We do not judge of the bent of men's minds by their raptures, any more than we judge of the natural direction of a tree during a storm. We rather suspect loud profession, for we have observed, that deep feeling is generally noiseless, and least seeks display.

We would not, by these remarks, be understood as wishing to exclude from religion warmth, and even transport. We honor, and highly value, true religious sensibility. We believe, that Christianity is intended to act powerfully on our whole nature, on the heart as well as the understanding and the conscience. We conceive of heaven as a state where the love of God will be exalted into an unbounded fervor and joy; and we desire, in our pilgrimage here, to drink into the spirit of that better world. But we think, that religious warmth is only to be valued, when it springs naturally from an improved character, when it comes unforced, when it is the recompense of obedience, when it is the warmth of a mind which understands God by being like him, and when, instead of disordering, it exalts the understanding, invigorates conscience, gives a pleasure to common duties, and is seen to exist in connexion with cheerfulness, judiciousness, and a reasonable frame of mind. When we observe a fervor, called religious, in men whose general character expresses little refinement and elevation, and whose piety seems at war with reason, we pay it little respect. We honor religion too much to give its sacred name to a feverish, forced, fluctuating zeal, which has little power over the life.

Another important branch of virtue, we believe to be love to Christ. The greatness of the work of Jesus, the spirit with which he executed it, and the sufferings which he bore for our salvation, we feel to be strong claims on our gratitude and veneration. We see in nature no beauty to be compared with the loveliness of his character, nor do we find on earth a benefactor to whom we owe an equal debt. We read his history with delight, and learn from it the perfection of our nature. We are particularly touched by his death, which was endured for our redemption, and by that strength of charity which triumphed over his pains. His resurrection is the foundation of our hope of immortality. His intercession gives us boldness to draw nigh to the throne of grace, and we look up to heaven with new desire, when we think, that, if we follow him here, we shall there see his benignant countenance, and enjoy his friendship for ever.

I need not express to you our views on the subject of the benevolent virtues. We attach such importance to these, that we are sometimes reproached with exalting them above piety. We regard the spirit of love, charity, meekness, forgiveness, liberality, and beneficence, as the badge and distinction of Christians, as the brightest image we can bear of God, as the best proof of piety. On this subject, I need not, and cannot enlarge; but there is one branch of benevolence which I ought not to pass over in silence, because we think that we conceive of it more highly and justly than many of our brethren. I refer to the duty of candor, charitable judgment, especially towards those who differ in religious opinion. We think, that in nothing have Christians so widely departed from their religion, as in this particular. We read with astonishment and horror, the history of the church; and sometimes when we look back on the fires of persecution, and on the zeal of Christians, in building up walls of separation, and in giving up one another to perdition, we feel as if we were reading the records of an infernal, rather than a heavenly kingdom. An enemy to every religion, if asked to describe a Christian, would, with some show of reason, depict him as an idolater of his own distinguishing opinions, covered with badges of party, shutting his eyes on the virtues, and his ears on the arguments, of his opponents, arrogating all excellence to his own sect and all saving power to his own creed, sheltering under the name of pious zeal the love of domination, the conceit of infallibility, and the spirit of intolerance, and trampling on men's rights under the pretence of saving their souls.

We can hardly conceive of a plainer obligation on beings of our frail and fallible nature, who are instructed in the duty of candid judgment, than to abstain from condemning men of apparent conscientiousness and sincerity, who are chargeable with no crime but that of differing from us in the interpretation of the Scriptures, and differing, too, on topics of great and acknowledged obscurity. We are astonished at the hardihood of those, who, with Christ's warnings sounding in their ears, take on them the responsibility of making creeds for his church, and cast out professors of virtuous lives for imagined errors, for the guilt of thinking for themselves

We know that zeal for truth is the cover for this usurpation of Christ's prerogative ; but we think that zeal for truth, as it is called, is very suspicious, except in men, whose capacities and advantages, whose patient deliberation, and whose improvements in humility, mildness, and candor, give them a right to hope that their views are more just than those of their neighbours. Much of what passes for a zeal for truth, we look upon with little respect, for it often appears to thrive most luxuriantly where other virtues shoot up thinly and feebly ; and we have no gratitude for those reformers, who would force upon us a doctrine which has not sweetened their own tempers, or made them better men than their neighbours.

We are accustomed to think much of the difficulties attending religious inquiries ; difficulties springing from the slow developement of our minds, from the power of early impressions, from the state of society, from human authority, from the general neglect of the reasoning powers, from the want of just principles of criticism and of important helps in interpreting Scripture, and from various other causes. We find, that on no subject have men, and even good men, ingrafted so many strange conceits, wild theories, and fictions of fancy, as on religion ; and remembering, as we do, that we ourselves are sharers of the common frailty, we dare not assume infallibility in the treatment of our fellow-Christians, or encourage in common Christians, who have little time for investigation, the habit of denouncing and contemning other denominations, perhaps more enlightened and virtuous than their own. Charity, forbearance, a delight in the virtues of different sects, a backwardness to censure and condemn, these are virtues, which, however poorly practised by us, we admire and recommend ; and we would rather join ourselves to the church in which they abound, than to any other communion, however elated with the belief of its own orthodoxy, however strict in guarding its creed, however burning with zeal against imagined error.

I have thus given the distinguishing views of those Christians in whose names I have spoken. We have embraced this system, not hastily or lightly, but after much deliberation ; and we hold it fast, not merely because we believe it to be true, but because we regard it as purifying truth, as a doctrine according to godliness, as able to " work mightily " and to " bring forth fruit " in them who believe. That we wish to spread it, we have no desire to conceal ; but we think, that we wish its diffusion, because we regard it as more friendly to practical piety and pure morals than the opposite doctrines, because it gives clearer and nobler views of duty, and stronger motives to its performance, because it recommends religion at once to the understanding and the heart, because it asserts the lovely and venerable attributes of God, because it tends to restore the benevolent spirit of Jesus to his divided and afflicted church, and because it cuts off every hope of God's favor, except that which springs from practical conformity to the life and precepts of Christ. We see nothing in our views to give offence, save their purity, and it is their purity, which makes us seek and hope their extension through the world.

My friend and brother ;—You are this day to take upon you important duties ; to be clothed with an office, which the Son of God did not disdain ; to devote your self to that religion, which the most hallowed lips have preached, and the most precious blood sealed. We trust that you will bring to this work a willing mind, a firm purpose, a martyr's spirit, a readiness to toil and suffer for the truth, a devotion of your best powers to the interests of piety and virtue. I have spoken of the doctrines which you will probably preach; but I do not mean, that you are to give yourself to controversy. You will remember, that good practice is the end of preaching, and will labor to make your people holy livers, rather than skilful disputants. Be careful, lest the desire of defending what you deem truth, and of repelling reproach and misrepresentation, turn you aside from your great business, which is to fix in men's minds a living conviction of the obligation, sublimity, and happiness of Christian virtue. The best way to vindicate your sentiments, is to show, in your preaching and life, their intimate connexion with Christian morals, with a high and delicate sense of duty, with candor towards your opposers, with inflexible integrity, and with an habitual reverence for God. If any light can pierce and scatter the clouds of prejudice, it is that of a pure example. My brother, may your life preach more loudly than your lips. Be to this people a pattern of all good works, and may your instructions derive authority from a well-grounded belief in your hearers, that you speak from the heart, that you preach from experience, that the truth which you dispense has wrought powerfully in your own heart, that God, and Jesus, and heaven, are not merely words on your lips, but most affecting realities to your mind, and springs of hope and consolation, and strength, in all your trials. Thus laboring, may you reap abundantly, and have a testimony of your faithfulness, not only in your own conscience, but in the esteem, love, virtues, and improvements of your people. To all who hear me, I would say, with the Apostle, Prove all things, hold fast that which is good. Do not, brethren, shrink from the duty of searching God's Word for yourselves, through fear of human censure and denunciation. Do not think, that you may innocently follow the opinions which prevail around you, without investigation, on the ground, that Christianity is now so purified from errors, as to need no laborious research. There is much reason to believe, that Christianity is at this moment dishonored by gross and cherished corruptions. If you remember the darkness which hung over the Gospel for ages; if you consider the impure union, which still subsists in almost every Christian country, between the church and state, and which enlists men's selfishness and ambition on the side of established error; if you recollect in what degree the spirit of intolerance has checked free inquiry, not only before, but since the Reformation; you will see that Christianity cannot have freed itself from all the human inventions, which disfigured it under the Papal tyranny. No. Much stubble is yet to be burned; much rubbish to be removed; many gaudy decorations, which a false taste has hung around Christianity, must be swept away; and the earth-born fogs, which have long shrouded it, must be scattered, before this divine fabric will rise before us in its native and awful majesty, in its harmonious proportions, in its mild and celestial splendors. This glorious reformation in the church, we hope, under God's blessing, from the progress of the human intellect, from the moral progress of society, from the consequent decline of prejudice and bigotry, and, though last not least, from the subversion of human authority in matters of religion, from the fall of those hierarchies, and other human institutions, by which the minds of individuals are oppressed under the weight of numbers, and a Papal dominion is perpetuated in the Protestant church. Our earnest prayer to God is, that he will overturn, and overturn, and overturn the strong-holds of spiritual usurpation, until HE shall come, whose right it is to rule the minds of men ; that the conspiracy of ages against the liberty of Christians may be brought to an end ; that the servile assent, so long yielded to human creeds, may give place to honest and devout inquiry into the Scriptures ; and that Christianity, thus purified from error, may put forth its almighty energy, and prove itself, by its ennobling influence on the mind, to be indeed " the power of God unto salvation."

THE
EVIDENCES OF REVEALED RELIGION.

DISCOURSE

BEFORE THE

UNIVERSITY IN CAMBRIDGE, AT THE DUDLEIAN LECTURE,

14th March, 1821.

John iii. 2: "The same came to Jesus by night, and said unto him, Rabbi, we know that thou art a teacher come from God; for no man can do these miracles that thou doest, except God be with him."

THE evidences of revealed religion are the subject of this lecture, a subject of great extent, as well as of vast importance. In discussing it, an immense variety of learning has been employed, and all the powers of the intellect been called forth. History, metaphysics, ancient learning, criticism, ethical science, and the science of human nature, have been summoned to the controversy, and have brought important contributions to the Christian cause. To condense into one discourse what scholars and great men have written on this point, is impossible, even if it were desirable; and I have stated the extent of speculation into which our subject has led, not because I propose to give an abstract of others' labors, but because I wish you to understand, that the topic is one not easily despatched, and because I would invite you to follow me in a discussion, which will require concentrated and continued attention. A subject more worthy of attention, than the claims of that religion which was impressed on our childhood, and which is acknowledged to be the only firm foundation of the hope of immortality; cannot be presented; and our minds must want the ordinary seriousness of human nature, if it cannot arrest us.

That Christianity has been opposed, is a fact, implied in the establishment of this lecture. That it has had adversaries of no mean intellect, you know. I propose in this discourse to make some remarks on what seems to me the great objection to Christianity, on the general principle on which its evidences rest, and on some of ts particular evidences.

The great objection to Christianity, the only one which has much influence at the present day, meets us at the very threshold. We cannot, if we would, evade t, for it is founded on a primary and essential attribute of this religion. The objection is oftener felt than expressed, and amounts to this, that miracles are incredible, and that the supernatural character of an alleged fact is proof enough of its falsehood. So strong is this propensity to doubt of departures from the order of nature, that there are sincere Christians, who incline to rest their religion wholly on its internal evidence, and to overlook the outward extraordinary interposition of God, by which it was at first established. But the difficulty cannot in this way be evaded ; for Christianity is not only confirmed by miracles, but is in itself, in its very essence, a miraculous religion. It is not a system which the human mind might have gathered, in the ordinary exercise of its powers, from the ordinary course of nature. Its doctrines, especially those which relate to its founder, claim for it the distinction of being a supernatural provision for the recovery of the human race. So that the objection which I have stated still presses upon us, and, if it be well grounded, it is fatal to Christianity.

It is proper, then, to begin the discussion with inquiring, whence the disposition to discredit miracles springs, and how far it is rational. A preliminary remark of some importance is, that this disposition is not a necessary part or principle of our mental constitution, like the disposition to trace effects to adequate causes. We are indeed so framed, as to expect a continuance of that order of nature which we have uniformly experienced; but not so framed as to revolt at alleged violations of that order, and to account them impossible or absurd. On the contrary, men at large discover a strong and incurable propensity to believe in miracles. Almost all histories, until within the two last centuries, reported seriously supernatural facts. Skepticism as to miracles is comparatively a new thing, if we except the Epicurean or Atheistical sect among the ancients; and so far from being founded in human nature, it is resisted by an almost infinite preponderance of belief on the other side.

Whence, then, has this skepticism sprung? It may be explained by two principal causes. 1. It is now an acknowledged fact, among enlightened men, that in past times and in our own, a strong disposition has existed and still exists to admit miracles without examination. Human credulity is found to have devoured nothing more eagerly than reports of prodigies. Now it is argued, that we discover here a principle of human nature, namely, the love of the supernatural and marvellous, which accounts sufficiently for the belief of miracles, wherever we find it; and that it is, consequently, unnecessary and unphilosophical to seek for other causes, and especially to admit that most improbable one, the actual existence of miracles. This sweeping conclusion is a specimen of that rash habit of generalizing, which rather distinguishes our times, and shows that philosophical reasoning has made fewer advances than we are apt to boast. It is true, that there is a principle of credulity as to prodigies in a considerable part of society, a disposition to believe without due scrutiny. But this principle, like every other in our nature, has its limits; acts according to fixed laws; is not omnipotent, cannot make the eyes see, and the ears hear, and the understanding credit delusions, under all imaginable circumstances; but requires the concurrence of various circumstances and of other principles of our nature in order to its operation. For example, the belief of spectral appearances has been very common; but under what circumstances and in what state of mind has it occurred? Do men see ghosts in broad day, and amidst cheerful society? Or in solitary places; in grave-yards in twilights or mists, where outward objects are so undefined, as easily to take a form from imagination; and in other circumstances favorable to terror, and associated with the delusion in question? The principle of credulity is as regular in its operation, as any other principle of the mind; and is so dependent on circumstances and so restrained and checked by other parts of human nature, that sometimes the most obstinate incredulity is found in that very class of people, whose easy belief on other occasions moves our contempt. It is well known, for example, that the efficacy of the vaccine inoculation has been encountered with much more unyielding skepticism among the vulgar, than among the improved ; and in general, it may be affirmed, that the credulity of the ignorant operates under the control of their strongest passions and impressions, and that no class of society yield a slower assent to positions, which manifestly subvert their old modes of thinking and most settled prejudices. It is, then, very unphilosophical to assume this principle as an explanation of all miracles whatever. [I grant that the fact, that accounts of supernatural agency so generally prove false, is a reason for looking upon them with peculiar distrust.] Miracles ought on this account to be sifted more than common facts. But if we find, that a belief in a series of supernatural works, has occurred under circumstances very different from those under which false prodigies have been received, under circumstances most unfavorable to the operation of credulity ; then this belief cannot be resolved into the common causes, which have blinded men in regard to supernatural agency. We must look for other causes, and if none can be found but the actual existence of the miracles, then true philosophy binds us to believe them. I close this head with ob serving, that the propensity of men to believe in what is strange and miraculous, though a presumption against particular miracles, is not a presumption against miracles universally, but rather the reverse ; for great principles of human nature have generally a foundation in truth, and one explanation of this propensity so common to mankind is obviously this, that in the earlier ages of the human race, miraculous interpositions, suited to man's infant state, were not uncommon, and, being the most striking facts of human history, they spread through all future times a belief and expectation of miracles.

I proceed now to the second cause of the skepticism in regard to supernatural agency, which has grown up, especially among the more improved, in later times. These later times are distinguished, as you well know, by successful researches into nature ; and the discoveries of science have continually added strength to that great principle, that the phenomena of the universe are regulated by general and permanent laws, or that the Author of the universe exerts his power according to an established order. Nature, the more it is explored, is found to be uniform. We observe an unbroken succession of causes and effects. Many phenomena, once denominated irregular, and ascribed to supernatural agency, are found to be connected with preceding circumstances, as regularly as the most common events. The comet, we learn, observes the same attraction as the sun and planets. When a new phenomenon now occurs, no one thinks it miraculous, but believes, that, when better understood, it may be reduced to laws already known, or is an example of a law not yet investigated.

Now this increasing acquaintance with the uniformity of nature begets a distrust of alleged violations of it, and a rational distrust too ; for, while many causes of mistake in regard to alleged miracles may be assigned, there is but one adequate cause of real miracles, that is, the power of God ; and the regularity of nature forms a strong presumption against the miraculous exertion of this power, except in extraordinary circumstances, and for extraordinary purposes, to which the established laws of the creation are not competent. But the observation of the uniformity of nature produces, in multitudes, not merely this rational distrust of alleged violations of it, but a secret feeling, as if such violations were impossible. That attention to the powers of nature, which is implied in scientific research, tends to weaken the practical conviction of a higher power; and the laws of the creation, instead of being regarded as the modes of Divine operation, come insensibly to be considered as fetters on his agency, as too sacred to be suspended even by their Author. This secret feeling, essentially atheistical, and at war with all sound philosophy, is the chief foundation of that skepticism, which prevails in regard to miraculous agency, and deserves our particular consideration.

To a man whose belief in God is strong and practical, a miracle will appear as possible as any other effect, as the most common event in life; and the argument against miracles, drawn from the uniformity of nature, will weigh with him, only as far as this uniformity is a pledge and proof of the Creator's disposition to accomplish his purposes by a fixed order or mode of operation. Now it is freely granted, that the Creator's regard or attachment to such an order may be inferred from the steadiness with which he observes it; and a strong presumption lies against any violation of it on slight occasions, or for purposes to which the established laws of nature are adequate. But this is the utmost which the order of nature authorizes us to infer respecting its Author. It forms no presumption against miracles universally, in all imaginable cases; but may even furnish a presumption in their favor.

We are never to forget, that God's adherence to the

order of the universe is not necessary and mechanical, but intelligent and voluntary.) He adheres to it, not for its own sake, or because it has a sacredness which compels him to respect it, but because it is most suited to accomplish his purposes. It is a means, and not an end ; and, like all other means, must give way when the end can best be promoted without it. It is the mark of a weak mind, to make an idol of order and method ; to cling to established forms of business, when they clog instead of advancing it. If, then, the great purposes of the universe can best be accomplished by departing from its established laws, these laws will undoubtedly be suspended ; and, though broken in the letter, they will be observed in their spirit, for the ends for which they were first instituted will be advanced by their violation. Now the question arises, (For what purposes were nature and its order appointed ? and there is no presumption in saying, that the highest of these is the improvement of intelligent beings. Mind (by which we mean both moral and intellectual powers) is God's first end. [The great purpose for which an order of nature is fixed, is plainly the formation of Mind.] In a creation without order, where events would follow without any regular succession, it is obvious, that Mind must be kept in perpetual infancy ; for, in such a universe, there could be no reasoning from effects to causes, no induction to establish general truths, no adaptation of means to ends ; that is, no science relating to God, or matter, or mind ; no action ; no virtue. The great purpose of God, then, I repeat it, in establishing the order of nature, is to form and advance the mind ; and if the case should occur, in which the interests of the mind could best be advanced by departing from this order, or by miraculous agency, then the great purpose of the creation, the great end of its laws and regularity, would demand such departure; and miracles, instead of warring against, would concur with nature.

Now, we Christians maintain, that such a case has existed. We affirm, that, when Jesus Christ came into the world, nature had failed to communicate instructions to men, in which, as intelligent beings, they had the deepest concern, and on which the full developement of their highest faculties essentially depended; and we affirm, that there was no prospect of relief from nature; so that an exigence had occurred, in which additional communications, supernatural lights, might rationally be expected from the Father of spirits. Let me state two particulars, out of many, in which men needed intellectual aids not given by nature. I refer to the doctrine of one God and Father, on which all piety rests; and to the doctrine of Immortality, which is the great spring of virtuous effort. Had I time to enlarge on the history of that period, I might show you under what heaps of rubbish and superstition these doctrines were buried. But I should repeat only what you know familiarly. The works of ancient genius, which form your studies, carry on their front the brand of polytheism, and of debasing error on subjects of the first and deepest concern. It is more important to observe, that the very uniformity of nature had some tendency to obscure the doctrines which I have named, or at least to impair their practical power, so that a departure from this uniformity was needed to fasten them on men's minds.

That a fixed order of nature, though a proof of the One God to reflecting and enlarged understandings, has yet a tendency to hide him from men in general, will appear, if we consider, first, that, as the human mind is constituted, what is regular and of constant occurrence, excites it feebly ; and benefits flowing to it through fixed, unchanging laws, seem to come by a kind of necessity, and are apt to be traced up to natural causes alone. Accordingly, religious convictions and feelings, even in the present advanced condition of society, are excited, not so much by the ordinary course of God's providence, as by sudden, unexpected events,—which rouse and startle the mind, and speak of a power higher than nature. — There is another way, in which a fixed order of nature seems unfavorable to just impressions respecting its Author. It discovers to us in the Creator, a regard to general good rather than an affection to individuals. The laws of nature, operating, as they do, with an inflexible steadiness, never varying to meet the cases and wants of individuals, and inflicting much private suffering in their stern administration for the general weal, give the idea of a distant, reserved sovereign, much more than of a tender parent ; and yet this last view of God is the only effectual security from superstition and idolatry. Nature, then, we fear, would not have brought back the world to its Creator. — And as to the doctrine of Immortality, the order of the natural world had little tendency to teach this, at least with clearness and energy. The natural world contains no provisions or arrangements for reviving the dead. The sun and the rain, which cover the tomb with verdure, send no vital influences to the mouldering body. The researches of science detect no secret processes for restoring the lost powers of life. If man is to live again, he is not to live through any known laws of nature, but by a power higher than nature ; and how, then, can we be assured of this truth, but by a manifestation of this power, that is, by miraculous agency, confirming a future life?

I have labored in these remarks to show, that the uniformity of nature is no presumption against miraculous agency, when employed in confirmation of such a religion as Christianity. Nature, on the contrary, furnishes a presumption in its favor. [Nature clearly shows to us a power above itself, so that it proves miracles to be possible. Nature reveals purposes and attributes in its Author, with which Christianity remarkably agrees. Nature too has deficiencies, which show that it was not intended by its Author to be his whole method of instructing mankind; and in this way it gives great confirmation to Christianity, which meets its wants, supplies its chasms, explains its mysteries, and lightens its heart-oppressing cares and sorrows.]

Before quitting the general consideration of miracles, I ought to take some notice of Hume's celebrated argument on this subject; not that it merits the attention which it has received, but because it is specious, and has derived weight from the name of its author. [The argument is briefly this, — "that belief is founded upon and regulated by experience. Now we often experience testimony to be false, but never witness a departure from the order of nature. That men may deceive us when they testify to miracles, is therefore more accordant with experience, than that nature should be irregular; and hence there is a balance of proof against miracles, a presumption so strong as to outweigh the strongest testimony."] The usual replies to this argument I have not time to repeat. Dr. Campbell's work, which is accessible to all, will show you that it rests on an equivocal use of terms, and will furnish you with many fine remarks on testimony and on the conditions or qualities which give it validity. I will only add a few remarks which seem to me worthy of attention.

1. This argument affirms, that the credibility of facts or statements is to be decided by their accordance with the established order of nature, and by this standard only. Now, if nature comprehended all existences and all powers, this position might be admitted. But if there is a Being higher than nature, the origin of all its powers and motions, and whose character falls under our notice and experience as truly as the creation, then there is an additional standard to which facts and statements are to be referred; and works which violate nature's order, will still be credible, if they agree with the known properties and attributes of its author; because for such works we can assign an adequate cause and sufficient reasons, and these are the qualities and conditions on which credibility depends.

2. This argument of Hume proves too much, and therefore proves nothing. It proves too much; for if I am to reject the strongest testimony to miracles, because testimony has often deceived me, whilst nature's order has never been found to fail, then I ought to reject a miracle, even if I should see it with my own eyes, and if all my senses should attest it; for all my senses have sometimes given false reports, whilst nature has never gone astray; and, therefore, be the circumstances ever so decisive or inconsistent with deception, still I must not believe what I see, and hear, and touch, what my senses, exercised according to the most deliberate judgment, declare to be true. All this the argument requires; and it proves too much; for disbelief, in the case supposed, is out of our power, and is instinctively

pronounced absurd ; and what is more, it would subvert that very order of nature on which the argument rests ; for this order of nature is learned only by the exercise of my senses and judgment, and if these fail me, in the most unexceptionable circumstances, then their testimony to nature is of little worth.

Once more ; this argument is built on an ignorance of the nature of testimony. Testimony, we are told, cannot prove a miracle. Now the truth is, that testimony of itself and immediately, proves no facts whatever, not even the most common. Testimony can do nothing more than show us the state of another's mind in regard to a given fact. It can only show us, that the testifier has a belief, a conviction, that a certain phenomenon or event has occurred. Here testimony stops ; and the reality of the event is to be judged altogether from the nature and degree of this conviction, and from the circumstances under which it exists. This conviction is an effect, which must have a cause, and needs to be explained ; and if no cause can be found but the real occurrence of the event, then this occurrence is admitted as true. Such is the extent of testimony. Now a man, who affirms a miraculous phenomenon or event, may give us just as decisive proofs, by his character and conduct, of the strength and depth of his conviction, as if he were affirming a common occurrence. Testimony, then, does just as much in the case of miracles, as of common events ; that is, it discloses to us the conviction of another's mind. Now this conviction in the case of miracles requires a cause, an explanation, as much as in every other ; and if the circumstances be such, that it could not have sprung up and been estab lished but by the reality of the alleged miracle, then that great and fundamental principle of human belief, namely, that every effect must have a cause, compels us to admit the miracle.

It may be observed of Hume and of other philosophical opposers of our religion, that they are much more inclined to argue against miracles in general, than against the particular miracles on which Christianity rests. And the reason is obvious. Miracles, when considered in a general, abstract manner, that is, when divested of all circumstances, and supposed to occur as disconnected facts, to stand alone in history, to have no explanations or reasons in preceding events, and no influence on those which follow, are indeed open to great objection, as wanton and useless violations of nature's order; and it is accordingly against miracles, considered in this naked, general form, that the arguments of infidelity are chiefly urged. But it is great disingenuity to class under this head the miracles of Christianity. They are palpably different. They do not stand alone in history; but are most intimately incorporated with it. They were demanded by the state of the world which preceded them, and they have left deep traces on all subsequent ages. In fact, the history of the whole civilized world, since their alleged occurrence, has been swayed and colored by them, and is wholly inexplicable without them. Now, such miracles are not to be met and disposed of by general reasonings, which apply only to insulated, unimportant, uninfluential prodigies.

I have thus considered the objections to miracles in general; and I would close this head with observing, that these objections will lose their weight, just in proportion as we strengthen our conviction of God's power over nature and of his parental interest in his creatures.

The great repugnance to the belief of miraculous agency is founded in a lurking atheism, which ascribes supremacy to nature, and which, whilst it professes to believe in God, questions his tender concern for the improvement of men. To a man, who cherishes a sense of God, the great difficulty is, not to account for miracles, but to account for their rare occurrence. One of the mysteries of the universe is this, that its Author retires so continually behind the veil of his works, that the great and good Father does not manifest himself more distinctly to his creatures. There is something like coldness and repulsiveness in instructing us only by fixed, inflexible laws of nature. The intercourse of God with Adam and the patriarchs suits our best conceptions of the relation which he bears to the human race, and ought not to surprise us more, than the expression of a human parent's tenderness and concern towards his offspring.

After the remarks now made to remove the objection to revelation in general, I proceed to consider the evidences of the Christian religion in particular; and these are so numerous, that should I attempt to compress them into the short space which now remains, I could give but a syllabus, a dry and uninteresting index. It will be more useful to state to you, with some distinctness, the general principle into which all Christian evidences may be resolved, and on which the whole religion rests, and then to illustrate it in a few striking particulars.

All the evidences of Christianity may be traced to this great principle, — that every effect must have an adequate cause. We claim for our religion a divine original, because no adequate cause for it can be found in the powers or passions of human nature, or in the circumstances under which it appeared; because it can only be accounted for by the interposition of that Being, to whom its first preachers universally ascribed it, and with whose nature it perfectly agrees.

Christianity, by which we mean not merely the doctrines of the religion, but every thing relating to it, its rise, its progress, the character of its author, the conduct of its propagators, — Christianity, in this broad sense, can only be accounted for in two ways. It either sprung from the principles of human nature, under the excitements, motives, impulses of the age in which it was first preached ; or it had its origin in a higher and supernatural agency. To which of these causes the religion should be referred, is not a question beyond our reach ; for being partakers of human nature, and knowing more of it than of any other part of creation, we can judge with sufficient accuracy of the operation of its principles, and of the effects to which they are competent. It is indeed true, that human powers are not exactly defined, nor can we state precisely the bounds beyond which they cannot pass ; but still, the disproportion between human nature and an effect ascribed to it, may be so vast and palpable, as to satisfy us at once, that the effect is inexplicable by human power. I know not precisely what advances may be made by the intellect of an unassisted savage; but that a savage in the woods could not compose the "Principia" of Newton, is about as plain as that he could not create the world. I know not the point at which bodily strength must stop ; but that a man cannot carry Atlas or Andes on his shoulders, is a safe position. The question, therefore, whether the principles of human nature, under the circumstances in which it was placed at Christ's birth, will explain his religion, is one to which we are competent, and is the great question on which the whole controversy turns.

Now we maintain, that a great variety of facts belonging to this religion, — such as the character of its Founder ; its peculiar principles ; the style and character of its records ; its progress; the conduct, circumstances, and sufferings of its first propagators ; the reception of it from the first on the ground of miraculous attestations ; the prophecies which it fulfilled and which it contains ; its influence on society, and other circumstances connected with it ; are utterly inexplicable by human powers and principles, but accord with, and are fully explained by, the power and perfections of God.

These various particulars I cannot attempt to unfold. One or two may be illustrated to show you the mode of applying the principles which I have laid down. I will take first the character of Jesus Christ. How is this to be explained by the principles of human nature ? — We are immediately struck with this peculiarity in the Author of Christianity, that, whilst all other men are formed in a measure by the spirit of the age, we can discover in Jesus no impression of the period in which he lived. We know with considerable accuracy the state of society, the modes of thinking, the hopes and expectations of the country in which Jesus was born and grew up ; and he is as free from them, and as exalted above them, as if he had lived in another world, or with every sense shut on the objects around him. His character has in it nothing local or temporary. It can be explained by nothing around him. His history shows him to us a solitary being, living for purposes which none but himself comprehended, and enjoying not so much as the sympathy of a single mind. His Apostles, his chosen companions, brought to him the spirit of the age; and nothing shows its strength more strikingly, than the slowness with which it yielded in these honest men to the instructions of Jesus.

Jesus came to a nation expecting a Messiah; and he claimed this character. But instead of conforming to the opinions which prevailed in regard to the Messiah, he resisted them wholly and without reserve. To a people anticipating a triumphant leader, under whom vengeance as well as ambition was to be glutted by the prostration of their oppressors, he came as a spiritual leader, teaching humility and peace. This undisguised hostility to the dearest hopes and prejudices of his nation; this disdain of the usual compliances, by which ambition and imposture conciliate adherents; this deliberate exposure of himself to rejection and hatred, cannot easily be explained by the common principles of human nature, and excludes the possibility of selfish aims in the Author of Christianity.

One striking peculiarity in Jesus is the extent, the vastness, of his views. Whilst all around him looked for a Messiah to liberate God's ancient people, whilst to every other Jew, Judea was the exclusive object of pride and hope, Jesus came, declaring himself to be the deliverer and light of the world, and in his whole teaching and life, you see a consciousness, which never forsakes him, of a relation to the whole human race. This idea of blessing mankind, of spreading a universal religion, was the most magnificent which had ever entered man's mind. All previous religions had been given to particular nations. No conqueror, legislator, philosopher, in the extravagance of ambition, had ever dreamed of subjecting all nations to a common faith. This conception of a universal religion, intended alike for Jew and Gentile, for all nations and climes, is wholly inexplicable by the circumstances of Jesus. He was a Jew, and the first and deepest and most constant impression on a Jew's mind, was that of the superiority conferred on his people and himself by the national religion introduced by Moses. The wall between the Jew and the Gentile seemed to reach to heaven. The abolition of the peculiarity of Moses, the prostration of the temple on Mount Zion, the erection of a new religion, in which all men would meet as brethren, and which would be the common and equal property of Jew and Gentile, these were of all ideas the last to spring up in Judea, the last for enthusiasm or imposture to originate.

Compare next these views of Christ with his station in life. He was of humble birth and education, with nothing in his lot, with no extensive means, no rank, or wealth, or patronage, to infuse vast thoughts and extravagant plans. The shop of a carpenter, the village of Nazareth, were not spots for ripening a scheme more aspiring and extensive than had ever been formed. It is a principle of human nature, that, except in case of insanity, some proportion is observed between the power of an individual, and his plans and hopes. The purpose, to which Jesus devoted himself, was as ill suited to his condition as an attempt to change the seasons, or to make the sun rise in the west. That a young man, in obscure life, belonging to an oppressed nation, should seriously think of subverting the time-hallowed and deep-rooted religions of the world, is a strange fact; but with this purpose we see the mind of Jesus thoroughly imbued; and, sublime as it is, he never falls below it in his language or conduct, but speaks and acts with a consciousness of superiority, with a dignity and authority, becoming this unparalleled destination.

In this connexion, I cannot but add another striking circumstance in Jesus, and that is, the calm confidence with which he always looked forward to the accomplishment of his design. He fully knew the strength of the passions and powers which were arrayed against him, and was perfectly aware that his life was to be shortened by violence; yet not a word escapes him implying a doubt of the ultimate triumphs of his religion. One of the beauties of the Gospels, and one of the proofs of their genuineness, is found in our Saviour's indirect and obscure allusions to his approaching sufferings, and to the glory which was to follow; allusions showing us the workings of a mind, thoroughly conscious of being appointed to accomplish infinite good through great calamity. This entire and patient relinquishment of immediate success, this ever present persuasion, that he was to perish before his religion would advance, and this calm, unshaken anticipation of distant and unbounded triumphs, are remarkable traits, throwing a tender and solemn grandeur over our Lord, and wholly inexplicable by human principles, or by the circumstances in which he was placed.

The views hitherto taken of Christ relate to his public character and office. If we pass to what may be called his private character, we shall receive the same impression of inexplicable excellence. The most strik ing trait in Jesus was, undoubtedly, benevolence; and, although this virtue had existed before, yet it had not been manifested in the same form and extent. Christ's benevolence was distinguished first by its expansiveness. At that age, an unconfined philanthropy, proposing and toiling to do good without distinction of country or rank, was unknown. Love to man as man, love comprehending the hated Samaritan and the despised publican, was a feature which separated Jesus from the best men of his nation and of the world. Another characteristic of the benevolence of Jesus, was its gentleness and tenderness, forming a strong contrast with the hardness and ferocity of the spirit and manners which then prevailed, and with that sternness and inflexibility, which the purest philosophy of Greece and Rome inculcated as the perfection of virtue. But its most distinguishing trait was its superiority to injury. Revenge was one of the recognised rights of the age in which he lived; and though a few sages, who had seen its inconsistency with man's dignity, had condemned it, yet none had inculcated the duty of regarding one's worst enemies with that kindness which God manifests to sinful men, and of returning curses with blessings and prayers. This form of benevolence, the most disinterested and divine form, was, as you well know, manifested by Jesus Christ in infinite strength, amidst injuries and indignities which cannot be surpassed. Now this singular eminence of goodness, this superiority to the degrading influences of the age, under which all other men suffered, needs to be explained; and one thing it demonstrates, that Jesus Christ was not an unprincipled deceiver, exposing not only his own life but the lives of confiding friends, in an enterprise next to desperate.

11*

I cannot enlarge on other traits of the character of Christ. I will only observe, that it had one distinction, which more than any thing, forms a perfect character. It was made up of contrasts; in other words, it was a union of excellences which are not easily reconciled, which seem at first sight incongruous, but which, when blended and duly proportioned, constitute moral harmony, and attract, with equal power, love and veneration. For example, we discover in Jesus Christ an unparalleled dignity of character, a consciousness of greatness, never discovered or approached by any other individual in history; and yet this was blended with a condescension, lowliness, and unostentatious simplicity, which had never before been thought consistent with greatness. In like manner, he united an utter superiority to the world, to its pleasures and ordinary interests, with suavity of manners and freedom from austerity He joined strong feeling and self-possession; an indignant sensibility to sin, and compassion to the sinner; an intense devotion to his work, and calmness under opposition and ill success; a universal philanthropy, and a susceptibility of private attachments; the authority which became the Saviour of the world, and the tenderness and gratitude of a son. Such was the author of our religion. And is his character to be explained by imposture or insane enthusiasm? Does it not bear the unambiguous marks of a heavenly origin?

Perhaps it may be said, this character never existed. Then the invention of it is to be explained, and the reception which this fiction met with; and these perhaps are as difficult of explanation on natural principles, as its real existence. Christ's history bears all the marks of reality; a more frank, simple, unlabored, unostentatious narrative was never penned. Besides, his character, if invented, must have been an invention of singular difficulty, because no models existed on which to frame it. He stands alone in the records of time. The conception of a being, proposing such new and exalted ends, and governed by higher principles than the progress of society had developed, implies singular intellectual power. That several individuals should join in equally vivid conceptions of this character; and should not merely describe in general terms the fictitious being to whom it was attributed, but should introduce him into real life, should place him in a great variety of circumstances, in connexion with various ranks of men, with friends and foes, and should in all preserve his identity, show the same great and singular mind always acting in harmony with itself; this is a supposition hardly credible, and, when the circumstances of the writers of the New Testament are considered, seems to be as inexplicable on human principles, as what I before suggested, the composition of Newton's "Principia" by a savage. The character of Christ, though delineated in an age of great moral darkness, has stood the scrutiny of ages; and, in proportion as men's moral sentiments have been refined, its beauty has been more seen and felt. To suppose it invented, is to suppose that its authors, outstripping their age, had attained to a singular delicacy and elevation of moral perception and feeling. But these attainments are not very reconcilable with the character of its authors, supposing it to be a fiction; that is, with the character of habitual liars and impious deceivers.

But we are not only unable to discover powers adequate to this invention. There must have been motives for it ; for men do not make great efforts, without strong motives ; and, in the whole compass of human incitements, we challenge the infidel to suggest any, which could have prompted to the work now to be explained.

Once more, it must be recollected, that this invention, if it were one, was received as real, at a period so near to the time ascribed to Christ's appearance, that the means of detecting it were infinite. That men should send out such a forgery, and that it should prevail and triumph, are circumstances not easily reconcilable with the principles of our nature.

The character of Christ, then, was real. Its reality is the only explanation of the mighty revolution produced by his religion. And how can you account for it, but by that cause to which he always referred it,—a mission from the Father ?

Next to the character of Christ, his religion might be shown to abound in circumstances which contradict and repel the idea of a human origin. For example, its representations of the paternal character of God ; its inculcation of a universal charity ; the stress which it lays on inward purity ; its substitution of a spiritual worship for the forms and ceremonies, which everywhere had usurped the name and extinguished the life of religion ; its preference of humility, and of the mild, unostentatious, passive virtues, to the dazzling qualities which had monopolized men's admiration ; its consistent and bright discoveries of immortality ; its adaptation to the wants of man as a sinner ; its adaptation to all the conditions, capacities, and sufferings of human nature ; its pure, sublime, yet practicable morality ; its high and generous motives ; and its fitness to form a character, which plainly prepares for a higher life than the present; these are peculiarities of Christianity, which will strike us more and more, in proportion as we understand distinctly the circumstances of the age and country in which this religion appeared, and for which no adequate human cause has been or can be assigned.

Passing over these topics, each of which might be enlarged into a discourse, I will make but one remark on this religion, which strikes my own mind very forcibly. Since its introduction, human nature has made great progress, and society experienced great changes; and in this advanced condition of the world, Christianity, instead of losing its application and importance, is found to be more and more congenial and adapted to man's nature and wants. Men have outgrown the other institutions of that period when Christianity appeared, its philosophy, its modes of warfare, its policy, its public and private economy; but Christianity has never shrunk as intellect has opened, but has always kept in advance of men's faculties, and unfolded nobler views in proportion as they have ascended. The highest powers and affections, which our nature has developed, find more than adequate objects in this religion. Christianity is indeed peculiarly fitted to the more improved stages of society, to the more delicate sensibilities of refined minds, and especially to that dissatisfaction with the present state, which always grows with the growth of our moral powers and affections. As men advance in civilization, they become susceptible of mental sufferings, to which ruder ages are strangers; and these Christianity is fitted to assuage. Imagination and intellect become more restless; and Christianity brings them tranquillity, by the eternal and magnificent truths, the solemn and unbounded prospects, which it unfolds. This fitness of our religion to more advanced stages of society than that in which it was introduced, to wants of human nature not then developed, seems to me very striking. The religion bears the marks of having come from a being who perfectly understood the human mind, and had power to provide for its progress. This feature of Christianity is of the nature of prophecy. It was an anticipation of future and distant ages; and, when we consider among whom our religion sprung, where, but in God, can we find an explanation of this peculiarity?

I have now offered a few hints on the character of Christ, and on the character of his religion; and, before quitting these topics, I would observe, that they form a strong presumption in favor of the miraculous facts of the Christian history. These miracles were not wrought by a man, whose character, in other respects, was ordinary. They were acts of a being, whose mind was as singular as his works, who spoke and acted with more than human authority, whose moral qualities and sublime purposes were in accordance with superhuman powers. Christ's miracles are in unison with his whole character, and bear a proportion to it, like that which we observe in the most harmonious productions of nature; and in this way they receive from it great confirmation. And the same presumption in their favor arises from his religion. That a religion, carrying in itself such marks of divinity, and so inexplicable on human principles, should receive outward confirmations from Omnipotence, is not surprising. The extraordinary character of the religion accords with and seems to demand extraordinary interpositions in its behalf. Its miracles are not solitary, naked, unexplained, disconnected events, but are bound up with a system, which is worthy of God, and impressed with God; which occupies a large space, and is operating, with great and increasing energy, in human affairs.

As yet I have not touched on what seem to many writers the strongest proofs of Christianity, I mean the direct evidences of its miracles; by which we mean the testimony borne to them, including the character, conduct, and condition of the witnesses. These I have not time to unfold; nor is this labor needed; for Paley's inestimable work, which is one of your classical books, has stated these proofs with great clearness and power. I would only observe, that they may all be resolved into this single principle, namely, that the Christian miracles were originally believed under such circumstances, that this belief can only be explained by their actual occurrence. That Christianity was received at first on the ground of miracles, and that its first preachers and converts proved the depth and strength of their conviction of these facts, by attesting them in sufferings and in death, we know from the most ancient records which relate to this religion, both Christian and Heathen; and, in fact, this conviction can alone explain their adherence to Christianity. Now, that this conviction could only have sprung from the reality of the miracles, we infer from the known circumstances of these witnesses, whose passions, interests, and strongest prejudices were originally hostile to the new religion; whose motives for examining with care the facts on which it rested, were as urgent and solemn, and whose means and opportunities of ascertaining their truth were as ample and unfailing, as can be conceived to conspire; so that the supposition of their falsehood cannot be admitted, without subverting our trust in human judgment and human testimony under the most favorable circumstances for discovering truth; that is, without introducing universal skepticism.

There is one class of Christian evidences, to which I have but slightly referred, but which has struck with peculiar force men of reflecting minds. I refer to the marks of truth and reality, which are found in the Christian Records; to the internal proofs, which the books of the New Testament carry with them, of having been written by men who lived in the first age of Christianity, who believed and felt its truth, who bore a part in the labors and conflicts which attended its establishment, and who wrote from personal knowledge and deep conviction. A few remarks to illustrate the nature and power of these internal proofs, which are furnished by the books of the New Testament, I will now subjoin.

The New Testament consists of histories and epistles. The historical books, namely, the Gospels and the Acts, are a continued narrative, embracing many years, and professing to give the history of the rise and progress of the religion. Now it is worthy of observation, that these writings completely answer their end; that they completely solve the problem, how this peculiar religion grew up and established itself in the world; that they furnish precise and adequate causes for this stupendous revolution in human affairs. It is also worthy of remark, that they relate a series of facts, which are not only connected with one another, but are intimately linked with the long series which has followed them, and agree accurately with subsequent history, so as to account for and sustain it. Now, that a collection of fictitious narratives, coming from different hands, comprehending many years, and spreading over many countries, should not only form a consistent whole, when taken by themselves; but should also connect and interweave themselves with real history so naturally and intimately, as to furnish no clue for detection, as to exclude the appearance of incongruity and discordance, and as to give an adequate explanation and the only explanation of acknowledged events, of the most important revolution in society; this is a supposition from which an intelligent man at once revolts, and which, if admitted, would shake a principal foundation of history.

I have before spoken of the unity and consistency of Christ's character as developed in the Gospels, and of the agreement of the different writers in giving us the singular features of his mind. Now there are the same marks of truth running through the whole of these narratives. For example, the effects produced by Jesus on the various classes of society; the different feelings of admiration, attachment, and envy, which he called forth; the various expressions of these feelings; the prejudices, mistakes, and gradual illumination of his disciples; these are all given to us with such marks of truth and reality as could not easily be counterfeited. The whole history is precisely such, as might be expected from the actual appearance of such a person as Jesus Christ, in such a state of society as then existed.

The Epistles, if possible, abound in marks of truth and reality even more than the Gospels. They are imbued thoroughly with the spirit of the first age of Christianity. They bear all the marks of having come from men plunged in the conflicts which the new religion excited, alive to its interests, identified with its fortunes. They betray the very state of mind which must have been generated by the peculiar condition of the first propagators of the religion. They are letters written on real business, intended for immediate effects, designed to meet prejudices and passions, which such a religion must at first have awakened. They contain not a trace of the circumstances of a later age, or of the feelings, impressions, and modes of thinking by which later times were characterized, and from which later writers could not easily have escaped. The letters of Paul have a remarkable agreement with his history. They are precisely such as might be expected from a man of a vehement mind, who had been brought up in the schools of Jewish literature, who had been converted by a sudden, overwhelming miracle, who had been intrusted with the preaching of the new religion to the Gentiles, and who was everywhere met by the prejudices and persecuting spirit of his own nation. They are full of obscurities growing out of these points of Paul's history and character, and out of the circumstances of the infant church, and which nothing but an intimate acquaintance with that early period can illustrate. This remarkable infusion of the spirit of the first age into the Christian Records, cannot easily be explained but by the fact, that they were written in that age by the real and zealous propagators of Christianity, and that they are records of real convictions and of actual events.

There is another evidence of Christianity, still more internal than any on which I have yet dwelt, an evidence to be felt rather than described, but not less real because founded on feeling. I refer to that conviction of the divine original of our religion, which springs up and continually gains strength, in those who apply it habitually to their tempers and lives, and who imbibe its spirit and hopes. In such men, there is a consciousness of the adaptation of Christianity to their noblest faculties; a consciousness of its exalting and consoling influences, of its power to confer the true happiness of human nature, to give that peace which the world cannot give; which assures them, that it is not of earthly origin, but a ray from the Everlasting Light, a stream from the Fountain of Heavenly Wisdom and Love. This is the evidence which sustains the faith of thousands, who never read and cannot understand the learned books of Christian apologists, who want, perhaps, words to explain the ground of their belief, but whose faith is of adamantine firmness, who hold the Gospel with a conviction more intimate and unwavering than mere argument ever produced.

But I must tear myself from a subject, which opens upon me continually as I proceed. — Imperfect as this discussion is, the conclusion, I trust, is placed beyond doubt, that Christianity is true. And, my hearers, if true, it is the greatest of all truths, deserving and demanding our reverent attention and fervent gratitude. This religion must never be confounded with our common blessings. It is a revelation of pardon, which, as sinners, we all need. Still more, it is a revelation of human immortality; a doctrine, which, however undervalued amidst the bright anticipations of inexperienced youth, is found to be our strength and consolation, and the only effectual spring of persevering and victorious virtue, when the realities of life have scattered our visionary hopes; when pain, disappointment, and temptation press upon us ; when this world's enjoyments are found unable to quench that deep thirst of happiness which burns in every breast ; when friends, whom we love as our own souls, die ; and our own graves open before us. — To all who hear me, and especially to my young hearers, I would say, let the truth of this religion be the strongest conviction of your understandings ; let its motives and precepts sway with an absolute power your characters and lives.

THE

DEMANDS OF THE AGE ON THE MINISTRY.

DISCOURSE

AT THE

ORDINATION OF THE REV. E. S. GANNETT.

Boston, 1824.

MATTHEW x. 16: " Behold I send you forth as sheep in tne midst of wolves : be ye therefore wise as serpents and harmless as doves."

THE communication of moral and religious truth is the most important office committed to men. The Son of God came into the world, not to legislate for nations, not to command armies, not to sit on the throne of universal monarchy ; but to teach religion, to establish truth and holiness. The highest end of human nature is duty, virtue, piety, excellence, moral greatness, spiritual glory ; and he who effectually labors for these, is taking part with God, in God's noblest work. The Christian ministry, then, which has for its purpose men's spiritual improvement and salvation, and which is intrusted for this end with weapons of heavenly temper and power, deserves to be ranked amongst God's most beneficent institutions and men's most honorable labors. ~he occasion requires that this institution should be our principal topic.

How happy a change has taken place since the words of Christ in the text were spoken! Ministers are no longer sent forth into the midst of wolves. Through the labors, sufferings, and triumphs of apostles, martyrs, and good and great men in successive ages, Christianity has become the professed and honored religion of the most civilized nations, and its preachers are exposed to very different temptations from those of savage persecution. Still our text has an application to the present time. We see our Saviour commanding his Apostles, to regard in their ministry the circumstances of the age in which they lived. Surrounded with foes, they were to exercise the wisdom or prudence of which the serpent was in ancient times the emblem, and to join with it the innocence and mildness of the dove. And, in like manner, the Christian minister is at all periods to regard the signs, the distinctive marks and character of the age to which he belongs, and must accommodate his ministry to its wants and demands. Accordingly, I propose to consider some of the leading traits of the present age, and the influence which they should have on a Christian teacher.

I. The state of the world, compared with the past, may be called enlightened, and requires an enlightened ministry. It hardly seems necessary to prove, that religion should be dispensed by men who at least keep pace with the intellect of the age in which they live. Some passages of Scripture, however, have been wrested to prove, that an unlearned ministry is that which God particularly honors. He always chooses, we are told.

"the foolish things of the world to confound the wise." But texts of this description are misunderstood, through the very ignorance which they are adduced to support. The wise, who are spoken of contemptuously in the New Testament, were not really enlightened men, but pretenders to wisdom, who substituted dreams of imagination and wild hypotheses for sober inquiry into God's works, and who knew comparatively nothing of nature or the human mind. The present age has a quite different illumination from that in which ancient philosophy prided itself. It is marked by great and obvious improvements in the methods of reasoning and inquiry, and by the consequent discovery and diffusion of a great mass of physical and moral truth, wholly unknown in the time of Christ. Now we affirm, that such an age demands an enlightened ministry. We want teachers, who will be able to discern and unfold the consistency of revealed religion with the new lights which are breaking in from nature ; and who will be able to draw, from all men's discoveries in the outward world and in their own souls, illustrations, analogies, and arguments for Christianity. We have reason to believe, that God, the author of nature and revelation, has established a harmony between them, and that their beams are intended to mingle and shed a joint radiance ; and, consequently, other things being equal, that teacher is best fitted to dispense Christianity, whose compass of mind enables him to compare what God is teaching in his Works and in his Word, and to present the truths of religion with those modifications and restraints which other acknowledged truths require. Christianity now needs dispensers, who will make history, nature, and the improvements of society, tributary to its elucidation and support ; who will show its adaptation to man as an ever progressive being ; who will be able to meet the objections to its truth, which will naturally be started in an active, stirring, inquiring age ; and, though last not least, who will have enough of mental and moral courage to detect and renounce the errors in the Church, on which such objections are generally built. In such an age, a ministry is wanted, which will furnish discussions of religious topics, not inferior at least in intelligence to those which people are accustomed to read and hear on other subjects. Christianity will suffer, if at a time when vigor and acuteness of thinking are carried into all other departments, the pulpit should send forth nothing but wild declamation, positive assertion, or dull commonplaces, with which even childhood is satiated. Religion must be seen to be the friend and quickener of intellect. It must be exhibited with clearness of reasoning and variety of illustration ; nor ought it to be deprived of the benefits of a pure and felicitous diction and of rich and glowing imagery, where these gifts fall to the lot of the teacher. It is not meant that every minister must be a man of genius ; for genius is one of God's rarest inspirations ; and of all the breathings of genius, perhaps the rarest is eloquence. I mean only to say, that the age demands of those, who devote themselves to the administration of Christianity, that they should feel themselves called upon for the highest cultivation and fullest developement of the intellectual nature. Instead of thinking, that the ministry is a refuge for dulness, and that whoever can escape from the plough is fit for God's spiritual husbandry, we ought to feel that no profession demands more enlarged thinking and more various acquisitions of truth.

In proportion as society becomes enlightened, talent acquires influence. In rude ages bodily strength is the most honorable distinction, and in subsequent times military prowess and skill confer mastery and eminence. But as society advances, mind, thought, becomes the sovereign of the world; and accordingly, at the present moment, profound and glowing thought, though breathing only from the silent page, exerts a kind of omnipotent and omnipresent energy. It crosses oceans and spreads through nations; and, at one and the same moment, the conceptions of a single mind are electrifying and kindling multitudes, through wider regions than the Roman eagle overshadowed. This agency of mind on mind, I repeat it, is the true sovereignty of the world, and kings and heroes are becoming impotent by the side of men of deep and fervent thought. In such a state of things, religion would wage a very unequal war, if divorced from talent and cultivated intellect, if committed to weak and untaught minds. God plainly intends, that it should be advanced by human agency; and does he not then intend, to summon to its aid the mightiest and noblest power with which man is gifted?

Let it not be said, that Christianity has an intrinsic glory, a native beauty, which no art or talent of man can heighten; that Christianity is one and the same, by whatever lips it is communicated, and that it needs nothing but the most naked exposition of its truths, to accomplish its saving purposes. Who does not know, that all truth takes a hue and form from the soul through which it passes, that in every mind it is invested with peculiar associations, and that, consequently, the same truth is quite a different thing, when exhibited by men of different habits of thought and feeling? Who does not know, that the sublimest doctrines lose in some hands all their grandeur, and the loveliest all their attractiveness? Who does not know, how much the diffusion and power of any system, whether physical, moral, or political, depend on the order according to which it is arranged, on the broad and consistent views which are given of it, on the connexions which it is shown to hold with other truths, on the analogies by which it is illustrated, adorned, and enforced, and, though last not least, on the clearness and energy of the style in which it is conveyed? "Nothing is needed in religion," some say, "but the naked truth." But I apprehend that there is no such thing as naked truth, at least as far as moral subjects are concerned. Truth which relates to God, and duty, and happiness, and a future state, is always humanized, if I may so use the word, by passing through a human mind; and, when communicated powerfully, it always comes to us in drapery thrown round it by the imagination, reason, and moral feelings of the teacher. It comes to us warm and living with the impressions and affections which it has produced in the soul from which it issues; and it ought so to come; for the highest evidence of moral truth is found in the moral principles and feelings of our nature, and therefore it fails of its best support, unless it is seen to accord with and to act upon these. The evidence of Christianity, which operates most universally, is not history nor miracles, but its correspondence to the noblest capacities, deepest wants, and purest aspirations of our nature, to the cravings of an immortal spirit; and when it comes to us from a mind, in which it has discovered nothing of this adaptation, and has touched none of these springs, it wants one of its chief signatures of divinity. Christianity is not, then, to be exhibited nakedly. It owes much of its power to the mind which communicates it; and the greater the enlargement and developement of the mind of which it has possessed itself, and from which it flows, the wider and deeper will be its action on other souls.

It may be said, without censoriousness, that the ordinary mode, in which Christianity has been exhibited in past times, does not suit the illumination of the present. That mode has been too narrow, technical, pedantic. Religion has been made a separate business, and a dull, unsocial, melancholy business, too, instead of being manifested as a truth which bears on and touches every thing human, as a universal spirit, which ought to breathe through and modify all our desires and pursuits, all our trains of thought and emotion. And this narrow, forbidden mode of exhibiting Christianity, is easily explained by its early history. Monks shut up in cells; a priesthood cut off by celibacy from the sympathies and most interesting relations of life; and universities enslaved to a scholastic logic, and taught to place wisdom in verbal subtilties and unintelligible definitions; these took Christianity into their keeping; and at their chilling touch, this generous religion, so full of life and affection, became a dry, frigid, abstract system. Christianity, as it came from their hands, and has been transmitted by a majority of Protestant divines, reminds us of the human form, compressed by swathing-bands, until every joint is rigid, every movement constrained, and almost all the beauty and grace of nature obliterated. Instead of regarding it as a heavenly institution, designed to perfect our whole nature, to offer awakening and purifying objects to the intellect, imagination, and heart, to develope every capacity of devout and social feeling, to form a rich, various, generous virtue, divines have cramped and tortured the Gospel into various systems, composed in the main of theological riddles and contradictions ; and this religion of love has been made to inculcate a monkish and dark-visaged piety, very hostile to the free expansion and full enjoyment of all our faculties and social affections. Great improvements indeed in this particular are taking place among Christians of almost every denomination. Religion has been brought from the cell of the monk, and the school of the verbal disputant, into life and society; and its connexions with all our pursuits and feelings have been made manifest. Still, Christianity, I apprehend, is not viewed in sufficiently broad lights to meet the spirit of an age, which is tracing connexions between all objects of thought and branches of knowledge, and which cannot but distrust an alleged revelation, in as far as it is seen to want harmonies and affinities with other parts of God's system, and especially with human nature and human life.

II. The age in which we live demands not only an enlightened but an earnest ministry, for it is an age of earnestness and excitement. Men feel and think at present with more energy than formerly. There is more of interest and fervor. We learn now from experience what might have been inferred from the purposes of our Creator, that civilization and refinement are not, as has been sometimes thought, inconsistent with sensibility ; that the intellect may grow without exhausting or overshadowing the heart. The human mind was never more in earnest than at the present moment. The political revolutions, which form such broad features and distinctions of our age, have sprung from a new and deep working in the human soul. Men have caught glimpses, however indistinct, of the worth, dignity, rights, and great interests of their nature; and a thirst for untried good, and impatience of long endured wrongs, have broken out wildly, like the fires of Etna, and shaken and convulsed the earth. It is impossible not to discern this increased fervor of mind in every department of life. A new spirit of improvement is abroad. The imagination can no longer be confined to the acquisitions of past ages, but is kindling the passions by vague but noble ideas of blessings never yet attained. Multitudes, unwilling to wait the slow pace of that great innovator, time, are taking the work of reform into their own hands. Accordingly, the reverence for antiquity and for age-hallowed establishments, and the passion for change and amelioration, are now arrayed against each other in open hostility, and all great questions, affecting human happiness, are debated with the eagerness of party. The character of the age is stamped very strongly on its literary productions. Who, that can compare the present with the past, is not struck with the bold and earnest spirit of the literature of our times. It refuses to waste itself on trifles, or to minister to mere gratification. Almost all that is written has now some bearing on great interests of human nature. Fiction is no longer a mere amusement; but transcendent genius, accommodating itself to the character of the age, has seized upon this province of literature, and turned fiction from a toy into a mighty engine, and, under the light tale, is breathing through the community either its reverence for the old or its thirst for the new, communicates the spirit and lessons of history, unfolds the operations of religious and civil institutions, and defends or assails new theories of education or morals by exhibiting them in life and action. The poetry of the age is equally characteristic. It has a deeper and more impressive tone than comes to us from what has been called the Augustan age of English literature. The regular, elaborate, harmonious strains, which delighted a former generation, are now accused, I say not how justly, of playing too much on the surface of nature and of the heart. Men want and demand a more thrilling note, a poetry which pierces beneath the exterior of life to the depths of the soul, and which lays open its mysterious workings, borrowing from the whole outward creation fresh images and correspondences, with which to illuminate the secrets of the world within us. So keen is this appetite, that extravagances of imagination, and gross violations both of taste and moral sentiment, are forgiven, when conjoined with what awakens strong emotion; and unhappily the most stirring is the most popular poetry, even though it issue from the desolate soul of a misanthrope and a libertine, and exhale poison and death.

Now, religion ought to be dispensed in accommodation to this spirit and character of our age. Men desire excitement, and religion must be communicated in a more exciting form. It must be seen not only to correspond and to be adapted to the intellect, but to furnish nutriment and appeals to the highest and profoundest sentiments of our nature. It must not be exhibited in the dry, pedantic divisions of a scholastic theology; nor must it be set forth and tricked out in the light drapery of an artificial rhetoric, in prettinesses of style, in measured sentences, with an insipid floridness, and in the form of elegantly feeble essays. No; it must come from the soul in the language of earnest conviction and strong feeling. Men will not now be trifled with. They listen impatiently to great subjects treated with apathy. They want a religion which will take a strong hold upon them; and no system, I am sure, can now maintain its ground, which wants the power of awakening real and deep interest in the soul. It is objected to Unitarian Christianity, that it does not possess this heart-stirring energy; and if so, it will, and still more, it ought to fall; for it does not suit the spirit of our times, nor the essential and abiding spirit of human nature. Men will prefer even a fanaticism which is in earnest, to a pretended rationality, which leaves untouched all the great springs of the soul, which never lays a quickening hand on our love and veneration, our awe and fear, our hope and joy.

It is obvious, I think, that the spirit of the age, which demands a more exciting administration of Christianity, begins to be understood and is responded to by preachers. Those of us, whose memory extends back but a little way, can see a revolution taking place in this country. "The repose of the pulpit" has been disturbed. In England, the Established Church gives broad symptoms of awaking; and the slumbering incumbents of a state religion, either roused by sympathy, or aware of the necessity of self-defence, are beginning to exhibit the energy of the freer and more zealous sects around them.

In such an age, earnestness should characterize the ministry; and by this I mean, not a louder voice or a more vehement gesture; I mean no tricks of oratory; but a solemn conviction that religion is a great concern, and a solemn purpose that its claims shall be felt by others. To suit such an age, a minister must communicate religion, not only as a result of reasoning, but as a matter of experience, with that inexpressible character of reality, that life and power, which accompany truths drawn from a man's own soul. We ought to speak of religion as something which we ourselves know. Its influences, struggles, joys, sorrows, triumphs, should be delineated from our own history. The life and sensibility which we would spread, should be strong in our own breasts. This is the only genuine, unfailing spring of an earnest ministry. Men may work themselves for a time into a fervor by artificial means; but the flame is unsteady, "a crackling of thorns" on a cold hearth; and, after all, it is hard for the most successful art to give, even for a time, that soul-subduing tone to the voice, that air of native feeling to the countenance, and that raciness and freshness to the conceptions, which come from an experimental conviction of religious truth; and, accordingly, I would suggest, that the most important part of theological education, even in this enlightened age, is not the communication of knowledge, essential as that is, but the conversion and exaltation of religious knowledge into a living, practical, and soul-kindling conviction. Much as the age requires intellectual culture in a minister, it requires still more, that his acquisitions of truth should be instinct with life and feeling; that he should deliver his message, not mechanically and "in the line of his profession," but with the sincerity and earnestness of a man bent on great effects; that he should speak of

God, of Christ, of the dignity and loveliness of Christian virtue, of heaven and redemption, not as of traditions and historical records, about which he has only read, but as of realities which he understands and feels in the very depths of his soul.

III. The present is an age of free and earnest inquiry on the subject of religion, and, consequently, an age in which the extremes of skepticism and bigotry, and a multiplicity of sects, and a diversity of interpretations of the Sacred Volume, must be expected; and these circumstances of the times influence and modify the duties of the ministry. Free inquiry cannot exist without generating a degree of skepticism; and against this influence, more disastrous than any error of any sect, a minister is bound to erect every barrier. The human mind, by a natural reaction, is undoubtedly tending, after its long vassalage, to licentious speculation. Men have begun to send keen, searching glances into old institutions, whether of religion, literature, or policy; and have detected so many abuses, that a suspicion of what is old has in many cases taken place of the veneration for antiquity. In such an age, Christianity must be subjected to a rigid scrutiny. Church establishments and state patronage cannot screen it from investigation; and its ministers, far from being called to remove it from the bar of reason, where God has chosen that it should appear, are only bound to see that its claims be fairly and fully made known; and to this they are solemnly bound; and, consequently, it is one of their first duties to search deeply and understand thoroughly the true foundations and evidences, on which the religion stands. Now it seems to me, that just in proportion as the human mind makes progress, the inward evidences of Christianity, the marks of divinity which it wears on its own brow, are becoming more and more important. I refer to the evidences which are drawn from its excellence, purity, and happy influences ; from its adaptation to the spiritual wants, to the weakness and the greatness of human nature ; from the original and unborrowed character, the greatness of soul, and the celestial loveliness of its Founder ; from its unbounded benevolence, corresponding with the spirit of the universe ; and from its views of God's parental character and purposes, of human duty and perfection, and of a future state ; views manifestly tending to the exaltation and perpetual improvement of our nature, yet wholly opposed to the character of the age in which they were unfolded. The historical and miraculous proofs of Christianity are indeed essential and impregnable ; but, without superseding these, the inward proofs, of which I speak, are becoming more and more necessary, and exert a greater power, in proportion as the moral discernment and sensibilities of men are strengthened and enlarged. And, if this be true, then Christianity is endangered, and skepticism fortified, by nothing so much as by representations of the religion, which sully its native lustre and darken its inward signatures of a heavenly origin ; and, accordingly, the first and most solemn duty of its ministers is, to rescue it from such perversions ; to see that it be not condemned for doctrines for which it is in no respect responsible ; and to vindicate its character as eminently a rational religion, that is, a religion consistent with itself, with the great principles of human nature, with God's acknowledged attributes, and with those indestructible convictions, which spring almost instinctively from our moral constitution, and which grow stronger and stronger as the human mind is developed. A professed revelation, carrying contradiction on its front, and wounding those sentiments of justice and goodness, which are the highest tests of moral truth, cannot stand ; and those who thus exhibit Christianity, however pure their aim, are shaking its foundations more deeply than its open and inveterate foes.

But free inquiry not only generates occasional skepticism, but much more a diversity of opinion among the believers of Christianity ; and to this the ministry must have a special adaptation. In such an age, the ministry must in a measure be controversial. In particular, a minister, who after serious investigation attaches himself to that class of Christians, to which we of this religious society are known to belong, cannot but feel that the painful office of conflict with other denominations is laid upon him ; for, whilst we deny the Christian name to none who acknowledge Jesus as their Saviour and Lord, we do deliberately believe, that, by many who confess him, his religion is mournfully disfigured. We believe, that piety at present is robbed in no small degree of its singleness, energy, and happiness, by the multiplication in the church of objects of supreme worship ; by the division of the One God into three persons, who sustain different relations to mankind ; and, above all, by the dishonorable views formed of the moral character and administration of the Deity. Errors relating to God seem to us among the most pernicious that can grow up among Christians ; for they darken, and, in the strong language of Scripture, " turn into blood," the Sun of the Spiritual Universe.

Around just views of the Divine character all truths and all virtues naturally gather; and although some minds of native irrepressible vigor may rise to greatness, in spite of dishonorable conceptions of God, yet, as a general rule, human nature cannot spread to its just and full proportions under their appalling, enslaving, heart-withering control. We discover very plainly, as we think, in the frequent torpor of the conscience and heart in regard to religious obligation, the melancholy influences of that system, so prevalent among us, which robs our heavenly Father of his parental attributes. Indeed it seems impossible for the conscience, under such injurious representations of the Divine character, to discharge intelligently its solemn office of enforcing love to God as man's highest duty; and, accordingly, when religious excitements take place under this gloomy system, they bear the marks of a morbid action, much more than of a healthy, restorative process of the moral nature.

These errors a minister of liberal views of Christianity will feel himself bound to withstand. But let me not be understood, as if I would have the ministry given chiefly to controversy, and would turn the pulpit into a battery for the perpetual assault of adverse sects. O, no. Other strains than those of warfare should predominate in this sacred place. A minister may be faithful to truth, without brandishing perpetually the weapons of controversy. Occasional discussions of disputed doctrines are indeed demanded by the zeal with which error is maintained. But it becomes the preacher to remember, that there is a silent, indirect influence, more sure and powerful than direct assault on false opinons. The most effectual method of expelling error, is, not to meet it sword in hand, but gradually to instil great truths, with which it cannot easily coexist, and by which the mind outgrows it. Men who have been recovered from false systems, will generally tell you, that the first step of their deliverance was the admission of some principle which seemed not to menace their past opinions, but which prepared the mind for the entrance of another and another truth, until they were brought, almost without suspecting it, to look on almost every doctrine of religion with other eyes, and in another and more generous light. The old superstitions about ghosts and dreams were not expelled by argument, for hardly a book was written against them; but men gradually outgrew them; and the spectres, which had haunted the terror-stricken soul for ages, fled before an improved philosophy, just as they were supposed to vanish before the rising sun. And, in the same manner, the errors which disfigure Christianity, and from which no creed is free, are to yield to the growth of the human mind. Instead of spending his strength in tracking and refuting error, let the minister, who would serve the cause of truth, labor to gain and diffuse more and more enlarged and lofty views of our religion, of its nature, spirit, and end. Let him labor to separate what is of universal and everlasting application, from the local and the temporary; to penetrate beneath the letter to the spirit; to detach the primary, essential, and all-comprehending principles of Christianity from the incrustations, accidental associations, and subordinate appendages by which they are often obscured; and to fix and establish these in men's minds as the standard by which more partial views are to be tried Let him especially set forth the great moral purpose of

Christianity, always teaching, that Christ came to deliver from the power still more than from the punishment of sin; that his most important operation is within us; and that the highest end of his mission is, the erection of God's throne in the soul, the inspiration of a fervent filial piety, a piety founded in confiding views of God's parental character, and manifested in a charity corresponding to God's unbounded and ever-active love. In addition to these efforts, let him strive to communicate the just principles of interpreting the Scriptures, that men, reading them more intelligently, may read them with new interest, and he will have discharged his chief duty in relation to controversy.

It is an interesting thought, that, through the influences now described, a sensible progress is taking place in men's conceptions of Christianity. It is a plain matter of fact, that the hard features of that religious system, which has been "received by tradition from our fathers," are greatly softened; and that a necessity is felt by those who hold it, of accommodating their representations of it more and more to the improved philosophy of the human mind, and to the undeniable principles of natural and revealed religion. Unconditional Election is seldom heard of among us. The Imputation of Adam's sin to his posterity, is hastening to join the exploded doctrine of Transubstantiation. The more revolting representations of man's state by nature, are judiciously kept out of sight; and, what is of still greater importance, preaching is incomparably more practical than formerly. And all these changes are owing, not to theological controversy so much as to the general progress of the human mind. This progress is especially discernible in the diminished importance now as cribed to the outward parts of Christianity. Christians, having grown up to understand that their religion is a spirit and not a form, are beginning to feel the puerility as well as guilt of breaking Christ's followers into factions, on such questions as these, How much a Bishop differs from a Presbyter? and, How great a quantity of water should be used in baptism? And, whilst they desire to ascertain the truth in these particulars, they look back on the uncharitable heat with which these and similar topics were once discussed, with something of the wonder which they feel, on recollecting the violence of the Papists during the memorable debate, Whether the Virgin Mary were born with original sin? It is a consoling and delightful thought, that God, who uses Christianity to advance civilization and knowledge, makes use of this very advancement to bring back Christianity to a purer state, thus binding together, and carrying forward by mutual action, the cause of knowledge and the cause of religion, and strengthening perpetually their blended and blessed influences on human nature.

IV. The age is in many respects a corrupt one, and needs and demands in the ministry a spirit of reform. The age, I say, is corrupt; not because I consider it as falling below the purity of past times, but because it is obviously and grossly defective, when measured by the Christian standard, and by the lights and advantages which it enjoys. I know nothing to justify the cry of modern degeneracy, but rather incline to the belief, that here at least the sense of religion was never stronger than at present. In comparing different periods as to virtue and piety, regard must be had to difference of circumstances. It would argue little wisdom or candor, to expect the same freedom from luxury and dissipation in this opulent and flourishing community, as marked the first settlement of our country, when the inhabitants, scarcely sheltered from the elements, and almost wholly cut off from intercourse with the civilized word, could command little more than the necessaries of life ; and yet it is through superficial comparisons in such particulars, that the past is often magnified at the expense of the present. I mean not to strike a balance between this age and former ones. I look on this age in the light of Christianity, as a minister ought to look upon it ; and whilst I see much to cheer and encourage, I see much to make a good man mourn, and to stir up Christ's servants to prayer and toil. That our increased comforts, improved arts, and overflowing prosperity are often abused to licentiousness ; that Christianity is with multitudes a mere name and form ; that a practical atheism, which ascribes to nature and fortune the gifts and operations of God, and a practical infidelity, which lives and cares and provides only for the present state, abound on every side of us ; that much which is called morality, springs from a prudent balancing of the passions, and a discreet regard to worldly interests ; that there is an insensibility to God, which, if our own hearts were not infected by it, would shock and amaze us ; that education, instead of guarding and rearing the moral and religious nature as its supreme care, often betrays and sacrifices it to accomplishments and acquisitions which relate only to the present life ; that there is a mournful prevalence of dissoluteness among the young, and of intemperance among the poor ; that the very religion of peace is made a torch of discord ; and that the fires of uncharitableness and bigotry, fires kindled from hell, often burn on altars consecrated to the true God;—that such evils exist, who does not know? What Christian can look round him and say, that the state of society corresponds to wnat men may and should be, under the light of the Gospel, and in an age of advanced intelligence? As for that man, who, on surveying the world, thinks its condition almost as healthy as can be desired or hoped; who sees but a few superficial blots on the general aspect of society; who thinks the ministry established for no higher end, than to perpetuate the present state of morals and religion; whose heart is never burdened and sorrow-smitten by the fearful doom to which multitudes around him are thoughtlessly hastening;— O, let not that man take on him the care of souls. The physician, who should enter a hospital to congratulate his dying patients on their pleasant sensations, and rapid convalescence, would be as faithful to his trust as the minister who sees no deep moral maladies around him. No man is fitted to withstand great evils with energy, unless he be impressed by their greatness. No man is fitted to enter upon that warfare with moral evil, to which the ministry is set apart, who is not pained and pierced by its extent and woes; who does not burn to witness and advance a great moral revolution in the world.

Am I told, that "romantic expectations of great changes in society will do more harm than good; that the world will move along in its present course, let the ministry do what it may; that we must take the present state as God has made it, and not waste our strength in useless lamentation for incurable evils." I hold this language, though it takes the name of philosophy, to be wholly unwarranted by experience and revelation. If there be one striking feature in human nature, it is its susceptibleness of improvement ; and who is authorized to say, that the limit of Christian improvement is reached ? that, whilst science and art, intellect and imagination, are extending their domains, the conscience and affections, the moral and religious principles of our nature, are incapable of increased power and elevation ? Have we not pledges, in man's admiration of disinterested, heroic love ; in his power of conceiving and thirsting for unattained heights of excellence ; and in the splendor and sublimity of virtue already manifested in not a few who "shine as lights" in the darkness of past ages, that man was created for perpetual moral and religious progress ? True, the minister should not yield himself to romantic anticipations ; for disappointment may deject him. Let him not expect to break in a moment chains of habit, which years have riveted, or to bring back to immediate intimacy with God souls which have wandered long and far from him. This is romance ; but there is something to be dreaded by the minister more than this ; I mean, that frigid tameness of mind, too common in Christian teachers, which confounds the actual and the possible ; which cannot burst the shackles of custom ; which never kindles at the thought of great improvements of human nature ; which is satisfied if religion receive an outward respect, and never dreams of enthroning it in men's souls; which looks on the strongholds of sin with despair ; which utters by rote the solemn and magnificent language of the Gospel, without expecting it to "work mightily" ; which sees in the ministry a part of the mechanism of society, a useful guardian of public order, but never suspects the powers with which it is armed by Christianity.

The ministry is indeed armed with great powers for great effects. The doctrines which Christianity commits to its teachers, are mighty engines. The perfect character of God; the tender and solemn attributes, which belong to him as our Father and Judge; his purposes of infinite and everlasting mercy towards the human race; the character and history of Christ; his entire, self-immolating devotion to the cause of mankind; his intimate union with his followers; his sufferings, and cross, his resurrection, ascension, and intercession; the promised aids of the Holy Spirit; the immortality of man; the retributions which await the unrepenting, and the felicities and glories of heaven, — here are truths, able to move the whole soul and to war victoriously with its host of passions. The teacher, to whom are committed the infinite realities of the spiritual world, the sanctions of eternity, "the powers of the life to come," has instruments to work with, which turn to feebleness all other means of influence. There is not heard on earth a voice so powerful, so penetrating, as that of an enlightened minister, who, under the absorbing influence of these mighty truths, devotes himself a living sacrifice, a whole burnt-offering, to the cause of enlightening and saving his fellow-creatures.

No; there is no romance in a minister's proposing, and hoping to forward, a great moral revolution on the earth; for the religion, which he is appointed to preach, was intended and is adapted to work deeply and widely, and to change the face of society. Christianity was not ushered into the world with such a stupendous preparation; it was not foreshown through so many ages by enraptured prophets; it was not proclaimed so joyfully by the songs of angels; it was not preached by such holy lips and sealed by such precious blood, to be only a pageant, a form, a sound, a show. O, no. It has come from heaven, with heaven's life and power, — come to "make all things new," to make "the wilderness glad and the desert blossom as the rose," to break the stony heart, to set free the guilt-burdened and earth-bound spirit, and to "present it faultless before God's glory with exceeding joy." With courage and hope becoming such a religion, let the minister bring to his work the concentrated powers of intellect and affection, and God, in whose cause he labors, will accompany and crown the labor with an almighty blessing.

My brother, you are now to be set apart to the Christian ministry. I bid you welcome to its duties, and implore for you strength to discharge them, a long and prosperous course, increasing success, and everlasting rewards. I also welcome you to the connexion which is this day formed between you and myself. I thank God for an associate, in whose virtues and endowments I have the promise of personal comfort and relief, and, still more, the pledges of usefulness to this people. I have lived too long, to expect unmingled good in this or in any relation of life ; nor am I ignorant of the difficulties and trials, which are thought to attend the union of different minds and different hands in the care of the same church. God grant us that singleness of purpose, that sincere concern for the salvation of our hearers, which will make the success of each the happiness of both. I know, for I have borne, the anxieties and sufferings which belong to the first years of the Christian ministry, and I beg you to avail yourself of whatever aid my experience can give you. But no human aid can lift every burden from your mind ; nor would the truest kindness desire for you exemption from the universal lot. May the discipline, which awaits you, give purity and loftiness to your motives ; give energy and tenderness to your character, and prepare you to minister to the wants of a tempted and afflicted world, with that sympathy and wisdom, which fellowship in suffering can alone bestow. May you grow in grace, and in the spirit of the ministry, as you grow in years ; and, when the voice which now speaks to you shall cease to be heard within these walls, may you, my brother, be left to enjoy and reward the confidence, to point out the path and the perils, to fortify the virtues, to animate the piety, to comfort the sorrows, to save the souls of this much loved people.

Brethren of this Christian Society ! I rejoice in the proof, which this day affords, of your desire to secure the administration of Christ's word and ordinances to yourselves and your children ; and I congratulate you on the prospects which it opens before you. The recollections, which rush upon my mind, of your sympathy and uninterrupted kindness through the vicissitudes of my health and the frequent suspensions of my labors, encourage me to anticipate for my young brother that kindness and candor, on which the happiness of a minister so much depends. I cannot ask for him sincerer attachment, than it has been my lot to enjoy. I remember, however, that the reciprocation of kind feelings is not the highest end of the ministry ; and, accordingly, my most earnest desire and prayer to God is, that, with a new pastor, he may send you new influences of his spirit, and that, through our joint labors, Christianity, being rooted in your understandings and hearts, may spring up into a rich harvest of universal goodness. May a more earnest concern for salvation, and a thirst for more generous improvement, be excited in your breasts. May a new life breathe through the worship of this house, and a new love join the hearts of the worshippers. May our ministry produce everlasting fruits; and on that great day, which will summon the teacher and the taught before the judgment-seat of Christ, may you, my much loved and respected people, be " our joy and crown"; and may we, when all hearts shall be revealed, be seen to have sought your good with unfeigned and disinterested love !

UNITARIAN CHRISTIANITY
MOST FAVORABLE TO PIETY.

DISCOURSE
AT THE
DEDICATION OF THE SECOND CONGREGATIONAL
UNITARIAN CHURCH.
NEW YORK, 1826.

MARK xii. 29, 30 : "And Jesus answered him, The first of all the commandments is, Hear, O Israel; The Lord our God is one Lord. And thou shalt love the Lord thy God with all thy heart, and with all thy soul, and with all thy mind, and with all thy strength. This is the first commandment."

WE have assembled to dedicate this building to the worship of the only living and true God, and to the teaching of the religion of his son, Jesus Christ. By this act we do not expect to confer on this spot of ground and these walls any peculiar sanctity or any mysterious properties. We do not suppose, that, in consequence of rites now performed, the worship offered here will be more acceptable than prayer uttered in the closet, or breathed from the soul in the midst of business; or that the instructions delivered from this pulpit will be more effectual, than if they were uttered in a private dwelling or the open air. By dedication we understand only a solemn expression of the purpose for which this building is reared, joined with prayer to Him, who alone can crown our enterprise with success, that our design may be accepted and fulfilled. For this religious act, we find indeed no precept in the New Testament, and on this account some have scrupled as to its propriety. But we are not among those who consider the written Word as a statute-book, by the letter of which every step in life must be governed. We believe, on the other hand, that one of the great excellences of Christianity is, that it does not deal in minute regulation, but that, having given broad views of duty, and enjoined a pure and disinterested spirit, it leaves us to apply these rules and express this spirit according to the promptings of the divine monitor within us, and according to the claims and exigencies of the ever varying conditions in which we are placed. We believe, too, that revelation is not intended to supersede God's other modes of instruction; that it is not intended to drown, but to make more audible, the voice of nature. Now, nature dictates the propriety of such an act as we are this day assembled to perform. Nature has always taught men, on the completion of an important structure, designed for public and lasting good, to solemnize its first appropriation to the purpose for which it was reared, by some special service. To us there is a sacredness in this moral instinct, in this law written on the heart; and in listening reverently to God's dictates, however conveyed, we doubt not that we shall enjoy his acceptance and blessing.

I have said, we dedicate this building to the teaching of the Gospel of Christ. But in the present state of the Christian church, these words are not as definite as they one day will be. This Gospel is variously interpreted. It is preached in various forms. Christendom is parcelled out into various sects. When, therefore, we see a new house of worship reared, the question immediately arises, To what mode of teaching Christianity is it to be devoted ? I need not tell you, my hearers, that this house has been built by that class of Christians, who are called Unitarians, and that the Gospel will here be taught, as interpreted by that body of believers. This you all know ; but perhaps all present have not attached a very precise meaning to the word, by which our particular views of Christianity are designated. Unitarianism has been made a term of so much reproach, and has been uttered in so many tones of alarm, horror, indignation, and scorn, that to many it gives only a vague impression of something monstrous, impious, unutterably perilous. To such, I would say, that this doctrine, which is considered by some as the last and most perfect invention of Satan, the consummation of his blasphemies, the most cunning weapon ever forged in the fires of hell, amounts to this, — That there is One God, even the Father ; and that Jesus Christ is not this One God, but his son and messenger, who derived all his powers and glories from the Universal Parent, and who came into the world not to claim supreme homage for himself, but to carry up the soul to his Father as the Only Divine Person, the Only Ultimate Object of religious worship. To us, this doctrine seems not to have sprung from hell, but to have descended from the throne of God, and to invite and attract us thither. To us it seems to come from the Scriptures, with a voice loud as the sound of many waters, and as articulate and clear as if Jesus, in a bodily form, were pronouncing it distinctly in our ears. To this doctrine, and to Christianity interpreted in consistency with it, we dedicate this building.

That we desire to propagate this doctrine, we do not conceal. It is a treasure, which we wish not to confine to ourselves, which we dare not lock up in our own breasts. We regard it as given to us for others, as well as for ourselves. We should rejoice to spread it through this great city, to carry it into every dwelling, and to send it far and wide to the remotest settlements of our country. Am I asked, why we wish this diffusion? We dare not say, that we are in no degree influenced by sectarian feeling; for we see it raging around us, and we should be more than men, were we wholly to escape an epidemic passion. We do hope, however, that our main purpose and aim is not sectarian, but to promote a purer and nobler piety than now prevails. We are not induced to spread our opinions by the mere conviction that they are true; for there are many truths, historical, metaphysical, scientific, literary, which we have no anxiety to propagate. We regard them as the highest, most important, most efficient truths, and therefore demanding a firm testimony, and earnest efforts to make them known. In thus speaking, we do not mean, that we regard our peculiar views as essential to salvation. Far from us be this spirit of exclusion, the very spirit of antichrist, the worst of all the delusions of Popery and of Protestantism. We hold nothing to be essential, but the simple and supreme dedication of the mind, heart, and life to God and to his will. This inward and practical devotedness to the Supreme Being, we are assured, is attained and accepted under all the forms of Christianity. We believe, however, that it is favored by that truth which we maintain, as by no other system of faith. We regard Unitarianism as peculiarly the friend of inward, living, practical religion. For this we value it. For this we would spread it; and we desire none to embrace it, but such as shall seek and derive from it this celestial influence.

This character and property of Unitarian Christianity, its fitness to promote true, deep, and living piety, being our chief ground of attachment to it, and our chief motive for dedicating this house to its inculcation, I have thought proper to make this the topic of my present discourse. I do not propose to prove the truth of Unitarianism by Scriptural authorities, for this argument would exceed the limits of a sermon, but to show its superior tendency to form an elevated religious character. If, however, this position can be sustained, I shall have contributed no weak argument in support of the truth of our views; for the chief purpose of Christianity undoubtedly is, to promote piety, to bring us to God, to fill our souls with that Great Being, to make us alive to him; and a religious system can carry no more authentic mark of a divine original, than its obvious, direct, and peculiar adaptation to quicken and raise the mind to its Creator. — In speaking thus of Unitarian Christianity as promoting piety, I ought to observe, that I use this word in its proper and highest sense. I mean not every thing which bears the name of piety, for under this title superstition, fanaticism, and formality are walking abroad and claiming respect. I mean not an anxious frame of mind, not abject and slavish fear, not a dread of hell, not a repetition of forms, not church-going, not loud profession, not severe censure of others' irreligion; but filial love and reverence towards God, habitual gratitude, cheerful trust, ready obedience, and, though last not least, an imitation of the ever-active and unbounded benevolence of the Creator.

The object of this discourse requires me to speak with great freedom of different systems of religion. But let me not be misunderstood. Let not the uncharitableness, which I condemn, be lightly laid to my charge. Let it be remembered, that I speak only of systems, not of those who embrace them. In setting forth with all simplicity what seem to me the good or bad tendencies of doctrines, I have not a thought of giving standards or measures by which to estimate the virtue or vice of their professors. Nothing would be more unjust, than to decide on men's characters from their peculiarities of faith; and the reason is plain. Such peculiarities are not the only causes which impress and determine the mind. Our nature is exposed to innumerable other influences. If indeed a man were to know nothing but his creed, were to meet with no human beings but those who adopt it, were to see no example and to hear no conversation, but such as were formed by it; if his creed were to meet him everywhere, and to exclude every other object of thought; then his character might be expected to answer to it with great precision. But our Creator has not shut us up in so narrow a school. The mind is exposed to an infinite variety of influences, and these are multiplying with the progress of society. Education, friendship, neighbourhood, public opinion, the state of society, "the genius of the place" where we live, books, events, the pleasures and business of life, the outward creation, our physical temperament, and innumerable other causes, are perpetually pouring in upon the soul thoughts, views, and emotions; and these influ ences are so complicated, so peculiarly combined in the case of every individual, and so modified by the original susceptibilities and constitution of every mind, that on no subject is there greater uncertainty, than on the formation of character. To determine the precise operation of a religious opinion amidst this host of influences, surpasses human power. A great truth may be completely neutralized by the countless impressions and excitements, which the mind receives from other sources ; and so a great error may be disarmed of much of its power, by the superior energy of other and better views, of early habits, and of virtuous examples. Nothing is more common than to see a doctrine believed without swaying the will. Its efficacy depends, not on the assent of the intellect, but on the place which it occupies in the thoughts, on the distinctness and vividness with which it is conceived, on its association with our common ideas, on its frequency of recurrence, and on its command of the attention, without which it has no life. Accordingly, pernicious opinions are not seldom held by men of the most illustrious virtue. I mean not, then, in commending or condemning systems, to pass sentence on their professors. I know the power of the mind to select from a multifarious system, for its habitual use, those features or principles which are generous, pure, and ennobling, and by these, to sustain its spiritual life amidst the nominal profession of many errors. I know that a creed is one thing, as written in a book, and another, as it exists in the minds of its advocates. In the book, all the doctrines appear in equally strong and legible lines. In the mind, many are faintly traced and seldom recurred to, whilst others are inscribed as with sunbeams, and are the chosen, constant lights of the soul. Hence, in good men of opposing denominations, a real agreement may subsist as to their vital principles of faith; and amidst the division of tongues, there may be unity of soul, and the same internal worship of God. By these remarks, I do not mean that error is not evil, or that it bears no pernicious fruit. Its tendencies are always bad. But I mean, that these tendencies exert themselves amidst so many counteracting influences; and that injurious opinions so often lie dead, through the want of mixture with the common thoughts, through the mind's not absorbing them, and changing them into its own substance; that the highest respect may, and ought to be cherished for men, in whose creed we find much to disapprove. In this discourse I shall speak freely, and some may say severely, of Trinitarianism; but I love and honor not a few of its advocates; and in opposing what I deem their error, I would on no account detract from their worth. After these remarks, I hope that the language of earnest discussion and strong conviction will not be construed into the want of that charity, which I acknowledge as the first grace of our religion.

I now proceed to illustrate and prove the superiority of Unitarian Christianity, as a means of promoting a deep and noble piety.

I. Unitarianism is a system most favorable to piety, because it presents to the mind One, and only one, Infinite Person, to whom supreme homage is to be paid. It does not weaken the energy of religious sentiment by dividing it among various objects. It collects and concentrates the soul on One Father of unbounded, undivided, unrivalled glory. To Him it teaches th' mind to rise through all beings. Around Him it gathers all the splendors of the universe. To Him it teaches us to ascribe whatever good we receive or behold, the beauty and magnificence of nature, the liberal gifts of Providence, the capacities of the soul, the bonds of society, and especially the riches of grace and redemption, the mission, and powers, and beneficent influences of Jesus Christ. All happiness it traces up to the Father, as the sole source; and the mind, which these views have penetrated, through this intimate association of every thing exciting and exalting in the universe with One Infinite Parent, can and does offer itself up to him with the intensest and profoundest love, of which human nature is susceptible. The Trinitarian indeed professes to believe in one God, and means to hold fast this truth. But three persons, having distinctive qualities and relations, of whom one is sent and another the sender, one is given and another the giver, of whom one intercedes and another hears the intercession, of whom one takes flesh and another never becomes incarnate, — three persons, thus discriminated, are as truly three objects of the mind, as if they were acknowledged to be separate divinities; and, from the principles of our nature, they cannot act on the mind as deeply and powerfully as one Infinite Person, to whose sole goodness all happiness is ascribed. To multiply infinite objects for the heart, is to distract it. To scatter the attention among three equal persons, is to impair the power of each. The more strict and absolute the unity of God, the more easily and intimately all the impressions and emotions of piety flow together, and are condensed into one glowing thought, one thrilling love. No language can express the absorbing energy of the thought of one Infinite Father. When vitally implanted in the soul, it grows and gains strength for ever. It enriches itself by every new view of God's word and works; gathers tribute from all regions and all ages; and attracts into itself all the rays of beauty, glory, and joy, in the material and spiritual creation.

My hearers, as you would feel the full influence of God upon your souls, guard sacredly, keep unobscured and unsullied, that fundamental and glorious truth, that there is One, and only One Almighty Agent in the universe, one Infinite Father. Let this truth dwell in me in its uncorrupted simplicity, and I have the spring and nutriment of an ever-growing piety. I have an object for my mind towards which all things bear me. I know whither to go in all trial, whom to bless in all joy, whom to adore in all I behold. But let three persons claim from me supreme homage, and claim it on different grounds, one for sending and another for coming to my relief, and I am divided, distracted, perplexed. My frail intellect is overborne. Instead of One Father, on whose arm I can rest, my mind is torn from object to object, and I tremble, lest among so many claimants of supreme love, I should withhold from one or another his due.

II. Unitarianism is the system most favorable to piety, because it holds forth and preserves inviolate the spirituality of God. "God is a spirit, and they that worship him must worship him in spirit and in truth." It is of great importance to the progress and elevation of the religious principle, that we should refine more and more our conceptions of God; that we should separate from him all material properties, and whatever is limited or imperfect in our own nature; that we should regard him as a pure intelligence, an unmixed and infinite Mind. When it pleased God to select the Jewish people and place them under miraculous interpositions, one of the first precepts given them was, that they should not represent God under any bodily form, any graven image, or the likeness of any creature. Next came Christianity, which had this as one of its great objects, to render religion still more spiritual, by abolishing the ceremonial and outward worship of former times, and by discarding those grosser modes of describing God, through which the ancient prophets had sought to impress an unrefined people.

Now, Unitarianism concurs with this sublime moral purpose of God. It asserts his spirituality. It approaches him under no bodily form, but as a pure spirit, as the infinite and the universal Mind. On the other hand, it is the direct influence of Trinitarianism to materialize men's conceptions of God ; and, in truth, this system is a relapse into the error of the rudest and earliest ages, into the worship of a corporeal God. Its leading feature is, the doctrine of a God clothed with a body, and acting and speaking through a material frame, — of the Infinite Divinity dying on a cross ; a doctrine, which in earthliness reminds us of the mythology of the rudest pagans, and which a pious Jew, in the twilight of the Mosaic religion, would have shrunk from with horror. It seems to me no small objection to the Trinity, that it supposes God to take a body in the later and more improved ages of the world, when it is plain, that such a manifestation, if needed at all, was peculiarly required in the infancy of the race. The effect of such a system in debasing the idea of God, in associating with the Divinity human passions and infirmities, is too obvious to need much elucidation. On the supposition that the second person of the Trinity became incarnate, God may be said to be a material being, on the same general ground, on which this is affirmed of man; for man is material only by the union of the mind with the body; and the very meaning of incarnation is, that God took a body, through which he acted and spoke, as the human soul operates through its corporeal organs. Every bodily affection may thus be ascribed to God. Accordingly the Trinitarian, in his most solemn act of adoration, is heard to pray in these appalling words : " Good Lord, deliver us; by the mystery of thy holy incarnation, by thy holy nativity and circumcision, by thy baptism, fasting, and temptation, by thine agony and bloody sweat, by thy cross and passion, good Lord, deliver us." Now I ask you to judge, from the principles of human nature, whether to worshippers, who adore their God for his wounds and tears, his agony, and blood, and sweat, the ideas of corporeal existence and human suffering will not predominate over the conceptions of a purely spiritual essence; whether the mind, in clinging to the man, will not lose the God; whether a surer method for depressing and adulterating the pure thought of the Divinity could have been devised. That the Trinitarian is unconscious of this influence of his faith, I know, nor do I charge it on him as a crime. Still it exists, and cannot be too much deplored.

The Roman Catholics, true to human nature and their creed, have sought, by painting and statuary, to bring their imagined God before their eyes; and have thus obtained almost as vivid impressions of him, as if they had lived with him on the earth. The Protestant condemns them for using these similitudes and representations in their worship ; but, if a Trinitarian, he does so to his own condemnation. For if, as he believes, it was once a duty to bow in adoration before the living body of his incarnate God, what possible guilt can there be in worshipping before the pictured or sculptured memorial of the same being ? Christ's body may as truly be represented by the artist, as any other human form ; and its image may be used as effectually and properly, as that of an ancient sage or hero, to recall him with vividness to the mind. — Is it said, that God has expressly forbidden the use of images in our worship ? But why was that prohibition laid on the Jews ? For this express reason, that God had not presented himself to them in any form, which admitted of representation. Hear the language of Moses : " Take good heed lest ye make you a graven image, for ye saw no manner of similitude on the day that the Lord spake unto you in Horeb out of the midst of the fire." * If, since that period, God has taken a body, then the reason of the prohibition has ceased ; and if he took a body, among other purposes, that he might assist the weakness of the intellect, which needs a material form, then a statue, which lends so great an aid to the conception of an absent friend, is not only justified, but seems to be required.

This materializing and embodying of the Supreme Being, which is the essence of Trinitarianism, cannot but be adverse to a growing and exalted piety. Human and divine properties, being confounded in one being, lose their distinctness. The splendors of the Godhead are dimmed. The worshippers of an incarnate Deity, through the frailty of their nature, are strongly tempted

* Deut. iv. 15, 16. — The arrangement of the text is a little changed, to put the reader immediately in possession of the meaning.

to fasten chiefly on his human attributes; and their devotion, instead of rising to the Infinite God, and taking the peculiar character which infinity inspires, becomes rather a human affection, borrowing much of its fervor from the ideas of suffering, blood, and death. It is indeed possible, that this God-man (to use the strange phraseology of Trinitarians) may excite the mind more easily, than a purely spiritual divinity; just as a tragedy, addressed to the eye and ear, will interest the multitude more than the contemplation of the most exalted character. But the emotions, which are the most easily roused, are not the profoundest or most enduring. This human love, inspired by a human God, though at first more fervid, cannot grow and spread through the soul, like the reverential attachment, which an infinite, spiritual Father awakens. Refined conceptions of God, though more slowly attained, have a more quickening and all-pervading energy, and admit of perpetual accessions of brightness, life, and strength.

True, we shall be told, that Trinitarianism has converted only one of its three persons into a human Deity, and that the other two remain purely spiritual beings. But who does not know, that man will attach himself most strongly to the God who has become a man? Is not this even a duty, if the Divinity has taken a body to place himself within the reach of human comprehension and sympathy? That the Trinitarian's views of the Divinity will be colored more by his visible, tangible, corporeal God, than by those persons of the Trinity, who remain comparatively hidden in their invisible and spiritual essence, is so accordant with the principles of our nature, as to need no labored proof.

My friends, hold fast the doctrine of a purely spiritual

Divinity. It is one of the great supports and instruments of a vital piety. It brings God near, as no other doctrine can. One of the leading purposes of Christianity is, to give us an ever-growing sense of God's immediate presence, a consciousness of him in our souls. Now, just as far as corporeal or limited attributes enter into our conception of him, we remove him from us. He becomes an outward, distant being, instead of being viewed and felt as dwelling in the soul itself. It is an unspeakable benefit of the doctrine of a purely spiritual God, that he can be regarded as inhabiting, filling our spiritual nature ; and, through this union with our minds, he can and does become the object of an intimacy and friendship, such as no embodied being can call forth.

III. Unitarianism is the system most favorable to piety, because it presents a distinct and intelligible object of worship, a being, whose nature, whilst inexpressibly sublime, is yet simple and suited to human apprehension. An infinite Father is the most exalted of all conceptions, and yet the least perplexing. It involves no incongruous ideas. It is illustrated by analogies from our own nature. It coincides with that fundamental law of the intellect, through which we demand a cause proportioned to effects. It is also as interesting as it is rational ; so that it is peculiarly congenial with the improved mind. The sublime simplicity of God, as he is taught in Unitarianism, by relieving the understanding from perplexity, and by placing him within the reach of thought and affection, gives him peculiar power over the soul. Trinitarianism, on the other hand, is a riddle. Men call it a mystery ; but it is mysterious, not like the great truths of religion, by its vastness and grandeur, but by the irreconcilable ideas which it involves. One God, consisting of three persons or agents, is so strange a being, so unlike our own minds, and all others with which we hold intercourse, is so misty, so incongruous, so contradictory, that he cannot be apprehended with that distinctness and that feeling of reality, which belong to the opposite system. Such a heterogeneous being, who is at the same moment one and many; who includes in his own nature the relations of Father and Son, or, in other words, is Father and Son to himself; who, in one of his persons, is at the same moment the Supreme God and a mortal man, omniscient and ignorant, almighty and impotent; such a being is certainly the most puzzling and distracting object ever presented to human thought. Trinitarianism, instead of teaching an intelligible God, offers to the mind a strange compound of hostile attributes, bearing plain marks of those ages of darkness, when Christianity shed but a faint ray, and the diseased fancy teemed with prodigies and unnatural creations. In contemplating a being, who presents such different and inconsistent aspects, the mind finds nothing to rest upon; and, instead of receiving distinct and harmonious impressions, is disturbed by shifting, unsettled images. To commune with such a being must be as hard, as to converse with a man of three different countenances, speaking with three different tongues. The believer in this system must forget it, when he prays, or he could find no repose in devotion. Who can compare it, in distinctness, reality, and power, with the simple doctrine of One Infinite Father?

IV. Unitarianism promotes a fervent and enlightened piety, by asserting the absolute and unbounded perfection of God's character. This is the highest service which can be rendered to mankind. Just and generous conceptions of the Divinity are the soul's true wealth. To spread these is to contribute more effectually, than by any other agency, to the progress and happiness of the intelligent creation. To obscure God's glory is to do greater wrong, than to blot out the sun. The character and influence of a religion must answer to the views which it gives of the Divinity; and there is a plain tendency in that system, which manifests the divine perfections most resplendently, to awaken the sublimest and most blessed piety.

Now, Trinitarianism has a fatal tendency to degrade the character of the Supreme Being, though its advocates, I am sure, intend no such wrong. By multiplying divine persons, it takes from each the glory of independent, all-sufficient, absolute perfection. This may be shown in various particulars. And in the first place, the very idea, that three persons in the Divinity are in any degree important, implies and involves the imperfection of each; for it is plain, that if one divine person possesses all possible power, wisdom, love, and happiness, nothing will be gained to himself or to the creation by joining with him two, or two hundred other persons. To say that he needs others for any purpose or in any degree, is to strip him of independent and all-sufficient majesty. If our Father in heaven, the God and Father of our Lord Jesus Christ, is not of himself sufficient to all the wants of his creation; if, by his union with other persons, he can accomplish any good to which he is not of himself equal; or if he thus acquires a claim to the least degree of trust or hope, to which he is not of himself entitled by his own independent attributes; then it is plain, he is not a being of infinite and absolute perfection. Now Trinitarianism teaches, that the highest good accrues to the human race from the existence of three divine persons, sustaining different offices and relations to the world; and it regards the Unitarian, as subverting the foundation of human hope, by asserting that the God and Father of our Lord Jesus is alone and singly God. Thus it derogates from his infinite glory.

In the next place, Trinitarianism degrades the character of the Supreme Being, by laying its disciples under the necessity of making such a distribution of offices and relations among the three persons, as will serve to designate and distinguish them; for in this way it interferes with the sublime conceptions of One Infinite Person, in whom all glories are concentred. If we are required to worship three persons, we must view them in different lights, or they will be mere repetitions of each other, mere names and sounds, presenting no objects, conveying no meaning to the mind. Some appropriate character, some peculiar acts, feelings, and relations must be ascribed to each. In other words, the glory of all must be shorn, that some special distinguishing lustre may be thrown on each. Accordingly, creation is associated peculiarly with the conception of the Father; satisfaction for human guilt with that of the Son; whilst sanctification, the noblest work of all, is given to the Holy Spirit as his more particular work. By a still more fatal distribution, the work of justice, the office of vindicating the rights of the Divinity, falls peculiarly to the Father, whilst the loveliness of interposing mercy clothes peculiarly the person of the Son. By this unhappy influence of Trinitarianism, from which common minds at least cannot escape, the splendors of the Godhead, being scattered among three objects, instead of being united in One Infinite Father, are dimmed ; and he, whose mind is thoroughly and practically possessed by this system, can hardly conceive the effulgence of glory in which the One God offers himself to a pious believer in his strict unity.

But the worst has not been told. I observe, then, in the third place, that if Three Divine Persons are believed in, such an administration or government of the world must be ascribed to them, as will furnish them with a sphere of operation. No man will admit three persons into his creed, without finding a use for them. Now it is an obvious remark, that a system of the universe, which involves and demands more than one Infinite Agent, must be wild, extravagant, and unworthy the perfect God ; because there is no possible or conceivable good, to which such an Agent is not adequate. Accordingly we find Trinitarianism connecting itself with a scheme of administration, exceedingly derogatory to the Divine character. It teaches, that the Infinite Father saw fit to put into the hands of our first parents the character and condition of their whole progeny ; and that, through one act of disobedience, the whole race bring with them into being a corrupt nature, or are born depraved. It teaches, that the offences of a short life, though begun and spent under this disastrous influence, merit endless punishment, and that God's law threatens this infinite penalty ; and that man is thus burdened with a guilt, which no sufferings of the created universe can expiate, which nothing but the sufferings of an Infinite Being can purge away. In this condition of human nature, Trinitarianism finds a sphere of action for its different persons. I am aware that some Trinitarians, on hearing this statement of their system, may reproach me with ascribing to them the errors of Calvinism, a system which they abhor as much as ourselves. But none of the peculiarities of Calvinism enter into this exposition. I have given what I understand to be the leading features of Trinitarianism all the world over; and the benevolent professors of that faith, who recoil from this statement, must blame not the preacher, but the creeds and establishments by which these doctrines are diffused. For ourselves, we look with horror and grief on the views of God's government, which are naturally and intimately united with Trinitarianism. They take from us our Father in heaven, and substitute a stern and unjust lord. Our filial love and reverence rise up against them. We say to the Trinitarian, touch any thing but the perfections of God. Cast no stain on that spotless purity and loveliness. We can endure any errors but those, which subvert or unsettle the conviction of God's paternal goodness. Urge not upon us a system, which makes existence a curse, and wraps the universe in gloom. Leave us the cheerful light, the free and healthful atmosphere, of a liberal and rational faith; the ennobling and consoling influences of the doctrine, which nature and revelation in blessed concord teach us, of One Father of unbounded and inexhaustible love.

V. Unitarianism is peculiarly favorable to piety, because it accords with nature, with the world around and the world within us; and through this accordance it gives aid to nature, and receives aid from it, in impressing the mind with God. We live in the midst of a glorious universe, which was meant to be a witness and a preacher of the Divinity; and a revelation from God may be expected to be in harmony with this system, and to carry on a common ministry with it in lifting the soul to God. Now, Unitarianism is in accordance with nature. It teaches One Father, and so does creation, the more it is explored. Philosophy, in proportion as it extends its views of the universe, sees in it, more and more, a sublime and beautiful unity, and multiplies proofs, that all things have sprung from one intelligence, one power, one love. The whole outward creation proclaims to the Unitarian the truth in which he delights. So does his own soul. But neither nature nor the soul bears one trace of Three Divine Persons. Nature is no Trinitarian. It gives not a hint, not a glimpse of a tri-personal author. Trinitarianism is a confined system, shut up in a few texts, a few written lines, where many of the wisest minds have failed to discover it. It is not inscribed on the heavens and the earth, not borne on every wind, not resounding and reëchoing through the universe. The sun and stars say nothing of a God of three persons. They all speak of the One Father whom *we* adore. To *our* ears, one and the same voice comes from God's word and works, a full and swelling strain, growing clearer, louder, more thrilling as we listen, and with one blessed influence lifting up our souls to the Almighty Father.

This accordance between nature and revelation increases the power of both over the mind. Concurring as they do in one impression, they make that impression deeper. To men of reflection, the conviction of the reality of religion is exceedingly heightened, by a perception of harmony in the views of it which they derive from various sources. Revelation is never received with so intimate a persuasion of its truth, as when it is seen to conspire to the same ends and impressions, for which all other things are made. It is no small objection to Trinitarianism, that it is an insulated doctrine, that it reveals a God whom we meet nowhere in the universe. Three Divine Persons, I repeat it, are found only in a few texts, and those so dark, that the gifted minds of Milton, Newton, and Locke, could not find them there. Nature gives them not a whisper of evidence. And can they be as real and powerful to the mind, as that One Father, whom the general strain and common voice of Scripture, and the universal voice of nature call us to adore?

VI. Unitarianism favors piety by opening the mind to new and ever-enlarging views of God. Teaching, as it does, the same God with nature, it leads us to seek him in nature. It does not shut us up in the written word, precious as that manifestation of the Divinity is. It considers revelation, not as independent of his other means of instruction; not as a separate agent; but as a part of the great system of God for enlightening and elevating the human soul; as intimately joined with creation and providence, and intended to concur with them; and as given to assist us in reading the volume of the universe. Thus Unitarianism, where its genuine influence is experienced, tends to enrich and fertilize the mind; opens it to new lights, wherever they spring up; and, by combining, makes more efficient, the means of religious knowledge. Trinitarianism, on the other hand, is a system which tends to confine the mind; to shut it up in what is written; to diminish its interest in the universe; and to disincline it to bright and enlarged views of God's works. — This effect will be explained, in the first place, if we consider, that the peculiarities of Trinitarianism differ so much from the teachings of the universe, that he who attaches himself to the one, will be in danger of losing his interest in the other. The ideas of Three Divine Persons, of God clothing himself in flesh, of the infinite Creator saving the guilty by transferring their punishment to an innocent being, these ideas cannot easily be made to coalesce in the mind with that which nature gives, of One Almighty Father and Unbounded Spirit, whom no worlds can contain, and whose vicegerent in the human breast pronounces it a crime, to lay the penalties of vice on the pure and unoffending.

But Trinitarianism has a still more positive influence in shutting the mind against improving views from the universe. It tends to throw gloom over God's works. Imagining that Christ is to be exalted, by giving him an exclusive agency in enlightening and recovering mankind, it is tempted to disparage other lights and influences ; and, for the purpose of magnifying his salvation, it inclines to exaggerate the darkness and desperateness of man's present condition. The mind thus impressed, naturally leans to those views of nature and of society, which will strengthen the ideas of desolation and guilt. It is tempted to aggravate the miseries of life, and to see in them only the marks of divine displeasure and punishing justice ; and overlooks their obvious fitness and design to awaken our powers, exercise our virtues, and strengthen our social ties. In like manner, it exaggerates the sins of men, that the need of an Infinite atonement may be maintained. Some of the most affecting tokens of God's love within and around us are obscured by this gloomy theology. The glorious faculties of the soul, its high aspirations, its sensibility to the great and good in character, its sympathy with disinterested and suffering virtue, its benevolent and religious instincts, its thirst for a happiness not found on earth, these are overlooked or thrown into the shade, that they may not disturb the persuasion of man's natural corruption. Ingenuity is employed to disparage what is interesting in the human character. Whilst the bursts of passion in the newborn child are gravely urged as indications of a native, rooted corruption; its bursts of affection, its sweet smile, its innocent and irrepressible joy, its loveliness and beauty, are not listened to, though they plead more eloquently its alliance with higher natures. The sacred and tender affections of home ; the unwearied watchings and cheerful sacrifices of parents ; the reverential, grateful assiduity of children, smoothing an aged father's or mother's descent to the grave ; woman's love, stronger than death; the friendship of brothers and sisters ; the anxious affection, which tends around the bed of sickness ; the subdued voice, which breathes comfort into the mourner's heart ; all the endearing offices, which shed a serene light through our dwellings ; these are explained away by the thorough advocates of this system, so as to include no real virtue, so as to consist with a natural aversion to goodness. Even the higher efforts of disinterested benevolence, and the most unaffected expressions of piety, if not connected with what is called "the true faith," are, by the most rigid disciples of the doctrine which I oppose, resolved into the passion for distinction, or some other working of "unsanctified nature." Thus, Trinitarianism and its kindred doctrines have a tendency to veil God's goodness, to sully his fairest works, to dim the lustre of those innocent and pure affections, which a divine breath kindles in the soul, to blight the beauty and freshness of creation, and in this way to consume the very nutriment of piety. We know, and rejoice to know, that in multitudes this tendency is counteracted by a cheerful temperament, a benevolent nature, and a strength of gratitude, which bursts the shackles of a melancholy system. But from the nature of the doctrine, the tendency exists and is strong; and an impartial observer will often discern it resulting in gloomy, depressing views of life and the universe.

Trinitarianism, by thus tending to exclude bright and enlarged views of the creation, seems to me not only to chill the heart, but to injure the understanding, as far as moral and religious truth is concerned. It does not send the mind far and wide for new and elevating objects; and we have here one explanation of the barrenness and feebleness, by which theological writings are so generally marked. It is not wonderful, that the prevalent theology should want vitality and enlargement of thought, for it does not accord with the perfections of God and the spirit of the universe. It has not its root in eternal truth; but is a narrow, technical, artificial system, the fabrication of unrefined ages, and consequently incapable of being blended with the new lights which are spreading over the most interesting subjects, and of being incorporated with the results and anticipations of original and progressive minds. It stands apart in the mind, instead of seizing upon new truths, and converting them into its own nutriment. With few exceptions, the Trinitarian theology of the present day is greatly deficient in freshness of thought, and in power to awaken the interest and to meet the intellectual and spiritual wants of thinking men. I see indeed superior minds and great minds among the adherents of the prevalent system ; but they seem to me to move in chains, and to fulfil poorly their high function of adding to the wealth of the human intellect. In theological discussion, they remind me more of Samson grinding in the narrow mill of the Philistines, than of that undaunted champion achieving victories for God's people, and enlarging the bounds of their inheritance. Now, a system which has a tendency to confine the mind, and to impair its sensibility to the manifestations of God in the universe, is so far unfriendly to piety, to a bright, joyous, hopeful, evergrowing love of the Creator. It tends to generate and nourish a religion of a melancholy tone, such, I apprehend, as now predominates in the Christian world.

VII. Unitarianism promotes piety, by the high place which it assigns to piety in the character and work of Jesus Christ. What is it which the Unitarian regards as the chief glory of the character of Christ ? I answer, his filial devotion, the entireness with which he surrendered himself to the will and benevolent purposes of God. The piety of Jesus, which, on the supposition of his Supreme Divinity, is a subordinate and incongruous, is, to us, his prominent and crowning, attribute. We place his " oneness with God," not in an unintelligible unity of essence, but in unity of mind and heart, in the strength of his love, through which he renounced every separate interest, and identified himself with his Father's designs. In other words, filial piety, the consecration of his whole being to the benevolent will of his Father, this is the mild glory in which he always offers himself to our minds ; and, of consequence, all our sympathies with him, all our love and veneration towards him, are so many forms of delight in a pious character, and our whole knowledge of him incites us to a like surrender of our whole nature and existence to God.

In the next place, Unitarianism teaches, that the highest work or office of Christ is, to call forth and strengthen piety in the human breast; and thus it sets before us this character as the chief acquisition and end of our being. To us, the great glory of Christ's mission consists in the power with which he "reveals the Father," and establishes the "kingdom or reign of God within" the soul. By the crown which he wears, we understand the eminence which he enjoys in the most beneficent work in the universe, that of bringing back the lost mind to the knowledge, love, and likeness of its Creator. With these views of Christ's office, nothing can seem to us so important as an enlightened and profound piety, and we are quickened to seek it, as the perfection and happiness to which nature and redemption jointly summon us.

Now we maintain, that Trinitarianism obscures and weakens these views of Christ's character and work; and this it does, by insisting perpetually on others of an incongruous, discordant nature. It diminishes the power of his piety. Making him, as it does, the Supreme Being, and placing him as an equal on his Father's throne, it turns the mind from him as the meekest worshipper of God; throws into the shade, as of very inferior worth, his self-denying obedience; and gives us other grounds for revering him, than his entire homage, his fervent love, his cheerful self-sacrifice to the Universal Parent. There is a plain incongruity in the belief of his Supreme Godhead with the ideas of filial piety and exemplary devotion. The mind, which has been taught to regard him as of equal majesty and authority with the Father, cannot easily feel the power of his character as the affectionate son, whose meat it was to do his Father's will. The mind, accustomed to make him the ultimate object of worship, cannot easily recognise in him the pattern of that worship, the guide to the Most High. The characters are incongruous, and their union perplexing, so that neither exerts its full energy on the mind.

Trinitarianism also exhibits the work as well as character of Christ, in lights less favorable to piety. It does not make the promotion of piety his chief end. It teaches, that the highest purpose of his mission was to reconcile God to man, not man to God. It teaches, that the most formidable obstacle to human happiness lies in the claims and threatenings of divine justice. Hence, it leads men to prize Christ more for answering these claims and averting these threatenings, than for awakening in the human soul sentiments of love towards its Father in heaven. Accordingly, multitudes seem to prize pardon more than piety, and think it a greater boon to escape, through Christ's sufferings, the fire of hell, than to receive, through his influence, the spirit of heaven, the spirit of devotion. Is such a system propitious to a generous and ever-growing piety?

If I may be allowed a short digression, I would conclude this head with the general observation, that we deem our views of Jesus Christ more interesting than those of Trinitarianism. We feel that we should lose much, by exchanging the distinct character and mild radiance with which he offers himself to our minds, for the confused and irreconcilable glories with which that system labors to invest him. According to Unitarianism, he is a being who may be understood, for he is one mind, one conscious nature. According to the opposite faith, he is an inconceivable compound of two most dissimilar minds, joining in one person a finite and infinite nature, a soul weak and ignorant, and a soul almighty and omniscient. And is such a being a proper object for human thought and affection?—I add, as another important consideration, that to us Jesus, instead of being the second of three obscure unintelligible persons, is first and preëminent in the sphere in which he acts, and is thus the object of a distinct attachment, which he shares with no equals or rivals. To us, he is first of the sons of God, the Son by peculiar nearness and likeness to the Father. He is first of all the ministers of God's mercy and beneficence, and through him the largest stream of bounty flows to the creation. He is first in God's favor and love, the most accepted of worshippers, the most prevalent of intercessors. In this mighty universe, framed to be a mirror of its Author, we turn to Jesus as the brightest image of God, and gratefully yield him a place in our souls, second only to the Infinite Father, to whom he himself directs our supreme affection.

VIII. I now proceed to a great topic. Unitarianism promotes piety, by meeting the wants of man as a sinner. The wants of the sinner may be expressed almost in one word. He wants assurances of mercy in his Creator. He wants pledges, that God is Love in its purest form, that is, that He has a goodness so disinterested, free, full, strong, and immutable, that the ingratitude and disobedience of his creatures cannot overcome it. This unconquerable love, which in Scripture is denominated grace, and which waits not for merit to call it forth, but flows out to the most guilty, is the sinner's only hope, and it is fitted to call forth the most devoted gratitude. Now, this grace or mercy of God, which seeks the lost, and receives and blesses the returning child, is proclaimed by that faith which we advocate, with a clearness and energy, which cannot be surpassed. Unitarianism will not listen for a moment to the common errors, by which this bright attribute is obscured. It will not hear of a vindictive wrath in God, which must be quenched by blood ; or of a justice, which binds his mercy with an iron chain, until its demands are satisfied to the full. It will not hear that God needs any foreign influence to awaken his mercy; but teaches, that the yearnings of the tenderest human parent towards a lost child, are but a faint image of God's deep and overflowing compassion towards erring man. This essential and unchangeable propensity of the Divine Mind to forgiveness, the Unitarian beholds shining forth through the whole Word of God, and especially in the mission and revelation of Jesus Christ, who lived and died to make manifest the inexhaustible plenitude of divine grace ; and, aided by revelation, he sees this attribute of God everywhere, both around him and within him. He sees it in the sun which shines, and the rain which descends on the evil and unthankful; in the peace, which returns to the mind in proportion to its return to God and duty ; in the sentiment of compassion, which springs up spontaneously in the human breast towards the fallen and lost ; and in the moral instinct, which teaches us to cherish this compassion as a sacred principle, as an emanation of God's infinite love. In truth, Unitarianism asserts so strongly the mercy of God, that the reproach thrown upon it is, that it takes from the sinner the dread of punishment, — a reproach wholly without foundation; for our system teaches that God's mercy is not an instinctive tenderness, which cannot inflict pain; but an all-wise love, which desires the true and lasting good of its object, and consequently desires first for the sinner that restoration to purity, without which, shame, and suffering, and exile from God and heaven are of necessity and unalterably his doom. Thus Unitarianism holds forth God's grace and forgiving goodness most resplendently; and, by this manifestation of him, it tends to awaken a tender and confiding piety; an ingenuous love, which mourns that it has offended; an ingenuous aversion to sin, not because sin brings punishment, but because it separates the mind from this merciful Father.

Now we object to Trinitarianism, that it obscures the mercy of God. It does so in various ways. We have already seen, that it gives such views of God's government, that we can hardly conceive of this attribute as entering into his character. Mercy to the sinner is the principle of love or benevolence in its highest form; and surely this cannot be expected from a being who brings us into existence burdened with hereditary guilt, and who threatens with endless punishment and woe the heirs of so frail and feeble a nature. With such a Creator, the idea of mercy cannot coalesce; and I will say more, that, under such a government, man would need no mercy; for he would owe no allegiance to such a maker, and could not of course contract the guilt of violating it; and, without guilt, no grace or pardon would be wanted. The severity of this system would place him on the ground of an injured being. The wrong would lie on the side of the Creator.

In the next place, Trinitarianism obscures God's mercy, by the manner in which it supposes pardon to be communicated. It teaches, that God remits the punishment of the offender, in consequence of receiving an equivalent from an innocent person; that the sufferings of the sinner are removed by a full satisfaction made to divine justice, in the sufferings of a substitute. And is this "the quality of mercy"? What means forgiveness, but the reception of the returning child through the strength of parental love? This doctrine invests the Saviour with a claim of merit, with a right to the remission of the sins of his followers; and represents God's reception of the penitent as a recompense due to the worth of his Son. And is mercy, which means free and undeserved love, made more manifest, more resplendent, by the introduction of merit and right as the ground of our salvation? Could a surer expedient be invented for obscuring its freeness, and for turning the sinner's gratitude from the sovereign who demands, to the sufferer who offers, full satisfaction for his guilt?

I know it is said, that Trinitarianism magnifies God's mercy, because it teaches, that he himself provided the substitute for the guilty. But I reply, that the work here ascribed to mercy is not the most appropriate, nor most fitted to manifest it and impress it on the heart. This may be made apparent by familiar illustrations. Suppose that a creditor, through compassion to certain debtors, should persuade a benevolent and opulent man to pay him in their stead. Would not the debtors see a greater mercy, and feel a weightier obligation, if they were to receive a free, gratuitous release? And will not their chief gratitude stray beyond the creditor to the benevolent substitute ? Or, suppose that a parent, unwilling to inflict a penalty on a disobedient but feeble child, should persuade a stronger child to bear it. Would not the offender see a more touching mercy in a free forgiveness, springing immediately from a parent's heart, than in this circuitous remission ? And will he not be tempted to turn with his strongest love to the generous sufferer ? In this process of substitution, of which Trinitarianism boasts so loudly, the mercy of God becomes complicated with the rights and merits of the substitute, and is a more distant cause of our salvation. These rights and merits are nearer, more visible, and more than divide the glory with grace and mercy in our rescue. They turn the mind from Divine Goodness, as the only spring of its happiness, and only rock of its hope. Now this is to deprive piety of one of its chief means of growth and joy. Nothing should stand between the soul and God's mercy. Nothing should share with mercy the work of our salvation. Christ's intercession should ever be regarded as an application to love and mercy, not as a demand of justice, not as a claim of merit. I grieve to say, that Christ, as now viewed by multitudes, hides the lustre of that very attribute which it is his great purpose to display. I fear, that, to many, Jesus wears the glory of a more winning, tender mercy, than his Father, and that he is regarded as the sinner's chief resource. Is this the way to invigorate piety ?

Trinitarians imagine, that there is one view of their system peculiarly fitted to give peace and hope to the sinner, and consequently to promote gratitude and love. It is this. They say, it provides an Infinite substitute for the sinner, than which nothing can give greater relief to the burdened conscience. Jesus, being the second person of the Trinity, was able to make infinite satisfaction for sin; and what, they ask, in Unitarianism, can compare with this? I have time only for two brief replies. And first, this doctrine of an Infinite satisfaction, or, as it is improperly called, of an Infinite atonement, subverts, instead of building up, hope; because it argues infinite severity in the government which requires it. Did I believe, what Trinitarianism teaches, that not the least transgression, not even the first sin of the dawning mind of the child, could be remitted without an infinite expiation, I should feel myself living under a legislation unspeakably dreadful, under laws written, like Draco's, in blood; and, instead of thanking the Sovereign for providing an infinite substitute, I should shudder at the attributes which render this expedient necessary. It is commonly said, that an infinite atonement is needed to make due and deep impressions of the evil of sin. But He who framed all souls, and gave them their susceptibilities, ought not to be thought so wanting in goodness and wisdom, as to have constituted a universe, which demands so dreadful and degrading a method of enforcing obedience, as the penal sufferings of a God. This doctrine, of an Infinite substitute suffering the penalty of sin, to manifest God's wrath against sin, and thus to support his government, is, I fear, so familiar to us all, that its severe character is overlooked. Let me, then, set it before you, in new terms, and by a new illustration; and if, in so doing, I may wound the feelings of some who hear me, I beg them to believe, that I do it with pain, and from no impulse but a desire to serve the cause of truth. —

Suppose, then, that a teacher should come among you, and should tell you, that the Creator, in order to pardon his own children, had erected a gallows in the centre of the universe, and had publicly executed upon it, in room of the offenders, an Infinite Being, the partaker of his own Supreme Divinity; suppose him to declare, that this execution was appointed, as a most conspicuous and terrible manifestation of God's justice, and of the infinite woe denounced by his law; and suppose him to add, that all beings in heaven and earth are required to fix their eyes on this fearful sight, as the most powerful enforcement of obedience and virtue. Would you not tell him, that he calumniated his Maker? Would you not say to him, that this central gallows threw gloom over the universe; that the spirit of a government, whose very acts of pardon were written in such blood, was terror, not paternal love; and that the obedience which needed to be upheld by this horrid spectacle, was nothing worth? Would you not say to him, that even you, in this infancy and imperfection of your being, were capable of being wrought upon by nobler motives, and of hating sin through more generous views; and that much more the angels, those pure flames of love, need not the gallows and an executed God to confirm their loyalty? You would all so feel, at such teaching as I have supposed; and yet how does this differ from the popular doctrine of atonement? According to this doctrine, we have an Infinite Being sentenced to suffer, as a substitute, the death of the cross, a punishment more ignominious and agonizing than the gallows, a punishment reserved for slaves and the vilest malefactors; and he suffers this punishment, that he may show forth the terrors of God's law, and strike a dread of sin through the universe. — I am indeed aware, that multitudes, who profess this doctrine, are not accustomed to bring it to their minds distinctly in this light; that they do not ordinarily regard the death of Christ as a criminal execution, as an infinitely dreadful infliction of justice, as intended to show, that, without an infinite satisfaction, they must hope nothing from God. Their minds turn, by a generous instinct, from these appalling views, to the love, the disinterestedness, the moral grandeur and beauty of the sufferer; and through such thoughts they make the cross a source of peace, gratitude, love, and hope; thus affording a delightful exemplification of the power of the human mind, to attach itself to what is good and purifying in the most irrational system. Not a few may shudder at the illustration which I have here given; but in what respects it is unjust to the popular doctrine of atonement, I cannot discern. I grieve to shock sincere Christians, of whatever name; but I grieve more for the corruption of our common faith, which I have now felt myself bound to expose.

I have a second objection to this doctrine of Infinite atonement. When examined minutely, and freed from ambiguous language, it vanishes into air. It is wholly delusion. The Trinitarian tells me, that, according to his system, we have an infinite substitute; that the Infinite God was pleased to bear our punishment, and consequently, that pardon is made sure. But I ask him, Do I understand you? Do you mean, that the Great God, who never changes, whose happiness is the same yesterday, to-day, and for ever, that this Eternal Being really bore the penalty of my sins, really suffered and died? Every pious man, when pressed by this question, answers, No. What, then, does the doctrine of Infinite atonement mean ? Why, this ; that God took into union with himself our nature, that is, a human body and soul ; and these bore the suffering for our sins ; and, through his union with these, God may be said to have borne it himself. Thus, this vaunted system goes out,—in words. The Infinite victim proves to be frail man, and God's share in the sacrifice is a mere fiction. I ask with solemnity, Can this doctrine give one moment's ease to the conscience of an unbiassed, thinking man ? Does it not unsettle all hope, by making the whole religion suspicious and unsure ? I am compelled to say, that I see in it no impression of majesty, or wisdom, or love, nothing worthy of a God ; and when I compare it with that nobler faith, which directs our eyes and hearts to God's essential mercy, as our only hope, I am amazed that any should ascribe to it superior efficacy, as a religion for sinners, as a means of filling the soul with pious trust and love. I know, indeed, that some will say, that, in giving up an infinite atonement, I deprive myself of all hope of divine favor. To such, I would say, You do wrong to God's mercy. On that mercy I cast myself without a fear. I indeed desire Christ to intercede for me. I regard his relation to me as God's kindest appointment. Through him, " grace and truth come " to me from Heaven, and I look forward to his friendship, as among the highest blessings of my whole future being. But I cannot, and dare not ask him, to offer an infinite satisfaction for my sins ; to appease the wrath of God ; to reconcile the Universal Father to his own offspring ; to open to me those arms of Divine mercy, which have encircled and borne me from the first moment of my being. The essential and unbounded mercy of my Creator, is the foundation of my hope, and a broader and surer the universe cannot give me.

IX. I now proceed to the last consideration, which the limits of this discourse will permit me to urge. It has been more than once suggested, but deserves to be distinctly stated. I observe, then, that Unitarianism promotes piety, because it is a rational religion. By this, I do not mean that its truths can be fully comprehended ; for there is not an object in nature or religion, which has not innumerable connexions and relations beyond our grasp of thought. I mean, that its doctrines are consistent with one another, and with all established truth. Unitarianism is in harmony with the great and clear principles of revelation ; with the laws and powers of human nature ; with the dictates of the moral sense ; with the noblest instincts and highest aspirations of the soul ; and with the lights which the universe throws on the character of its author. We can hold this doctrine without self-contradiction, without rebelling against our rational and moral powers, without putting to silence the divine monitor in the breast. And this is an unspeakable benefit ; for a religion thus coincident with reason, conscience, and our whole spiritual being, has the foundations of universal empire in the breast ; and the heart, finding no resistance in the intellect, yields itself wholly, cheerfully, without doubts or misgivings, to the love of its Creator.

To Trinitarianism we object, what has always been objected to it, that it contradicts and degrades reason, and thus exposes the mind to the worst delusions. Some of its advocates, more courageous than prudent, have even recommended " the prostration of the understanding," as preparatory to its reception. Its chief doctrine is an outrage on our rational nature. Its three persons who constitute its God, must either be frittered away into three unmeaning distinctions, into sounds signifying nothing ; or they are three conscious agents, who cannot, by any human art or metaphysical device, be made to coalesce into one being ; who cannot be really viewed as one mind, having one consciousness and one will. Now a religious system, the cardinal principle of which offends the understanding, very naturally conforms itself throughout to this prominent feature, and becomes prevalently irrational. He who is compelled to defend his faith in any particular, by the plea, that human reason is so depraved through the fall, as to be an inadequate judge of religion, and that God is honored by our reception of what shocks the intellect, seems to have no defence left against accumulated absurdities. According to these principles, the fanatic who exclaimed, " I believe, because it is impossible," had a fair title to canonization. Reason is too godlike a faculty, to be insulted with impunity. Accordingly, Trinitarianism, as we have seen, links itself with several degrading errors ; and its most natural alliance is with Calvinism, that cruel faith, which, stripping God of mercy and man of power, has made Christianity an instrument of torture to the timid, and an object of doubt or scorn to hardier spirits. I repeat it, a doctrine which violates reason like the Trinity, prepares its advocates, in proportion as it is incorporated into the mind, for worse and worse delusions. It breaks down the distinctions and barriers between truth and falsehood. It creates a diseased taste for prodigies, fictions, and exaggerations, for startling mysteries, and wild dreams of enthusiasm. It destroys the relish for the simple, chaste, serene beauties of truth. Especially when the prostration of understanding is taught as an act of piety, we cannot wonder, that the grossest superstitions should be devoured, and that the credulity of the multitude should keep pace with the forgeries of imposture and fanaticism. The history of the Church is the best comment on the effects of divorcing reason from religion; and if the present age is disburdened of many of the superstitions under which Christianity and human nature groaned for ages, it owes its relief in no small degree to the reinstating of reason in her long-violated rights.

The injury to religion, from irrational doctrines when thoroughly believed, is immense. The human soul has a unity. Its various faculties are adapted to one another. One life pervades it; and its beauty, strength, and growth depend on nothing so much, as on the harmony and joint action of all its principles. To wound and degrade it in any of its powers, and especially in the noble and distinguishing power of reason, is to inflict on it universal injury. No notion is more false, than that the heart is to thrive by dwarfing the intellect; that perplexing doctrines are the best food of piety; that religion flourishes most luxuriantly in mist and darkness. Reason was given for God as its great object; and for him it should be kept sacred, invigorated, clarified, protected from human usurpation, and inspired with a meek self-reverence.

The soul never acts so effectually or joyfully, as when all its powers and affections conspire; as when thought and feeling, reason and sensibility, are called forth together by one great and kindling object. It will never devote itself to God with its whole energy, whilst its guiding faculty sees in him a being to shock and confound it. We want a harmony in our inward nature. We want a piety, which will join light and fervor, and on which the intellectual power will look benignantly. We want religion to be so exhibited, that, in the clearest moments of the intellect, its signatures of truth will grow brighter ; that, instead of tottering, it will gather strength and stability from the progress of the human mind. These wants we believe to be met by Unitarian Christianity, and therefore we prize it as the best friend of piety.

I have thus stated the chief grounds, on which I rest the claim of Unitarianism to the honor of promoting an enlightened, profound, and happy piety.

Am I now asked, why we prize our system, and why we build churches for its inculcation ? If I may be allowed to express myself in the name of conscientious Unitarians, who apply their doctrine to their own hearts and lives, I would reply thus : We prize and would spread our views, because we believe that they reveal God to us in greater glory, and bring us nearer to him, than any other. We are conscious of a deep want, which the creation cannot supply, the want of a Perfect Being, on whom the strength of our love may be centred, and of an Almighty Father, in whom our weaknesses, imperfections, and sorrows may find resource ; and such a Being and Father, Unitarian Christianity sets before us. For this we prize it above all price. We can part with every other good. We can endure the darkening of life's fairest prospects. But this bright, consoling doctrine of One God, even the Father, is dearer than life, and we cannot let it go. — Through this faith, every thing grows brighter to our view. Born of such a Parent, we esteem our existence an inestimable gift. We meet everywhere our Father, and his presence is as a sun shining on our path. We see him in his works, and hear his praise rising from every spot which we tread. We feel him near in our solitudes, and sometimes enjoy communion with him more tender than human friendship. We see him in our duties, and perform them more gladly, because they are the best tribute we can offer our Heavenly Benefactor. Even the consciousness of sin, mournful as it is, does not subvert our peace; for, in the mercy of God, as made manifest in Jesus Christ, we see an inexhaustible fountain of strength, purity, and pardon, for all who, in filial reliance, seek these heavenly gifts. — Through this faith, we are conscious of a new benevolence springing up to our fellow-creatures, purer and more enlarged than natural affection. Towards all mankind we see a rich and free love flowing from the common Parent, and, touched by this love, we are the friends of all. We compassionate the most guilty, and would win them back to God. — Through this faith, we receive the happiness of an ever-enlarging hope. There is no good too vast for us to anticipate for the universe or for ourselves, from such a Father as we believe in. We hope from him, what we deem his greatest gift, even the gift of his own Spirit, and the happiness of advancing for ever in truth and virtue, in power and love, in union of mind with the Father and the Son. — We are told, indeed, that our faith will not prove an anchor in the last hour. But we have known those, whose departure it has brightened; and our experience of its power, in trial and peril, has proved it to be equal to all the wants of human nature

We doubt not, that, to its sincere followers, death will be a transition to the calm, pure, joyful mansions, prepared by Christ for his disciples. There we expect to meet that great and good Deliverer. With the eye of faith, we already see him looking round him with celestial love on all of every name, who have imbibed his spirit. His spirit; his loyal and entire devotion to the will of his Heavenly Father; his universal, unconquerable benevolence, through which he freely gave from his pierced side his blood, his life for the salvation of the world; this divine love, and not creeds, and names, and forms, will then be found to attract his supreme regard. This spirit we trust to see in multitudes of every sect and name; and we trust, too, that they, who now reproach us, will at that day recognise, in the dreaded Unitarian, this only badge of Christ, and will bid him welcome to the joy of our common Lord. — I have thus stated the views with which we have reared this building. We desire to glorify God, to promote a purer, nobler, happier piety. Even if we err in doctrine, we think that these motives should shield us from reproach; should disarm that intolerance, which would exclude us from the church on earth, and from our Father's house in heaven.

We end, as we began, by offering up this building to the Only Living and True God. We have erected it amidst our private habitations, as a remembrancer of our Creator. We have reared it in this busy city, as a retreat for pious meditation and prayer. We dedicate it to the King and Father Eternal, the King of kings and Lord of lords. We dedicate it to his Unity, to his unrivalled and undivided Majesty. We dedicate it to the praise of his free, unbought, unmerited grace.

We dedicate it to Jesus Christ, to the memory of his love, to the celebration of his divine virtue, to the preaching of that truth, which he sealed with blood. We dedicate it to the Holy Spirit, to the sanctifying influence of God, to those celestial emanations of light and strength, which visit and refresh the devout mind. We dedicate it to prayers and praises, which, we trust, will be continued and perfected in heaven. We dedicate it to social worship, to Christian intercourse, to the communion of saints. We dedicate it to the cause of pure morals, of public order, of temperance, uprightness, and general good will. We dedicate it to Christian admonition, to those warnings, remonstrances, and earnest and tender persuasions, by which the sinner may be arrested, and brought back to God. We dedicate it to Christian consolation, to those truths which assuage sorrow, animate penitence, and lighten the load of human anxiety and fear. We dedicate it to the doctrine of Immortality, to sublime and joyful hopes which reach beyond the grave. In a word, we dedicate it to the great work of perfecting the human soul, and fitting it for nearer approach to its Author. Here may heart meet heart. Here may man meet God. From this place may the song of praise, the ascription of gratitude, the sigh of penitence, the prayer for grace, and the holy resolve, ascend as fragrant incense to Heaven; and, through many generations, may parents bequeath to their children this house, as a sacred spot, where God had "lifted upon them his countenance," and given them pledges of his everlasting love.

THE

GREAT PURPOSE OF CHRISTIANITY.

DISCOURSE

AT THE

INSTALLATION OF THE REV. M. I. MOTTE.

BOSTON, 1828.

2 TIMOTHY i. 7: "For God hath not given us the spirit of fear; but of power, and of love, and of a sound mind."

WHY was Christianity given? Why did Christ seal it with his blood? Why is it to be preached? What is the great happiness it confers? What is the chief blessing for which it is to be prized? What is its preeminent glory, its first claim on the gratitude of mankind? These are great questions. I wish to answer them plainly, according to the light and ability which God has given me. I read the answer to them in the text. There I learn the great good which God confers through Jesus Christ. "He hath given us, not the spirit of fear, but of power, and of love, and of a sound mind." The glory of Christianity is, the pure and lofty action which it communicates to the human mind. It does not breathe a timid, abject spirit. If it did, it would deserve no praise. It gives power, energy, courage, constancy to the will ; love, disinterestedness, enlarged affection to the heart ; soundness, clearness, and vigor to the understanding. It rescues him, who receives it, from sin, from the sway of the passions ; gives him the full and free use of his best powers ; brings out and brightens the divine image in which he was created ; and, in this way, not only bestows the promise, but the beginning, of heaven. This is the excellence of Christianity.

This subject I propose to illustrate. Let me begin it with one remark, which I would willingly avoid, but which seems to me to be demanded by the circumstances in which I am placed. I beg you to remember, that in this discourse I speak in my own name, and in no other. I am not giving you the opinions of any sect or body of men, but my own. I hold myself alone responsible for what I utter. Let none listen to me for the purpose of learning what others think. I indeed belong to that class of Christians, who are distinguished by believing that there is one God, even the Father, and that Jesus Christ is not this one God, but his dependent and obedient Son. But my accordance with these is far from being universal, nor have I any desire to extend it. What other men believe, is to me of little moment. Their arguments I gratefully hear. Their conclusions I am free to receive or reject. I have no anxiety to wear the livery of any party. I indeed take cheerfully the name of a Unitarian, because unwearied efforts are used to raise against it a popular cry ; and I have not so learned Christ, as to shrink poses. I wish to regard myself as belonging, not to a sect, but to the community of free minds, of lovers of truth, of followers of Christ, both on earth and in heaven. I desire to escape the narrow walls of a particular church, and to live under the open sky, in the broad light, looking far and wide, seeing with my own eyes, hearing with my own ears, and following truth meekly, but resolutely, however arduous or solitary be the path in which she leads. I am, then, no organ of a sect, but speak from myself alone ; and I thank God that I live at a time, and under circumstances, which make it my duty to lay open my whole mind with freedom and simplicity.

I began with asking, What is the main design and glory of Christianity ? and I repeat the answer, that its design is to give, not a spirit of fear, but of power, of love, and of a sound mind. In this its glory chiefly consists. In other words, the influence, which it is intended to exert on the human mind, constitutes its supreme honor and happiness. Christ is a great Saviour, as he redeems or sets free the mind, cleansing it from evil, breathing into it the love of virtue, calling forth its noblest faculties and affections, enduing it with moral power, restoring it to order, health, and liberty. Such was his great aim. To illustrate these views will be the object of the present discourse.

In reading the New Testament, I everywhere meet the end here ascribed to Jesus Christ. He came, as I am there taught, not to be an outward, but inward deliverer ; not to rear an outward throne, but to establish his kingdom within us. He came, according to the express language and plain import of the sacred writers, " to save us from sin," " to bless us by turning us from our iniquities," " to redeem us " from corruptions "handed down by tradition," to form "a glorious and spotless church" or community, to "create us anew after the image of God," to make us by his " promises partakers of a divine nature," and to give us pardon and heaven by calling us to repentance and a growing virtue. In reading the New Testament, I everywhere learn, that Christ lived, taught, died, and rose again, to exert a purifying and ennobling influence on the human character; to make us victorious over sin, over ourselves, over peril and pain; to join us to God by filial love, and, above all, by likeness of nature, by participation of his spirit. This is plainly laid down in the New Testament as the supreme end of Christ.

Let me now ask, Can a nobler end be ascribed to Jesus? I affirm, that there is, and can be, no greater work on earth, than to purify the soul from evil, and to kindle in it new light, life, energy, and love. I maintain, that the true measure of the glory of a religion is to be found in the spirit and power, which it communicates to its disciples. This is one of the plain teachings of reason. The chief blessing to an intelligent being, that which makes all other blessings poor, is the improvement of his own mind. Man is glorious and happy, not by what he has, but by what he is. He can receive nothing better or nobler than the unfolding of his own spiritual nature. The highest existence in the universe is Mind; for God is mind; and the developement of that principle which assimilates us to God, must be our supreme good. The omnipotent Creator, we have reason to think, can bestow nothing greater than intelligence, love, rectitude, energy of will and of benevolent action; for these are the splendors of his own nature. We adore him for these. In imparting these, he imparts, as it were, himself. We are too apt to look abroad for good. But the only true good is within. In this outward universe, magnificent as it is, in the bright day and the starry night, in the earth and the skies, we can discover nothing so vast as thought, so strong as the unconquerable purpose of duty, so sublime as the spirit of disinterestedness and self-sacrifice. A mind which withstands all the powers of the outward universe, all the pains which fire and sword and storm can inflict, rather than swerve from uprightness, is nobler than the universe. Why will we not learn the glory of the soul? We are seeking a foreign good. But we all possess within us what is of more worth than the external creation. For this outward system is the product of Mind. All its harmony, beauty, and beneficent influences are the fruits and manifestations f Thought and Love; and is it not nobler and happier, to be enriched with these energies, from which the universe springs, and to which it owes its magnificence, than to possess the universe itself? It is not what we have, but what we are, which constitutes our glory and felicity. The only true and durable riches belong to the mind. A soul, narrow and debased, may extend its possessions to the ends of the earth, but is poor and wretched still. It is through inward health that we enjoy all outward things. Philosophers teach us, that the mind creates the beauty which it admires in nature; and we all know, that, when abandoned to evil passions, it can blot out this beauty, and spread over the fairest scenes the gloom of a dungeon. We all know, that by vice it can turn the cup of social happiness into poison, and the most prosperous condition of life into a curse. From these views we learn, that the true friend and Saviour, is not he who acts for us abroad, but who acts within, who sets the soul free, touches the springs of thought and affection, binds us to God, and, by assimilating us to the Creator, brings us into harmony with the creation. Thus the end, which we have ascribed to Christ, is the most glorious and beneficent which can be accomplished by any power on earth or in heaven.

That the highest purpose of Christianity is such as has now been affirmed, might easily be shown from a survey of all its doctrines and precepts. It might be shown, that every office with which Jesus Christ is invested, was intended to give him power over the human character; and that his great distinction consists in the grandeur and beneficence of his influence on the soul. But a discussion of this extent cannot be comprehended in a single discourse. Instead of a general survey o˜ the subject, I shall take one feature of it, a primary and most important one, and shall attempt to show, that the great aim of this is to call forth the soul to a higher life, to a nobler exercise of its power and affections.

This leading feature of Christianity is, the knowledge which it gives of the character of God. Jesus Christ came to reveal the Father. In the prophecies concerning him in the Old Testament, no characteristic is so frequently named, as that he should spread the knowledge of the true God. Now I ask, What constitutes the importance of such a revelation? Why has the Creator sent his Son to make himself known? I answer, God is most worthy to be known, because he is the most quickening, purifying, and ennobling object for the mind; and his great purpose in revealing himself is, that he may exalt and perfect human nature. God, as he is manifested by Christ, is another name for intellectual and moral excellence; and, in the knowledge of him, our intellectual and moral powers find their element, nutriment, strength, expansion, and happiness. To know God is to attain to the sublimest conception in the universe. To love God, is to bind ourselves to a being, who is fitted, as no other being is, to penetrate and move our whole hearts; in loving whom, we exalt ourselves; in loving whom, we love the great, the good, the beautiful, and the infinite; and under whose influence, the soul unfolds itself as a perennial plant under the cherishing sun. This constitutes the chief glory of religion. It ennobles the soul. In this its unrivalled dignity and happiness consist.

I fear, that the world at large think religion a very different thing from what has now been set forth. Too many think it a depressing, rather than an elevating service, that it breaks rather than ennobles the spirit, that it teaches us to cower before an almighty and irresistible being; and I must confess, that religion, as it has been generally taught, is any thing but an elevating principle. It has been used to scare the child, and appal the adult. Men have been virtually taught to glorify God by flattery, rather than by becoming excellent and glorious themselves, and thus doing honor to their Maker. Our dependence on God has been so taught, as to extinguish the consciousness of our free nature and moral power. Religion, in one or another form, has always been an engine for crushing the human soul. But such is not the religion of Christ. If it were, it would deserve no respect. We are not, we cannot be bound to prostrate ourselves before a deity who makes us abject and base. That moral principle within us, which calls us to watch over and to perfect our own souls, is an inspiration, which no teaching can supersede or abolish. But I cannot bear, even in way of argument, to speak of Christianity as giving views of God depressing and debasing to the human mind. Christ hath revealed to us God as The Father, and as a Father in the noblest sense of that word. He hath revealed him, as the author and lover of all souls, desiring to redeem all from sin, and to impress his likeness more and more resplendently on all; as proffering to all that best gift in the universe, his "holy spirit"; as having sent his beloved Son to train us up, and to introduce us to an "inheritance, incorruptible, undefiled, and unfading in the heavens." Such is the God of Jesus Christ; a being not to break the spirit, but to breathe trust, courage, constancy, magnanimity, in a word, all the sentiments which form an elevated mind.

This sentiment, that the knowledge of God, as given by Christ, is important and glorious, because quickening and exalting to the human soul, needs to be taught plainly and forcibly. The main ground of the obligation of being religious, I fear, is not understood among the multitude of Christians. Ask them, why they must know and worship God? and I fear, that, were the heart to speak, the answer would be, Because he can do with us what he will, and consequently our first concern is to secure his favor. Religion is a calculation of interest, a means of safety. God is worshipped too often on the same principle on which flattery and personal attentions are lavished on human superiors, and the worshipper cares not how abjectly he bows, if he may win to his side the power which he cannot resist. I look with deep sorrow on this common perversion of the highest principle of the soul. My friends, God is not to be worshipped, because he has much to give, for on this principle a despot, who should be munificent to his slaves, would merit homage. He is not to be adored for mere power; for power, when joined with selfishness and crime, ought to be withstood, and the greater the might of an evil agent, the holier and the loftier is the spirit which will not bend to him. True religion is the worship of a perfect being, who is the author of perfection to those who adore him. On this ground, and on no other, religion rests.

Why is it, my hearers, that God has discoverd such solicitude, if I may use the word, to make himself known and obtain our worship? Think you, that he calls us to adore him from a love of homage or service? Has God man's passion for ruling, man's thirst for applause, man's desire to have his name shouted by crowds? Could the acclamations of the universe, though concentrated into one burst of praise, give our Creator a new or brighter consciousness of his own majesty and goodness? O! no. He has manifested himself to us, because, in the knowledge and adoration of his perfections, our own intellectual and moral perfection is found. What he desires, is, not our subjection, out our excellence. He has no love of praise. He calls us as truly to honor goodness in others as in himself, and only claims supreme honor, because he transcends all others, and because he communicates to the mind which receives him, a light, strength, purity, which no other being can confer. God has no love of empire. It could give him no pleasure to have his footstool worn by the knees of infinite hosts. It is to make us his children in the highest sense of that word, to make us more and more the partakers of his own nature, not to multiply slaves, that he hath sent his Son to make himself known. God indeed is said to seek his own glory; but the glory of a creator must consist in the glory of his works; and we may be assured, that he cannot wish any recognition of himself, but that which will perfect his noblest, highest work, the immortal mind.

Do not, my friends, forget the great end for which Christ enjoins on us the worship of God. It is not, that we may ingratiate ourselves with an almighty agent, whose frown is destruction. It is, that we may hold communion with an intelligence and goodness, infinitely surpassing our own; that we may rise above imperfect and finite natures; that we may attach ourselves by love and reverence to the best Being in the universe; and that, through veneration and love, we may receive into our own minds the excellence, disinterestedness, wisdom, purity, and power, which we adore. This reception of the divine attributes, I desire especially to hold forth, as the most glorious end for which God reveals himself. To praise him is not enough. That homage, which has no power to assimilate us to him, is of little or no worth. The truest admiration is that by which we receive other minds into our own. True praise is a sympathy with excellence, gaining strength by utterance. Such is the praise which God demands. Then only is the purpose of Christ's revelation of God accomplished, when, by reception of the doctrine of a Paternal Divinity, we are quickened to "follow him, as dear children," and are "filled with his fulness," and become "his temples," and "dwell in God, and have God dwelling in ourselves."

I have endeavoured to show the great purpose of the Christian doctrine respecting God, or in what its importance and glory consist. Had I time, I might show, that every other doctrine of our religion has the same end. I might particularly show how wonderfully fitted are the character, example, life, death, resurrection, and all the offices of Christ, to cleanse the mind from moral evil, to quicken, soften, elevate, and transform it into the divine image ; and I might show that these are the influences which true faith derives from him, and through which he works out our salvation. But I cannot enter on this fruitful subject. Let me only say, that I see everywhere in Christianity, this great design of liberating and raising the human mind, on which I have enlarged. I see in Christianity nothing narrowing or depressing, nothing of the littleness of the systems which human fear, and craft, and ambition have engendered. I meet there no minute legislation, no descending to precise details, no arbitrary injunctions, no yoke of ceremonies, no outward religion. Every thing breathes freedom, liberality, enlargement. I meet there, not a formal, rigid creed, binding on the intellect, through all ages, the mechanical, passive repetition of the same words, and the same ideas ; but I meet a few grand, all-comprehending truths, which are given to the soul, to be developed and applied by itself ; given to it, as seed to the sower, to be cherished and expanded by its own thought, love, and obedience into more and more glorious fruits of wisdom and virtue. I see it everywhere inculcating an enlarged spirit of piety and philanthropy, leaving each of us to manifest this spirit according to the monitions of his individual conscience. I hear it everywhere calling the soul to freedom and power, by calling it to guard against the senses, the passions, the appetites, through which it is chained, enfeebled, destroyed. I see it everywhere aiming to give the mind power over the outward world, to make it superior to events, to suffering, to material nature, to persecution, to death. I see it everywhere aiming to give the mind power over itself, to invest it with inward sovereignty, to call forth within us a mighty energy for our own elevation. I meet in Christianity only discoveries of a vast, bold, illimitable character; fitted and designed to give energy and expansion to the soul. By its doctrine of a Universal Father, it sweeps away all the barriers of sect, party, rank, and nation, in which men have labored to shut up their love; makes us members of an unbounded family; and establishes sympathies between man and the whole intelligent creation. In the character of Christ, it sets before us moral perfection, that greatest and most quickening miracle in human history, a purity, which shows no stain or touch of the earth, an excellence unborrowed, unconfined, bearing no impress of any age or any nation, the very image of the Universal Father; and it encourages us, by assurances of God's merciful aid, to propose this enlarged, unsullied virtue, as the model and happiness of our moral nature. By the cross of Christ, it sets forth the spirit of self-sacrifice with an energy never known before, and, in thus crucifying selfishness, frees the mind from its worst chain. By Christ's resurrection, it links this short life with eternity, discovers to us in the fleeting present, the germ of an endless future, reveals to us the human mind ascending to other worlds, breathing a freer air, forming higher connexions, and summons us to a force of holy purpose becoming such a destination. To conclude, Christianity everywhere sets before us God in the character of infinitely free, rich, boundless Grace, in a clemency which is "not overcome by evil, but overcomes evil with good;" and a more animating and ennobling truth, who of us can conceive? I have hardly glanced at what Christianity contains. But who does not see that it was sent from Heaven, to call forth and exalt human nature, and that this is its great glory?

It has been my object in this discourse to lay open a great truth, a central, all-comprehending truth of Christianity. Whoever intelligently and cordially embraces it, obtains a standard by which to try all other doctrines, and to measure the importance of all other truths. Is it so embraced? I fear not. I apprehend that it is dimly discerned by many who acknowledge it, whilst on many more it has hardly dawned. I see other views prevailing, and prevailing in a greater or less degree among all bodies of Christians, and they seem to me among the worst errors of our times. Some of these I would now briefly notice.

1. There are those, who, instead of placing the glory of Christianity in the pure and powerful action which it gives to the human mind, seem to think, that it is rather designed to substitute the activity of another for our own. They imagine the benefit of the religion to be, that it enlists on our side an almighty being who does every thing for us. To disparage human agency, seems to them the essence of piety. They think Christ's glory to consist, not in quickening free agents to act powerfully on themselves, but in changing them by an irresistible energy. They place a Christian's happiness, not so much in powers and affections unfolded in his own breast, as in a foreign care extended over him, in a foreign wisdom which takes the place of his own intelligence. Now,

the great purpose of Christianity is, not to procure or offer to the mind a friend on whom it may passively lean, but to make the mind itself wise, strong, and efficient. Its end is, not that wisdom and strength, as subsisting in another, should do every thing for us, but that these attributes should grow perpetually in our own souls. According to Christianity, we are not carried forward as a weight by a foreign agency; but God, by means suited to our moral nature, quickens and strengthens us to walk ourselves. The great design of Christianity is, to build up in our own souls a power to withstand, to endure, to triumph. Inward vigor is its aim. That we should do most for ourselves and most for others, this is the glory it confers, and in this its happiness is found.

2. I pass to another illustration of the insensibility of men to the great doctrine, that the happiness and glory of Christianity consist in the healthy and lofty frame to which it raises the mind. I refer to the propensity of multitudes to make a wide separation between religion or Christian virtue, and its rewards. That the chief reward lies in the very spirit of religion, they do not dream. They think of being Christians for the sake of something beyond the Christian character, and something more precious. They think that Christ has a greater good to give, than a strong and generous love towards God and mankind; and would almost turn from him with scorn, if they thought him only a benefactor to the mind. It is this low view, which dwarfs the piety of thousands. Multitudes are serving God for wages distinct from the service, and hence superstition, slavishness, and formality are substituted for inward energy and spiritual worship.

3. Men's ignorance of the great truth stated in this

discourse, is seen in the low ideas attached by multitudes to the word, salvation. Ask multitudes, what is the chief evil from which Christ came to save them, and they will tell you, " From hell, from penal fires, from future punishment." Accordingly, they think that salvation is something which another may achieve for them, very much as a neighbour may quench a conflagration that menaces their dwellings and lives. That word, hell, which is used so seldom in the sacred pages, which, in a faithful translation, would not once occur in the writings of Paul, and Peter, and John, which we meet only in four or five discourses of Jesus, and which all persons, acquainted with Jewish geography, know to be a metaphor, a figure of speech, and not a literal expression, this word, by a perverse and exaggerated use, has done unspeakable injury to Christianity. It has possessed and diseased men's imaginations with outward tortures, shrieks, and flames; given them the idea of an outward ruin as what they have chiefly to dread; turned their thoughts to Jesus, as an outward deliverer; and thus blinded them to his true glory, which consists in his setting free and exalting the soul. Men are flying from an outward hell, when in truth they carry within them the hell which they should chiefly dread. The salvation which man chiefly needs, and that which brings with it all other deliverance, is salvation from the evil of his own mind. There is something far worse than outward punishment. It is sin; it is the state of a soul, which has revolted from God, and cast off its allegiance to conscience and the divine word; which renounces its Father, and hardens itself against Infinite Love; which, endued with divine powers, enthralls itself to animal lusts; which makes gain its god; which has capacities of boundless and ever-growing love, and shuts itself up in the dungeon of private interests; which, gifted with a self-directing power, consents to be a slave, and is passively formed by custom, opinion, and changing events; which, living under God's eye, dreads man's frown or scorn, and prefers human praise to its own calm consciousness of virtue; which tamely yields to temptation, shrinks with a coward's baseness from the perils of duty, and sacrifices its glory and peace in parting with self-control. No ruin can be compared to this. This the impenitent man carries with him beyond the grave, and there meets its natural issue, and inevitable retribution, in remorse, self-torture, and woes unknown on earth. This we cannot too strongly fear. To save, in the highest sense of that word, is to lift the fallen spirit from this depth, to heal the diseased mind, to restore it to energy and freedom of thought, conscience, and love. This was chiefly the salvation for which Christ shed his blood. For this the holy spirit is given; and to this all the truths of Christianity conspire.

4. Another illustration of the error which I am laboring to expose, and which places the glory and importance of Christianity in something besides its quickening influence on the soul, is afforded in the common apprehensions formed of heaven, and of the methods by which it may be obtained. Not a few, I suspect, conceive of heaven as a foreign good. It is a distant country, to which we are to be conveyed by an outward agency. How slowly do men learn, that heaven is the perfection of the mind, and that Christ gives it now just as far as he raises the mind to celestial truth and virtue. It is true, that this word is often used to ex-

press a future felicity; but the blessedness of the future world is only a continuance of what is begun here. There is but one true happiness, that of a mind unfolding its best powers, and attaching itself to great objects; and Christ gives heaven, only in proportion as he gives this elevation of character. The disinterestedness, and moral strength, and filial piety of the Christian, are not mere means of heaven, but heaven itself, and heaven now.

The most exalted idea we can form of the future state is, that it brings and joins us to God. But is not approach to this great being begun on earth? Another delightful view of heaven is, that it unites us with the good and great of our own race, and even with higher orders of beings. But this union is one of spirit, not of mere place; it is accordance of thought and feeling, not an outward relation; and does not this harmony begin even now? and is not virtuous friendship on earth essentially the pleasure which we hope hereafter? What place would be drearier than the future mansions of Christ, to one who should want sympathy with their inhabitants, who could not understand their language, who would feel himself a foreigner there, who would be taught, by the joys which he could not partake, his own loneliness and desolation? These views, I know, are often given with greater or less distinctness; but they seem to me not to have brought home to men the truth, that the fountain of happiness must be in our own souls. Gross ideas of futurity still prevail. I should not be surprised if to some among us the chief idea of heaven were that of a splendor, a radiance, like that which Christ wore on the Mount of Transfiguration. Let us all consider, and it is a great truth, that heaven has no lustre surpassing that of intellectua and moral worth; and that, were the effulgence of the sun and stars concentrated in the Christian, even this would be darkness, compared with the pure beamings of wisdom, love, and power from his mind. Think not, then, that Christ has come to give heaven as something distinct from virtue. Heaven is the freed and sanctified mind, enjoying God through accordance with his attributes, multiplying its bonds and sympathies with excellent beings, putting forth noble powers, and ministering, in union with the enlightened and holy, to the happiness and virtue of the universe.

My friends, I fear I have been guilty of repetition. But I feel the greatness of the truth which I deliver, and I am anxious to make it plain. Men need to be taught it perpetually. They have always been inclined to look to Christ for something better, as they have dreamed, than the elevation of their own souls. The great purpose of Christianity to unfold and strengthen and lift up the mind, has been perpetually thrown out of sight. In truth, this purpose has been more than overlooked. It has been reversed. The very religion given to exalt human nature, has been used to make it abject. The very religion which was given to create a generous hope, has been made an instrument of servile and torturing fear. The very religion which came from God's goodness to enlarge the human soul with a kindred goodness, has been employed to narrow it to a sect, to rear the Inquisition, and to kindle fires for the martyr. The very religion given to make the understanding and conscience free, has, by a criminal perversion, served to break them into subjection to priests, ministers, and human creeds. Ambition and craft have seized on the solemn doctrines of an omnipotent God and of future punishment, and turned them into engines against the child, the trembling female, the ignorant adult, until the skeptic has been emboldened to charge on religion the chief miseries and degradation of human nature. It is from a deep and sorrowful conviction of the injuries inflicted on Christianity and on the human soul, by these perversions and errors, that I have reiterated the great truth of this discourse. I would rescue our holy faith from this dishonor. Christianity has no tendency to break the human spirit, or to make man a slave. It has another aim; and as far as it is understood, it puts forth another power. God sent it from heaven, Christ sealed it with his blood, that it might give force of thought and purpose to the human mind, might free it from all fear but the fear of wrong-doing, might make it free of its fellow-beings, might break from it every outward and inward chain.

My hearers, I close with exhorting you to remember this great purpose of our religion. Receive Christianity as given to raise you in the scale of spiritual being. Expect from it no good, any farther than it gives strength and worth to your characters. Think not, as some seem to think, that Christ has a higher gift than purity to bestow, even pardon to the sinner. He does bring pardon. But once separate the idea of pardon from purity; once imagine that forgiveness is possible to him who does not forsake sin; once make it an exemption from outward punishment, and not the admission of the reformed mind to favor and communion with God; and the doctrine of pardon becomes your peril, and a system so teaching it, is fraught with evil. Expect no good from Christ, any farther than you are exalted by his character and teaching. Expect nothing from his cross, unless a power comes from it, strengthening you to "bear his cross," to "drink his cup," with his own unconquerable love. This is its highest influence. Look not abroad for the blessings of Christ. His reign and chief blessings are within you. The human soul is his kingdom. There he gains his victories, there rears his temples, there lavishes his treasures. His noblest monument is a mind redeemed from iniquity, brought back and devoted to God, forming itself after the perfection of the Saviour, great through its power to suffer for truth, lovely through its meek and gentle virtues. No other monument does Christ desire; for this will endure and increase in splendor, when earthly thrones shall have fallen, and even when the present order of the outward universe shall have accomplished its work, and shall have passed away.

LIKENESS TO GOD.

DISCOURSE

AT THE

ORDINATION OF THE REV. F. A. FARLEY.

PROVIDENCE, R. I. 1828.

EPHESIANS v. 1: "Be ye therefore followers of God, as dear children."

To promote true religion is the purpose of the Christian ministry. For this it was ordained. On the present occasion, therefore, when a new teacher is to be given to the church, a discourse on the character of true religion will not be inappropriate. I do not mean, that I shall attempt, in the limits to which I am now confined, to set before you all its properties, signs, and operations; for in so doing I should burden your memories with divisions and vague generalities, as uninteresting as they would be unprofitable. My purpose is, to select one view of the subject, which seems to me of primary dignity and importance; and I select this, because it is greatly neglected, and because I attribute to this neglect much of the inefficacy, and many of the corruptions, of religion.

[The text calls us to follow or imitate God,] to seek accordance with or likeness to him; and to do this, not fearfully and faintly, but with the spirit and hope of beloved children. The doctrine which I propose to illustrate, is derived immediately from these words, and is incorporated with the whole New Testament. I affirm, and would maintain, [that true religion consists in proposing, as our great end, a growing likeness to the Supreme Being.] Its noblest influence consists in making us more and more partakers of the Divinity For this it is to be preached. (Religious instruction should aim chiefly to turn men's aspirations and efforts to that perfection of the soul, which constitutes it a bright image of God.] Such is the topic now to be discussed; and I implore Him, whose glory I seek, to aid me in unfolding and enforcing it with simplicity and clearness, with a calm and pure zeal, and with unfeigned charity.

I begin with observing, what all indeed will understand, that the likeness to God, of which I propose to speak, belongs to man's higher or spiritual nature. It has its foundation in the original and essential capacities of the mind.) In proportion as these are unfolded by right and vigorous exertion, it is extended and brightened. In proportion as these lie dormant, it is obscured. In proportion as they are perverted and overpowered by the appetites and passions, it is blotted out. In truth, moral evil, if unresisted and habitual, may so blight and lay waste these capacities, that the image of God in man may seem to be wholly destroyed.

The importance of this assimilation to our Creator, is a topic which needs no labored discussion. All men, of whatever name. or sect, or opinion, will meet me on this ground. All, I presume, will allow, that no good in the compass of the universe, or within the gift of omnipotence, can be compared to a resemblance of God, or to a participation of his attributes. I fear no contradiction here. Likeness to God is the supreme gift. He can communicate nothing so precious, glorious, blessed, as himself. To hold intellectual and moral affinity with the Supreme Being, to partake his spirit, to be his children by derivations of kindred excellence, to bear a growing conformity to the perfection which we adore, this is a felicity which obscures and annihilates all other good.

It is only in proportion to this likeness, that we can enjoy either God or the universe. That God can be known and enjoyed only through sympathy or kindred attributes, is a doctrine which even Gentile philosophy discerned. That the pure in heart can alone see and commune with the pure Divinity, was the sublime instruction of ancient sages as well as of inspired prophets. It is indeed the lesson of daily experience. To understand a great and good being, we must have the seeds of the same excellence. How quickly, by what an instinct, do accordant minds recognise one another! No attraction is so powerful as that which subsists between the truly wise and good; whilst the brightest excellence is lost on those who have nothing congenial in their own breasts. God becomes a real being to us, in proportion as his own nature is unfolded within us. To a man who is growing in the likeness of God, faith begins even here to change into vision. He carries within himself a proof of a Deity, which can only be understood by experience. He more than believes, he feels the Divine presence; and gradually rises to an intercourse with his Maker, to which it is not irreverent to apply the name of friendship and intimacy. The Apostle John intended to express this truth, when he tells us, that he, in whom a principle of divine charity or benevolence has become a habit and life, "dwells in God and God in him."

It is plain, too, that likeness to God is the true and only preparation for the enjoyment of the universe. In proportion as we approach and resemble the mind of God, we are brought into harmony with the creation; for, in that proportion, we possess the principles from which the universe sprung; we carry within ourselves the perfections, of which its beauty, magnificence, order, benevolent adaptations, and boundless purposes, are the results and manifestations. God unfolds himself in his works to a kindred mind. It is possible, that the brevity of these hints may expose to the charge of mysticism, what seems to me the calmest and clearest truth. I think, however, that every reflecting man will feel, that likeness to God must be a principle of sympathy or accordance with his creation; for the creation is a birth and shining forth of the Divine Mind, a work through which his spirit breathes. In proportion as we receive this spirit, we possess within ourselves the explanation of what we see. We discern more and more of God in every thing, from the frail flower to the everlasting stars. Even in evil, that dark cloud which hangs over the creation, we discern rays of light and hope, and gradually come to see, in suffering and temptation, proofs and instruments of the sublimest purposes of Wisdom and Love.

I have offered these very imperfect views, that I may show the great importance of the doctrine which I am solicitous to enforce. I would teach, that likeness to God is a good so unutterably surpassing all other good, that whoever admits it as attainable, must acknowledge it to be the chief aim of life. I would show, that the highest and happiest office of religion is, to bring the mind into growing accordance with God; and that by the tendency of religious systems to this end, their truth and worth are to be chiefly tried.

I am aware that it may be said, that the Scriptures, in speaking of man as made in the image of God, and in calling us to imitate him, use bold and figurative language. It may be said, that there is danger from too literal an interpretation; that God is an unapproachable being; that I am not warranted in ascribing to man a like nature to the Divine; that we and all things illustrate the Creator by contrast, not by resemblance; that religion manifests itself chiefly in convictions and acknowledgments of utter worthlessness; and that to talk of the greatness and divinity of the human soul, is to inflate that pride through which Satan fell, and through which man involves himself in that fallen spirit's ruin.

I answer, that, to me, Scripture and reason hold a different language. In Christianity particularly, I meet perpetual testimonies to the divinity of human nature. This whole religion expresses an infinite concern of God for the human soul, and teaches that he deems no methods too expensive for its recovery and exaltation. Christianity, with one voice, calls me to turn my regards and care to the spirit within me, as of more worth than the whole outward world. It calls us to "be perfect as our Father in heaven is perfect;" and everywhere, in the sublimity of its precepts, it implies and recognises the sublime capacities of the being to whom they are addressed. It assures us that human virtue is "in the sight of God of great price," and speaks of the return of a human being to virtue as an event which increases the joy of heaven. In the New Testament, Jesus Christ, the Son of God, the brightness of his glory, the express and unsullied image of the Divinity, is seen mingling with men as a friend and brother, offering himself as their example, and promising to his true followers a share in all his splendors and joys. In the New Testament, God is said to communicate his own spirit, and all his fulness to the human soul. In the New Testament man is exhorted to aspire after "honor, glory, and immortality"; and Heaven, a word expressing the nearest approach to God, and a divine happiness, is everywhere proposed as the end of his being. In truth, the very essence of Christian faith is, that we trust in God's mercy, as revealed in Jesus Christ, for a state of celestial purity, in which we shall grow for ever in the likeness, and knowledge, and enjoyment of the Infinite Father. Lofty views of the nature of man are bound up and interwoven with the whole Christian system. Say not, that these are a war with humility; for who was ever humbler than Jesus, and yet who ever possessed such a consciousness of greatness and divinity? Say not that man's business is to think of his sin, and not of his dignity; for great sin implies a great capacity; it is the abuse of a noble nature; and no man can be deeply and rationally contrite, but he who feels, that in wrong-doing he has resisted a divine voice, and warred against a divine principle, in his own soul. — I need not, I trust, pursue the argument from revelation. There is an argument from nature and reason, which seems to me so convincing, and is at the same time so fitted to explain what I mean by man's possession of a like nature to God, that I shall pass at once to its exposition.

That man has a kindred nature with God, and may bear most important and ennobling relations to him, seems to me to be established by a striking proof. This proof you will understand, by considering, for a moment, how we obtain our ideas of God. Whence come the conceptions which we include under that august name? Whence do we derive our knowledge of the attributes and perfections which constitute the Supreme Being? I answer, we derive them from our own souls. The divine attributes are first developed in ourselves, and thence transferred to our Creator. The idea of God, sublime and awful as it is, is the idea of our own spiritual nature, purified and enlarged to infinity. In ourselves are the elements of the Divinity. God, then, does not sustain a figurative resemblance to man. It is the resemblance of a parent to a child, the likeness of a kindred nature.

We call God a Mind. He has revealed himself as a Spirit. But what do we know of mind, but through the unfolding of this principle in our own breasts? That unbounded spiritual energy which we call God, is conceived by us only through consciousness, through the knowledge of ourselves. — We ascribe thought or intelligence to the Deity, as one of his most glorious attributes. And what means this language? These terms we have framed to express operations or faculties of our own souls. The Infinite Light would be for ever hidden from us, did not kindred rays dawn and brighten within us. God is another name for human intelligence raised above all error and imperfection, and extended to all possible truth.

The same is true of God's goodness. How do we understand this, but by the principle of love implanted in the human breast ? Whence is it, that this divine attribute is so faintly comprehended, but from the feeble developement of it in the multitude of men ? Who can understand the strength, purity, fulness, and extent of divine philanthropy, but he in whom selfishness has been swallowed up in love ?

The same is true of all the moral perfections of the Deity. These are comprehended by us, only through our own moral nature. It is conscience within us, which, by its approving and condemning voice, interprets to us God's love of virtue and hatred of sin ; and without conscience, these glorious conceptions would never have opened on the mind. It is the lawgiver in our own breasts, which gives us the idea of divine authority, and binds us to obey it. The soul, by its sense of right, or its perception of moral distinctions, is clothed with sovereignty over itself, and through this alone, it understands and recognises the Sovereign of the Universe. Men, as by a natural inspiration, have agreed to speak of conscience as the voice of God, as the Divinity within us. This principle, reverently obeyed, makes us more and more partakers of the moral perfection of the Supreme Being, of that very excellence, which constitutes the rightfulness of his sceptre, and enthrones him over the universe. Without this inward law, we should be as incapable of receiving a law from Heaven, as the brute. Without this, the thunders of Sinai might startle the outward ear, but would have no meaning, no authority to the mind. I have expressed here a great truth. Nothing teaches so encouragingly our relation and resemblance to God; for the glory of the Supreme Being is eminently moral. We blind ourselves to his chief splendor, if we think only or mainly of his power, and overlook those attributes of rectitude and goodness, to which he subjects his omnipotence, and which are the foundations and very substance of his universal and immutable Law. And are these attributes revealed to us through the principles and convictions of our own souls? Do we understand through sympathy God's perception of the right, the good, the holy, the just? Then with what propriety is it said, that in his own image he made man!

I am aware, that it may be objected to these views, that we receive our idea of God from the universe, from his works, and not so exclusively from our own souls. The universe, I know, is full of God. The heavens and earth declare his glory. In other words, the effects and signs of power, wisdom, and goodness, are apparent through the whole creation. But apparent to what? Not to the outward eye; not to the acutest organs of sense; but to a kindred mind, which interprets the universe by itself. It is only through that energy of thought, by which we adapt various and complicated means to distant ends, and give harmony and a common bearing to multiplied exertions, that we understand the creative intelligence which has established the order, dependencies, and harmony of nature. We see God around us, because he dwells within us. It is by a kindred wisdom, that we discern his wisdom in his works. The brute, with an eye as piercing as ours, looks on the universe; and the page, which to us is radiant with characters of greatness and goodness, is to him a blank. In truth, the beauty and glory of God's works, are revealed to the mind by a light beaming from itself. We discern the impress of God's attributes in the universe, by accordance of nature, and enjoy them through sympathy. — I hardly need observe, that these remarks in relation to the universe apply with equal, if not greater force, to revelation.

I shall now be met by another objection, which to many may seem strong. It will be said, that these various attributes of which I have spoken, exist in God in Infinite Perfection, and that this destroys all affinity between the human and the Divine mind. To this I have two replies. In the first place, an attribute, by becoming perfect, does not part with its essence. Love, wisdom, power, and purity do not change their nature by enlargement. If they did, we should lose the Supreme Being through his very infinity. Our ideas of him would fade away into mere sounds. For example, if wisdom in God, because unbounded, have no affinity with that attribute in man, why apply to him that term? It must signify nothing. Let me ask what we mean, when we say that we discern the marks of intelligence in the universe? We mean, that we meet there the proofs of a mind like our own. We certainly discern proofs of no other; so that to deny this doctrine would be to deny the evidences of a God, and utterly to subvert the foundations of religious belief. What man can examine the structure of a plant or an animal, and see the adaptation of its parts to each other and to common ends, and not feel, that it is the work of an intelligence akin to his own, and that he traces these marks of design by the same spiritual energy in which they had their origin?

But I would offer another answer to this objection,

that God's infinity places him beyond the resemblance and approach of man. I affirm, and trust that I do not speak too strongly, that there are traces of infinity in the human mind; and that, in this very respect, it bears a likeness to God. The very conception of infinity, is the mark of a nature to which no limit can be prescribed. This thought, indeed, comes to us, not so much from abroad, as from our own souls. We ascribe this attribute to God, because we possess capacities and wants, which only an unbounded being can fill, and because we are conscious of a tendency in spiritual faculties to unlimited expansion. We believe in the Divine infinity, through something congenial with it in our own breasts. I hope I speak clearly, and if not, I would ask those to whom I am obscure, to pause before they condemn. To me it seems, that the soul, in all its higher actions, in original thought, in the creations of genius, in the soarings of imagination, in its love of beauty and grandeur, in its aspirations after a pure and unknown joy, and especially in disinterestedness, in the spirit of self-sacrifice, and in enlightened devotion, has a character of infinity. There is often a depth in human love, which may be strictly called unfathomable. There is sometimes a lofty strength in moral principle, which all the power of the outward universe cannot overcome. There seems a might within, which can more than balance all might without. There is, too, a piety, which swells into a transport too vast for utterance, and into an immeasurable joy. I am speaking, indeed, of what is uncommon, but still of realities. We see, however, the tendency of the soul to the infinite, in more familiar and ordinary forms. Take, for example, the delight which we find in the vast scenes of nature, in prospects which spread around us without limits, in the immensity of the heavens and the ocean, and especially in the rush and roar of mighty winds, waves, and torrents, when, amidst our deep awe, a power within seems to respond to the omnipotence around us. The same principle is seen in the delight ministered to us by works of fiction or of imaginative art, in which our own nature is set before us in more than human beauty and power. In truth, the soul is always bursting its limits. It thirsts continually for wider knowledge. It rushes forward to untried happiness. It has deep wants, which nothing limited can appease. Its true element and end is an unbounded good. Thus, God's infinity has its image in the soul; and through the soul, much more than through the universe, we arrive at this conception of the Deity.

In these remarks I have spoken strongly. But I have no fear of expressing too strongly the connexion between the Divine and the human mind. My only fear is, that I shall dishonor the great subject. The danger to which we are most exposed, is that of severing the Creator from his creatures. The propensity of human sovereigns to cut off communication between themselves and their subjects, and to disclaim a common nature with their inferiors, has led the multitude of men, who think of God chiefly under the character of a king, to conceive of him as a being who places his glory in multiplying distinctions between himself and all other beings. The truth is, that the union between the Creator and the creature surpasses all other bonds in strength and intimacy. He penetrates all things, and delights to irradiate all with his glory. Nature, in all its lowest and inanimate forms, is pervaded by his power; and, when quickened by the mysterious property of life, how wonderfully does it show forth the perfections of its Author! How much of God may be seen in the structure of a single leaf, which, though so frail as to tremble in every wind, yet holds connexions and living communications with the earth, the air, the clouds, and the distant sun, and, through these sympathies with the universe, is itself a revelation of an omnipotent mind! God delights to diffuse himself everywhere. Through his energy, unconscious matter clothes itself with proportions, powers, and beauties, which reflect his wisdom and love. How much more must he delight to frame conscious and happy recipients of his perfections, in whom his wisdom and love may substantially dwell, with whom he may form spiritual ties, and to whom he may be an everlasting spring of moral energy and happiness! How far the Supreme Being may communicate his attributes to his intelligent offspring, I stop not to inquire. But that his almighty goodness will impart to them powers and glories, of which the material universe is but a faint emblem, I cannot doubt. That the soul, if true to itself and its Maker, will be filled with God, and will manifest him, more than the sun, I cannot doubt. Who can doubt it, that believes and understands the doctrine of human immortality?.

The views which I have given in this discourse, respecting man's participation of the Divine nature, seem to me to receive strong confirmation, from the title or relation most frequently applied to God in the New Testament; and I have reserved this as the last corroboration of this doctrine, because, to my own mind, it is singularly affecting. In the New Testament God is made known to us as a Father; and a brighter feature of that book cannot be named. Our worship is to be directed to him as our Father. Our whole religion is to take its character from this view of the Divinity. In this he is to rise always to our minds. And what is it to be a Father? It is to communicate one's own nature, to give life to kindred beings; and the highest function of a Father is to educate the mind of the child, and to impart to it what is noblest and happiest in his own mind. God is our Father, not merely because he created us, or because he gives us enjoyment; for he created the flower and the insect, yet we call him not their Father. This bond is a spiritual one. This name belongs to God, because he frames spirits like himself, and delights to give them what is most glorious and blessed in his own nature. Accordingly, Christianity is said, with special propriety, to reveal God as the Father, because it reveals him as sending his Son to cleanse the mind from every stain, and to replenish it for ever with the spirit and moral attributes of its Author. Separate from God this idea of his creating and training up beings after his own likeness, and you rob him of the paternal character. This relation vanishes, and with it vanishes the glory of the Gospel, and the dearest hopes of the human soul.

The greatest use which I would make of the principles laid down in this discourse, is to derive from them just and clear views of the nature of religion. What, then, is religion? I answer; it is not the adoration of a God with whom we have no common properties; of a distinct, foreign, separate being; but of an all-communicating Parent. It recognises and adores God, as a being whom we know through our own souls, who has made man in his own image, who is the perfection of our own spiritual nature, who has sympathies with us as kindred beings, who is near us, not in place only like this all-surrounding atmosphere, but by spiritual influence and love, who looks on us with parental interest, and whose great design it is to communicate to us for ever, and in freer and fuller streams, his own power, goodness, and joy. The conviction of this near and ennobling relation of God to the soul, and of his great purposes towards it, belongs to the very essence of true religion; and true religion manifests itself chiefly and most conspicuously in desires, hopes, and efforts corresponding to this truth. It desires and seeks supremely the assimilation of the mind to God, or the perpetual unfolding and enlargement of those powers and virtues by which it is constituted his glorious image. The mind, in propor tion as it is enlightened and penetrated by true religion, thirsts and labors for a godlike elevation. What else, indeed, can it seek, if this good be placed within its reach? If I am capable of receiving and reflecting the intellectual and moral glory of my Creator, what else in comparison shall I desire? Shall I deem a property in the outward universe as the highest good, when I may become partaker of the very mind from which it springs, of the prompting love, the disposing wisdom, the quickening power, through which its order, beauty, and beneficent influences subsist? True religion is known by these high aspirations, hopes, and efforts. And this is the religion which most truly honors God. To honor him, is not to tremble before him as an unapproachable sovereign, not to utter barren praise which leaves us as it found us. It is to become what we praise. It is to approach God as an inexhaustible Fountain of light, power, and purity. It is to feel the quickening and transforming energy of his perfections. It is to thirst for the growth and invigoration of the divine principle within us. It is to seek the very spirit of God. It is to trust in, to bless, to thank him for that rich grace, mercy, love, which was revealed and proffered by Jesus Christ, and which proposes as its great end the perfection of the human soul.

I regard this view of religion as infinitely important It does more than all things to make our connexion with our Creator ennobling and happy ; and, in proportion as we want it, there is danger that the thought of God may itself become the instrument of our degradation. That religion has been so dispensed as to depress the human mind, I need not tell you ; and it is a truth which ought to be known, that the greatness of the Deity, when separated in our thoughts from his parental character, especially tends to crush human energy and hope. To a frail, dependent creature, an omnipotent Creator easily becomes a terror, and his worship easily degenerates into servility, flattery, self-contempt, and selfish calculation. Religion only ennobles us, in as far as it reveals to us the tender and intimate connexion of God with his creatures, and teaches us to see in the very greatness which might give alarm, the source of great and glorious communications to the human soul. You cannot, my hearers, think too highly of the majesty of God. But let not this majesty sever him from you. Remember, that his greatness is the infinity of attributes which yourselves possess. Adore his infinite wisdom ; but remember that this wisdom rejoices to diffuse itself, and let an exhilarating hope spring up, at the thought of the immeasurable intelligence which such a Father must communicate to his children. In like manner adore his power. Let the boundless creation fill you with awe and admiration of the energy which sustains it. But remember that God has a nobler work than the outward creation, even the spirit within yourselves; and that it is his purpose to replenish this with his own energy, and to crown it with growing power and triumphs over the material universe. Above all, adore his unutterable goodness. But remember, that this attribute is particularly proposed to you as your model; that God calls you, both by nature and revelation, to a fellowship in his philanthropy; that he has placed you in social relations, for the very end of rendering you ministers and representatives of his benevolence; that he even summons you to espouse and to advance the sublimest purpose of his goodness, the redemption of the human race, by extending the knowledge and power of Christian truth. It is through such views, that religion raises up the soul, and binds man by ennobling bonds to his Maker.

To complete my views of this topic, I beg to add an important caution. (I have said that the great work of religion is, to conform ourselves to God, or to unfold the divine likeness within us.) Let none infer from this language, that I place religion in unnatural effort, in straining after excitements which do not belong to the present state, or in any thing separate from the clear and simple duties of life. I exhort you to no extravagance. I reverence human nature too much to do it violence I see too much divinity in its ordinary operations, to urge on it a forced and vehement virtue. To grow in the likeness of God, we need not cease to be men. This likeness does not consist in extraordinary or miraculous gifts, in supernatural additions to the soul, or in any thing foreign to our original constitution; but in our essential faculties, unfolded by vigorous and conscientious exertion in the ordinary circumstances assigned by God. To resemble our Creator, we need not fly from society, and entrance ourselves in lonely contemplation and prayer. Such processes might give a feverish strength to one class of emotions, but would result in disproportion, distortion, and sickliness of mind. /Our proper work is to approach God by the free and natural unfolding of our highest powers, of understanding, conscience, love, and the moral will.(

Shall I be told that, by such language, I ascribe to nature the effects which can only be wrought in the soul by the Holy Spirit? I anticipate this objection, and wish to meet it by a simple exposition of my views. I would on no account disparage the gracious aids and influences which God imparts to the human soul. The promise of the Holy Spirit is among the most precious in the Sacred Volume. Worlds could not tempt me to part with the doctrine of God's intimate connexion with the mind, and of his free and full communications to it. But these views are in no respect at variance with what I have taught, of the method by which we are to grow in the likeness of God. Scripture and experience concur in teaching, that, by the Holy Spirit, we are to understand a divine assistance adapted to our moral freedom, and accordant with the fundamental truth, that virtue is the mind's own work. By the Holy Spirit, I understand an aid, which must be gained and made effectual by our own activity; an aid, which no more interferes with our faculties, than the assistance which we receive from our fellow-beings; an aid, which silently mingles and conspires with all other helps and means of goodness; an aid, by which we unfold our natural powers in a natural order, and by which we are strengthened to understand and apply the resources derived from our munificent Creator. This aid we cannot prize too much, or pray for too earnestly. But wherein, let me ask, does it war with the doctrine, that God is to be approached by the exercise and unfolding of our highest powers and affections, in the ordinary circumstances of human life?

I repeat it, to resemble our Maker we need not quarrel with our nature or our lot. Our present state, made up, as it is, of aids and trials, is worthy of God, and may be used throughout to assimilate us to him. For example, our domestic ties, the relations of neighbourhood and country, the daily interchanges of thoughts and feelings, the daily occasions of kindness, the daily claims of want and suffering, these and the other circumstances of our social state, form the best sphere and school for that benevolence, which is God's brightest attribute; and we should make a sad exchange, by substituting for these natural aids, any self-invented artificial means of sanctity. Christianity, our great guide to God, never leads us away from the path of nature, and never wars with the unsophisticated dictates of conscience. We approach our Creator by every right exertion of the powers he gives us. Whenever we invigorate the understanding by honestly and resolutely seeking truth, and by withstanding whatever might warp the judgment; whenever we invigorate the conscience by following it in opposition to the passions; whenever we receive a blessing gratefully, bear a trial patiently, or encounter peril or scorn with moral courage; whenever we perform a disinterested deed; whenever we lift up the heart in true adoration to God; whenever we war against a habit or desire which is strengthening itself against our higher principles; whenever we think, speak, or act, with moral energy, and resolute devotion to duty, be the occasion ever so humble, obscure, familiar; then the divinity is growing within us, and we are ascending towards our Author. True religion thus blends itself with common life. We are thus to draw nigh to God, without forsaking men. We are thus, without parting with our human nature, to clothe ourselves with the divine.

My views on the great subject of this discourse have now been given. I shall close with a brief consideration of a few objections, in the course of which I shall offer some views of the Christian ministry, which this occasion and the state of the world, seem to me to demand. — I anticipate from some an objection to this discourse, drawn as they will say from experience. I may be told, that, I have talked of the godlike capacities of human nature, and have spoken of man as a divinity; and where, it will be asked, are the warrants of this high estimate of our race? I may be told that I dream, and that I have peopled the world with the creatures of my lonely imagination. What! Is it only in dreams, that beauty and loveliness have beamed on me from the human countenance, that I have heard tones of kindness, which have thrilled through my heart, that I have found sympathy in suffering, and a sacred joy in friendship? Are all the great and good men of past ages only dreams? Are such names as Moses, Socrates, Paul, Alfred, Milton, only the fictions of my disturbed slumbers? Are the great deeds of history, the discoveries of philosophy, the creations of genius, only visions?

O ! no. I do not dream when I speak of the divine capacities of human nature. It is a real page in which I read of patriots and martyrs, of Fenelon and Howard, of Hampden and Washington. And-tell me not that these were prodigies, miracles, immeasurably separated from their race ; for the very reverence, which has treasured up and hallowed their memories, the very sentiments of admiration and love with which their names are now heard, show that the principles of their greatness are diffused through all your breasts. The germs of sublime virtue are scattered liberally on our earth. How often have I seen in the obscurity of domestic life, a strength of love, of endurance, of pious trust, of virtuous resolution, which in a public sphere would have attracted public homage. I cannot but pity the man, who recognises nothing godlike in his own nature. I see the marks of God in the heavens and the earth, but how much more in a liberal intellect, in magnanimity, in unconquerable rectitude, in a philanthropy which forgives every wrong, and which never despairs of the cause of Christ and human virtue. I do and I must reverence human nature. Neither the sneers of a worldly skepticism, nor the groans of a gloomy theology, disturb my faith in its godlike powers and tendencies. I know how it is despised, how it has been oppressed, how civil and religious establishments have for ages- conspired to crush it. I know its history. I shut my eyes on none of its weaknesses and crimes. I understand the proofs, by which despotism demonstrates, that man is a wild beast, in want of a master, and only safe in chains. But, injured, trampled on, and scorned as our nature is, I still turn to it with intense sympathy and strong hope. The signatures of its origin and its end are impressed too deeply to be ever wholly effaced. I bless it for its kind affections, for its strong and tender love. I honor it for its struggles against oppression, for its growth and progress under the weight of so many chains and prejudices, for its achievements in science and art, and still more for its examples of heroic and saintly virtue. These are marks of a divine origin and the pledges of a celestial inheritance; and I thank God that my own lot is bound up with that of the human race.

But another objection starts up. It may be said, "Allow these views to be true; are they fitted for the pulpit? fitted to act on common minds? They may be prized by men of cultivated intellect and taste; but can the multitude understand them? Will the multitude feel them? On whom has a minister to act? On men immersed in business, and buried in the flesh; on men, whose whole power of thought has been spent on pleasure or gain; on men chained by habit and wedded to sin. Sooner may adamant be riven by a child's touch, than the human heart be pierced by refined and elevated sentiment. Gross instruments will alone act on gross minds. Men sleep, and nothing but thunder, nothing but flashes from the everlasting fire of hell, will thoroughly wake them."

I have all along felt that such objections would be made to the views I have urged. But they do not move me. I answer, that I think these views singularly adapted to the pulpit, and I think them full of power. The objection is that they are refined. But I see God accomplishing his noblest purposes by what may be called refined means. All the great agents of nature, attraction, heat, and the principle of life, are refined, spiritual, invisible, acting gently, silently, imperceptibly; and yet brute matter feels their power, and is transformed by them into surpassing beauty. The electric fluid, unseen, unfelt, and everywhere diffused, is infinitely more efficient, and ministers to infinitely nobler productions, than when it breaks forth in thunder. Much less can I believe, that in the moral world, noise, menace, and violent appeals to gross passions, to fear and selfishness, are God's chosen means of calling forth spiritual life, beauty, and greatness. It is seldom that human nature throws off all susceptibility of grateful and generous impressions, all sympathy with superior virtue; and here are springs and principles to which a generous teaching, if simple, sincere, and fresh from the soul, may confidently appeal.

It is said, men cannot understand the views which seem to me so precious. This objection I am anxious to repel, for the common intellect has been grievously kept down and wronged through the belief of its incapacity. The pulpit would do more good, were not the mass of men looked upon and treated as children. Happily for the race, the time is passing away, in which intellect was thought the monopoly of a few, and the majority were given over to hopeless ignorance. Science is leaving her solitudes to enlighten the multitude. How much more may religious teachers take courage to speak to men on subjects, which are nearer to them than the properties and laws of matter, I mean their own souls. The multitude, you say, want capacity to receive great truths relating to their spiritual nature. But what, let me ask you, is the Christian religion? A spiritual system, intended to turn men's minds upon themselves, to frame them to watchfulness over thought, imagination, and passion, to establish them in an intimacy with their own souls. What are all the Christian virtues, which men are exhorted to love and seek? I answer, pure and high motions or determinations of the mind. That refinement of thought, which, I am told, transcends the common intellect, belongs to the very essence of Christianity. In confirmation of these views, the human mind seems to me to be turning itself more and more inward, and to be growing more alive to its own worth, and its capacities of progress. The spirit of education shows this, and so does the spirit of freedom. There is a spreading conviction that man was made for a higher purpose than to be a beast of burden, or a creature of sense. The divinity is stirring within the human breast, and demanding a culture and a liberty worthy of the child of God. Let religious teaching correspond to this advancement of the mind. Let it rise above the technical, obscure, and frigid theology which has come down to us from times of ignorance, superstition, and slavery. Let it penetrate the human soul, and reveal it to itself. No preaching, I believe, is so intelligible, as that which is true to human nature, and helps men to read their own spirits.

But the objection which I have stated not only represents men as incapable of understanding, but still more of being moved, quickened, sanctified, and saved, by such views as I have given. If by this objection nothing more is meant, than that these views are not alone or of themselves sufficient, I shall not dispute it; for true and glorious as they are, they do not constitute the whole truth, and I do not expect great moral effects from narrow and partial views of our nature. I have spoken of the godlike capacities of the soul. But other and very different elements enter into the human being. Man has animal propensities as well as intellectual and moral powers. He has a body as well as mind. He has passions to war with reason, and self-love with conscience. He is a free being, and a tempted being, and thus constituted he may and does sin, and often sins grievously. To such a being, religion, or virtue, is a conflict, requiring great spiritual effort, put forth in habitual watchfulness and prayer; and all the motives are needed, by which force and constancy may be communicated to the will. I exhort not the preacher, to talk perpetually of man as " made but a little lower than the angels." I would not narrow him to any class of topics. Let him adapt himself to our whole and various nature. Let him summon to his aid all the powers of this world, and the world to come. Let him bring to bear on the conscience and the heart, God's milder and more awful attributes, the promises and threatenings of the divine word, the lessons of history, the warnings of experience. Let the wages of sin here and hereafter be taught clearly and earnestly. But amidst the various motives to spiritual effort, which belong to the minister, none are more quickening than those drawn from the soul itself, and from God's desire and purpose to exalt it, by every aid consistent with its freedom. These views I conceive are to mix with all others, and without them all others fail to promote a generous virtue. Is it said, that the minister's proper work is, to preach Christ, and not the dignity of human nature? I answer, that Christ's greatness is manifested in the greatness of the nature which he was sent to redeem; and that his chief glory consists in this, that he came to restore God's image where it was obscured or effaced, and to give an everlasting impulse and life to what is divine within us. Is it said, that the malignity of sin is to be the minister's great theme? I answer, that this malignity can only be understood and felt, when sin is viewed as the ruin of God's noblest work, as darkening a light brighter than the sun, as carrying discord, bondage, disease, and death into a mind framed for perpetual progress towards its Author. Is it said, that terror is the chief instrument of saving the soul? I answer, that if by terror, be meant a rational and moral fear, a conviction and dread of the unutterable evil incurred by a mind which wrongs, betrays, and destroys itself, then I am the last to deny its importance. But a fear like this, which regards the debasement of the soul as the greatest of evils, is plainly founded upon and proportioned to our conceptions of the greatness of our nature. The more common terror, excited by vivid images of torture and bodily pain, is a very questionable means of virtue. When strongly awakened, it generally injures the character, breaks men into cowards and slaves, brings the intellect to cringe before human authority, makes man abject before his Maker, and, by a natural reaction of the mind, often terminates in a presumptuous confidence, altogether distinct from virtuous self-respect, and singularly hostile to the unassuming, charitable spirit of Christianity. The preacher should rather strive to fortify the soul against physical pains, than to bow it to their mastery, teaching it to dread nothing in comparison with sin, and to dread sin as the ruin of a noble nature.

Men, I repeat it, are to be quickened and raised by appeals to their highest principles. Even the convicts of a prison may be touched by kindness, generosity, and especially by a tone, look, and address, expressing hope and respect for their nature. I know, that the doctrine of ages has been, that terror, restraint, and bondage are the chief safeguards of human virtue and peace. But we have begun to learn, that affection, confidence, respect, and freedom are mightier as well as nobler agents. Men can be wrought upon by generous influences. I would that this truth were better understood by religious teachers. From the pulpit, generous influences too seldom proceed. In the church, men too seldom hear a voice to quicken and exalt them. Religion, speaking through her public organs, seems often to forget her natural tone of elevation. The character of God, the principles of his government, his relations to the human family, the purposes for which he brought us into being, the nature which he has given us, and the condition in which he has placed us, these and the like topics, though the sublimest which can enter the mind, are not unfrequently so set forth as to narrow and degrade the hearers, disheartening and oppressing with gloom the timid and sensitive, and infecting coarser minds with the unhallowed spirit of intolerance, presumption, and exclusive pretension to the favor of God. I know, and re-rejoice to know, that preaching in its worst forms does good; for so bright and piercing is the light of Christianity, that it penetrates in a measure the thickest clouds in which men contrive to involve it. But that evil mixes with the good, I also know; and I should be unfaithful to my deep convictions, did I not say, that human nature requires for its elevation, more generous treatment from the teachers of religion.

I conclude with saying, let the minister cherish a reverence for his own nature. Let him never despise it even in its most forbidding forms. Let him delight in its beautiful and lofty manifestations. Let him hold fast as one of the great qualifications for his office, a faith in the greatness of the human soul, that faith, which looks beneath the perishing body, beneath the sweat of the laborer, beneath the rags and ignorance of the poor, beneath the vices of the sensual and selfish, and discerns in the depths of the soul a divine principle, a ray of the Infinite Light, which may yet break forth and " shine as the sun " in the kingdom of God. Let him strive to awaken in men a consciousness of the heavenly treasure within them, a consciousness of possessing what is of more worth than the outward universe. Let hope give life to all his labors. Let him speak to men, as to beings liberally gifted, and made for God. Let him always look round on a congregation with the encouraging trust, that he has hearers prepared to respond to the simple, unaffected utterance of great truths, and to the noblest workings of his own mind. Let him feel deeply for those, in whom the divine nature is overwhelmed by the passions. Let him sympathize tenderly with those, in whom it begins to struggle, to mourn for sin, to thirst for a new life. Let him guide and animate to higher and diviner virtue, those in whom it has gained strength. Let him strive to infuse courage, enterprise, devout trust, and an inflexible will, into men's labors for their own perfection. In one word, let him cherish an unfaltering and growing faith in God as the Father and quickener of the human mind, and in Christ as its triumphant and immortal friend. That by such preaching he is to work miracles, I do not say. That he will rival in sudden and outward effects what is wrought by the preachers of a low and terrifying theology, I do not expect or desire. That all will be made better, I am far from believing.

His office is, to act on free beings, who, after all, must determine themselves ; who have power to withstand all foreign agency ; who are to be saved, not by mere preaching, but by their own prayers and toil. Still I believe that such a minister will be a benefactor beyond all praise to the human soul. I believe, and know, that, on those who will admit his influence, he will work deeply, powerfully, gloriously. His function is the sublimest under heaven ; and his reward will be, a growing power of spreading truth, virtue, moral strength, love, and happiness, without limit and without end.

THE CHRISTIAN MINISTRY.

DISCOURSE

AT

THE DEDICATION OF DIVINITY HALL,

CAMBRIDGE, 1826.

LUKE iv. 32: "His word was with power."

WE are assembled to set apart and consecrate this building to the education of teachers of the Christian religion. Regarding, as we do, this religion as God's best gift to mankind, we look on these simple walls, reared for this holy and benevolent work, with an interest, which more splendid edifices, dedicated to inferior purposes, would fail to inspire. We thank God for the zeal which has erected them. We thank him for the hope, that here will be trained, and hence will go forth, able ministers of the New Testament. God accept our offering and fulfil our trust. May he shed on this spot the copious dew of his grace, and compass it with his favor as with a shield.

To what end do we devote this building? How may this end be accomplished? These questions will guide our present reflections.

To what end is this edifice dedicated? The answer to this question may be given in various forms or expanded into various particulars. From this wide range of topics, I shall select one, which from its comprehensiveness and importance, will be acknowledged to deserve peculiar attention. I say, then, that this edifice is dedicated to the training of ministers, whose word, like their Master's, shall be "*with power.*" Power, energy, efficiency, that is the endowment to be communicated most assiduously by a theological institution. Such is the truth, which I would now develope. My meaning may easily be explained. By the power, of which I have spoken, I mean that strong action of the understanding, conscience, and heart, on moral and religious truth, through which the preacher is quickened and qualified to awaken the same strong action in others. I mean energy of thought and feeling in the minister, creating for itself an appropriate expression, and propagating itself to the hearer. What this power is all men understand by experience. All know, how the same truth differs, when dispensed by different lips; how doctrines, inert and uninteresting as expounded by one teacher, come fraught with life from another; arrest attention, rouse emotion, and give a new spring to the soul. In declaring this power to be the great object of a theological institution, I announce no discovery. I say nothing new. But this truth, like many others, is too often acknowledged only to be slighted. It needs to be brought out, to be made prominent, to become the living, guiding principle of education for the ministry. Power, then, I repeat it, is the great good to be communicated by theological institutions. To impart knowledge is indeed their indispensable duty, but not their whole, nor most arduous, nor highest work. Knowledge is the means, power the end. The former, when accumulated, as it often is, with no strong action of the intellect, no vividness of conception, no depth of conviction, no force of feeling, is of little or no worth to the preacher. It comes from him as a faint echo, with nothing of that mysterious energy, which strong conviction throws into style and utterance. His breath, which should kindle, chills his hearers, and the nobler the truth with which he is charged, the less he succeeds in carrying it far into men's souls. We want more than knowledge. We want force of thought, feeling, and purpose. What profits it to arm the pupil with weapons of heavenly temper, unless his hands be nerved to wield them with vigor and success? The word of God is indeed " quick and powerful, and sharper than any two-edged sword;" but when committed to him who has no kindred energy, it does not and cannot penetrate the mind. Power is the attribute, which crowns all a minister's accomplishments. It is the centre and grand result, in which all his studies, meditations, and prayers should meet, and without which his office becomes a form and a show. And yet how seldom is it distinctly and earnestly proposed as the chief qualification for the sacred office! How seldom do we meet it! How often does preaching remind us of a child's arrows shot against a fortress of adamant. How often does it seem a mock fight. We do not see the earnestness of real warfare; of men bent on the accomplishment of a great good. We want powerful ministers, not graceful declaimers, not elegant essayists, but men fitted to act on men, to make themselves *felt* in society.

I have said that the communication of power is the

great end of a theological institution. Let not this word give alarm. I mean by it, as you must have seen, a very different power from that which ministers once possessed, and which some still covet. There have been times, when the clergy were rivals in dominion with kings; when the mitre even towered above the diadem; when the priest, shutting God's word on the people, and converting its threatenings and promises into instruments of usurpation, was able to persuade men, that the soul's everlasting doom hung on his ministry, and even succeeded in establishing a sway over fiery and ferocious spirits, which revolted against all other control. This power, suited to barbarous times, and, as some imagine, a salutary element of society in rude, lawless ages, has been shaken almost everywhere by the progress of intellect; and in Protestant countries, it is openly reprobated and renounced. It is not to reëstablish this, that these walls have been reared. We trust, that they are to be bulwarks against its encroachments, and that they are to send forth influences more and more hostile to every form of spiritual usurpation.

Am I told that this kind of power is now so fallen and so contemned, that to disclaim or to oppose it seems a waste of words? I should rejoice to yield myself to this belief. But unhappily the same enslaving and degrading power may grow up under Protestant as under Catholic institutions. In all ages and all churches, terror confers a tremendous influence on him who can spread it; and, through this instrument, the Protestant minister, whilst disclaiming Papal pretensions, is able, if so minded, to build up a spiritual despotism. That this means of subjugating the mind should be too freely used and dreadfully perverted, we cannot wonder, when we consider that no talent is required to spread a panic, and that coarse minds and hard hearts are signally gifted for this work of torture. The progress of intelligence is undoubtedly narrowing the power, which the minister gains by excessive appeals to men's fears, but has by no means destroyed it; for as yet the intellect, even in Protestant countries, has exerted itself comparatively little on religion; and, ignorance begetting a passive, servile state of mind, the preacher, if so disposed, finds little difficulty in breaking some, if not many, spirits by terror. The effects of this ill-gotten power are mournful on the teacher and the taught. The panic-smitten hearer, instructed that safety is to be found in bowing to an unintelligible creed, and too agitated for deliberate and vigorous thought, resigns himself a passive subject to his spiritual guides, and receives a faith by which he is debased. Nor does the teacher escape unhurt; for all usurpation on men's understandings begets, in him who exercises it, a dread and resistance of the truth which threatens its subversion. Hence ministers have so often fallen behind their age, and been the chief foes of the master spirits who have improved the world. They have felt their power totter at the tread of an independent thinker. By a kind of instinct, they have fought against the light, before which the shades of superstition were vanishing, and have received their punishment in the darkness and degradation of their own minds. To such power as we have described, we do not dedicate these walls. We would not train here, if we could, agents of terror, to shake weak nerves, to disease the imagination, to lay a spell on men's faculties, to guard a creed by fires more consuming than those which burned on Sinai.

Believing that this method of dominion is among the chief obstructions to an enlightened faith, and abhorring tyranny in the pulpit as truly as on the throne, we would consecrate this edifice to the subversion, not the participation, of this unhallowed power.

Is it then asked, what I mean by the power which this institution should aim to communicate? I mean power to act on intelligent and free beings, by means proportioned to their nature. I mean power to call into healthy exertion the intellect, conscience, affections, and moral will of the hearer. I mean force of conception, and earnestness of style and elocution. I mean, that truth should be a vital principle in the soul of the teacher, and should come from him as a reality. I mean, that his whole moral and intellectual faculties should be summoned to his work; that a tone of force and resolution should pervade his efforts; that, throwing his soul into his cause, he should plead it with urgency, and should concentrate on his hearers all the influences which consist with their moral freedom.

Every view which we can take of the ministry will teach us, that nothing less than the whole amount of power in the individual can satisfy its demands. This we learn, if we consider, first, the weight and grandeur of the subjects which the minister is to illustrate and enforce. He is to speak of God, the King and Father Eternal, whose praise no tongue of men or angels can worthily set forth. He is to speak of the soul, that ray of the Divinity, the partaker of God's own immortality, to which the outward universe was made to minister, and which, if true to itself, will one day be clad with a beauty and grandeur such as nature's loveliest and sublimest scenery never wears. He is to speak, not of this world only, but of invisible and more advanced states of being; of a world too spiritual for the fleshly eye to see, but of which a presage and earnest may be found in the enlightened and purified mind. He has to speak of virtue, of human perfection, of the love which is due to the Universal Father and to fellow-beings, of the intercourse of the soul with its Creator, and of all the duties of life as hallowed and elevated by a reference to God and to the future world. He has to speak of sin, that essential evil, that only evil, which, by its unutterable fearfulness, makes all other calamities unworthy of the name. He is to treat, not of ordinary life, nor of the most distinguished agents in ordinary history, but of God's supernatural interpositions; of his most sensible and immediate providence; of men inspired and empowered to work the most important revolutions in society; and especially of Jesus Christ, the Son of God, the theme of prophecy, the revealer of grace and truth, the Saviour from sin, the conqueror of death, who hath left us an example of immaculate virtue, whose love passeth knowledge, and whose history, combining the strange and touching contrasts of the cross, the resurrection, and a heavenly throne, surpasses all other records in interest and grandeur. He has to speak, not of transitory concerns but of happiness and misery transcending in duration and degree the most joyful and suffering condition of the present state. He has to speak of the faintly shadowed, but solemn consummation of this world's eventful history; of the coming of the Son of Man, the resurrection, the judgment, the retributions of the last day. Here are subjects of intense interest. They claim and should call forth the mind's whole power, and are infinitely wronged when uttered with cold lips and from an unmoved heart.

If we next consider the effects, which, through these truths, the minister is to produce, we shall see that his function demands and should be characterized by power. The first purpose of a minister's function, which is to enlighten the understanding on the subject of religion, is no easy task; for all religious truth is not obvious, plain, shining with an irresistible evidence, so that a glance of thought will give the hearer possession of the teacher's mind. We sometimes talk, indeed, of the simplicity of religion, as if it were as easy as a child's book, as if it might be taught with as little labor as the alphabet. But all analogy forbids us to believe, that the sublimest truths can be imparted or gained with little thought or effort, and the prevalent ignorance confirms this presumption. Obstacles neither few nor small to a clear apprehension of religion, are found in the invisibleness of its objects; in the disproportion between the Infinite Creator and the finite mind; in the proneness of human beings to judge of superior natures by their own, and to transfer to the spiritual world the properties of matter and the affections of sense; in the perpetual pressure of outward things upon the attention; in the darkness which sin spreads over the intellect; in the ignorance which yet prevails in regard to the human mind; and, though last not least, in the errors and superstitions which have come down to us from past ages, and which exert an unsuspected power on our whole modes of religious thinking. These obstacles are strengthened by the general indisposition to investigate religion freely and thoroughly. The tone of authority with which it has been taught, the terror and obscure phraseology in which it has been shrouded, and the unlovely aspect which it has been made to wear, have concurred to repel from it deliberate and earnest attention, and to reconcile men to a superficial mode of thinking which they would scorn on every other subject. Add to this, that the early inculcation and frequent repetition of religion, by making it familiar, expose it to neglect. The result of all these unfavorable influences, is, that religious truth is more indistinctly apprehended, is more shadowy and unreal to the multitude, than any other truth; and, unhappily, this remark applies with almost equal truth to all ranks of society and all orders of intellect. The loose conceptions of Christianity which prevail among the high as well as the low, do not deserve the name of knowledge. The loftiest minds among us seldom put forth their strength on the very subject, for which intelligence was especially given. A great revolution is needed here. The human intellect is to be brought to act on religion with new power. It ought to prosecute this inquiry with an intenseness, with which no other subject is investigated. And does it require no energy in the teacher, to awaken this power and earnestness of thought in others, to bring religion before the intellect as its worthiest object, to raise men's traditional, lifeless, superficial faith into deliberate, profound conviction?

That the ministry should be characterized by power and energy, will be made more apparent, if we consider that it is instituted to quicken, not only the intellect but the conscience; to enforce the obligations, as well as illustrate the truth, of religion. It is an important branch of the minister's duty, to bring home the general principles of duty to the individual mind; to turn it upon itself; to rouse it to a resolute, impartial survey of its whole responsibilities and ill deserts. And is not energy needed to break through the barriers of pride and self-love, and to place the individual before a tribunal in his own breast, as solemn and searching as that which awaits him at the last day? It is not indeed so difficult to rouse, in the timid and susceptible, a morbid susceptibility of conscience, to terrify weak people into the idea, that they are to answer for sins inherited from the first fallen pair, and entailed upon them by a stern necessity. But this feverish action of the conscience is its weakness, not its strength; and the teacher who would rouse the moral sense to discriminating judgment and healthful feeling, has need of a vastly higher kind of power than is required to darken and disease it.

Another proof that the ministry should be characterized by power, is given to us by the consideration, that it is intended to act on the affections; to exhibit religion in its loveliness and venerableness, as well as in its truth and obligation; to concentrate upon it all the strength of moral feeling. The Christian teacher has a great work to do in the human heart. His function has, for its highest aim, to call forth towards God the profoundest awe, attachment, trust, and joy, of which human nature is capable. Religion demands, that He who is supreme in the universe, should be supreme in the human soul. God, to whom belongs the mysterious and incommunicable attribute of Infinity; who is the fulness and source of life and thought, of beauty and power, of love and happiness; on whom we depend more intimately than the stream on the fountain, or the plant on the earth in which it is rooted,—this Great Being ought to call forth peculiar emotions, and to move and sway the soul, as he pervades creation, with unrivalled energy. It is his distinction, that he unites in his nature infinite majesty and infinite benignity, the most awful with the most endearing attributes, the tenderest relations to the individual with the grandeur of the universal sovereign; and, through this nature, he is fitted to act on the mind as no other being can, — to awaken a love more intense, a veneration more profound, a sensibility of which the soul knows not its capacity until it is penetrated and touched by God. To bring the created mind into living union with the Infinite Mind, so that it shall respond to him through its whole being, is the noblest function, which this harmonious and beneficent universe performs. For this, revelation was given. For this, the ministry was instituted. The Christian teacher is to make more audible, and to interpret, the voice in which the beauty and awfulness of nature, the heavens, the earth, fruitful seasons, storms and thunders, recall men to their Creator. Still more, he is to turn them to the clearer, milder, more attractive splendors, in which the Divinity is revealed by Jesus Christ. His great purpose, I repeat it, is, to give vitality to the thought of God in the human mind; to make his presence felt; to make him a reality, and the most powerful reality to the soul. And is not this a work requiring energy of thought and utterance? Is it easy, in a world of matter and sense, amidst crowds of impressions rushing in from abroad, amidst the constant and visible agency of second causes, amidst the anxieties, toils, pleasures, dissipations, and competitions of life, in the stir and bustle of society, and in an age when luxury wars with spirituality, and the developement of nature's resources is turning men's trust from the Creator, — is it easy, amidst these gross interests and distracting influences, to raise men's minds to the invisible Divinity, to fix impressions of God deeper and more enduring than those which are received from all other beings, to make him the supreme object, spring, and motive of the soul?

We have seen how deep and strong are the affections which the minister is to awaken towards God. But *strength* of religious impression is not his whole work. From the imperfections of our nature, this very strength has its dangers. Religion, in becoming fervent, often becomes morbid. It is the minister's duty to inculcate a piety characterized by wisdom as much as by warmth; to meditate, if I may so speak, between the reason and the affections, so that, with joint energy and in blessed harmony, they may rise together and offer up the undivided soul to God. Whoever understands the strength of emotion in man's nature, and how hardly the balance of the soul is preserved, need not be told of the arduousness of this work. Devout people, through love of excitement, and through wrong views of the love of God, are apt to cherish the devotional feelings, at the expense, if not to the exclusion, of other parts of our nature. They seem to imagine that piety, like the Upas tree, makes a desert where it grows; that the mind, if not the body, needs a cloister. The natural movements of the soul are repressed; the social affections damped; the grace, and ornament, and innocent exhilarations of life frowned upon; and a gloomy, repulsive religion is cultivated, which, by way of compensation for its privations, claims a monopoly of God's favor, abandoning all to his wrath who will not assume its own sad livery and echo its own sepulchral tones. Through such exhibitions, religion has lost its honor; and, though the most ennobling of all sentiments, dilating the soul with vast thoughts and an unbounded hope, has been thought to contract and degrade it. The minister is to teach an earnest but enlightened religion ; a piety, which, far from wasting or eradicating, will protect, nourish, freshen the mind's various affections and powers ; which will add force to reason, as well as ardor to the heart ; which will at once bind us to God, and cement and multiply our ties to our families, our country, and mankind ; which will heighten the relish of life's pleasures, whilst it kindles an unquenchable thirst for a purer happiness in the life to come. Religion does not mutilate our nature. It does not lay waste our human interests and affections, that it may erect for God a throne amidst cheerless and solitary ruins, but widens the range of thought, feeling, and enjoyment. Such is religion ; and the Christian ministry, having for its end the communication of this healthful, well-proportioned, and all-comprehending piety, demands every energy of thought, feeling, and utterance, which the individual can bring to the work.

The time would fail me to speak of the other affections and sentiments which the ministry is instituted to excite and cherish, and I hasten to another object of the Christian teacher, which, to those who know themselves, will peculiarly illustrate the power which his office demands. It is his duty to rouse men to self-conflict, to warfare with the evil in their own hearts. This is in truth the supreme evil. The sorest calamities of life, sickness, poverty, scorn, dungeons, and death, form a less amount of desolation and suffering than is included in that one word, sin, — in revolt from God, in disloyalty to conscience, in the tyranny of the passions, in the thraldom of the soul's noblest powers. To redeem men from sin was Christ's great end. To pierce them with a new consciousness of sin, so that they shall groan under it, and strive against it, and through prayer and watching master it, is an essential part of the minister's work. Let him not satisfy himself with awakening, by his eloquence, occasional emotions of gratitude or sympathy. He must rouse the soul to solemn, stern resolve against its own deep and cherished corruptions, or he only makes a show of assault, and leaves the foe intrenched and unbroken within. We see, then, the arduousness of the minister's work. He is called to war with the might of the human passions, with the whole power of moral evil. He is to enlist men, not for a crusade, nor for extermination of heretics, but to fight a harder battle within, to expel sin in all its forms, and especially their besetting sins, from the strongholds of the heart. I know no task so arduous, none which demands equal power.

I shall take but one more view of the objects for which the Christian ministry was instituted, and from which we infer that it should be fraught with energy. It is the duty of the Christian teacher to call forth in the soul a conviction of its immortality, a thirst for a higher existence, and a grandeur and elevation of sentiment, becoming a being who is to live, enjoy, and advance for ever. His business is with men, not as inhabitants of this world, but as related to invisible beings, and to purer and happier worlds. The minister should look with reverence on the human soul as having within itself the germ of heaven. He should recognise, in the ignorant and unimproved, vast spiritual faculties given for perpetual enlargement, just as the artist of genius sees in the unhewn marble the capacity of being transformed into a majesty and grace, which will command the admiration of ages. In correspondence with these views, let him strive to quicken men to a consciousness of their inward nature and of its affinity with God, and to raise their steadfast aim and hope to its interminable progress and felicity. Such is his function. Perhaps I may be told, that men are incapable of rising, under the best instruction, to this height of thought and feeling. But let us never despair of our race. There is, I am sure, in the human soul, a deep consciousness, which responds to him who sincerely, and with the language of reality, speaks to it of the great and everlasting purposes for which it was created. There are sublime instincts in man. There is in human nature, a want which the world cannot supply ; a thirst for objects on which to pour forth more fervent admiration and love, than visible things awaken ; a thirst for the unseen, the infinite, and the everlasting. Most of you who hear have probably had moments, when a new light has seemed to dawn, a new life to stir within you ; when you have aspired after an unknown good ; when you have been touched by moral greatness and disinterested love ; when you have longed to break every chain of selfishness and sensuality, and enjoy a purer being. It is on this part of our nature that religion is founded. To this Christianity is addressed. The power to speak to this, is the noblest which God has imparted to man or angel, and should be coveted above all things by the Christian teacher.

The need of power in the ministry has been made apparent, from the greatness of the truths to be dispensed and the effects to be wrought by the Christian teacher. The question then comes, How may the student of theology be aided in gaining or cherishing this power? Under what influences should he be placed? What are the springs or foundations of the energy which he needs? How may he be quickened and trained to act most efficiently on the minds of men? In answering these questions, we of course determine the character which belongs to a theological institution, the spirit which it should cherish, the discipline, the mode of teaching, the excitements, which it should employ. From this wide range, I shall select a few topics which are recommended at once by their own importance and by the circumstances in which we are now placed.

1. To train the student to power of thought and utterance, let him be left, and, still more, encouraged, to free investigation. Without this a theological institution becomes a prison to the intellect and a nuisance to the church. The mind grows by free action. Confine it to beaten paths, prescribe to it the results in which all study must end, and you rob it of elasticity and life. It will never spread to its full dimensions. Teach the young man, that the instructions of others are designed to quicken, not supersede his own activity; that he has a divine intellect for which he is to answer to God, and that to surrender it to another, is to cast the crown from his head, and to yield up his noblest birthright. Encourage him, in all great questions, to hear both sides, and to meet fairly the point of every hostile argument. Guard him against tampering with his own mind, against silencing its whispers and objections, that he may enjoy a favorite opinion undisturbed. Do not give him the shadow for the substance of freedom, by telling him to inquire, but prescribing to him

the convictions at which he must stop. Better show him honestly his chains, than mock the slave with the show of liberty.

I know the objection to this course. It puts to hazard, we are told, the religious principles of the young. The objection is not without foundation. The danger is not unreal. But I know no method of forming a manly intellect, or a manly character, without danger. Peril is the element in which power is developed. Remove the youth from every hazard, keep him in leading-strings lest he should stray into forbidden paths, surround him with down lest he should be injured by a fall, shield him from wind and storms, and you doom him to perpetual infancy. All liberty is perilous, as the despot truly affirms; but who would therefore seek shelter under a despot's throne? Freedom of will is almost a tremendous gift; but still, a free agent, with all his capacity of crime, is infinitely more interesting and noble than the most harmonious and beautiful machine. Freedom is the nurse of intellectual and moral vigor. Better expose the mind to error, than rob it of hardihood and individuality. Keep not the destined teacher of mankind from the perilous field, where the battle between Truth and Falsehood is fought. Let him grapple with difficulty, sophistry, and error Truth is a conquest, and no man holds her so fast as he who has won her by conflict.

That cases of infidelity may occur in institutions conducted on free principles, is very possible, though our own experience gives no ground for fear. But the student, who, with all the aids to Christian belief which are furnished in a theological seminary, still falls a prey to skepticism, is not the man to be trusted with the cause of Christ. He is radically deficient. He wants that congeniality with spiritual and lofty truths, without which the evidences of religion work no deep conviction, and without which the faith that might be instilled by a slavish institution, would be of little avail. An upright mind may indeed be disturbed and shaken for a time by the arguments of skepticism; but these will be ultimately repelled, and, like conquered foes, will strengthen the principle by which they have been subdued.

Nothing, I am sure, can give power like a free action of the mind. Accumulate teachers and books, for these are indispensable. But the best teacher is he who awakens in his pupils the power of thought, and aids them to go alone. It is possible to weaken and encumber the mind by too much help. The very splendor of a teacher's talents may injure the pupil; and a superior man, who is more anxious to spread his own creed and his own praise, than to nourish a strong intellect in others, will only waste his life in multiplying poor copies, and in sending forth into the churches tame mimics of himself.

To free inquiry, then, we dedicate these walls. We invite into them the ingenuous young man, who prizes liberty of mind more than aught within the gift of sects or of the world. Let Heaven's free air circulate, and Heaven's unobstructed light shine here, and let those who shall be sent hence, go forth, not to echo with servility a creed imposed on their weakness, but to utter, in their own manly tones, what their own free investigation and deep conviction urge them to preach as the truth of God.

2. In the second place, to give power to the teacher,

he should be imbued, by all possible inculcation and excitement, with a supreme and invincible love of truth. This is at once the best defence against the perils of free inquiry, and the inspirer of energy both in thought and utterance. The first duty of a rational being is to his own intellect ; for it is through soundness and honesty of intellect that he is to learn all other duties. I know no virtue more important and appropriate to a teacher, and especially a religious teacher, than fairness and rectitude of understanding, than a love of truth stronger than the love of gain, honor, life ; and yet, so far from being cherished, this virtue has been warred against, hunted down, driven to exile, or doomed to the stake, in almost every Christian country, by ministers, churches, religious seminaries, or a maddened populace. In the glorious company of heroes and martyrs, a high rank belongs to him, who, superior to the frowns or the sneers, the pity or the wrath, which change of views would bring upon him, and in opposition to the warping influences of patronage, of private friendship, or ambition, keeps his mind chaste, inviolate, a sacred temple for truth, ever open to new light from Heaven ; and who, faithful to his deliberate convictions, speaks simply, and firmly, what his uncorrupted mind believes. This love of truth gives power, for it secures a growing knowledge of truth ; and truth is the mighty weapon by which the victories of religion are to be wrought out. This endures, whilst error carries with it the seeds of decay. Truth is an emanation from God, a beam of his wisdom, and immutable as its source ; and, although its first influences may seem to be exceeded by those of error, it grows stronger, and strikes deeper root, amidst the fluctuations and ruins of false opinions. Besides, this loyalty to truth not only leads to its acquisition, but, still more, begets a vital acquaintance with it, a peculiar conviction, which gives directness, energy, and authority to teaching. A minister, who has been religiously just to his own understanding, speaks with a tone of reality, of calm confidence, of conscious uprightness, which cannot be caught by the servile repeater of other men's notions, or by the passionate champion of an unexamined creed. A look, an accent, a word, from a single-hearted inquirer after truth, expressing his deliberate convictions, has a peculiar power in fortifying the convictions of others. To the love of truth, then, be these walls consecrated, and here may every influence be combined to build it up in the youthful heart.

3. To train powerful ministers, let an institution avail itself of the means of forming a devotional spirit, and imbuing the knowledge of the student with religious sensibility. Every man knows, that a cultivated mind, under strong and generous emotion, acquires new command of its resources, new energy and fulness of thought and expression; whilst, in individuals of a native vigor of intellect, feeling almost supplies the place of culture, inspiring the unlettered teacher with a fervid, resistless eloquence, which no apparatus of books, teachers, criticism, ancient languages, and general literature can impart. This power of sensibility to fertilize and vivify the intellect is not difficult of explanation. A strong and pure affection concentrates the attention on its objects, fastens on them the whole soul, and thus gives vividness of conception. It associates, intimately, all the ideas which are congenial with itself, and thus causes a rush of thought into the mind in moments of excitement. Indeed, a strong emotion seems to stir up the

soul from its foundations, and to attract to itself, and to impregnate with its own fire, whatever elements, conceptions, illustrations, can be pressed into its own service. Hence it is, that even ordinary men, strongly moved, abound in arguments, analogies, and fervent appeals, which nothing but sensibility could have taught. Every minister can probably recollect periods, when devotional feeling has seemed to open a new fountain of thought in the soul. Religious affection instinctively seeks and seizes the religious aspect of things. It discerns the marks of God, and proofs and illustrations of divine truth, in all nature and providence; and seems to surround the mind with an atmosphere which spreads its own warm hues on every object which enters it. This attraction, or affinity, if I may so say, which an emotion establishes among the thoughts which accord with itself, is one of the very important laws of the mind, and is chiefly manifested in poetry, eloquence, and all the higher efforts of intellect, by which man sways his fellow-beings. Religious feeling, then, is indispensable to a powerful minister. Without it, learning and fancy may please, but cannot move men profoundly and permanently. It is this, which not only suggests ideas, but gives felicity and energy of expression. It prompts "the words that burn"; those mysterious combinations of speech, which send the speaker's soul like lightning through his hearers, which breathe new life into old and faded truths, and cause an instantaneous gush of thought and feeling in susceptible minds.

We dedicate this institution, then, to religious feeling. Here let the heart muse, till the fire burns. Here let prayer, joined with meditation on nature and Scripture, and on the fervid writings of devout men, awaken the whole strength of the affections. But on no point is caution more needed than on this. Let it never be forgotten, that we want genuine feeling; not its tones, looks, and gestures, not a forced ardor and factitious zeal. Woe to that institution, where the young man is expected to repeat the language of emotion, whether he feel it or not; where perpetual pains are taken, to chafe the mind to a warmth which it cannot sustain. The affections are delicate and must not be tampered with. They cannot be compelled. Hardly any thing is more blighting to genuine sensibility, than to assume its tones and badge where it does not exist. Exhort the student to cherish devout feeling, by intercourse with God, and with those whom God has touched. But exhort him as strenuously, to abstain from every sign of emotion which the heart does not prompt. Teach him that nothing grieves more the Holy Spirit, or sooner closes the mind against heavenly influences, than insincerity. Teach him to be simple, ingenuous, true to his own soul. Better be cold, than affect to feel. In truth, nothing is so cold as an assumed, noisy enthusiasm. Its best emblem is the northern blast of winter, which freezes as it roars. Be this spot sacred to Christian ingenuousness and sincerity. Let it never be polluted by pretence, by affected fervor, by cant and theatric show.

4. Another source of power in the ministry, is Faith; by which we mean, not a general belief in the truths of Christianity, but a confidence in the great results, which this religion and the ministry are intended to promote. It has often been observed, that a strong faith tends to realize its objects; that all things become possible to him who thinks them so. Trust and hope breathe

animation and force. He, who despairs of great effects, never accomplishes them. All great works have been the results of a strong confidence, inspiring and sustaining strong exertion. The young man, who cannot conceive of higher effects of the ministry than he now beholds, who thinks that Christianity has spent all its energies in producing the mediocrity of virtue which characterizes Christendom, and to whom the human soul seems to have put forth its whole power and to have reached its full growth in religion, has no call to the ministry. Let not such a man put forth his nerveless hands in defence of the Christian cause. A voice of confidence has been known to rally a retreating army, and to lead it back to victory; and this spirit-stirring tone be longs to the leaders of the Christian host. The minister, indeed, ought to see and feel, more painfully than other men, the extent and power of moral evil in individuals, in the church, and in the world. Let him weep over the ravages of sin. But let him feel, too, that the mightiest power of the universe is on the side of truth and virtue; and with sorrow and fear let him join an unfaltering trust in the cause of human nature. Let him look on men, as on mysterious beings, endued with a spiritual life, with a deep central principle of holy and disinterested love, with an intellectual and moral nature which was made to be receptive of God. To nourish this hopeful spirit, this strengthening confidence, it is important that the minister should understand and feel, that he is not acting alone in his efforts for religion, but in union with God and Christ, and good beings on earth and in heaven. Let him regard the spiritual renovation of mankind, as God's chief purpose, for which nature and providence are leagued in holy coöperation. Let him feel himself joined in counsel and labor, with tha great body of which Christ is the head, with the noble brotherhood of apostles and martyrs, of the just made perfect, and, I will add, of angels ; and, speaking with a faith becoming this sublime association, he will not speak in vain. To this faith, to prophetic hope, to a devout trust in the glorious issues of Christianity, we dedicate these walls ; and may God here train up teachers, worthy to mingle and bear a part, with the holy of both worlds, in the cause of man's redemption.

5. Again, that the ministry may be imbued with new power, it needs a spirit of enterprise and reform. They who enter it should feel that it may be improved. We live in a stirring, advancing age ; and shall not the noblest function on earth partake of the general progress ? Why is the future ministry to be a servile continuation of the past ? Have all the methods of operating on human beings been tried and exhausted ? Are there no unessayed passages to the human heart ? If we live in a new era, must not religion be exhibited under new aspects, or in new relations ? Is not skepticism taking a new form ? Has not Christianity new foes to contend with ? And are there no new weapons and modes of warfare, by which its triumphs are to be insured ? If human nature is manifesting itself in new lights, and passing through a new and most interesting stage of its progress, shall it be described by the commonplaces, and appealed to exclusively by the motives, which belonged to earlier periods of society ? May not the mind have become susceptible of nobler incitements than those which suited ruder times ? Shall the minister linger behind his age, and be dragged along, as he often has been, in the last ranks of improvement ? Let those who are

to assume the ministry be taught, that they have something more to do than to handle old topics in old ways, and to walk in beaten and long-worn paths. Let them inquire, if new powers and agents may not be brought to bear on the human character. Is it incredible, that the progress of intellect and knowledge should develope new resources for the teacher of religion, as well as for the statesman, the artist, the philosopher? Are there no new combinations and new uses of the elements of thought, as well as of the elements of nature? Is it impossible that in the vast compass of Scripture, of nature, of Providence, and of the soul, there should be undisclosed or dimly defined truths, which may give a new impulse to the human mind? We dedicate this place, not only to the continuance, but to the improvement of the ministry; and let this improvement begin, at once, in those particulars, where the public, if not the clergy, feel it to be wanted. Let those, who are to be educated here, be admonished against the frigid eloquence, the school-boy tone, the inanimate diction, too common in the pulpit, and which would be endured nowhere else. Let them speak in tones of truth and nature, and adopt the style and elocution of men, who have an urgent work in hand, and who are thirsting for the regeneration of individuals and society.

6. Another source of power, too obvious to need elucidation, yet too important to be omitted, is, an independent spirit. By which I mean, not an unfeeling defiance of the opinions and usages of society, but that moral courage, which, through good report and evil report, reverently hears, and fearlessly obeys, the voice of conscience and God. He who would instruct men, must not fear them. He who is to reform society, must

not be anxious to keep its level. Dread of opinion effeminates preaching, and takes from truth its pungency. The minister so subdued, may flourish his weapons in the air, to the admiration of spectators, but will never pierce the conscience. The minister, like the good knight, should be without fear. Let him cultivate that boldness of speech, for which Paul prayed. Let him not flatter great or small. Let him not wrap up reproof in a decorated verbiage. Let him make no compromise with evil because followed by a multitude, but, for this very cause, lift up against it a more earnest voice. Let him beware of the shackles which society insensibly fastens on the mind and the tongue. Moral courage is not the virtue of our times. The love of popularity is the all-tainting vice of a republic. Besides, the increasing connexion between a minister and the community, whilst it liberalizes the mind, and counteracts professional prejudices, has a tendency to enslave him to opinion, to wear away the energy of virtuous resolution, and to change him from an intrepid guardian of virtue and foe of sin, into a merely elegant and amiable companion. Against this dishonorable cowardice, which smoothes the thoughts and style of the teacher, until they glide through the ear and the mind without giving a shock to the most delicate nerves, let the young man be guarded. We dedicate this institution to Christian independence. May it send forth brave spirits to the vindication of truth and religion.

7. I shall now close, with naming the chief source of power to the minister; one, indeed, which has been in a measure anticipated, and all along implied, but which ought not to be dismissed without a more distinct annunciation. I refer to that spirit, or frame, or

sentiment, in which the love of God, the love of men, the love of duty, meet as their highest result, and in which they are perfected and most gloriously displayed; I mean the spirit of self-sacrifice, — the spirit of martyrdom. This was the perfection of Christ, and it is the noblest inspiration which his followers derive from him. Say not that this is a height to which the generality of ministers must not be expected to rise. This spirit is of more universal obligation than many imagine. It enters into all the virtues which deeply interest us. In truth, there is no thorough virtue without it. Who is the upright man? He, who would rather die than defraud. Who the good parent? He, to whom his children are dearer than life. Who the good patriot? He, who counts not life dear in his country's cause. Who the philanthropist? He, who forgets himself in an absorbing zeal for the mitigation of human suffering, for the freedom, virtue, and illumination of men. It is not Christianity alone which has taught self-sacrifice. Conscience and the divinity within us, have in all ages borne testimony to its loveliness and grandeur, and history borrows from it her chief splendors. But Christ on his cross has taught it with a perfection unknown before, and his glory consists in the power with which he breathes it. Into this spirit, Christ's meanest disciple is expected to drink. How much more the teachers and guides of his church! He who is not moved with this sublime feature of our religion, who cannot rise above himself, who cannot, by his own consciousness, comprehend the kindling energy and solemn joy, which pain or peril in a noble cause has often inspired, — he, to whom this language is a mystery, wants one great mark of his vocation to the sacred office. Let him enlist under any standard rather than the cross. To preach with power, a man must feel Christianity to be worthy of the blood which it has cost; and, espousing it as the chief hope of the human race, must contemn life's ordinary interests, compared with the glory and happiness of advancing it. This spirit of self-exposure and self-surrender, throws into preachers an energy which no other principle can give. In truth, such power resides in disinterestedness, that no man can understand his full capacity of thought and feeling, his strength to do and suffer, until he gives himself, with a single heart, to a great and holy cause. New faculties seem to be created, and more than human might sometimes imparted, by a pure fervent love. Most of us are probably strangers to the resources of power in our own breasts, through the weight and pressure of the chains of selfishness. We consecrate this institution, then, to that spirit of martyrdom, of disinterested attachment to the Christian cause, through which it first triumphed, and for want of which its triumphs are now slow. In an age of luxury and self-indulgence, we would devote these walls to the training of warm, manly, generous spirits. May they never shelter the self-seeking slaves of ease and comfort, pupils of Epicurus rather than of Christ. God send from this place devoted and efficient friends of Christianity and the human race.

My friends, I have insisted on the need, and illustrated the sources, of power in the ministry. To this end, may the institution, in whose behalf we are now met together, be steadily and sacredly devoted. I would say to its guardians and teachers, Let this be your chief aim. I would say to the students, Keep this in sight in all your studies. Never forget your great vocation ; that you are to prepare yourselves for a strong, deep, and beneficent agency on the minds of your fellow-beings. Everywhere I see a demand for the power on which I have now insisted. The cry comes to me from society and from the church. The condition of society needs a more efficient administration of Christianity. Great and radical changes are needed in the community to make it Christian. There are those indeed, who, mistaking the courtesies and refinements of civilized life for virtue, see no necessity of a great revolution in the world. But civilization, in hiding the grossness, does not break the power of evil propensities. Let us not deceive ourselves. Multitudes are living with few thoughts of God, and of the true purpose and glory of their being. Among the nominal believers in a Deity and in a judgment to come, sensuality, and ambition, and the love of the world, sit on their thrones, and laugh to scorn the impotence of preaching. Christianity has yet a hard war to wage, and many battles to win ; and it needs intrepid, powerful ministers, who will find courage and excitement, not dismay, in the strength and number of their foes.

Christians, you have seen in this discourse, the purposes and claims of this theological institution. Offer your fervent prayers for its prosperity. Besiege the throne of mercy in its behalf. Cherish it as the dearest hope of our churches. Enlarge its means of usefulness, and let your voice penetrate its walls, calling aloud and importunately for enlightened and powerful teachers. Thus joining in effort with the directors and instructors of this seminary, doubt not that God will here train up ministers worthy to bear his truth to present and future generations. If on the contrary you and they slumber, you will have erected these walls, not to nourish energy, but to be its tomb, not to bear witness to your zeal, but to be a melancholy monument of fainting effort and betrayed truth.

But let me not cast a cloud over the prospects of this day. In hope I began, — with hope I will end. This institution has noble distinctions, and has afforded animating pledges. It is eminently a free institution, an asylum from the spiritual despotism, which, in one shape or another, overspreads the greatest part of Christendom. It has already given to the churches a body of teachers, who, in theological acquisitions and ministerial gifts, need not shrink from comparison with their predecessors or contemporaries. I see in it means and provisions, nowhere surpassed, for training up enlightened, free, magnanimous, self-sacrificing friends of truth. In this hope, let us then proceed to the work, which has brought us together. With trust in God, with love to mankind, with unaffected attachment to Christian truth, with earnest wishes for its propagation through all lands and its transmission to remotest ages, let us now, with one heart and one voice, dedicate this edifice to the One living and true God, to Christ and his Church, to the instruction and regeneration of the human soul.

THE DUTIES OF CHILDREN.

DISCOURSE

DELIVERED

TO THE RELIGIOUS SOCIETY IN FEDERAL-STREET,

BOSTON.

EPHESIANS vi. 1, 2: "Children, obey your parents in the Lord: for this is right. Honor thy father and thy mother, which is the first commandment with promise."

FROM these words I propose to point out the duties of children to their parents. My young friends, let me ask your serious attention. I wish to explain to you the honor and obedience which you are required to render your parents; and to impress you with the importance, excellence, and happiness of this temper and conduct.

It will be observed, in the progress of this discourse, that I have chiefly in view the youngest part of my hearers; but I would not on this account be supposed to intimate, that those who have reached more advanced periods of life, are exempted from the obligation of honoring their parents. However old we may be, we should never forget that tenderness which watched over our infancy, which listened to our cries before we could articulate our wants, and was never weary with ministering to our comfort and enjoyments. There is scarcely any thing more interesting than to see the *man* retaining the respect and gratitude which belong to the *child*; than to see persons, who have come forward into life, remembering with affection the guides and friends of their youth, and laboring by their kind and respectful attention to cheer the declining years, and support the trembling infirmities, of those whose best days were spent in solicitude and exertion for their happiness and improvement. He who suffers any objects or pursuits to shut out a parent from his heart, who becomes so weaned from the breast which nourished and the arms which cherished him, as coldly to forsake a parent's dwelling, and neglect a parent's comfort, not only renounces the dictates of religion and morality, but deserves to be cast out from society as a stranger to the common sensibilities of human nature.

In the observations I am now to make, all who have parents should feel an interest; for some remarks will apply to all. But I shall principally confine myself to those, who are so young as to depend on the care and to live under the eye of their parents; who surround a parent's table, dwell beneath a parent's roof, and hear continually a parent's voice. To such the text addresses itself, " Honor and obey your father and mother."

I shall now attempt to explain and enforce what is here required of you.

First, you are required to view and treat your parents with *respect*. Your tender, inexperienced age requires that you think of yourselves with humility, and conduct yourselves with modesty; that you respect the superior age and wisdom and improvements of your parents, and observe towards them a submissive deportment. Nothing is more unbecoming in you, nothing will render you more unpleasant in the eyes of others, than froward or contemptuous conduct towards your parents. There are children, and I wish I could say there are only a few, who speak to their parents with rudeness, grow sullen at their rebukes, behave in their presence as if they deserved no attention, hear them speak without noticing them, and rather ridicule than honor them. There are many children at the present day, who think more highly of themselves than of their elders; who think that their own wishes are first to be gratified; who abuse the condescension and kindness of their parents, and treat them as servants rather than superiors.

Beware, my young friends, lest you grow up with this assuming and selfish spirit. Regard your parents as kindly given you by God, to support, direct, and govern you in your present state of weakness and inexperience. Express your respect for them in your manner and conversation. Do not neglect those outward signs of dependence and inferiority which suit your age. You are young, and you should therefore take the lowest place, and rather retire than thrust yourselves forward into notice. You have much to learn, and you should therefore hear instead of seeking to be heard. You are dependent, and you should therefore *ask* instead of *demanding* what you desire; and you should receive every thing from your parents as a favor, and not as a debt. I do not mean to urge upon you a slavish fear of your parents. Love them, and love them ardently; but mingle a sense of their superiority with your love. Feel a confidence in their kindness; but let not this confidence make you rude and presumptuous, and lead to indecent familiarity. Talk to them with openness and freedom; but never contradict with violence; never answer with passion or contempt.

The Scriptures say, "Cursed be he that setteth light by his father or his mother." "The eye that mocketh at his father, the ravens of the valley shall pluck it out, and the young ravens shall eat it.". The sacred history teaches us, that when Solomon, on his throne, saw his mother approaching him, he rose to meet her, and bowed himself unto her, and caused a seat to be set for her on his right hand. Let this wise and great king teach you to respect your parents.

Secondly, You should be grateful to your parents. Consider how much you owe them. The time has been, and it was not a long time past, when you depended wholly on their kindness, when you had no strength to make a single effort for yourselves, when you could neither speak, nor walk, and knew not the use of any of your powers. Had not a parent's arm supported you, you must have fallen to the earth and perished. Observe with attention the infants which you so often see, and consider that a little while ago you were as feeble as they are; you were only a burden and a care, and you had nothing with which you could repay your parents' affection. But did they forsake you? How many sleepless nights have they been disturbed by your cries! When you were sick, how tenderly did they hang over you! With what pleasure have they seen you grow up in health to your present state! and what do you now possess, which you have not received from their hands? God indeed is your great parent, your best friend, and from him every good gift descends; but God is pleased to bestow every thing upon you through the kindness of your parents. To your parents you owe every comfort; you owe to them the shelter you enjoy from the rain and cold, the raiment which covers and the food which nourishes you. While you are seeking amusement, or are employed in gaining knowledge at school, your parents are toiling that you may be happy, that your wants be supplied, that your minds may be improved, that you may grow up and be useful in the world. And when you consider how often you have forfeited all this kindness, and yet how ready they have been to forgive you, and to continue their favors, ought you not to look upon them with the tenderest gratitude? What greater monster can there be than an unthankful child, whose heart is never warmed and melted by the daily expressions of parental solicitude; who, instead of requiting his best friend by his affectionate conduct, is sullen and passionate, and thinks that his parents have done nothing for him, because they will not do all he desires? My young friends, your parents' hearts have ached enough for you already; you should strive from this time, by your expressions of gratitude and love, to requite their goodness. Do you ask how you may best express these feelings of respect and gratitude, which have been enjoined? In answer, I would observe,

Thirdly, That you must make it your study to obey your parents, to do what they command, and do it cheerfully. Your own hearts will tell you that this is a most natural and proper expression of honor and love. For how often do we see children opposing their wills to the will of their parents; refusing to comply with absolute commands; growing more obstinate, the more they are required to do what they dislike ; and at last sullenly and unwillingly obeying, because they can no longer refuse without exposing themselves to punishment. Consider, my young friends, that by such conduct you very much displease God, who has given you parents, that they may control your passions and train you up in the way you should go. Consider how much better they can decide for you, than you can for yourselves. You know but little of the world in which you live. You hastily catch at every thing which promises you pleasure ; and unless the authority of a parent should restrain you, you would soon rush into ruin, without a thought or a fear. In pursuing your own inclinations, your health would be destroyed, your minds would run waste, you would grow up slothful, selfish, a trouble to others, and burdensome to yourselves. Submit, then, cheerfully to your parents. Have you not experienced their goodness long enough to know that they wish to make you happy, even when their commands are most severe ? Prove, then, your sense of their goodness by doing cheerfully what they require. When they oppose your wishes, do not think that you have more knowledge than they. Do not receive their commands with a sour, angry, sullen look, which says louder than words, that you obey only because you dare not rebel. If they deny your requests, do not persist in urging them ; but consider how many requests they have already granted you. Consider that you have no claim upon them, and that it will be base and ungrateful for you, after all their tenderness, to murmur and complain. Do not expect that your parents are to give up every thing to your wishes ; but study to give up every thing to theirs. Do not wait for them to threaten ; but, when a look tells you what they want, fly to perform it. This is the way in which you can best reward them for all their pains and labors. In this way you will make their houses pleasant and cheerful. But if you are disobedient, perverse, and stubborn, you will be uneasy yourselves, and will make all around you unhappy. You will make home a place of contention, noise, and anger; and your best friends will have reason to wish that you had never been born. A disobedient child almost always grows up ill-natured and disobliging to all with whom he is connected. None love him, and he has no heart to love any but himself. If you would be amiable in your temper and manner, and desire to be beloved, let me advise you to begin life with giving up your wills to your parents.

Fourthly, You must further express your respect, affection, and gratitude, by doing all in your power to assist and oblige your parents. Children can very soon make some return for the kindness they receive. Every day you can render your parents some little service, and often save them many cares, and sometimes not a little expense. There have been children, who in early life have been great supports to their sick, poor, and helpless parents. This is the most honorable way in which you can be employed. You must never think too highly of yourselves to be unwilling to do any thing for those who have done so much for you. You should never let your amusements take such a hold of your minds, as to make you slothful, backward, and unwilling, when you are called to serve your parents. Some children seem to think that they have nothing to seek but their own pleasure. They will run from every task which is imposed on them; and leave their parents to want many comforts, rather than expose themselves to a little trouble. But consider, had they loved you no better than you loved them, how wretched would have been your state! There are some children, who not only refuse to exert themselves for their parents, but add very much to their cares, give them unnecessary trouble, and, by carelessness, by wasting, by extravagance, help to keep them in poverty and toil. Such children, as they grow up, instead of seeking to provide for themselves, generally grow more and more burdensome to their friends, and lead useless, sluggish, and often profligate lives. My young friends, you should be ashamed, after having given your parents so much pain, to multiply their cares and labors unnecessarily. You should learn very early, to be active in pleasing them, and active in doing what you can for yourselves. Do not waste all your spirit upon play; but learn to be useful. Perhaps the time is coming, when your parents will need as much attention from you as you have received from them; and you should endeavour to form such industrious, obliging habits, that you may render their last years as happy as they have rendered the first years of your existence.

Fifthly, You should express your respect for your parents, and your sense of their kindness and superior wisdom, by placing unreserved confidence in them. This is a very important part of your duty. Children should learn to be honest, sincere, and open-hearted to their parents. An artful, hypocritical child is one of the most unpromising characters in the world. You should have no secrets which you are unwilling to disclose to your parents. If you have done wrong, you should openly confess it, and ask that forgiveness which

THE DUTIES OF CHILDREN. 295

a parent's heart is ready to bestow. If you wish to undertake any thing, ask their consent. Never begin any thing in the hope that you can conceal your design. If you once strive to impose on your parents, you will be led on, from one step to another, to invent falsehoods, to practise artifice, till you will become contemptible and hateful. You will soon be detected, and then none will trust you. Sincerity in a child will make up for many faults. Of children, he is the worst, who watches the eyes of his parents, pretends to obey as long as they see him, but as soon as they have turned away, does what they have forbidden. Whatever else you do, never deceive. Let your parents always learn your faults from your own lips; and be assured they will never love you the less for your openness and sincerity.

Lastly, You must prove your respect and gratitude to your parents by attending seriously to their instructions and admonitions, and by improving the advantages they afford you for becoming wise, useful, good, and happy for ever. I hope, my young friends, that you have parents who take care, not only of your bodies, but your souls; who instruct you in your duty, who talk to you of your God and Saviour, who teach you to pray and to read the Scriptures, and who strive to give you such knowledge, and bring you up in such habits, as will lead you to usefulness on earth, and to happiness in heaven. If you have not, I can only pity you; I have little hope that I can do you good by what I have here said. But if your parents are faithful in instructing and guiding you, you must prove your gratitude to them and to God, by listening respectfully and attentively to what they say; by shunning the temptations of which they warn you, and by walking in the paths they mark out before you. You must labor to answer their hopes and wishes, by improving in knowledge ; by being industrious at school; by living peaceably with your companions ; by avoiding all profane and wicked language ; by fleeing bad company ; by treating all persons with respect ; by being kind and generous and honest, and by loving and serving your Father in heaven. This is the happiest and most delightful way of repaying the kindness of your parents. Let them see you growing up with amiable tempers and industrious habits; let them see you delighting to do good, and fearing to offend God ; and they will think you have never been a burden. Their fears and anxieties about you, will give place to brighter views. They will hope to see you prosperous, respected, and beloved in the present world. But if in this they are to be disappointed, if they are soon to see you stretched on the bed of sickness and death, they will still smile amidst their tears, and be comforted by the thought that you are the children of God, and that you are going to a Father that loves you better than they. If, on the contrary, you slight and despise their instructions, and suffer your youth to run waste, you will do much to embitter their happiness and shorten their days. Many parents have gone to the grave broken-hearted by the ingratitude, perverseness, impiety, and licentiousness of their children. My young friends, listen seriously to parental admonition. Beware, lest you pierce with anguish that breast on which you have so often leaned. Beware, lest by early contempt of instruction, you bring yourselves to shame and misery in this world, and draw on your heads still heavier ruin in the world beyond the grave.

Children, I have now set before you your duties. Let me once more beseech you to honor your father and mother. Ever cling to them with confidence and love. Be to them an honor, an ornament, a solace, and a support. Be more than they expect, and if possible be all that they desire. To you they are now looking with an affection which trembles for your safety. So live, that their eyes may ever fix on you with beams of hope and joy. So live, that the recollection of you may soothe their last hours. May you now walk by their side in the steps of the holy Saviour, and through his grace may you meet again in a better and happier world. Amen.

HONOR DUE TO ALL MEN.

1 Peter ii. 17: "Honor all men."

Among the many and inestimable blessings of Christianity, I regard, as not the least, the new sentiment with which it teaches man to look upon his fellow-beings; the new interest which it awakens in us towards every thing human; the new importance which it gives to the soul; the new relation which it establishes between man and man. In this respect, it began a mighty revolution, which has been silently spreading itself through society, and which, I believe, is not to stop, until new ties shall have taken place of those which have hitherto, in the main, connected the human race. Christianity has as yet but begun its work of reformation. Under its influences, a new order of society is advancing, surely though slowly; and this beneficent change it is to accomplish in no small measure by revealing to men their own nature, and teaching them to "honor all" who partake it.

As yet Christianity has done little, compared with what it is to do, in establishing the true bond of union between man and man. The old bonds of society still continue in a great degree. They are instinct, interest, force. The true tie, which is mutual respect, calling forth mutual, growing, never-failing acts of love, is as yet little known. A new revelation, if I may so speak, remains to be made; or rather, the truths of the old revelation in regard to the greatness of human nature, are to be brought out from obscurity and neglect. The soul is to be regarded with a religious reverence, hitherto unfelt; and the solemn claims of every being to whom this divine principle is imparted, are to be established on the ruins of those pernicious principles, both in church and state, which have so long divided mankind into the classes of the abject Many and the self-exalting Few.

(There is nothing of which men know so little, as themselves.) They understand incomparably more of the surrounding creation, of matter, and of its laws, than of that spiritual principle, to which matter was made to be the minister, and without which the outward universe would be worthless. Of course, no man can be wholly a stranger to the soul, for the soul is himself, and he cannot but be conscious of its most obvious workings. But it is to most a chaos, a region shrouded in ever-shifting mists, baffling the eye and bewildering the imagination. The affinity of the mind with God, its moral power, the purposes for which its faculties were bestowed, its connexion with futurity, and the dependence of its whole happiness on its own right action and progress, — these truths, though they might be expected to absorb us, are to most men little more than sounds, and to none of us those living realities, which, I trust, they are to become. That conviction, without which we are all poor, of the unlimited and immortal nature of the soul, remains in a great degree to be developed. (Men have as yet no just respect for themselves, and of consequence no just respect for others.) The true bond of society is thus wanting; and accordingly there is a great deficiency of Christian benevolence. There is indeed much instinctive, native benevolence, and this is not to be despised; but the benevolence of Jesus Christ, which consists in a calm purpose to suffer, and, if need be, to die, for our fellow-creatures, the benevolence of Christ on the cross, which is the true pattern to the Christian, this is little known; and what is the cause? It is this. We see nothing in human beings to entitle them to such sacrifices; we do not think them worth suffering for. Why should we be martyrs for beings, who awaken in us little more of moral interest than the brutes?

(I hold, that nothing is to make man a true lover of man, but the discovery of something interesting and great in human nature.) We must see and feel, that a human being is something important and of immeasurable importance. We must see and feel the broad distance between the spiritual life within us, and the vegetable or animal life which acts around us. I cannot love the flower, however beautiful, with a disinterested affection, which will make me sacrifice to it my own prosperity. You will in vain exhort me to attach myself, with my whole strength of affection, to the inferior animals, however useful or attractive; and why not? They want the capacity of truth, virtue, and progress. They want that principle of duty, which alone gives permanence to a being; and accordingly they soon lose their individual nature, and go to mingle with the general mass. A human being deserves a different affection from what we bestow on inferior creatures, for he has a rational and moral nature, by which he is to endure for ever, by which he may achieve an unutterable happiness, or sink into an unutterable woe. He is more interesting through what is in him, than the earth or heavens ; and the only way to love him aright, is to catch some glimpse of this immortal power within him. Until this is done, all charity is little more than instinct ; we shall embrace the great interests of human nature with coldness.

It may be said, that Christianity has done much to awaken benevolence, and that it has taught men to call one another brethren. Yes, to *call* one another so ; but has it as yet given the true feeling of brotherhood ? We undoubtedly feel ourselves to be all of one race, and this is well. We trace ourselves up to one pair, and feel the same blood flowing in our veins. But do we understand our spiritual Brotherhood ? Do we feel ourselves to be derived from one Heavenly Parent, in whose image we are all made, and whose perfection we may constantly approach ? Do we feel that there is one divine life in our own and in all souls ? This seems to me the only true bond of man to man. Here is a tie more sacred, more enduring, than all the ties of this earth. Is it felt, and do we in consequence truly honor one another ?

Sometimes, indeed, we see men giving sincere, profound, and almost unmeasured respect to their fellow-creatures ; but to whom ? To great men ; to men distinguished by a broad line from the multitude ; to men preëminent by genius, force of character, daring effort, high station, brilliant success. To such, honor is given; but this is not to "honor all men" ; and the homage paid to such, is generally unfriendly to that Christian estimate of human beings for which I am now pleading. The great are honored at the expense of their race. They absorb and concentrate the world's admiration, and their less gifted fellow-beings are thrown by their brightness into a deeper shade, and passed over with a colder contempt. Now I have no desire to derogate from the honor paid to great men, but I say, Let them not rise by the depression of the multitude. I say, that great men, justly regarded, exalt our estimate of the human race, and bind us to the multitude of men more closely ; and when they are not so regarded, when they are converted into idols, when they serve to wean our interest from ordinary men, they corrupt us, they sever the sacred bond of humanity which should attach us to all, and our characters become vitiated by our very admiration of greatness. (The true view of great men is, that they are only examples and manifestations of our common nature, showing what belongs to all souls, though unfolded as yet only in a few.) The light which shines from them is, after all, but a faint revelation of the power which is treasured up in every human being. They are not prodigies, not miracles, but natural developements of the human soul. They are indeed as men among children, but the children have a principle of growth which leads to manhood.

That great men and the multitude of minds are of one family, is apparent, I think, in the admiration which the great inspire into the multitude. A sincere, enlightened admiration always springs from something congenial in him who feels it with him who inspires it. He that can understand and delight in greatness, was created to partake of it ; the germ is in him ; and sometimes this admiration, in what we deem inferior minds, discovers a nobler spirit than belongs to the great man who awakens it; for sometimes the great man is so absorbed in his own greatness as to admire no other; and I should not hesitate to say, that a common mind, which is yet capable of a generous admiration, is destined to rise higher than the man of eminent capacities, who can enjoy no power or excellence but his own. When I hear of great men, I wish not to separate them from their race, but to blend them with it. I esteem it no small benefit of the philosophy of mind, that it teaches us that the elements of the greatest thoughts of the man of genius, exist in his humbler brethren; and that the faculties which the scientific exert in the profoundest discoveries, are precisely the same with those which common men employ in the daily labors of life.

To show the grounds on which the obligation to honor all men rests, I might take a minute survey of that human nature which is common to all, and set forth its claims to reverence. But, leaving this wide range, I observe that there is one principle of the soul, which makes all men essentially equal, which places all on a level as to means of happiness, which may place in the first rank of human beings those who are the most depressed in worldly condition, and which therefore gives the most depressed a title to interest and respect. I refer to the Sense of Duty, to the power of discerning and doing right, to the moral and religious principle, to the inward monitor which speaks in the name of God, to the capacity of virtue or excellence. This is the great gift of God. We can conceive no greater. In seraph and archangel, we can conceive no higher energy than the power of virtue, or the power of forming themselves after the will and moral perfections of God. This power breaks down all barriers between the seraph and the lowest human being; it makes them brethren. Whoever has derived from God this perception and capacity of rectitude, has a bond of union with the spiritual world, stronger than all the ties of nature. He possesses a principle which, if he is faithful to it, must carry him forward for ever, and insures to him the improvement and happiness of the highest order of beings.

It is this moral power, which makes all men essentially equal, which annihilates all the distinctions of this world. Through this, the ignorant and the poor may become the greatest of the race; for the greatest is he who is most true to the principle of duty. It is not improbable, that the noblest human beings are to be found in the least favored conditions of society, among those, whose names are never uttered beyond the narrow circle in which they toil and suffer, who have but "two mites" to give away, who have perhaps not even that, but who "desire to be fed with the crumbs which fall from the rich man's table;" for in this class may be found those, who have withstood the severest temptation, who have practised the most arduous duties, who have confided in God under the heaviest trials, who have been most wronged and have forgiven most; and these are the great, the exalted. It matters nothing, what the particular duties are to which the individual is called, — how minute or obscure in their outward form. Greatness in God's sight lies, not in the extent of the sphere which is filled, or of the effect which is produced, but altogether in the power of virtue in the soul, in the en ergy with which God's will is chosen, with which trial is borne, and goodness loved and pursued.

The sense of duty is the greatest gift of God. The Idea of Right is the primary and the highest revelation of God to the human mind, and all outward revelations are founded on and addressed to it. All mysteries of science and theology fade away before the grandeur of the simple perception of duty, which dawns on the mind of the little child. That perception brings him into the moral kingdom of God. That lays on him an everlasting bond. He, in whom the conviction of duty is unfolded, becomes subject from that moment to a law, which no power in the universe can abrogate. He forms a new and indissoluble connexion with God, that of an accountable being. He begins to stand before an inward tribunal, on the decisions of which his whole happiness rests; he hears a voice, which, if faithfully followed, will guide him to perfection, and in neglecting which he brings upon himself inevitable misery. We little understand the solemnity of the moral principle in every human mind. We think not how awful are its functions. We forget that it is the germ of immortality. Did we understand it, we should look with a feeling of reverence on every being to whom it is given.

Having shown in the preceding remarks, that there is a foundation in the human soul for the honor enjoined in our text towards all men, I proceed to observe, that, if we look next into Christianity, we shall find this duty enforced by new and still more solemn considerations. This whole religion is a testimony to the worth of man in the sight of God, to the importance of human nature, to the infinite purposes for which we were framed. God is there set forth, as sending to the succour of his human family, his Beloved Son, the bright image and representative of his own perfections; and sending him, not simply to roll away a burden of pain and punishment (for this, however magnified in systems of theology, is not his highest work), but to create men after that divine image which he himself bears, to purify the soul from every stain, to communicate to it new power over evil, and to open before it Immortality as its aim and destination, — Immortality, by which we are to understand, not merely a perpetual, but an ever-improving and celestial being. Such are the views of Christianity. And these blessings it proffers, not to a few, not to the educated, not to the eminent, but to all human beings, to the poorest, and the most fallen; and we know, that, through the power of its promises, it has in not a few instances raised the most fallen to true greatness, and given them in their present virtue and peace, an earnest of the Heaven which it unfolds. Such is Christianity. Men, viewed in the light of this religion, are beings cared for by God, to whom he has given his Son, on whom he pours forth his Spirit, and whom he has created for the highest good in the universe, for participation in his own perfections and happiness. My friends, such is Christianity. Our skepticism as to our own nature cannot quench the bright light which that religion sheds on the soul and on the prospects of mankind; and just as far as we receive its truth, we shall honor all men.

I know I shall be told that Christianity speaks of man as a sinner, and thus points him out to abhorrence and scorn. I know it speaks of human sin, but it does not speak of this as indissolubly bound up with the soul, as entering into the essence of human nature, but as a temporary stain, which it calls on us to wash away. Its greatest doctrine is, that the most lost are recoverable, that the most fallen may rise, and that there is no height of purity, power, felicity in the universe, to which the guiltiest mind may not, through penitence, attain. Christianity indeed gives us a deeper, keener feeling of the guilt of mankind, than any other religion. By the revelation of perfection in the character of Jesus Christ, it shows us how imperfect even the best men are. But it reveals perfection in Jesus, not for our discouragement, but as our model, reveals it only that we may thirst for and approach it. From Jesus I learn what man is to become, that is, if true to this new light ; and true he may be.

Christianity, I have said, shows man as a sinner, but I nowhere meet in it those dark views of our race which would make us shrink from it as from a nest of venomous reptiles. According to the courteous style of theology, man has been called half brute and half devil. But this is a perverse and pernicious exaggeration. The brute, as it is called, that is, animal, appetite is indeed strong in human beings ; but is there nothing within us but appetite ? Is there nothing to war with it ? Does this constitute the essence of the soul ? Is it not rather an accident, the result of the mind's union with matter ? Is not its spring in the body, and may it not be expected to perish with the body ? In addition to animal propensities, I see the tendency to criminal excess in all men's passions. I see not one only, but many Tempters in every human heart. Nor am I insensible to the fearful power of these enemies to our virtue. But is there nothing in man but temptation, but propensity to sin ? Are there no counterworking powers ? no attractions in virtue ? no tendencies to God ?

no sympathies with sorrow? no reverence for greatness? no moral conflicts? no triumphs of principle? This very strength of temptation seems to me to be one of the indications of man's greatness. It shows a being framed to make progress through difficulty, suffering, and conflict; that is, it shows a being designed for the highest order of virtues; for we all feel by an unerring instinct, that virtue is elevated in proportion to the obstacles which it surmounts, to the power with which it is chosen and held fast. I see men placed by their Creator on a field of battle; but compassed with peril that they may triumph over it; and, though often overborne, still summoned to new efforts, still privileged to approach the Source of all power, and to seek "grace in time of need," and still addressed in tones of encouragement by a celestial Leader, who has himself fought and conquered, and holds forth to them his own crown of righteousness and victory.

From these brief views of human nature and of Christianity, you will see the grounds of the solemn obligation of honoring all men, of attaching infinite importance to human nature, and of respecting it, even in its present infant, feeble, tottering state. This sentiment of honor or respect for human beings, strikes me more and more as essential to the Christian character. I conceive that a more thorough understanding and a more faithful culture of this, would do very much to carry forward the church and the world. In truth, I attach to this sentiment such importance, that I measure by its progress the progress of society. I judge of public events very much by their bearing on this. I estimate political revolutions, chiefly by their tendency to exalt men's conceptions of their nature, and to inspire them with respect for one another's claims. The present stupendous movements in Europe naturally suggest, and almost force upon me, this illustration of the importance which I have given to the sentiment enjoined in our text. Allow me to detain you a few moments on this topic.

What is it, then, I ask, which makes the present revolutionary movement abroad so interesting ? I answer, that I see in it the principle of respect for human nature and for the human race, developing itself more powerfully, and this to me constitutes its chief interest. I see in it proofs, indications, that the mind is awakening to a consciousness of what it is, and of what it is made for. In this movement I see man becoming to himself a higher object. I see him attaining to the conviction of the equal and indestructible rights of every human being. I see the dawning of that great principle, that the individual is not made to be the instrument of others, but to govern himself by an inward law, and to advance towards his proper perfection ; that he belongs to himself and to God, and to no human superior. I know, indeed, that, in the present state of the world, these conceptions are exceedingly unsettled and obscure ; and in truth, little effort has hitherto been made to place them in a clear light, and to give them a definite and practical form in men's minds. The multitude know not with any distinctness what they want. Imagination, unschooled by reason and experience, dazzles them with bright but baseless visions. They are driven onward with a perilous violence, by a vague consciousness of not having found their element ; by a vague yet noble faith in a higher good than they have attained ; by impatience under restraints, which they feel to be degrading. In this violence, however, there is nothing strange, nor ought it to discourage us. It is, I believe, universally true, that great principles, in their first developement, manifest themselves irregularly. It is so in religion. In history we often see religion, especially after long depression, breaking out in vehemence and enthusiasm, sometimes stirring up bloody conflicts, and through struggles establishing a calmer empire over society. In like manner, political history shows us, that men's consciousness of their rights and essential equality has at first developed itself passionately. Still the consciousness is a noble one, and the presage of a better social state.

Am I asked, what I hope from the present revolutionary movements in Europe? I answer, that I hope a good which includes all others, and which almost hides all others from my view. I hope the subversion of institutions, by which the true bond between man and man has been more or less dissolved, by which the will of one or a few has broken down the will, the heart, the conscience of the many; and I hope that, in the place of these, are to grow up institutions, which will express, cherish, and spread far and wide a just respect for human nature, which will strengthen in men a consciousness of their powers, duties, and rights, which will train the individual to moral and religious independence, which will propose as their end the elevation of all orders of the community, and which will give full scope to the best minds in this work of general improvement. I do not say, that I expect it to be suddenly realized. The sun, which is to bring on a brighter day, is rising in thick and threatening clouds. Perhaps the minds of men were never more unquiet than at the present moment

Still I do not despair. That a higher order of ideas or principles is beginning to be unfolded; that a wider philanthropy is beginning to triumph over the distinctions of ranks and nations; that a new feeling of what is due to the ignorant, poor, and depraved, has sprung up; that the right of every human being to such an education as shall call forth his best faculties, and train him more and more to control himself, is recognised as it never was before; and that government is more and more regarded as intended not to elevate the few, but to guard the rights of all; that these great revolutions in principle have commenced and are spreading, who can deny? and to me they are prophetic of an improved condition of human nature and human affairs.— O, that this melioration might be accomplished without blood! As a Christian, I feel a misgiving, when I rejoice in any good, however great, for which this fearful price has been paid. In truth, a good so won is necessarily imperfect and generally transient. War may subvert a despotism, but seldom builds up better institutions. Even when joined, as in our own history, with high principles, it inflames and leaves behind it passions, which make liberty a feverish conflict of jealous parties, and which expose a people to the tyranny of faction under the forms of freedom. Few things impair men's reverence for human nature, more than war; and did I not see other and holier influences than the sword, working out the regeneration of the race, I should indeed despair.

In this discourse I have spoken of the grounds and importance of that honor or respect which is due from us, and enjoined on us, towards all human beings. The various forms, in which this principle is to be exercised or manifested, I want time to enlarge on. I would only say, "Honor all men." Honor man, from the beginning to the end of his earthly course. Honor the child. Welcome into being the infant, with a feeling of its mysterious grandeur, with the feeling, that an immortal existence has begun, that a spirit has been kindled which is never to be quenched. Honor the child. On this principle, all good education rests. Never shall we learn to train up the child, till we take it in our arms, as Jesus did, and feel distinctly that "of such is the kingdom of heaven." In that short sentence is taught the spirit of the true system of education; and for want of understanding it, little effectual aid, I fear, is yet given to the heavenly principle in the infant soul. — Again. Honor the poor. This sentiment of respect is essential to improving the connexion between the more and less prosperous conditions of society. This alone makes beneficence truly godlike. Without it, almsgiving degrades the receiver. We must learn how slight and shadowy are the distinctions between us and the poor; and that the last in outward condition may be first in the best attributes of humanity. A fraternal union, founded on this deep conviction, and intended to lift up and strengthen the exposed and tempted poor, is to do infinitely more for that suffering class, than all our artificial associations; and till Christianity shall have breathed into us this spirit of respect for our nature, wherever it is found, we shall do them little good. I conceive, that in the present low state of Christian virtue, we little apprehend the power which might be exerted over the fallen and destitute, by a benevolence which should truly, thoroughly recognise in them the image of God.

Perhaps none of us have yet heard or can comprehend the tone of voice, in which a man, thoroughly impressed with this sentiment, would speak to a fellow-creature. It is a language hardly known on earth; and no eloquence, I believe, has achieved such wonders as it is destined to accomplish. I must stop, though I have but begun the application of the principle which I have urged. I will close as I began, with saying, that the great revelation which man now needs, is a revelation of man to himself. The faith which is most wanted, is a faith in what we and our fellow-beings may become, a faith in the divine germ or principle in every soul. In regard to most of what are called the mysteries of religion, we may innocently be ignorant. But the mystery within ourselves, the mystery of our spiritual, accountable, immortal nature, it behoves us to explore. Happy are they who have begun to penetrate it, and in whom it has awakened feelings of awe towards themselves, and of deep interest and honor towards their fellow-creatures.

EVIDENCES OF CHRISTIANITY.

ROMANS i. 16: "I am not ashamed of the Gospel of Christ."

PART I.

THESE words of Paul are worthy of his resolute and disinterested spirit. In uttering them he was not an echo of the multitude, a servile repeater of established doctrines. The vast majority around him were ashamed of Jesus. The cross was then coupled with infamy. Christ's name was scorned as a malefactor's, and to profess his religion was to share his disgrace. Since that time what striking changes have occurred! The cross now hangs as an ornament from the neck of beauty. It blazes on the flags of navies, and the standards of armies. Millions bow before it in adoration, as if it were a shrine of the divinity. Of course, the temptation to be ashamed of Jesus is very much diminished. Still it is not wholly removed. Much of the homage now paid to Christianity is outward, political, worldly, and paid to its corruptions much more than to its pure and lofty spirit; and accordingly its conscientious and intrepid friends must not think it a strange thing to be encountered with occasional coldness or reproach. We may still be tempted to be ashamed of our religion, by being thrown among skeptics, who deny and deride it. We may be tempted to be ashamed of the simple and rational doctrines of Christ, by being brought into connexion with narrow zealots, who enforce their dark and perhaps degrading peculiarities as essential to salvation. We may be tempted to be ashamed of his pure, meek, and disinterested precepts, by being thrown among the licentious, self-seeking, and vindictive. Against these perils we should all go armed. To be loyal to truth and conscience under such trials, is one of the signal proofs of virtue. No man deserves the name of Christian, but he who adheres to his principles amidst the unbelieving, the intolerant, and the depraved.

"I am not ashamed of the gospel of Christ." So said Paul. So would I say. Would to God that I could catch the spirit as well as the language of the Apostle, and bear my testimony to Christianity with the same heroic resolution. Do any ask, why I join in this attestation to the gospel? Some of my reasons I propose now to set before you; and in doing so, I ask the privilege of speaking, as the Apostle has done, in the first person; of speaking in my own name, and of laying open my own mind in the most direct language. There are cases, in which the ends of public discourse may be best answered by the frank expression of individual feeling; and this mode of address, when adopted with such views, ought not to be set down to the account of egotism.

I proceed to state the reasons why I am not ashamed of the gospel of Christ; and I begin with one so important, that it will occupy the present discourse.

I am not ashamed of the gospel of Christ, because it is *true*. This is my first reason. The religion is *true*, and no consideration but this could induce me to defend it. I adopt it, not because it is popular, for false and ruinous systems have enjoyed equal reputation; nor because it is thought to uphold the order of society, for I believe that nothing but truth can be permanently useful. It is *true*; and I say this not lightly, but after deliberate examination. I am not repeating the accents of the nursery. I do not affirm the truth of Christianity, because I was so taught before I could inquire, or because I was brought up in a community pledged to this belief. It is not unlikely, that my faith and zeal will be traced by some to these sources; and believing such imputations to be groundless, fidelity to the cause of truth binds me to repel them. The circumstance of having been born and educated under Christianity, so far from disposing me to implicit faith, has often been to me the occasion of serious distrust of our religion. On observing how common it is for men of all countries and names, whether Christians, Jews, or Mahometans, to receive the religion of their fathers, I have again and again asked myself, whether I too was not a slave, whether I too was not blindly walking in the path of tradition, and yielding myself as passively as others to an hereditary faith. I distrust and fear the power of numbers and of general opinion over my judgment; and few things incite me more to repel a doctrine than intolerant attempts to force it on my understanding. Perhaps my Christian education and connexions have inclined me to skepticism, rather than bowed my mind to authority.

It may still be said, that the pride and prejudices

and motives of interest, which belong to my profession as a Christian minister, throw a suspiciousness over my reasoning and judgment on the present subject. I reply, that to myself I seem as free from biases of this kind, as the most indifferent person. I have no priestly prepossessions. I know and acknowledge the corruptions and perversions of the ministerial office from the earliest age of the church. I reprobate the tyranny which it exercises so often over the human mind. I recognise no peculiar sanctity in those who sustain it. I think, then, that I come to the examination of Christianity with as few blinding partialities as any man. I indeed claim no exemption from error; I ask no implicit faith in my conclusions; I care not how jealously and thoroughly my arguments are sifted. I only ask, that I may not be prejudged as a servile or interested partisan of Christianity. I ask that I may be heard as a friend of truth, desirous to aid my fellow-creatures in determining a question of great and universal concern. I appear as the advocate of Christianity, solely because it approves itself to my calmest reason as a revelation from God, and as the purest, brightest light which He has shed on the human mind. I disclaim all other motives. No policy, no vassalage to opinion, no dread of reproach even from the good, no private interest, no desire to uphold a useful superstition, nothing in short but a deliberate conviction of the truth of Christianity, induces me to appear in its ranks. I should be ashamed of it, did I not believe it true.

In discussing this subject, I shall express my convictions strongly; I shall speak of infidelity as a gross and perilous error. But in so doing, I beg not to be understood as passing sentence on the character of individual unbelievers. I shall show that the Christian religion is true, is from God; but I do not therefore conclude, that all who reject it are the enemies of God, and are to be loaded with reproach. I would uphold the truth without ministering to uncharitableness. The criminality, the damnable guilt of unbelief in all imaginable circumstances, is a position which I think untenable; and persuaded as I am, that it prejudices the cause of Christianity, by creating an antipathy between its friends and opposers, which injures both, and drives the latter into more determined hostility to the truth, I think it worthy of a brief consideration in this stage of the discussion.

I lay it down as a principle, that unbelief, considered in itself, has no moral quality, is neither a virtue nor a vice, but must receive its character, whether good or bad, from the dispositions or motives which produce or pervade it. Mere acts of the understanding are neither right nor wrong. When I speak of faith as a holy or virtuous principle, I extend the term beyond its primitive meaning, and include in it not merely the assent of the intellect, but the disposition or temper by which this assent is determined, and which it is suited to confirm; and I attach as broad a signification to unbelief, when I pronounce it a crime. The truth is, that the human mind, though divided by our philosophy into many distinct capacities, seldom or never exerts them separately, but generally blends them in one act. Thus in forming a judgment, it exerts the will and affections, or the moral principles of our nature, as really as the power of thought. Men's passions and interests mix with, and are expressed in, the decisions of the intellect. In the Scriptures, which use language freely, and not with philosophical strictness, faith and unbelief are mental acts of this complex character, or joint products of the understanding and heart; and on this account alone, they are objects of approbation or reproof. In these views, I presume, reflecting Christians of every name agree.

According to these views, opinions cannot be laid down as unerring and immutable signs of virtue and vice. The very same opinion may be virtuous in one man and vicious in another, supposing it, as is very possible, to have originated in different states of mind. For example, if through envy and malignity I should rashly seize on the slightest proofs of guilt in my neighbour, my judgment of his criminality would be morally wrong. Let another man arrive at the same conclusion, in consequence of impartial inquiry and love of truth, and his decision would be morally right. Still more, according to these views, it is possible for the belief of Christianity to be as criminal as unbelief. Undoubtedly the reception of a system, so pure in spirit and tendency as the gospel, is to be regarded in general as a favorable sign. But let a man adopt this religion, because it will serve his interest and popularity; let him shut his mind against objections to it, lest they should shake his faith in a gainful system; let him tamper with his intellect, and for base and selfish ends exhaust its strength in defence of the prevalent faith, and he is just as criminal in believing, as another would be in rejecting Christianity under the same bad impulses. Our religion is at this moment adopted, and passionately defended by vast multitudes, on the ground of the very same pride, worldliness, love of popularity, and blind devotion to hereditary prejudices, which led the Jews and Heathens to reject it in the primitive age; and the faith of the first is as wanting in virtue, as was the infidelity of the last.

To judge of the character of faith and unbelief, we must examine the times and the circumstances in which they exist. At the first preaching of the gospel, to believe on Christ was a strong proof of an upright mind; to enlist among his followers, was to forsake ease, honor, and wordly success; to confess him was an act of signal loyalty to truth, virtue, and God. To believe in Christ at the present moment has no such significance. To confess him argues no moral courage. It may even betray a servility and worldliness of mind. These remarks apply in their spirit to unbelief. At different periods, and in different conditions of society, unbelief may express very different states of mind. Before we pronounce it a crime, and doom it to perdition, we ought to know the circumstances under which it has sprung up, and to inquire with candor whether they afford no palliation or defence. When Jesus Christ was on earth, when his miracles were wrought before men's eyes, when his voice sounded in their ears, when not a shade of doubt could be thrown over the reality of his supernatural works, and not a human corruption had mingled with his doctrine, there was the strongest presumption against the uprightness and the love of truth of those who rejected him. He knew too the hearts and the lives of those who surrounded him, and saw distinctly in their envy, ambition, worldliness, sensuality, the springs of their unbelief; and accordingly he pronounced it a crime. Since that period, what changes have taken place! Jesus Christ has left the world. His miracles are events of a remote age, and the proofs of them though abundant, are to many perfectly unknown ; and, what is incomparably more important, his religion has undergone corruption, adulteration, disastrous change, and its likeness to its Founder is in no small degree effaced. The clear, consistent, quickening truth, which came from the lips of Jesus, has been exchanged for a hoarse jargon and vain babblings. The stream, so pure at the fountain, has been polluted and poisoned through its whole course. Not only has Christianity been overwhelmed by absurdities, but by impious doctrines, which have made the Universal Father, now a weak and vain despot, to be propitiated by forms and flatteries, and now an almighty torturer, foreordaining multitudes of his creatures to guilt, and then glorifying his justice by their everlasting woe. When I think what Christianity has become in the hands of politicians and priests, how it has been shaped into a weapon of power, how it has crushed the human soul for ages, how it has struck the intellect with palsy and haunted the imagination with superstitious phantoms, how it has broken whole nations to the yoke, and frowned on every free thought ; when I think how, under almost every form of this religion, its ministers have taken it into their own keeping, have hewn and compressed it into the shape of rigid creeds, and have then pursued by menaces of everlasting woe whoever should question the divinity of these works of their hands ; when I consider, in a word, how, under such influences, Christianity has been and still is exhibited, in forms which shock alike the reason, conscience, and heart, I feel deeply, painfully, what a different system it is from that which Jesus taught, and I dare not apply to unbelief the terms of condemnation which belonged to the infidelity of the primitive age.

Perhaps I ought to go further. Perhaps I ought to say, that to reject Christianity under some of its corruptions is rather a virtue than a crime. At the present moment, I would ask, whether it is a vice to doubt the truth of Christianity, as it is manifested in Spain and Portugal? When a patriot in those benighted countries, who knows Christianity only as a bulwark of despotism, as a rearer of inquisitions, as a stern jailer immuring wretched women in the convent, as an executioner stained and reeking with the blood of the friends of freedom; I say, when the patriot, who sees in our religion the instrument of these crimes and woes, believes and affirms that it is not from God, are we authorized to charge his unbelief on dishonesty and corruption of mind, and to brand him as a culprit? May it not be that the spirit of Christianity in his heart emboldens him to protest with his lips against what bears the name? And if he thus protest, through a deep sympathy with the oppression and sufferings of his race, is he not nearer the kingdom of God than the priest and inquisitor who boastingly and exclusively assume the Christian name? Jesus Christ has told us, that "this is the condemnation" of the unbelieving, "that they love darkness rather than light;" and who does not see, that this ground of condemnation is removed, just in proportion as the light is quenched, or Christian truth is buried in darkness and debasing error?

I know I shall be told that a man in the circumstances now supposed, would still be culpable for his unbelief, because the Scriptures are within his reach, and these are sufficient to guide him to the true doctrines of Christ. But in the countries of which I have spoken, the Scriptures are not common; and if they were, I apprehend that we should task human strength too severely, in requiring it, under every possible disadvantage, to gain the truth from this source alone. A man, born and brought up in the thickest darkness, and amidst the grossest corruptions of Christianity, accustomed to hear the Scriptures disparaged, accustomed to connect false ideas with their principal terms, and wanting our most common helps of criticism, can hardly be expected to detach from the mass of error which bears the name of the Gospel, the simple principles of the primitive faith. Let us not exact too much of our fellow-creatures. In our zeal for Christianity, let us not forget its spirit of equity and mercy. — In these remarks I have taken an extreme case. I have supposed a man subjected to the greatest disadvantages in regard to the knowledge of Christianity. But obstacles less serious may exculpate the unbeliever. In truth, none of us can draw the line which separates between innocence and guilt in this particular. To measure the responsibility of a man, who doubts or denies Christianity, we must know the history of his mind, his capacity of judgment, the early influences and prejudices to which he was exposed, the forms under which the religion and its proofs first fixed his thoughts, and the opportunities since enjoyed of eradicating errors, which struck root before the power of trying them was unfolded. We are not his judges. At another and an unerring tribunal he must give account.

I cannot, then, join in the common cry against infidelity as the sure mark of a corrupt mind. That unbelief often has its origin in evil dispositions, I cannot doubt. The character of the unbeliever often forces us to acknowledge, that he rejects Christianity to escape its rebukes; that its purity is its chief offence; that he seeks infidelity as a refuge from fear and virtuous restraint. But to impute these unholy motives to a man of pure life, is to judge rashly, and it may be unrighteously. I cannot look upon unbelief as essentially and unfailingly a crime. But I do look upon it as among the greatest of calamities. It is the loss of the chief aid of virtue, of the mightiest power over temptation, of the most quickening knowledge of God, of the only unfailing light, of the only sure hope. The unbeliever would gain unspeakably by parting with every possession for the truth which he doubts or rejects. And how shall we win him to the faith? Not by reproach, by scorn, by tones of superiority; but by paying due respect to his understanding, his virtues, and his right of private judgment; by setting before him Christianity in its simple majesty, its reasonableness, and wonderful adaptation to the wants of our spiritual nature; by exhibiting its proofs without exaggeration, yet in their full strength; and, above all, by showing in our own characters and lives, that there is in Christianity a power to purify, elevate, and console, which can be found in no human teaching. These are the true instruments of conversion. The ignorant and superstitious may indeed be driven into a religion by menace and reproach. But the reflecting unbeliever cannot but distrust a cause which admits such weapons. He must be reasoned with as a man, an equal, and a brother. Perhaps we may silence him for a time, by spreading through the community a fanatical excitement, and a persecuting hatred of infidelity. But as by such processes Christianity would be made to take a more unlovely and irrational form, its secret foes would be multiplied; its brightest evidence would be dimmed, its foundation sapped, its energy impaired ; and whenever the time should arrive for throwing off the mask (and that time would come), we should learn, that in the very ranks of its nominal disciples, there had been trained a host of foes, who would burn to prostrate the intolerant faith, which had so long sealed their lips, and trampled on the rights and freedom of the human mind.

According to these views, I do not condemn the unbeliever, unless he bear witness against himself by an immoral and irreligious life. It is not given me to search his heart. But this power is given to himself, and as a friend, I call upon him to exert it ; I ask him to look honestly into his own mind, to question his past life, and to pronounce impartial sentence on the causes of his unbelief. Let him ask himself, whether he has inquired into the principles and proofs of Christianity deliberately and in the love of truth ; whether the desire to discover and fulfil his duties to God and his fellow-creatures has governed his examination ; whether he has surrendered himself to no passions or pursuits which religion and conscience rebuke, and which bar the mind and sear the heart against the truth. If, thus self-questioned, his heart acquit him, let no man condemn him, and let him heed no man's condemnation. But if conscience bear witness against him, he has cause to suspect and dread his unbelief. He has reason to fear, that it is the fruit of a depraved mind, and that it will ripen and confirm the depravity from which it sprung.

I know that there are those, who will construe what they will call my lenity towards unbelief, into treachery towards Christianity. There are those who think, that unless skepticism be ranked among the worst crimes, and the infidel be marked out for abhorrence and dread, the multitude of men will lose their hold on the gospel. An opinion more discreditable to Christianity cannot easily be advanced by its friends. It virtually admits, that the proofs of our religion, unless examined under the influence of terror, cannot work conviction; that the gospel cannot be left, like other subjects, to the calm and unbiassed judgment of mankind. It discovers a distrust of Christianity, with which I have no sympathy. And here I would remark, that the worst abuses of our religion have sprung from this cowardly want of confidence in its power. Its friends have feared, that it could not stand without a variety of artificial buttresses. They have imagined, that men must now be bribed into faith by annexing to it temporal privileges, now driven into it by menaces and inquisitions, now attracted by gorgeous forms, now awed by mysteries and superstitions; in a word, that the multitude must be imposed upon, or the religion will fall. I have no such distrust of Christianity; I believe in its invincible powers. It is founded in our nature. It meets our deepest wants. Its proofs as well as principles are adapted to the common understandings of men, and need not to be aided by appeals to fear or any other passion, which would discourage inquiry or disturb the judgment. I fear nothing for Christianity, if left to speak in its own tones, to approach men with its unveiled, benignant countenance. I do fear much from the weapons of policy and intimidation, which are framed to uphold the imagined weakness of Christian truth.

I now come to the great object of this discourse,— an exhibition of the proofs of Christianity;— and I begin with a topic which is needed to prepare some, if not many, to estimate these proofs fairly, and according to their true weight. I begin with the position, That there is nothing in the general idea of Revelation at which Reason ought to take offence; nothing inconsistent with any established truth, or with our best views of God and Nature. This topic meets a prejudice not very rare. I repeat it then, Revelation is nothing incredible, nothing which carries contradiction on its face, nothing at war with any great principles of reason or experience. On hearing of God's teaching us by some other means than the fixed order of nature, we ought not to be surprised, nor ought the suggestion to awaken resistance in our minds.

Revelation is not at war with nature. From the necessity of the case, the earliest instruction must have come to human beings from this source. If our race had a beginning (and nothing but the insanity of Atheism can doubt this), then its first members, created as they were without human parentage, and having no resource in the experience of fellow-creatures who had preceded them, required an immediate teaching from their Creator; they would have perished without it. Revelation was the very commencement of human history, the foundation of all later knowledge and improvement. It was an essential part of the course of Providence, and must not then be regarded as a discord in God's general system.

Revelation is not at war with nature. Nature prompts us to expect it from the relation which God bears to the human race. The relation of Creator is the most intimate which can subsist; and it leads us to anticipate a free and affectionate intercourse with the creature.

That the Universal Father should be bound by a parental interest to his offspring, that he should watch over and assist the progress of beings whom he has enriched with the divine gifts of reason and conscience, is so natural a doctrine, so accordant with his character, that various sects, both philosophical and religious, both anterior and subsequent to Christianity, have believed, not only in general revelation, but that God reveals himself to every human soul. When I think of the vast capacities of the human mind, of God's nearness to it, and unbounded love towards it, I am disposed to wonder, not that revelations have been made, but that they have not been more variously vouchsafed to the wants of mankind.

Revelation has a striking agreement with the chief method which God has instituted for carrying forward individuals and the race, and is thus in harmony with his ordinary operations. Whence is it, that we all acquire our chief knowledge ? Not from the outward universe ; not from the fixed laws of material nature ; but from intelligent beings, more advanced than ourselves. The teachings of the wise and good are our chief aids. Were our connexion with superior minds broken off, had we no teacher but nature with its fixed laws, its unvarying revolutions of night and day and seasons, we should remain for ever in the ignorance of childhood. Nature is a volume, which we can read only by the help of an intelligent interpreter. The great law under which man is placed, is, that he shall receive illumination and impulse from beings more improved than himself. Now revelation is only an extension of this universal method of carrying forward mankind. In this case, God takes on himself the office to which all rational beings are called. He becomes an immediate teacher to a few, communicating to them a higher order of truths than had before been attained, which they in turn are to teach to their race. Here is no new power or element introduced into the system, but simply an enlargement of that agency on which the progress of man chiefly depends.

Let me next ask you to consider, Why or for what end God has ordained, as the chief means of human improvement, the communication of light from superior to inferior minds; and if it shall then appear, that revelation is strikingly adapted to promote a similar though more important end, you will have another mark of agreement between revelation and his ordinary Providence. Why is it that God has made men's progress dependent on instruction from their fellow-beings? Why are the more advanced commissioned to teach the less informed? A great purpose, I believe the chief purpose, is, to establish interesting relations among men, to bind them to one another by generous sentiments, to promote affectionate intercourse, to call forth a purer love than could spring from a communication of mere outward gifts. Now it is rational to believe, that the Creator designs to bind his creatures to Himself as truly as to one another, and to awaken towards himself even stronger gratitude, confidence, and love; for these sentiments towards God are more happy and ennobling than towards any other being; and it is plain that revelation, or immediate divine teaching, serves as effectually to establish these ties between God and man, as human teaching to attach men to one another. We see, then, in revelation an end corresponding to what the Supreme Being adopts in his common providence.

That the end here affirmed is worthy of his interposition, who can doubt? His benevolence can propose no higher purpose, than that of raising the minds and hearts of his creatures to himself. His parental character is a pledge that he must intend this ineffable happiness for his rational offspring; and Revelation is suited to this end, not only by unfolding new doctrines in relation to God, but by the touching proof which it carries in itself of the special interest which he takes in his human family. There is plainly an expression of deeper concern, a more affectionate character, in this mode of instruction, than in teaching us by the fixed order of nature. Revelation is God speaking to us in our own language, in the accents which human friendship employs. It shows a love, breaking through the reserve and distance, which we all feel to belong to the method of teaching us by his works alone. It fastens our minds on him. We can look on nature, and not think of the Being whose glory it declares; but God is indissolubly connected with, and indeed is a part of, the idea of revelation. How much nearer does this direct intercourse bring him to the mass of mankind! On this account revelation would seem to me important, were it simply to repeat the teachings of nature. This reiteration of great truths in a less formal style, in kinder, more familiar tones, is peculiarly fitted to awaken the soul to the presence and benignity of its heavenly Parent. I see, then, in revelation a purpose corresponding with that for which human teaching was instituted. Both are designed to bring together the teacher and the taught in pure affections.

Let me next ask you to consider, what is the kind of instruction which the higher minds among men are chiefly called to impart to the inferior. You will here see another agreement between revelation and that ordinary human teaching, which is the great instrument of improving the race. What kind of instruction is it, which parents, which the aged and experienced, are most anxious to give to the young, and on which the safety of this class mainly depends? It is instruction in relation to the Future, to their adult years, such as is suited to prepare them for the life that is opening before them. It is God's will, when he gives us birth, that we should be forewarned of the future stages of our being, of approaching manhood or womanhood, of the scenes, duties, labors, through which we are to pass; and for this end he connects us with beings, who have traversed the paths on which we are entering, and whose duty it is to train us for a more advanced age. Instruction in regard to Futurity is the great means of improvement. Now the Christian revelation has for its aim to teach us on this very subject; to disclose the life which is before us, and to fit us for it. A Future state is its constant burden. That God should give us light in regard to that state, if he designs us for it, is what we should expect from his solicitude to teach us in regard to what is future in our earthly existence. Nature thirsts for, and analogy almost promises, some illumination on the subject of human destiny. This topic I shall insist on more largely hereafter. I wish now simply to show you the agreement of revelation, in this particular, with the ordinary providence of God.

I proceed to another order of reflections, which to my own mind is particularly suited to meet the vague idea, that revelation is at war with nature. To judge of nature, we should look at its highest ranks of beings. We should inquire of the human soul, which we all fee to be a higher existence than matter. Now I maintain, that there are in the human soul wants, deep wants, which are not met by the influences and teachings, which the ordinary course of things affords. I am aware that this is a topic to provoke distrust, if not derision, in the low-minded and sensual; but I speak what I do know; and nothing moves me so little as the scoffs of men who despise their own nature. One of the most striking views of human nature, is the disproportion between what it conceives and thirsts for, and what it finds or can secure in the range of the present state. It is prone to stretch beyond its present bounds. Ideas of excellence and happiness spring up, which it cannot realize now. It carries within itself a standard, of which it daily and hourly falls short. This self-contradiction is the source of many sharp pains. There is, in most men, a dim consciousness, at least, of being made for something higher than they have gained, a feeling of internal discord, a want of some stable good, a disappointment in merely outward acquisitions; and in proportion as these convictions and wants become distinct, they break out in desires of illumination and aids from God not found in nature. I am aware, that the wants of which I have spoken are but faintly developed in the majority of men. Accustomed to give their thoughts and strength to the outward world, multitudes do not penetrate and cannot interpret their own souls. They impute to outward causes the miseries which spring from an internal fountain. They do not detain, and are scarcely conscious of the better thoughts and feelings, which sometimes dart through their minds. Still there are few, who are not sometimes dissatisfied with themselves, who do not feel the wrong which they have done to themselves, and who do not desire a purer and nobler state of mind. The suddenness, with which the multitude are thrilled by the voice of fervent eloquence, when it speaks to them of the spiritual world in tones of reality, shows the deep wants of human nature even amidst ignorance and degradation. But all men do not give themselves wholly to outward things. There are those, and not a few, who are more true to their nature, and ought therefore to be regarded as its more faithful representatives; and in such, the wants, of which I have spoken, are unfolded with energy. There are those, who feel painfully the weight of their present imperfection; who are fired by rare examples of magnanimity and devotion; who desire nothing so intensely as power over temptation, as elevation above selfish passions, as conformity of will to the inward law of duty, as the peace of conscious rectitude and religious trust; who would rejoice to lay down the present life for that spotless, bright, disinterested virtue, of which they have the type or germ in their own minds. Such men can find no resource but in God, and are prepared to welcome a revelation of his merciful purposes as an unspeakable gift. I say, then, that the human mind has wants which nature does not answer. And these are not accidental feelings, unaccountable caprices, but are deep, enduring, and reproduced in all ages under one or another form. They breathe through the works of genius; they burn in the loftiest souls. Here are principles implanted by God in the highest order of his creatures on earth, to which revelation is adapted; and I say, then, that revelation is any thing but hostility to nature.

I will offer but one more view in illustration of this topic. I ask you to consider, on what Principle of human nature the Christian revelation is intended to bear and to exert influence, and then to inquire whether the peculiar importance of this principle be not a foundation for peculiar interposition in its behalf. If so, revelation may be said to be a demand of the human soul, and its imagined incongruity with nature will disappear. For what principle or faculty of the mind, then, was Christianity intended ? It was plainly not given to enrich the intellect by teaching philosophy, or to perfect the imagination and taste by furnishing sublime and beautiful models of composition. It was not meant to give sagacity in public life, or skill and invention in common affairs. It was undoubtedly designed to develope all these faculties, but secondarily, and through its influence on a higher principle. It addresses itself primarily, and is especially adapted, to the Moral power in man. It regards and is designed for man as a moral being, endued with conscience or the principle of duty, who is capable of that peculiar form of excellence which we call righteousness or virtue, and exposed to that peculiar evil, guilt. Now the question offers itself, Why does God employ such extraordinary means for promoting virtue rather than science, for aiding conscience rather than intellect and our other powers ? Is there a foundation in the moral principle for peculiar interpositions in its behalf ? I affirm that there is. I affirm that a broad distinction exists between our moral nature and our other capacities. Conscience is the Supreme power within us. Its essence, its grand characteristic, is Sovereignty. It speaks with a divine authority. Its office is to command, to rebuke, to reward ; and happiness and honor depend on the reverence with which we listen to it. All our other powers become useless and worse than useless, unless controlled by the principle of duty. Virtue is the supreme good, the supreme beauty, the divinest of God's gifts, the healthy and harmonious unfolding of the soul, and the germ of immortality. It is worth every sacrifice, and has power to transmute sacrifices and sufferings into crowns of glory and rejoicing. Sin, vice, is an evil of its own kind, and not to be confounded with any other. Who does not feel at once the broad distinction between misfortune and crime, between disease of body and turpitude of soul? Sin, vice, is war with the highest power in our own breasts, and in the universe. It makes a being odious to himself, and arms against him the principle of rectitude in God and in all pure beings. It poisons or dries up the fountains of enjoyment, and adds unspeakable weight to the necessary pains of life. It is not a foreign evil, but a blight and curse in the very centre of our being. Its natural associates are fear, shame, and self-torture; and, whilst it robs the present of consolation, it leaves the future without hope. Now I say, that in this peculiar ruin wrought by moral evil, and in this peculiar worth of moral goodness, we see reasons for special interpositions of God in behalf of virtue, in resistance of sin. It becomes the Infinite Father to manifest peculiar interest in the moral condition and wants of his creatures. Their great and continued corruption is an occasion for peculiar methods of relief; and a revelation given to restore them, and carry them forward to perfection, has an end which justifies, if it does not demand, this signal expression of parental love.

The preceding views have been offered, not as sufficient to prove that a revelation has been given, but for the purpose of removing the vague notion that it is at war with nature, and of showing its consistency with the spirit and principles of the divine administration. I proceed now to consider the direct and positive proofs of Christianity, beginning with some remarks on the nature and sufficiency of the evidence on which it chiefly relies.

Christianity sprung up about eighteen hundred years ago. Of course its evidences are to be sought in history. We must go back to the time of its birth, and understand the condition in which it found the world, as well as the circumstances of its origin, progress, and establishment; and happily, on these points, we have all the light necessary to a just judgment. We must not imagine, that a religion, which bears the date of so distant an age, must therefore be involved in obscurity. We know enough of the earliest times of Christianity to place the question of its truth within our reach. The past may be known as truly as the present; and I deem this principle so important in the present discussion that I ask your attention to it.

The past, I have said, may be known; nor is this all; we derive from it our most important knowledge. Former times are our chief instructors. Our political, as well as religious institutions, our laws, customs, modes of thinking, arts of life, have come down from earlier ages, and most of them are unintelligible without a light borrowed from history.

Not only are we able to know the nearest of past ages, or those which touch on our own times, but those which are remote. No educated man doubts any more of the victories of Alexander or Cæsar, before Christ, than of Napoleon's conquests in our own day. So open is our communication with some ages of antiquity, so many are the records which they have transmitted, that we know them even better than nearer times ; and a religion which grew up eighteen hundred years ago, may be more intelligible and accompanied with more decisive proofs of truth or falsehood, than one which is not separated from us by a fourth part of that duration.

From the nature of things, we may and must know much of the past ; for the present has grown out of the past, is its legacy, fruit, representative, and is deeply impressed with it. Events do not expire at the moment of their occurrence. Nothing takes place without leaving traces behind it ; and these are in many cases so distinct and various, as to leave not a doubt of their cause. We all understand, how, in the material world, events testify of themselves to future ages. Should we visit an unknown region, and behold masses of lava covered with soil of different degrees of thickness, and surrounding a blackened crater, we should have as firm a persuasion of the occurrence of remote and successive volcanic eruptions, as if we had lived through the ages in which they took place. The chasms of the earth would report how terribly it had been shaken, and the awful might of long-extinguished fires would be written in desolations which ages had failed to efface. Now conquest, and civil and religious revolutions, leave equally their impressions on society, leave institutions, manners, and a variety of monuments, which are inexplicable without them, and which, taken together, admit not a doubt of their occurrence. The past stretches into the future; the present is crowded with it, and can be interpreted only by the light of history.

But besides these effects and remains of earlier times, we have other and more distinct memorials of the past, which, when joined with the former, place it clearly within our knowledge. I refer to books. A book is more than a monument of a preceding age. It is a voice coming to us over the interval of centuries. Language, when written, as truly conveys to us another's mind as when spoken. It is a species of personal intercourse. By it the wise of former times give us their minds as really, as if by some miracle they were to rise from the dead and communicate with us by speech.

From these remarks we learn that Christianity is not placed beyond the reach of our investigations by the remoteness of its origin ; and they are particularly applicable to the age in which the gospel was first given to the world. Our religion did not spring up before the date of authentic history. Its birth is not hidden in the obscurity of early and fabulous times. We have abundant means of access to its earliest stages ; and, what is very important, the deep and peculiar interest which Christianity has awakened, has fixed the earnest attention of the most learned and sagacious men on the period of its original publication, so that no age of antiquity is so thoroughly understood. Christianity sprung up at a time, when the literature and philosophy of Greece was spread far and wide, and had given a great impulse to the human mind ; and when Rome by unexampled conquests had become a centre and bond of union to the civilized world and to many half civilized regions, and had established a degree of communication between distant countries before unknown. We are not, then, left to grope our way by an unsteady light. Our means of information are various and great. We have incontestable facts in relation to the origin of our religion, from which its truth may be easily deduced. A few of these facts, which form the first steps of our reasoning on this subject, I will now lay before you.

1. First, then, we know with certainty the *time* when Christianity was founded. As to this fact, there is and can be no doubt. Heathen and Christian historians speak on this point with one voice. Christianity was first preached in the age of Tiberius. Not a trace of it exists before that period, and afterwards the marks and proofs of its existence are so obvious and acknowledged as to need no mention. Here is one important fact placed beyond doubt.

2. In the next place, we know the *place* where Christianity sprung up. No one can dispute the country of its birth. Its Jewish origin is not only testified by all history, but is stamped on its front and woven into its frame. The language in which it is conveyed, carries us at once to Judea. Its name is derived from Jewish prophecy. None but Jews could have written the New Testament. So natural, undesigned, and perpetual are the references and allusions of the writers to the opinions and manners of that people, so accustomed are they to borrow from the same source the metaphors, similitudes, types, by which they illustrate their doctrines, that Christianity, as to its outward form, may be said to be steeped in Judaism. We have, then, another established fact. We know where it was born.

3. Again, we know the individual by whom Christianity was founded. We know its Author, and from the nature of the case this fact cannot but be known. The founder of a religion is naturally and necessarily the object of general inquiry. Wherever the new faith

is carried, the first and most eager questions are, "From whom does it come? On whose authority does it rest?" Curiosity is never more intense, than in regard to the individual, who claims a divine commission and sends forth a new religion. He is the last man to be overlooked or mistaken. In the case of Christianity especially, its founder may be said to have been forced on men's notice, for his history forms an essential part of his religion. Christianity is not an abstract doctrine, which keeps its author out of sight. He is its very soul. It rests on him, and finds its best illustration in his life. These reflections however may be spared. The simple consideration, that Christianity must have had an author, and that it has been always ascribed to Jesus, and to no one else, places the great fact, which I would establish, beyond doubt.

4. I next observe, that we not only know the founder of Christianity, but the ministers by whom he published and spread it through the world. A new religion must have propagators, first teachers, and with these it must become intimately associated. A community can no more be ignorant as to the teachers who converted it to a new faith, than as to the conqueror who subjected it to a new government; and where the art of writing is known and used for recording events, the latter fact will not more certainly be transmitted to posterity than the former. We have the testimony of all ages, that the men called Apostles were the first propagators of Christianity, nor have any others been named as sustaining this office; and it is impossible that, on such a point, such testimony should be false.

5. Again; we know not only when, and where, and by whom Christianity was introduced;—we know, from

a great variety of sources, what in the main this religion was, as it came from the hands of its founder. To assure ourselves on this point, we need not recur to any sacred books. From the age following that of Christ and the Apostles, down to the present day, we have a series, and an almost numberless host, of writers on the subject of Christianity; and whilst we discover in them a great diversity of opinions, and opposite interpretations of some of Christ's teachings, yet on the whole they so far agree in the great facts of his history, and in certain great principles of his religion, that we cannot mistake as to the general character of the system which he taught. There is not a shadow of reason for the opinion that the original system which Jesus taught was lost, and a new one substituted and fastened on the world in his name. The many and great corruptions of Christianity did not and could not hide its principal features. The greatest corruptions took place in the century which followed the death of the Apostles, when certain wild and visionary sects endeavoured to establish a union between the new religion and the false philosophy to which they had been wedded in their heathen state. You may judge of their character and claims, when I tell you, that they generally agreed in believing, that the God who made the world, and who was worshipped by the Jews, was not the supreme God, but an inferior and imperfect Deity, and that matter had existed from eternity, and was essentially and unchangeably evil. Yet these sects endeavoured to sustain themselves on the writings which the great body of Christians received and honored as the works of the Apostles; and, amidst their delusions they recognised and taught the miracles of Christ, his resurrection, and the most important principles of his religion ; so that the general nature of Christianity, as it came from its Founder, may be ascertained beyond a doubt. Here another great point is fixed.

6. I have now stated to you several particulars relating to Christianity, which admit no doubt ; and these indisputable facts are of great weight in a discussion of the Christian evidences. There is one point more, of importance, which cannot be settled so expeditiously as these. I hope, however, enough may be said to place it beyond doubt, without exceeding the limits of a discourse ; and I invite to it your serious attention. I say, then, that we not only know in general what Christianity was at its first promulgation ; but we know precisely what its first propagators taught, for we have their writings. We have their religion under their own hands. We have particularly four narratives of the life, works, and words of their Master, which put us in possession of his most private as well as public teaching. It is true, that without those writings we should still have strong arguments for the truth of Christianity ; but we should be left in doubt as to some of its important principles ; and its internal evidence, which corroborates, and, as some think, exceeds the external, would be very much impaired. The possession of the writings of the first propagators of the gospel, must plainly render us great aid in judging of its claims. These writings, I say, we have, and this point I would now establish.

I am aware that the question, to which I now ask your attention, is generally confined to professed students. But it is one on which men of good sense are competent to judge, and its great importance gives it a claim to the serious consideration of every Christian.

The question is, whether the four Gospels are genuine, that is, whether they were written by those to whom they are ascribed. To answer it, let us consider how we determine the genuineness of books in general. I begin with the obvious remark, that to know the author of a work, it is not necessary that we should be eye-witnesses of its composition. Perhaps of the numberless publications of the present day, we have not seen one growing under the pen of the writer. By far the greater number come to us across the ocean, and yet we are as confident in regard to their authors as if we had actually seen them first committed to paper. The ascription of a book to an individual, during his life, by those whe are interested in him, and who have the best means of knowing the truth, removes all doubts as to its author. A strong and wide-spread conviction of this kind must have a cause, and can only be explained by the actual production of the work by the reputed writer. It should here be remembered that there is a strong disposition in men to ascertan the author of an important and interesting work. We have had a remarkable illustration of this in our own times. The author of "Waverley" saw fit to wrap himself for a time in mystery; and what was the consequence? No subject in politics or science was agitated more generally than the question to whom the work belonged. It was not only made a topic in almost every periodical publication, but one book was expressly written to solve the problem. The instance, I know, was remarkable; but this inquisitiveness in regard to books is a principle of our nature, and is particularly active, when the book in debate is a work of singular authority.

I have spoken of the confidence which we feel as to

he authors of books published in our own times. But our certainty is not confined to these. Every reading man is as sure that Hume and Robertson wrote the histories which bear their names, as that Scott has in our own time sent out the " Life of Bonaparte." Those eminent men were born more than a hundred years ago, and they died before the birth of most to whom I speak. But the communication between their times and our own is so open and various, that we know their literary labors as well as those of the present day. Not a few persons now living have had intercourse with some of the contemporaries of these historians; and through this channel in particular, we of this generation have the freest access to the preceding, and know its convictions in regard to the authors of interesting books as fully as if we had lived in it ourselves. That the next age will have the same communication with the present as the present has with the past, and that these convictions of our predecessors will be transmitted by us to our immediate successors, you will easily comprehend; and you will thus learn the respect which is due to the testimony of the third generation on such a subject.

In what has now been said, we see with what confidence and certainty we determine the authors of writings published in our own age or in the times nearest our own. These remarks may be easily applied to the productions of antiquity. When the question arises, whether an ancient book was written by the individual whose name it bears, we must inquire into the opinion of his contemporaries, or of those who succeeded his contemporaries so nearly as to have intimate communication with them. The competency of these to a just judgment on the subject, we have seen ; and if they have transmitted their convictions to us in undisputed writings, it ought to be decisive. On this testimony, we ascribe many ancient books to their authors with the firmest faith ; and, in truth, we receive as genuine many works of antiquity on far inferior proofs. There are many books of which no notice can be found for several ages after the time of their reputed authors. Still the fact, that, as soon as they are named, they are ascribed undoubtingly, and by general consent, to certain authors, is esteemed a sufficient reason for regarding them as their productions, unless some opposite proof can be adduced. This general reception of a work as having come from a particular writer, is an effect which requires a cause ; and the most natural and obvious explanation of his being named, rather than any other man, is, that he actually composed it.

I now proceed to apply these principles to the four histories of Christ, commonly called Gospels. The question is, what testimony respecting their authors has come down to us from the age of their reputed authors, or from times so near it and so connected with it, as to be faithful representatives of its convictions. By this testimony, as we have seen, the genuineness of the books must be decided. And I begin with admitting that no evidence on the subject is to be derived from contemporary writers. No author, living in the age of the first propagators of Christianity, has named the Gospels. The truth is, that no undisputed writings of their immediate converts have been preserved. A few tracts, bearing the name of men acquainted with the Apostles, have indeed come down to us ; but so much uncertainty hangs over their origin, that I am unwilling to ground on them any reasoning. Nor ought we to wonder that the works of private Christians of the primitive age are wanting to us; for that was an age of persecution, when men were called to *die* rather than *write* for their religion. I suppose too, that during the times of the Apostles, little importance was attached to any books but such as were published or authorized by these eminent men; and, of course, what was written by others was little circulated, and soon passed away.

The undisputed writings of the early Christians begin about seventy years after the times of the Apostles. At that period there probably remained none of the first converts or contemporaries of the Apostles. But there were living not a few, who had been acquainted with the last survivors of that honored generation. When the Apostles died, they must have left behind a multitude who had known them; and of these not a few must have continued many years, and must have had intercourse with the new generation which sprung up after the apostolic age. Now in the times of this generation, the series of Christian authors begins. Although, then, we have no productions of the apostolic age to bear witness to the Gospels, we have writings from the ages which immediately followed it, and which, from their connexion with it, ought, as we have seen, to be regarded as most credible witnesses on such a subject. What, then, do these writings teach? I answer, Their testimony is clear and full. We learn from them, not only that the Gospels existed in those times, but that they were widely diffused, that they were received as the writings of the men whose names they bear, and that they were regarded with a confidence and veneration yielded to no other books. They are quoted as books given by their revered authors to the Christian community, to be public and enduring records of the religion; and they are spoken of as read in the assemblies which were held for the inculcation and extension of the faith. I ask you to weigh this testimony. It comes to us from times connected intimately with the first age. Had the Gospels been invented and first circulated among the generation which succeeded the Apostles, could that generation have received them, as books known and honored before their time, and as the most authoritative and precious records transmitted to them from their fathers and predecessors? The case may seem too plain to require explanation; but as many are unaccustomed to inquiries of this kind, I will offer an example. You well know, that nearly a century ago a great religious excitement was spread through this country chiefly by the ministry of Whitefield. Suppose now that four books were at this moment to come forth, bearing the names of four of the most distinguished men of that period, of Whitefield, of the venerable Edwards, and of two others intimately associated with them in their religious labors; and suppose these books not only to furnish narratives of what then took place, but to contain principles and rules urged with all possible earnestness and authority on the disciples or admirers of these religious leaders. Do you think it possible that their followers of the present day, and the public, could be made to believe, that these books had been published by their pretended authors, had been given as standards to a religious community, and had been handed down as venerated books, when no such works had been heard of before? This is but a faint illustration; for Whitefield and Edwards are names of little weight or authority, compared with what the Apostles possessed in the primitive church.

We have, then, strong and sufficient reasons for believing that the histories called Gospels were received, in the times of the Apostles, as works of those whose names they bear ; and were handed down as theirs with veneration by their contemporaries. Will any say that all this may be true, but that, during the lives of the Apostles, books forged in their names may have obtained general currency ? To this extravagant supposition it would be sufficient to reply, according to my previous remarks, that the general ascription of a book to an author during his life, is the ground on which the genuineness of the most unquestioned works depends. But I would add, that this evidence is singularly conclusive in the present case. The original propagators of Christianity, to whom the Gospels were ascribed, were, from their office, among the public men of their age. They must have travelled extensively. They must have been consulted by inhabitants of various countries on the subject of the new religion. They must have been objects of deep interest to the first converts. They lived in the world's eye. Their movements, visits, actions, words, and writings, must have awakened attention. Books from their hands must have produced a great sensation. We cannot conceive a harder task, than to impose writings, forged in their name, on Christians and Christian communities, thus intimately connected with them, and so alive to their efforts for the general cause. The opportunities of detecting the falsehood were abundant ; and to imagine falsehood to prosper under such circumstances, argues a strange ignorance of literary history and of human nature.

Let me add, that the motives of the first Christians, to ascertain distinctly whether writings ascribed to the

Apostles were truly theirs, were the strongest which can be conceived. I have mentioned, in my previous remarks, the solicitude of the world to learn the author of "Waverley." The motive was mere curiosity; and yet to what earnest inquiries were multitudes impelled. The name of the author was of little or no moment. The book was the same, its portraits equally vivid, its developements of the human heart equally true and powerful, whether the author were known or not. So it is with most works. Books of science, philosophy, morals, and polite literature, owe their importance and authority, not to their writers, but to their contents. Now, the four Gospels were different in this respect. They were not the same to the first converts, come from whom they might. If written by Apostles or by their associates, they had an authority and sacredness, which could belong to them on no other condition. They became books of laws to the Christian community, became binding on their consciences and lives. To suppose such books received blindly and without inquiry, by great numbers who had all the means of ascertaining their true origin, is to suppose the first converts insane or idiots, a charge which I believe their worst enemies will not think of urging against them, and which the vast superiority of their religious and moral system to all the philosophical systems of the times abundantly disproves.

I have now finished what is called the historical or external evidence of the genuineness of the four Gospels; that is, the evidence drawn from their being received and revered as the writings of the Apostles in the first and succeeding ages of Christianity. But before leaving this head, I would notice a difficulty which may press on some minds. I suppose, that many of you have heard, that very early, probably about the beginning of the second century, writings were forged in the name of the Apostles ; and some may ask why the four Gospels may not belong to this description. The answer is, that the Gospels, as we have seen, were received and honored by the great body of Christians, in the first and succeeding ages of Christianity, as writings of Apostles or their associates. The forgeries are known to be forgeries, because they were not so received, because they were held in no veneration, but were rejected as fictitious by the Christian community. Here is a broad line of distinction. It must not surprise us, that in the great excitement produced by the first publication and triumphs of Christianity, a variety of extravagant notions should spring up, and that attempts should be made to blend the new religion with established systems ; and as the names of the first propagators of the Gospel were held in peculiar reverence, we cannot wonder that the leaders of sects should strive to attach an apostolic sanction to their opinions, by sending abroad partly true and partly false accounts of the preaching of these eminent men. Whether these writings were sent forth as compositions of the Apostles, or only as records of their teaching, made by their hearers, is a question open to debate ; but as to their origin there can be little doubt. We can account for their existence, and for the degree of favor which they obtained. They were generally written to give authority to the dreams or speculations of some extravagant sects, to which they were very much confined, and with which most of them passed away. There is not a shadow of reason for confounding with these our Gospels, which were spread from the beginning through the Christian world, and were honored and transmitted as the works of the venerated men by whose names they were called.

Having now given the historical argument in favor of the genuineness of the Gospels, that is, in favor of their being written by their reputed authors, I now add, that there are several presumptive and internal proofs of the same truth, which, taken alone, have great weight, and when connected with the preceding, form an amount of evidence not easily withstood. I have time to glance at only a few of these.

It is a presumption in favor of the claims of an author, that the book ascribed to him has never been assigned to any other individual. Now I am not aware, that unbelief has in any age named any individuals, to whom the Gospels may be traced rather than to those whose names they bear. We are not called upon to choose between different writers. In common cases, this absence of rival claims is considered as decisive in favor of the reputed author, unless the books themselves give ground to suspect another hand. Why shall not this principle be applied to the Gospels as well as to all other works?

Another presumption in favor of the belief that these histories were written by the first propagators of Christianity, arises from the consideration, that such books were to be expected from them. It is hardly conceivable that the Apostles, whose zeal carried abroad their system through so many nations, and who lived in an age of reading and writing, should leave their doctrines to tradition, should neglect the ordinary precaution of embodying them in the only permanent form, the only one in which they could be accurately transmitted, and by which all other systems were preserved. It is reasonable to suppose that they wrote what they taught; and if so, it is hardly possible that their writings should be lost. Their accounts must have been received and treasured up just as we know the Gospels were cherished; and hence arises a strong presumption in favor of the genuineness of these books.

Again; these books carry one strong mark of having been written in the time of the Apostles. They contain no trace of later times, nothing to indicate that the authors belonged to another age. Now to those of you, who are acquainted with such subjects, it is hardly necessary to observe, how difficult it is for a writer to avoid betraying the period in which he lives; and the cause is very obvious. Every age has its peculiarities, has manners, events, feelings, words, phrases of its own; and a man brought up among these falls so naturally under their influence, and incorporates them so fully with his own mind, that they break out and manifest themselves, almost necessarily and without his consciousness, in his words and writings. The present makes an impression incomparably more vivid than the past, and accordingly traces of the real age of a writer may almost always be discovered by a critical eye, however anxious he may be to assume the style and character of a preceding age. Now the Gospels betray no marks of the feelings, manners, contentions, events of a period later than that in which the Apostles lived; and when we consider, that, with the exception of Luke's history, they have all the appearance of having come from plain men, unused to composition, this argument applies to them with peculiar force. Under this head, I might place before you the evidence of the genuineness of these books derived from the language, dialect, idiom, in which they are written. You can easily understand, that by these helps the country and age of a writing may often be traced; but the argument belongs to the learned. It may however be satisfactory to know, that the profoundest scholars see in the dialect and idiom of the Gospels, a precise accordance with what might be expected of Jews, writing in the age of the Apostles.

Another internal proof, and one within the reach of all, may be gathered from the style and character of the evangelical narratives. They are written with the simplicity, minuteness, and ease, which are the natural tones of truth, which belong to writers thoroughly acquainted with their subjects, and writing from reality. You discover in them nothing of the labor, caution, and indistinctness, which can scarcely be escaped by men who are assuming a character not their own, and aiming to impose on the world. There is a difference which we have all discerned and felt, though we cannot describe it, between an honest, simple-hearted witness, who tells what he has seen or is intimately acquainted with, and the false witness, who affects an intimate knowledge of events and individuals, which are in whole or in part his own fabrication. Truth has a native frankness, an unaffected freedom, a style and air of its own, and never were narratives more strongly characterized by these than the Gospels. It is a striking circumstance in these books, that whilst the life and character which they portray, are the most extraordinary in history, the style is the most artless. There is no straining for epithets or for elevation of language to suit the dignity of the great personage who is the subject. You hear plain men telling you what they know, of a character which they venerated too much to think of adorning or extolling. It is also worthy of remark, that the character of Jesus, though the most peculiar and exalted in history, though the last to be invented and the hardest to be sustained, is yet unfolded through a great variety of details and conditions, with perfect unity and consistency. The strength of this proof can only be understood by those who are sufficiently acquainted with literary history, to appreciate the difficulty of accomplishing a consistent and successful forgery Such consistency is, in the present case, an almost infallible test. Suppose four writers, of a later age, to have leagued together in the scheme of personating the first propagators of Christianity, and of weaving, in their name, the histories of their Master's life. Removed as these men would have been from the original, and having no model or type of his character in the elevation of their own minds, they must have portrayed him with an unsteady hand, must have marred their work with incongruous features, must have brought down their hero on some occasion to the ordinary views and feelings of men, and in particular must have been warped in their selection and representation of incidents by the private purpose which led them to this singular coöperation. That four writers, under such circumstances, should sustain throughout so peculiar and elevated a character as Jesus, and should harmonize with each other in the delineation, would be a prodigy which no genius, however preëminent, could achieve. I say, then, that the narratives bear strong internal marks of having been drawn from the living original, by those who had the best means of knowing his character and life.

So various, strong, sufficient are the proofs that the four Gospels are the works of the first preachers of Christianity, whose name they bear. I will only add, that the genuineness of few ancient books is supported by proofs equally strong. Most of the works, which have come down to us from antiquity, and which are ascribed to their reputed writers with undoubting confidence, are so ascribed on evidence inferior to that on which the claims of the Evangelists rest. On this point therefore not a doubt should remain.

Here I pause. The proofs of Christianity, which are involved in or founded on the facts now established, will be the subjects of future discussion.

PART II.

I HAVE now stated some of the great facts relating to the origin of Christianity, of which we have clear and full proof. We know when and where this religion sprung up. We know its Author, and the men whom he employed as the first propagators of his doctrine. We know the great features of the religion as it was originally taught; and still more, we have the writings of its first teachers, by which its precise character is placed beyond doubt. I now proceed to lay before you some of the arguments in support of Christianity, which are involved in or are founded on these facts. I must confine myself to a few, and will select those to which some justice may be done in the compass of a discourse.

I. I believe Christianity to be true, or to have come from God, because it seems to me impossible to trace it to any other origin. It must have had a cause, and no other adequate cause can be assigned. The incongruity between this religion and all the circumstances amidst which it grew up, is so remarkable, that we are compelled to look beyond and above this world for its explanation. When I go back to the origin of Christianity, and place myself in the age and country of its birth, I can find nothing in the opinions of men, or in the state of society, which can account for its beginning or diffusion. There was no power on earth to create or uphold such a system. There was nothing congenial with it in Judaism, in heathenism, or in the state of society among the most cultivated communities. If you study the religions, governments, and philosophical systems of that age, you will discover in them not even a leaning towards Christianity. It sprung up in opposition to all, making no compromise with human prejudice or passion; and it sprung up, not only superior to all, but possessing at its very beginning a perfection, which has been the admiration of ages, and which, instead of being dimmed by time, has come forth more brightly, in proportion to the progress of the human mind.

I know, indeed, that, at the origin of our religion, the old heathen worship had fallen into disrepute among the enlightened classes through the Roman Empire, and was gradually losing its hold on the populace. Accordingly some have pretended that Christianity grew from the ruins of the ancient faith. But this is not true; for the decline of the heathen systems was the product of causes singularly adverse to the origination of such a system as Christianity. One cause was the monstrous depravity of the age, which led multitudes to an utter scorn of religion in all its forms and restraints, and which prepared others to exchange their old worship for still grosser and more licentious superstitions, particularly for the magical arts of Egypt. Surely this corruption of manners, this wide-wasting moral pestilence, will not be considered by any as a germ of the Christian religion. Another principal agent in loosening the foundations of the old systems, was Philosophy, a noble effort indeed of the human intellect, but one which did nothing to prepare the way for Christianity

The most popular systems of philosophy at the birth of Christianity were the Skeptical and the Epicurean, the former of which turned religion into a jest, denied the possibility of arriving at truth, and cast the mind on an ocean of doubt in regard to every subject of inquiry; whilst the latter placed happiness in ease, inculcated a calm indifference both as to this world and the next, and would have set down the Christian doctrine of self-sacrifice, of suffering for truth and duty, as absolute insanity. Now I ask in what single point do these systems touch Christianity, or what impulse could they have given to its invention. There was indeed another philosophical sect of a nobler character; I mean the Stoical. This maintained that virtue was the supreme good, and it certainly nurtured some firm and lofty spirits amidst the despotism which then ground all classes in the dust. But the self-reliance, sternness, apathy, and pride of the Stoic, his defiance and scorn of mankind, his want of sympathy with human suffering, and his extravagant exaggerations of his own virtue, placed this sect in singular opposition to Christianity; so that our religion might as soon have sprung from Skepticism and Epicureanism, as from Stoicism. There was another system, if it be worthy of the name, which prevailed in Asia, and was not unknown to the Jews, often called the Oriental philosophy. But this, though certainly an improvement on the common heathenism, was visionary and mystical, and placed happiness in an intuition or immediate perception of God, which was to be gained by contemplation and ecstasies, by emaciation of the body, and desertion of the world. I need not tell you how infinitely removed was the practical, benevolent spirit of Christianity, from this spurious sanctity and profitless enthusiasm. I repeat it, then, that the various causes which were silently operating against the established heathen systems in the time of Christ, had no tendency to suggest and spread such a religion as he brought, but were as truly hostile to it as the worst forms of heathenism.

We cannot find, then, the origin of Christianity in the heathen world. Shall we look for it in the Jewish? This topic is too familiar to need much exposition. You know the character, feelings, expectations of the descendants of Abraham at the appearing of Jesus; and you need not be told, that a system, more opposed to the Jewish mind than that which he taught, cannot be imagined. There was nothing friendly to it in the soil or climate of Judea. As easily might the luxuriant trees of our forest spring from the sands of an Arabian desert. There was never perhaps a national character so deeply stamped as the Jewish. Ages after ages of unparalleled suffering have done little to wear away its indelible features. In the time of Jesus the whole influence of education and religion was employed to fix it in every member of the state. In the bosom of this community, and among its humblest classes, sprung up Christianity, a religion as unfettered by Jewish prejudices, as untainted by the earthly, narrow views of the age, as if it had come from another world. Judaism was all around it, but did not mar it by one trace, or sully its brightness by a single breath. Can we find, then, the cause of Christianity in the Jewish any more than in the heathen world?

Christianity, I maintain, was not the growth of any of the circumstances, principles, or feelings of the age in which it appeared. In truth, one of the great distinctions of the Gospel is, that it did not *grow*. The conception, which filled the mind of Jesus, of a religion more spiritual, generous, comprehensive, and unworldly than Judaism, and destined to take its place, was not of gradual formation. We detect no signs of it, and no efforts to realize it, before his time; nor is there an appearance of its having been gradually matured by Jesus himself. Christianity was delivered from the first in its full proportions, in a style of singular freedom and boldness, and without a mark of painful elaboration. This suddenness with which this religion broke forth, this maturity of the system at the very moment of its birth, this absence of gradual developement, seems to me a strong mark of its divine original. If Christianity be a human invention, then I can be pointed to something in the history of the age which impelled and fitted the mind of its author to its production; then I shall be able to find some germ of it, some approximation to it, in the state of things amidst which it first appeared. How was it, that from thick darkness there burst forth at once meridian light? Were I told that the sciences of the civilized world had sprung up to perfection at once, amidst a barbarous horde, I should pronounce it incredible. Nor can I easily believe, that Christianity, the religion of unbounded love, a religion which broke down the barrier between Jew and Gentile, and the barriers between nations, which proclaimed one Universal Father, which abolished forms and substituted the worship of the soul, which condemned alike the false greatness of the Roman and the false holiness of the Jew, and which taught an elevation of virtue, that the growing knowledge of succeeding ages has made more admirable;— I say, I cannot easily believe that such a religion was suddenly immediately struck out by human ingenuity, among a people distinguished by bigotry and narrowness of spirit, by superstitious reliance on outward worship, by hatred and scorn of other nations, and by the proud, impatient hope of soon bending all nations to their sway.

Christianity, I repeat it, was not the growth of the age in which it appeared. It had no sympathy with that age. It was the echo of no sect or people. It stood alone at the moment of its birth. It used not a word of conciliation. It stooped to no error or passion. It had its own tone, the tone of authority and superiority to the world. It struck at the root of what was everywhere called glory, reversed the judgments of all former ages, passed a condemning sentence on the idols of this world's admiration, and held forth, as the perfection of human nature, a spirit of love, so pure and divine, so free and full, so mild and forgiving, so invincible in fortitude yet so tender in its sympathies, that even now few comprehend it in its extent and elevation. Such a religion had not its origin in this world.

I have thus sought to unfold one of the evidences of Christianity. Its incongruity with the age of its birth, its freedom from earthly mixtures, its original, unborrowed, solitary greatness, and the suddenness with which it broke forth amidst the general gloom, these are to me strong indications of its divine descent. I cannot reconcile them with a human origin.

II. Having stated the argument in favor of Christianity, derived from the impossibility of accounting for it by the state of the world at the time of its birth, I proceed, in the second place, to observe, that it cannot be accounted for by any of the motives which instigate men to the fabrication of religions. Its aims and objects are utterly irreconcilable with imposture. They are pure, lofty, and worthy of the most illustrious delegate of heaven. This argument deserves to be unfolded with some particularity.

Men act from Motives. The inventors of religions have purposes to answer by them. Some systems have been framed by legislators to procure reverence to their laws, to bow the minds of the people to the civil power; and some have been forged by priests, to establish their sway over the multitude, to form themselves into a dominant caste, and to extort the wealth of the industrious. Now I affirm, that Christianity cannot be ascribed to any selfish, ambitious, earthly motive. It is suited to no private end. Its purpose is generous and elevated, and thus bears witness to its heavenly origin.

The great object which has seduced men to pretend to inspiration, and to spread false religions, has been Power, in one form or another, sometimes political power, sometimes spiritual, sometimes both. Is Christianity to be explained by this selfish aim? I answer, No. I affirm that the love of power is the last principle to be charged on the Founder of our religion. Christianity is distinguished by nothing more than by its earnest enforcement of a meek and humble spirit, and by its uncompromising reprobation of that passion for dominion, which had in all ages made the many the prey of the few, and had been worshipped as the attribute and impulse of the greatest minds. Its tone on this subject was original, and altogether its own. Jesus felt, as none had felt before, and as few feel now, the baseness of selfish ambition, and the grandeur of that benevolence which waves every mark of superiority, that it may more effectually bless mankind. He taught this lesson, not only in the boldest language, but, accommodating himself to the emblematical mode of religious instruction prevalent in the East, he set before his disciples a little child as their pattern, and himself washed their feet. His whole life was a commentary on his teaching. Not a trace of the passion for distinction and sway can be detected in the artless narratives of his historians. He wore no badge of superiority, exacted no signs of homage, coveted no attentions, resented no neglect. He discouraged the ruler who prostrated himself before him with flattering salutations, but received with affectionate sensibility the penitent who bathed his feet with her tears. He lived with his obscure disciples as a friend, and mixed freely with all ranks of the community. He placed himself in the way of scorn, and advanced to meet a death, more suited than any other imaginable event, to entail infamy on his name. Stronger marks of an infinite superiority to what the world calls glory, cannot be conceived than we meet in the history of Jesus.

I have named two kinds of power, Political and Spiritual, as the ordinary objects of false religions. I wish to show you more particularly the elevation of Christianity above these aims. That the Gospel was not framed for political purposes, is too plain to require proof; but its peculiarity in this respect is not sufficiently considered. In ancient times, religion was everywhere a national concern. In Judea the union between religion and government was singularly close, and political sovereignty was one of the chief splendors, with which the Jewish imagination had surrounded the expected Messiah. That in such an age and country, a religion should arise, which hardly seems to know that government exists; which makes no reference to it except in a few general inculcations of obedience to the civil powers; which says not a word nor throws out a hint of allying itself with the state; which assumes to itself no control of political affairs, and intermeddles with no public concerns; which has no tendency, however indirect, to accumulate power in particular hands; which provides no form of national worship as a substitute for those which it was intended to destroy; and which treats the distinctions of rank and office as worthless in comparison with moral influence and an unostentatious charity; — that such a religion should spring up in such a state of the world is a remarkable fact. We here see a broad line between Christianity and other systems, and a striking proof of its originality and elevation. Other systems were framed for communities; Christianity approached men as Individuals. It proposed, not the glory of the state, but the perfection of the individual mind. So far from being contrived to build up political power, Christianity tends to reduce and gradually to supplant it, by teaching men to substitute the sway of truth and love for menace and force, by spreading through all ranks a feeling of brotherhood altogether opposed to the spirit of domination, and by establishing principles which nourish self-respect in every human being, and teach the obscurest to look with an undazzled eye on the most powerful of their race.

Christianity bears no mark of the hands of a politician. One of its main purposes is to extinguish the very spirit which the ambitious statesman most anxiously cherishes, and on which he founds his success. It proscribes a narrow patriotism, shows no mercy to the spirit of conquest, requires its disciples to love other countries as truly as their own, and enjoins a spirit of peace and forbearance in language so broad and earnest, that not a few of its professors consider war in every shape and under all circumstances as a crime. The hostility between Christianity and all the political maxims of that age, cannot easily be comprehended at the present day. No doctrines were then so rooted, as, that conquest was the chief interest of a nation, and that an exclusive patriotism was the first and noblest of social virtues. Christianity, in loosening the tie which bound man to the state, that it might connect him with his race, opposed itself to what was deemed the vital principle of national safety and grandeur, and commenced a political revolution as original and unsparing as the religious and moral reform at which it aimed.

Christianity, then, was not framed for political purposes. But I shall be asked, whether it stands equally clear of the charge of being intended to accumulate Spiritual power. Some may ask, whether its founder was not instigated by the passion for religious domination, whether he did not aim to subdue men's minds, to dictate to the faith of the world, to make himself the leader of a spreading sect, to stamp his name as a prophet on human history, and thus to secure the prostration of multitudes to his will, more abject and entire than kings and conquerors can achieve.

To this I might reply by what I have said of the character of Jesus, and of the spirit of his religion. It is plain, that the founder of Christianity had a perception, quite peculiar to himself, of the moral beauty and greatness of a disinterested, meek, and self-sacrificing spirit, and such a person was not likely to meditate the subjugation of the world to himself. But, leaving this topic, I observe, that on examining Christianity we discover none of the features of a religion framed for spiritual domination. One of the infallible marks of such a system is, that it makes some terms with the passions and prejudices of men. It does not, cannot provoke and ally against itself all the powers, whether civil or religious, of the world. Christianity was throughout uncompromising and exasperating, and threw itself in the way of hatred and scorn. Such a system was any thing but a scheme for seizing the spiritual empire of the world.

There is another mark of a religion which springs from the love of spiritual domination. It infuses a servile spirit. Its author, desirous to stamp his name and image on his followers, has an interest in curbing the free action of their minds, imposes on them arbitrary doctrines, fastens on them badges which may separate them from others, and besets them with rules, forms, and distinctive observances, which may perpetually remind them of their relation to their chief. Now I see nothing in Christianity of this enslaving legislation. It has but one aim, which is, not to exalt its teacher, but to improve the disciple; not to fasten Christ's name on mankind, but to breathe into them his spirit of universal love. Christianity is not a religion of forms. It has but two ceremonies, as simple as they are expressive; and these hold so subordinate a place in the New Testament, that some of the best Christians question or deny their permanent obligation.

Neither is it a narrow creed, or a mass of doctrines which find no support in our rational nature. It may be summed up in a few great, universal, immutable principles, which reason and conscience, as far as they are unfolded, adopt and rejoice in, as their own everlasting laws, and which open perpetually enlarging views to the mind. As far as I am a Christian, I am free. My religion lays on me not one chain. It does not prescribe a certain range for my mind, beyond which nothing can be learned. It speaks of God as the Universal Father, and sends me to all his works for instruction. It does not hem me round with a mechanical ritual, does not enjoin forms, attitudes, and hours of prayer, does not descend to details of dress and food, does not put on me one outward badge. It teaches and enkindles love to God, but commands no precise expressions of this sentiment. It prescribes prayer; but lays the chief stress on the prayer of the closet, and treats all worship as worthless but that of the mind and heart. It teaches us to do good, but leaves us to devise for ourselves the means by which we may best serve mankind. In a word, the whole religion of Christ may be summed up in the love of God and of mankind, and it leaves the individual to cherish and express this spirit by the methods most accordant with his own condition and peculiar mind. Christianity is eminently the religion of freedom. The views which it gives of the parental, impartial, universal goodness of God, and of the equal right of every human being to inquire into his will, and its inculcations of candor, forbearance, and mutual respect, contribute alike to freedom of thought and enlargement of the heart. I repeat it, Christianity lays on me no chains. It is any thing but a contrivance for spiritual domination.

I am aware that I shall be told, that Christianity, if judged by its history, has no claim to the honorable title of a religion of liberty. I shall be told, that no system of heathenism ever weighed more oppressively on men's souls ; that the Christian ministry has trained tyrants, who have tortured, now the body with material fire, and now the mind with the dread of fiercer flames, and who have proscribed and punished free thought and free speech as the worst of crimes. I have no disposition to soften the features of priestly oppression ; but I say, let not Christianity be made to answer for it. Christianity gives its ministers no such power. They have usurped it in the face of the sternest prohibitions, and in opposition to the whole spirit of their Master. Christianity institutes no priesthood, in the original and proper sense of that word. It has not the name of priest among its officers ; nor does it confer a shadow of priestly power. It invests no class of men with peculiar sanctity, ascribing to their intercessions a special influence over God, or suspending the salvation of the private Christian on ceremonies which they alone can administer. Jesus indeed appointed twelve of his immediate disciples to be the great instruments of propagating his religion ; but nothing can be simpler than their office. They went forth to make known through all nations the life, death, resurrection, and teachings of Jesus Christ; and this truth they spread freely and without reserve. They did not give it as a mystery to a few who were to succeed them in their office, and according to whose direction it was to be imparted to others. They communicated it to the whole body of converts, to be their equal and common property, thus securing to all the invaluable rights of the mind. It is true, they appointed ministers or teachers in the various congregations which they formed; and in that early age, when the religion was new and unknown, and when oral teaching was the only mode of communicating it, there seems to have been no way for its diffusion but this appointment of the most enlightened disciples to the work of instruction. But the New Testament nowhere intimates, that these men were to monopolize the privilege of studying their religion, or of teaching it to others. Not a single man can claim under Christianity the right to interpret it exclusively, or to impose his interpretation on his brethren. The Christian minister enjoys no nearer access to God, and no promise of more immediate illumination, than other men. He is not intrusted with the Christian records more than they, and by these records it is both their right and duty to try his instructions. I have here pointed out a noble peculiarity of Christianity. It is the religion of liberty. It is in no degree tainted with the passion for spiritual power. "Call no man master, for ye are all brethren," is its free and generous inculcation, and to every form of freedom it is a friend and defence.

We have seen that Christianity is not to be traced to the love of power, that master passion in the authors of false religions. I add, that no other object of a selfish nature could have led to its invention. The Gospel is not of this world. At the time of its origin no ingenuity could have brought it to bear on any private or worldly interest. Its spirit is self-denial. Wealth, ease, and honor, it counts among the chief perils of life, and it insists on no duty more earnestly than on that of putting them to hazard and casting them from us, if the cause of truth and humanity so require. And these maxims were not mere speculations or rhetorical commonplaces in the times of Christ and his Apostles The first propagators of Christianity were called upon to practise what they preached, to forego every interest on its account. They could not but foreknow, that a religion so uncompromising and pure would array against them the world. They did not merely take the chance of suffering, but were sure that the whole weight of scorn, pain, and worldly persecution would descend on their heads. How inexplicable, then, is Christianity by any selfish object, or any low aim?

The Gospel has but one object, and that too plain to be mistaken. In reading the New Testament, we see the greatest simplicity of aim. There is no lurking purpose, no by-end, betraying itself through attempts to disguise it. A perfect singleness of design runs through the records of the religion, and is no mean evidence of their truth. This end of Christianity is the moral perfection of the human soul. It aims and it tends, in all its doctrines, precepts, and promises, to rescue men from the power of moral evil; to unite them to God by filial love, and to one another in the bonds of brotherhood; to inspire them with a philanthropy as meek and unconquerable as that of Christ; and to kindle intense desire, hope, and pursuit of celestial and immortal virtue.

And now, I ask, what is the plain inference from these views? If Christianity can be traced to no selfish or worldly motive, if it was framed, not for dominion, not to compass any private purpose, but to raise men above themselves, and to conform them to God, can we help pronouncing it worthy of God? And to whom but to God can we refer its origin? Ought we not to recognise in the first propagators of such a faith the holiest of men, the friends of their race, and the messengers of Heaven? Christianity, from its very nature, repels the charge of imposture. It carries in itself the proof of pure intention. Bad men could not have conceived it, much less have adopted it as the great object of their lives. The supposition of selfish men giving up every private interest to spread a system which condemned themselves, and which tended only to purify mankind, is an absurdity as gross as can be found in the most irrational faith. Christianity, therefore, when tried by its Motives, approves itself to be of God.

III. I now proceed to another and very important ground of my belief in the divine origin of Christianity. Its truth was attested by miracles. Its first teachers proved themselves the ministers of God by supernatural works. They did what man cannot do, what bore the impress of a divine power, and what thus sealed the divinity of their mission. A religion so attested must be true. This topic is a great one, and I ask your patient attention to it.

I am aware that a strong prejudice exists in some minds against the kind of evidence which I have now adduced. Miracles seem to them to carry a confutation in themselves. The presumption against them seems next to infinite. In this respect, the present times differ from the past. There have been ages, when men believed any thing and every thing; and the more monstrous the story, the more eagerly was it received by the credulous multitude. In the progress of knowledge men have come to see, that most of the prodigies and supernatural events in which their forefathers believed, were fictions of fancy, or fear, or imposture. The light of knowledge has put to flight the ghosts and witches which struck terror into earlier times. We now know, that not a few of the appearances in the heavens, which appalled nations, and were interpreted as precursors of divine vengeance, were natural effects. We have learned, too, that a highly excited imagination can work some of the cures once ascribed to magic ; and the lesson taught us by these natural solutions of apparent miracles, is, that accounts of supernatural events are to be sifted with great jealousy and received with peculiar care.

But the result of this new light thrown on nature and history is, that some are disposed to discredit all miracles indiscriminately. So many having proved groundless, a sweeping sentence of condemnation is passed on all. The human mind, by a natural reaction, has passed from extreme credulousness, to the excess of incredulity. Some persons are even hardy enough to deride the very idea of a miracle. They pronounce the order of nature something fixed and immutable, and all suspensions of it incredible. This prejudice, for such it is, seems to deserve particular attention ; for, until it is removed, the evidences of Christian miracles will have little weight. Let us examine it patiently and impartially.

The skeptic tells me, that the order of nature is fixed. I ask him, By whom or by what is it fixed ? By an iron fate ? By an inflexible necessity ? Does not nature bear the signatures of an intelligent Cause ? Does not the very idea of its order imply an ordaining or disposing Mind ? Does not the universe, the more t is explored, bear increasing testimony to a Being superior to itself? Then the order of nature is fixed by a Will which can reverse it. Then a power equal to miracles exists. Then miracles are not incredible.

It may be replied, that God indeed *can* work miracles, but that he *will* not. He will not? And how does the skeptic know this? Has God so told him? This language does not become a being of our limited faculties; and the presumptuousness which thus makes laws for the Creator, and restricts his agency to particular modes, is as little the spirit of true philosophy as of religion.

The skeptic sees nothing in miracles, but ground of offence. To me, they seem to involve in their very nature a truth so great, so vital, that I am not only reconciled to them, but am disposed to receive joyfully any sufficient proofs of their having been performed. To the skeptic, no principle is so important as the uniformity of nature, the constancy of its laws. To me, there is a vastly higher truth, to which miracles bear witness, and to which I welcome their aid. What I wish chiefly to know is, that Mind is the supreme power in the universe; that matter is its instrument and slave; that there is a Will to which nature can offer no obstruction; that God is unshackled by the laws of the universe, and controls them at his pleasure. This absolute sovereignty of the Divine Mind over the universe, is the only foundation of hope for the triumph of the human mind over matter, over physical influences, over imperfection and death. Now it is plain, that the strong impressions which we receive through the senses from the material creation, joined to our experience of its regularity, and to our instinctive trust in its future uniformity, do obscure this supremacy of God, do tempt us to ascribe a kind of omnipotence to nature's laws, and to limit our hopes to the good which is promised by these. There is a strong tendency in men to attach the idea of necessity to an unchanging regularity of operation, and to imagine bounds to a being who keeps one undeviating path, or who repeats himself perpetually. Hence, I say that I rejoice in miracles. They show and assert the supremacy of Mind in the universe. They manifest a spiritual power, which is in no degree enthralled by the laws of matter. I rejoice in these witnesses to so great a truth. I rejoice in whatever proves, that this order of nature, which so often weighs on me as a chain, and which contains no promise of my perfection, is not supreme and immutable, and that the Creator is not restricted to the narrow modes of operation with which I am most familiar.

Perhaps the form in which the objection to miracles is most frequently expressed, is the following ; "It is derogatory," says the skeptic, "to the perfect wisdom of God, to suppose him to break in upon the order of his own works. It is only the unskilful artist who is obliged to thrust his hand into the machine for the purpose of supplying its defects, and of giving it a new impulse by an immediate agency." To this objection I reply, that it proceeds on false ideas of God and of the creation. God is not an artist, but a Moral Parent and Governor ; nor is the creation a machine. If it were, it might be urged with greater speciousness, that miracles cannot be needed or required. One of the most striking views of the creation, is the contrast or opposition of the elements of which it consists. It in eludes not only matter but mind, not only lifeless and unconscious masses, but rational beings, free agents; and these are its noblest parts and ultimate objects The material universe was framed not for itself, but for these. Its order was not appointed for its own sake, but to instruct and improve a higher rank of beings, the intelligent offspring of God; and whenever a departure from this order, that is, whenever miraculous agency can contribute to the growth and perfection of his intelligent creatures, it is demanded by his wisdom, goodness, and all his attributes. If the Supreme Being proposed only such ends as mechanism can produce, then he might have framed a machinery so perfect and sure as to need no suspension of its ordinary movements. But he has an incomparably nobler end. His great purpose is to educate, to rescue from evil, to carry forward for ever the free, rational mind or soul; and who that understands what a free mind is, and what a variety of teaching and discipline it requires, will presume to affirm, that no lights or aids, but such as come to it through an invariable order of nature, are necessary to unfold it?

Much of the difficulty in regard to miracles, as I apprehend, would be removed, if we were to consider more particularly, that the chief distinction of intelligent beings is Moral Freedom, the power of determining themselves to evil as well as good, and consequently the power of involving themselves in great misery. When God made man, he framed not a machine, but a free being, who was to rise or fall according to his use or abuse of his powers. This capacity, at once the most glorious and the most fearful which we can conceive, shows us how the human race may have come into a condition, to which the illumination of nature was inadequate. In truth, the more we consider the freedom of intelligent beings, the more we shall question the possibility of establishing an unchangeable order which will meet fully all their wants; for such beings, having of necessity a wide range of action, may bring themselves into a vast variety of conditions, and of course may come to need a relief not contained in the resources of nature. The history of the human race illustrates these truths. At the introduction of Christianity, the human family were plunged into gross and debasing error, and the light of nature had not served for ages to guide them back to truth. Philosophy had done its best, and failed. A new element, a new power seems to have been wanting to the progress of the race. That in such an exigence miraculous aid should be imparted, accords with our best views of God. I repeat it; were men mechanical beings, an undeviating order of nature might meet all their wants. They are free beings, who bear a moral relation to God, and as such may need, and are worthy of, a more various and special care than is extended over the irrational creation.

When I examine nature, I see reasons for believing that it was not intended by God to be the only method of instructing and improving mankind. I see reasons, as I think, why its order or regular course should be occasionally suspended, and why revelation should be joined to it in the work of carrying forward the race. I can offer only a few considerations on this point, but they seem to me worthy of serious attention. — The first is, that a fixed, invariable order of nature does not give us some views of God which are of great interest and importance, or at least it does not give them with that distinctness which we all desire. It reveals him as the Universal Sovereign who provides for the whole or for the general weal, but not, with sufficient clearness, as a tender father, interested in the Individual. I see, in this fixed order, his care of the race, but not his constant, boundless concern for myself. Nature speaks of a general Divinity, not of the friend and benefactor of each living soul. This is a necessary defect attending an inflexible, unvarying administration by general laws; and it seems to require that God, to carry forward the race, should reveal himself by some other manner than by general laws. No conviction is more important to human improvement than that of God's paternal interest in every human being; and how can he communicate this persuasion so effectually, as by suspending nature's order, to teach, through an inspired messenger, his paternal love?

My second remark is, that, whilst nature teaches many important lessons, it is not a direct, urgent teacher. Its truths are not prominent, and consequently men may neglect it, and place themselves beyond its influence. For example, nature holds out the doctrine of One God, but does not compel attention to it. God's name is not written in the sky in letters of light, which all nations must read, nor sounded abroad in a voice, deep and awful as thunders, so that all must hear. Nature is a gentle, I had almost said, a reserved teacher, demanding patient thought in the learner, and may therefore be unheeded. Men may easily shut their ears and harden their hearts against its testimony to God. Accordingly we learn, that, at Christ's coming, almost all nations had lost the knowledge of the true glory of the Creator, and given themselves up to gross superstitions

EVIDENCES OF CHRISTIANITY. 379

To such a condition of the world, nature's indirect and unimposing mode of instruction is not fitted, and thus it furnishes a reason for a more immediate and impressive teaching. In such a season of moral darkness, was it not worthy of God to kindle another and more quickening beam ? When the long repeated and almost monotonous language of creation was not heard, was it unworthy of God to speak with a new and more startling voice? What fitter method was there for rousing those whom nature's quiet regularity could not teach, than to interrupt its usual course ?

I proceed to another reason for expecting revelation to be added to the light of nature. Nature, I have said, is not a direct or urgent teacher, and men may place themselves beyond its voice. I say, thirdly, that there is one great point, on which we are deeply concerned to know the truth, and which is yet taught so indistinctly by nature, that men, however disposed to learn, cannot by that light alone obtain full conviction. What, let me ask, is the question in which each man has the deepest interest ? It is this, Are we to live again ; or is this life all ? Does the principle of thought perish with the body ; or does it survive ? And if it survive, where ? how ? in what condition ? under what law ? There is an inward voice which speaks of judgment to come. Will judgment indeed come ? and if so, what award may we hope or fear ? The Future state of man, this is the great question forced on us by our changing life, and by approaching death. I will not say, that on this topic nature throws no light. I think it does ; and this light continually grows brighter to them whose eyes revelation has couched and made strong to see But nature alone does not meet our wants. I might prove this by referring you to the ages preceding Christ, when the anxious spirit of man constantly sought to penetrate the gloom beyond the grave, when imagination and philosophy alike plunged into the future, but found no resting-place. But every man must feel, that, left to nature as his only guide, he must wander in doubt as to the life to come. Where, but from God himself, can I learn my destination? I ask at the mouth of the tomb for intelligence of the departed, and the tomb gives me no reply. I examine the various regions of nature, but I can discover no process for restoring the mouldering body, and no sign or track of the spirit's ascent to another sphere. I see the need of a power above nature to restore or perpetuate life after death; and if God intended to give assurance of this life, I see not how he can do it but by supernatural teaching, by a miraculous revelation. Miracles are the appropriate, and would seem to be the only mode of placing beyond doubt man's future and immortal being; and no miracles can be conceived so peculiarly adapted to this end as the very ones which hold the highest place in Christianity, — I mean the resurrection of Lazarus, and, still more, the resurrection of Jesus. No man will deny, that, of all truths, a future state is most strengthening to virtue and consoling to humanity. Is it then unworthy of God to employ miracles for the awakening or the confirmation of this hope? May they not even be expected, if nature, as we have seen, sheds but a faint light on this most interesting of all verities?

I add one more consideration in support of the position, that nature was not intended to be God's only method of teaching mankind. In surveying the human mind, we discover a principle which singularly fits it to be wrought upon and benefited by miraculous agency, and which might therefore lead us to expect such interposition. I refer to that principle of our nature, by which we become in a measure insensible or indifferent to what is familiar, but are roused to attention and deep interest by what is singular, strange, supernatural. This principle of wonder is an important part of our constitution; and that God should employ it in the work of our education, is what reason might anticipate. I see, then, a foundation for miracles in the human mind; and, when I consider that the mind is God's noblest work, I ought to look to this as the interpreter of his designs. We are plainly so constituted, that the order of nature, the more it is fixed, excites us the less. Our interest is blunted by its ceaseless uniformity. On the contrary, departures from this order powerfully stir the soul, break up its old and slumbering habits of thought, turn it with a new solicitude to the Almighty Interposer, and prepare it to receive with awe the communications of his will. Was it unworthy of God, who gave us this sensibility to the wonderful, to appeal to it for the recovery of his creatures to himself?

I here close my remarks on the great objection of skepticism, that miracles are inconsistent with the divine perfections; that the Supreme Being, having established an order of operation, cannot be expected to depart from it. To me, such reasoning, if reasoning it may be called, is of no weight. When I consider God's paternal and moral relation to mankind, and his interest in their progress; when I consider how accordant it is with his character that he should make himself known to them by methods most fitted to awaken the mind and heart to his goodness; when I consider the need we have of illumination in regard to the future life, more distinct and full than the creation affords ; when I consider the constitution and condition of man, his free agency, and the corruption into which he had fallen; when I consider how little benefit a being so depraved was likely to derive from an order of nature to which he had grown familiar, and how plainly the mind is fitted to be quickened by miraculous interposition ; — I say, when I take all these things into view, I see, as I think, a foundation in nature for supernatural light and aid, and I discern in a miraculous revelation, such as Christianity, a provision suited at once to the frame and wants of the human soul, and to the perfections of its Author.

There are other objections to miracles, though less avowed, than that which I have now considered, yet perhaps not less influential, and probably operating on many minds so secretly as to be unperceived. At two of these I will just glance. Not a few, I am confident, have doubts of the Christian miracles, because they see none *now*. Were their skepticism to clothe itself in language, it would say, " Show us miracles, and we will believe them. We suspect them, because they are confined to the past." Now this objection is a childish one. It may be resolved into the principle, that nothing in the past is worthy of belief, which is not repeated in the present. Admit this, and where will incredulity stop ? How many forms and institutions of society, recorded in ancient history, have passed away. Has history, then, no title to respect ? If indeed the human race were standing still, if one age were merely a copy of preceding ones, if each had precisely the same wants, then the miracles required at one period would be reproduced in all. But who does not know that there is a progress in human affairs ? that formerly mankind were in a different stage from that through which they are now passing ? that of course the education of the race must be varied ? and that miracles, important once, may be superfluous now ? Shall we bind the Creator to invariable modes of teaching and training a race whose capacities and wants are undergoing a perpetual change ? Because in periods of thick darkness God introduced a new religion by supernatural works, shall we expect these works to be repeated, when the darkness is scattered and their end attained ? Who does not see that miracles, from their very nature, must be rare, occasional, limited ? Would not their power be impaired by frequency ? and would it not wholly cease, were they so far multiplied as to seem a part of the order of nature ?

The objection I am now considering, shows us the true character of skepticism. Skepticism is essentially a narrowness of mind, which makes the present moment the measure of the past and future. It is the creature of sense. In the midst of a boundless universe, it can conceive no mode of operation but what falls under its immediate observation. The visible, the present, is every thing to the unbeliever. Let him but enlarge his views ; let him look round on the immensity of the universe ; let him consider the infinity of resources which are comprehended in omnipotence ; let him represent to himself the manifold stages through which the human race is appointed to pass ; let him remember that the education of the ever-growing mind must require a great variety of discipline ; and especially let him admit the sublime thought, of which the germ is found in nature, that man was created to be trained for, and to ascend to, an incomparably higher order of existence than the present, — and he will see the childishness of making his narrow experience the standard of all that is past and is to come in human history.

It is strange, indeed, that men of science should fall into this error. The improved science of the present day teaches them, that this globe of ours, which seems so unchangeable, is not now what it was a few thousand years ago. They find proofs by digging into the earth, that this globe was inhabited before the existence of the human race, by classes of animals which have perished, and the ocean peopled by races now unknown, and that the human race are occupying a ruined and restored world. Men of science should learn to free themselves from the vulgar narrowness which sees nothing in the past but the present, and should learn the stupendous and infinite variety of the dispensations of God.

There is another objection to miracles, and the last to be now considered, which is drawn from the well-known fact, that pretended miracles crowd the pages of ancient history. No falsehoods, we are told, have been more common than accounts of prodigies, and therefore the miraculous character of Christianity is a presumption against its truth. I acknowledge that this argument has its weight; and I am ready to say, that, did I know nothing of Christianity, but that it was a religion full of miracles; did I know nothing of its doctrines, its purpose, its influences, and whole history, I should suspect it as much as the unbeliever. There is a strong presumption against miracles, considered nakedly, or separated from their design and from all circumstances which explain and support them. There s a like presumption against events not miraculous, but of an extraordinary character. But this is only a reason for severe scrutiny and slow belief, not for resisting strong and multiplied proofs. I blame no man for doubting a report of miracles when first brought to his ears. Thousands of absurd prodigies have been created by ignorance and fanaticism, and thousands more been forged by imposture. I invite you, then, to try scrupulously the miracles of Christianity; and, if they bear the marks of the superstitious legends of false religions, do not spare them. I only ask for them a fair hearing and calm investigation.

It is plainly no sufficient argument for rejecting all miracles, that men have believed in many which are false. If you go back to the times when miraculous stories were swallowed most greedily, and read the books then written on history, geography, and natural science, you will find all of them crowded with error; but do they therefore contain nothing worthy your trust? Is there not a vein of truth running through the prevalent falsehood? And cannot a sagacious mind very often detach the real from the fictitious, explain the origin of many mistakes, distinguish the judicious and honest from the credulous or interested narrator, and by a comparison of testimonies detect the latent truth? Where will you stop, if you start with believing nothing on points where former ages have gone astray? You must pronounce all religion and all morality to be delusion, for on both topics men have grossly erred. Nothing is more unworthy of a philosopher, than to found a universal censure on a limited number of unfavorable facts. This is much like the reasoning of the misanthrope, who, because he sees much vice, infers that there is no virtue, and, because he has sometimes been deceived, pronounces all men hypocrites.

I maintain that the multiplicity of false miracles, far from disproving, gives support to those on which Christianity rests; for, first, there is generally some foundation for falsehood, especially when it obtains general belief. The love of truth is an essential principle of human nature; men generally embrace error on account of some precious ingredient of truth mixed with it, and for the time inseparable from it. The universal belief of past ages in miraculous interpositions, is to me a presumption that miracles have entered into human history. Will the unbeliever say, that it only shows the insatiable thirst of the human mind for the supernatural? I reply, that, in this reasoning, he furnishes a weapon against himself; for a strong principle in the human mind, impelling men to seek for and to cling to miraculous agency, affords a presumption that the Author of our being, by whom this thirst for the supernatural was given, intended to furnish objects for it, and to assign it a place in the education of the race.

But I observe, in the next place, and it is an observation of great importance, that the exploded miracles of ancient times, if carefully examined, not only furnish a general presumption in favor of the existence of genuine ones, but yield strong proof of the truth of those in particular upon which Christianity rests. I say to the skeptic, You affirm nothing but truth in declaring history to abound in false miracles; I agree with you in exploding by far the greater part of the supernatural accounts of which ancient religions boast. But how do we know these to be false? We do not so judge without proofs. We discern in them the marks of delusion. Now I ask you to examine these marks, and then to answer me honestly, whether you find them in the miracles of Christianity. Is there not a broad line between Christ's works and those which we both agree in rejecting ? I maintain that there is, and that nothing but ignorance can confound the Christian miracles with the prodigies of heathenism. The contrast between them is so strong as to forbid us to refer them to a common origin. The miracles of superstition carry the brand of falsehood in their own nature, and are disproved by the circumstances under which they were imposed on the multitude. The objects, for which they are said to have been wrought, are such as do not require or justify a divine interposition. Many of them are absurd, childish, or extravagant, and betray a weak intellect or diseased imagination. Many can be explained by natural causes. Many are attested by persons who lived in different countries and ages, and enjoyed no opportunities of inquiring into their truth. We can see the origin of many in the self-interest of those who forged them, and can account for their reception by the condition of the world. In other words, these spurious miracles were the natural growth of the ignorance, passions, prejudices, and corruptions of the times, and tended to confirm them. Now it is not enough to say, that these various marks of falsehood cannot be found in the Christian miracles. We find in them characters directly the reverse. They were wrought for an end worthy of God ; they were wrought in an age of improvement ; they are marked by a majesty, beneficence, unostentatious simplicity, and wisdom, which separate them immeasurably from the dreams of a disordered fancy or the contrivances of imposture.

They can be explained by no interests, passions, or prejudices of men. They are parts of a religion, which was singularly at variance with established ideas and expectations, which breathes purity and benevolence, which transcended the improvements of the age, and which thus carries with it the presumption of a divine original. Whence this immense distance between the two classes of miracles ? Will you trace both to one source, and that a polluted one ? Will you ascribe to one spirit, works as different as light and darkness, as earth and heaven ? I am not, then, shaken in my faith by the false miracles of other religions. I have no desire to keep them out of sight ; I summon them as my witnesses. They show me how naturally imposture and superstition leave the stamp of themselves on their fictions. They show how man, when he aspires to counterfeit God's agency, betrays more signally his impotence and folly. When I place side by side the mighty works of Jesus and the prodigies of heathenism, I see that they can no more be compared with one another, than the machinery and mock thunders of the theatre can be likened to the awful and beneficent powers of the universe.

In the preceding remarks on miracles, I have aimed chiefly to meet those general objections by which many are prejudiced against supernatural interpositions universally, and are disinclined to weigh any proof in their support. Hoping that this weak skepticism has been shown to want foundation in nature and reason, I proceed now to state more particularly the principal grounds on which I believe that the miracles ascribed to Jesus and the first propagators of Christianity, were actually wrought in attestation of its truth.

The evidences of facts are of two kinds, presumptive

and direct, and both meet in support of Christian miracles. First, there are strong presumptions in its favor. To this class of proofs, belong the views already given of the accordance of revelation and miracles with the wants and principles of human nature, with the perfections of God, with his relations to his human family, and with his ordinary providence. These I need not repeat. I will only observe, that a strong presumption in support of the miracles arises from the importance of the religion to which they belong. If I were told of supernatural works performed to prove, that three are more than one, or that human life requires food for its support, I should know that they were false. The presumption against them would be invincible. The author of nature could never supersede its wise and stupendous order to teach what falls within the knowledge of every child. Extraordinary interpositions of God suppose that truths of extraordinary dignity and beneficence are to be imparted. Now, in Christianity, I find truths of transcendent importance, which throw into shade all the discoveries of science, and which give a new character, aim, and interest, to our existence. Here is a fit occasion for supernatural interposition. A presumption exists in favor of miracles, by which a religion so worthy of God is sustained.

But a presumption in favor of facts, is not enough. It indeed adds much force to the direct proofs ; still these are needed, nor are they wanting to Christianity. The direct proofs of facts are chiefly of two kinds ; they consist of testimony, oral or written, and of effects, traces, monuments, which the facts have left behind them. The Christian miracles are supported by both. — We have first the most unexceptionable Testimony, nothing less than that of contemporaries and eye-witnesses, of the companions of Jesus and the first propagators of his religion. We have the testimony of men who could not have been deceived as to the facts which they report; who bore their witness amidst perils and persecutions; who bore it on the very spot where their Master lived and died; who had nothing to gain, and every thing to lose, if their testimony were false; whose writings breathe the sincerest love of virtue and of mankind; and who at last sealed their attestations with their blood. More unexceptionable witnesses to facts cannot be produced or conceived.

Do you say, "These witnesses lived ages ago; could we hear these accounts from their own lips, we should be satisfied"? I answer, You have something better than their own lips, or than their own word taken alone. You have, as has been proved, their writings. Perhaps you hear with some surprise that a book may be a better witness than its author; but nothing is more true, and I will illustrate it by an imaginary case in our own times.

Suppose, then, that a man claiming to be an eye-witness should relate to me the events of the three memorable days of July, in which the last revolution of France was achieved; suppose next, that a book, a history of that revolution, published and received as true in France, should be sent to me from that country. Which is the best evidence of the facts? I say the last. A single witness may deceive; but that a writer should publish in France the history of a revolution, which never occurred there, or which differed essentially from the true one, is, in the highest degree, improbable; and that such a history should obtain currency, that it should not be instantly branded as a lie, is utterly impossible. A history received by a people as true, not only gives us the testimony of the writer, but the testimony of the nation among whom it obtains credit. It is a concentration of thousands of voices, of many thousand witnesses. I say, then, that the writings of the first teachers of Christianity, received as they were by the multitude of Christians in their own times and in those which immediately followed, are the testimonies of that multitude as well as of the writers. Thousands, nearest to the events, join in bearing testimony to the Christian miracles.

But there is another class of evidence, sometimes more powerful than direct witnesses, and this belongs to Christianity. Facts are often placed beyond doubt by the effects which they leave behind them. This is the case with the miracles of Christ. Let me explain this branch of evidence. I am told, when absent and distant from your city, that on a certain day, a tide, such as had never been known, rose in your harbour, overflowed your wharves, and rushed into your streets; I doubt the fact; but hastening here, I see what were once streets, strewed with sea-weed, and shells, and the ruins of houses, and I cease to doubt. A witness may deceive, but such effects cannot lie. All great events leave effects, and these speak directly of the cause. What, I ask, are the proofs of the American revolution? Have we none but written or oral testimony? Our free constitution, the whole form of our society, the language and spirit of our laws, all these bear witness to our English origin, and to our successful conflict for independence. Now the miracles of Christianity have left effects, which equally attest their reality, and cannot be explained without them. I go back to the age of Jesus Christ, and I am immediately struck with the commencement and rapid progress of the most remarkable revolution in the annals of the world. I see a new religion, of a character altogether its own, which bore no likeness to any past or existing faith, spreading in a few years through all civilized nations, and introducing a new era, a new state of society, a change of the human mind, which has broadly distinguished all following ages. Here is a plain fact, which the skeptic will not deny, however he may explain it. I see this religion issuing from an obscure, despised, hated people. Its founder had died on the cross, a mode of punishment as disgraceful as the pillory or gallows of the present day. Its teachers were poor men, without rank, office, or education, taken from the fishing-boat and other occupations which had never furnished teachers to mankind. I see these men beginning their work on the spot where their Master's blood had been shed, as of a common malefactor; and I hear them summoning first his murderers, and then all nations and all ranks, the sovereign on the throne, the priest in the temple, the great and the learned, as well as the poor and the ignorant, to renounce the faith and the worship which had been hallowed by the veneration of all ages, and to take the yoke of their crucified Lord. I see passion and prejudice, the sword of the magistrate, the curse of the priest, the scorn of the philosopher, and the fury of the populace, joined to crush this common enemy; and yet, without a human weapon and in opposition to all human power, I see the humble Apostles of Jesus winning their way, overpowering prejudice, breaking the ranks of their opposers, changing enemies into friends, breathing into multitudes a calm spirit of martyrdom, and carrying to the bounds of civilization, and even into half-civilized regions, a religion which has contributed to advance society more than all other causes combined. Here is the effect. Here is a monument more durable than pillars or triumphal arches. Now I ask for an explanation of these effects. If Jesus Christ and his Apostles were indeed sent and empowered by God, and wrought miracles in attestation of their mission, then the establishment of Christianity is explained. Suppose them, on the other hand, to have been insane enthusiasts, or selfish impostors, left to meet the whole strength of human opposition, with nothing but their own power or rather their own weakness, and you have no cause for the stupendous effect I have described. Such men could no more have changed the face of the world, than they could have turned back rivers to their sources, sunk mountains into valleys, or raised valleys to the skies. Christianity, then, has not only the evidence of unexceptionable witnesses, but that of effects; a proof which will grow stronger by comparing its progress with that of other religions, such as Mahometanism, which sprung from human passions, and were advanced by human power.

IV. Having given my views on the subject of Christian miracles, I now pass to the last topic of this discourse. Its extent and importance will lead me to enlarge upon it in a subsequent discourse; but a discussion of Christian evidences, in which it should find no place, would be essentially defective. I refer to the proof of Christianity derived from the Character of its Author.

The character of Jesus was Original. He formed a new era in the moral history of the human race. His perfection was not that of his age, nor a copy of the greatness which had long engrossed the world's admiration. Jesus stood apart from other men. He borrowed from none and leaned on none. Surrounded by men of low thoughts, he rose to the conception of a higher form of human virtue than had yet been realized or imagined, and deliberately devoted himself to its promotion, as the supreme object of his life and death. Conscious of being dedicated to this great work, he spoke with a calm dignity, an unaffected elevation, which separated him from all other teachers. Unsupported, he never wavered; sufficient to himself, he refused alliance with wealth or power. Yet, with all this self-subsistence and uncompromising energy, his character was the mildest, the gentlest, the most attractive, ever manifested among men. It could not have been a fiction, for who could have conceived it, or who could have embodied the conception in such a life as Jesus is said to have led, in actions, words, manners, so natural and unstudied, so imbued with reality, so worthy of the Son of God?

The great distinction of Jesus was a philanthropy without mixture and without bounds; a philanthropy, uniting grandeur and meekness in beautiful proportions; a philanthropy, as wise as it was fervent, which comprehended the true wants and the true good of man, which compassionated, indeed, his sufferings from abroad, but which saw in the soul the deep fountain of his miseries, and labored, by regenerating this, to bring him to a pure and enduring happiness. So peculiar, so unparalleled was the benevolence of Jesus, that it has impressed itself on all future times. There went forth a virtue, a beneficent influence from his character, which operates even now. Since the death of Christ, a spirit of humanity, unknown before, has silently diffused itself over a considerable portion of the earth. A new standard of virtue has gradually possessed itself of the veneration of men. A new power has been acting on society, which has done more than all other causes combined, to disarm the selfish passions, and to bind men strongly to one another and to God. What a monument have we here to the virtue of Jesus! and if Christianity has such a Founder, it must have come from Heaven.

There are other remarkable proofs of the power and elevation of the character of Christ. It has touched and conciliated not a few of the determined adversaries of his religion. Infidelity, whilst it has laid unsparing hands on the system, has generally shrunk from offering violence to its Author. In truth, unbelievers have occasionally borne eloquent testimony to the benignant and celestial virtues of Jesus; and I record this with pleasure, not only as honorable to Christianity, but as showing that unbelief does not universally sear the moral feelings, or breathe hostility to goodness. Nor is this all. The character of Christ has withstood the most deadly and irresistible foe of error and unfounded claims, I mean, Time. It has lost nothing of its elevation by the improvements of ages. Since he appeared, society has gone forward, men's views have become enlarged, and philosophy has risen to conceptions of far purer virtues than were the boast of antiquity. But, however the human mind may have advanced, it must still look upward, if it would see and understand Christ. He is still above it. Nothing purer, nobler, has yet dawned on human thoughts. Then Christianity is true. The delineation of Jesus in the Gospels, so warm with life, and so unrivalled in loveliness and grandeur, required the existence of an original. To suppose that this character was invented by unprincipled men, amidst Jewish and heathen darkness, and was then imposed as a reality in the very age of the founder of Christianity, argues an excess of credulity, and a strange ignorance of the powers and principles of human nature. The character of Jesus was real; and if so, Jesus must have been what he professed to be, the Son of God and the revealer of his mercy and his will to mankind.

I have now completed what I proposed in this discourse. I have laid before you some of the principal evidences of Christianity. I have aimed to state them without exaggeration. That an honest mind, which thoroughly comprehends them, can deny their force, seems to me hardly possible. Stronger proofs may indeed be conceived; but it is doubtful, whether these could be given in consistency with our moral nature, and with the moral government of God. Such a government requires, that truth should not be forced on the mind, but that we should be left to gain it, by an upright use of our understandings, and by conforming ourselves to what we have already learned. God might indeed shed on us an overpowering light, so that it would be impossible for us to lose our way; but in so doing, he would annihilate an important part of our present probation. It is then no objection to Christianity, that its evidences are not the very strongest which might be given, and that they do not extort universal assent. In this respect, it accords with other great truths. These are not forced on our belief. Whoever will, may shut his eyes on their proofs, and array against them objections. In the measure of evidence with which Christianity is accompanied, I see a just respect for the freedom of the mind, and a wise adaptation to that moral nature, which it is the great aim of this religion to carry forward to perfection.

I close as I began. I am not ashamed of the gospel of Christ; for it is True. It is true; and its truth is to break forth more and more gloriously. Of this I have not a doubt. I know indeed that our religion has been questioned even by intelligent and good men; but this does not shake my faith in its divine original or in its ultimate triumphs. Such men have questioned it, because they have known it chiefly by its corruptions. In proportion as its original simplicity shall be restored, the doubts of the well-disposed will yield. I have no fears from infidelity; especially from that form of it, which some are at this moment laboring to spread through our country; I mean, that insane, desperate unbelief, which strives to quench the light of nature as well as of revelation, and to leave us, not only without Christ, but without God. This I dread no more than I should fear the efforts of men to pluck the sun from his sphere, or to storm the skies with the artillery of the earth. We were made for religion; and unless the enemies of our faith can change our nature, they will leave the foundation of religion unshaken. The human soul was created to look above material nature. It wants a Deity for its love and trust, an Immortality for its hope. It wants consolations not found in philosophy, wants strength in temptation, sorrow, and death, which human wisdom cannot minister; and knowing as I do, that Christianity meets these deep wants of men, I have no fear or doubt as to its triumphs. Men cannot long live without

VOL. III.

religion. In France there is a spreading dissatisfaction with the skeptical spirit of the past generation. A philosopher in that country would now blush to quote Voltaire as an authority in religion. Already Atheism is dumb where once it seemed to bear sway. The greatest minds in France are working back their way to the light of truth. Many of them indeed cannot yet be called Christians; but their path, like that of the wise men of old who came star-guided from the East, is towards Christ. I am not ashamed of the Gospel of Christ. It has an immortal life, and will gather strength from the violence of its foes. It is equal to all the wants of men. The greatest minds have found in it the light which they most anxiously desired. The most sorrowful and broken spirits have found in it a healing balm for their woes. It has inspired the sublimest virtues and the loftiest hopes. For the corruptions of such a religion I weep, and I should blush to be their advocate; but of the Gospel itself, I can never be ashamed.

END OF VOL. III.

THE

WORKS

OF

WILLIAM E. CHANNING, D. D.

NINETEENTH COMPLETE EDITION.

WITH

AN INTRODUCTION.

VOL. IV.

BOSTON:
AMERICAN UNITARIAN ASSOCIATION.
1869.

Entered according to Act of Congress, in the year 1841 by
GEORGE G. CHANNING,
In the Clerk's Office of the District Court for the District of Massachusetts

CONTENTS OF VOL. IV.

	PAGE
CHARACTER OF CHRIST.	7
CHRISTIANITY A RATIONAL RELIGION.	31
SPIRITUAL FREEDOM: DISCOURSE AT THE ANNUAL ELECTION, MAY 26, 1830.	67
SELF-DENIAL.	123
THE IMITABLENESS OF CHRIST'S CHARACTER.	135
THE EVIL OF SIN.	151
IMMORTALITY.	169
LOVE TO CHRIST.	183
LOVE TO CHRIST.	199
THE FUTURE LIFE.	217
WAR.	237
MINISTRY FOR THE POOR: DISCOURSE BEFORE THE BENEVOLENT FRATERNITY OF CHURCHES.	265
CHRISTIAN WORSHIP: DISCOURSE AT THE DEDICATION OF THE UNITARIAN CONGREGATIONAL CHURCH, NEWPORT, RHODE ISLAND.	303
THE SUNDAY-SCHOOL: DISCOURSE PRONOUNCED BEFORE THE SUNDAY-SCHOOL SOCIETY.	355
THE PHILANTHROPIST: A TRIBUTE TO THE MEMORY OF THE REV. NOAH WORCESTER, D. D.	387

DISCOURSES.

CHARACTER OF CHRIST.

MATTHEW xvii. 5: "This is my beloved Son, in whom I am well pleased."

THE character of Christ may be studied for various purposes. It is singularly fitted to call forth the heart, to awaken love, admiration, and moral delight. As an example, it has no rival. As an evidence of his religion, perhaps it yields to no other proof; perhaps no other has so often conquered unbelief. It is chiefly to this last view of it, that I now ask your attention. The character of Christ is a strong confirmation of the truth of his religion. As such, I would now place it before you. I shall not, however, think only of confirming your faith; the very illustrations, which I shall adduce for this purpose, will show the claims of Jesus to our reverence, obedience, imitation, and fervent love.

The more we contemplate Christ's character, as exhibited in the Gospel, the more we shall be impressed with its genuineness and reality. It was plainly drawn from the life. The narratives of the Evangelists bear the marks of truth, perhaps beyond all other histories. They set before us the most extraordinary being who ever appeared on earth, and yet they are as artless as the stories of childhood. The authors do not think of themselves. They have plainly but one aim, to show us their Master ; and they manifest the deep veneration which he inspired, by leaving him to reveal himself, by giving us his actions and sayings without comment, explanation, or eulogy. You see in these narratives no varnishing, no high coloring, no attempts to make his actions striking, or to bring out the beauties of his character. We are never pointed to any circumstance as illustrative of his greatness. The Evangelists write with a calm trust in his character, with a feeling that it needed no aid from their hands, and with a deep veneration, as if comment or praise of their own were not worthy to mingle with the recital of such a life.

It is the effect of our familiarity with the history of Jesus, that we are not struck by it as we ought to be. We read it before we are capable of understanding its excellence. His stupendous works become as familiar to us as the events of ordinary life, and his high offices seem as much matters of course, as the common relations which men bear to each other. On this account, it is fit for the ministers of religion to do what the Evangelists did not attempt, to offer comments on Christ's character, to bring out its features, to point men to its higher beauties, to awaken their awe by unfolding its wonderful majesty. Indeed, one of our most important functions, as teachers, is to give freshness and vividness to truths which have become worn, I had almost said tarnished, by long and familiar handling. We have to fight with the power of habit. Through habit, men look on this glorious creation with insensibility, and are less moved by the all-enlightening sun than by a show of fire-works. It is the duty of a moral and religious teacher, almost to create a new sense in men, that they may learn in what a world of beauty and magnificence they live. And so in regard to Christ's character; men become used to it, until they imagine, that there is something more admirable in a great man of their own day, a statesman or a conqueror, than in Him, the latchet of whose shoes statesmen and conquerors are not worthy to unloose.

In this discourse, I wish to show that the character of Christ, taken as a whole, is one which could not have entered the thoughts of man, could not have been imagined or feigned; that it bears every mark of genuineness and truth; that it ought therefore to be acknowledged as real and of divine original.

It is all-important, my friends, if we would feel the force of this argument, to transport ourselves to the times when Jesus lived. We are very apt to think, that he was moving about in such a city as this, or among a people agreeing with ourselves in modes of thinking and habits of life. But the truth is, he lived in a state of society singularly remote from our own. Of all nations, the Jewish was the most strongly marked. The Jew hardly felt himself to belong to the human family. He was accustomed to speak of himself as chosen by God, holy, clean; whilst the Gentiles were sinners, dogs, polluted, unclean. His common dress, the phylactery on his brow or arm, the hem of his garment, his food, the ordinary circumstances of his life, as well as his temple, his sacrifices, his ablutions, all held him up to himself, as a peculiar favorite of God, and all separated him from the rest of the world. With other nations he could not eat or marry. They were unworthy of his communion. Still, with all these notions of superiority, he saw himself conquered by those whom he despised. He was obliged to wear the shackles of Rome, to see Roman legions in his territory, a Roman guard near his temple, and a Roman tax-gatherer extorting, for the support of an idolatrous government and an idolatrous worship, what he regarded as due only to God. The hatred which burned in the breast of the Jew towards his foreign oppressor, perhaps never glowed with equal intenseness in any other conquered state. He had, however, his secret consolation. The time was near, the prophetic age was at hand, when Judea was to break her chains and rise from the dust. Her long-promised king and deliverer was near, and was coming to wear the crown of universal empire. From Jerusalem was to go forth his law, and all nations were to serve the chosen people of God. To this conqueror the Jews indeed ascribed the office of promoting religion; but the religion of Moses, corrupted into an outward service, was to them the perfection of human nature. They clung to its forms with the whole energy of their souls. To the Mosaic institution, they ascribed their distinction from all other nations. It lay at the foundation of their hopes of dominion. I believe no strength of prejudice ever equalled the intense attachment of the Jew to his peculiar national religion. You may judge of its power by the fact of its having been transmitted through so many ages, amidst persecution and sufferings which would have subdued any spirit but that of a Jew. You must bring these things to your mind. You must place yourselves in the midst of this singular people.

Among this singular people, burning with impatient

expectation, appeared Jesus of Nazareth. His first words were, " Repent, for the kingdom of heaven is at hand." These words we hear with little emotion; but to the Jews, who had been watching for this kingdom for ages, and who were looking for its immediate manifestation, they must have been awakening as an earthquake. Accordingly we find Jesus thronged by multitudes which no building could contain. He repairs to a mountain, as affording him advantages for addressing the crowd. I see them surrounding him with eager looks, and ready to drink in every word from his lips. And what do I hear? Not one word of Judea, of Rome, of freedom, of conquest, of the glories of God's chosen people, and of the thronging of all nations to the temple on Mount Zion. Almost every word was a death-blow to the hopes and feelings, which glowed through the whole people, and were consecrated under the name of religion. He speaks of the long-expected Kingdom of Heaven; but speaks of it as a felicity promised to, and only to be partaken by, the humble and pure in heart. The righteousness of the Pharisees, that which was deemed the perfection of religion, and which the new deliverer was expected to spread far and wide, he pronounces worthless, and declares the kingdom of Heaven, or of the Messiah, to be shut against all who do not cultivate a new, spiritual, and disinterested virtue. Instead of war and victory, he commands his impatient hearers to love, to forgive, to bless their enemies; and holds forth this spirit of benignity, mercy, peace, as the special badge of the people of the true Messiah. Instead of national interests and glories, he commands them to seek first a spirit of impartial charity and love, unconfined by the bounds of tribe or nation, and proclaims this to be the happiness and honor of the reign for which they hoped. Instead of this world's riches, which they expected to flow from all lands into their own, he commands them to lay up treasures in heaven, and directs them to an incorruptible, immortal life, as the true end of their being. Nor is this all. He does not merely offer himself as a spiritual deliverer, as the founder of a new empire of inward piety and universal charity; he closes with language announcing a more mysterious office. "Many will say unto me in that day, Lord, Lord, have we not prophesied in thy name? and in thy name done many wonderful works? And then will I profess unto them, I never knew you; depart from me, ye that work iniquity." Here I meet the annunciation of a character as august as it must have been startling. I hear him foretelling a dominion to be exercised in the future world. He begins to announce, what entered largely into his future teaching, that his power was not bounded to this earth. These words I better understand, when I hear him subsequently declaring, that, after a painful death, he was to rise again and ascend to heaven, and there, in a state of preëminent power and glory, was to be the advocate and judge of the human race.

Such are some of the views given by Jesus, of his character and reign, in the Sermon on the Mount. Immediately afterwards, I hear another lesson from him, bringing out some of these truths still more strongly. A Roman centurion makes application to him for the cure of a servant, whom he particularly valued; and on expressing, in a strong manner, his conviction of the power of Jesus to heal at a distance, Jesus, according to the historian, "marvelled, and said to those that followed, Verily I say unto you, I have not found so gieat faith in Israel; and I say unto you, that many shall come from the east and west, and shall sit down with Abraham, and Isaac, and Jacob in the kingdom of heaven; but the children of the kingdom" (that is, the Jews) "shall be cast out." Here all the hopes which the Jews had cherished of an exclusive or peculiar possession of the Messiah's kingdom, were crushed; and the reception of the despised Gentile world to all his blessings, or, in other words, the extension of his pure religion to the ends of the earth, began to be proclaimed.

Here I pause for the present, and I ask you, whether the character of Jesus be not the most extraordinary in history, and wholly inexplicable on human principles. Review the ground over which we have gone. Recollect that he was born and grew up a Jew, in the midst of Jews, a people burning with one passion, and throwing their whole souls into the expectation of a national and earthly deliverer. He grew up among them in poverty, seclusion, and labors fitted to contract his thoughts, purposes, and hopes; and yet we find him escaping every influence of education and society. We find him as untouched by the feelings which prevailed universally around him, which religion and patriotism concurred to consecrate, which the mother breathed into the ear of the child, and which the teacher of the synagogue strengthened in the adult, as if he had been brought up in another world. We find him conceiving a sublime purpose, such as had never dawned on sage or hero, and see him possessed with a consciousness of sustaining a relation to God and mankind, and of being invested with powers in this world and the world to come, such as had never entered the human mind. Whence now, I ask, came the conception of this character?

Will any say it had its origin in imposture; that it was a fabrication of a deceiver? I answer, the character claimed by Christ excludes this supposition, by its very nature. It was so remote from all the ideas and anticipations of the times, so unfit to awaken sympathy, so unattractive to the heathen, so exasperating to the Jew, that it was the last to enter the mind of an impostor. A deceiver of the dullest vision must have foreseen, that it would expose him to bitter scorn, abhorrence, and persecution, and that he would be left to carry on his work alone, just as Jesus always stood alone, and could find not an individual to enter into his spirit and design. What allurements an unprincipled, self-seeking man could find to such an enterprise, no common ingenuity can discover.

I affirm next, that the sublimity of the character claimed by Christ forbids us to trace it to imposture. That a selfish, designing, depraved mind could have formed the idea and purpose of a work unparalleled in beneficence, in vastness, and in moral grandeur, would certainly be a strange departure from the laws of the human mind. I add, that if an impostor could have lighted on the conception of so sublime and wonderful a work as that claimed by Jesus, he could not, I say, he *could* not have thrown into his personation of it the air of truth and reality. The part would have been too high for him. He would have overacted it or fallen short of it perpetually. His true character would have rebelled against his assumed one. We should have seen something strained, forced, artificial, awkward, showing that he was not in his true sphere. To act up to a character so singular and grand, and one for which no precedent could be found, seems to me utterly impossible for a man who had not the true spirit of it, or who was only wearing it as a mask.

Now, how stands the case with Jesus? Bred a Jewish peasant or carpenter, he issues from obscurity, and claims for himself a divine office, a superhuman dignity, such as had not been imagined; and in no instance does he fall below the character. The peasant, and still more the Jew, wholly disappears. We feel that a new being, of a new order of mind, is taking a part in human affairs. There is a native tone of grandeur and authority in his teaching. He speaks as a being related to the whole human race. His mind never shrinks within the ordinary limits of human agency. A narrower sphere than the world never enters his thoughts. He speaks in a natural, spontaneous style, of accomplishing the most arduous and important change in human affairs. This unlabored manner of expressing great thoughts is particularly worthy of attention. You never hear from Jesus that swelling, pompous, ostentatious language, which almost necessarily springs from an attempt to sustain a character above our powers. He talks of his glories as one to whom they were familiar, and of his intimacy and oneness with God, as simply as a child speaks of his connexion with his parents. He speaks of saving and judging the world, of drawing all men to himself, and of giving everlasting life, as we speak of the ordinary powers which we exert. He makes no set harangues about the grandeur of his office and character. His consciousness of it gives a hue to his whole language, breaks out in indirect, undesigned expressions, showing that it was the deepest and most familiar of his convictions. This argument is only to be understood by reading the Gospels with a wakeful mind and heart. It does not lie on their surface, and it is the stronger for lying beneath it. When I read these books with care, when I trace the unaffected majesty which runs through the life of Jesus, and see him never falling below his sublime claims amidst poverty, and scorn, and in his last agony ; I have a feeling of the reality of his character which I cannot express. I feel that the Jewish carpenter could no more have conceived and sustained this character under motives of imposture, than an infant's arm could repeat the deeds of Hercules, or his unawakened intellect comprehend and rival the matchless works of genius.

Am I told that the claims of Jesus had their origin, not in imposture but in enthusiasm ; that the imagination, kindled by strong feeling, overpowered the judgment so far as to give him the notion of being destined to some strange and unparalleled work ? I know that enthusiasm, or a kindled imagination, has great power ; and we are never to lose sight of it, in judging of the claims of religious teachers. But I say first, that, except in cases where it amounts to insanity, enthusiasm works, in a greater or less degree, according to a man's previous conceptions and modes of thought. In Judea, where the minds of men were burning with feverish expectation of a Messiah, I can easily conceive of a Jew imagining that in himself this ardent conception, this ideal of glory, was to be realized. I can conceive of his seating himself in fancy on the throne of David, and secretly pondering the means of his appointed triumphs. But that a Jew should fancy himself the Messiah, and at the same time should strip that character of all the attributes which had fired his youthful imagination and heart, — that he should start aside from all the feelings and hopes of his age, and should acquire a consciousness of being destined to a wholly new career, and one as unbounded as it was new, this is exceedingly improbable ; and one thing is certain, that an imagination so erratic, so ungoverned, and able to generate the conviction of being destined to a work so immeasurably disproportioned to the power of the individual, must have partaken of insanity. Now, is it conceivable, that an individual, mastered by so wild and fervid an imagination, should have sustained the dignity claimed by Christ, should have acted worthily the highest part ever assumed on earth ? Would not his enthusiasm have broken out amidst the peculiar excitements of the life of Jesus, and have left a touch of madness on his teaching and conduct ? Is it to such a man that we should look for the inculcation of a new and perfect form of virtue, and for the exemplification of humanity in its fairest form ?

The charge of an extravagant, self-deluding enthusiasm is the last to be fastened on Jesus. Where can we find the traces of it in his history ? Do we detect them in the calm authority of his precepts ; in the mild, practical, and beneficent spirit of his religion ; in the unlabored simplicity of the language with which he unfolds his high powers, and the sublime truths of religion ; or in the good sense, the knowledge of human nature, which he always discovers in his estimate and treatment of the different classes of men with whom he acted ? Do we discover this enthusiasm in the singular fact, that whilst he claimed power in the future world, and always turned men's minds to Heaven, he never indulged his own imagination, or stimulated that of his disciples, by giving vivid pictures, or any minute description, of that unseen state? The truth is, that, remarkable as was the character of Jesus, it was distinguished by nothing more than by calmness and self-possession. This trait pervades his other excellences. How calm was his piety! Point me, if you can, to one vehement, passionate expression of his religious feelings. Does the Lord's Prayer breathe a feverish enthusiasm? The habitual style of Jesus on the subject of religion, if introduced into many churches of his followers at the present day, would be charged with coldness. The calm and the rational character of his piety is particularly seen in the doctrine which he so earnestly inculcates, that disinterested love and self-denying service to our fellow-creatures are the most acceptable worship we can offer to our Creator. His benevolence, too, though singularly earnest and deep, was composed and serene. He never lost the possession of himself in his sympathy with others; was never hurried into the impatient and rash enterprises of an enthusiastic philanthropy; but did good with the tranquillity and constancy which mark the providence of God. The depth of his calmness may best be understood by considering the opposition made to his claims. His labors were everywhere insidiously watched and industriously thwarted by vindictive foes, who had even conspired to compass, through his death, the ruin of his cause. Now, a feverish enthusiasm, which fancies itself to be intrusted with a great work of God, is singularly liable to impatient indignation under furious and malignant opposition. Obstacles increase its vehemence; it becomes more eager and hurried in the accomplishment of its purposes, in proportion as they are withstood. Be it therefore remembered, that the malignity of Christ's foes, though never surpassed, and for the time triumphant, never robbed him of self-possession, roused no passion, and threw no vehemence or precipitation into his exertions. He did not disguise from himself or his followers the impression made on the multitude by his adversaries. He distinctly foresaw the violent death towards which he was fast approaching. Yet, confiding in God, and in the silent progress of his truth, he possessed his soul in peace. Not only was he calm, but his calmness rises into sublimity when we consider the storms which raged around him, and the vastness of the prospects in which his spirit found repose. I say, then, that serenity and self-possession were peculiarly the attributes of Jesus. I affirm, that the singular and sublime character claimed by Jesus, can be traced neither to imposture, nor to an ungoverned, insane imagination. It can only be accounted for by its truth, its reality.

I began with observing how our long familiarity with Jesus blunts our minds to his singular excellence. We probably have often read of the character which he claimed, without a thought of its extraordinary nature. But I know nothing so sublime. The plans and labors of statesmen sink into the sports of children, when compared with the work which Jesus announced, and to which he devoted himself in life and death, with a thorough consciousness of its reality. The idea of changing the moral aspect of the whole earth, of recovering all nations to the pure and inward worship of one God, and to a spirit of divine and fraternal love, was one of which we meet not a trace in philosopher or legislator before him. The human mind had given no promise of this extent of view. The conception of this enterprise, and the calm, unshaken expectation of success, in one who had no station and no wealth, who cast from him the sword with abhorrence, and who forbade his disciples to use any weapons but those of love, discover a wonderful trust in the power of God and the power of love; and when to this we add, that Jesus looked not only to the triumph of his pure faith in the present world, but to a mighty and beneficent power in Heaven, we witness a vastness of purpose, a grandeur of thought and feeling, so original, so superior to the workings of all other minds, that nothing but our familiarity can prevent our contemplation of it with wonder and profound awe. I confess, when I can escape the deadening power of habit, and can receive the full import of such passages as the following, — "Come unto me, all ye that labor and are heavy laden, and I will give you rest," — "I am come to seek and to save that which was lost," — "He that confesseth me before men, him will I confess before my Father in Heaven," — "Whosoever shall be ashamed of me before men, of him shall the Son of Man be ashamed when he cometh in the glory of the Father with the holy angels," — "In my Father's house are many mansions; I go to prepare a place for you:" — I say, when I can succeed in realizing the import of such passages, I feel myself listening to a being, such as never before and never since spoke in human language. I am awed by the consciousness of greatness which these simple words express; and when I connect this greatness with the proofs of Christ's miracles which I gave you in a former discourse, I am compelled to exclaim with the centurion, "Truly, this was the Son of God."

I have thus, my friends, set before you one view of Jesus Christ, which shows him to have been the most extraordinary being who ever lived. I invite your attention to another; and I am not sure, but that it is still more striking. You have seen the consciousness of greatness which Jesus possessed; I now ask you to consider, how, with this consciousness, he lived among men. To convey my meaning more distinctly, let me avail myself of an imaginary case. Suppose you had never heard the particulars of Christ's history, but were told in general, that, ages ago, an extraordinary man appeared in the world, whose mind was wholly possessed with the idea of having come from God, who regarded himself as clothed with divine power and charged with the sublimest work in the universe, who had the consciousness of sustaining a relation of unexampled authority and beneficence, not to one nation or age, but to all nations and all times, — and who anticipated a spiritual kingdom and everlasting power beyond the grave. Suppose you should be told, that, on entering the world, he found not one mind able to comprehend his views, and felt himself immeasurably exalted in thought and purpose above all around him, and suppose you should then be asked what appearance, what mode of life, what tone, what air, what deportment, what intercourse with the multitude seemed to you to suit such a character, and were probably adopted by him; how would you represent him to your minds? Would you not suppose, that, with this peculiar character; he adopted some peculiar mode of life, expressive of his superiority to and separation from all other men? Would you not expect something distinctive in his appearance? Would you not expect him to assume some badge, and to exact some homage? Would you not expect, that, with a mind revolving such vast thoughts, and raised above the earth, he would look coldly on the ordinary gratifications of men ? that, with a mind spreading itself over the world, and meditating its subjection to his truth, he would take little interest in ordinary individuals ? and that, possessing, in his own doctrine and character, a standard of sublime virtue, he would attach little importance to the low attainments of the ignorant and superstitious around him ? Would you not make him a public character, and expect to see him laboring to establish his ascendency among public men ? Would you not expect to see his natural affections absorbed in his universal philanthropy ; and would not private attachments seem to you quite inconsistent with his vast superiority, and the immensity of his purposes ? Would you not expect him to avail himself of the best accommodations the world could afford ? Would you not expect the great Teacher to select the most sacred spots for his teaching, and the Lord of all to erect some conspicuous seat, from which should go forth the laws which were to reach the ends of the earth ? Would you not, in a word, expect this extraordinary personage to surround himself with extraordinary circumstances, and to maintain a separation from the degraded multitude around him ?

Such, I believe, would be the expectation of us all ; and what was the case with Jesus ? Read his history. He comes with the consciousness of more than human greatness, to accomplish an infinite work ; and where do you find him ? What is his look ? what his manner? How does he converse, how live with men ? His appearance, mode of life, and intercourse are directly the reverse of what we should have supposed. He comes in the ordinary dress of the class of society in which he had grown up. He retreats to no solitude, like John, to strike awe, nor seeks any spot which had been consecrated in Jewish history. Would you find him? Go to the house of Peter, the fisherman. Go to the well of Samaria, where he rests after the fatigues of his journey. Would you hear him teach? You may find him, indeed, sometimes in the temple, for that was a place of general resort; but commonly you may find him instructing in the open air, now from a boat on the Galilean lake, now on a mount, and now in the streets of the crowded city. He has no place wherein to lay his head, nor will he have one. A rich ruler comes and falls at his feet. He says, "Go, sell what thou hast, and give to the poor, and then come and follow me." Nor was this all. Something more striking remains to be told. He did not merely live in the streets, and in the houses of fishermen. In these places, had he pleased, he might have cleared a space around him, and raised a barrier between himself and others. But in these places, and everywhere, he lived with men as a man, a brother, a friend, sometimes a servant; and entered, with a deep, unexampled sympathy, into the feelings, interests, wants, sorrows of individuals, of ordinary men, and even of the most depressed, despised, and forsaken of the race. Here is the most striking view of Jesus. This combination of the spirit of humanity, in its lowliest, tenderest form, with the consciousness of unrivalled and divine glories, is the most wonderful distinction of this wonderful character. Here we learn the chief reason, why he chose poverty, and refused every peculiarity of manner and appearance. He did this because he desired to come near to the multitude of men, to make himself accessible to all, to pour out the fullness of his sympathy upon all, to know and weep over their sorrows and sins, and to manifest his interest in their affections and joys.

I can offer but a few instances of this sympathy of Christ with human nature in all its varieties of character and condition. But how beautiful are they! At the very opening of his ministry, we find him present at a marriage, to which he and his disciples had been called. Among the Jews this was an occasion of peculiar exhilaration and festivity; but Jesus did not therefore decline it. He knew what affections, joys, sorrows, and moral influences are bound up in this institution, and he went to the celebration, not as an ascetic, to frown on its bright hopes and warm congratulations, but to sanction it by his presence, and to heighten its enjoyments. How little does this comport with the solitary dignity which we should have pronounced most accordant with his character, and what a spirit of humanity does it breathe! But this event stands almost alone in his history. His chief sympathy was not with them that rejoice, but with the ignorant, sinful, sorrowful; and with these we find him cultivating an habitual intimacy. Though so exalted in thought and purpose, he chose uneducated men to be his chief disciples; and he lived with them, not as a superior, giving occasional and formal instruction, but became their companion, travelled with them on foot, slept in their dwellings, sat at their tables, partook their plain fare, communicated to them his truth in the simplest form; and though they constantly misunderstood him, and never received his full meaning, he was never wearied with teaching them. So familiar was his intercourse, that we find Peter reproving him with an affectionate zeal, for announcing his approaching death, and we find John leaning on his bosom. Of his last discourse to these disciples I need not speak. It stands alone among all writings for the union of tenderness and majesty. His own sorrows are forgotten in his solicitude to speak peace and comfort to his humble followers.

The depth of his human sympathies was beautifully manifested when children were brought to him. His disciples, judging as all men would judge, thought that he who was sent to wear the crown of universal empire, had too great a work before him to give his time and attention to children, and reproved the parents who brought them ; but Jesus, rebuking his disciples, called to him the children. Never, I believe, did childhood awaken such deep love as at that moment. He took them in his arms and blessed them, and not only said that " of such was the kingdom of heaven," but added, " He that receiveth a little child in my name, receiveth me ; " so entirely did he identify himself with this primitive, innocent, beautiful form of human nature.

There was no class of human beings so low as to be beneath his sympathy. He not merely taught the publican and sinner, but, with all his consciousness of purity, sat down and dined with them, and, when reproved by the malignant Pharisee for such companionship, answered by the touching parables of the Lost Sheep and the Prodigal Son, and said, " I am come to seek and to save that which was lost."

No personal suffering dried up this fountain of love in his breast. On his way to the cross, he heard some women of Jerusalem bewailing him, and at the sound, forgetting his own grief, he turned to them and said,

"Women of Jerusalem, weep not for me, but weep for yourselves and your children." On the cross, whilst his mind was divided between intense suffering, and the contemplation of the infinite blessings in which his sufferings were to issue, his eye lighted on his mother and John, and the sensibilities of a son and a friend mingled with the sublime consciousness of the universal Lord and Saviour. Never before did natural affection find so tender and beautiful an utterance. To his mother he said, directing her to John, "*Behold thy son;* I leave my beloved disciple to take my place, to perform my filial offices, and to enjoy a share of that affection with which you have followed me through life;" and to John he said, "*Behold thy mother;* I bequeath to you the happiness of ministering to my dearest earthly friend." Nor is this all. The spirit of humanity had one higher triumph. Whilst his enemies surrounded him with a malignity unsoftened by his last agonies, and, to give the keenest edge to insult, reminded him scoffingly of the high character and office which he had claimed, his only notice of them was the prayer, "Father, forgive them, they know not what they do."

Thus Jesus lived with men; with the consciousness of unutterable majesty, he joined a lowliness, gentleness, humanity, and sympathy, which have no example in human history. I ask you to contemplate this wonderful union. In proportion to the superiority of Jesus to all around him, was the intimacy, the brotherly love, with which he bound himself to them. I maintain, that this is a character wholly remote from human conception. To imagine it to be the production of imposture or enthusiasm, shows a strange unsoundness of mind. I contemplate it with a veneration second only to the profound awe with which I look up to God. It bears no mark of human invention. It was real. It belonged to and it manifested the beloved Son of God.

But I have not done. May I ask your attention a few moments more ? We have not yet reached the depth of Christ's character. We have not touched the great principle, on which his wonderful sympathy was founded, and which endeared to him his office of universal Saviour. Do you ask what this deep principle was ? I answer, it was his conviction of the greatness of the human soul. He saw in man the impress and image of the divinity, and therefore thirsted for his redemption, and took the tenderest interest in him, whatever might be the rank, character, or condition in which he was found. This spiritual view of man pervades and distinguishes the teaching of Christ. Jesus looked on men with an eye which pierced beneath the material frame. The body vanished before him. The trappings of the rich, the rags of the poor, were nothing to him. He looked through them, as though they did not exist, to the soul ; and there, amidst clouds of ignorance and plague-spots of sin, he recognised a spiritual and immortal nature, and the germs of power and perfection which might be unfolded for ever. In the most fallen and depraved man, he saw a being who might become an angel of light. Still more, he felt that there was nothing in himself to which men might not ascend. His own lofty consciousness did not sever him from the multitude ; for he saw in his own greatness the model of what men might become. So deeply was he thus impressed, that again and again, in speaking of his future glories, he announced, that in these his true followers were to share. They were to sit on his throne, and partake of his beneficent power.

Here I pause, and indeed I know not what can be added to heighten the wonder, reverence, and love, which are due to Jesus. When I consider him, not only as possessed with the consciousness of an unexampled and unbounded majesty, but as recognising a kindred nature in human beings, and living and dying to raise them to a participation of his divine glories; and when I see him under these views allying himself to men by the tenderest ties, embracing them with a spirit of humanity, which no insult, injury, or pain could for a moment repel or overpower, I am filled with wonder as well as reverence and love. I feel that this character is not of human invention, that it was not assumed through fraud, or struck out by enthusiasm; for it is infinitely above their reach. When I add this character of Jesus to the other evidences of his religion, it gives to what before seemed so strong, a new and a vast accession of strength; I feel as if I could not be deceived. The Gospels must be true; they were drawn from a living original; they were founded on reality. The character of Jesus is not a fiction; he was what he claimed to be, and what his followers attested. Nor is this all. Jesus not only *was*, he is still, the Son of God, the Saviour of the world. He exists now; he has entered that Heaven, to which he always looked forward on earth. There he lives and reigns. With a clear, calm faith, I see him in that state of glory; and I confidently expect, at no distant period, to see him face to face. We have indeed no absent friend whom we shall so surely meet. Let us then, my hearers, by imitation of his virtues and obedience to his word, prepare ourselves to join him in those pure mansions, where he is surrounding himself with the good and pure of our race, and will communicate to them for ever his own spirit, power, and joy.

CHRISTIANITY A RATIONAL RELIGION.

ROMANS i. 16: "I am not ashamed of the Gospel of Christ."

SUCH was the language of Paul; and every man will respond to it, who comprehends the character and has felt the influence of Christianity. In a former discourse, I proposed to state to you some reasons for adopting as our own the words of the Apostle, for joining in this open and resolute testimony to the gospel of Christ. I observed, that I was not ashamed of the gospel, first because it is True, and to this topic the discourse was devoted. I wish now to continue the subject, and to state another ground of undisguised and unshaken adherence to Christianity. I say, then, I am not ashamed of the gospel of Christ, because it is a *rational* religion. It agrees with reason; therefore I count it worthy of acceptation, therefore I do not blush to enrol myself among its friends and advocates. The object of the present discourse will be the illustration of this claim of Christianity. I wish to show you the harmony which subsists between the light of God's word, and that primitive light of reason, which he has kindled within us to be our perpetual guide. If, in treating this subject, I shall come into conflict with any class of Christians, I trust I shall not be considered as imputing to them any moral or intellectual defect. I judge men by their motives, dispositions, and lives, and not by their speculations or peculiar opinions; and I esteem piety and virtue equally venerable, whether found in friend or foe.

Christianity is a Rational religion. Were it not so, I should be ashamed to profess it. I am aware that it is the fashion with some to decry reason, and to set up revelation as an opposite authority. This error though countenanced by good men, and honestly maintained for the defence of the Christian cause, ought to be earnestly withstood; for it virtually surrenders our religion into the hands of the unbeliever. It saps the foundation to strengthen the building. It places our religion in hostility to human nature, and gives to its adversaries the credit of vindicating the rights and noblest powers of the mind.

We must never forget that our rational nature is the greatest gift of God. For this we owe him our chief gratitude. It is a greater gift than any outward aid or benefaction, and no doctrine which degrades it can come from its Author. The developement of it is the end of our being. Revelation is but a means, and is designed to concur with nature, providence, and God's spirit, in carrying forward reason to its perfection. I glory in Christianity because it enlarges, invigorates, exalts my rational nature. If I could not be a Christian without ceasing to be rational, I should not hesitate as to my choice. I feel myself bound to sacrifice to Christianity property, reputation, life; but I ought not to sacrifice to any religion, that reason which lifts me above the brute and constitutes me a man. I can conceive no sacrilege greater than to prostrate or renounce the highest faculty which we have derived from God. In so doing we should offer violence to the divinity within us. Christianity wages no war with reason, but is one with it, and is given to be its helper and friend.

I wish, in the present discourse, to illustrate and confirm the views now given. My remarks will be arranged under two heads. I propose, first, to show that Christianity is founded on, and supposes, the authority of reason, and cannot therefore oppose it without subverting itself. My object in this part of the discourse will be to expose the error of those who hope to serve revelation by disparaging reason. I shall then, in the second place, compare Christianity and the light of reason, to show their accordance; and shall prove, by descending to particulars, that Christianity is eminently a rational religion. My aim, under this head, will be to vindicate the Gospel from the reproaches of the unbeliever, and to strengthen the faith and attachment of its friends. — Before I begin, let me observe that this discussion, from the nature of the subject, must assume occasionally an abstract form, and will demand serious attention. I am to speak of Reason, the chief faculty of the mind; and no simplicity of language in treating such a topic can exempt the hearer from the necessity of patient effort of thought.

I am to begin with showing that the Christian revelation is founded on the authority of reason, and consequently cannot oppose it; and here it may be proper to settle the meaning of the word Reason. One of the most important steps towards the truth is to determine the import of terms. Very often fierce controversies have sprung from obscurity of language, and the parties.

on explaining themselves, have discovered that they have been spending their strength in a war of words. What, then, is reason?

The term Reason is used with so much latitude, that to fix its precise limits is not an easy task. In this respect it agrees with the other words which express the intellectual faculties. One idea, however, is always attached to it. All men understand by reason the highest faculty or energy of the mind. Without laboring for a philosophical definition that will comprehend all its exercises, I shall satisfy myself with pointing out two of its principal characteristics or functions.

First, it belongs to reason to comprehend Universal truths. This is among its most important offices. There are particular and there are universal truths. The last are the noblest, and the capacity of perceiving them is the distinction of intelligent beings; and these belong to reason. Let me give my meaning by some illustrations. I see a stone falling to the ground. This is a particular truth; but I do not stop here. I believe that not only this particular stone falls towards the earth, but that every particle of matter, in whatever world, tends, or, as is sometimes said, is attracted towards all other matter. Here is a universal truth, a principle extending to the whole material creation, and essential to its existence. This truth belongs to reason.— Again, I see a man producing some effect, a manufacture, a house. Here is a particular truth. But I am not only capable of seeing particular causes and effects; I am sure that every thing which begins to exist, no matter when or where, must have a cause, that no change ever has taken place or ever will take place without a cause. Here is a universal truth, something true here and everywhere, true now and through eternity ; and this truth belongs to reason. — Again, I see with my eyes, I traverse with my hands, a limited space ; but this is not all. I am sure, that, beyond the limits which my limbs or senses reach, there is an unbounded space ; that, go where I will, an infinity will spread around me. Here is another universal truth, and this belongs to reason. The idea of Infinity is indeed one of the noblest conceptions of this faculty. — Again, I see a man conferring a good on another. Here is a particular truth or perception. But my mind is not confined to this. I see and feel that it is right for all intelligent beings, exist when or where they may, to do good, and wrong for them to seek the misery of others. Here is a universal truth, a law extending from God to the lowest human being ; and this belongs to reason. I trust I have conveyed to you my views in regard to the first characteristic of this highest power of the soul. Its office is to discern universal truths, great and eternal principles. But it does not stop here. Reason is also exercised in applying these universal truths to particular cases, beings, events. For example, reason teaches me, as we have seen, that all changes without exception require a cause ; and in conformity to this principle, it prompts me to seek the particular causes of the endless changes and appearances which fall under my observation. Thus reason is perpetually at work on the ideas furnished us by the senses, by consciousness, by memory, associating them with its own great truths, or investing them with its own universality.

I now proceed to the second function of reason, which is indeed akin to the first. Reason is the power which ends, and is perpetually striving, to reduce our various thoughts to Unity or Consistency. Perhaps the most fundamental conviction of reason is, that all truths agree together; that inconsistency is the mark of error. Its intensest, most earnest effort is to bring concord into the intellect, to reconcile what seem to be clashing views. On the observation of a new fact, reason strives to incorporate it with former knowledge. It can allow nothing to stand separate in the mind. It labors to bring together scattered truths, and to give them the strength and beauty of a vital order. Its end and delight is harmony. It is shocked by an inconsistency in belief, just as a fine ear is wounded by a discord. It carries within itself an instinctive consciousness, that all things which exist are intimately bound together; and it cannot rest until it has connected whatever we witness with the infinite whole. Reason, according to this view, is the most glorious form or exercise of the intellectual nature. It corresponds to the unity of God and the universe, and seeks to make the soul the image and mirror of this sublime unity.

I have thus given my views of reason; but, to prevent all perversion, before I proceed to the main discussion, let me offer a word or two more of explanation. In this discourse, when I speak of the accordance of revelation with reason, I suppose this faculty to be used deliberately, conscientiously, and with the love of truth. Men often baptize with the name of reason their prejudices, unexamined notions, or opinions adopted through interest, pride, or other unworthy biasses. It is not uncommon to hear those who sacrifice the plainest dictates of the rational nature to impulse and passion, setting themselves up as oracles of reason. Now when I say revelation must accord with reason, I do not mean by the term the corrupt and superficial opinions of men who have betrayed and debased their rational powers. I mean reason, calmly, honestly exercised for the acquisition of truth and the invigoration of virtue.

After these explanations, I proceed to the discussion of the two leading principles to which this Discourse is devoted.

First, I am to show that revelation is founded on the authority of reason, and cannot therefore oppose or disparage it without subverting itself. Let me state a few of the considerations which convince me of the truth of this position. The first is, that reason alone makes us capable of receiving a revelation. It must previously exist and operate, or we should be wholly unprepared for the communications of Christ. Revelation, then, is built on reason. You will see the truth of these remarks if you will consider to whom revelation is sent. Why is it given to men rather than to brutes? Why have not God's messengers gone to the fields to proclaim his glad tidings to bird and beast? The answer is obvious. These want reason; and, wanting this, they have no capacity or preparation for revealed truth. And not only would revelation be lost on the brute; let it speak to the child, before his rational faculties have been awakened, and before some ideas of duty and his own nature have been developed, and it might as well speak to a stone. Reason is the preparation and ground of revelation.

This truth will be still more obvious, if we consider, not only to whom, but in what way, the Christian revelation is communicated. How is it conveyed? In words. Did it make these words? No. They were in use ages before its birth. Again I ask, Did it make the ideas or thoughts which these words express? No. If the hearers of Jesus had not previously attached ideas to the terms which he employed, they could not have received his meaning. He might as well have spoken to them in a foreign tongue. Thus the ideas which enter into Christianity subsisted before. They were ideas of reason; so that to this faculty revelation owes the materials of which it is composed.

Revelation, we must remember, is not our earliest teacher. Man is not born with the single power of reading God's word, and sent immediately to that guide His eyes open first on another volume, that of the creation. Long before he can read the Bible, he looks round on the earth and sky. He reads the countenances of his friends, and hears and understands their voices. He looks, too, by degrees within himself, and acquires some ideas of his own soul. Thus his first school is that of nature and reason, and this is necessary to prepare him for a communication from Heaven. Revelation does not find the mind a blank, a void, prepared to receive unresistingly whatever may be offered; but finds it in possession of various knowledge from nature and experience, and, still more, in possession of great principles, fundamental truths, moral ideas, which are derived from itself, and which are the germs of all its future improvement. This last view is peculiarly important. The mind does not receive every thing from abroad. Its great ideas arise from itself, and by those native lights it reads and comprehends the volumes of nature and revelation. We speak, indeed, of nature and revelation as making known to us an intelligent First Cause; but the ideas of intelligence and causation we derive originally from our own nature. The elements of the idea of God we gather from ourselves. Power, wisdom, love, virtue, beauty, and happiness, words which contain all that is glorious in the universe and interesting in our existence, express attributes of the mind, and are understood by us only through consciousness. It is true, these ideas or principles of reason are often obscured by thick clouds, and mingled with many and deplorable errors. Still they are never lost. Christianity recognises them, is built on them, and needs them as its interpreters. If an illustration of these views be required, I would point you to what may be called the most fundamental idea of religion. I mean the idea of right, of duty. Do we derive this originally and wholly from sacred books? Has not every human being, whether born within or beyond the bounds of revelation, a sense of the distinction between right and wrong? Is there not an earlier voice than revelation, approving or rebuking men according to their deeds? In barbarous ages is not conscience heard? And does it not grow more articulate with the progress of society? Christianity does not create, but presupposes the idea of duty; and the same may be said of other great convictions. Revelation, then, does not stand alone, nor is it addressed to a blank and passive mind. It was meant to be a joint worker with other teachers, with nature, with Providence, with conscience, with our rational powers; and as these all are given us by God, they cannot differ from each other. God must agree with himself. He has but one voice. It is man who speaks with jarring tongues. Nothing but harmony can come from the Creator; and, accordingly, a religion claiming to be from God, can give no surer proof of falsehood than by contradicting those previous truths which God is teaching by our very nature. We have thus seen that reason prepares us for a divine communication, and that it furnishes the ideas or materials of which revelation consists. This is my first consideration.

I proceed to a second. I affirm, then, that revelation rests on the authority of reason, because to this faculty it submits the evidences of its truth, and nothing but the approving sentence of reason binds us to receive and obey it. This is a very weighty consideration. Christianity, in placing itself before the tribunal of reason and in resting its claims on the sanction of this faculty, is one of the chief witnesses to the authority and dignity of our rational nature. That I have ascribed to this faculty its true and proper office, may be easily made to appear. I take the New Testament in hand, and on what ground do I receive its truths as divine? I see nothing on its pages but the same letters in which other books are written. No miraculous voice from Heaven assures me that it is God's word, nor does any mysterious voice within my soul command me to believe the supernatural works of Christ. How, then, shall I settle the question of the origin of this religion? I must examine it by the same rational faculties by which other subjects are tried. I must ask what are its evidences, and I must lay them before reason, the only power by which evidence can be weighed. I have not a distinct faculty given me for judging a revelation. I have not two understandings, one for inquiring into God's word and another into his works. As with the same bodily eye I now look on the earth, now on the heavens, so with the same power of reason I examine now nature, now revelation. Reason must collect and weigh the various proofs of Christianity. It must especially compare this system with those **great** moral convictions, which are written by the finger of God on the heart, and which make man a law to himself. A religion subverting these, it must not hesitate to reject, be its evidences what they may. A religion, for example, commanding us to hate and injure society, reason must instantly discard, without even waiting to examine its proofs. From these views we learn, not only that it is the province of reason to judge of the truth of Christianity, but, what is still more important, that the rules or tests by which it judges are of its own dictation. The laws which it applies in this case have their origin in itself. No one will pretend, that revelation can prescribe the principles by which the question of its own truth should be settled; for, until proved to be true, it has no authority. Reason must prescribe the tests or standards, to which a professed communication from God should be referred; and among these none are more important than that moral law, which belongs to the very essence, and is the deepest conviction, of the rational nature. Revelation, then, rests on reason, and, in opposing it, would act for its own destruction.

I have given two views. I have shown that revelation draws its ideas or materials from reason, and that it appeals to this power as the judge of its truth. I now assert, thirdly, that it rests on the authority of reason, because it needs and expects this faculty to be its interpreter, and without this aid would be worse than useless. How is the right of interpretation, the real meaning, of Scriptures to be ascertained? I answer, By reason. I know of no process by which the true sense of the New Testament is to pass from the page into my mind without the use of my rational faculties. It will not be pretended that this book is so exceedingly plain, its words so easy, its sentences so short, its meaning so exposed on the surface, that the whole truth may be received in a moment and without any intellectual effort. There is no such miraculous simplicity in the Scriptures. In truth, no book can be written so simply as to need no exercise of reason. Almost every word has more than one meaning, and judgment is required to select the particular sense intended by the writer. Of all books, perhaps the Scriptures need most the use of reason for their just interpretation ; and this, not from any imperfection, but from the strength, boldness, and figurative character of their style, and from the distance of the time when they were written. I open the New Testament and my eye lights on this passage ; "If thy hand offend thee, cut it off and cast it from thee." Is this language to be interpreted in its plainest and most obvious sense? Then I must mutilate my body, and become a suicide. I look again, and I find Jesus using these words to the Jews ; "Fill ye up the measure of your iniquities." Am I to interpret this according to the letter, or the first ideas which it suggests? Then Jesus commanded his hearers to steep themselves in crime, and was himself a minister of sin. It is only by a deliberate use of reason, that we can penetrate beneath the figurative, hyperbolical, and often obscure style of the New Testament, to the real meaning. Let me go to the Bible, dismissing my reason and taking the first impression which the words convey, and there is no absurdity, however gross, into which I shall not fall. I shall ascribe a limited body to God, and unbounded knowledge to man, for I read of God having limbs, and of man knowing all things. Nothing is plainer, than that I must compare passage with passage, and limit one by another, and especially limit all by those plain and universal principles of reason, which are called common sense, or I shall make revelation the patron of every folly and vice. So essential is reason to the interpretation of the Christian records. Revelation rests upon its authority. Can it then oppose it, or teach us to hold it in light esteem?

I have now furnished the proofs of my first position, that revelation is founded on reason; and in discussing this, I have wished not only to support the main doctrine, but to teach you to reverence, more perhaps than you have done, your rational nature. This has been decried by theologians, until men have ceased to feel its sacredness and dignity. It ought to be regarded as God's greatest gift. It is his image within us. To renounce it would be to offer a cruel violence to ourselves, to take our place among the brutes. Better pluck out the eye, better quench the light of the body, than the light within us. We all feel, that the loss of reason, when produced by disease, is the most terrible calamity of life, and we look on a hospital for the insane as the receptacle for the most pitiable of our race. But, in one view, insanity is not so great an evil as the prostration of reason to a religious sect or a religious chief; for the first is a visitation of Providence, the last is a voluntary act, the work of our own hands.

I am aware, that those who have spoken most contemptuously of human reason, have acted from a good motive; their aim has been to exalt revelation. They have thought that by magnifying this as the only means of divine teaching, they were adding to its dignity. But truth gains nothing by exaggeration; and Christianity, as we have seen, is undermined by nothing more effectu ally, than by the sophistry which would bring discredit on our rational powers. Revelation needs no such support. For myself I do not find, that, to esteem Christianity, I must think it the only source of instruction to which I must repair. I need not make nature dumb, to give power or attraction to the teaching of Christ. The last derives new interest and confirmation from its harmony with the first. Christianity would furnish a weapon against itself, not easily repelled, should it claim the distinction of being the only light vouchsafed by God to men ; for, in that case, it would represent a vast majority of the human race as left by their Creator without guidance or hope. I believe, and rejoice to believe, that a ray from Heaven descends on the path of every fellow-creature. The heathen, though in darkness when compared with the Christian, has still his light ; and it comes from the same source as our own, just as the same sun dispenses, now the faint dawn, and now the perfect day. Let not nature's teaching be disparaged. It is from God as truly as his word. It is sacred, as truly as revelation. Both are manifestations of one infinite mind, and harmonious manifestations ; and without this agreement the claims of Christianity could not be sustained.

In offering these remarks, I have not forgotten that they will expose me to the reproach of ministering to " the pride of reason" ; and I may be told, that there is no worse form of pride than this. The charge is so common, as to deserve a moment's attention. It will appear at once to be groundless, if you consider, that pride finds its chief nourishment and delight in the idea of our own superiority. It is built on something peculiar and distinctive, on something which separates us from others and raises us above them, and not on powers which we share with all around us. Now, in speaking, as I have done, of the worth and dignity of reason, I have constantly regarded and represented this faculty as the common property of all human beings. I have spoken of its most important truths as universal and unconfined, such as no individual can monopolize or make the grounds of personal distinction or elevation. I have given, then, no occasion and furnished no nutriment to pride. I know, indeed, that the pride of reason or of intellect exists; but how does it chiefly manifest itself? Not in revering that rational nature, which all men have derived from God; but in exaggerating our particular acquisitions or powers, in magnifying our distinctive views, in looking contemptuously on other minds, in making ourselves standards for our brethren, in refusing new lights, and in attempting to establish dominion over the understandings of those who are placed within our influence. Such is the most common form of the pride of intellect. It is a vice confined to no sect, and perhaps will be found to prevail most where it is most disclaimed.

I doubt not that they who insist so continually on the duty of exalting Scripture above reason, consider themselves as particularly secured against the pride of reason. Yet none, I apprehend, are more open to the charge. Such persons are singularly prone to enforce their own interpretations of Scripture on others, and to see peril and crime in the adoption of different views from their own. Now, let me ask, by what power do these men interpret revelation? Is it not by their reason? Have they any faculties but the rational ones, by which to compare Scripture with Scripture, to explain figurative language, to form conclusions as to the will of God ? Do they not employ on God's word the same intellect as on his works ? And are not their interpretations of both equally results of reason ? It follows, that in imposing on others their explications of the Scriptures, they as truly arrogate to themselves a superiority of reason, as if they should require conformity to their explanations of nature. Nature and Scripture agree in this, that they cannot be understood at a glance. Both volumes demand patient investigation, and task all our powers of thought. Accordingly it is well known, that as much intellectual toil has been spent on theological systems as on the natural sciences ; and unhappily it is not less known, that as much intellectual pride has been manifested in framing and defending the first as the last. I fear, indeed, that this vice has clung with peculiar obstinacy to the students of revelation. Nowhere, I fear, have men manifested such infatuated trust in their own infallibility, such overweening fondness for their own conclusions, such positiveness, such impatience of contradiction, such arrogance towards the advocates of different opinions, as in the interpretation of the Scriptures; and yet these very men, who so idolize their own intellectual powers, profess to humble reason, and consider a criminal reliance on it as almost exclusively chargeable on others. The true defence against the pride of reason, is, not to speak of it contemptuously, but to reverence it as God's inestimable gift to every human being, and as given to all for never-ceasing improvements of which we see but the dawn in the present acquisitions of the noblest mind.

I have now completed my views of the first principle, which I laid down in this discourse; namely, that the Christian revelation rests on the authority of reason Of course, it cannot oppose reason without undermining and destroying itself. I maintain, however, that it does not oppose, that it perfectly accords with reason. It is a rational religion. This is my second great position, and to this I ask your continued attention. This topic might easily be extended to a great length. I might state, in succession, all the principles of Christianity, and show their accordance with reason. But I believe that more general views will be more useful, and such only can be given within the compass of a discourse.

In the account which I gave you of reason, in the beginning of this discourse, I confined myself to two of its functions, namely, its comprehension of universal truths, and the effort it constantly makes to reduce the thoughts to harmony or consistency. Universality and Consistency are among the chief attributes of reason. Do we find these in Christianity? If so, its claim to the character of a rational religion will be established. These tests I will therefore apply to it, and I will begin with Consistency.

That a religion be rational, nothing more is necessary than that its truths should consist or agree with one another, and with all other truths, whether derived from outward nature or our own souls. Now I affirm, that the Christian doctrines have this agreement; and the more we examine, the more brightly this mark of truth will appear. I go to the Gospel, and I first compare its various parts with one another. Among these I find perfect harmony; and what makes this more remarkable is, that Christianity is not taught systematically, or like a science. Jesus threw out, if I may so speak, his precepts and doctrines incidentally, or as they were required by the occasion, and yet, when they are brought together, they form a harmonious whole. I do not think it necessary to enlarge on this topic, because I believe it is not questioned by infidelity. I will name but one example of this harmony in Christianity. All its doctrines and all its precepts have that species of unity, which is most essential in a religion, that is, they all tend to one object. They all agree in a single aim or purpose, and that is to exalt the human character to a height of virtue never known before. Let the skeptic name, if he can, one Christian principle which has not a bearing on this end. A consistency of this kind is the strongest mark of a rational religion which can be conceived. Let me observe, in passing, that, besides this harmony of the Christian doctrines with one another, there is a striking and beautiful agreement between the teachings of Jesus and his character, which gives confirmation to both. Whatever Jesus taught, you may see embodied in himself. There is perfect unity between the system and its Founder. His life republished what fell from his lips. With his lips he enjoined earnestly, constantly a strong and disinterested philanthropy; and how harmoniously and sublimely did his cross join with his word in enforcing this exalted virtue! With his lips he taught the mercy of God to sinners; and of this attribute he gave a beautiful illustration in his own deep interest in the sinful, in his free intercourse with the most fallen, and in his patient efforts to recover them to virtue and to filial reliance on their Father in Heaven. So, his preaching turned much on the importance of raising the mind above the world; and his own life was a constant renunciation of worldly interests, a cheerful endurance of poverty that he might make many truly rich. So, his discourses continually revealed to man the doctrine of immortality; and in his own person he brought down this truth to men's senses, by rising from the dead and ascending to another state of being.—I have only glanced at the unity which subsists between Jesus and his religion. Christianity, from every point of view, will be found a harmonious system. It breathes throughout one spirit and one purpose. Its doctrines, precepts, and examples have the consistency of reason.

But this is not enough. A rational religion must agree not only with itself, but with all other truths, whether revealed by the outward creation or our own souls. I take, then, Christianity into the creation, I place it by the side of nature. Do they agree? I say, Perfectly. I can discover nothing, in what claims to be God's word, at variance with his works. This is a bright proof of the reasonableness of Christianity. When I consult nature with the lights modern science affords, I see continually multiplying traces of the doctrine of One God. The more I extend my researches into nature, the more I see that it is a whole, the product of one wisdom, power, and goodness. It bears witness to one Author, nor has its testimony been without effect; for although the human mind has often multiplied its objects of worship, still it has always tended towards the doctrine of the divine unity, and has embraced it more and more firmly in the course of human improvement. The Heathen, while he erected many altars, generally believed in one Supreme Divinity, to whom the inferior deities were subjected and from whom they sprung. Need I tell you of the harmony which subsists between nature and revelation in this particular? To Christianity belongs the glory of having proclaimed this primitive truth with new power, and of having spread it over the whole civilized world. — Again. Nature gives intimation of another truth, I mean of the universal, impartial goodness of God. When I look round on the creation, I see nothing to lead me to suspect that its Author confines his love to a few. The sun sends no brighter beam into the palace of the proudest king, than into the hut of the meanest peasant. The clouds select not one man's fields rather than his neighbour's, but shed down their blessings on rich and poor, and, still more, on the just and the unjust. True, there is a variety of conditions among men; but this takes place, not by any interposition of God, but by fixed and general laws of nature. Impartial, universal goodness is the character in which God is revealed by his works, when they are properly understood; and need I tell you how brightly this truth shines in the pages of Christianity, and how this religion has been the great means of establishing it among men? — Again. When I look through nature, nothing strikes me more than the union which subsists among all its works. Nothing stands alone in the creation. The humblest plant has intimate connexions with the air, the clouds, the sun. Harmony is the great law of nature, and how strikingly does Christianity coincide here with God's works; for what is the design of this religion, but to bring the human race, the intelligent creation of God, into a harmony, union, peace, like that which knits together the outward universe? I will give another illustration. It is one of the great laws of nature, that good shall come to us through agents of God's appointment; that beings shall receive life, support, knowledge, and safety through the interposition and labors and sufferings of others. Sometimes whole communities are rescued from oppression and ruin chiefly by the efforts and sacrifices of a wise, disinterested, and resolute individual. How accordant with this ordination of nature is the doctrine of Christianity, that our Heavenly Father, having purposed our recovery from sin and death, has instituted for this end the agency and mediation of his Son; that he has given an illustrious deliverer to the world, through whose toils and sufferings we may rise to purity and immortal life. — I say, then, that revelation is consistent with nature, when nature is truly interpreted by reason. I see it bringing out with noonday brightness the truths which dawn in nature; so that it is reason in its most perfect form.

I have thus carried Christianity abroad into nature. I now carry it within, and compare it with the human soul; and is it consistent with the great truths of reason which I discover there? I affirm, that it is. When I look into the soul, I am at once struck with its immeasurable superiority to the body. I am struck with the contrast between these different elements of my nature, between this active, soaring mind, and these limbs and material organs which tend perpetually to the earth, and are soon to be resolved into dust. How consistent is Christianity with this inward teaching! In Christianity, with what strength, with what bold relief, is the supremacy of the spiritual nature brought out! What contempt does Jesus cast on the body and its interests, when compared with the redemption of the soul! —

Another great truth dawns on me when I look within. I learn more and more, that the great springs of happiness and misery are in the mind, and that the efforts of men to secure peace by other processes than by inward purification, are vain strivings; and Christianity is not only consistent with, but founded on, this great truth; teaching us, that the kingdom of heaven is within us, and proposing, as its great end, to rescue the mind from evil, and to endue it with strength and dignity worthy its divine origin. — Again, when I look into the soul I meet intimations of another great truth. I discern in it capacities which are not fully unfolded here. I see desires which find no adequate good on earth. I see a principle of hope always pressing forward into futurity. Here are marks of a nature not made wholly for this world; and how does Christianity agree with this teaching of our own souls? Its great doctrine is that of a higher life, where the spiritual germ within us will open for ever, and where the immortal good after which the mind aspires will prove a reality. — Had I time, I might survey distinctly the various principles of the soul, the intellectual, moral, social, and active, and might show you how Christianity accords with them all, enlarging their scope and energy, proposing to them nobler objects, and aiding their developement by the impulse of a boundless hope. But, commending these topics to your private meditation, I will take but one more view of the soul. When I look within, I see stains of sin, and fears and forebodings of guilt; and how adapted to such a nature is Christianity, a religion which contains blood-sealed promises of forgiveness to the penitent, and which proffers heavenly strength to fortify us in our conflict with moral evil. — I say, then,

Christianity consists with the nature within us, as well as with nature around us. The highest truths in respect to the soul are not only responded to, but are carried out by Christianity, so that it deserves to be called the perfection of reason.

I have now shown, in a variety of particulars, that Christianity has the character of Consistency, and thus satisfies the first demand of reason. It does not divide the mind against itself, does not introduce discord into the intellect, by proposing doctrines which our consciousness and experience repel. But these views do not exhaust the present topic. It is not enough to speak of Christianity as furnishing views which harmonize with one another, and with all known truth. It gives a new and cheering consistency to the views with which we are furnished by the universe. Nature and providence, with all their beauty, regularity, and beneficence, have yet perplexing aspects. Their elements are often seen in conflict with one another. Sunshine and storms, pleasure and pain, success and disaster, abundance and want, health and sickness, life and death, seem to ordinary spectators to be mixed together confusedly and without aim. Reason desires nothing so earnestly, so anxiously, as to solve these discordant appearances, as to discover some great, central, reconciling truth, around which they may be arranged, and from which they may borrow light and harmony. This deep want of the rational nature, Christianity has supplied. It has disclosed a unity of purpose in the seemingly hostile dispensations of providence, and opened to the mind a new world of order, beauty, and benevolent design. Christianity, revealing, as it does, the unbounded mercy of God to his sinful creatures; revealing an endless futurity, in which the inequalities of the present state are to be redressed, and which reduces by its immensity the sorest pains of life to light and momentary evils; revealing a Moral Perfection, which is worth all pain and conflicts, and which is most effectually and gloriously won amidst suffering and temptation; revealing in Jesus Christ the sublimity and rewards of tried and all-enduring virtue; revealing in Him the founder of a new moral kingdom or power, which is destined to subdue the world to God; and proffering the Holy Spirit to all who strive to build up in themselves and others the reign of truth and virtue; Christianity, I say, by these revelations, has poured a flood of light over nature and providence, and harmonized the infinite complexity of the works and ways of God. Thus it meets the first want of the rational nature, the craving for consistency of views. It is reason's most effectual minister and friend. Is it not, then, eminently a Rational Faith?

Having shown that Christianity has the character of consistency, I proceed to the second mark or stamp of reason on a religion, that is, Universality; and this I claim for Christianity. This indeed is one of the most distinguishing features of our religion, and so obvious and striking as to need little illustration. When I examine the doctrines, precepts, and spirit of Christianity, I discover, in them all, this character of Universality. I discover nothing narrow, temporary, local. The Gospel bears the stamp of no particular age or country. It does not concern itself with the perishable interests of communities or individuals; but appeals to the Spiritual, Immortal, Unbounded principle in human nature. Its aim is to direct the mind to the Infinite Being, and to an Infinite good. It is not made up, like other reigions, of precise forms and details; but it inculcates immutable and all-comprehending principles of duty, leaving every man to apply them for himself to the endless variety of human conditions. It separates from God the partial, limited views of Judaism and heathenism, and holds him forth in the sublime attributes of the Universal Father. In like manner, it inculcates philanthropy without exceptions or bounds; a love to man as man, a love founded on that immortal nature of which all men partake, and which binds us to recognise in each a child of God and a brother. The spirit of bigotry, which confines its charity to a sect, and the spirit of aristocracy, which looks on the multitude as an inferior race, are alike rebuked by Christianity; which, eighteen hundred years ago, in a narrow and superstitious age, taught, what the present age is beginning to understand, that all men are essentially equal, and that all are to be honored, because made for immortality and endued with capacities of ceaseless improvement. The more I examine Christianity, the more I am struck with its universality. I see in it a religion made for all regions and all times, for all classes and all stages of society. It is fitted, not to the Asiatic or the European, but to the essential principles of human nature, to man under the tropical or polar skies, to all descriptions of intellect and condition. It speaks a language which all men need and all can understand; enjoins a virtue, which is man's happiness and glory in every age and clime; and ministers consolations and hopes which answer to man's universal lot, to the sufferings, the fear, and the self-rebuke, which cleave to our nature in every outward change. I see in it the light, not of one nation, but of the world ; and a light reaching beyond the world, beyond time, to higher modes of existence and to an interminable futurity. Other religions have been intended to meet the exigencies of particular countries or times, and therefore society in its progress has outgrown them ; but Christianity meets more and more the wants of the soul in proportion to the advancement of our race, and thus proves itself to be Eternal Truth. After these remarks, may I not claim for Christianity that character of universality which is the highest distinction of reason ? To understand fully the confirmation which these views give to the Gospel, you must compare it with the religions prevalent in the age of Christ, all of which bore the marks of narrow, local, temporary institutions. How striking the contrast ! And how singular the fact, that amid this darkness there sprung up a religion so consistent and universal, as to deserve to be called the perfection of reason !

I do and must feel, my friends, that the claim of Christianity to the honor of being a rational religion, is fully established. As such I commend it to you. As such it will more and more approve itself, in proportion as you study and practise it. You will never find cause to complain, that by adopting it you have enslaved or degraded your highest powers. Here, then, I might stop, and might consider my work as done But I am aware that objections have been made to the rational character of our religion, which may still linger in the minds of some of my hearers. A brief notice of these may aid the purpose, and will form a proper conclusion, of this discourse.

I imagine that were some who are present to speak

they would tell me, that if Christianity be judged by its fruits, it deserves any character but that of rational. I should be told that no religion has borne a more abundant harvest of extravagance and fanaticism. I should be told that reason is a calm, reflecting, sober principle, and I should be asked whether such is the character of the Christianity which has overspread the world. Perhaps some of you will remind me of the feverish, wild, passionate religion, which is now systematically dispersed through our country, and I shall be asked whether a system under which such delusions prevail can be a rational one.

To these objections I answer, You say much that is true. I grant that reason is a calm and reflecting principle, and I see little calmness or reflection among many who take exclusively the name of Christ. But I say, you have no right to confound Christianity with its professors. This religion, as you know, has come down to us through many ages of darkness, during which it must have been corrupted and obscured. Common candor requires that you should judge of it as it came from its Founder. Go, then, to its original records; place yourselves near Jesus; and tell me if you ever found yourselves in the presence of so calm a teacher. We indeed discern in Jesus great earnestness, but joined with entire self-control. Sensibility breathes through his whole teaching and life, but always tempered with wisdom. Amidst his boldest thoughts and expressions, we discover no marks of ungoverned feeling or a diseased imagination. Take, as an example, his longest discourse, the Sermon on the Mount. How weighty the thoughts! How grave and dignified the style! You recollect, that the multitude were astonished, not at the passionate vehemence, but at the authority, with which he spoke. Read next the last discourse of Jesus to his disciples in St. John's Gospel. What a deep, yet mild and subdued tenderness mingles with conscious greatness in that wonderful address. Take what is called the Lord's Prayer, which Jesus gave as the model of all prayer to God. Does that countenance fanatical fervor, or violent appeals to our Creator ? Let me further ask, Does Jesus anywhere place religion in tumultuous, ungoverned emotion ? Does he not teach us, that obedience, not feeling, marks and constitutes true piety, and that the most acceptable offering to God is to exercise mercy to our fellow-creatures ? When I compare the clamorous preaching and passionate declamation, too common in the Christian world, with the composed dignity, the deliberate wisdom, the freedom from all extravagance, which characterized Jesus, I can imagine no greater contrast ; and I am sure that the fiery zealot is no representative of Christianity.

I have done with the first objection ; but another class of objections is often urged against the reasonable character of our religion. It has been strenuously maintained, that Christianity contains particular doctrines which are irrational, and which involve the whole religion to which they are essential, in their own condemnation. To this class of objections I have a short reply. I insist that these offensive doctrines do not belong to Christianity, but are human additions, and therefore do not derogate from its reasonableness and truth. What is the doctrine most frequently adduced to fix the charge of irrationality on the Gospel ? It is the Trinity. This is pronounced by the unbeliever a gross offence to reason It teaches that there is one God, and yet that there are three divine persons. According to the doctrine, these three persons perform different offices, and sustain different relations to each other. One is Father, another his Son. One sends, another is sent. They love each other, converse with each other, and make a covenant with each other; and yet, with all these distinctions, they are, according to the doctrine, not different beings, but one being, one and the same God. Is this a rational doctrine? has often been the question of the objector to Christianity. I answer, No. I can as easily believe that the whole human race are one man, as that three infinite persons, performing such different offices, are one God. But I maintain, that, because the Trinity is irrational, it does not follow that the same reproach belongs to Christianity; for this doctrine is no part of the Christian religion. I know, there are passages which are continually quoted in its defence; but allow me to prove doctrines in the same way, that is, by detaching texts from their connexion and interpreting them without reference to the general current of Scripture, and I can prove any thing and every thing from the Bible. I can prove, that God has human passions. I can prove transubstantiation, which is taught much more explicitly than the Trinity. Detached texts prove nothing. Christ is called God; the same title is given to Moses and to rulers. Christ has said, "I and my Father are one;" so he prayed that all his disciples might be one, meaning not one and the same being, but one in affection and purpose. I ask you, before you judge on this point, to read the Scriptures as a whole, and to inquire into their general strain and teaching in regard to Christ. I find him uniformly distinguishing between himself and God, calling himself, not God the Son, but the Son of God, continually speaking of himself as sent by God, continually referring his power and miracles to God. I hear him saying, that of himself he can do nothing, and praying to his Father under the character of the only true God. Such I affirm to be the tenor, the current, the general strain of the New Testament; and the scattered passages, on which a different doctrine is built, should have no weight against this host of witnesses. Do not rest your faith on a few texts. Sometimes these favorite texts are no part of Scripture. For example, the famous passage on which the Trinity mainly rests, " There are three that bear record in Heaven, the Father, the Word, and the Holy Ghost, and these three are one," — this text, I say, though found at present in John's Epistle, and read in our churches, has been pronounced by the ablest critics a forgery; and a vast majority of the educated ministers of this country are satisfied, that it is not a part of Scripture. Suffer no man, then, to select texts for you as decisive of religious controversies. Read the whole record for yourselves, and possess yourselves of its general import. I am very desirous to separate the doctrine in question from Christianity, because it fastens the charge of irrationality on the whole religion. It is one of the great obstacles to the propagation of the Gospel. The Jews will not hear of a Trinity. I have seen in the countenance, and heard in the tones of the voice, the horror with which that people shrink from the doctrine, that God died on the cross. Mahometans, too, when they hear this opinion from Christian missionaries, repeat the first article of their faith, " There is one God;" and look with pity or scorn on the disciples of Jesus, as deserters of the plainest and greatest truth of religion. Even the Indian of our wilderness, who worships the Great Spirit, has charged absurdity on the teacher who has gone to indoctrinate him in a Trinity. How many, too, in Christian countries, have suspected the whole religion for this one error. Believing, then, as I do, that it forms no part of Christianity, my allegiance to Jesus Christ calls me openly to withstand it. In so doing I would wound no man's feelings. I doubt not, that they who adopt this doctrine intend, equally with those who oppose it, to render homage to the truth and service to Christianity. They think that their peculiar faith gives new interest to the character and new authority to the teaching of Jesus. But they grievously err. The views, by which they hope to build up love towards Christ, detract from the perfection of his Father; and I fear, that the kind of piety, which prevails now in the Christian world, bears witness to the sad influence of this obscuration of the true glory of God. We need not desert reason or corrupt Christianity, to insure the purest, deepest love towards the only true God, or towards Jesus Christ, whom he has sent for our redemption.

I have named one doctrine, which is often urged against Christianity as irrational. There is one more on which I would offer a few remarks. Christianity has often been reproached with teaching, that God brings men into life totally depraved, and condemns immense multitudes to everlasting misery for sins to which their nature has irresistibly impelled them. This is said to be irrational, and consequently such must be the religion which teaches it. I certainly shall not attempt to vindicate this theological fiction. A more irrational doctrine could not, I think, be contrived; and it is something worse; it is as immoral in its tendency, as it is unreasonable. It is suited to alienate men from God and from one another. Were it really believed (which it cannot be), men would look up with dread and detestation to the Author of their being, and look round with horror on their fellow-creatures. It would dissolve society. Were men to see in one another wholly corrupt beings, incarnate fiends, without one genuine virtue, society would become as repulsive as a den of lions or a nest of vipers. All confidence, esteem, love, would die; and without these, the interest, charm, and worth of existence would expire. What a pang would shoot through a parent's heart, if he were to see in the smiling infant a moral being continually and wholly propense to sin, in whose mind were thickly sown the seeds of hatred to God and goodness, and who had commenced his existence under the curse of his Creator? What good man could consent to be a parent, if his offspring were to be born to this infinitely wretched inheritance? I say, the doctrine is of immoral tendency; but I do not say that they who profess it are immoral. The truth is, that none do or can hold it in its full and proper import. I have seen its advocates smile as benignantly on the child whom their creed has made a demon, as if it were an angel; and I have seen them mingling with their fellow-creatures as cordially and confidingly as if the doctrine of total depravity had never entered their ears. Perhaps the most mischievous effect of the doctrine is the dishonor which it has thrown on Christianity. This dishonor I would wipe away. Christianity teaches no such doctrine. Where do you find it in the New Testament? Did Jesus teach it, when he took little children in his arms and blessed them, and said "Of such is the kingdom of God"? Did Paul teach it, when he spoke of the Gentiles, who have not the law, or a written revelation, but who do by nature the things contained in the law? Christainity indeed speaks strongly of human guilt, but always treats men as beings who have the power of doing right, and who have come into existence under the smile of their Creator.

I have now completed my vindication of the claim of the Gospel to the character of a rational religion; and my aim has been, not to serve a party, but the cause of our common Christianity. At the present day, one of the most urgent duties of its friends is, to rescue it from the reproach of waging war with reason. The character of our age demands this. There have been times when Christianity, though loaded with unreasonable doctrines, retained its hold on men's faith; for men had not learned to think. They received their religion as children learn the catechism; they substituted the priest for their own understandings, and cared neither what nor why they believed. But that day is gone by, and the spirit of freedom, which has succeeded it, is subjecting Christianity to a scrutiny more and more severe; and if this religion cannot vindicate itself to the reflecting, the calm, the wise, as a reasonable service, it cannot stand. Fanatical sects may, for a time, spread an intolerant excitement through a community, and impose silence on the objections of the skeptical. But fanaticism is the epidemic of a season; it wastes itself by its own violence. Sooner or later the voice of reflection will be heard. Men will ask, What are the claims of Christianity? Does it bear the marks of truth? And if it be found to war with nature and reason, it will be, and it ought to be abandoned. On this ground, I am anxious that Christianity should be cleared from all human additions and corruptions. If indeed irrational doctrines belong to it, then I have no desire to separate them from it. I have no desire, for the sake of upholding the Gospel, to wrap up and conceal, much less to deny, any of its real principles. Did I think that it was burdened with one irrational doctrine, I would say so, and I would leave it, as I found it, with this millstone round its neck. But I know none such. I meet, indeed, some difficulties in the narrative part of the New Testament; and there are arguments in the Epistles, which, however suited to the Jews, to whom they were first addressed, are not apparently adapted to men at large; but I see not a principle of the religion, which my reason, calmly and impartially exercised, pronounces inconsistent with any great truth. I have the strongest conviction, that Christianity is reason in its most perfect form, and therefore I plead for its disengagement from the irrational additions with which it has been clogged for ages.

With these views of Christianity, I do and I must hold it fast. I cannot surrender it to the cavils or scoffs of infidelity. I do not blush to own it, for it is a rational religion. It satisfies the wants of the intellect as well as those of the heart. I know that men of strong minds have opposed it. But, as if Providence intended that their sophistry should carry a refutation on its own front, they have generally fallen into errors so gross and degrading, as to prove them to be any thing rather than the apostles of reason. When I go from the study of Christianity to their writings, I feel as if I were passing from the warm, bright sun into a chilling twilight, which too often deepens into utter darkness. I am not, then, ashamed of the Gospel. I see it glorified by the hostile systems which are reared for its destruction. I follow Jesus, because he is eminently "the Light"; and I doubt not, that, to his true disciples, he will be a guide to that world, where the obscurities of our present state will be dispersed, and where reason as well as virtue will be unfolded under the quickening influence and in the more manifest presence of God.

6*

SPIRITUAL FREEDOM.

DISCOURSE
PREACHED AT THE ANNUAL ELECTION,
MAY 26, 1830.

JOHN viii. 31, 32. 36: "Then said Jesus to those Jews which believed on him, If ye continue in my word, then are ye my disciples indeed; and ye shall know the truth, and the truth shall make you free." "If the Son therefore shall make you free, ye shall be free indeed."

THE Scriptures continually borrow from nature and social life, illustrations and emblems of spiritual truth. The character, religion, and blessings of Jesus Christ, are often placed before us by sensible images. His influences on the mind are shadowed forth by the light of the sun, by the vital union of the head with the members, by the shepherd bringing back the wandering flock, by the vine which nourishes and fructifies the branches, by the foundation sustaining the edifice, by bread and wine invigorating the animal frame. In our text we have a figurative illustration of his influence or religion, peculiarly intelligible and dear to this community. He speaks of himself as giving freedom, that great good of individuals and states; and by this similitude he undoubtedly intended to place before men, in a strong and attractive light, that spiritual and inward liberty which his truth confers on its obedient disciples. Inward, spiritual liberty, this is the great gift of Jesus Christ. This will be the chief topic of the present discourse. I wish to show, that this is the supreme good of men, and that civil and political liberty has but little worth, but as it springs from and invigorates this.

From what I have now said, the general tone of this discourse may be easily anticipated. I shall maintain, that the highest interest of communities, as well as individuals, is a spiritual interest; that outward and earthly goods are of little worth, but as bearing on the mind, and tending to its liberation, strength, and glory. And I am fully aware that in taking that course, I lay myself open to objection. I shall be told, that I show my ignorance of human nature, in attempting to interest men by such refined views of society; that I am too speculative; that spiritual liberty is too unsubstantial and visionary to be proposed to statesmen as an end in legislation; that the dreams of the closet should not be obtruded on practical men; that gross and tangible realities can alone move the multitude; and that to talk to politicians of the spiritual interests of society as of supreme importance, is as idle as to try to stay with a breath the force of the whirlwind.

I anticipate such objections. But they do not move me. I firmly believe, that the only truth which is to do men lasting good, is that which relates to the soul, which carries them into its depths, which reveals to them its powers and the purposes of its creation. The progress of society is retarded, by nothing more than by the low views which its leaders are accustomed to take of human nature. Man has a mind as well as a body, and this he ought to know; and till he knows it, feels it, and is deeply penetrated by it, he knows nothing aright. His body should, in a sense, vanish away before his mind; or, in the language of Christ, he should hate his animal life in comparison with the intellectual and moral life which is to endure for ever. This doctrine, however, is pronounced too refined. Useful and practical truth, according to its most improved expositors, consists in knowing that we have an animal nature, and in making this our chief care; in knowing that we have mouths to be filled, and limbs to be clothed; that we live on the earth, which it is our business to till; that we have a power of accumulating wealth, and that this power is the measure of the greatness of the community! For such doctrines I have no respect. I know no wisdom but that which reveals man to himself, and which teaches him to regard all social institutions, and his whole life, as the means of unfolding and exalting the spirit within him. All policy which does not recognise this truth, seems to me shallow. The statesman who does not look at the bearing of his measures on the mind of a nation, is unfit to touch one of men's great interests. Unhappily, statesmen have seldom understood the sacredness of human nature and human society. Hence, policy has become almost a contaminated word. Hence, government has so often been the scourge of mankind.

I mean not to disparage political science. The best constitution and the best administration of a state, are subjects worthy of the profoundest thought. But there are deeper foundations of public prosperity than these.

The statesman who would substitute these for that virtue which they ought to subserve and exalt, will only add his name to the long catalogue which history preserves of baffled politicians. It is idle to hope, by our short-sighted contrivances, to insure to a people a happiness which their own character has not earned. The everlasting laws of God's moral government we cannot repeal; and parchment constitutions, however wise, will prove no shelter from the retributions which fall on a degraded community.

With these convictions, I feel that no teaching is so practical as that which impresses on a people the importance of their spiritual interests. With these convictions, I feel that I cannot better meet the demands of this occasion, than by leading you to prize, above all other rights and liberties, that inward freedom which Christ came to confer. To this topic I now solicit your attention.

And first, I may be asked what I mean by Inward, Spiritual Freedom. The common and true answer is, that it is freedom from sin. I apprehend, however, that to many, if not to most, these words are too vague to convey a full and deep sense of the greatness of the blessing. Let me, then, offer a brief explanation; and the most important remark in illustrating this freedom, is that it is not a negative state, not the mere absence of sin; for such a freedom may be ascribed to inferior animals, or to children before becoming moral agents. Spiritual freedom is the attribute of a mind, in which reason and conscience have begun to act, and which is free through its own energy, through fidelity to the truth, through resistance of temptation. I cannot therefore better give my views of spiritual freedom, than by say

SPIRITUAL FREEDOM. 71

ing, that it is moral energy or force of holy purpose put forth against the senses, against the passions, against the world, and thus liberating the intellect, conscience, and will, so that they may act with strength and unfold themselves for ever. The essence of spiritual freedom is power. A man liberated from sensual lusts by a palsy, would not therefore be inwardly free. He only is free, who, through self-conflict and moral resolution, sustained by trust in God, subdues the passions which have debased him, and, escaping the thraldom of low objects, binds himself to pure and lofty ones. That mind alone is free, which, looking to God as the inspirer and rewarder of virtue, adopts his law, written on the heart and in his word, as its supreme rule, and which, in obedience to this, governs itself, reveres itself, exerts faithfully its best powers, and unfolds itself by well-doing, in whatever sphere God's providence assigns.

It has pleased the All-wise Disposer to encompass us from our birth by difficulty and allurement, to place us in a world where wrong-doing is often gainful, and duty rough and perilous, where many vices oppose the dictates of the inward monitor, where the body presses as a weight on the mind, and matter, by its perpetual agency on the senses, becomes a barrier between us and the spiritual world. We are in the midst of influences, which menace the intellect and heart; and to be free, is to withstand and conquer these.

I call that mind free, which masters the senses, which protects itself against animal appetites, which contemns pleasure and pain in comparison with its own energy, which penetrates beneath the body and recognises its own reality and greatness, which passes life, not in asking what it shall eat or drink, but in hungering, thirsting, and seeking after righteousness.

I call that mind free, which escapes the bondage of matter, which, instead of stopping at the material universe and making it a prison wall, passes beyond it to its Author, and finds in the radiant signatures which it everywhere bears of the Infinite Spirit, helps to its own spiritual enlargement.

I call that mind free, which jealously guards its intellectual rights and powers, which calls no man master, which does not content itself with a passive or hereditary faith, which opens itself to light whencesoever it may come, which receives new truth as an angel from heaven, which, whilst consulting others, inquires still more of the oracle within itself, and uses instructions from abroad, not to supersede but to quicken and exalt its own energies.

I call that mind free, which sets no bounds to its love, which is not imprisoned in itself or in a sect, which recognises in all human beings the image of God and the rights of his children, which delights in virtue and sympathizes with suffering wherever they are seen, which conquers pride, anger, and sloth, and offers itself up a willing victim to the cause of mankind.

I call that mind free, which is not passively framed by outward circumstances, which is not swept away by the torrent of events, which is not the creature of accidental impulse, but which bends events to its own improvement, and acts from an inward spring, from immutable principles which it has deliberately espoused.

I call that mind free, which protects itself against the usurpations of society, which does not cower to human opinion, which feels itself accountable to a higher tribunal than man's, which respects a higher law than fashion, which respects itself too much to be the slave or tool of the many or the few.

I call that mind free, which, through confidence in God and in the power of virtue, has cast off all fear but that of wrong-doing, which no menace or peril can enthrall, which is calm in the midst of tumults, and possesses itself though all else be lost.

I call that mind free, which resists the bondage of habit, which does not mechanically repeat itself and copy the past, which does not live on its old virtues, which does not enslave itself to precise rules, but which forgets what is behind, listens for new and higher monitions of conscience, and rejoices to pour itself forth in fresh and higher exertions.

I call that mind free, which is jealous of its own freedom, which guards itself from being merged in others, which guards its empire over itself as nobler than the empire of the world.

In fine, I call that mind free, which, conscious of its affinity with God, and confiding in his promises by Jesus Christ, devotes itself faithfully to the unfolding of all its powers, which passes the bounds of time and death, which hopes to advance for ever, and which finds inexhaustible power, both for action and suffering, in the prospect of immortality.

Such is the spiritual freedom which Christ came to give. It consists in moral force, in self-control, in the enlargement of thought and affection, and in the unrestrained action of our best powers. This is the great good of Christianity, nor can we conceive a greater within the gift of God. I know that to many, this will seem too refined a good to be proposed as the great end of society and government. But our skepticism cannot change the nature of things. I know how little this freedom is understood or enjoyed, how enslaved men are to sense, and passion, and the world ; and I know, too, that through this slavery they are wretched, and that while it lasts no social institution can give them happiness.

I now proceed, as I proposed, to show, that civil or political liberty is of little worth, but as it springs from, expresses, and invigorates this spiritual freedom. I account civil liberty as the chief good of states, because it accords with, and ministers to, energy and elevation of mind. Nor is this a truth so remote or obscure as to need laborious proof or illustration. For consider what civil liberty means. It consists in the removal of all restraint, but such as the public weal demands. And what is the end and benefit of removing restraint? It is that men may put forth their powers, and act from themselves. Vigorous and invigorating action is the chief fruit of all outward freedom. Why break the chains from the captive, but that he may bring into play his liberated limbs? Why open his prison, but that he may go forth, and open his eyes on a wide prospect, and exert and enjoy his various energies? Liberty, which does not minister to action and the growth of power, is only a name, is no better than slavery.

The chief benefit of free institutions is clear and unutterably precious. Their chief benefit is, that they aid freedom of mind, that they give scope to man's faculties, that they throw him on his own resources, and summon him to work out his own happiness. It is, that, by removing restraint from intellect, they favor force, originality, and enlargement of thought. It is, that, by removing restraint from worship, they favor the ascent of the soul to God. It is, that, by removing restraint from industry, they stir up invention and enterprise to explore and subdue the material world, and thus rescue the race from those sore physical wants and pains, which narrow and blight the mind. It is, that they cherish noble sentiments, frankness, courage, and self-respect.

Free institutions contribute in no small degree to freedom and force of mind, by teaching the essential equality of men, and their right and duty to govern themselves; and I cannot but consider the superiority of an elective government, as consisting very much in the testimony which it bears to these ennobling truths. It has often been said, that a good code of laws, and not the form of government, is what determines a people's happiness. But good laws, if not springing from the community, if imposed by a master, would lose much of their value. The best code is that which has its origin in the will of the people who obey it; which, whilst it speaks with authority, still recognises self-government as the primary right and duty of a rational being; and which thus cherishes in the individual, be his condition what it may, a just self-respect.

We may learn, that the chief good and the most precious fruit of civil liberty, is spiritual freedom and power, by considering what is the chief evil of tyranny. I know that tyranny does evil by invading men's outward interests, by making property and life insecure, by robbing the laborer to pamper the noble and king. But its worst influence is *within*. Its chief curse is, that it breaks and tames the spirit, sinks man in his own eyes, takes away vigor of thought and action, substitutes for conscience an outward rule, makes him abject, cowardly, a parasite and a cringing slave. This is the curse of tyranny. It wars with the soul, and thus it wars with God. We read in theologians and poets, of angels fighting against the Creator, of battles in heaven. But God's throne in heaven is unassailable. The only war against God is against his image, against the divine principle in the soul, and this is waged by tyranny in all its forms. We here see the chief curse of tyranny; and this should teach us that civil freedom is a blessing, chiefly as it reverences the human soul, and ministers to its growth and power.

Without this inward, spiritual freedom, outward liberty is of little worth. What boots it, that I am crushed by no foreign yoke, if through ignorance and vice, through selfishness and fear, I want the command of my own mind? The worst tyrants are those which establish themselves in our own breast. The man who wants force of principle and purpose, is a slave, however free the air he breathes. The mind, after all, is our only possession, or, in other words, we possess all things through its energy and enlargement; and civil institutions are to be estimated by the free and pure minds to which they give birth.

It will be seen from these remarks, that I consider the freedom or moral strength of the individual mind, as the supreme good, and the highest end of government. I am aware that other views are often taken. It is said that government is intended for the public, for the community, not for the individual. The idea of a national interest prevails in the minds of statesmen, and to this it is thought that the individual may be sacrificed. But I would maintain, that the individual is not made for the state, so much as the state for the individual. A man is not created for political relations as his highest end, but for indefinite spiritual progress, and is placed in political relations as the means of his progress. The human soul is greater, more sacred, than the state, and must never be sacrificed to it. The human soul is to outlive all earthly institutions. The distinction of nations is to pass away. Thrones, which have stood for ages, are to meet the doom pronounced upon all man's works. But the individual mind survives, and the obscurest subject, if true to God, will rise to a power never wielded by earthly potentates.

A human being is a member of the community, not as a limb is a member of the body, or as a wheel is a part of a machine, intended only to contribute to some general, joint result. He was created, not to be merged in the whole, as a drop in the ocean, or as a particle of sand on the sea-shore, and to aid only in composing a mass. He is an ultimate being, made for his own perfection as the highest end, made to maintain an individual existence, and to serve others only as far as consists with his own virtue and progress. Hitherto governments have tended greatly to obscure this importance of the individual, to depress him in his own eyes, to give him the idea of an outward interest more important than the invisible soul, and of an outward authority more sacred than the voice of God in his own secret conscience. Rulers have called the private man the property of the state, meaning generally by the state themselves, and thus the many have been immolated to the few, and have even believed that this was their highest destination. These views cannot be too earnestly withstood. Nothing seems to me so needful as to give to the mind the consciousness, which governments have done so much to suppress, of its own separate worth. Let the individual feel, that, through his immortality, he may concentrate in his own being a greater good than that of nations. Let him feel that he is placed in the community, not to part with his individuality, or to become a tool, but that he should find a sphere for his various powers, and a preparation for, immortal glory. To me, the progress of society consists in nothing more, than in bringing out the individual, in giving him a consciousness of his own being, and in quickening him to strengthen and elevate his own mind.

In thus maintaining that the individual is the end of social institutions, I may be thought to discourage public efforts and the sacrifice of private interests to the state. Far from it. No man, I affirm, will serve his fellow-beings so effectually, so fervently, as he who is not their slave; as he who, casting off every other yoke, subjects himself to the law of duty in his own mind. For this law enjoins a disinterested and generous spirit, as man's glory and likeness to his Maker. Individuality, or moral self-subsistence, is the surest foundation of an all-comprehending love. No man so multiplies his bonds with the community, as he who watches most jealously over his own perfection. There is a beautiful harmony between the good of the state and the moral freedom and dignity of the individual. Were it not so, were these interests in any case discordant, were an individual ever called to serve his country by acts debasing his own mind, he ought not to waver a moment as to the good which he should prefer. Property, life, he should joyfully surrender to the state. But his soul he must never stain or enslave. From poverty, pain, the rack, the gibbet, he should not recoil; but for no good of others ought he to part with self-control, or violate the inward law. We speak of the patriot as sacrificing himself to the public weal Do we mean, that he sacrifices what is most properly himself, the principle of piety and virtue? Do we not feel, that, however great may be the good, which, through his sufferings, accrues to the state, a greater and purer glory redounds to himself, and that the most precious fruit of his disinterested services, is the strength of resolution and philanthropy which is accumulated in his own soul?

I have thus endeavoured to illustrate and support the doctrine, that spiritual freedom, or force and elevation of soul, is the great good to which civil freedom is subordinate, and which all social institutions should propose as their supreme end.

I proceed to point out some of the means by which this spiritual liberty may be advanced; and, passing over a great variety of topics, I shall confine myself to two;—Religion and Government.

I begin with Religion, the mightiest agent in human affairs. To this belongs preëminently the work of freeing and elevating the mind. All other means are comparatively impotent. The sense of God is the only spring, by which the crushing weight of sense, of the world, and temptation, can be withstood. Without a consciousness of our relation to God, all other relations will prove adverse to spiritual life and progress. I have spoken of the religious sentiment as the mightiest agent on earth. It has accomplished more, it has strengthened men to do and suffer more, than all other principles. It can sustain the mind against all other powers. Of all principles it is the deepest, the most ineradicable. In its perversion, indeed, it has been fruitful of crime and woe; but the very energy which it has given to the passions, when they have mixed with and corrupted it, teaches us the omnipotence with which it is imbued.

Religion gives life, strength, elevation to the mind, by connecting it with the Infinite Mind; by teaching it to regard itself as the offspring and care of the Infinite Father, who created it that he might communicate to it his own spirit and perfections, who framed it for truth and virtue, who framed it for himself, who subjects it to sore trials, that by conflict and endurance it may grow strong, and who has sent his Son to purify it from every sin, and to clothe it with immortality. It is religion alone, which nourishes patient, resolute hopes and efforts for our own souls. Without it, we can hardly escape self-contempt, and the contempt of our race. Without God, our existence has no support, our life no aim, our improvements no permanence, our best labors no sure and enduring results, our spiritual weakness no power to lean upon, and our noblest aspirations and desires no pledge of being realized in a better state. Struggling virtue has no friend; suffering virtue no promise of victory. Take away God, and life becomes mean, and man poorer than the brute.— I am accustomed to speak of the greatness of human nature; but it is great only through its parentage; great, because descended from God, because connected with a goodness and power from which it is to be enriched for ever; and nothing but the consciousness of this connexion, can give that hope of elevation, through which alone the mind is to rise to true strength and liberty.

All the truths of religion conspire to one end, spiritual liberty. All the objects which it offers to our thoughts are sublime, kindling, exalting. Its fundamental truth is the existence of one God, one Infinite and Everlasting Father; and it teaches us to look on the universe as pervaded, quickened, and vitally joined into one harmonious and beneficent whole, by his ever-present and omnipotent love. By this truth it breaks the power of matter and sense, of present pleasure and pain, of anxiety and fear. It turns the mind from the visible, the outward and perishable, to the Unseen, Spiritual, and Eternal, and, allying it with pure and great objects, makes it free.

I well know, that what I now say, may seem to some to want the sanction of experience. By many, religion is perhaps regarded as the last principle to give inward energy and freedom. I may be told of its threatenings, and of the bondage which they impose. I acknowledge that religion has threatenings, and it *must* have them; for evil, misery, is necessarily and unchangeably bound up with wrong-doing, with the abuse of moral power. From the nature of things, a mind disloyal to God and duty, must suffer; and religion, in uttering this, only re-echoes the plain teaching of conscience. But let it be remembered, that the single end of the threatenings of religion, is to make us spiritually free. They are all directed against the passions which enthrall and degrade us. They are weapons given to conscience, with which to fight the good fight, and to establish its throne within us. When not thus used, they are turned from their end; and if by injudicious preaching they engender superstition, let not the fault be laid at the door of religion.

I do not indeed wonder that so many doubt the power of religion to give strength, dignity, and freedom to the mind. What bears this name too often yields no such fruits. Here, religion is a form, a round of prayers and rites, an attempt to propitiate God by flattery and fawning. There, it is terror and subjection to a minister or priest; and there, it is a violence of emotion, bearing away the mind like a whirlwind, and robbing it of self-direction. But true religion disclaims connexion with these usurpers of its name. It is a calm, deep conviction of God's paternal interest in the improvement, happiness, and honor of his creatures; a practical persuasion, that he delights in virtue and not in forms and flatteries, and that he especially delights in resolute effort to conform ourselves to the disinterested love and rectitude which constitute his own glory. It is for this religion, that I claim the honor of giving dignity and freedom to the mind.

The need of religion to accomplish this work, is in no degree superseded by what is called the progress of society. I should say that civilization, so far from being able of itself to give moral strength and elevation, includes causes of degradation, which nothing but the religious principle can withstand. It multiplies, undoubtedly, the comforts and enjoyments of life; but in these I see sore trials and perils to the soul. These minister to the sensual element in human nature, to that part of our constitution, which allies, and too often enslaves us, to the earth. Of consequence, civilization needs, that proportional aid should be given to the spiritual element in man, and I know not where it is to be found but in religion. Without this, the civilized man, with all his properties and refinements, rises little in true dignity above the savage whom he disdains. You tell me of civilization, of ts arts and sciences, as the sure instruments of human elevation. You tell me, how by these man masters and bends to his use the powers of nature. I know he masters them, but it is to become in turn their slave He explores and cultivates the earth, but it is to grow more earthly. He explores the hidden mine, but it is to forge himself chains. He visits all regions, but therefore lives a stranger to his own soul. In the very progress of civilization, I see the need of an antagonist principle to the senses, of a power to free man from matter, to recall him from the outward to the inward world ; and religion alone is equal to so great a work.

The advantages of civilization have their peril. In such a state of society, opinion and law impose salutary restraint, and produce general order and security. But the power of opinion grows into a despotism, which more than all things, represses original and free thought, subverts individuality of character, reduces the community to a spiritless monotony, and chills the love of perfection. Religion, considered simply as the principle, which balances the power of human opinion, which takes man out of the grasp of custom and fashion, and teaches him to refer himself to a higher tribunal, is an infinite aid to moral strength and elevation.

An important benefit of civilization, of which we hear much from the political economist, is the division of labor, by which arts are perfected. But this, by confining the mind to an unceasing round of petty operations, tends to break it into littleness. We possess improved fabrics, but deteriorated men. Another advantage of civilization is, that manners are refined, and accomplishments multiplied ; but these are continually seen to supplant simplicity of character, strength of feeling, the love of nature, the love of inward beauty and glory. Under **outward** courtesy, we see a cold selfishness, a spirit of calculation, and little energy of love.

I confess I look round on civilized society with many fears, and with more and more earnest desire, that a regenerating spirit from heaven, from religion, may descend upon and pervade it. I particularly fear, that various causes are acting powerfully among ourselves, to inflame and madden that enslaving and degrading principle, the passion for property. For example, the absence of hereditary distinctions in our country, gives prominence to the distinction of wealth, and holds up this as the chief prize to ambition. Add to this the epicurean, self-indulgent habits, which our prosperity has multiplied, and which crave insatiably for enlarging wealth as the only means of gratification. This peril is increased by the spirit of our times, which is a spirit of commerce, industry, internal improvements, mechanical invention, political economy, and peace. Think not that I would disparage commerce, mechanical skill, and especially pacific connexions among states. But there is danger that these blessings may by perversion issue in a slavish love of lucre. It seems to me, that some of the objects which once moved men most powerfully, are gradually losing their sway, and thus the mind is left more open to the excitement of wealth. For example, military distinction is taking the inferior place which it deserves; and the consequence will be, that the energy and ambition, which have been exhausted in war, will seek new directions; and happy shall we be if they do not flow into the channel of gain. So I think that political eminence is to be less and less coveted; and there is danger that the energies absorbed by it will be spent in seeking another kind of dominion, the dominion of property. And if such be the result, what shall we gain by what is called the progress of society? What shall we gain by national peace, if men, instead of meeting on the field of battle, wage with one another the more inglorious strife of dishonest and rapacious traffic? What shall we gain by the waning of political ambition, if the intrigues of the exchange take place of those of the cabinet, and private pomp and luxury be substituted for the splendor of public life? I am no foe to civilization. I rejoice in its progress. But I mean to say, that, without a pure religion to modify its tendencies, to inspire and refine it, we shall be corrupted, not ennobled by it. It is the excellence of the religious principle, that it aids and carries forward civilization, extends science and arts, multiplies the conveniences and ornaments of life, and at the same time spoils them of their enslaving power, and even converts them into means and ministers of that spiritual freedom, which, when left to themselves, they endanger and destroy.

In order, however, that religion should yield its full and best fruits, one thing is necessary; and the times require that I should state it with great distinctness. It is necessary that religion should be held and professed in a liberal spirit. Just as far as it assumes an intolerant, exclusive, sectarian form, it subverts, instead of strengthening, the soul's freedom, and becomes the heaviest and most galling yoke which is laid on the intellect and conscience. Religion must be viewed, not as a monopoly of priests, ministers, or sects, not as conferring on any man a right to dictate to his fellow-beings, not as an instrument by which the few may awe the many, not as bestowing on one a prerogative which is not enjoyed by all, but as the property of every human being, and as the great subject for every human mind. It must be regarded as the revelation of a common Father, to whom all have equal access, who invites all to the like immediate communion, who has no favorites, who has appointed no infallible expounders of his will, who opens his works and word to every eye, and calls upon all to read for themselves, and to follow fearlessly the best convictions of their own understandings. Let religion be seized on by individuals or sects, as their special province; let them clothe themselves with God's prerogative of judgment; let them succeed in enforcing their creed by penalties of law, or penalties of opinion; let them succeed in fixing a brand on virtuous men, whose only crime is free investigation; and religion becomes the most blighting tyranny which can establish itself over the mind. You have all heard of the outward evils, which religion, when thus turned into tyranny, has inflicted; how it has dug dreary dungeons, kindled fires for the martyr, and invented instruments of exquisite torture. But to me all this is less fearful than its influence over the mind. When I see the superstitions which it has fastened on the conscience, the spiritual terrors with which it has haunted and subdued the ignorant and susceptible, the dark, appalling views of God which it has spread far and wide, the dread of inquiry which it has struck into superior understandings, and the servility of spirit which it has made to pass for piety, — when I see all this, the fire, the scaffold, and the outward inquisition, terrible as they are, seem to me inferior evils. I look with a solemn joy on the heroic spirits, who have met freely and fearlessly pain and death in the cause of truth and human rights. But there are other victims of intolerance, on whom I look with unmixed sorrow. They are those, who, spell-bound by early prejudice, or by intimidations from the pulpit and the press, dare not think; who anxiously stifle every doubt or misgiving in regard to their opinions, as if to doubt were a crime; who shrink from the seekers after truth as from infection; who deny all virtue, which does not wear the livery of their own sect; who, surrendering to others their best powers, receive unresistingly a teaching which wars against reason and conscience; and who think it a merit to impose on such as live within their influence, the grievous bondage, which they bear themselves. How much to be deplored is it, that religion, the very principle which is designed to raise men above the judgment and power of man, should become the chief instrument of usurpation over the soul.

Is it said, that in this country, where the rights of private judgment, and of speaking and writing according to our convictions, are guarantied with every solemnity by institutions and laws, religion can never degenerate into tyranny; that here its whole influence must conspire to the liberation and dignity of the mind? I answer, we discover little knowledge of human nature, if we ascribe to constitutions the power of charming to sleep the spirit of intolerance and exclusion. Almost every other bad passion may sooner be put to rest; and for this plain reason, that intolerance always shelters itself under the name and garb of religious zeal. Be cause we live in a country, where the gross, outward, visible chain is broken, we must not conclude that we are necessarily free. There are chains not made of iron, which eat more deeply into the soul. An espionage of bigotry may as effectually close our lips and chill our hearts, as an armed and hundred-eyed police.

There are countless ways by which men in a free country may encroach on their neighbours' rights. In religion, the instrument is ready made and always at hand. I refer to opinion, combined and organized in sects, and swayed by the clergy. We say we have no Inquisition. But a sect skilfully organized, trained to utter one cry, combined to cover with reproach whoever may differ from themselves, to drown the free expression of opinion by denunciations of heresy, and to strike terror into the multitude by joint and perpetual menace, — such a sect is as perilous and palsying to the intellect as the Inquisition. It serves the ministers as effectually as the sword. The present age is notoriously sectarian, and therefore hostile to liberty. One of the strongest features of our times, is the tendency of men to run into associations, to lose themselves in masses, to think and act in crowds, to act from the excitement of numbers, to sacrifice individuality, to identify themselves with parties and sects. At such a period, we ought to fear, and cannot too much dread, lest a host should be marshalled under some sectarian standard, so numerous and so strong, as to overawe opinion, stifle inquiry, compel dissenters to a prudent silence, and thus accomplish the end, without incurring the odium, of penal laws. We have indeed no small protection against this evil, in the multiplicity of sects. But let us not forget, that coalitions are as practicable and as perilous in church as in state; and that minor differences, as they are called, may be sunk, for the purpose of joint exertion against a common foe. Happily, the spirit of this people, in spite of all narrowing influences, is essentially liberal. Here lies our safety. The liberal spirit of the people, I trust, is more and more to temper and curb that exclusive spirit, which is the besetting sin of their religious guides.

In this connexion I may be permitted to say, and I say it with heartfelt joy, that the government of this Commonwealth has uniformly distinguished itself by the spirit of religious freedom. Intolerance, however rife abroad, has found no shelter in our halls of legislation. As yet, no sentence of proscription has been openly or indirectly passed on any body of men for religious opinions. A wise and righteous jealousy has watched over our religious liberties, and been startled by the first movement, the faintest sign, of sectarian ambition. Our Commonwealth can boast no higher glory. May none of us live to see it fade away.

I have spoken with great freedom of the sectarian and exclusive spirit of our age. I would earnestly recommend liberality of feeling and judgment towards men of different opinions. But, in so doing, I intend not to teach, that opinions are of small moment, or that we should make no effort for spreading such as we deem the truth of God. I do mean, however, that we are to spread them by means which will not enslave ourselves to a party, or bring others into bondage. We must respect alike our own and others' minds. We must not demand a uniformity in religion which exists nowhere else, but expect, and be willing, that the religious principle, like other principles of our nature, should manifest itself in different methods and degrees. Let us not forget, that spiritual, like animal life, may subsist and grow under various forms. Whilst earnestly recommending what we deem the pure and primitive faith, let us remember, that those who differ in word or speculation, may agree in heart; that the spirit of Christianity, though mixed and encumbered with error, is still divine ; and that sects which assign different ranks to Jesus Christ, may still adore that godlike virtue, which constituted him the glorious representative of his Father. Under the disguises of Papal and Protestant Creeds, let us learn to recognise the lovely aspect of Christianity, and rejoice to believe, that, amidst dissonant forms and voices, the common Father discerns and accepts the same deep filial adoration. This is true freedom and enlargement of mind, a liberty which he who knows it would not barter for the widest dominion which priests and sects have usurped over the human soul.

I have spoken of Religion ; I pass to Government, another great means of promoting that spiritual liberty, that moral strength and elevation, which we have seen to be our supreme good. I thus speak of government, not because it always promotes this end, but because it may and should thus operate. Civil institutions should be directed chiefly to a moral or spiritual good, and, until this truth is felt, they will continue, I fear, to be perverted into instruments of crime and misery. Other views of their design, I am aware, prevail. We are sometimes told, that government has no purpose but an earthly one ; that, whilst religion takes care of the soul, government is to watch over outward and bodily interests. This separation of our interests into earthly and spiritual, seems to me unfounded. There is a unity in our whole being. There is one great end for which body and mind were created, and all the relations of life were ordained ; one central aim, to which our whole being should tend ; and this is the unfolding of our intellectual and moral nature ; and no man thoroughly understands government, but he who reverences it as a part of God's stupendous machinery for this sublime design. I do not deny that government is instituted to watch over our present interests. But still it has a spiritual or moral purpose, because present interests are, in an important sense, spiritual; that is, they are instruments and occasions of virtue, calls to duty, sources of obligation, and are only blessings when they contribute to the health of the soul. For example, property, the principal object of legislation, is the material, if I may so speak, on which justice acts, or through which this cardinal virtue is exercised and expressed; and property has no higher end than to invigorate, by calling forth, the principle of impartial rectitude.

Government is the great organ of civil society, and we should appreciate the former more justly, if we better understood the nature and foundation of the latter. I say, then, that society is throughout a moral institution. It is something very different from an assemblage of animals feeding in the same pasture. It is the combination of rational beings for the security of right. Right, a moral idea, lies at the very foundation of civil communities; and the highest happiness which they confer, is the gratification of moral affections. We are sometimes taught, that society is the creature of compact, and selfish calculation; that men agree to live together for the protection of private interests. But no. Society is of earlier and higher origin. It is God's ordinance, and answers to what is most godlike in our nature. The chief ties that hold men together in communities, are not self-interests, or compacts, or positive institutions, or force. They are invisible, refined, spiritual ties, bonds of the mind and heart. Our best powers and affections crave instinctively for society as the sphere in which they are to find their life and happiness. That men may greatly strengthen and improve society by written constitutions, I readily grant. There is, however, a constitution which precedes all of men's making, and after which all others are to be formed; a constitution, the great lines of which are drawn in our very nature; a primitive law of justice, rectitude, and philanthropy, which all other laws are bound to enforce, and from which all others derive their validity and worth.

Am I now asked, how government is to promote energy and elevation of moral principle? I answer, not by making the various virtues matters of legislation, not by preaching morals, not by establishing religion; for these are not its appropriate functions. It is to serve the cause of spiritual freedom, not by teaching or persuasion, but by action; that is, by rigidly conforming itself, in all its measures, to the moral or Christian law; oy the most public and solemn manifestations of reverence for right, for justice, for the general weal, for the principles of virtue. Government is the most conspicuous of human institutions, and were moral rectitude written on its front, stamped conspicuously on all its operations, an immense power would be added to pure principle in the breasts of individuals.

To be more particular, a government may, and should, ennoble the mind of the citizen, by continually holding up to him the idea of the general good. This idea should be impressed in characters of light on all legislation; and a government directing itself resolutely and steadily to this end, becomes a minister of virtue. It teaches the citizen to attach a sanctity to the public weal, carries him beyond selfish regards, nourishes magnanimity, and the purpose of sacrificing himself, as far as virtue will allow, to the commonwealth. On the other hand, a government which wields its power for selfish interests, which sacrifices the many to a few, or the state to a party, becomes a public preacher of crime, taints the mind of the citizen, does its utmost to make him base and venal, and prepares him, by its example, to sell or betray that public interest for which he should be ready to die.

Again, on government, more than on any institution, depends that most important principle, the sense of justice in the community. To promote this, it should express, in all its laws, a reverence for right, and an equal reverence for the rights of high and low, of rich and poor. It should choose to sacrifice the most dazzling advantages, rather than break its own faith, rather than unsettle the fixed laws of property, or in any way shock the sentiment of justice in the community.

Let me add one more method by which government is to lift up and enlarge the minds of its citizens. In its relations to other governments, it should inviolably adhere to the principles of justice and philanthropy. By its moderation, sincerity, uprightness, and pacific spirit towards foreign states, by abstaining from secret arts and unfair advantages, by cultivating free and mutually beneficial intercourse, it should cherish among its citizens the ennobling consciousness of belonging to the human family, and of having a common interest with the whole human race Government only fulfils its end, when it thus joins with Christianity in inculcating the law of universal love.

Unhappily, governments have seldom recognised as the highest duty, the obligation of strengthening pure and noble principle in the community. I fear, they are even to be numbered among the chief agents in corrupting nations. Of all the doctrines by which vice has propagated itself, I know none more pernicious than the maxim, that statesmen are exempted from the common restraints of morality, that nations are not equally bound with individuals by the eternal laws of justice and philanthropy. Through this doctrine, vice has lifted its head unblushingly in the most exalted stations. Vice has seated itself on the throne. The men who have wielded the power and riveted the gaze of nations, have lent the sanction of their greatness to crime. In the very heart of nations, in the cabinet of rulers, has been bred a moral pestilence, which has infected and contaminated all orders of the state. Through the example of rulers, private men have learned to regard the everlasting law as a temporary conventional rule, and been blinded to the supremacy of virtue.

That the prosperity of a people is intimately connected with this reverence for virtue, which I have inculcated on legislators, is most true, and cannot be too deeply felt. There is no foundation for the vulgar doctrine, that a state may flourish by arts and crimes. Nations and individuals are subjected to one law. The moral principle is the life of communities. No calamity can befall a people so great, as temporary success through a criminal policy, as the hope thus cherished of trampling with impunity on the authority of God. Sooner or later, insulted virtue avenges itself terribly on states as well as on private men. We hope, indeed, security and the quiet enjoyment of our wealth, from our laws and institutions. But civil laws find their chief sanction in the law written within by the finger of God. In proportion as a people enslave themselves to sin, the fountain of public justice becomes polluted. The most wholesome statutes, wanting the support of public opinion, grow impotent. Self-seekers, unprincipled men, by flattering bad passions, and by darkening the public mind, usurp the seat of judgment and places of power and trust, and turn free institutions into lifeless forms or instruments of oppression. I especially believe, that communities suffer sorely by that species of immorality which the herd of statesmen have industriously cherished as of signal utility, I mean, by hostile feeling towards other countries. The common doctrine has been, that prejudice and enmity towards foreign states, are means of fostering a national spirit, and of confirming union at home. But bad passions, once instilled into a people, will never exhaust themselves abroad. Vice never yields the fruits of virtue. Injustice to strangers does not breed justice to our friends. Malignity, in every form, is a fire of hell, and the policy which feeds it, is infernal. Domestic feuds and the madness of party are its natural and necessary issues; and a people hostile to others, will demonstrate in its history, that no form of inhumanity or injustice, escapes its just retribution.

Our great error as a people is, that we put an idolatrous trust in our free institutions; as if these, by some magic power, must secure our rights, however we enslave ourselves to evil passions. We need to learn that the forms of liberty are not its essence; that, whilst the letter of a free constitution is preserved, its spirit may be lost; that even its wisest provisions and most guarded powers may be made weapons of tyranny. In a country called free, a majority may become a faction, and a proscribed minority may be insulted, robbed, and oppressed. Under elective governments, a dominant party may become as truly a usurper, and as treasonably conspire against the state, as an individual who forces his way by arms to the throne.

I know that it is supposed, that political wisdom can so form institutions, as to extract from them freedom, notwithstanding a people's sins. The chief expedient for this purpose has been, to balance, as it is called, men's passions and interests against each other, to use one man's selfishness as a check against his neighbour's, to produce peace by the counteraction and equilibrium of hostile forces. This whole theory I distrust. The vices can by no management or skilful poising be made to do the work of virtue. Our own history has already proved this. Our government was founded on the doctrine of checks and balances; and what does experience teach us? It teaches, what the principles of our nature might have taught, that, whenever the country is divided into two great parties, the dominant party will possess itself of both branches of the legislature, and of the different departments of the state, and will move towards its objects with as little check, and with as determined purpose, as if all powers were concentrated in a single body. There is no substitute for virtue. Free institutions secure rights, only when secured by, and when invigorating that spiritual freedom, that moral power and elevation, which I have set before you as the supreme good of our nature.

According to these views, the first duty of a statesman is to build up the moral energy of a people. This is their first interest; and he who weakens it, inflicts an injury which no talent can repair; nor should any splendor of services, or any momentary success, avert from him the infamy which he has earned. Let public men learn to think more reverently of their function. Let them feel that they are touching more vital interests than property. Let them fear nothing so much as to sap the moral convictions of a people, by unrighteous legislation, or a selfish policy. Let them cultivate in themselves the spirit of religion and virtue, as the first requisite to public station. Let no apparent advantage to the community, any more than to themselves, seduce them to the infraction of any moral law. Let them put faith in virtue as the strength of nations. Let them not be disheartened by temporary ill success in upright exertion. Let them remember, that while they and their contemporaries live but for a day, the state is to live for ages; and that Time, the unerring arbiter, will vindicate the wisdom as well as the magnanimity of the public man, who, confiding in the power of truth, justice, and philanthropy, asserts their claims, and reverently follows their monitions, amidst general disloyalty and corruption.

I have hitherto spoken of the general influence which government should exert on the moral interests of a people, by expressing reverence for the moral law in its whole policy and legislation. It is also bound to exert a more particular and direct influence. I refer to its duty of preventing and punishing crime. This is one of the chief ends of government, but it has received as yet very little of the attention which it deserves. Government, indeed, has not been slow to punish crime, nor has society suffered for want of dungeons and gibbets. But the prevention of crime and the reformation of the offender have nowhere taken rank among the first objects of legislation. Penal codes, breathing vengeance, and too often written in blood, have been set in array against the violence of human passions, and the legislator's conscience has been satisfied with enacting these. Whether by shocking humanity he has not multiplied offenders, is a question into which he would do wisely to inquire.

On the means of preventing crime, I want time, and still more ability, to enlarge. I would only say, that this object should be kept in view through the whole of legislation. For this end, laws should be as few and as simple as may be; for an extensive and obscure code multiplies occasions of offence, and brings the citizen unnecessarily into collision with the state. Above all, let the laws bear broadly on their front the impress of justice and humanity, so that the moral sense of the community may become their sanction. Arbitrary and oppressive laws invite offence, and take from disobedience the consciousness of guilt. It is even wise to abstain from laws, which, however wise and good in themselves, have the semblance of inequality, which find no response in the heart of the citizen, and which will be evaded with little remorse. The wisdom of legislation is especially seen in grafting laws on conscience. I add, what seems to me of great importance, that the penal code should be brought to bear with the sternest impartiality on the rich and exalted, as well as on the poor and fallen. Society suffers from the crimes of the former, not less than by those of the latter. It has been truly said, that the amount of property taken by theft and forgery, is small compared with what is taken by dishonest insolvency. Yet the thief is sent to prison, and the dishonest bankrupt lives perhaps in state. The moral sentiment of the community is thus corrupted; and, for this and other solemn reasons, a reform is greatly needed in the laws which respect insolvency. I am shocked at the imprisonment of the honest debtor; and the legislation, which allows a creditor to play the tyrant over an innocent man, would disgrace, I think, a barbarous age. I am not less shocked by the impunity with which criminal insolvents continually escape, and by the lenity of the community towards these transgressors of its most essential laws.

Another means of preventing crime, is to punish it wisely; and by wise punishment, I mean that which aims to reform the offender. I know that this end of punishment has been questioned by wise and good men. But what higher or more practicable end can be proposed? You say, we must punish for example. But history shows that what is called examplary punishment cannot boast of great efficiency. Crime thrives under severe penalties, thrives on the blood of offenders. The frequent exhibition of such punishments hardens a people's heart, and produces defiance and reaction in the guilty. Until recently, government seems to have labored to harden the criminal by throwing him into a crowd of offenders, into the putrid atmosphere of a common prison. Humanity rejoices in the reform, which, in this respect, is spreading through our country. To remove the convict from bad influences is an essential step to his moral restoration. It is however but a step. To place him under the aid of good influence is equally important; and here individual exertion must come to the aid of legislative provisions. Private Christians, selected at once for their judiciousness and philanthropy, must connect themselves with the solitary prisoner, and by manifestations of a sincere fraternal interest, by conversation, books, and encouragement, must touch within him chords which have long ceased to vibrate ; must awaken new hopes ; must show him that all is not lost, that God, and Christ, and virtue, and the friendship of the virtuous, and honor, and immortality, may yet be secured. Of this glorious ministry of private Christianity, I do not despair. I know I shall be told of the failure of all efforts to reclaim criminals. They have not always failed. And besides, has philanthropy, has genius, has the strength of humanity, been fairly and fervently put forth in this great concern ? I find in the New Testament no class of human beings whom charity is instructed to forsake. I find no exception made by Him who came to seek and save that which was lost. I must add, that the most hopeless subjects are not always to be found in prisons. That convicts are dreadfully corrupt, I know ; but not more corrupt than some who walk at large, and are not excluded from our kindness. The rich man who defrauds is certainly as criminal as the poor man who steals. The rich man who drinks to excess contracts deeper guilt, than he who sinks into this vice under the pressure of want. The young man who seduces innocence, deserves more richly the House of Correction, than the unhappy female whom he allured into the path of destruction. Still more, I cannot but remember how much the guilt of the convict results from the general corruption of society. When I reflect, how much of the responsibility for crimes rests on the state, how many of the offences, which are most severely punished, are to be traced to neglected education, to early squalid want, to temptations and exposures which society might do much to relieve, — I feel that a spirit of mercy should temper legislation; that we should not sever ourselves so widely from our fallen brethren; that we should recognise in them the countenance and claims of humanity; that we should strive to win them back to God.

I have thus spoken of the obligation of government to contribute by various means to the moral elevation of a people. I close this head with expressing sorrow, that an institution, capable of such purifying influences, should so often be among the chief engines of a nation's corruption.

In this discourse I have insisted on the supreme importance of virtuous principle, of moral force, and elevation in the community; and I have thus spoken, not that I might conform to professional duty, but from deep personal conviction. I feel, as I doubt not many feel, that the great distinction of a nation, the only one worth possessing, and which brings after it all other blessings, is the prevalence of pure principle among the citizens. I wish to belong to a state, in the character and institutions of which I may find a spring of improvement, which I can speak of with an honest pride, in whose records I may meet great and honored names, and which is making the world its debtor by its discoveries of truth, and by an example of virtuous freedom. O save me from a country which worships wealth, and cares not for true glory; in which intrigue bears rule; in which patriotism borrows its zeal from the prospect of office; in which hungry sycophants besiege with supplication all the departments of state; in which public men bear the brand of vice, and the seat of government is a noisome sink of private licentiousness and political corruption. Tell me not of the honor of belonging to a free country. I ask, does our liberty bear generous fruits? Does it exalt us in manly spirit, in public virtue, above countries trodden under foot by despotism? Tell me not of the extent of our territory. I care not how large it is, if it multiply degenerate men. Speak not of our prosperity. Better be one of a poor people, plain in manners, revering God and respecting themselves, than belong to a rich country which knows no higher good than riches. Earnestly do I desire for this country, that, instead of copying Europe with an undiscerning servility, it may have a character of its own, corresponding to the freedom and equality of our institutions. One Europe is enough. One Paris is enough. How much to be desired is it, that, separated as we are from the eastern continent by an ocean, we should be still more widely separated by simplicity of manners, by domestic purity, by inward piety, by reverence for human nature, by moral independence, by withstanding that subjection to fashion and that debilitating sensuality, which characterize the most civilized portions of the old world.

Of this country I may say with peculiar emphasis, that its happiness is bound up in its virtue. On this our union can alone stand firm. Our union is not like that of other nations, confirmed by the habits of ages, and riveted by force. It is a recent, and still more, a voluntary union. It is idle to talk of force as binding us together. Nothing can retain a member of this confederacy, when resolved on separation. The only bonds that can permanently unite us, are moral ones. That there are repulsive powers, principles of discord, in these States, we all feel. The attraction which is to counteract them, is only to be found in a calm wis dom, controlling the passions, in a spirit of equity and regard to the common weal, and in virtuous patriotism, clinging to union as the only pledge of freedom and peace. The union is threatened by sectional jealousies, and collisions of local interests, which can be reconciled only by a magnanimous liberality. It is endangered by the prostitution of executive patronage, through which the public treasury is turned into a fountain of corruption, and by the lust for power, which perpetually convulses the country for the sake of throwing office into new hands ; and the only remedy for these evils, is to be found in the moral indignation of the community, in a pure, lofty spirit, which will overwhelm with infamy this selfish ambition.

To the Chief Magistrate of this Commonwealth, and to those associated with him in the Executive and Legislative departments, I respectfully commend the truths which have now been delivered ; and, with the simplicity becoming a minister of Jesus Christ, I would remind them of their solemn obligations to God, to their fellow-creatures, and to the interests of humanity, freedom, virtue, and religion. We trust that in their high stations, they will seek, not themselves, but the public weal, and will seek it by inflexible adherence to the principles of the Constitution, and still more to the principles of God's Everlasting Law.

SELF-DENIAL.

MATTHEW xvi. 24: "Then said Jesus unto his disciples, if any man will come after me, let him deny himself, and take up his cross, and follow me."

THIS passage is an example of our Saviour's mode of teaching. He has given us his truth in the costume of the age; and this style is so common in the New Testament, that an acquaintance with the usages of those times is necessary to the understanding of a large part of his instructions. The cross was then a mode of punishment reserved for the greatest criminals, and was intended to inflict the deepest disgrace as well as sorest pain. "To take up the cross" had therefore become a proverbial expression of the most dreaded suffering and shame. By this phrase in the text, Jesus intended to teach, that no man could become his disciple without such a deep conviction of the truth and excellence of his religion, as would fortify the mind against persecution, reproach, and death. The command "to deny ourselves" is more literal, but is an instance of what is very common in our Saviour's teaching, I mean, of the use of unlimited expressions, which require to be restrained by the good sense of the hearer, and which, if taken without considerable modification, may lead into pernicious error. We know that this precept, for want of a wise caution, has driven men to self-inflicted penance and to the austerities of the cloister and wilderness; and it is one among many proofs of the necessity of a calm and sober judgment to a beneficial use of Christianity.

In this discourse I shall offer remarks on the limits or just extent of Christian Self-denial, and on the design of Providence in so constituting us, as to make self-denial necessary; and in discussing these topics I shall set before you its obligation, necessity, and excellence.

We are to deny ourselves; but how far? to what extent? This is our first inquiry. Are we to deny ourselves wholly? To deny ourselves in every power, faculty, and affection of our nature? Has the duty no bounds? For example, are we to deny the highest part of our nature, I mean conscience, or the moral faculty? Are we to oppose our sense of right, or desire of virtue? Every Christian says, No. Conscience is sacred; and revelation is intended to quicken, not resist it.

Again, are we to deny reason, the intellectual faculty, by which we weigh evidence, trace out causes and effects, ascend to universal truths, and seek to establish harmony among all our views? The answer to this question seems as plain as to the former. Yet many good men have seemed to dread reason, have imagined an inconsistency between faith and a free use of our intellectual powers, and have insisted that it is a religious duty " to prostrate our understandings." To some this may even seem a principal branch of Christian self-denial. The error I think is a great one; and believing that the honor, progress, and beneficial influence of Christianity are involved in its removal, I wish to give it a brief consideration.

I am told that I must deny reason. I ask, Must I deny it, when it teaches me that there is a God? if so, the very foundation of religion is destroyed, and I am abandoned to utter unbelief. Again, must I deny reason when it forbids the literal interpretation of the text, which commands us to hate father and mother and our own lives? If so, I must rupture the most sacred ties of domestic life, and must add to social vices the crime of self-murder. Surely reason, in its teachings on these great subjects, is not to be denied, but revered and obeyed; and if revered here, where ought it to be contemned and renounced?

I am told, that we have a better guide than reason, even God's word, and that this is to be followed and the other denied. But I ask, How do I know that Christianity is God's word? Are not the evidences of this religion submitted to reason? and if this faculty be unworthy of trust, is not revelation necessarily involved in the same condemnation? The truth is, and it ought not to be disguised, that our ultimate reliance is, and must be, on our own reason. Faith in this power lies at the foundation of all other faith. No trust can be placed in God, if we discredit the faculty by which God is discerned. — I have another objection to the doctrine, that we must deny reason in order to follow revelation. Reason is the very faculty to which revelation is addressed, and by which alone it can be explained. Without it we should be incapable of divine teaching, just as without the eye we should lose the happiest influences of the sun; and they who would discourage the use of reason, that we may better receive revelation, are much like those, who should bind up or pluck out the eye, that we might enjoy to the full the splendor of day.

Perhaps I shall be pointed to the many and gross errors into which reason has fallen on almost every subject, and shall be told that here are motives for distrusting and denying it. I reply, first, by asking how we detect these errors. By what power do we learn that reason so often misguides us? Is it not by reason itself? and shall we renounce it on account of its capacity of rectifying its own wrong judgments?— Consider next, that on no subject has reason gone more astray than in the interpretation of the Scriptures ; so that if it is to be denied on account of its errors, we must especially debar it from the study of revelation ; in other words, we must shut the word of God in despair, a consequence which, to a Protestant, is a sufficient refutation of the doctrine from which it flows.

A common method of enforcing the denial of reason, is to contrast it with the Infinite Intelligence of God, and then to ask whether it can be prostrated too submissively, or renounced too humbly, before Him. I acknowledge reverently the immeasurable superiority of God to human reason ; but I do not therefore contemn or renounce it; for, in the first place, it is as true of the "rapt seraph" as of man, that his intelligence is most narrow, compared with the Divine. Is no honor therefore due to angelic wisdom? In the next place, I observe that human reason, imperfect though it be, is still the offspring of God, allied to him intimately, and worthy of its divine Parent. There is no extravagance in calling it, as is sometimes done, "a beam of the infinite light"; for it involves in its very essence those immutable and everlasting principles of truth and rectitude, which constitute the glory of the Divine Mind. It ascends to the sublime idea of God by possessing kindred attributes, and knows him only through its affinity with him. It carries within itself the germ of that spiritual perfection, which is the great end of the creation. Is it not, then, truly a "partaker of a divine nature"? Can we think or speak of it too gratefully or with too much respect?— The Infinity of God, so far from calling on me to prostrate and annihilate reason, exalts my conception of it. It is my faith in this perfection of the Divine Mind, that inspires me with reverence for the human, for they are intimately connected, the latter being a derivation from the former, and endued with the power of approaching its original more and more through eternity. Severed from God, reason would lose its grandeur. In his infinity it has at once a source and a pledge of endless and unbounded improvement. God delights to communicate himself; and therefore his greatness, far from inspiring contempt for human reason, gives it a sacredness, and opens before it the most elevating hopes. The error of men is, not that they exaggerate, but that they do not know or suspect, the worth and dignity of their rational nature.

Perhaps I shall be told, that reason is not to be denied universally, but only in cases where its teachings are contradicted by revelation. To this I reply, that a contradiction between reason and a genuine revelation cannot exist. A doctrine claiming a divine origin would refute itself, by opposing any of the truths which reason intuitively discerns, or which it gathers from nature. God is the "Father of lights" and the "Author of concord," and he cannot darken and distract the human mind by jarring and irreconcilable instructions. He cannot subvert the authority of the very faculty through which we arrive at the knowledge of himself. A revelation from the Author of our rational nature, will certainly be adapted to its fundamental laws. I am aware, that it is very possible to give the name of reason to rash prejudices and corrupt opinions, and that on this ground we may falsely pronounce a genuine revelation to be inconsistent with reason; and our liableness to this delusion binds us to judge calmly, cautiously, and in the fear of God. But if, after a deliberate and impartia. use of our best faculties, a professed revelation seems to us plainly to disagree with itself or to clash with great principles which we cannot question, we ought not to hesitate to withhold from it our belief. I am surer that my rational nature is from God, than that any book is an expression of his will. This light in my own breast is his primary revelation, and all subsequent ones must accord with it, and are in fact intended to blend with and brighten it. My hearers, as you value Christianity, never speak of it as in any thing opposed to man's rational nature. Join not its foes in casting on it this reproach. It was given, not to supersede our rational faculties, but to quicken and invigorate them, to open a wider field to thought, to bring peace into the intellect as well as into the heart, to give harmony to all our views. We grievously wrong Christianity, by supposing it to raise a standard against reason, or to demand the sacrifice of our noblest faculties. These are her allies, friends, kindred. With these she holds unalterable concord. Whenever doctrines are taught you from the Christian records, opposing any clear conviction of reason and conscience, be assured that it is not the teaching of Christ which you hear. Some rash human expounder is subsituting his own weak, discordant tones for the voice of God, which they no more resemble than the rattling chariot-wheel does Heaven's awful thunder. — Never, never do violence to your rational nature. He who in any case admits doctrines which contradict reason, has broken down the great barrier between truth and falsehood, and lays open his mind to every delusion. The great mark of error, which is inconsistency, ceases to shock him. He has violated the first law of the intellect, and must pay the fearful penalty. Happy will it be for him, if, by the renunciation of reason, he be not prepared for the opposite extreme, and do not, through a natural reaction, rush into the excess of incredulity. In the records of individuals and of the race, it is not uncommon for an era of intellectual prostration to be followed by an era of proud and licentious philosophy ; nor will this alternation cease to form this history of the human mind, till the just rights of reason be revered.

I will notice one more, and a very common one, in which the duty of denying reason is urged. We are told, that there is one case in which we ought to prostrate our understandings, and that is, the case of mysteries, whenever they are taught in the word of God. The answer to this popular language is short. Mysteries, *continuing such*, cannot, from their very nature, be believed, and of consequence reason incurs no blame in refusing them assent. This will appear by considering what a mystery is. In the language of Scripture, and in its true sense, it is a secret, something unknown. I say, then, that from its nature it cannot be an object of belief ; for to know and to believe are expressions of the same act of the mind, differing chiefly in this, that the former is more applicable to what admits of demonstration, the latter to probable truth. I have no disposition to deny the existence of mysteries. Every truth involves them. Every object which falls under our notice, the most common and simple, contains much that we do not know and cannot now penetrate. We know not, for example, what it is which holds together the particles of the meanest stone beneath our feet, nor the manner in which the humblest plant grows. That there are mysteries, secrets, things unknown without number, I should be the last to deny. I only maintain, and in so doing I utter an identical proposition, that what is mysterious, secret, unknown, cannot at the same time be known or an object of faith. It is a great and common error, to confound facts which we understand, with the mysteries which lurk under them, and to suppose that in believing the first we believe the last. But no two things are more distinct, nor does the most thorough knowledge of the one imply the least perception of the other. For example, my hand is moved by the act of my will. This is a plain fact. The words which convey it are among the most intelligible. I believe it without doubt. But under this fact, which I so well know, lies a great mystery. The *manner* in which the will acts on the hand, or the process which connects them, is altogether unknown. The fact and the mystery, as you see, have nothing in common. The former is so manifest, that I cannot, if I would, withhold from it my faith. Of the latter not even a glimpse is afforded me ; not an idea of it has dawned on the mind ; and without ideas, there can, of course, be no knowledge or belief. These remarks apply to revelation as well as to nature. The subjects of which revelation treats, God, Christ, human nature, holiness, heaven, contain infinite mysteries. What is revealed n regard to them is indeed as nothing compared with what remains secret. But "secret things belong to God," and the pride of reason is manifested, not in declining, but in professing, to make them objects of faith. — It is the influence of time and of intellectual improvement to bring mysteries to light, both in nature and religion; and just as far as this process goes on, the belief of them becomes possible and right. Thus, the cause of eclipses, which was once a mystery, is now disclosed, and who of us does not believe it? In like manner Christ revealed "the mysteries of the kingdom of heaven," or the purposes and methods of God which had been kept secret for ages, in relation to the redemption of the world from sin, death, and woe. Being now revealed, or having ceased to be mysteries, these have become objects of faith, and reason ranks them among its most glorious truths.

From what has been said, we see, that to deny reason is no part of religion. Never imagine yourselves called to prostrate and contemn this noble nature. Reverence conscience. Foster, extend, enlighten intellect. Never imagine that you are forsaking God, in reposing a trust in the faculties he has given you. Only exercise them with impartiality, disinterestedness, and a supreme love of truth, and their instructions will conspire with revelation, and a beautiful harmony will more and more manifest itself in the lessons which God's book and God's works, which Christ and conscience teach.

But, if Reason and Conscience are not to be denied, what is? I answer, that there are other principles in our nature. Man is not wholly reason and conscience. He has various appetites, passions, desires, resting on present gratification and on outward objects; some of which we possess in common with inferior animals, such as sensual appetites and anger; and others belong more to the mind, such as love of power, love of honor, love of property, love of society, love of amusement, or a taste for literature and elegant arts; but all referring to our present being, and terminating chiefly on ourselves, or on a few beings who are identified with ourselves. These are to be denied or renounced; by which I mean not exterminated, but renounced as masters, guides, lords, and brought into strict and entire subordination to our moral and intellectual powers. It is a false idea, that religion requires the extermination of any principle, desire, appetite, or passion, which our Creator has implanted. Our nature is a whole, a beautiful whole, and no part can be spared. You might as properly and innocently lop off a limb from the body, as eradicate any natural desire from the mind. All our appetites are in themselves innocent and useful, ministering to the general weal of the soul. They are like the elements of the natural world, parts of a wise and beneficent system, but, like those elements, are beneficent only when restrained.

There are two remarks relating to our appetites and desires, which will show their need of frequent denial and constant control. In the first place, it is true of them all, that they do not carry within themselves their own rule. They are blind impulses. Present their objects, and they are excited as easily when gratification would be injurious as when it would be useful. We are not so constituted, for example, that we hunger and thirst for those things only which will be nutritive and wholesome, and lose all hunger and thirst at the moment when we have eaten or drunk enough. We are not so made, that the desire of property springs up only when property can be gained by honest means, and that it declines and dies as soon as we have acquired a sufficiency for ourselves and for usefulness. Our desires are undiscerning instincts, generally directed to what is useful, but often clamoring for gratification, which would injure health, debilitate the mind, or oppose the general good ; and this blindness of desire makes the demand for self-denial urgent and continual.

I pass to a second remark. Our appetites and desires carry with them a principle of growth or tendency to enlargement. They expand by indulgence, and, if not restrained, they fill and exhaust the soul, and hence are to be strictly watched over and denied. Nature has set bounds to the desires of the brute, but not to human desire, which partakes of the illimitableness of the soul to which it belongs. In brutes, for example, the animal appetites impel to a certain round of simple gratifications, beyond which they never pass. But man, having imagination and invention, is able by these noble faculties, to whet his sensual desires indefinitely. He is able to form new combinations of animal pleasures, and to provoke appetite by stimulants. The East gives up its spices, and the South holds not back its vintage. Sea and land are rifled for luxuries. Whilst the animal finds its nourishment in a few plants, perhaps in a single blade, man's table groans under the spoils of all regions ; and the consequence is, that in not a few cases the whole strength of the soul runs into appetite, just as some rich soil shoots up into poisonous weeds, and man, the rational creature of God, degenerates into the most thorough sensualist. — As another illustration of the ten dency of our desires to grow and usurp the whole mind, take the love of property. We see this every day gaining dangerous strength, if left to itself, if not denied or curbed. It is a thirst which is inflamed by the very copiousness of its draughts. Anxiety grows with possession. Riches become dearer by time. The love of money, far from withering in life's winter, strikes deeper and deeper root in the heart of age. He who has more than he can use or manage, grows more and more eager and restless for new gains, muses by day and dreams by night of wealth; and in this way the whole vigor of his soul, of intellect and affection, shoots up into an intense, unconquerable, and almost infinite passion for accumulation.

It is an interesting and solemn reflection, that the very nobleness of human nature may become the means and instrument of degradation. The powers which ally us to God, when pressed into the service of desire and appetite, enlarge desire into monstrous excess, and irritate appetite into fury. The rapidity of thought, the richness of imagination, the resources of invention, when enslaved to any passion, give it an extent and energy unknown to inferior natures; and just in proportion as this usurper establishes its empire over us, all the nobler attainments and products of the soul perish. Truth, virtue, honor, religion, hope, faith, charity, die. Here we see the need of self-denial. The lower principles of our nature not only act blindly, but, if neglected, grow indefinitely, and overshadow and blight and destroy every better growth. Without self-restraint and self-denial, the proportion, order, beauty, and harmony of the spiritual nature are subverted, and the soul becomes as monstrous and deformed, as the body would become, were all the nutriment to flow into a few organs and these the least valuable, and to break out into loathsome excrescences, whilst the eye, the ear, and the active limbs should pine, and be palsied, and leave us without guidance or power.

Do any of you now ask, how it comes to pass that we are so constituted ; why we are formed with desires so blind and strong, and tending so constantly to enlargement and dominion ; and how we can reconcile this constitution with God's goodness ? This is our second question. Some will answer it, by saying, that this constitution is a sinful nature derived from our first parents ; that it comes not from God, but from Adam ; that it is a sad inheritance from the first fallen pair ; and that God is not to be blamed for it, but our original progenitor. But, I confess, this explanation does not satisfy me. Scripture says, it was God who made me, not Adam. What I was at birth, I was by the ordinance of God. Make the connexion between Adam and his posterity as close as you will, God must have intended it, and God has carried it into effect. My soul, at the moment of its creation, was as fresh from the hands of the Deity, as if no human parent had preceded me ; and I see not how to shift off on any other being the reproach of my nature, if it deserve reproach. But does it merit blame ? Is the tendency to excess and growth, which we are conscious of in our passions and appetites, any derogation from the goodness or wisdom of our Maker ? Can we find only evil in such a constitution ? Perhaps it may minister to the highest purpose of God.

It is true, that as we are now made, our appetites and desires often war against reason, conscience, and religion. But why is this warfare appointed ? Not to extinguish these high principles ; but to awaken and invigorate them. It is meant to give them a field for action, occasion for effort, and means of victory. True, virtue is thus opposed and endangered ; but virtue owes its vigor and hardihood to obstacles, and wins its crown by conflict. I do not say, that God can find no school for character but temptation, and trial, and strong desire ; but I do say, that the present state is a fit and noble school. You, my hearers, would have the path of virtue, from the very beginning, smooth and strewed with flowers ; and would this train the soul to energy ? You would have pleasure always coincide with duty ; and how, then, would you attest your loyalty to duty ? You would have conscience and desire always speak the same language, and prescribe the same path ; and how, then, would conscience assert its supremacy ? God has implanted blind desires, which often rise up against reason and conscience, that he may give to these high faculties the dignity of dominion and the joy of victory. He has surrounded us with rivals to himself, that we may love him freely, and by our own unfettered choice erect his throne in our souls. He has given us strong desires of inferior things, that the desire of excellence may grow stronger than all. Make such a world as you wish, let no appetite or passion ever resist God's will, no object of desire ever come in competition with duty ; and where would be the resolution, and energy, and constancy, and effort, and purity, the trampling under foot of low interests, the generous self-surrender, the heroic devotion, all the sublimities of virtue, which now throw lustre over man's nature and speak of his immortality ? You would blot the precept of self-denial from the

Scriptures, and the need of it from human life, and, in so doing, you would blot out almost every interesting passage in man's history. Let me ask you, when you read that history, what is it which most interests and absorbs you, which seizes on the imagination and memory, which agitates the soul to its centre ? Who is the man whom you select from the records of time as the object of your special admiration ? Is it he, who lived to indulge himself ? whose current of life flowed most equably and pleasurably ? whose desires were crowned most liberally with means of gratification ? whose table was most luxuriantly spread ? and whom fortune made the envy of his neighbourhood by the fulness of her gifts ? Were such the men to whom monuments have been reared, and whose memories, freshened with tears of joy and reverence, grow and flourish and spread through every age ? O no ! He whom we love, whose honor we most covet, is he who has most denied and subdued himself ; who has made the most entire sacrifice of appetites and passions and private interest to God, and virtue, and mankind ; who has walked in a rugged path, and clung to good and great ends in persecution and pain ; who, amidst the solicitations of ambition, ease, and private friendship, and the menaces of tyranny and malice, has listened to the voice of conscience, and found a recompense for blighted hopes and protracted suffering, in conscious uprightness and the favor of God. Who is it that is most lovely in domestic life ? It is the Martyr to domestic affection, the mother forgetting herself, and ready to toil, suffer, die for the happiness and virtue of her children. Who is it that we honor in public life ? It is the Martyr to his country, he who serves her, not when she has honors for his brow and wealth for his coffers, but who clings to her in her danger and falling glories, and thinks life a cheap sacrifice to her safety and freedom. Whom does the church retain in most grateful remembrance, and pronounce holy and blessed? The self-denying, self-immolating apostle, the fearless confessor, the devoted martyr, men who have held fast the truth even in death, and bequeathed it to future ages amidst blood. Above all, to what moment of the life of Jesus does the Christian turn, as the most affecting and sublime illustration of his divine character? It is that moment, when, in the spirit of self-sacrifice, denying every human passion, and casting away every earthly interest, he bore the agony and shame of the cross. Thus all great virtues bear the impress of self-denial; and were God's present constitution of our nature and life so reversed as to demand no renunciation of desire, the chief interest and glory of our present being would pass away. There would be nothing in history to thrill us with admiration. We should have no consciousness of the power and greatness of the soul. We should love feebly and coldly, for we should find nothing in one another to love earnestly. Let us not, then, complain of Providence because it has made self-denial necessary; or complain of religion because it summons us to this work. Religion and nature here hold one language. Our own souls bear witness to the teaching of Christ, that it is the " narrow way " of self-denial " which leadeth unto life."

My friends, at death, if reason is spared to us and memory retains its hold on the past, will it gratify us to see, that we have lived, not to deny, but to indulge ourselves, that we have bowed our souls to any passion, that we gave the reins to lust, that we were palsied by sloth, that, through love of gain, we hardened ourselves against the claims of humanity, or, through love of man's favor, parted with truth and moral independence, or that in any thing reason and conscience were sacrificed to the impulse of desire, and God forgotten for present good? Shall we then find comfort in remembering our tables of luxury, our pillows of down, our wealth amassed and employed for private ends, or our honors won by base compliance with the world? Did any man at his death ever regret his conflicts with himself, his victories over appetite, his scorn of impure pleasures, or his sufferings for righteousness' sake? Did any man ever mourn, that he had impoverished himself by integrity, or worn out his frame in the service of mankind? Are these the recollections which harrow the soul, and darken and appall the last hour? To whom is the last hour most serene and full of hope? Is it not to him, who, amidst perils and allurements, has denied himself, and taken up the cross with the holy resolution of Jesus Christ?

SELF-DENIAL.

MATTHEW xvi. 24: "Then said Jesus unto his disciples, if any man will come after me, let him deny himself, and take up his cross, and follow me."

In the preceding discourse, I spoke of the just limits and moral dignity of self-denial. I resume the subject, because it throws much light on the nature of true virtue, and helps us to distinguish moral goodness from qualities which resemble it. Clear conceptions on this point are inestimable. To love and seek excellence, we must know what it is, and separate it from counterfeits. For want of just views of virtue and piety, men's admiration and efforts are often wasted, and sometimes carry them wide of the great object of human life. Perhaps truth on this subject cannot be brought out more clearly than by considering the nature of Self-denial. Such will be the aim of this discourse.

To deny ourselves, is to deny, to withstand, to renounce whatever, within or without, interferes with our conviction of right, or with the will of God. It is to suffer, to make sacrifices, for duty or our principles. The question now offers itself, What constitutes the singular merit of this suffering? Mere suffering, we all know, is not virtue. Evil men often endure pain as well as the good, and are evil still. This and this alone constitutes the worth and importance of the sacrifice, suffering, which enters into self-denial, that it springs from and manifests Moral Strength, power over ourselves, force of purpose, or the mind's resolute determination of itself to duty. It is the proof and result of inward energy. Difficulty, hardship, suffering, sacrifices, are tests and measures of Moral Force, and the great means of its enlargement. To withstand these is the same thing as to put forth power. Self-denial, then, is the will acting with power in the choice and prosecution of duty. Here we have the distinguishing glory of self-denial, and here we have the essence and distinction of a good and virtuous man.

The truth to which these views lead us, and which I am now solicitous to enforce, is this, that the great characteristic of a virtuous or religious mind is strength of Moral purpose. This force is the measure of excellence. . The very idea of Duty implies that we are bound to adopt and pursue it with a stronger and more settled determination than any other object, and virtue consists in fidelity to this primary dictate of conscience. We have virtue only as far as we exert inward energy, or as far as we put forth a strong and overcoming will in obeying the law of God and of our own minds. Let this truth be deeply felt. Let us not confide in good emotions, in kind feelings, in tears for the suffering, or in admiration of noble deeds. These are not goodness, in the moral and Christian sense of that word. It is force of upright and holy purpose, attested and approved by withstanding trial, temptation, allurement, and suffering; it is this, in which virtues consists. I know nothing else which an enlightened conscience approves, nothing else which God will accept.

I am aware, that if I were called upon to state my ideas of a perfect character, I should give an answer that would seem at first to contradict the doctrine just expressed, or to be inconsistent with the stress which I have laid on strength of moral purpose. I should say, that perfection of mind, like that of the body, consists of two elements, of strength and beauty; that it consists of firmness and mildness, of force and tenderness, of vigor and grace. It would ill become a teacher of Christianity to overlook the importance of sympathy, gentleness, humility, and charity, in his definition of moral excellence. The amiable, attractive, mild attributes of the mind are recommended as of great price in the sight of God, by Him who was emphatically meek and lowly in heart. Still I must say, that all virtue lies in strength of character or of moral purpose; for these gentle, sweet, winning qualities rise into virtue only when pervaded and sustained by moral energy. On this they must rest, by this they must be controlled and exalted, or they have no moral worth. I acknowledge love, kindness, to be a great virtue; but what do I mean by love, when I thus speak? Do I mean a constitutional tenderness? an instinctive sympathy? the natural and almost necessary attachment to friends and benefactors? the kindness which is inseparable from our social state, and which is never wholly extinguished in the human breast? In all these emotions of our nature, I see the kind design of God; I see a beauty; I see the germ and capacity of an ever-growing charity. But they are not virtues, they are not proper objects of moral approbation, nor do they give any sure pledge of improvement. This natural amiableness I too often see in company with sloth, with uselessness, with the contemptible vanity and dissipation of fashionable life. It is no ground of trust, no promise of fidelity, in any of the great exigencies of life. The love, the benevolence, which I honor as virtue, is not the gift of nature or condition, but the growth and manifestation of the soul's moral power. It is a spirit chosen as excellent, cherished as divine, protected with a jealous care, and especially fortified by the resistance and subjection of opposite propensities. It is the soul, determining itself to break every chain of selfishness, to enlarge and to invigorate the kind affections, to identify itself with other beings, to sympathize, not with a few, but with all the living and rational children of God, to honor others' worth, to increase and enjoy their happiness, to partake in the universal goodness of the Creator, and to put down within itself every motion of pride, anger, or sensual desire, inconsistent with this pure charity. In other words, it is strength of holy purpose, infused into the kind affections, which raises them into virtues, or gives them a moral worth, not found in constitutional amiableness.

I read in the Scriptures the praises of meekness. But when I see a man meek or patient of injury through tameness, or insensibility, or want of self-respect, passively gentle, meek through constitution or fear, I look on him with feelings very different from veneration. It 's the meekness of principle; it is mildness replete with energy; it is the forbearance of a man who feels a wrong, but who curbs anger, who though injured resolves to be just, who voluntarily remembers that his foe is a man and a brother, who dreads to surrender himself to his passions, who in the moment of provocation subjects himself to reason and religion, and who holds fast the great truth, that the noblest victory over a foe is to disarm and subdue him by equity and kindness, — it is this meekness which I venerate, and which seems to me one of the divinest virtues. It is moral power, the strength of virtuous purpose, pervading meekness, which gives it all its title to respect.

It is worthy of special remark, that without this moral energy, resisting passion and impulse, our tenderest attachments degenerate more or less into weaknesses and immoralities; sometimes prompting us to sympathize with those whom we love, in their errors, prejudices, and evil passions; sometimes inciting us to heap upon them injurious praises and indulgences : sometimes urging us to wrong or neglect others, that we may the more enjoy or serve our favorites; and sometimes poisoning our breasts with jealousy or envy, because our affection is not returned with equal warmth. The principle of love, whether exercised towards our relatives or our country, whether manifested in courtesy or compassion, can only become virtue, can only acquire purity, consistency, serenity, dignity, when imbued, swayed, cherished, enlarged by the power of a virtuous will, by a self-denying energy. It is Inward Force, power over ourselves, which is the beginning and the end of virtue.

What I have now said of the kind affections is equally true of the religious ones. These have virtue in them, only as far as they are imbued with self-denying strength. I know that multitudes place religion in feeling. Ardent sensibility is the measure of piety. He who is wrought up by preaching or sympathy into extraordinary fervor, is a saint; and the less he governs himself in his piety, the more he is looked upon as inspired.

But I know of no religion which has moral worth or is acceptable to God, but that which grows from and is nourished by our own spiritual, self-denying energy. Emotion towards God, springing up without our own thought or care, grateful feelings at the reception of signal benefits, the swelling of the soul at the sight of nature, tenderness awakened by descriptions of the love and cross of Christ, these, though showing high capacities, though means and materials of piety, are not *of themselves* acceptable religion. The religious character which has true virtue, and which is built upon a rock, is that which has been deliberately and resolutely adopted and cherished, as our highest duty, and as the friend and strengthener of all other duties ; and which we have watched over and confirmed by suppressing inconsistent desires and passions, by warring against selfishness and the love of the world.

There is one fact very decisive on this subject. It is not uncommon to see people with strong religious feeling, who are not made better by it ; who at church or in other meetings are moved perhaps to tears, but who make no progress in self-government or charity, and who gain nothing of elevation of mind in their common feelings and transactions. They take pleasure in religious excitement, just as others delight to be interested by a fiction or a play. They invite these emotions because they suppose them to aid or insure salvation, and soon relapse into their ordinary sordidness or other besetting infirmities. Now to give the name of Religion to this mockery, is the surest way to dishonor it. True religion is not mere emotion, is not something communicated to us without our own moral effort. It involves much self-denial. Its great characteristic is, not feeling, but the subjection of our wills, desires, habits, lives, to the will of God, from a conviction that what he wills is the perfection of virtue, and the true happiness of our nature. In genuine piety the mind chooses as its supreme good, the moral excellence enjoined by its Author, and resolutely renounces whatever would sully this divine image, and so disturb its communion with God. This religion, though its essence be not emotion, will gradually gather and issue in a sensibility, deeper, intenser, more glowing, than the blind enthusiast ever felt ; and then only does it manifest itself in its perfect form, when, through a self-denying and self-purifying power, it rises to an overflowing love, gratitude, and joy towards the Universal Father.

In insisting on the great principle, that religion, or virtue, consists in strength of moral purpose, in the soul's resolute determination of itself to duty, I am satisfied that I express a truth, which has a witness and confirmation in the breast of every reflecting man. We all of us feel, that virtue is not something adopted from necessity, something to which feeling impels us, something which comes to us from constitution, or accident, or outward condition ; but that it has its origin in our moral freedom, that it consists in moral energy ; and accordingly we all measure virtue by the trials and difficulties which it overcomes, for these are the tests and measures of the force with which the soul adopts it. Every one of us, who has adhered to duty, when duty brought no recompense but the conviction of well-doing, who has faced the perils of a good but persecuted cause with unshrinking courage, who has been conscious of an inward triumph over temptation, conscious of having put down bad motives and exalted good ones in his own breast, must remember the clear, strong, authentic voice, the accents of peculiar encouragement and joy, with which the inward judge has at such seasons pronounced its approving sentence. This experience is universal, and it is the voice of nature and of God, in confirmation of the great truth of this discourse.

I fear, that the importance of strength in the Christian character has been in some degree obscured by the habit of calling certain Christian graces of singular worth by the name of *passive* virtues. This name has been given to humility, patience, resignation ; and I fear, that the phrase has led some to regard these noble qualities as allied to inaction, as wanting energy and determination. Now the truth is, that the mind never puts forth greater power over itself, than when, in great trials, it yields up calmly its desires, affections, interests to God. There are seasons, when to be *still* demands immeasurably higher strength than to act. Composure is often the highest result of power. Think you it demands no power to calm the stormy elements of passion, to moderate the vehemence of desire, to throw off the load of dejection, to suppress every repining thought, when the dearest hopes are withered, and to turn the wounded spirit from dangerous reveries and wasting grief, to the quiet discharge of ordinary duties ? Is there no power put forth, when a man, stripped of his property, of the fruits of a life's labor, quells discontent and gloomy forebodings, and serenely and patiently returns to the tasks which Providence assigns ? I doubt not, that the all-seeing eye of God sometimes discerns the sublimest human energy under a form and countenance, which by their composure and tranquillity indicate to the human spectator only passive virtues.

The doctrine of this discourse is in every view interesting. To me it goes further than all others to explain the present state. If moral strength, if inward power in the choice and practice of duty, constitute excellence and happiness, then I see why we are placed in a world of obstructions, perils, hardships, why duty is so often a "narrow way," why the warfare of the passions with conscience is so subtle and unceasing; why within and without us are so many foes to rectitude; for this is the very state to call forth and to build up moral force. In a world where duty and inclination should perfectly agree, we should indeed never err, but the living power of virtue could not be developed. Do not complain, then, of life's trials. Through these you may gain incomparably higher good, than indulgence and ease. This view reveals to us the impartial goodness of God in the variety of human conditions. We sometimes see individuals, whose peculiar trials are thought to make their existence to them an evil. But among such may be found the most favored children of God. If there be a man on earth to be envied, it is he, who, amidst the sharpest assaults from his own passions, from fortune, from society, never falters in his allegiance to God and the inward monitor. So peculiar is the excellence of this moral strength, that I believe the Creator regards one being who puts it forth, with greater complacency than he would look on a world of beings, innocent and harmless through the necessity of constitution. I know not that human wisdom has arrived at a juster or higher view of the present state, than that it is intended to call forth power by obstruction, the power of intellect by the difficulties of knowledge, the power of conscience and virtue by temptation, allurement, pleasure, pain, and the alternations of prosperous and adverse life. When I see a man holding faster his uprightness in proportion as it is assailed, fortifying his religious trust in proportion as Providence is obscure, hoping in the ultimate triumphs of virtue, more surely in proportion to its present afflictions; cherishing philanthropy amidst the discouraging experience of men's unkindness and unthankfulness; extending to others a sympathy which his own sufferings need, but cannot obtain; growing milder and gentler amidst what tends to exasperate and harden; and through inward principle converting the very incitements to evil into the occasions of a victorious virtue, — I see an explanation, and a noble explanation, of the present state. I see a good produced, so transcendent in its nature as to justify all the evil and suffering under which it grows up. I should think the formation of a few such minds worth all the apparatus of the present world. I should say, that this earth, with its continents and oceans, its seasons and harvests, and its successive generations, was a work worthy of God, even were it to accomplish no other end than the training and manifestation of the illustrious characters which are scattered through history. And when I consider, how small a portion of human virtue is recorded by history, how superior in dignity, as well as in number, are the unnoticed, unhonored saints and heroes of domestic and humble life, I see a light thrown over the present state which more than reconciles me to all its evils.

The views given in this discourse of the importance of moral power, manifested in great trials, may be employed to shed a glorious and perhaps a new light on the character and cross of Christ. But this topic can now be only suggested to your private meditation. There is, however, one practical application of our subject, which may be made in a few words, and which I cannot omit. I wish to ask the young who hear me, and especially of my own sex, to use the views now offered in judging and forming their characters. Young man, remember that the only test of goodness, virtue, is moral strength, self-denying energy. You have generous and honorable feelings, you scorn mean actions, your heart beats quick at the sight or hearing of courageous, disinterested deeds, and all these are interesting qualities; but, remember, they are the gifts of nature, the endowments of your susceptible age. They are not virtue. God and the inward monitor ask for more. The question is, Do you strive to confirm, into permanent principles, the generous sensibilities of the heart? Are you watchful to suppress the impetuous emotions, the resentments, the selfish passionateness, which are warring against your honorable feelings? Especially do you subject to your moral and religious convictions, the love of pleasure, the appetites, the passions, which form the great trials of youthful virtue? Here is the field of conflict to which youth is summoned. Trust not to occasional impulses of benevolence, to constitutional courage, frankness, kindness, if you surrender yourselves basely to the temptations of your age. No man who has made any observation of life, but will tell you how often he has seen the promise of youth blasted; intellect, genius, honorable feeling, kind affection, overpowered and almost extinguished, through the want of moral strength, through a tame yielding to pleasure and the passions. Place no trust in your good propensities, unless these are fortified, and upheld, and improved by moral energy and self-control. — To all of us, in truth, the same lesson comes. If any man will be Christ's disciple, sincerely good, and worthy to be named among the friends of virtue, if he will have inward peace and the consciousness of progress towards Heaven, he must deny himself, he must take the cross, and follow Christ in the renunciation of every gain and pleasure inconsistent with the will of God.

THE IMITABLENESS OF CHRIST'S CHARACTER.

1 Peter ii. 21: " Christ also suffered for us, leaving us an example, that ye should follow his steps."

The example of Jesus is our topic. To incite you to follow it, is the aim of this discourse. Christ came to give us a religion, — but this is not all. By a wise and beautiful ordination of Providence, he was sent to show forth his religion in himself. He did not come to sit in a hall of legislation, and from some commanding eminence to pronounce laws and promises. He is not a mere channel through which certain communications are made from God; not a mere messenger appointed to utter the words which he had heard, and then to disappear, and to sustain no further connexion with his message. He came, not only to teach with his lips, but to be a living manifestation of his religion, — to be, in an important sense, the religion itself.

This is a peculiarity worthy of attention. Christianity is not a mere code of laws, not an abstract system such as theologians frame. It is a living, embodied religion. It comes to us in a human form; it offers itself to our eyes as well as ears; it breathes, it moves in our sight. It is more than precept; it is example and action.

The importance of example, who does not understand? How much do most of us suffer from the presence, conversation, spirit, of men of low minds by whom we are surrounded! The temptation is strong, to take as our standard, the average character of the society in which we live, and to satisfy ourselves with decencies and attainments which secure to us among the multitude the name of respectable men. On the other hand, there is a power (have you not felt it?) in the presence, conversation, and example of a man of strong principle and magnanimity, to lift us, at least for the moment, from our vulgar and tame habits of thought, and to kindle some generous aspirations after the excellence which we were made to attain. I hardly need say to you, that it is impossible to place ourselves under any influence of this nature so quickening as the example of Jesus. This introduces us to the highest order of virtues. This is fitted to awaken the whole mind. Nothing has equal power to neutralize the coarse, selfish, and sensual influences, amidst which we are plunged, to refine our conception of duty, and to reveal to us the perfection on which our hopes and most strenuous desires should habitually fasten.

There is one cause, which has done much to defeat this good influence of Christ's character and example, and which ought to be exposed. It is this. Multitudes, I am afraid great multitudes, think of Jesus as a being to be admired, rather than approached. They have some vague conceptions of a glory in his nature and character which makes it presumption to think of proposing him as their standard. He is thrown so far from them, that he does them little good. Many feel that a close resemblance of Jesus Christ is not to be expected;

that this, like many other topics, may serve for declamation in the pulpit, but is utterly incapable of being reduced to practice. I think I am touching here an error, which exerts a blighting influence on not a few minds. Until men think of the religion and character of Christ as truly applicable to them, as intended to be brought into continual operation, as what they must incorporate with their whole spiritual nature, they will derive little good from Christ. Men think indeed to honor Jesus, when they place him so high as to discourage all effort to approach him. They really degrade him. They do not understand his character; they throw a glare over it, which hides its true features. This vague admiration is the poorest tribute which they can pay him.

The manner in which Jesus Christ is conceived and spoken of by many, reminds me of what is often seen in Catholic countries, where a superstitious priesthood and people imagine that they honor the Virgin Mary by loading her image with sparkling jewels and the gaudiest attire. A Protestant of an uncorrupted taste is at first shocked, as if there was something like profanation in thus decking out, as for a theatre, the meek, modest, gentle, pure, and tender mother of Jesus. It seems to me, that something of the same superstition is seen in the indefinite epithets of admiration heaped upon Jesus; and the effect is, that the mild and simple beauty of his character is not seen. Its sublimity, which had nothing gaudy or dazzling, which was plain and unaffected, is not felt; and its suitableness as an example to mankind, is discredited or denied.

I wish, in this discourse, to prevent the discouraging influence of the greatness of Jesus Christ; to show, that, however exalted, he is not placed beyond the reach of our sympathy and imitation.

I begin with the general observation, that real greatness of character, greatness of the highest order, far from being repulsive and discouraging, is singularly accessible and imitable, and, instead of severing a being from others, fits him to be their friend and model. A man who stands apart from his race, who has few points of contact with other men, who has a style and manner which strike awe, and keep others far from him, whatever rank he may hold in his own and others' eyes, wants, after all, true grandeur of mind; and the spirit of this remark, I think, may be extended beyond men to higher orders of beings, to angels and to Jesus Christ. A great soul is known by its enlarged, strong, and tender sympathies. True elevation of mind does not take a being out of the circle of those who are below him, but binds him faster to them, and gives them advantages for a closer attachment and conformity to him.

Greatness of character is a communicable attribute; I should say, singularly communicable. It has nothing exclusive in its nature. It cannot be the monopoly of an individual, for it is the enlarged and generous action of faculties and affections which enter into and constitute all minds, I mean reason, conscience, and love, so that its elements exist in all. It is not a peculiar or exclusive knowledge, which can be shut up in one or a few understandings; but the comprehension of great and universal truths, which are the proper objects of every rational being. It is not a devotion to peculiar, exclusive objects, but the adoption of public interests, the consecration of the mind to the cause of virtue and happiness in the creation, that is, to the very cause which all intelligent beings are bound to espouse. Greatness is not a secret, solitary principle, working by itself and refusing participation, but frank and open-hearted, so large in its views, so liberal in its feelings, so expansive in its purposes, so beneficent in its labors, as naturally and necessarily to attract sympathy and coöperation. It is selfishness that repels men; and true greatness has not a stronger characteristic than its freedom from every selfish taint. So far from being imprisoned in private interests, it covets nothing which it may not impart. So far from being absorbed in its own distinctions, it discerns nothing so quickly and joyfully as the capacities and pledges of greatness in others, and counts no labor so noble as to call forth noble sentiments, and the consciousness of a divine power, in less improved minds.

I know that those who call themselves great on earth, are apt to estrange themselves from their inferiors; and the multitude, cast down by their high bearing, never think of proposing them as examples. But this springs wholly from the low conceptions of those whom we call the great, and shows a mixture of vulgarity of mind with their superior endowments. Genuine greatness is marked by simplicity, unostentatiousness, self-forgetfulness, a hearty interest in others, a feeling of brotherhood with the human family, and a respect for every intellectual and immortal being as capable of progress towards its own elevation. A superior mind, enlightened and kindled by just views of God and of the creation, regards its gifts and powers as so many bonds of union with other beings, as given it, not to nourish self-elation, but to be employed for others, and still more to be communicated to others. Such greatness has no reserve, and especially no affected dignity of deportment. It is too conscious of its own power, to need, and too benevolent to desire, to entrench itself behind forms and ceremonies ; and when circumstances permit such a character to manifest itself to inferior beings, it is beyond all others the most winning, and most fitted to impart itself, or to call forth a kindred elevation of feeling. I know not in history an individual so easily comprehended as Jesus Christ, for nothing is so intelligible as sincere, disinterested love. I know not any being who is so fitted to take hold on all orders of minds ; and accordingly he drew after him the unenlightened, the publican, and the sinner. It is a sad mistake, then, that Jesus Christ is too great to allow us to think of intimacy with him, and to think of making him our standard.

Let me confirm this truth by another order of reflections. You tell me, my hearers, that Jesus Christ is so high that he cannot be your model ; I grant the exaltation of his character. I believe him to be a more than human being. In truth, all Christians so believe him. Those who suppose him not to have existed before his birth, do not regard him as a mere man, though so reproached. They always separate him by broad distinctions from other men. They consider him as enjoying a communion with God, and as having received gifts, endowments, aid, lights from him, granted to no other, and as having exhibited a spotless purity, which is the highest distinction of Heaven. All admit, and joyfully admit, that Jesus Christ, by his greatness and goodness, throws all other human attainments into obscurity. But on this account he is not less a standard, nor is he to discourage us, but on the contrary to breathe into us a more exhilarating hope ; for though so far above us, he is still one of us, and is only an illustration of the capacities which we all possess. This is a great truth. Let me strive to unfold it. Perhaps I cannot better express my views, than by saying, that I regard all minds as of one family. When we speak of higher orders of beings, of angels and archangels, we are apt to conceive of distinct kinds or races of beings, separated from us and from each other by impassable barriers. But it is not so. All minds are of one family. There is no such partition in the spiritual world as you see in the material. In material nature, you see wholly distinct classes of beings. A mineral is not a vegetable, and makes no approach to it ; these two great kingdoms of nature are divided by immeasurable spaces. So, when we look at different races of animals, though all partake of that mysterious property, life, yet, what an immense and impassable distance is there between the insect and the lion. They have no bond of union, no possibility of communication. During the lapse of ages, the animalcules which sport in the sunbeams a summer's day and then perish, have made no approximation to the king of the forests. But in the intellectual world there are no such barriers. All minds are essentially of one origin, one nature, kindled from one divine flame, and are all tending to one centre, one happiness. This great truth, to us the greatest of truths, which lies at the foundation of all religion and of all hope, seems to me not only sustained by proofs which satisfy the reason, but to be one of the deep instincts of our nature. It mingles, unperceived, with all our worship of God, which uniformly takes for granted that he is a Mind having thought. affection, and volition like ourselves. It runs through false religions ; and whilst, by its perversion, it has made them false, it has also given to them whatever purifying power they possess. But passing over this instinct, which is felt more and more to be unerring as the intellect is improved, this great truth of the unity or likeness of all minds, seems to me demonstrable from this consideration, that Truth, the object and nutriment of mind, is one and immutable, so that the whole family of intelligent beings must have the same views, the same motives, and the same general ends. For example, a truth of mathematics, is not a truth only in this world, a truth to our minds, but a truth everywhere, a truth in heaven, a truth to God, who has indeed framed his creation according to the laws of this universal science. So, happiness and misery, which lie at the foundation of morals, must be to all intelligent beings what they are to us, the objects, one of desire and hope, and the other of aversion ; and who can doubt that virtue and vice are the same everywhere as on earth, that in every community of beings, the mind which devotes itself to the general weal, must be more reverenced than a mind which would subordinate the general interest to its own. Thus all souls are one in nature, approach one another, and have grounds and bonds of communion with one another. I am not only one of the human race ; I am one of the great intellectual family of God. There is no spirit so exalted, with which I have not common thoughts and feelings. That conception which I have gained, of One Universal Father, whose love is the fountain and centre of all things, is the dawn of the highest and most magnificent views in the universe, and if I look up to this being with filial love, I have the spring and beginning of the noblest sentiments and joys which are known in the universe. No greatness, therefore, of a being, separates me from him or makes him unapproachable by me. The mind of Jesus Christ, my hearer, and your mind are of one family ; nor was there any thing in his, of which you have not the principle, the capacity, the promise in yourself. This is the very impression which he intends to give. He never held himself up as an inimitable and unapproachable being ; but directly the reverse. He always spoke of himself as having come to communicate himself to others. He always invited men to believe on and adhere to him, that they might receive that very spirit, that pure, celestial spirit, by which he was himself actuated. " Follow me," is his lesson. The relation which he came to establish between himself and mankind, was not that of master and slave, but that of friends. He compares himself, in a spirit of divine benevolence, to a vine, which, you know, sends its own sap, that by which it is itself nourished, into all its branches. We read, too, these remarkable words in his prayer for his disciples, " I have given to them the glory thou gavest me ; " and I am persuaded that there is not a glory, a virtue, a power, a joy, possessed by Jesus Christ, to which his disciples will not successively rise. In the spirit of these remarks, the Apostles say, " Let the same mind be in you which was also in Christ."

I have said, that all minds being of one family, the greatness of the mind of Christ is no discouragement to our adoption of him as our model. I now observe, that there is one attribute of mind to which I have alluded, that should particularly animate us to propose to ourselves a sublime standard, as sublime as Jesus Christ. I refer to the principle of growth in human nature. We were made to grow. Our faculties are germs, and given for an expansion, to which nothing authorizes us to set bounds. The soul bears the impress of illimitableness, in the thirst, the unquenchable thirst, which it brings with it into being, for a power, knowledge, happiness, which it never gains, and which always carry it forward into futurity. The body soon reaches its limit. But intellect, affection, moral energy, in proportion to their growth, tend to further enlargement, and every acquisition is an impulse to something higher. When I consider this principle or capacity of the human soul, I cannot restrain the hope which it awakens. The partition-walls which imagination has reared between men and higher orders of beings vanish. I no longer see aught to prevent our becoming whatever was good and great in Jesus on earth. In truth, I feel my utter inability to conceive what a mind is to attain which is to advance for ever. Add but that element, eternity, to man's progress, and the results of his existence surpass, not only human, but angelic thought. Give me this, and the future glory of the human mind becomes to me as incomprehensible as God himself. To encourage these thoughts and hopes, our Creator has set before us delightful exemplifications, even now, of this principle of growth both in outward nature and in the human mind. We meet them in nature. Suppose you were to carry a man, wholly unacquainted with vegetation, to the most majestic tree in our forests, and, whilst he was admiring its extent and proportions, suppose you should take from the earth at its root a little downy substance, which a breath might blow away, and say to him, That tree was once such a seed as this; it was wrapped up here; it once lived only within these delicate fibres, this narrow compass. With what incredulous wonder would he regard you! And if by an effort of imagination, somewhat Oriental, we should suppose this little seed to be suddenly endued with thought, and to be told that it was one day to become this mighty tree, and to cast out branches which would spread an equal shade, and wave with equal grace, and withstand the winter winds; with what amazement may we suppose it to anticipate its future lot! Such growth we witness in nature. A nobler hope we Christians are to cherish; and still more striking examples of the growth of mind are set before us in human history. We wonder indeed when we are told, that one day we shall be as the angels of God. I apprehend that as great a wonder has been realized already on the earth. I apprehend that the distance between the mind of Newton and of a Hottentot may have been as great as between Newton and an angel. There is another view still more striking. This Newton, who lifted his calm, sublime eye to the heavens, and read among the planets and the stars, the great law of the material universe, was, forty or fifty years before, an infant, without one clear perception, and unable to distinguish his nurse's arm from the pillow on which he slept. Howard, too, who, under the strength of an all-sacrificing benevolence, explored the depths of human suffering, was, forty or fifty years before, an infant wholly absorbed in himself, grasping at all he saw, and almost breaking his little heart with fits of passion, when the idlest toy was withheld. Has not man already traversed as wide a space as separates him from angels? And why must he stop? There is no extravagance in the boldest anticipation. We may truly become one with Christ, a partaker of that celestial mind. He is truly our brother, one of our family. Let us make him our constant model.

I know not that the doctrine now laid down, is liable but to one abuse. It may unduly excite susceptible minds, and impel to a vehemence of hope and exertion unfavorable in the end to the very progress which is proposed. To such I would say, Hasten to conform yourselves to Christ, but hasten according to the laws of your nature. As the body cannot by the concentration of its whole strength into one bound, scale the height of a mountain, neither can the mind free every obstacle and achieve perfection by an agony of the will. Great effort is indeed necessary; but such as can be sustained, such as fits us for greater, such as will accumulate, not exhaust, our spiritual force. The soul may be overstrained as truly as the body, and it often is so in seasons of extraordinary religious excitement; and the consequence is, an injury to the constitution of the intellect and the heart, which a life may not be able to repair. I rest the hopes for human nature, which I have now expressed, on its principle of growth; and growth, as you well know, is a gradual process, not a convulsive start, accomplishing the work of years in a moment. All great attainments are gradual. As easily might a science be mastered by one struggle of thought, as sin be conquered by a spasm of remorse. Continuous, patient effort, guided by wise deliberation, is the true means of spiritual progress. In religion, as in common life, mere force of vehemence will prove a fallacious substitute for the sobriety of wisdom.

The doctrine which I have chiefly labored to maintain in this discourse, that minds are all of one family, are all brethren, and may be more and more nearly united to God, seems to me to have been felt peculiarly by Jesus Christ ; and if I were to point out the distinction of his greatness, I should say it lay in this. He felt his superiority, but he never felt as if it separated him from mankind. He did not come among us as some great men would visit a colliery, or any other resort of the ignorant and corrupt, with an air of greatness, feeling himself above us, and giving benefits as if it were an infinite condescension. He came and mingled with us as a friend and a brother. He saw in every human being a mind which might wear his own brightest glory. He was severe only towards one class of men, and they were those who looked down on the multitude with contempt. Jesus respected human nature ; he felt it to be his own. This was the greatness of Jesus Christ. He felt, as no other felt, a union of mind with the human race, felt that all had a spark of that same intellectual and immortal flame which dwelt in himself.

I insist on this view of his character, not only to encourage us to aspire after a likeness to Jesus ; I consider it as peculiarly fitted to call forth love towards him. If I regard Jesus as an august stranger, belonging to an entirely different class of existence from myself, having no common thoughts or feelings with me, and looking down upon me with only such a sympathy as I have with an inferior animal, I should regard him with a vague awe ; but the immeasurable space between us would place him beyond friendship and affection. But when I feel, that all minds form one family, that I have the same nature with Jesus, and that he came to communicate to me, by his teaching, example, and intercession, his own mind, to bring me into communion with what was sublimest, purest, happiest in himself, then I can love him as I love no other being, excepting only Him who is the Father alike of Christ and of the Christian. With these views, I feel that, though ascended to Heaven, he is not gone beyond the reach of our hearts; that he has now the same interest in mankind as when he entered their dwellings, sat at their tables, washed their feet; and that there is no being so approachable, none with whom such unreserved intercourse is to be enjoyed in the future world.

Believing, as I do, that I have now used no inflated language, but have spoken the words of truth and soberness, I exhort you with calmness, but earnestness, to choose and adopt Jesus Christ as your example, with the whole energy of your wills. I exhort you to resolve on following him, not, as perhaps you have done, with a faint and yielding purpose, but with the full conviction, that your whole happiness is concentrated in the force and constancy of your adherence to this celestial guide. My friends, there is no other happiness. Let not the false views of Christianity which prevail in the world, seduce you into the belief, that Christ can bless you in any other way than by assimilating you to his own virtue, than by breathing into you his own mind. Do not imagine that any faith or love towards Jesus can avail you, but that which quickens you to conform yourselves to his spotless purity and unconquerable rectitude. Settle it as an immovable truth, that neither in this world nor in the next can you be happy, but in proportion to the sanctity and elevation of your characters. Let no man imagine, that through the patronage or protection of Jesus Christ, or any other being, he can find peace or any sincere good, but in the growth of an enlightened, firm, disinterested, holy mind. Expect no good from Jesus, any farther than you clothe yourselves with excellence. He can impart to you nothing so precious as himself, as his own mind; and believe me, my hearers, this mind may dwell in you. His sublimest virtues may be yours. Admit, welcome this great truth. Look up to the illustrious Son of God, with the conviction that you may become one with him in thought, in feeling, in power, in holiness. His character will become a blessing, just as far as it shall awaken in you this consciousness, this hope. The most lamentable skepticism on earth, and incomparably the most common, is a skepticism as to the greatness, powers, and high destinies of human nature. In this greatness I desire to cherish an unwavering faith. Tell me not of the universal corruption of the race. Humanity has already, in not a few instances, borne conspicuously the likeness of Christ and God. The sun grows dim, the grandeur of outward nature shrinks, when compared with the spiritual energy of men, who, in the cause of truth, of God, of charity, have spurned all bribes of ease, pleasure, renown, and have withstood shame, want, persecution, torture, and the most dreaded forms of death. In such men I learn that the soul was made in God's image, and made to conform itself to the loveliness and greatness of his Son.

My Friends, we may all approach Jesus Christ. For all of us he died, to leave us an example that we should follow his steps. By earnest purpose, by self-conflict, by watching and prayer, by faith in the Christian promises, by those heavenly aids and illuminations, which he that seeketh shall find, we may all unite ourselves, in living bonds, to Christ, may love as he loved, may act from his principles, may suffer with his constancy, may enter into his purposes, may sympathize with his self-devotion to the cause of God and mankind, and, by likeness of spirit, may prepare ourselves to meet him as our everlasting friend.

THE EVIL OF SIN.

Proverbs xiv. 9: "Fools make a mock at sin."

My aim in this discourse is simple, and may be expressed in a few words. I wish to guard you against thinking lightly of sin. No folly is so monstrous, and yet our exposure to it is great. Breathing an atmosphere tainted with moral evil, seeing and hearing sin in our daily walks, we are in no small danger of overlooking its malignity. This malignity I would set before you with all plainness, believing that the effort which is needed to resist this enemy of our peace, is to be called forth by fixing on it our frequent and serious attention.

I feel as if a difficulty lay at the very threshold of this discussion, which it is worth our while to remove. The word Sin, I apprehend, is to many obscure, or not sufficiently plain. It is a word seldom used in common life. It belongs to theology and the pulpit. By not a few people, sin is supposed to be a property of our nature, born with us; and we sometimes hear of the child as being sinful before it can have performed any action. From these and other causes, the word gives to many confused notions. Sin, in its true sense, is the violation of duty, and cannot, consequently, exist, before conscience has begun to act, and before power to obey it is unfolded. To sin is to resist our sense of right, to oppose known obligation, to cherish feelings, or commit deeds, which we know to be wrong. It is, to withhold from God the reverence, gratitude, and obedience, which our own consciences pronounce to be due to that great and good Being. It is, to transgress those laws of equity, justice, candor, humanity, disinterestedness, which we all feel to belong and to answer to our various social relations. It is, to yield ourselves to those appetites which we know to be the inferior principles of our nature, to give the body a mastery over the mind, to sacrifice the intellect and heart to the senses, to surrender ourselves to ease and indulgence, or to prefer outward accumulation and power to strength and peace of conscience, to progress towards perfection. Such is sin. It is voluntary wrong-doing. Any gratification injurious to ourselves, is sin. Any act injurious to our neighbours, is sin. Indifference to our Creator, is sin. The transgression of any command which this excellent Being and rightful Sovereign has given us, whether by conscience or revelation, is sin. So broad is this term. It is as extensive as duty. It is not some mysterious thing wrought into our souls at birth. It is not a theological subtilty. It is choosing and acting in opposition to our sense of right, to known obligation.

Now, according to the Scriptures, there is nothing so evil, so deformed, so ruinous as sin. All pain, poverty, contempt, affliction, ill success, are light, and not to be named with it. To do wrong is more pernicious than to incur all the calamities which nature or human malice can heap upon us. According to the Scriptures, I am not to fear those who would kill this body, and have nothing more that they can do. Such enemies are impotent, compared with that sin which draws down the displeasure of God, and draws after it misery and death to the soul. According to the Scriptures, I am to pluck out even a right eye, or cut off even a right arm, which would ensnare or seduce me into crime. The loss of the most important limbs and organs, is nothing compared to the loss of innocence. Such you know is the whole strain of Scripture. Sin, violated duty, the evil of the heart, this is the only evil of which Scripture takes account. It was from this that Christ came to redeem us. It is to purify us from this stain, to set us free from this yoke, that a new and supernatural agency was added to God's other means of promoting human happiness.

It is the design of these representations of Scripture, to lead us to connect with sin or wrong-doing the ideas of evil, wretchedness, and debasement, more strongly than with any thing else; and this deep, deliberate conviction of the wrong and evil done to ourselves by sin, is not simply a command of Christianity. It is not an arbitrary, positive precept, which rests solely on the word of the lawgiver, and of which no account can be given but that he wills it. It is alike the dictate of natural and revealed religion, an injunction of conscience and reason, founded in our very souls, and confirmed by constant experience. To regard sin, wrong-doing, as the greatest of evils, is God's command, proclaimed from within and without, from Heaven and earth; and he who does not hear it, has not learned the truth on which his whole happiness rests. This I propose to illustrate.

1. If we look within, we find in our very nature a testimony to the doctrine, that sin is the chief of evils, a testimony which, however slighted or smothered, will be recognised, I think, by every one who hears me. To understand this truth better, it may be useful to inquire into and compare the different kinds of evil. Evil has various forms, but these may all be reduced to two great divisions, called by philosophers *natural* and *moral*. By the first, is meant the pain or suffering which springs from outward condition and events, or from causes independent of the will. The latter, that is, moral evil, belongs to character and conduct, and is commonly expressed by the words sin, vice, transgression of the rule of right. Now I say, that there is no man, unless he be singularly hardened and an exception to his race, who, if these two classes or divisions of evil should be clearly and fully presented him in moments of calm and deliberate thinking, would not feel, through the very constitution of his mind, that sin or vice is worse and more to be dreaded than pain. I am willing to take from among you, the individual who has studied least the great questions of morality and religion, whose mind has grown up with least discipline. If I place before such a hearer two examples in strong contrast, one of a man gaining great property by an atrocious crime, and another exposing himself to great suffering through a resolute purpose of duty, will he not tell me at once, from a deep moral sentiment, which leaves not a doubt on his mind, that the last has chosen the better part, that he is more to be envied than the first? On these great questions, What is the chief good? and What the chief evil? we are instructed by our own nature. An inward voice has

told men, even in heathen countries, that excellence of character is the supreme good, and that baseness of soul and of action involves something worse than suffering. We have all of us, at some periods of life, had the same conviction; and these have been the periods when the mind has been healthiest, clearest, least perturbed by passion. Is there any one here who does not feel, that what the divine faculty of conscience enjoins as right, has stronger claims upon him than what is recommended as merely agreeable or advantageous; that duty is something more sacred than interest or pleasure; that virtue is a good of a higher order than gratification; that crime is something worse than outward loss? What means the admiration with which we follow the conscientious and disinterested man, and which grows strong in proportion to his sacrifices to duty? Is it not the testimony of our whole souls to the truth and greatness of the good he has chosen? What means the feeling of abhorrence, which we cannot repress if we would, towards him who, by abusing confidence, trampling on weakness, or hardening himself against the appeals of mercy, has grown rich or great? Do we think that such a man has made a good bargain in bartering principle for wealth? Is prosperous fortune a balance for vice? In our deliberate moments, is there not a voice which pronounces his craft folly, and his success misery?

And, to come nearer home, what conviction is it, which springs up most spontaneously in our more reflecting moments, when we look back without passion on our own lives? Can vice *stand* that calm look? Is there a single wrong act, which we would not then rejoice to expunge from the unalterable records of our deeds? Do we ever congratulate ourselves on having despised the inward monitor, or revolted against God? To what portions of our history do we return most joyfully? Are they those in which we gained the world and lost the soul, in which temptation mastered our principles, which levity and sloth made a blank, or which a selfish and unprincipled activity made worse than a blank, in our existence? or are they those in which we suffered, but were true to conscience, in which we denied ourselves for duty, and sacrificed success through unwavering rectitude? In these moments of calm recollection, do not the very transgressions at which perhaps we once mocked, and which promised unmixed joy, recur to awaken shame and remorse? And do not shame and remorse involve a consciousness that we have sunk beneath our proper good? that our highest nature, what constitutes our true self, has been sacrificed to low interests and pursuits? I make these appeals confidently. I think my questions can receive but one answer. Now, these convictions and emotions, with which we witness moral evil in others, or recollect it in ourselves, these feelings towards guilt, which mere pain and suffering never excite, and which manifest themselves with more or less distinctness in all nations and all stages of society, these inward attestations that sin, wrong-doing, is a peculiar evil, for which no outward good can give adequate compensation, surely these deserve to be regarded as the voice of nature, the voice of God. They are accompanied with a peculiar consciousness of truth. They are felt to be our ornament and defence. Thus our nature teaches the doctrine of Christianity, that sin, or moral evil, ought of all evils to inspire most abhorrence and fear.

Our first argument has been drawn from Sentiment

from deep and almost instinctive feeling, from the handwriting of the Creator on the soul. Our next, may be drawn from experience. We have said, that even when sin or wrong-doing is prosperous, and duty brings suffering, we feel that the suffering is a less evil than sin. I now add, in the second place, that sin, though it sometimes prospers, and never meets its full retribution on earth, yet, on the whole, produces more present suffering than all things else ; so that experience warns us against sin or wrong-doing as the chief evil we can incur. Whence come the sorest diseases and acutest bodily pains ? Come they not from the lusts warring in our members, from criminal excess ? What chiefly generates poverty and its worst sufferings ? Is it not to evils of character, to the want of self-denying virtue, that we must ascribe chiefly the evils of our outward condition ? The pages of history, how is it that they are so dark and sad ? Is it not, that they are stained with crime ? If we penetrate into private life, what spreads most misery through our homes ? Is it sickness, or selfishness ? Is it want of outward comforts, or want of inward discipline, of the spirit of love ? What more do we need to bring back Eden's happiness, than Eden's sinlessness ? How light a burden would be life's necessary ills, were they not aided by the crushing weight of our own and others' faults and crimes ? How fast would human woe vanish, were human selfishness, sensuality, injustice, pride, impiety, to yield to the pure and benign influences of Christian truth ? How many of us know, that the sharpest pains we have ever suffered, have been the wounds of pride, the paroxysms of passion, the stings of remorse ; and where this is not the case, who of us, if he were to know his own soul, would not see.

that the daily restlessness of life, the wearing uneasiness of the mind, which, as a whole, brings more suffering than acute pains, is altogether the result of undisciplined passions, of neglect or disobedience of God? Our discontents and anxieties have their origin in moral evil. The lines of suffering on almost every human countenance have been deepened, if not traced there, by unfaithfulness to conscience, by departures from duty. To do wrong is the surest way to bring suffering; no wrong deed ever failed to bring it. Those sins which are followed by no palpable pain, are yet terribly avenged even in this life. They abridge our capacity of happiness, impair our relish for innocent pleasure, and increase our sensibility to suffering. They spoil us of the armour of a pure conscience, and of trust in God, without which we are naked amidst hosts of foes, and are vulnerable by all the changes of life. Thus, to do wrong is to inflict the surest injury on our own peace. No enemy can do us equal harm with what we do ourselves, whenever or however we violate any moral or religious obligation.

I have time but for one more view of moral evil or sin, showing that it is truly the greatest evil. It is this. The miseries of disobedience to conscience and God are not exhausted in this life. Sin deserves, calls for, and will bring down Future, greater misery. This Christianity teaches, and this nature teaches. Retribution is not a new doctrine brought by Christ into the world. Though darkened and corrupted, it was spread everywhere before he came. It carried alarm to rude nations, which nothing on earth could terrify. It mixed with all the false religions of antiquity, and it finds a response now in every mind not perverted by sophistry. That we shall carry with us into the future world our present minds, and that a character, formed in opposition to our highest faculties and to the will of God, will produce suffering in our future being, these are truths, in which revelation, reason, and conscience remarkably conspire.

I know, indeed, that this doctrine is sometimes questioned. It is maintained by some among us, that punishment is confined to the present state; that in changing worlds we shall change our characters; that moral evil is to be buried with the body in the grave. As this opinion spreads industriously, and as it tends to diminish the dread of sin, it deserves some notice. To my mind, a more irrational doctrine was never broached. In the first place, it contradicts all our experience of the nature and laws of the mind. There is nothing more striking in the mind, than the connexion of its successive states. Our present knowledge, thoughts, feelings characters, are the results of former impressions, passions, and pursuits. We are this moment what the past has made us; and to suppose, that at death the influences of our whole past course are to cease on our minds, and that a character is to spring up altogether at war with what has preceded it, is to suppose the most important law or principle of the mind to be violated, is to destroy all analogy between the present and future, and to substitute for experience the wildest dreams of fancy. In truth, such a sudden revolution in the character, as is here supposed, seems to destroy a man's identity. The individual thus transformed, can hardly seem to himself or to others the same being. It is equivalent to the creation of a new soul.

Let me next ask, what fact can be adduced in proof or illustration of the power ascribed to death, of changing and purifying the mind ? What is death ? It is the dissolution of certain limbs and organs by which the soul now acts. But these, however closely connected with the mind, are entirely distinct from its powers, from thought and will, from conscience and affection. Why should the last grow pure from the dissolution of the first ? Why shall the mind put on a new character, by laying aside the gross instruments through which it now operates ? At death, the hands, the feet, the eye, and the ear perish. But they often perish during life ; and does character change with them ? It is true that our animal appetites are weakened and sometimes destroyed by the decay of the bodily organs on which they depend. But our deeper principles of action, and the moral complexion of the mind, are not therefore reversed. It often happens, that the sensualist, broken down by disease, which excess has induced, comes to loathe the luxuries to which he was once enslaved ; but do his selfishness, his low habits of thought, his insensibility to God, decline and perish with his animal desires ? Lop off the criminal's hands ; does the disposition to do mischief vanish with them ? When the feet mortify, do we see a corresponding mortification of the will to go astray ? The loss of sight or hearing is a partial death ; but is a single vice plucked from the mind, or one of its strong passions palsied, by this destruction of its chief corporeal instruments ?

Again ; the idea that by dying, or changing worlds, a man may be made better or virtuous, shows an ignorance of the nature of moral goodness or virtue. This belongs to free beings ; it supposes moral liberty. A man cannot be made virtuous, as an instrument may be put in tune, by a foreign hand, by an outward force. Virtue is that to which the man himself contributes. It is the fruit of exertion. It supposes conquest of temptation. It cannot be given from abroad to one who has wasted life, or steeped himself in crime. To suppose moral goodness breathed from abroad into the guilty mind, just as health may be imparted to a sick body, is to overlook the distinction between corporeal and intellectual natures, and to degrade a free being into a machine.

I will only add, that to suppose no connexion to exist between the present and the future character, is to take away the use of the present state. Why are we placed in a state of discipline, exposed to temptation, encompassed with suffering, if, without discipline, and by a sovereign act of omnipotence, we are all of us, be our present characters what they may, soon and suddenly to be made perfect in virtue, and perfect in happiness?

Let us not listen for a moment to a doctrine so irrational, as that our present characters do not follow us into a future world. If we are to live again, let us settle it as a sure fact, that we shall carry with us our present minds, such as we now make them; that we shall reap good or ill according to their improvement or corruption; and, of consequence, that every act, which affects character, will reach in its influence beyond the grave, and have a bearing on our future weal or woe. We are now framing our future lot. He who does a bad deed says, more strongly than words can utter, "I cast away a portion of future good, I resolve on future pain."

I proceed now to an important and solemn remark, in illustration of the evil of sin. It is plainly implied in Scripture, that we shall suffer much more from sin, evil tempers, irreligion, in the future world, than we suffer here. This is one main distinction between the two states. In the present world, sin does indeed bring with it many pains, but not full or exact retribution, and sometimes it seems crowned with prosperity; and the cause of this is obvious. The present world is a state for the formation of character. It is meant to be a state of trial, where we are to act freely, to have opportunities of wrong as well as right action, and to become virtuous amidst temptation. Now such a purpose requires, that sin, or wrong-doing, should not regularly and infallibly produce its full and immediate punishment. For, suppose, my hearers, that, at the very instant of a bad purpose or a bad deed, a sore and awful penalty were unfailingly to light upon you; would this be consistent with trial? would you have moral freedom? would you not live under compulsion? Who would do wrong, if judgment were to come like lightning after every evil deed? In such a world, fear would suspend our liberty and supersede conscience. Accordingly sin, though, as we have seen, it produces great misery, is still left to compass many of its objects, often to prosper, often to be gain. Vice, bad as it is, has often many pleasures in its train. The worst men partake, equally with the good, the light of the sun, the rain, the harvest, the accommodations and improvements of civilized life, and sometimes accumulate more largely outward goods. And thus sin has its pleasures, and escapes many of its natural and proper fruits. We live in a world where, if we please, we may forget ourselves, may delude ourselves, may intoxicate our minds with false hopes, and may find for a time a deceitful joy in an evil course. In this respect the future will differ from the present world. After death, character will produce its full effect. According to the Scriptures, the color of our future existence will be wholly determined by the habits and principles which we carry into it. The circumstances which in this life prevent vice, sin, wrong-doing, from inflicting pain, will not operate hereafter. There the evil mind will be exposed to its own terrible agency, and nothing, nothing will interfere between the transgressor and his own awakened conscience. I ask you to pause, and weigh this distinction between the present and future. In the present life, we have, as I have said, the means of escaping, amusing, and forgetting ourselves. Once, in the course of every daily revolution of the sun, we all of us find refuge, and many a long refuge, in sleep; and he who has lived without God, and in violation of his duty, hears not, for hours, a whisper of the monitor within. But sleep is a function of our present animal frame, and let not the transgressor anticipate this boon in the world of retribution before him. It may be, and he has reason to fear, that in that state repose will not weigh down his eyelids, that conscience will not slumber there, that night and day the same reproaching voice is to cry within, that unrepented sin will fasten with unrelaxing grasp on the ever-waking soul. What an immense change in condition would the removal of this single alleviation of suffering produce?

Again; in the present state, how many pleasant sights, scenes, voices, motions, draw us from ourselves; and he who has done wrong, how easily may he forget it, perhaps mock at it, under the bright light of this sun, on this fair earth, at the table of luxury, and amidst cheerful associates. In the state of retribution, he who has abused the present state, will find no such means of escaping the wages of sin. The precise mode in which such a man is to exist hereafter, I know not. But I know, that it will offer nothing to amuse him, to dissipate thought, to turn him away from himself; nothing to which he can fly for refuge from the inward penalties of transgression.

In the present life, I have said, the outward creation, by its interesting objects, draws the evil man from himself. It seems to me probable, that, in the future, the whole creation will, through sin, be turned into a source of suffering, and will perpetually throw back the evil mind on its own transgressions. I can briefly state the reflections which lead to this anticipation. The Scriptures strongly imply, if not positively teach, that in the future life we shall exist in connexion with some material frame; and the doctrine is sustained by reason; for it can hardly be thought, that in a creation which is marked by gradual change and progress, we should make at once the mighty transition from our present state into a purely spiritual or unembodied existence. Now in the present state we find, that the mind has an immense power over the body, and, when diseased, often communicates disease to its sympathizing companion. I believe, that, in the future state, the mind will have this power of conforming its outward frame to itself, incomparably more than here. We must never forget, that in that world mind or character is to exert an all-powerful sway; and accordingly, it is rational to believe, that the corrupt and deformed mind, which wants moral goodness, or a spirit of concord with God and with the universe, will create for itself, as its fit dwelling, a deformed body, which will also want concord or harmony with all things around it. Suppose this to exist, and the whole creation which now amuses, may become an instrument of suffering, fixing the soul with a more harrowing consciousness on itself. You know that even now, in consequence of certain derangements of the nervous system, the beautiful light gives acute pain, and sounds, which once delighted us, become shrill and distressing. How often this excessive irritableness of the body has its origin in moral disorders, perhaps few of us suspect. I apprehend, indeed, that we should be all amazed, were we to learn to what extent the body is continually incapacitated for enjoyment, and made susceptible of suffering, by sins of the heart and life. That delicate part of our organization, on which sensibility, pain, and pleasure depend, is, I believe, peculiarly alive to the touch of moral evil. How easily, then, may the mind hereafter frame the future body according to itself, so that, in proportion to its vice, it will receive, through its organs and senses, impressions of gloom, which it will feel to be the natural productions of its own depravity, and which will in this way give a terrible energy to conscience! For myself, I see no need of a local hell for the sinner after death. When I reflect, how, in the present world, a guilty mind has power to deform the countenance, to undermine health, to poison pleasure, to darken the fairest scenes of nature, to turn prosperity into a curse, I can easily understand how, in the world to come, sin, working without obstruction according to its own nature, should spread the gloom of a dungeon over the whole creation, and wherever it goes, should turn the universe into a hell.

In these remarks I presume not to be the prophet of the future world. I only wish you to feel how terribly sin is hereafter to work its own misery, and how false and dangerous it is to argue from your present power of escaping its consequences, that you may escape them in the life to come. Let each of us be assured, that by abusing this world, we shall not earn a better. The Scriptures announce a state of more exact and rigorous retribution than the present. Let this truth sink into our hearts. It shows us, what I have aimed to establish, that to do wrong is to incur the greatest of calamities, that sin is the chief of evils. May I not say, that nothing else deserves the name ? No other evil will follow us beyond the grave. Poverty, disease, the world's scorn, the pain of bereaved affection, these cease at the grave. The purified spirit lays down there every burden. One and only one evil can be carried from this world to the next, and that is, the evil within us, moral evil, guilt, crime, ungoverned passion, the depraved mind, the memory of a wasted or ill-spent life, the character which has grown up under neglect of God's voice in the soul and in his word. This, this will go with us, to stamp itself on our future frames, to darken our future being, to separate us like an impassable gulf from our Creator and from pure and happy beings, to be as a consuming fire and an undying worm.

I have spoken of the pains and penalties of moral evil, or of wrong-doing, in the world to come. How long they will endure, I know not. Whether they will issue in the reformation and happiness of the sufferer, or will terminate in the extinction of his conscious being, is a question on which Scripture throws no clear light. Plausible arguments may be adduced in support of both these doctrines. On this and on other points revelation aims not to give precise information, but to fix in us a deep impression, that great suffering awaits a disobedient, wasted, immoral, irreligious life. To fasten this impression, to make it a deliberate and practical conviction, is more needful than to ascertain the mode or duration of future suffering. May the views this day given, lead us all to self-communion, and to new energy, watchfulness, and prayer against our sins. May they teach us, that to do wrong, to neglect or violate any known duty, is of all evils the most fearful. Let every act, or feeling, or motive, which bears the brand of guilt, seem to us more terrible than the worst calamities of life. Let us dread it more than the **agonies** of the most painful death.

IMMORTALITY.

2 Timothy i. 10: "Our Saviour Jesus Christ, who hath abolished death, and hath brought life and immortality to light through the Gospel."

Immortality is the glorious discovery of Christianity. I say discovery, not because a future life was wholly unknown before Christ, but because it was so revealed by him as to become, to a considerable extent, a new doctrine. Before Christ, immortality was a conjecture or a vague hope. Jesus, by his teaching and resurrection, has made it a certainty. Again, before Christ, a future life lent little aid to virtue. It was seized upon by the imagination and passions, and so perverted by them as often to minister to vice. In Christianity this doctrine is wholly turned to a moral use; and the Future is revealed only to give motives, resolution, force, to self-conflict and to a holy life.

My aim in this discourse is, to strengthen, if I may, your conviction of immortality; and I have thought that I may do this by showing, that this great truth is also a dictate of nature; that reason, though unable to establish it, yet accords with and adopts it; that it is written alike in God's word and in the soul. It is plainly rational to expect, that, if man was made for immortality, the marks of this destination will be found in his very constitution, and that these marks will grow stronger in proportion to the unfolding of his faculties. I would show, that this expectation proves just, that the teaching of revelation, in regard to a future life, finds a strong response in our own nature.

This topic is the more important, because to some men there seem to be appearances in nature unfavorable to immortality. To many, the constant operation of decay in all the works of creation, the dissolution of all the forms of animal and vegetable nature, gives a feeling, as if destruction were the law to which we and all beings are subjected.

It has often been said by the skeptic, that the *races* or classes of being are alone perpetual, that all the *individuals* which compose them are doomed to perish. Now I affirm, that the more we know of the Mind, the more we see reason to distinguish it from the animal and vegetable races which grow and decay around us; and that in its very nature we see reason for exempting it from the universal law of destruction. To this point, I now ask your attention.

When we look round us on the earth, we do indeed see every thing changing, decaying, passing away; and so inclined are we to reason from analogy or resemblance, that it is not wonderful that the dissolution of all the organized forms of matter should seem to us to announce our own destruction. But we overlook the distinctions between matter and mind; and these are so immense as to justify the directly opposite conclusion. Let me point out some of these distinctions.

1. When we look at the organized productions of nature, we see that they require only a limited time and most of them a very short time, to reach their perfection, and accomplish their end. Take, for example, that noble production, a tree. Having reached a certain height and borne leaves, flowers, and fruit, it has nothing more to do. Its powers are fully developed ; it has no hidden capacities, of which its buds and fruit are only the beginnings and pledges. Its design is fulfilled ; the principle of life within it can effect no more. Not so the mind. We can never say of this, as of the full-grown tree in autumn, It has answered its end, it has done its work, its capacity is exhausted. On the contrary, the nature, powers, desires, and purposes of the mind are all undefined. We never feel, when a great intellect has risen to an original thought, or a vast discovery, that it has now accomplished its whole purpose, reached its bound, and can yield no other or higher fruits. On the contrary, our conviction of its resources is enlarged ; we discern more of its affinity to the inexhaustible intelligence of its Author. In every step of its progress, we see a new impulse gained and the pledge of nobler acquirements. So, when a pure and resolute mind has made some great sacrifice to truth and duty, has manifested its attachment to God and man in singular trials, we do not feel as if the whole energy of virtuous principle were now put forth, as if the measure of excellence were filled, as if the maturest fruits were now borne, and henceforth the soul could only repeat itself. We feel, on the contrary, that virtue by illustrious efforts replenishes instead of wasting its life ; that the mind by perseverence in well-doing, instead of sinking into a mechanical tameness, is able to conceive of higher duties, is

armed for a nobler daring, and grows more efficient in charity. The mind, by going forward, does not reach insurmountable prison-walls, but learns more and more the boundlessness of its powers, and of the range for which it was created.

Let me place this topic in another light, which may show, even more strongly, the contrast of the mind with the noblest productions of matter. My meaning may best be conveyed by reverting to the tree. We consider the tree as having answered its highest purpose, when it yields a particular fruit. We judge of its perfection by a fixed, positive, definite product. The mind, however, in proportion to its improvement, becomes conscious that its perfection consists not in fixed, prescribed effects, not in exact and defined attainments, but in an original, creative, unconfinable energy, which yields new products, which carries it into new fields of thought and new efforts for religion and humanity. This truth indeed is so obvious, that even the least improved may discern it. You all feel, that the most perfect mind is not that which works in a prescribed way, which thinks and acts according to prescribed rules, but that which has a spring of action in itself, which combines anew the knowledge received from other minds, which explores its hidden and multiplied relations, and gives it forth in fresh and higher forms. The perfection of the tree, then, lies in a precise or definite product. That of the mind lies in an indefinite and boundless energy. The first implies limits. To set limits to the mind, would destroy that original power in which its perfection consists. Here, then, we observe a distinction between material forms and the mind; and from the destruction of the first, which, as we see, attain perfection and fulfil their purpose in a limited duration, we cannot argue to the destruction of the last, which plainly possesses the capacity of a progress without end.

2. We have pointed out one contrast between the mind and material forms. The latter, we have seen, by their nature have bounds. The tree in a short time, and by rising and spreading a short distance, accomplishes its end. I now add, that the system of nature to which the tree belongs, requires that it should stop where it does. Were it to grow for ever, it would be an infinite mischief. A single plant, endued with the principle of unlimited expansion, would in the progress of centuries overshadow nations and exclude every other growth, would exhaust the earth's whole fertility. Material forms, then, must have narrow bounds, and their usefulness requires that their life and growth should often be arrested even before reaching the limits prescribed by nature. But the indefinite expansion of the mind, instead of warring with and counteracting the system of creation, harmonizes with and perfects it. One tree, should it grow for ever, would exclude other forms of vegetable life. One mind, in proportion to its expansion, awakens and in a sense creates other minds. It multiplies, instead of exhausting, the nutriment which other understandings need. A mind, the more it has of intellectual and moral life, the more it spreads life and power around it. It is an ever-enlarging source of thought and love. Let me here add, that the mind, by unlimited growth, not only yields a greater amount of good to other beings, but it produces continually new forms of good. This is an important distinction. Were the tree to spread indefinitely, it would abound more in fruit, but in fruit of the same

kind; and, by excluding every other growth, it would destroy the variety of products, which now contribute to health and enjoyment. But the mind, in its progress, is perpetually yielding new fruits, new forms of thought and virtue and sanctity. It always contains within itself the germs of higher influences than it has ever put forth, the buds of fruits which it has never borne. Thus the very reason which requires the limitation of material forms, I mean the good of the whole system, seems to require the unlimited growth of mind.

3. Another distinction between material forms and the mind is, that to the former destruction is no loss. They exist for others wholly, in no degree for themselves; and others only can sorrow for their fall. The mind, on the contrary, has a deep interest in its own existence. In this respect, indeed, it is distinguished from the animal as well as the vegetable. To the animal, the past is a blank, and so is the future. The present is every thing. But to the mind the present is comparatively nothing. Its great sources of happiness are memory and hope. It has power over the past, not only the power of recalling it, but of turning to good all its experience, its errors and sufferings as well as its successes. It has power over the future, not only the power of anticipating it, but of bringing the present to bear upon it, and of sowing for it the seeds of a golden harvest. To a mind capable of thus connecting itself with all duration, of spreading itself through times past and to come, existence becomes infinitely dear, and, what is most worthy of observation, its interest in its own being increases with its progress in power and virtue. An improved mind understands the greatness of its own nature, and the worth of existence,

as these cannot be understood by the unimproved. The thought of its own destruction suggests to it an extent of ruin, which the latter cannot comprehend. The thought of such faculties as reason, conscience, and moral will, being extinguished, — of powers, akin to the divine energy, being annihilated by their Author, — of truth and virtue, those images of God, being blotted out, — of progress towards perfection, being broken off almost at its beginning, — this is a thought fitted to overwhelm a mind, in which the consciousness of its own spiritual nature is in a good degree unfolded. In other words, the more the mind is true to itself and to God, the more it clings to existence, the more it shrinks from extinction as an infinite loss. Would not its destruction, then, be a very different thing from the destruction of material beings, and does the latter furnish an analogy or presumption in support of the former? To me, the undoubted fact, that the mind thirsts for continued being, just in proportion as it obeys the will of its Maker, is a proof, next to irresistible, of its being destined by him for immortality.

4. Let me add one more distinction between the mind and material forms. I return to the tree. We speak of the tree as *destroyed*. We say that destruction is the order of nature, and some say that man must not hope to escape the universal law. Now we deceive ourselves in this use of words. There is in reality no destruction in the material world. True, the tree is resolved into its elements. But its elements survive, and, still more, they survive to fulfil the same end which they before accomplished. Not a power of nature is lost. The particles of the decayed tree are only left at liberty to form

new, perhaps more beautiful and useful combinations. They may shoot up into more luxuriant foliage, or enter into the structure of the highest animals. But were mind to perish, there would be absolute, irretrievable destruction; for mind, from its nature, is something individual, an uncompounded essence, which cannot be broken into parts, and enter into union with other minds. I am myself, and can become no other being. My experience, my history, cannot become my neighbour's. My consciousness, my memory, my interest in my past life, my affections, cannot be transferred. If in any instance I have withstood temptation, and through such resistance have acquired power over myself and a claim to the approbation of my fellow-beings, this resistance, this power, this claim are my own; I cannot make them another's. I can give away my property, my limbs; but that which makes myself, in other words, my consciousness, my recollections, my feelings, my hopes, these can never become parts of another mind. In the extinction of a thinking, moral being, who has gained truth and virtue, there would be an absolute destruction. This event would not be as the setting of the sun, which is a transfer of light to new regions; but a quenching of the light. It would be a ruin such as nature nowhere exhibits, a ruin of what is infinitely more precious than the outward universe, and is not, therefore, to be inferred from any of the changes of the material world.

I am aware, that views of this nature, intended to show us that immortality is impressed on the soul itself, fail to produce conviction from various causes. There are not a few, who are so accustomed to look on the errors and crimes of society, that human nature seems to them little raised above the brutal; and they hear, with a secret incredulity, of those distinctions and capacities of the mind which point to its perpetual existence. To such men, I might say, that it is a vicious propensity which leads them to fasten continually and exclusively on the sins of human nature; just as it is criminal to fix the thoughts perpetually on the miseries of human life, and to see nothing but evil in the order of creation and the providence of God. But, passing over this, I allow that human nature abounds in crime. But this does not destroy my conviction of its greatness and immortality. I say, that I see in crime itself the proofs of human greatness and of an immortal nature. The position may seem extravagant, but it may be fully sustained.

I ask you first to consider, what is implied in crime. Consider in what it originates. It has its origin in the noblest principle that can belong to any being; I mean, in moral freedom. There can be no crime without liberty of action, without moral power. Were man a machine, were he a mere creature of sensation and impulse, like the brute, he could do no wrong. It is only because he has the faculties of reason and conscience, and a power over himself, that he is capable of contracting guilt. Thus great guilt is itself a testimony to the high endowments of the soul.

In the next place, let me ask you to consider, whence it is that man sins. He sins by being exposed to temptation. Now the great design of temptation plainly is, that the soul, by withstanding it, should gain strength, should make progress, should become a proper object of divine reward. That is, man sins through an exposure which is designed to carry him forward to perfection, so that the cause of his guilt points to a continued and improved existence.

In the next place, I say, that guilt has a peculiar consciousness belonging to it, which speaks strongly of a future life. It carries with it intimations of retribution. Its natural associate is fear. The connexion of misery with crime is anticipated by a kind of moral instinct; and the very circumstance, that the unprincipled man sometimes escapes present suffering, suggests more strongly a future state, where this apparent injustice will be redressed, and where present prosperity will become an aggravation of woe. Guilt sometimes speaks of a future state even in louder and more solemn tones than virtue. It has been known to overwhelm the spirit with terrible forebodings, and has found through its presentiments the hell which it feared. Thus guilt does not destroy, but corroborates, the proofs contained in the soul itself of its own future being.

Let me add one more thought. The sins, which abound in the world, and which are so often adduced to chill our belief in the capacities and vast prospects of human nature, serve to place in stronger relief, and in brighter light, the examples of piety and virtue, which all must acknowledge, are to be found among the guilty multitude. A mind which, in such a world, amidst so many corrupting influences, holds fast to truth, duty, and God, is a nobler mind than any which could be formed in the absence of such temptation. Thus the great sinfulness of the world makes the virtue which exists in it more glorious; and the very struggles which the good man has to maintain with its allurements and persecutions, prepare him for a brighter reward. To me such views are singularly interesting and encouraging. I delight to behold the testimony which sin itself furnishes to man's greatness and immortality. I indeed see great guilt on earth ; but I see it giving occasion to great moral strength, and to singular devotion and virtue in the good, and thus throwing on human nature a lustre which more than compensates for its own deformity. I do not shut my eyes on the guilt of my race. I see, in history, human malignity, so aggravated, so unrelenting, as even to pursue with torture, and to doom to the most agonizing death, the best of human beings. But when I see these beings unmoved by torture ; meek, and calm, and forgiving in their agonies ; superior to death, and never so glorious as in the last hour, — I forget the guilt which persecutes them, in my admiration of their virtue. In their sublime constancy, I see a testimony to the worth and immortality of human nature, that outweighs the wickedness of which they seem to be the victims ; and I feel an assurance, which nothing can wrest from me, that the godlike virtue, which has thus been driven from earth, will find a home, an everlasting home, in its native heaven. Thus sin itself becomes a witness to the future life of man.

I have thus, my hearers, endeavoured to show, that our nature, the more it is inquired into, discovers more clearly the impress of immortality. I do not mean, that this evidence supersedes all other. From its very nature it can only be understood thoroughly by improved and purified minds. The proof of immortality, which is suited to all understandings, is found in the Gospel, sealed by the blood and confirmed by the resurrection of Christ. But this, I think, is made more impressive, by a demonstration of its harmony with the teachings of nature. To me, nature and revelation speak with one voice on the great theme of man's future being. Let not their joint witness be unheard.

How full, how bright, are the evidences of this grand truth. How weak are the common arguments, which skepticism arrays against it. To me there is but one objection against immortality, if objection it may be called, and this arises from the very greatness of the truth. My mind sometimes sinks under its weight, is lost in its immensity; I scarcely dare believe that such a good is placed within my reach. When I think of myself, as existing through all future ages, as surviving this earth and that sky, as exempted from every imperfection and error of my present being, as clothed with an angel's glory, as comprehending with my intellect and embracing in my affections an extent of creation compared with which the earth is a point; when I think of myself, as looking on the outward universe with an organ of vision that will reveal to me a beauty and harmony and order not now imagined, and as having an access to the minds of the wise and good, which will make them in a sense my own; when I think of myself, as forming friendships with innumerable beings of rich and various intellect and of the noblest virtue, as introduced to the society of heaven, as meeting there the great and excellent, of whom I have read in history, as joined with " the just made perfect " in an ever-enlarging ministry of benevolence, as conversing with Jesus Christ with the familiarity of friendship, and especially as having an immediate intercourse with God, such as the closest intimacies of earth dimly shadow forth; — when this thought of my future being comes to me, whilst I hope, I also fear; the blessedness seems too great; the consciousness of present weakness and unworthiness is almost too strong for hope. But when, in this frame of mind, I look round on the creation, and see there the marks of an omnipotent goodness, to which nothing is impossible, and from which every thing may be hoped; when I see around me the proofs of an Infinite Father, who must desire the perpetual progress of his intellectual offspring; when I look next at the human mind, and see what powers a few years have unfolded, and discern in it the capacity of everlasting improvement; and especially when I look at Jesus, the conqueror of death, the heir of immortality, who has gone as the forerunner of mankind into the mansions of light and purity, I can and do admit the almost overpowering thought of the everlasting life, growth, felicity of the human soul.

To each of us, my friends, is this felicity offered; a good which turns to darkness and worthlessness the splendor and excellence of the most favored lot on earth. I say, it is *offered*. It cannot be forced on us; from its nature, it must be won. Immortal happiness is nothing more than the unfolding of our own minds, the full, bright exercise of our best powers; and these powers are never to be unfolded here or hereafter, but through our own free exertion. To anticipate a higher existence whilst we neglect our own souls, is a delusion on which reason frowns no less than revelation. Dream not of a heaven into which you may enter, live here as you may. To such as waste the present state, the future will not, cannot, bring happiness. There is no concord between them and that world of purity. A human being, who has lived without God, and without self-improvement, can no more enjoy Heaven, than a mouldering body, lifted from the tomb, and placed amidst beautiful prospects, can enjoy the light through its decayed eyes, or feel the balmy air which blows away its dust. My hearers, immortality is a glorious doctrine; but not given us for speculation or amusement. Its happiness is to be realized only through our own struggles with ourselves, only through our own reaching forward to new virtue and piety. To be joined with Christ in Heaven, we must be joined with him now in spirit, in the conquest of temptation, in charity and well-doing. Immortality should begin here. The seed is now to be sown, which is to expand for ever. "Be not weary then in well-doing; for in due time we shall reap, if we faint not."

LOVE TO CHRIST.

Ephesians vi. 24: "Grace be with all them that love our Lord Jesus Christ in sincerity."

I propose in this discourse, to speak of Love to Christ, and especially of the foundations on which it rests. I will not detain you by remarks on the importance of the subject. I trust, that you feel it, and that no urgency is needed to secure your serious attention.

Love to Christ is said, and said with propriety, to be a duty, not of Natural, but of Revealed religion. Other precepts of Christianity are dictates of nature as well as of revelation. They result from the original and permanent relations which we bear to our Creator and our fellow-creatures; and are written by God on the mind, as well as in the Bible. For example, gratitude towards the Author of our being, and justice and benevolence towards men, are inculcated with more or less distinctness by our moral faculties; they are parts of the inward law which belongs to a rational mind; and accordingly, wherever men are found, you find some conviction of these duties, some sense of their obligation to a higher power and to one another. But the same is not true of the duty of love to Jesus Christ; for as the knowledge of him is not communicated by nature, as his name is not written, like that of God, on the heavens and earth, but is confined to countries where his Gospel is preached, it is plain that no sense of obligation to him can be felt beyond these bounds. No regard is due or can be paid to him beyond these. It is commonly said, therefore, that love to Christ is a duty of revealed, not natural religion, and this language is correct; but let it not mislead us. Let us not imagine, that attachment to Jesus is an arbitrary duty, that it is unlike our other duties, that it is separate from common virtue, or that it is not founded, like all virtues, in our constitution, or not recognised and enforced by natural conscience. We say, that nature does not enjoin this regard to the Saviour, simply because it does not make him known; but, as soon as he is made known, nature enjoins love and veneration towards him as truly as towards God or towards excellent men. Reason and conscience teach us to regard him with a strong and tender interest. Love to him is not an arbitrary precept. It is not unlike our other affections; it requires for its culture no peculiar influences from heaven; it stands on the same ground with all our duties; it is to be strengthened by the same means. It is essentially the same sentiment, feeling, or principle, which we put forth towards other excellent beings, whether in heaven or on earth.

I make these remarks, because I apprehend that the duty of loving Jesus Christ has been so urged, as to seem to many particularly mysterious and obscure; and the consequence has been, that by some it has been neglected as unnatural, unreasonable, and unconnected with common life; whilst others, in seeking to cherish it, have rushed into wild, extravagant, and feverish emotions. I would rescue, if I can, this duty from neglect on the one hand, and from abuse on the other; and to do this, nothing is necessary, but to show the true ground and nature of love to Christ. You will then see, not only that it is an exalted and generous sentiment, but that it blends with, and gives support to, all the virtuous principles of the mind, and to all the duties, even the most common, of active life.

There is another great good, which may result from a just explanation of the love due to Christ. You will see, that this sentiment has no dependence, at least no necessary dependence, on the opinions we may form about his place, or rank, in the universe. This topic has convulsed the church for ages. Christians have cast away the spirit, in settling the precise dignity, of their Master. That this question is unimportant, I do not say. That some views are more favorable to love towards him than others, I believe; but I maintain that all opinions, adopted by different sects, include the foundation, on which veneration and attachment are due to our common Lord. This truth, for I hold it to be a plain truth, is so fitted to heal the wounds and allay the uncharitable fervors of Christ's divided church, that I shall rejoice, if I can set it forth to others as clearly as it rises to my own mind.

To accomplish the ends now expressed, I am led to propose to you one great but simple question. What is it that constitutes Christ's claim to love and respect? What is it that is to be loved in Christ? Why are we to hold him dear? I answer, There is but one ground for virtuous affection, in the universe, but one object worthy of cherished and enduring love in heaven or on earth, and that is, Moral Goodness. I make no exceptions. My principle applies to all beings, to the Creator as well as to his creatures. The claim of God to the love of his rational offspring rests on the rectitude and benevolence of his will. It is the moral beauty and grandeur of his character, to which alone we are bound to pay homage. The only power, which can and ought to be loved, is a beneficent and righteous power. The creation is glorious, and binds us to supreme and everlasting love to God, only because it sprung from and shows forth this energy of goodness; nor has any being a claim on love, any farther than this same energy dwells in him, and is manifested in him. I know no exception to this principle. I can conceive of no being, who can have any claim to affection but what rests on his character, meaning by this the spirit and principles which constitute his mind, and from which he acts; nor do I know but one character which entitles a being to our hearts, and it is that which the Scriptures express by the word Righteousness; which in man is often called Virtue, in God, Holiness; which consists essentially in supreme reverence for and adoption of what is right; and of which benevolence, or universal charity, is the brightest manifestation.

After these remarks, you will easily understand what I esteem the ground of love to Christ. It is his spotless purity, his moral perfection, his unrivalled goodness. It is the spirit of his religion, which is the spirit of God, dwelling in him without measure. Of consequence to love Christ is to love the perfection of virtue, of righteousness, of benevolence; and the great excellence of this love is, that, by cherishing it, we imbibe, we strengthen in our own souls, the most illustrious virtue, and through Jesus become like to God.

From the view now given, you see that love to Jesus Christ is a perfectly natural sentiment; I mean, one which our natural sense of right enjoins and approves, and which our minds are constituted to feel and to cherish, as truly as any affection to the good whom we know on earth. It is not a theological, mysterious feeling, which some supernatural and inexplicable agency must generate within us. It has its foundation or root in the very frame of our minds, in that sense of right by which we are enabled to discern, and bound to love, perfection. I observe next, that, according to this view, it is, as I have said, an exalted and generous affection; for it brings us into communion and contact with the sublimest character ever revealed among men. It includes and nourishes great thoughts and high aspirations, and gives us here on earth the benefit of intercourse with celestial beings.

Do you not also see, that the love of Christ, according to the view now given of it, has no dependence on any particular views which are formed of his nature by different sects? According to all sects, is he not perfect, spotless in virtue, the representative and resplendent image of the moral goodness and rectitude of God? However contending sects may be divided as to other points, they all agree in the moral perfection of his character. All recognise his most glorious peculiarity, his sublime and unsullied goodness. All therefore see in him that which alone deserves love and veneration.

I am aware, that other views are not uncommon. It is said, that a true love to Christ requires just opinions concerning him, and that they who form different opinions of him, however they may use the same name, do not love the same being. We must *know* him, it is said, in order to esteem him as we ought. Be it so. To love Christ we must know him. But what must we know respecting him? Must we know his countenance and form, must we know the manner in which he existed before his birth, or the manner in which he now exists? Must we know his precise rank in the universe, his precise power and influence? On all these points, indeed, just views would be gratifying and auxiliary to virtue. But love to Christ may exist, and grow strong without them. What we need to this end, is the knowledge of his mind, his virtues, his principles of action. No matter how profoundly we speculate about Christ, or how profusely we heap upon him epithets of praise and admiration; if we do not understand the distinguishing virtues of his character, and see and feel their grandeur, we are as ignorant of him as if we had never heard his name, nor can we offer him an acceptable love. I desire indeed to know Christ's rank in the universe; but rank is nothing, except as it proves and manifests superior virtue. High station only degrades a being who fills it unworthily. It is the mind which gives dignity to the office, not the office to the mind. All glory is of the soul. Accordingly we know little or nothing of another until we look into his soul. I cannot be said to know a being of a singularly great character, because I have learned from what region he came, to what family he belongs, or what rank he sustains. I can only know him as far as I discern the greatness of his spirit, the unconquerable strength of his benevolence, his loyalty to God and duty, his power to act and suffer in a good and righteous cause, and his intimate communion with God. Who knows Christ best? I answer, It is he who, in reading his history, sees and feels most distinctly and deeply the perfection by which he was distinguished. Who knows Jesus best? It is he, who, not resting in general and almost unmeaning praises, becomes acquainted with what was peculiar, characteristic, and individual in his mind, and who has thus framed to himself, not a dim image called Jesus, but a living being, with distinct and glorious features, and with all the reality of a wellknown friend. Who best knows Jesus? I answer, It is he, who deliberately feels and knows, that his character is of a higher order than all other characters which have appeared on earth, and who thirsts to commune with and resemble it. I hope I am plain. When I hear, as I do, men disputing about Jesus, and imagining that they know him by settling some theory as to his generation in time or eternity, or as to his rank in the scale of being, I feel that their knowledge of him is about as great as I should have of some saint or hero, by studying his genealogy. These controversies have built up a technical theology, but give no insight into the mind and heart of Jesus; and without this the true knowledge of him cannot be enjoyed. And here I would observe, not in the spirit of reproach, but from a desire to do good, that I know not a more effectual method of hiding Jesus from us, of keeping us strangers to him, than the inculcation of the doctrine which makes him the same being with his Father, makes him God himself. This doctrine throws over him a mistiness. For myself, when I attempt to bring it home, I have not a real being before me, not a soul which I can understand and sympathize with, but a vague, shifting image, which gives nothing of the stability of knowledge. A being, consisting of two natures, two souls, one Divine and another human, one finite and another infinite, is made up of quali ties which destroy one another, and leave nothing for distinct apprehension. This compound of different minds, and of contradictory attributes, I cannot, if I would, regard as one conscious person, one intelligent agent. It strikes me almost irresistibly as a fiction. On the other hand, Jesus, contemplated as he is set before us in the Gospel, as one mind, one heart, answering to my own in all its essential powers and affections, but purified, enlarged, exalted; so as to constitute him the unsullied image of God and a perfect model, is a being who bears the marks of reality, whom I can understand, whom I can receive into my heart as the best of friends, with whom I can become intimate, and whose society I can and do anticipate among the chief blessings of my future being.

My friends, I have now stated, in general, what knowledge of Christ is most important, and is alone required in order to a true attachment to him. Let me still farther illustrate my views, by descending to one or two particulars. Among the various excellences of Jesus, he was distinguished by a benevolence so deep, so invincible, that injury and outrage had no power over it. His kindness towards men was in no degree diminished by their wrong-doing. The only intercession which he offered in his sufferings, was for those who at that very moment were wreaking on him their vengeance; and, what is more remarkable, he not only prayed for them, but with an unexampled generosity and candor, urged in their behalf the only extenuation which their conduct would admit. Now, to know Jesus Christ, is to understand this attribute of his mind, to understand the strength and triumph of the benevolent principle in this severest trial, to understand the energy with which he then held fast the virtue which he had enjoined. It is to see in the mind of Jesus at that moment a moral grandeur which raised him above all around him. This is to know him. I will suppose now a man to have studied all the controversies about Christ's nature, and to have arrived at the truest notions of his rank in the universe. But this incident in Christ's history, this discovery of his character, has never impressed him; the glory of a philanthropy which embraces one's enemies, has never dawned upon him. With all his right opinions about the Unity, or the Trinity, he lives, and acts towards others, very much as if Jesus had never lived or died. Now I say, that such a man does not know Christ. I say, that he is a stranger to him. I say, that the great truth is hidden from him; that his skill in religious controversy is of little more use to him than would be the learning by rote of a language which he does not understand. He knows the name of Christ, but the excellence which that name imports, and which gives it its chief worth, is to him as an unknown tongue.

I have referred to one view of Christ's character. I might go through his whole life. I will only observe, that in the New Testament, the crucifixion of Jesus is always set forth as the most illustrious portion of his history. The spirit of self-sacrifice, of deliberate self-immolation, of calm, patient endurance of the death of the cross, in the cause of truth, piety, virtue, human happiness, — this particular manifestation of love is always urged upon us in the New Testament, as the crowning glory of Jesus Christ. To understand this part of his character; to understand him when he gave himself up to the shame and anguish of crucifixion; to understand that sympathy with human misery, that love of human nature, that thirst for the recovery of the human soul, that zeal for human virtue, that energy of moral principle, that devotion to God's purposes, through which the severest suffering was chosen and borne, and into which no suffering, or scorn, or desertion, or ingratitude, could infuse the least degree of selfishness, unkindness, doubt, or infirmity, — to understand this, is to understand Jesus; and he who wants sensibility to this, be his speculations what they may, has every thing to learn respecting the Saviour.

You will see, from the views now given, that I consider love to Christ as requiring nothing so much, as that we fix our thoughts on the excellence of his character, study it, penetrate our minds with what was peculiar in it, and cherish profound veneration for it; and consequently I fear, that attachment to him has been diminished by the habit of regarding other things in Christ as more important than his lovely and sublime virtues.

Christians have been prone to fix on something mysterious in his nature, or else on the dignity of his offices, as his chief claim; and in this way his supreme glory has been obscured. His nature and offices I, of course, would not disparage; but let them not be exalted above his Moral Worth. I maintain that this gives to his nature and offices all their claims to love and veneration, and that we understand them only as far as we see this to pervade them. This principle I would uphold against Christians of very different modes of faith.

First, there are Christians who maintain that Jesus Christ is to be loved as the Son of God, understanding by this title some mysterious connexion and identity with the Father. Far be it from me to deny, that the Divine Sonship of Jesus constitutes his true claim on our affection; but I do deny, that the mysterious properties of this relation form any part of this claim; for it is very clear that love to a being must rest on what we know of him, and not on unknown and unintelligible attributes. In saying that the Divine Sonship of Jesus is the great foundation of attachment to him, I say nothing inconsistent with the doctrine of this discourse, that the moral excellence of Jesus is the great object and ground of the love which is due to him. Indeed, I only repeat the principle, that he is to be loved exclusively for the virtues of his character; for what, I ask, is the great idea involved in his filial relation to God? To be the Son of God, in the chief and highest sense of that term, is to bear the likeness, to possess the spirit, to be partaker of the moral perfections of God. This is the essential idea. To be God's Son is to be united with him by consent and accordance of mind. Jesus was the only begotten Son, because he was the perfect image and representative of God, especially of divine philanthropy; because he espoused as his own the benevolent purposes of God towards the human race, and yielded himself to their accomplishment with an entire self-sacrifice. To know Jesus as the Son of God, is not to understand what theologians have written about his eternal generation, or about a mystical, incomprehensible union between Christ and his Father. It is something far higher and more instructive. It is to see in Christ, if I may say so, the lineaments of the Universal Father. It is to discern in him a godlike purity and goodness. It is to understand his harmony with the Divine Mind, and the entireness and singleness of love with which he devoted himself to the purposes of God, and the interests of the human race. Of consequence, to love

Jesus as the Son of God, is to love the spotless purity and godlike charity of his soul.

There are other Christians who differ widely from those of whom I have now spoken, but who conceive that Christ's Offices, Inspiration, Miracles, are his chief claims to veneration, and who, I fear, in extolling these, have overlooked what is incomparably more glorious, the moral dignity of his mind, the purity and inexhaustibleness of his benevolence. It is possible, that to many who hear me, Christ seems to have been more exalted when he received from his Father supernatural light and truth, or when with superhuman energy he quelled the storm and raised the dead, than when he wept over the city which was in a few days to doom him to the most shameful and agonizing death; and yet, his chief glory consisted in the spirit through which these tears were shed. Christians have yet to learn that inspiration, and miracles, and outward dignities, are nothing compared with the soul. We all need to understand better than we have done, that noble passage of Paul, " Though I speak with the tongues of men and of angels, and understand all mysteries, and have all faith, so that I could remove mountains, and have not charity [disinterestedness, love], I am nothing;" and this is as true of Christ as of Paul. Indeed it is true of all beings, and yet, I fear, it is not felt as it should be by the multitude of Christians.

You tell me, my friends, that Christ's unparalleled inspiration, his perpetual reception of light from God, that this was his supreme distinction; and a great distinction undoubtedly it was: but I affirm, that Christ's inspiration, though conferred on him without measure, gives him no claim to veneration or love, any farther than it found within him a virtue, which accorded with, welcomed, and adopted it; any farther than his own heart responded to the truths he received; any farther than he sympathized with, and espoused as his own, the benevolent purposes of God, which he was sent to announce; any farther than the spirit of the religion which he preached was his own spirit, and was breathed from his life as well as from his lips. In other words, his inspiration was made glorious through his virtues. Mere inspiration seems to me a very secondary thing. Suppose the greatest truths in the universe to be revealed supernaturally to a being who should take no interest in them, who should not see and feel their greatness, but should repeat them mechanically, as they were put into his mouth by the Deity. Such a man would be inspired, and would teach the greatest verities, and yet he would be nothing, and would have no claim to reverence.

The excellence of Jesus did not consist in his mere inspiration, but in the virtue and love which prepared him to receive it, and by which it was made effectual to the world. He did not passively hear, and mechanically repeat, certain doctrines from God, but his whole soul accorded with what he heard. Every truth which he uttered came warm and living from his own mind; and it was this pouring of his own soul into his instructions, which gave them much of their power. Whence came the authority and energy, the conscious dignity, the tenderness and sympathy, with which Jesus taught? They came not from inspiration, but from the mind of him who was inspired. His personal virtues gave power to his teachings; and without these no inspiration could have made him the source of such light and strength as he now communicates to mankind.

My friends, I have aimed to show in this discourse, that the virtue, purity, rectitude of Jesus Christ, is his most honorable distinction, and constitutes his great claim to veneration and love. I can direct you to nothing in Christ, more important than his tried, and victorious, and perfect goodness. Others may love Christ for mysterious attributes; I love him for the rectitude of his soul and his life. I love him for that benevolence, which went through Judea, instructing the ignorant, healing the sick, giving sight to the blind. I love him for that universal charity, which comprehended the despised publican, the hated Samaritan, the benighted heathen, and sought to bring a world to God and to happiness. I love him for that gentle, mild, forbearing spirit, which no insult, outrage, injury could overpower; and which desired as earnestly the repentance and happiness of its foes, as the happiness of its friends. I love him for the spirit of magnanimity, constancy, and fearless rectitude, with which, amidst peril and opposition, he devoted himself to the work which God gave him to do. I love him for the wise and enlightened zeal with which he espoused the true, the spiritual interests of mankind, and through which he lived and died to redeem them from every sin, to frame them after his own godlike virtue. I love him, I have said, for his moral excellence; I know nothing else to love. I know nothing so glorious in the Creator or his creatures. This is the greatest gift which God bestows, the greatest to be derived from his Son.

You see why I call you to cherish the love of Christ. This love I do not recommend as a luxury of feeling, as an ecstasy bringing immediate and overflowing joy. I view it in a nobler light. I call you to love Jesus, that you may bring yourselves into contact and communion with perfect virtue, and may become what you love. I know no sincere, enduring good but the moral excellence which shines forth in Jesus Christ. Your wealth, your outward comforts and distinctions, are poor, mean, contemptible, compared with this; and to prefer them to this is self-debasement, self-destruction. May this great truth penetrate our souls; and may we bear witness in our common lives, and especially in trial, n sore temptation, that nothing is so dear to us as the virtue of Christ.

17*

LOVE TO CHRIST.

EPHESIANS vi. 24: "Grace be with all them that love our Lord Jesus Christ in sincerity."

IN the preceding discourse, I considered the nature and ground of love to Christ. The subject is far from being exhausted. I propose now, after a few remarks on the importance and happiness of this attachment, to call your attention to some errors in relation to it, which prevail in the Christian world.

A virtuous attachment purifies the heart. In loving the excellent, we receive strength to follow them. It is happy for us when a pure affection springs up within us, when friendship knits us with holy and generous minds. It is happy for us when a being of noble sentiments and beneficent life enters our circle, becomes an object of interest to us, and by affectionate intercourse takes a strong hold on our hearts. Not a few can trace the purity and elevation of their minds, to connexion with an individual who has won them by the beauty of his character to the love and practice of righteousness. These views show us the service which Jesus Christ has done to mankind, simply in offering himself before them as an object of attachment and affection. In inspiring love, he is a benefactor. A man brought to see and feel the godlike virtues of Jesus Christ, who understands his character and is attracted and won by it, has gained, in this sentiment, immense aid in his conflict with evil and in his pursuit of perfection. And he has not only gained aid, but happiness; for a true love is in itself a noble enjoyment. It is the proper delight of a rational and moral being, leaving no bitterness or shame behind, not enervating like the world's pleasures, but giving energy and a lofty consciousness to the mind.

Our nature was framed for virtuous attachments. How strong and interesting are the affections of domestic life, the conjugal, parental, filial ties. But the heart is not confined to our homes, or even to this world. There are more sacred attachments than these, in which instinct has no part, which have their origin in our highest faculties, which are less tumultuous and impassioned than the affections of nature, but more enduring, more capable of growth, more peaceful, far happier, and far nobler. Such is love to Jesus Christ, the most purifying, and the happiest attachment, next to the love of our Creator, which we can form. I wish to aid you in cherishing this sentiment, and for this end I have thought, that in the present discourse it would be well to point out some wrong views, which I think have obstructed it, and obscured its glory.

I apprehend, that, among those Christians who bear the name of Rational, from the importance which they give to the exercise of reason in religion, love to Christ has lost something of its honor, in consequence of its perversion It has too often been substituted for practical religion. Not a few have professed a very fervent attachment to Jesus, and have placed great confidence in this feeling, who, at the same time, have seemed to think little of his precepts, and have even spoken of them as unimportant, compared with certain doctrines about his person or nature. Gross errors of this kind have led, as it seems to me, to the opposite extreme. They have particularly encouraged among calm and sober people the idea, that the great object of Christ was to give a religion, to teach great and everlasting truth, and that our concern is with his religion rather than with himself. The great question, as such people say, is, not what Jesus *was*, but what he *revealed*. In this way a distinction has been made between Jesus and his religion; and, whilst some sects have done little but talk of Christ and his person, others have dwelt on the principles he taught, to the neglect, in a measure, of the Divine Teacher. I consider this as an error, to which some of us may be exposed, and which therefore deserves consideration.

Now, I grant, that Jesus Christ came to give a religion, to reveal truth. This is his great office; but I maintain, that this is no reason for overlooking Jesus; for his religion has an intimate and peculiar connexion with himself. It derives authority and illustration from his character. Jesus is his religion embodied, and made visible. The connexion between him and his system is peculiar. It differs altogether from that which ancient philosophers bore to their teachings. An ancient sage wrote a book, and the book is of equal value to us, whether we know its author or not. But there is no such thing as Christianity without Christ. We cannot know it separately from him. It is not a book which Jesus wrote. It is his conversation, his character, his history, his life, his death, his resurrection. He pervades it throughout. In loving him, we love his religion; and a just interest in this cannot be awakened, but by contemplating it as it shone forth in himself.

Christ's religion, I have said, is very imperfect without himself; and therefore they who would make an abstract of his precepts, and say that it is enough to follow these without thinking of their author, grievously mistake, and rob the system of much of its energy. I mean not to disparage the precepts of Christ, considered in themselves. But their full power is only to be understood and felt, by those who place themselves near the Divine Teacher, who see the celestial fervor of his affection whilst he utters them, who follow his steps from Bethlehem to Calvary, and witness the expression of his precepts in his own life. These come to me almost as new precepts, when I associate them with Jesus. His command to love my enemies, becomes intelligible and bright, when I stand by his cross and hear his prayer for his murderers. I understand what he meant by the self-denial which he taught, when I see him foregoing the comforts of life, and laying down life itself, for the good of others. I learn the true character of that benevolence, by which human nature is perfected, how it unites calmness and earnestness, tenderness and courage, condescension and dignity, feeling and action; this I learn in the life of Jesus as no words could teach me. So I am instructed in the nature of piety by the same model. The command to love God with all my heart, if only written, might have led me into extravagance, enthusiasm, and neglect of common duties; for religious excitement has a peculiar tendency to excess; but in Jesus I see a devotion to God, entire, perfect, never remitted, yet without the least appearance of passion, as calm and self-possessed as the love which a good mind bears to a parent; and in him I am taught, as words could not teach, how to join supreme regard to my Creator, with active charity and common duties towards my fellow-beings.

And not only the precepts, but the great doctrines of Christianity, are bound up with Jesus, and cannot be truly understood without him. For example, one of the great doctrines of Christianity, perhaps its chief, is the kind interest of God in all his creatures, not only in the good but in the evil; his placable, clement, merciful character; his desire to recover and purify and make for ever happy even those who have stained themselves with the blackest guilt. The true character of God in this respect I see indeed in his providence, I read it in his word, and for every manifestation of it I am grateful. But when I see his spotless and beloved Son, to whom his power was peculiarly delegated, and in whom he peculiarly dwelt, giving singular attention to the most fallen and despised men, casting away all outward pomp that he might mingle familiarly with the poor and neglected; when I see him sitting at table with the publican and the sinner, inviting them to approach him as a friend, suffering the woman whose touch was deemed pollution, to bedew his feet with tears; and when I hear him in the midst of such a concourse saying, "I am come to seek and to save that which was lost,"—I have a conviction of the lenity, benignity, grace, of that God whose representative and chosen minister he was, such as no abstract teaching could have given me. Let me add one more doctrine, that of immortality. I prize every evidence of this great truth; I look within and without me, for some pledge that I am not to perish in the grave, that this mind, with its thoughts and affections, is to live, and improve, and be perfected, and to find that joy for which it thirsts and which it cannot find on earth. Christ's teaching on this subject is invaluable; but what power does this teaching gain, when I stand by his sepulchre, and see the stone rolled away, and behold the great revealer of immortality, rising in power and triumph, and ascending to the life and happiness he had promised!

Thus Christianity, from beginning to end, is intimately connected with its Divine teacher. It is not an abstract system. The rational Christian who would think of it as such, who, in dwelling on the religion, overlooks its Revealer, is unjust to it. Would he see and feel its power, let him see it warm, living, breathing, acting in the mind, heart, and life of its Founder. Let him love it there. In other words, let him love the character of Jesus, justly viewed, and he will love the religion in the way most fitted to make it the power of God unto salvation.

I have said that love to Christ, when he is justly viewed, that is, when it is an enlightened and rational affection, includes the love of his whole religion; but I beg you to remember that I give this praise only to an enlightened affection; and such is not the most common, nor is it easily acquired. I apprehend that there is no sentiment, which needs greater care in its culture than this. Perhaps, in the present state of the world, no virtue is of more difficult acquisition than a pure and intelligent love towards Jesus. There is undoubtedly much of fervent feeling towards him in the Christian world. But let me speak plainly. I do it from no uncharitableness. I do it only to warn my fellow Christians. The greater part of this affection to Jesus seems to me of very doubtful worth. In many cases, it is an irregular fervor, which impairs the force and soundness of the mind, and which is substituted for obedience to his precepts, for the virtues which ennoble the soul. Much of what is called love to Christ I certainly do not desire you or myself to possess. I know of no sentiment which needs more to be cleared from error and abuse, and I therefore feel myself bound to show you some of its corruptions.

In the first place, I am persuaded that a love to Christ of quite a low character is often awakened by an injudicious use of his sufferings. I apprehend, that if the affection which many bear to Jesus were analyzed, the chief ingredient in it would be found to be a tenderness awakened by his cross. In certain classes of Christians, it is common for the religious teacher to delineate the bleeding, dying Saviour, and to detail his agonies, until men's natural sympathy is awakened; and when assured that this deep woe was borne for themselves, they almost necessarily yield to the softer feelings of their nature. I mean not to find fault with this sensibility. It is happy for us that we are made to be touched by others' pains. Woe to him, who has no tears for mortal agony. But in this emotion there is no virtue, no moral worth; and we dishonor Jesus, when this is the chief tribute we offer him. I say there is no moral goodness in this feeling. To be affected, overpowered by a crucifixion, is the most natural thing in the world. Who of us, let me ask, whether religious or not, ever went into a Catholic church, and there saw the picture of Jesus hanging from his cross, his head bending under the weight of exhausting suffering, his hands and feet pierced with nails, and his body stained with his open wounds, and has not been touched by the sight ? Suppose that, at this moment, there were lifted up among us a human form, transfixed with a spear, and from which the warm life-blood was dropping in the midst of us. Who would not be deeply moved ? and when a preacher, gifted with something of an actor's power, places the cross, as it were, in the midst of a people, is it wonderful that they are softened and subdued ? I mean not to censure all appeals of this kind to the human heart. There is something interesting and encouraging in the tear of compassion. There was wisdom in the conduct of the Moravian Missionaries in Greenland, who, finding that the rugged and barbarous natives were utterly insensible to general truth, depicted, with all possible vividness, the streaming blood and dying agonies of Jesus, and thus caught the attention of the savage through his sympathies, whom they could not interest through his reason or his fears. But sensibility thus awakened, is quite a different thing from true, virtuous love to Jesus Christ ; and, when viewed and cherished as such, it takes the place of higher affections. I have often been struck by the contrast between the use made of the cross in the pulpit, and the calm, unimpassioned manner in which the sufferings of Jesus are detailed by the Evangelists. These witnesses of Christ's last moments, give you in simple language the particulars of that scene, without one remark, one word of emotion ; and if you read the Acts and Epistles, you will not find a single instance, in which the Apostles strove to make a moving picture of his crucifixion. No ; they honored Jesus too much, they felt too deeply the greatness of his character, to be moved as many are by the circumstances of his death. Reverence, admiration, sympathy with his sublime spirit, these swallowed up, in a great measure, sympathy with his sufferings. The cross was to them the last, crowning manifestation of a celestial mind; they felt that it was endured to communicate the same mind to them and the world; and their emotion was a holy joy in this consummate and unconquerable goodness. To be touched by suffering is a light thing. It is not the greatness of Christ's sufferings on the cross which is to move our whole souls, but the greatness of the spirit with which he suffered. There, in death, he proved his entire consecration of himself to the cause of God and mankind. There his love flowed forth towards his friends, his enemies, and the human race. It is moral greatness, it is victorious love, it is the energy of principle, which gives such interest to the cross of Christ. We are to look through the darkness which hung over him, through his wounds and pains, to his unbroken, disinterested, confiding spirit. To approach the cross for the purpose of weeping over a bleeding, dying friend, is to lose the chief influence of the crucifixion. We are to visit the cross, not to indulge a natural softness, but to acquire firmness of spirit, to fortify our minds for hardship and suffering in the cause of duty and of human happiness. To live as Christ lived, to die as Christ died, to give up ourselves as sacrifices to God, to conscience, to whatever good interest we can advance, — these are the lessons written with the blood of Jesus. His cross is to inspire us with a calm courage, resolution, and superiority to all temptation. I fear (is my fear groundless?) that a sympathy which enervates rather than fortifies, is the impression too often received from the crucifixion. The depression with which the Lord's table is too often approached, and too often left, shows, I apprehend, that the chief use of his sufferings is little understood, and that he is loved, not as a glorious sufferer who died to spread his own sublime spirit, but as a man of sorrows, a friend bowed down with the weight of grief.

In the second place, love to Christ of a very defective kind, is cherished in many, by the views which they are accustomed to take of themselves. They form irrational ideas of their own guilt, supposing it to have its origin in their very creation, and then represent to their imaginations an abyss of fire and torment, over which they hang, into which the anger of God is about to precipitate them, and from which nothing but Jesus can rescue them. Not a few, I apprehend, ascribe to Jesus Christ a greater compassion towards them than God is supposed to feel. His heart is tenderer than that of the Universal Parent, and this tenderness is seen in his plucking them by a mighty power from tremendous and infinite pain, from everlasting burnings. Now, that Jesus, under such circumstances should excite the mind strongly, should become the object of a very intense attachment, is almost necessary; but the affection so excited is of very little worth. Let the universe seem to me wrapped in darkness, let God's throne send forth no light but blasting flashes, let Jesus be the only bright and cheering object to my affrighted and desolate soul, and a tumultuous gratitude will carry me towards him just as irresistibly as natural instinct carries the parent animal to its young. I do and must grieve at the modes commonly used to make Jesus Christ an interesting be ing. Even the Infinite Father is stripped of his glory for the sake of throwing a lustre round the Son. The condition of man is painted in frightful colors which cast unspeakable dishonor on his Creator, for the sake of magnifying the greatness of Christ's salvation. Man is stripped of all the powers which make him a responsible being, his soul harrowed with terrors, and the future illumined only by the flames which are to consume him, that his deliverer may seem more necessary; and when the mind, in this state of agitation, in this absence of self-control, is wrought up into a fervor of gratitude to Jesus, it is thought to be sanctified. This selfish, irrational gratitude, is called a virtue. Much of the love given to Jesus, having the origin of which I now speak, seems to me of no moral worth. It is not the soul's free gift, not a sentiment nourished by our own care from a conviction of its purity and nobleness, but an instinctive, ungoverned, selfish feeling. Suppose, my friends, that in a tempestuous night you should find yourselves floating towards a cataract, the roar of which should announce the destruction awaiting you, and that a fellow-being of great energy, should rush through the darkness, and bring you to the shore; could you help embracing him with gratitude? And would this emotion imply any change of character? Would you not feel it towards your deliverer, even should he have acted from mere impulse, and should his general character be grossly defective? Is not this a necessary working of nature, a fruit of terror changed into joy? I mean not to condemn it; I only say it is not virtue. It is a poor tribute to Jesus; he deserves something far purer and nobler.

The habit of exaggerating the wretchedness of man's condition, for the purpose of rendering Jesus more necessary, operates very seriously to degrade men's **love** to Jesus, by accustoming them to ascribe to him a low and commonplace character. I wish this to be weighed. They who represent to themselves the whole human race as sinking by an hereditary corruption into an abyss of flame and perpetual woe, very naturally think of Jesus as a being of overflowing compassion, as impelled by a resistless pity to fly to the relief of these hopeless victims; for this is the emotion that such a sight is fitted to produce. Now this overpowering compassion, called forth by the view of exquisite misery, is a very ordinary virtue; and yet, I apprehend, it is the character ascribed above all others to Jesus. It certainly argues no extraordinary goodness, for it is an almost necessary impulse of nature. Were you, my friends, to see millions and millions of the human race on the edge of a fiery gulf, where ages after ages of torture awaited them, and were the shrieks of millions who had already been plunged into the abyss to pierce your ear, — could you refrain from an overpowering compassion, and would you not willingly endure hours and days of exquisite pain to give these wretched millions release? Is there any man who has not virtue enough for this? I have known men of ordinary character hazard their lives under the impulse of compassion, for the rescue of fellow-beings from infinitely lighter evils than are here supposed. To me it seems, that to paint the misery of human beings in these colors of fire and blood, and to ascribe to Christ the compassion which such misery must awaken, and to make this the chief attribute of his mind, is the very method to take from his character its greatness, and to weaken his claim on our love. I see nothing in Jesus of the overpowering compassion which is often ascribed o him. His character rarely exhibited strong emotion. It was distinguished by calmness, firmness, and conscious dignity. Jesus had a mind too elevated to be absorbed and borne away by pity, or any other passion. He felt indeed deeply for human suffering and grief; but his chief sympathy was with the Mind, with its sins and moral diseases, and especially with its capacity of improvement and everlasting greatness and glory. He felt himself commissioned to quicken and exalt immortal beings. The thought which kindled and sustained him, was that of an immeasurable virtue to be conferred on the mind, even of the most depraved; a good, the very conception of which implies a lofty character, a good, which as yet has only dawned on his most improved disciples. It is his consecration to this sublime end, which constitutes his glory; and no farther than we understand this, can we yield him the love which his character claims and deserves.

I have endeavoured to show the circumstances which have contributed to depress and degrade men's affections towards Jesus Christ. To me the influence of these causes seems to be great. I know of no feeling more suspicious than the common love to Christ. A true affection to him, indeed, is far from being of easy acquisition. As it is the purest and noblest we can cherish, with the single exception of love to God, so it requires the exercise of our best powers. You all must feel, that an indispensable requisite or preparation for this love is to understand the character of Jesus. But this is no easy thing. It not only demands that we carefully read and study his history; there is another process more important. We must begin in earnest to convert into practice our present imperfect knowledge of Christ, and to form ourselves upon him as far as he is now discerned. Nothing so much brightens and strengthens the eye of the mind to understand an excellent being, as likeness to him. We never know a great character until something congenial to it has grown up within ourselves. No strength of intellect and no study can enable a man of a selfish and sensual mind to comprehend Jesus. Such a mind is covered with a mist; and just in proportion as it subdues evil within itself, the mist will be scattered, Jesus will rise upon it with a sun-like brightness, and will call forth its most fervent and most enlightened affection.

I close with two remarks. You see, by this discourse, how important to the love of Christ it is, to understand with some clearness the purpose for which he came into the world. The low views prevalent on this subject, seem to me to exert a disastrous influence on the whole character, and particularly on our feelings towards Christ. Christ is supposed to have come to rescue us from an outward hell, to bear the penalties of an outward law. Such benevolence would indeed be worthy of praise; but it is an inferior form of benevolence. The glory of Christ's character, its peculiar brightness, seems to me to consist in his having given himself to accomplish an inward, moral, spiritual deliverance of mankind. He was alive to the worth and greatness of the human soul. He looked through what men were, looked through the thick shades of their idolatry, superstition, and vice, and saw in every human being a spirit of divine origin and godlike faculties, which might be recovered from all its evil, which might become an image and a temple of God. The greatness of Jesus consisted in his devoting himself to call forth a mighty power in the human breast, to kindle in us a celestial flame, to breathe into us an inexhaustible hope, and to lay within us the foundation of an immovable peace. His greatness consists in the greatness and sublimity of the action which he communicates to the human soul. This is his chief glory. To avert pain and punishment is a subordinate work. Through neglect of these truths, I apprehend that the brightness of Christ's character is even now much obscured, and perhaps least discerned by some who think they understand him best.

My second remark is, that, if the leading views of this discourse be just, then love to Jesus Christ depends very little on our conception of his rank in the scale of being. On no other topic have Christians contended so earnestly, and yet it is of secondary importance. To know Jesus Christ is not to know the precise place he occupies in the universe. It is something more ; it is to look into his mind ; to approach his soul ; to comprehend his spirit ; to see how he thought, and felt, and purposed, and loved ; to understand the workings of that pure and celestial principle within him, through which he came among us as our friend, and lived and died for us. I am persuaded that controversies about Christ's person, have in one way done great injury. They have turned attention from his character. Suppose, that, as Americans, we should employ ourselves in debating the questions, where Washington was born, and from what spot he came when he appeared at the head of our armies ; and that, in the fervor of these contentions, we should overlook the character of his mind, the spirit that moved within him, the virtues which distinguished him, the beamings of a noble, magnanimous soul, — how unprofitably should we be employed! Who is it that understands Washington? Is it he, that can settle his rank in the creation, his early history, his present condition? or he, to whom the soul of that great man is laid open, who comprehends and sympathizes with his generous purposes, who understands the energy with which he espoused the cause of freedom and his country, and who receives through admiration a portion of the same divine energy? So in regard to Jesus, the questions which have been agitated about his rank and nature are of inferior moment. His greatness belonged not to his condition, but to his mind, his spirit, his aim, his disinterestedness, his calm, sublime consecration of himself to the high purpose of God.

My hearers, it is the most interesting event in human history, that such a being as Jesus has entered our world, to accomplish the deliverance of our minds from all evil, to bring them to God, to open heaven within them, and thus to fit them for heaven. It is our greatest privilege that he is brought within our view, offered to our imitation, to our trust, to our love. A sincere and enlightened attachment to him is at once our honor and our happiness, a spring of virtuous action, of firmness in suffering, of immortal hope. But remember, it will not grow up of itself. You must resolve upon it, and cherish it. You must bring Jesus near, as he lives and moves in the Gospel. You should meet him in the institution, which he especially appointed for the commemoration of himself. You should seek, by prayer, God's aid in strengthening your love to the Saviour. You should learn his greatness and beneficence by learning the greatness and destination of the souls which he came to rescue and bless. In the last place, you should obey his precepts, and through this obedience should purify and invigorate your minds to know and love him more. "Grace be with all them that love our Lord Jesus Christ in sincerity."

THE FUTURE LIFE.

DISCOURSE

PREACHED

ON EASTER SUNDAY, 1834, AFTER THE DEATH OF AN EXCELLENT AND VERY DEAR FRIEND.

EPHESIANS i. 20: "He raised him from the dead, and set him at his own right hand in the heavenly places."

THIS day is set apart by the Christian world to the commemoration of Christ's resurrection. Many uses may be made of this event, but it is particularly fitted to confirm the doctrine of another life, and to turn our thoughts, desires, hopes towards another world. I shall employ it to give this direction to our minds.

There is one method in which Christ's resurrection gives aid to our faith in another life, which is not often dwelt on, and which seems to me worthy of attention. Our chief doubts and difficulties in regard to that state, spring chiefly from the senses and the imagination, and not from the reason. The eye, fixed on the lifeless body, on the wan features and the motionless limbs, — and the imagination, following the frame into the dark tomb, and representing to itself the stages of decay and ruin, are apt to fill and oppress the mind with discouraging and appalling thoughts. The senses can detect in the pale corse not a trace of the activity of that spirit which lately moved it. Death seems to have achieved an entire victory; and when reason and revelation speak of continued and a higher life, the senses and imagination, pointing to the disfigured and mouldering body, obscure by their sad forebodings the light which reason and revelation strive to kindle in the bereaved soul.

Now the resurrection of Christ meets, if I may so say, the senses and imagination on their own ground, contends with them with their own weapons. It shows us the very frame, on which death, in its most humiliating form, had set its seal, and which had been committed in utter hopelessness to the tomb, rising, breathing, moving with new life, and rising not to return again to the earth, but, after a short sojourn, to ascend from the earth to a purer region, and thus to attest man's destination to a higher life. These facts, submitted to the very senses, and almost necessarily kindling the imagination to explore the unseen world, seem to me particularly suited to overcome the main difficulties in the way of Christian faith. Reason is not left to struggle alone with the horrors of the tomb. The assurance that Jesus Christ, who lived on the earth, who died on the cross, and was committed a mutilated, bleeding frame to the receptacle of the dead, rose uninjured, and then exchanged an earthly for a heavenly life, puts to flight the sad auguries, which rise like spectres from the grave, and helps us to conceive, as in our present weakness we could not otherwise conceive, of man's appointed triumph over death.

Such is one of the aids given by the resurrection,

to faith in immortality. Still this faith is lamentably weak in the multitude of men. To multitudes, Heaven is almost a world of fancy. It wants substance. The idea of a world, in which beings exist without these gross bodies, exist as pure spirits, or clothed with refined and spiritual frames, strikes them as a fiction. What cannot be seen or touched, appears unreal. This is mournful, but not wonderful; for how can men, who immerse themselves in the body and its interests, and cultivate no acquaintance with their own souls and spiritual powers, comprehend a higher, spiritual life? There are multitudes who pronounce a man a visionary, who speaks distinctly and joyfully of his future being, and of the triumph of the mind over bodily decay.

This skepticism as to things spiritual and celestial, is as irrational and unphilosophical as it is degrading. We have more evidence that we have souls or spirits, than that we have bodies. We are surer that we think, and feel, and will, than that we have solid and extended limbs and organs. Philosophers have said much to disprove the existence of matter and motion, but they have not tried to disprove the existence of thought; for it is by thought they attempt to set aside the reality of material nature.

Farther, how irrational is it, to imagine that there are no worlds but this, and no higher modes of existence than our own! Who that sends his eye through this immense creation, can doubt that there are orders of beings superior to ourselves, or can see any thing unreasonable in the doctrine, that there are states in which mind exists less circumscribed and clogged by matter than on earth; in other words, that there is a spiritual world? It is childish to make this infant life of ours the model of existence in all other worlds. The philosopher, especially, who sees a vast chain of beings and an infinite variety of life on this single globe, which is but a point in creation, should be ashamed of that narrowness of mind, which can anticipate nothing nobler in the universe of God than his present mode of being.

How, now, shall the doctrine of a future, higher life, the doctrine both of reason and revelation, be brought to bear more powerfully on the mind, to become more real, and effectual? Various methods might be given. — I shall confine myself to one. This method is, to seek some clearer, more definite conception of the future state. That world seems less real, for want of some distinctness in its features. We should all believe it more firmly if we conceived of it more vividly. It seems unsubstantial, from its vagueness and dimness. I think it right, then, to use the aids of Scripture and Reason in forming to ourselves something like a sketch of the life to come. The Scriptures, indeed, give not many materials for such a delineation, but the few they furnish are invaluable, especially when we add to these the lights thrown over futurity by the knowledge of our own spiritual nature. Every new law of the mind, which we discover, helps us to comprehend its destiny; for its future life must correspond to its great laws and essential powers.

These aids we should employ to give distinctness to the spiritual state; and it is particularly useful so to do, when excellent beings, whom we have known and loved, pass from earth into that world. Nature prompts us to follow them to their new abode, to inquire into their new life, to represent to ourselves their new happiness;

and perhaps the spiritual world never becomes so near and real to us, as when we follow into it dear friends, and sympathize with them in the improvements and enjoyments of that blessed life. Do not say that there is danger here of substituting imagination for Truth. There is no danger if we confine ourselves to the spiritual views of Heaven; given us in the New Testament, and interpret these by the principles and powers of our own souls. To me the subject is too dear and sacred to allow me to indulge myself in dreams. I want reality; I want truth; and this I find in God's word and in the human soul.

When our virtuous friends leave the world, we know not the place where they go. We can turn our eyes to no spot in the universe, and say they are there. Nor is our ignorance here of any moment. It is unimportant what region of space contains them. Whilst we know not to what place they go, we know what is infinitely more interesting, to what beings they go. We know not where Heaven is, but we know Whom it contains, and this knowledge opens to us an infinite field for contemplation and delight.

I. Our virtuous friends, at death, go to Jesus Christ. This is taught in the text. "God raised him from the dead, and exalted him to Heaven." The New Testament always speaks of Jesus as existing now in the spiritual world; and Paul tells us that it is the happiness of the holy, when absent from the body, to be present with the Lord. Here is one great fact in regard to futurity. The good, on leaving us here, meet their Saviour; and this view alone assures us of their unutterable happiness. In this world, they had cherished acquaintance with Jesus through the records of the Evangelists. They had followed him through his eventful life with veneration and love, had treasured in their memories his words, works, and life-giving promises, and, by receiving his spirit, had learned something of the virtues and happiness of a higher world. Now they meet him, they see him. He is no longer a faint object to their mind, obscured by distance and by the mists of sense and the world. He is present to them, and more intimately present than we are to each other. Of this we are sure; for whilst the precise mode of our future existence is unknown, we do know, that spiritual beings in that higher state must approach and commune with each other more and more intimately in proportion to their progress. Those who are newly born into Heaven meet Jesus, and meet from him the kindest welcome. The happiness of the Saviour, in receiving to a higher life a human being who has been redeemed, purified, inspired with immortal goodness by his influence, we can but imperfectly comprehend. You can conceive what would be your feelings, on welcoming to shore your best friend, who had been tossed on a perilous sea; but the raptures of earthly reunion are faint compared with the happiness of Jesus, in receiving the spirit for which he died, and which under his guidance has passed with an improving virtue through a world of sore temptation. We on earth meet after our long separations to suffer as well as enjoy, and soon to part again. Jesus meets those who ascend from earth to Heaven, with the consciousness that their trial is past, their race is run, that death is conquered. With his far-reaching prophetic eye he sees them entering a career of joy and glory never to end. And his benevolent welcome is expressed with a power which belongs only to the utterance of Heaven, and which communicates to them an immediate, confiding, overflowing joy. You know that on earth we sometimes meet human beings, whose countenances, at the first view, scatter all distrust, and win from us something like the reliance of a long-tried friendship. One smile is enough to let us into their hearts, to reveal to us a goodness on which we may repose. That smile with which Jesus will meet the new-born inhabitant of Heaven, that joyful greeting, that beaming of love from him who bled for us, that tone of welcome, — all these I can faintly conceive, but no language can utter them. The joys of centuries will be crowded into that meeting. This is not fiction. It is truth founded on the essential laws of the mind.

Our friends, when they enter Heaven, meet Jesus Christ, and their intercourse with him will be of the most affectionate and ennobling character. There will be nothing of distance in it. Jesus is indeed sometimes spoken of as reigning in the future world, and sometimes imagination places him on a real and elevated throne. Strange that such conceptions can enter the minds of Christians. Jesus will indeed reign in Heaven, and so he reigned on earth. He reigned in the fishing-boat, from which he taught ; in the humble dwelling, where he gathered round him listening and confiding disciples. His reign is not the vulgar dominion of this world. It is the empire of a great, godlike, disinterested being, over minds capable of comprehending and loving him. In Heaven, nothing like what we call government on earth can exist, for government here is founded in human weakness and guilt. The voice of command is never heard among the spirits of the just. Even on earth, the most perfect government is that of a family, where parents employ no tone but that of affectionate counsel, where filial affection reads its duty in the mild look and finds its law and motive in its own pure impulse. Christ will not be raised on a throne above his followers. On earth he sat at the same table with the publican and sinner. Will he recede from the excellent whom he has fitted for celestial mansions? How minds will communicate with one another in that world, we know not; but we know that our closest embraces are but types of the spiritual nearness which will then be enjoyed; and to this intimacy with Jesus the new-born inhabitant of Heaven is admitted.

But we have not yet exhausted this source of future happiness. The excellent go from earth not only to receive a joyful welcome and assurances of eternal love from the Lord. There is a still higher view. They are brought by this new intercourse to a new comprehension of his mind, and to a new reception of his spirit. It is indeed a happiness to know that we are objects of interest and love to an illustrious being; but it is a greater happiness, to know deeply the sublime and beautiful character of this being, to sympathize with him, to enter into his vast thoughts and pure designs, and to become associated with him in the great ends for which he lives. Even here in our infant and dim state of being, we learn enough of Jesus, of his divine philanthropy triumphant over injuries and agonies, to thrill us with affectionate admiration. But those in Heaven look into that vast, godlike soul, as we have never done. They approach it, as we cannot approach the soul of the most confiding friend; and this nearness to the mind of Jesus awakens in themselves a power of love and virtue, which they little suspected during their earthly being. I trust I speak to those, who, if they have ever been brought into connexion with a noble human being, have felt, as it were, a new spirit, and almost new capacities of thought and life, expanded within them. We all know, how a man of mighty genius and of heroic feeling, can impart himself to other minds, and raise them for a time to something like his own energy; and in this we have a faint delineation of the power to be exerted on the minds of those who approach Jesus after death. As nature at this season springs to a new life under the beams of the sun, so will the human soul be warmed and expanded under the influence of Jesus Christ. It will then become truly conscious of the immortal power treasured up in itself. His greatness will not overwhelm it, but will awaken a corresponding grandeur.

Nor is this topic yet exhausted. The good, on approaching Jesus, will not only sympathize with his spirit, but will become joint workers, active, efficient ministers, in accomplishing his great work of spreading virtue and happiness. We must never think of Heaven as a state of inactive contemplation, or of unproductive feeling. Even here on earth, the influence of Christ's character is seen in awakening an active, self-sacrificing goodness. It sends the true disciples to the abodes of the suffering. It binds them by new ties to their race. It gives them a new consciousness of being created for a ministry of beneficence; and can they, when they approach more nearly this divine Philanthropist, and learn, by a new alliance with him, the fulness of his love, can they fail to consecrate themselves to his work and to kindred labors, with an energy of will unknown on earth? In truth, our sympathy with Christ could not be per fect, did we not act with him. Nothing so unites beings as coöperation in the same glorious cause, and to this union with Christ the excellent above are received.

There is another very interesting view of the future state, which seems to me to be a necessary consequence of the connexion to be formed there with Jesus Christ. Those who go there from among us, must retain the deepest interest in this world. Their ties to those they have left are not dissolved, but only refined. On this point, indeed, I want not the evidence of revelation; I want no other evidence than the essential principles and laws of the soul. If the future state is to be an improvement on the present, if intellect is to be invigorated and love expanded there, then memory, the fundamental power of the intellect, must act with new energy on the past, and all the benevolent affections, which have been cherished here, must be quickened into a higher life. To suppose the present state blotted out hereafter from the mind, would be to destroy its use, would cut off all connexion between the two worlds, and would subvert responsibility; for how can retribution be awarded for a forgotten existence? No; we must carry the present with us, whether we enter the world of happiness or woe. The good will indeed form new, holier, stronger ties above; but under the expanding influence of that better world, the human heart will be capacious enough to retain the old whilst it receives the new, to remember its birth-place with tenderness whilst enjoying a maturer and happier being. Did I think of those who are gone, as dying to those they left, I should honor and love them less. The man who forgets his home when he quits it, seems to want the best sensibilities of our nature; and if the good were to forget their brethren on earth in their new abode, were to cease to intercede for them in their nearer approach to their common Father, could we think of them as improved by the change ?

All this I am compelled to infer from the nature of the human mind. But when I add to this, that the newborn heirs of heaven go to Jesus Christ, the great lover of the human family, who dwelt here, suffered here, who moistened our earth with his tears and blood, who has gone not to break off but to continue and perfect his beneficent labors for mankind, whose mind never for a moment turns from our race, whose interest in the progress of his truth and the salvation of the tempted soul, has been growing more and more intense ever since he left our world, and who has thus bound up our race with his very being, — when I think of all this, I am sure that they cannot forget our world. Could we hear them, I believe they would tell us that they never truly loved the race before ; never before knew, what it is to sympathize with human sorrow, to rejoice in human virtue, to mourn for human guilt. A new fountain of love to man is opened within them. They now see what before dimly gleamed on them, the capacities, the mysteries of a human soul. The significance of that word Immortality is now apprehended, and every being destined to it rises into unutterable importance. They love human nature as never before, and human friends are prized as above all price.

Perhaps it may be asked, whether those born into Heaven, not only remember with interest, but have a present immediate knowledge of those whom they left on earth ? On this point, neither Scripture nor the principles of human nature give us light, and we are of course left to uncertainty. I will only say, that I know nothing to prevent such knowledge. We are indeed accustomed to think of Heaven as distant; but of this we have no proof. Heaven is the union, the society of spiritual, higher beings. May not these fill the universe, so as to make Heaven everywhere? are such beings probably circumscribed, as we are, by material limits Milton has said, —

> "Millions of spiritual beings walk the earth
> Both when we wake and when we sleep."

It is possible that the distance of Heaven lies wholly in the veil of flesh, which we now want power to penetrate. A new sense, a new eye, might show the spiritual world compassing us on every side.

But suppose Heaven to be remote. Still we on earth may be visible to its inhabitants; still in an important sense they may be present; for what do we mean by presence? Am I not present to those of you who are beyond the reach of my arm, but whom I distinctly see? And is it at all inconsistent with our knowledge of nature, to suppose that those in Heaven, whatever be their abode, may have spiritual senses, organs, by which they may discern the remote as clearly as we do the near? This little ball of sight can see the planets at the distance of millions of miles, and by the aids of science, can distinguish the inequalities of their surfaces. And it is easy for us to conceive of an organ of vision so sensitive and piercing, that from our earth the inhabitants of those far-rolling worlds might be discerned. Why, then, may not they who have entered a higher state, and are clothed with spiritual frames, survey our earth as distinctly as when it was their abode?

This may be the truth; but if we receive it as such, let us not abuse it. It is liable to abuse. Let us not think of the departed, as looking on us with earthly, partial affections. They love us more than ever, but with a refined and spiritual love. They have now but one wish for us, which is, that we may fit ourselves to join them in their mansions of benevolence and piety. Their spiritual vision penetrates to our souls. Could we hear their voice, it would not be an utterance of personal attachment, so much as a quickening call to greater effort, to more resolute self-denial, to a wider charity, to a meeker endurance, a more filial obedience of the will of God. Nor must we think of them as appropriated to ourselves. They are breathing now an atmosphere of divine benevolence. They are charged with a higher mission than when they trod the earth. And this thought of the enlargement of their love should enlarge ours, and carry us beyond selfish regards to a benevolence akin to that with which they are inspired.

It is objected, I know, to the view I have given of the connexion of the inhabitants of Heaven with this world, that it is inconsistent with their happiness. It is said, that if they retain their knowledge of this state, they must suffer from the recollection or sight of our sins and woes; that to enjoy Heaven, they must wean themselves from the earth. This objection is worse than superficial. It is a reproach to Heaven and the good. It supposes, that the happiness of that world is founded in ignorance, that it is the happiness of the blind man, who, were he to open his eye on what exists around him, would be filled with horror. It makes Heaven an Elysium, whose inhabitants perpetuate their joy by shutting themselves up in narrow bounds, and hiding themselves from the pains of their fellow-creatures. But the good, from their very nature, cannot thus be confined. Heaven would be a prison, did it cut them off from sympathy with the suffering. Their benevolence is too pure, too divine, to shrink from the sight of evil. Let me add, that the objection before us casts reproach on God. It supposes that there are regions of his universe, which must be kept out of sight, which, if seen, would blight the happiness of the virtuous. But this cannot be true. There are no such regions, no secret places of woe which these pure spirits must not penetrate. There is impiety in the thought. In such a universe there could be no Heaven.

Do you tell me that according to these views, suffering must exist in that blessed state? I reply, I do and must regard Heaven as a world of sympathy. Nothing, I believe, has greater power to attract the regards of its benevolent inhabitants, than the misery into which any of their fellow-creatures may have fallen. The suffering which belongs to a virtuous sympathy, I cannot, then, separate from Heaven. But that sympathy, though it has sorrow, is far from being misery. Even in this world, a disinterested compassion, when joined with power to minister to suffering, and with wisdom to comprehend its gracious purposes, is a spirit of peace, and often issues in the purest delight. Unalloyed as it will be in another world, by our present infirmities, and enlightened by comprehensive views of God's perfect government, it will give a charm and loveliness to the sublimer virtues of the blessed, and, like all other forms of excellence, will at length enhance their felicity.

II. You see how much of Heaven is taught us in the single truth, that they who enter it, meet and are united to Jesus Christ. There are other interesting views at which I can only glance. The departed go not to Jesus only. They go to the great and blessed society which is gathered round him, to the redeemed from all regions of earth, " to the city of the living God, to an innumerable company of angels, to the church of the first-born, to the spirits of the just made perfect." Into what a glorious community do they enter! And how they are received you can easily understand. We are told, there is joy in heaven over the sinner who repenteth ; and will not his ascension to the abode of perfect virtue, communicate more fervent happiness ? Our friends who leave us for that world, do not find themselves cast among strangers. No desolate feeling springs up of having exchanged their home for a foreign country. The tenderest accents of human friendship never approached in affectionateness the voice of congratulation, which bids them welcome to their new and everlasting abode. In that world, where minds have surer means of revealing themselves than here, the newly arrived immediately see and feel themselves encompassed with virtue and goodness ; and through this insight into the congenial spirits which surround them, intimacies stronger than years can cement on earth, may be created in a moment.

It seems to me accordant with all the principles of human nature, to suppose that the departed meet peculiar congratulation from friends who had gone before them to that better world ; and especially from all who had in any way given aids to their virtue ; from parents who had instilled into them the first lessons of love to God and man ; from associates, whose examples had won them to goodness, whose faithful counsels deterred them from sin. The ties created by such benefits must be eternal. The grateful soul must bind itself with peculiar affection to such as guided it to immortality.

In regard to the happiness of the intercourse of the future state, all of you, I trust, can form some apprehensions of it. If we have ever known the enjoyments of friendship, of entire confidence, of coöperation in honorable and successful labors with those we love, we can comprehend something of the felicity of a world, where souls, refined from selfishness, open as the day, thirsting for new truth and virtue, endued with new power of enjoying the beauty and grandeur of the universe, allied in the noblest works of benevolence, and continually discovering new mysteries of the Creator's power and goodness, communicate themselves to one another with the freedom of perfect love. The closest attachments of this life are cold, distant, stranger-like, compared with theirs. How they communicate themselves, by what language or organs, we know not. But this we know, that in the progress of the mind, its power of imparting itself must improve. The eloquence, the thrilling, inspiring tones, in which the good and noble sometimes speak to us on earth, may help us to conceive the expressiveness, harmony, energy of the language in which superior beings reveal themselves above. Of what they converse we can better judge. They who enter that world, meet beings whose recollections extend through ages, who have met together perhaps from various worlds, who have been educated amidst infinite varieties of condition, each of whom has passed through his own discipline and reached his own peculiar form of perfection, and each of whom is a peculiar testimony to the providence of the Universal Father. What treasures of memory, observation, experience, imagery, illustration, must enrich the intercourse of Heaven! One angel's history may be a volume of more various truth, than all the records of our race. — After all, how little can our present experience help us to understand the intercourse of Heaven, a communion marred by no passion, chilled by no reserve, depressed by no consciousness of sin, trustful as childhood, and overflowing with innocent joy, a communion in which the noblest feelings flow fresh from the heart, in which pure beings give familiar utterance to their divinest inspirations, to the Wonder which perpetually springs up amidst this ever-unfolding and ever-mysterious universe, to the raptures of adoration and pious gratitude, and to the swellings of a sympathy which cannot be confined.

But it would be wrong to imagine that the inhabitants of Heaven only converse. They who reach that world, enter on a state of action, life, effort. We are apt to think of the future world as so happy that none need the aid of others, that effort ceases, that the good have nothing to do, but to enjoy. The truth is, that all action on earth, even the intensest, is but the sport of childhood, compared with the energy and activity of that higher life. It must be so. For what principles are so active as intellect, benevolence, the love of truth, the thirst for perfection, sympathy with the suffering, and devotion to God's purposes; and these are the ever-expanding principles of the future life. It is true, the labors which are now laid on us for food, raiment, outward interests, cease at the grave. But far deeper wants than those of the body are developed in Heaven. There it is that the spirit first becomes truly conscious of its capacities; that truth opens before us in its infinity; that the universe is seen to be a boundless sphere for discovery, for science, for the sense of beauty, for beneficence, and for adoration. There new objects to live for, which reduce to nothingness present interests, are constantly unfolded. We must not think of Heaven as a stationary community. I think of it as a world of stupendous plans and efforts for its own improvement. I think of it, as a society passing through successive stages of developement, virtue, knowledge, power, by the energy of its own members. Celestial genius is always active to explore the great laws of the creation and the everlasting principles of the mind, to disclose the beautiful in the universe, and to discover the means by which every soul may be carried forward. In that world, as in this, there are diversities of intellect, and the highest minds find their happiness and progress in elevating the less improved. There the work of education, which began here, goes on without end; and a diviner philosophy than is taught on earth, reveals the spirit to itself, and awakens it to earnest, joyful effort for its own perfection.

And not only will they who are born into Heaven, enter a society full of life and action for its own developement. Heaven has connexion with other worlds. Its inhabitants are God's messengers through the creation. They have great trusts. In the progress of their endless being, they may have the care of other worlds. But I pause, lest to those unused to such speculations, I seem to exceed the bounds of calm anticipation. What I have spoken seems to me to rest on God's word and the laws of the mind, and these laws are everlasting.

On one more topic I meant to enlarge, but I must forbear. They who are born into Heaven, go not only to Jesus, and an innumerable company of pure beings.

They go to God. They see Him with a new light in all his works. Still more, they see Him, as the Scriptures teach, face to face, that is, by Immediate Communion. These new relations of the ascended spirit to the Universal Father, how near! how tender! how strong! how exalting! But this is too great a subject for the time which remains. And yet it is the chief element of the felicity of Heaven.

The views now given of the future state, should make it an object of deep interest, earnest hope, constant pursuit. Heaven is, in truth, a glorious reality. Its attraction should be felt perpetually. It should overcome the force with which this world draws us to itself. Were there a country on earth uniting all that is beautiful in nature, all that is great in virtue, genius, and the liberal arts, and numbering among its citizens, the most illustrious patriots, poets, philosophers, philanthropists of our age, how eagerly should we cross the ocean to visit it! And how immeasurably greater is the attraction of Heaven! There live the elder brethren of the creation, the sons of the morning, who sang for joy at the creation of our race; there the great and good of all ages and climes; the friends, benefactors, deliverers, ornaments of their race; the patriarch, prophet, apostle, and martyr; the true heroes of public, and still more of private, life; the father, mother, wife, husband, child, who, unrecorded by man, have walked before God in the beauty of love and self-sacrificing virtue. There are all who have built up in our hearts the power of goodness and truth, the writers from whose pages we have received the inspiration of pure and lofty sentiments, the friends whose countenances have shed light through our dwellings, and peace and strength through our hearts. There they are gathered together, safe from every storm, triumphant over evil;—and they say to us, Come and join us in our everlasting blessedness; Come and bear part in our song of praise; Share our adoration, friendship, progress, and works of love. They say to us, Cherish now in your earthly life, that spirit and virtue of Christ which is the beginning and dawn of Heaven, and we shall soon welcome you, with more than human friendship, to our own immortality. Shall that voice speak to us in vain? Shall our worldliness and unforsaken sins, separate us, by a gulf which cannot be passed, from the society of Heaven?

WAR.

DISCOURSE

DELIVERED JANUARY 25, 1835.

JAMES iv. 1: "Whence come wars and fightings among you?"

I ASK your attention to the subject of public war. I am aware, that to some this topic may seem to have political bearings, which render it unfit for the pulpit; but to me it is eminently a moral and religious subject. In approaching it, political parties and interest vanish from my mind. They are forgotten amidst the numerous miseries and crimes of war. To bring war to an end was one of the purposes of Christ, and his ministers are bound to concur with him in the work. The great difficulty on the present occasion, is, to select some point of view from the vast field which opens before us. After some general remarks, I shall confine myself to a single topic, which at present demands peculiar attention.

Public war is not an evil which stands alone, or has nothing in common with other evils. It belongs, as the text intimates, to a great family. It may be said, that society, through its whole extent, is deformed by war.

Even in families we see jarring interests and passions, invasions of rights, resistance of authority, violence, force ; and in common life, how continually do we see men struggling with one another for property or distinction, injuring one another in word or deed, exasperated against one another by jealousies, neglects, and mutual reproach. All this is essentially war, but war restrained, hemmed in, disarmed by the opinions and institutions of society. To limit its ravages, to guard reputation, property, and life, society has instituted government, erected the tribunal of justice, clothed the legislator with the power of enacting equal laws, put the sword into the hand of the magistrate, and pledged its whole force to his support. Human wisdom has been manifested in nothing more conspicuously than in civil institutions for repressing war, retaliation, and passionate resort to force, among the citizens of the same state. But here it has stopped. Government, which is ever at work to restrain the citizen at home, often lets him loose, and arms him with fire and sword against other communities, sends out hosts for desolation and slaughter, and concentrates the whole energies of a people in the work of spreading misery and death. Government, the peace-officer at home, breathes war abroad, organizes it into a science, reduces it to a system, makes it a trade, and applauds it as if it were the most honorable work of nations. Strange that the wisdom which has so successfully put down the wars of individuals, has never been inspired and emboldened to engage in the task of bringing to an end the more gigantic crimes and miseries of public war. But this universal pacification, until of late, has hardly been thought of ; and in reading history we are almost tempted to believe, that the chief end of govern ment in promoting internal quiet, has been to accumulate greater resources for foreign hostilities. Bloodshed is the staple of history, and men have been butchered and countries ravaged, as if the human frame had been constructed with such exquisite skill only to be mangled, and the earth covered with fertility only to attract the spoiler.

These reflections, however, it is not my intention to pursue. The miseries of war are not my present subject. One remark will be sufficient to place them in their true light. What gives these miseries preëminence among human woes, — what should compel us to look on them with peculiar horror, — is, not their awful amount, but their origin, their source. They are miseries inflicted by man on man. They spring from depravity of will. They bear the impress of cruelty, of hardness of heart. The distorted features, writhing frames, and shrieks of the wounded and dying, — these are not the chief horrors of war : they sink into unimportance compared with the infernal passions which work this woe. Death is a light evil when not joined with crime. Had the countless millions destroyed by war, been swallowed up by floods or yawning earthquakes, we should look back awe-struck, but submissive, on the mysterious providence which had thus fulfilled the mortal sentence originally passed on the human race. But that man, born of woman, bound by ties of brotherhood to man, and commanded by an inward law and the voice of God to love and do good, should, through selfishness, pride, revenge, inflict these agonies, shed these torrents of human blood, — here is an evil which combines with exquisite suffering fiendish guilt. All other evils fade before it.

Such are the dark features of war. I have spoken of them strongly, because humanity and religion demand from us all a new and sterner tone on this master evil. But it is due to human nature to observe, that whilst war is, in the main, the offspring and riot of the worst passions, better principles often mix with it and throw a veil over its deformity. Nations fight not merely for revenge or booty. Glory is often the stirring word; and glory, though often misinterpreted and madly pursued by crime, is still an impulse of great minds, and shows a nature made to burn with high thoughts, and to pour itself forth in noble deeds. Many have girded themselves for battle from pure motives; and, as if to teach us that unmingled evil cannot exist in God's creation, the most ferocious conflicts have been brightened by examples of magnanimous and patriotic virtue. In almost all wars, there is some infusion of enthusiasm; and in all enthusiasm, there is a generous element.

Still war is made up essentially of crime and misery, and to abolish it is one great purpose of Christianity, and should be the earnest labor of philanthropy; nor is this enterprise to be scoffed at as hopeless. The tendencies of civilization are decidedly towards peace. The influences of progressive knowledge, refinement, arts, and national wealth, are pacific. The old motives for war are losing power. Conquest, which once maddened nations, hardly enters now into the calculation of statesmen. The disastrous and disgraceful termination of the last career of conquest which the world has known, is reading a lesson not soon to be forgotten. It is now thoroughly understood, that the developemer of a nation's resources in peace is the only road to prosperity; that even successful war makes a people poor, crushing them with taxes and crippling their progress in industry and useful arts. We have another pacific influence at the present moment, in the increasing intelligence of the middle and poorer classes of society, who, in proportion as they learn their interests and rights, are unwilling to be used as materials of war, to suffer and bleed in serving the passions and glory of a privileged few. Again; science, commerce, religion, foreign travel, new facilities of intercourse, new exchanges of literature, new friendships, new interests, are overcoming the old antipathies of nations, and are silently spreading the sentiment of human brotherhood, and the conviction that the welfare of each is the happiness of all. Once more; public opinion is continually gaining strength in the civilized and Christian world; and to this tribunal all states must in a measure bow. Here are pacific influences. Here are encouragements to labor in the cause of peace.

At the present day, one of the chief incitements to war is to be found in false ideas of honor. Military prowess and military success are thought to shed peculiar glory on a people; and many, who are too wise to be intoxicated with these childish delusions, still imagine that the honor of a nation consists peculiarly in the spirit which repels injury, in sensibility to wrongs, and is therefore peculiarly committed to the keeping of the sword. These opinions I shall now examine, beginning with the glory attached to military achievements.

That the idea of glory should be associated strongly with military exploits, ought not to be wondered at. From the earliest ages, ambitious sovereigns and states have sought to spread the military spirit, by loading it with rewards. Badges, ornaments, distinctions, the most flattering and intoxicating, have been the prizes of war. The aristocracy of Europe, which commenced in barbarous ages, was founded on military talent and success; and the chief education of the young noble, was for a long time little more than a training for battle, — hence the strong connexion between war and honor. All past ages have bequeathed us this prejudice, and the structure of society has given it a fearful force. Let us consider it with some particularity.

The idea of honor is associated with war. But to whom does the honor belong? If to any, certainly not to the mass of the people, but to those who are particularly engaged in it. The mass of a people, who stay at home, and hire others to fight, — who sleep in their warm beds, and hire others to sleep on the cold and damp earth, — who sit at their well-spread board, and hire others to take the chance of starving, who nurse the slightest hurt in their own bodies, and hire others to expose themselves to mortal wounds and to linger in comfortless hospitals; — certainly this mass reap little honor from war; the honor belongs to those immediately engaged in it. Let me ask, then, what is the chief business of war? It is to destroy human life; to mangle the limbs; to gash and hew the body; to plunge the sword into the heart of a fellow-creature; to strew the earth with bleeding frames, and to trample them under foot with horses' hoofs. It is to batter down and burn cities; to turn fruitful fields into deserts; to level the cottage of the peasant and the magnificent abode of opulence; to scourge nations with famine; to multiply widows and orphans. Are these honorable deeds? Were you called to name exploits worthy of demons, would you not naturally select such as these? Grant that a necessity for them may exist; it is a dreadful necessity, such as a good man must recoil from with instinctive horror; and though it may exempt them from guilt, it cannot turn them into glory. We have thought that it was honorable to heal, to save, to mitigate pain, to snatch the sick and sinking from the jaws of death. We have placed among the revered benefactors of the human race, the discoverers of arts which alleviate human sufferings, which prolong, comfort, adorn, and cheer human life; and if these arts be honorable, where is the glory of multiplying and aggravating tortures and death?

It will be replied, that the honorableness of war consists not in the business which it performs, but in the motives from which it springs, and in the qualities which it indicates. It will be asked, Is it not honorable to serve one's country, and to expose one's life in its cause? Yes, our country deserves love and service; and let her faithful friends, her loyal sons, who under the guidance of duty and disinterested zeal, have poured out their blood in her cause, live in the hearts of a grateful posterity. But who does not know, that this moral heroism is a very different thing from the common military spirit? Who is so simple as to believe, that this all-sacrificing patriotism of principle is the motive which fills the ranks of war, and leads men to adopt the profession of arms? Does this sentiment reign in the common soldier, who enlists because driven from all other modes of support, and hires himself to be shot at for a few cents a-day? Or does it reign in the officer, who, for pay and promotion, from the sense of reputation, or dread of disgrace, meets the foe with a fearless front? There is, indeed, a vulgar patriotism nourished by war; I mean that which burns to humble other nations, and to purchase for our own the exultation of triumph and superior force. But as for true patriotism, which has its root in benevolence, and which desires the real and enduring happiness of our country, nothing is more adverse to it than war, and no class of men have less of it than those engaged in war. Perhaps in no class is the passion for display and distinction so strong; and in accordance with this infirmity, they are apt to regard as the highest interest of the state, a career of conquests, which makes a show and dazzles the multitude, however desolating or unjust in regard to foreign nations, or however blighting to the prosperity of their own.

The motives which generally lead to the choice of a military life, strip it of all claim to peculiar honor. There are employments, which from their peculiar character, should be undertaken only from high motives. This is peculiarly the case with the profession of arms. Its work is bloodshed, destruction, the infliction of the most dreaded evils, not only on wrong-doers, oppressors, usurpers, but on the innocent, weak, defenceless. From this task humanity recoils, and nothing should reconcile us to it but the solemn conviction of duty to God, to our country, to mankind. The man who undertakes this work solely or chiefly to earn money or an epaulette, commits, however unconsciously, a great wrong. Let it be conceded, that he who engages in military life, is bound, as in other professions, to insure from his employers the means of support, and that he may innocently seek the honor which is awarded to faithful and successful service. Still, from the peculiar character of the profession, from the solemnity and terribleness of its agency, no man can engage in it innocently or honorably, who does not deplore its necessity, and does not adopt it from generous motives, from the power of moral and public considerations. That these are not the motives which now fill armies, is too notorious to need proof. How common is it for military men to desire war, as giving rich prizes and as advancing them in their profession. They are willing to slaughter their fellow-creatures for money and distinction ; — and is the profession of such men peculiarly glorious ? I am not prepared to deny that human life may sometimes be justly taken ; but it ought to be taken under the solemn conviction of duty and for great public ends. To destroy our fellow-creatures for profit or promotion, is to incur a guilt from which most men would shrink, could it be brought distinctly before their minds. That there may be soldiers of principle, men who abhor the thought of shedding human blood, and who consent to the painful office only because it seems to them imposed by their country and the best interests of mankind, is freely granted. Such men spring up especially in periods of revolution, when the liberties of a nation are at stake. But that this is not the spirit of the military profession, you know. That men generally enter this profession from selfish motives, that they hire themselves to kill for personal remuneration, you know. That they are ready to slay a fellow-creature, from inducements not a whit more disinterested than those which lead other men to fell an ox or crush a pernicious insect, you know ; and, of consequence, the profession has no peculiar title to respect. It is particularly degraded by the offer of prize-money. The power of this inducement is well understood. But is it honorable to kill a fellow-creature for a share of his spoils ? A nation which offers prize-money, is chargeable with the crime of tainting the mind of the soldier. It offers him a demoralizing motive to the destruction of his fellow-creatures. It saps high principle in the minds of those who are susceptible of generous impulses. It establishes the most inhuman method of getting rich which civilized men can pursue. I know that society views this subject differently, and more guilt should be attached to society than to the soldier; but still the character of the profession remains degraded by the motives which most commonly actuate its members; and war, as now carried on, is certainly among the last vocations to be called honorable.

Let not these remarks be misconstrued. I mean not to deny to military men equal virtue with other classes of society. All classes are alike culpable in regard to war, and the burden presses too heavily on all, to allow any to take up reproaches against others. Society has not only established and exalted the military profession, but studiously allures men into it by bribes of vanity, cupidity, and ambition. They who adopt it, have on their side the suffrage of past ages, the sanction of opinion and law, and the applauding voice of nations; so that justice commands us to acquit them of peculiar deviations from duty, or of falling below society in moral worth or private virtue.

Much of the glare thrown over the military profession, is to be ascribed to the false estimate of courage, which prevails through the Christian world. Men are dazzled by this quality. On no point is popular opinion more perverted and more hostile to Christianity, and to this point I would therefore solicit particular attention. The truth is, that the delusion on this subject has come down to us from remote ages, and has been from the beginning a chief element of the European character. Our northern ancestors, who overwhelmed the Roman empire, were fanatical to the last degree in respect to military courage. They made it the first of virtues. One of the chief articles of their creed was, that a man dying on the field of battle, was transported at once to the hall of their god Odin, a terrible paradise, where he was to quaff for ever delicious draughts from the skulls of his enemies. So rooted was this fanaticism, that it was thought a calamity to die of disease or old age ; and death by violence, even if inflicted by their own hands, was thought more honorable than to expire by the slow, inglorious processes of nature. This spirit, aided by other causes, broke out at length into chivalry, the strangest mixture of good and evil, of mercy and cruelty, of insanity and generous sentiment, to be found in human history. This whole institution breathed an extravagant estimation of courage. To be without fear was the first attribute of a good knight. Danger was thirsted for, when it might innocently be shunned. Life was sported with wantonly. Amusements full of peril, exposing even to mortal wounds, were pursued with passionate eagerness. The path to honor lay through rash adventures, the chief merit of which was the scorn of suffering and of death which they expressed. This fanaticism has yielded in a measure to good sense, and still more to the spirit of Christianity. But still it is rife ; and not a few imagine fearless courage to be the height of glory.

That courage is of no worth, I have no disposition to affirm. It ought to be prized, sought, cherished. Though not of itself virtuous, it is an important aid to virtue. It gives us the command of our faculties when needed most. It converts the dangers which palsy the weak, into springs of energy. Its firm look often awes the injurious, and silences insult. All great enterprises demand it, and without it virtue cannot rise into magnanimity. Whilst it leaves us exposed to many vices, it saves us from one class peculiarly ignominious,—from the servility, deceit, and base compliance, which belong to fear. It is accompanied too with an animated consciousness of power, which is one of the high enjoyments of life. We are bound to cherish it as the safeguard of happiness and rectitude; and when so cherished it takes rank among the virtues.

Still, courage considered in itself, or without reference to its origin and motives, and regarded in its common manifestations, is not virtue, is not moral excellence; and the disposition to exalt it above the spirit of Christianity, is one of the most ruinous delusions which have been transmitted to us from barbarous times. In most men, courage has its origin in a happy organization of the body. It belongs to the nerves rather than the character. In some, it is an instinct bordering on rashness. In one man, it springs from strong passions obscuring the idea of danger. In another, from the want of imagination or from the incapacity of bringing future evils near. The courage of the uneducated may often be traced to stupidity; to the absence of thought and sensibility. Many are courageous from the dread of the infamy absurdly attached to cowardice. One terror expels another. A bullet is less formidable than a sneer To show the moral worthlessness of mere courage, of contempt of bodily suffering and pain, one consideration is sufficient;— the most abandoned have possessed it in perfection. The villain often hardens into the thorough hero, if courage and heroism be one. The more complete his success in searing conscience and defying God, the more dauntless his daring. Long-continued vice and exposure naturally generate contempt of life and a reckless encounter of peril. Courage, considered in itself or without reference to its causes, is no virtue and deserves no esteem. It is found in the best and the worst, and is to be judged according to the qualities from which it springs and with which it is conjoined. There is in truth a virtuous, glorious courage; but it happens to be found least in those who are most admired for bravery. It is the courage of principle, which dares to do right in the face of scorn, which puts to hazard reputation, rank, the prospects of advancement, the sympathy of friends, the admiration of the world, rather than violate a conviction of duty. It is the courage of benevolence and piety, which counts not life dear in withstanding error, superstition, vice, oppression, injustice, and the mightiest foes of human improvement and happiness. It is moral energy, that force of will in adopting duty, over which menace and suffering have no power. It is the courage of a soul, which reverences itself too much to be greatly moved about what befalls the body; which thirsts so intensely for a pure inward life, that it can yield up the animal life without fear; in which the idea of moral, spiritual, celestial good has been unfolded so brightly as to obscure all worldly interests; which aspires after immortality, and therefore heeds little the pains or pleasures of a day; which has so concentred its whole power and life in the love of godlike virtue, that it even finds a joy in the perils and sufferings by which its loyalty to God and virtue may be approved. This courage may be called the perfection of humanity, for it is the exercise, result, and expression of the highest attributes of our nature. Need I tell you, that this courage has hardly any thing in common with what generally bears the name, and has been lauded by the crowd to the skies ? Can any man, not wholly blinded to moral distinctions, compare or confound with this divine energy, the bravery derived from constitution, nourished by ambition, and blazing out in resentment, which forms the glory of military men and of men of the world ? The courage of military and ordinary life, instead of resting on high and unchangeable principles, finds its chief motive in the opinions of the world, and its chief reward in vulgar praise. Superior to bodily pain, it crouches before censure, and dares not face the scorn which faithfulness to God and unpopular duty must often incur. It wears the appearance of energy, because it conquers one strong passion, fear ; but the other passions it leaves unmastered, and thus differs essentially from moral strength or greatness, which consists is subjecting all appetites and desires to a pure and high standard of rectitude. Brilliant courage, as it is called, so far from being a principle of universal self-control, is often joined with degrading pleasures, with a lawless spirit, with general licentiousness of manners, with a hardihood which defies God as well as man, and which, not satisfied with scorning death, contemns the judgment that is to follow. So wanting in moral worth is the bravery which has so long been praised, sung, courted, adored. It is time that it should be understood. It is time that the old, barbarous, indiscriminate worship of mere courage should give place to a wise moral judgment. This fanaticism has done much to rob Christianity of its due honor. Men, who give their sympathies and homage to the fiery and destructive valor of the soldier, will see little attraction in the mild and peaceful spirit of Jesus. His unconquerable forbearance, the most genuine and touching expression of his divine philanthropy, may even seem to them a weakness. We read of those who, surrounding the cross, derided the meek sufferer. They did it in their ignorance. More guilty, more insensible are those, who, living under the light of Christianity, and yielding it their assent, do not see in that cross a glory which pours contempt on the warrior. Will this delusion never cease ? Will men never learn to reverence disinterested love ? Shall the desolations and woes of ages bear their testimony in vain against the false glory which has so long dazzled the world ? Shall Christ, shall moral perfection, shall the spirit of heaven, shall God manifest in his Son, be for ever insulted by the worship paid to the spirit of savage hordes ? Shall the cross ostentatiously worn on the breast, never come to the heart, a touching emblem and teacher of all-suffering love ?— I do not ask these questions in despair. Whilst we lament the limited triumphs of Christianity over false notions of honor, we see and ought to recognise its progress. War is not now the only or chief path to glory. The greatest names are not now written in blood. The purest fame is the meed of genius, philosophy, philanthropy, and piety, devoting themselves to the best interests of humanity. The passion for military glory is no longer, as once, able of itself to precipitate nations into war. In all this let us rejoice.

In the preceding remarks, I aimed to show that the glory awarded to military prowess and success, is unfounded, — to show the deceitfulness of the glare which seduces many into the admiration of war. I proceed to another topic, which is necessary to give us a ful. understanding of the pernicious influence exerted by the idea of honor in exciting nations to hostility. There are many persons who have little admiration of warlike achievements, and are generally inclined to peace, but who still imagine that the honor of a nation consists peculiarly in quickness to feel and repel injury, and who, consequently, when their country has been wronged, are too prone to rush into war. Perhaps its interests have been slightly touched. Perhaps its wellbeing imperiously demands continued peace. Still its honor is said to call for reparation, and no sacrifice is thought too costly to satisfy the claim. That rational honor should be dear, and guarded with jealous care, no man will deny ; but in proportion as we exalt it, we should be anxious to know precisely what it means, lest we set up for our worship a false, unjust, merciless deity, and instead of glory shall reap shame. I ask, then, in what does the honor of a nation consist ? What are its chief elements or constituents ? The common views of it are narrow and low. Every people should study it ; and in proportion as we understand it, we shall learn that it has no tendency to precipitate nations into war. What, I ask again, is this national honor from which no sacrifice must be withheld ?

The first element of a nation's honor is undoubtedly justice. A people, to deserve respect, must lay down the maxim, as the foundation of its intercourse with other communities, that justice, — a strict regard to the rights of other states, — shall take rank of its interests. A nation without reverence for right, can never plead in defence of a war, that this is needed to maintain its honor, for it has no honor to maintain. It bears a brand of infamy, which oceans of human blood cannot wash away. With these views, we cannot be too much shocked by the language of a chief magistrate recently addressed to a legislative body in this country.

"No community of men," he says, "in any age or nation, under any dispensation, political or religious, has been governed by justice in its negotiations or conflicts with other states. It is not justice and magnanimity, but interest and ambition, dignified under the name of State policy, that has governed, and ever will govern, masses of men acting as political communities. Individuals may be actuated by a sense of justice; but what citizen in any country would venture to contend for justice to a foreign and rival community, in opposition to the prevailing policy of his state, without forfeiting the character of a patriot?"

Now, if this be true of our country, and to our own country it was applied, then, I say, we have no honor to fight for. A people systematically sacrificing justice to its interests, is essentially a band of robbers, and receives but the just punishment of its profligacy in the assaults of other nations. But it is not true that nations are so dead to moral principles. The voice of justice is not always drowned by the importunities of interest; nor ought we, as citizens, to acquiesce in an injurious act, on the part of our rulers, towards other states, as if it were a matter of course, a necessary working of human selfishness. It ought to be reprobated as indignantly as the wrongs of private men. A people strictly just has an honor independent of opinion, and to which opinion must pay homage. Its glory is purer and more enduring than that of a thousand victories. Let not him who prefers for his country the renown of military spirit and success to that of justice, talk of his zeal for its honor. He does not know the meaning of the word. He belongs to a barbarous age, and desires for his country no higher praise than has been gained by many a savage horde.

The next great element of a nation's honor is a spirit of philanthropy. A people ought to regard itself as a member of the human family, and as bound to bear part in the work of human improvement and happiness. The obligation of benevolence, belonging to men as individuals, belongs to them in their associated capacities. We have indeed no right to form an association of whatever kind, which severs us from the human race. I care not though men of loose principles scoff at the idea of a nation respecting the claims of humanity. Duty is eternal, and too high for human mockery; and this duty in particular, so far from being a dream, has been reduced to practice. Our own country, in framing its first treaties, proposed to insert an article prohibiting privateering; and this it did in the spirit of humanity to diminish the crimes and miseries of war. England, from philanthropy, abolished the slave trade and slavery. No nation stands alone; and each is bound to consecrate its influence to the promotion of equitable, pacific, and beneficent relations among all countries, and to the diffusion of more liberal principles of intercourse and national law. This country is intrusted by God with a mission for humanity. Its office is to commend to all nations free institutions, as the sources of public prosperity and personal dignity; and I trust we desire to earn the thanks and honor of nations by fidelity o our trust. A people reckless of the interest of the world, and profligately selfish in its policy, incurs far deeper disgrace than by submission to wrongs ; and whenever it is precipitated into war by its cupidity, its very victories become monuments of its guilt, and deserve the execration of present and coming times.

I now come to another essential element of a nation's honor ; and that is, the existence of institutions which tend, and are designed, to elevate all classes of its citizens. As it is the improved character of a people which alone gives it an honorable place in the world, its dignity is to be measured chiefly by the extent and efficiency of its provisions and establishments for national improvement, — for spreading education far and wide, — for purifying morals and refining manners, — for enlightening the ignorant and succouring the miserable, — for building up intellectual and moral power, and breathing the spirit of true religion. The degree of aid given to the individual in every condition, for unfolding his best powers, determines the rank of a nation. Mere wealth adds nothing to a people's glory ; it is the nation's soul which constitutes its greatness. Nor is it enough for a country to possess a select class of educated, cultivated men ; for the nation consists of the many, not the few ; and where the mass are sunk in ignorance and sensuality ; there you see a degraded community, even though an aristocracy of science be lodged in its bosom. It is the moral and intellectual progress of the people, to which the patriot should devote himself as the only dignity and safeguard of the state. How needed this truth ! In all ages, nations have imagined that they were glorifying themselves by triumphing over foreign foes, whilst at home they have been denied every ennobling institution; have been trodden under foot by tyranny, defrauded of the most sacred rights of humanity, enslaved by superstition, buried in ignorance, and cut off from all the means of rising to the dignity of men. They have thought that they were exalting themselves, in fighting for the very despots who ground them in the dust. Such has been the common notion of national honor; nor is it yet effaced. How many among ourselves are unable to stifle their zeal for our honor as a people, who never spent a thought on the institutions and improvements which ennoble a community, and whose character and examples degrade and taint their country, as far as their influence extends?

I have now given you the chief elements of national honor; and a people cherishing these can hardly be compelled to resort to war. I shall be told, however, that an enlightened and just people though less exposed to hostilities, may still be wronged, insulted, and endangered; and I shall be asked, if in such a case its honor do not require it to repel injury, — if submission be not disgrace? I answer, that a nation which submits to wrong from timidity, or a sordid love of ease or gain, forfeits its claim to respect. A faint-hearted, self-indulgent people, cowering under menace, shrinking from peril, and willing to buy repose by tribute or servile concession, deserves the chains which it cannot escape. But to bear much and long from a principle of humanity, from reverence for the law of love, is noble; and nothing but moral blindness and degradation induce men to see higher glory in impatience of injury and quickness to resent.

Still I may be asked, whether a people, however forbearing, may not sometimes owe it to its own dignity and safety to engage in war? I answer, yes. When the spirit of justice, humanity, and forbearance, instead of spreading peace, provokes fresh outrage, this outrage must be met and repressed by force. I know that many sincere Christians oppose to this doctrine the precept of Christ, " Resist not evil." But Christianity is wronged and its truth exposed to strong objections, when these and the like precepts are literally construed. The whole legislation of Christ is intended to teach us the spirit from which we should act, not to lay down rules for outward conduct. The precept, " Resist not evil," if practised to the letter, would annihilate all government in the family and the state; for it is the great work of government to resist evil passions and evil deeds. It is indeed our duty, as Christians, to love our worst enemy, and to desire his true good; but we are to love not only our enemy, but our families, friends, and country, and to take a wise care of our own rights and happiness; and when we abandon to the violence of a wrong-doer these fellow-beings, and these rights, commended by God to our love and care, we are plainly wanting in that expanded benevolence which Christianity demands. A nation, then, may owe it to its welfare and dignity to engage in war; and its honor demands that it should meet the trial with invincible resolution. It ought, at such a moment, to dismiss all fear, except the fear of its own passions,— the fear of the crimes to which the exasperations and sore temptations of public hostilities expose a state.

I have admitted that a nation's honor may require its citizens to engage in war; but it requires them to engage in it wisely,— with a full consciousness of rectitude and with unfeigned sorrow. On no other conditions does war comport with national dignity; and these deserve a moment's attention. A people must engage in war wisely; for rashness is dishonorable, especially in so solemn and tremendous a concern. A nation must propose a wise end in war; and this remark is the more important, because the end or object which, according to common speech, a people is bound by its honor to propose, is generally disowned by wisdom. How common it is to hear, that the honor of a nation requires it to seek redress of grievances,— reparation of injuries. Now, as a general rule, war does not and cannot repair injuries. Instead of securing compensation for past evils, it almost always multiplies them. As a general rule, a nation loses incomparably more by war than it has previously lost by the wrong-doer. Suppose, for example, a people to have been spoiled by another state of "five millions of dollars." To recover this by war, it must expend fifty or a hundred millions more, and will, almost certainly, come forth from the contest burdened with debt. Nor is this all. It loses more than wealth. It loses many lives. Now, life and property are not to be balanced against each other. If a nation, by slaying a single innocent man, could possess itself of the wealth of worlds, it would have no right to destroy him for that cause alone. A human being cannot be valued by silver and gold; and, of consequence, a nation can never be authorized to sacrifice or expose thousands of lives, for the mere recovery of property of which it has been spoiled. To secure compensation for the past, is very seldom a sufficient object for war. The true end is, security for the future. An injury inflicted by one nation on another, may manifest a lawless, hostile spirit, from which, if unresisted, future and increasing outrages are to be feared, which would embolden other communities in wrong-doing, and against which neither property, nor life, nor liberty, would be secure. To protect a state from this spirit of violence and unprincipled aggression, is the duty of rulers ; and protection may be found only in war. Here is the legitimate occasion and the true end of an appeal to arms. Let me ask you to apply this rule of wisdom to a case, the bearings of which will be easily seen. Suppose, then, an injury to have been inflicted on us by a foreign nation a quarter of a century ago. Suppose it to have been inflicted by a government which has fallen through its lawlessness, and which can never be restored. Suppose this injury to have been followed, during this long period, by not one hostile act, and not one sign of a hostile spirit. Suppose a disposition to repair it to be expressed by the head of the new government of the injurious nation ; and suppose further, that our long endurance has not exposed us to a single insult from any other power since the general pacification of Europe. Under these circumstances, can it be pretended, with any show of reason, that threatened wrong, or that future security, requires us to bring upon ourselves and the other nation the horrors and miseries of war ? Does not wisdom join with humanity in reprobating such a conflict ?

I have said that the honor of a nation requires it to engage in a war for a wise end. I add, as a more important rule, that its dignity demands of it to engage in no conflict without a full consciousness of rectitude. It must not appeal to arms for doubtful rights. It must not think it enough to establish a probable claim. The true principle for a nation, as for an individual, is, that it will suffer rather than do wrong. It should prefer being injured, to the hazard of doing injury. To secure to itself this full consciousness of rectitude, a nation should always desire to refer its disputes to an impartial umpire. It cannot too much distrust its own judgment in its own cause. That same selfish partiality which blinds the individual to the claims of a rival or foe, and which has compelled society to substitute public and disinterested tribunals for private war, disqualifies nations, more or less, to determine their own rights, and should lead them to seek a more dispassionate decision. The great idea which should rise to the mind of a country on meditating war, is rectitude. In declaring war, it should listen only to the voice of duty. To resolve on the destruction of our fellow-creatures without a command from conscience, — a commission from God, — is to bring on a people a load of infamy and crime. A nation, in declaring war, snould be lifted above its passions by the fearfulness and solemnity of the act. It should appeal with unfeigned confidence to Heaven and earth for its uprightness of purpose. It should go forth as the champion of truth and justice, as the minister of God, to vindicate and sustain that great moral and national law, without which life has no security, and social improvements no defence. It should be inspired with invincible courage, not by its passions, but by the dignity and holiness of its cause. Nothing in the whole compass of legislation is so solemn as a declaration of war. By nothing do a people incur such tremendous responsibility. Unless justly waged, war involves a people in the guilt of murder. The state which, without the command of justice and God, sends out fleets and armies to slaughter fellow-creatures, must answer for the blood it sheds, as truly as the assassin for the death of his victim. Oh, how loudly does the voice of blood cry to Heaven from the field of battle! Undoubtedly, the men whose names have come down to us with the loudest shouts of ages, stand now before the tribunal of eternal justice condemned as murderers; and the victories which have been thought to encircle a nation with glory, have fixed the same brand on multitudes in the sight of the final and Almighty Judge. How essential is it to a nation's honor that it should engage in war with a full conviction of rectitude!

But there is one more condition of an honorable war. A nation should engage in it with unfeigned sorrow. It should beseech the throne of grace with earnest supplication, that the dreadful office of destroying fellow-beings may not be imposed on it. War concentrates all the varieties of human misery, and a nation which can inflict these without sorrow, contracts deeper infamy than from cowardice. It is essentially barbarous; and will be looked back upon by more enlightened and Christian ages, with the horror with which we recall the atrocities of savage tribes. Let it be remembered that the calamities of war, its slaughter, famine, and desolation, instead of being confined to its criminal authors, fall chiefly on multitudes who have had no share in provoking and no voice in proclaiming it; and let not a nation talk of its honor, which has no sympathy with these woes, which is steeled to the most terrible sufferings of humanity.

I have now spoken, my friends, of the sentiments with which war should be regarded. Is it so regarded? When recently the suggestion of war was thrown out to this people, what reception did it meet? Was it viewed at once in the light in which a Christian nation should immediately and most earnestly consider it? Was it received as a proposition to slaughter thousands of our fellow-creatures? Did we feel as if threatened with a calamity more fearful than earthquakes, famine, or pestilence? The blight which might fall on our prosperity, drew attention; but the thought of devoting as a people, our power and resources to the destruction of mankind, of those whom a common nature, whom reason, conscience, and Christianity command us to love and save, did this thrill us with horror? Did the solemn inquiry break forth through our land, is the dreadful necessity indeed laid upon us to send abroad death and woe? No. There was little manifestation of the sensibility with which men and Christians should look such an evil in the face. As a people, we are still seared and blinded to the crimes and miseries of war. The principles of honor, to which the barbarism and infatuation of dark ages gave birth, prevail among us. The generous, merciful spirit of our religion is little understood. The law of love preached from the cross and written in the blood of the Saviour, is trampled on by public men. The true dignity of man, which consists in breathing and cherishing God's spirit of justice and philanthropy towards every human being, is counted folly in comparison with that spirit of vindictiveness and self-aggrandizement, which turns our earth into an image of the abodes of the damned. How long will the friends of humanity, of religion, of Christ, silently, passively, uncomplainingly, suffer the men of this world, the ambitious, vindictive, and selfish, to array them against their brethren in conflicts which they condemn and abhor? Shall not truth, humanity, and the mild and holy spirit of Christianity, find a voice to rebuke and awe the wickedness which precipitates nations into war, and to startle and awaken nations to their fearful responsibility in taking arms against the children of their Father in heaven? Prince of Peace! Saviour of men! speak in thine own voice of love, power, and fearful warning; and redeem the world for which thou hast died, from lawless and cruel passions, from the spirit of rapine and murder, from the powers of darkness and hell!

MINISTRY FOR THE POOR.

DISCOURSE
DELIVERED
BEFORE THE BENEVOLENT FRATERNITY OF CHURCHES,
Boston, April 9, 1835.

Luke iv. 18: "The spirit of the Lord is upon me, because he hath anointed me to preach the Gospel to the poor."

We are met together on the first anniversary of the Benevolent Fraternity of Churches, an institution formed for the purpose of providing a ministry for the poor, and of thus communicating moral and spiritual blessings to the most destitute portion of the community. We may well thank God for living in a state of society, in which such a design finds cordial support. We should rejoice in this token of human progress. Man has always felt for the outward wants and sufferings of man. This institution shows, that he is alive to the higher capacities, the deeper cravings of his fellow-beings. This institution is one of the forms in which the spirit of Christianity is embodied, a spirit of reverence and love for the human soul, of sympathy with its fall, of intense desire for its redemption.

On this occasion there is but one topic of which I can speak, and that is the claims of the poor as Moral, Spiritual beings; and it is a topic on which I enter with a consciousness of insufficiency. The claims of outward and worldly things I can comprehend. I can look through wealth, pomp, rank. I can meet unmoved the most imposing forms of earthly dignity; but the immortal principle in the heart of the poorest human being, I approach with awe. There I see a mystery in which my faculties are lost. I see an existence, before which the duration of the world and the outward heavens is a span. I say that I see it. I am not surrendering myself to imagination; I have a consciousness of truth, or rather a consciousness of falling beneath the truth. I feel, then, my incompetency to be just to this subject. But we must do what we can. No testimony, however feeble, if lifted up in sincerity in behalf of great principles, is ever lost. Through weak man, if sanctified by a simple, humble love of truth, a higher power than man's is pleased to work. May that power overshadow us, and work within us, and open every soul to truth.

To awaken a Spiritual interest in the poor, this is my object. I wish not to diminish your sympathy with their outward condition; I would increase it. But their physical sufferings are not their chief evils. The great calamity of the poor is not their poverty, understanding this word in the usual sense, but the tendency of their privations, and of their social rank, to degradation of mind. Give them the Christian spirit, and their lot would not be intolerable. Remove from them the misery which they bring on themselves by evil-doing, and separate from their inevitable sufferings the aggravations which come from crime, and their burden would be light compared with what now oppresses them.

The outward condition of the poor is a hard one. I mean not to criticize it with the apathy of the stoic, to deny that pain is an evil, privation a loss of good. But when I compare together different classes as existing at this moment in the civilized world, I cannot think the difference between the rich and the poor, in regard to mere physical suffering, so great as is sometimes imagined. That some of the indigent among us die of scanty food, is undoubtedly true; but vastly more in this community die from eating too much, than from eating too little; vastly more from excess, than starvation. So as to clothing, many shiver from want of defences against the cold; but there is vastly more suffering among the rich from absurd and criminal modes of dress, which fashion has sanctioned, than among the poor from deficiency of raiment. Our daughters are oftener brought to the grave by their rich attire, than our beggars by their nakedness. So the poor are often over-worked, but they suffer less than many among the rich who have no work to do, no interesting object to fill up life, to satisfy the infinite cravings of man for action. According to our present modes of education, how many of our daughters are victims of *ennui*, a misery unknown to the poor, and more intolerable than the weariness of excessive toil! The idle young man spending the day in exhibiting his person in the street, ought not to excite the envy of the overtasked poor, and this cumberer of the ground is found exclusively among the rich.

I repeat it, the condition of the poor deserves sympathy; but let us not, by exaggeration of its pains, turn away our minds from the great inward sources of their misery. In this city, the condition of a majority of the indigent is such as would be thought eligible elsewhere. Insure to a European peasant an abundance of wheaten bread through every season of the year, and he would bless his easy lot. Among us, many a poor family, if doomed to live on bread, would murmur at its hard fare; and accordingly the table of the indigent is daily spread with condiments and viands hardly known in the cottage of the transatlantic laborer. The Greenlander and Laplander dwelling in huts and living on food compared with which the accommodations of our poor are abundant, are more than content. They would not exchange their wastes for our richest soils and proudest cities. It is not, then, the physical suffering of the poor, but their relation to the rest of society, the want of means of inward life, the degrading influences of their position, to which their chief misery is to be traced.

Let not the condition of the poor be spoken of as necessarily wretched. Give them the Christian spirit, and they would find in their lot the chief elements of good. For example, the domestic affections may and do grow up among the poor, and these are to all of us the chief springs of earthly happiness. And it deserves consideration, that the poor have their advantages as well as disadvantages in respect to domestic ties. Their narrow condition obliges them to do more for one another, than is done among the rich; and this necessity, as is well known, sometimes gives a vigor and tenderness to the love of parents and children, brothers and sisters, not always found in the luxurious classes, where wealth destroys this mutual dependence, this need of mutual help. Nor let it be said, that the poor cannot enjoy domestic happiness for want of the means of educating their children. A sound moral judgment is of more value in education, than all wealth and all talent. For want of this, the children of men of genius and opulence are often the worst trained in the community ; and if, by our labors, we can communicate this moral soundness to the poor, we shall open among them the fountain of the only pure domestic felicity.

In this country, the poor might enjoy the most important advantages of the rich, had they the moral and religious cultivation consistent with their lot. Books find their way into every house, however mean ; and especially that book which contains more nutriment for the intellect, imagination, and heart, than all others ; I mean, of course, the Bible. And I am confident, that among the poor are those, who find in that one book, more enjoyment, more awakening truth, more lofty and beautiful imagery, more culture to the whole soul, than thousands of the educated find in their general studies, and vastly more than millions among the rich find in that superficial, transitory literature, which consumes all their reading hours.

Even the pleasures of a refined taste are not denied to the poor, but might easily be opened to them by a wise moral culture. True, their rooms are not lined with works of art ; but the living beauty of nature opens on the eyes of all her children ; and we know from the history of self-educated genius, that sometimes the inhabitant of a hovel, looking out on the serene sky, the illumined cloud, the setting sun, has received into his rapt spirit, impressions of divine majesty and loveliness, to which the burning words of poetry give but faint utterance. True, the rich may visit distant scenery, and feed their eyes on the rarest and most stupendous manifestations of creative power ; but the earth and common sky reveal, in some of their changeful aspects, a grandeur as awful as Niagara or the Andes; and nothing is wanting to the poor man in his ordinary walks, but a more spiritual eye to discern a beauty which has never yet been embodied in the most inspired works of sculpture or painting.

Thus for the poor, as for all men, there are provisions for happiness; and it deserves remark, that their happiness has a peculiar dignity. It is more honorable to be content with few outward means, than with many; to be cheerful amidst privation, than amidst overflowing plenty. A poor man, living on bread and water, because he will not ask for more than bare sustenance requires, and leading a quiet, cheerful life through his benevolent sympathies, his joy in duty, his trust in God, is one of the true heroes of the race, and understands better the meaning of happiness, than we, who cannot be at ease unless we clothe ourselves "in purple, and fare sumptuously every day," unless we surround, defend, and adorn ourselves with all the products of nature and art. His scantiness of outward means is a sign of inward fulness, whilst the slavery in which most of us live, to luxuries and accommodations, shows the poverty within.

I have given the fair side of the poor man's lot. I have shown the advantages placed within his reach; but I do not therefore call him happy. His advantages are too commonly lost through want of inward culture. The poor are generally wretched, with many means of good. Think not that I mean to throw one false color on their actual state. It is miserable enough to awaken deep sympathy; but their misery springs not so much from physical causes, which cannot be withstood, as from moral want. The moral influences of their condit'on, of their rank in society, of their connexion with other classes, these are more terrible than hunger or cold, and to these I desire to turn your chief-regard.

What, then, are the moral influences of poverty, its influences on character, which deserve our chief attention? As one of its most fatal effects, I would observe, in the first place, that it impairs, often destroys, self-respect. I know, and rejoice to know, that the institutions of this country do much to counteract this influence of poverty; but still it exists and works frequent debasement. It is hard for any of us to interpret justly our own nature, and how peculiarly hard for the poor! Uninstructed in the import and dignity of their rational and moral powers, they naturally measure themselves by their outward rank. Living amidst the worshippers of wealth, they naturally feel as if degraded by the want of it. They read in the looks, tones, and manners of the world, the evidences of being regarded as an inferior race, and want inward force to repel this cruel, disheartening falsehood. They hear the word *respectable* confined to other conditions, and the word *low* applied to their own. Now, habitual subjection to slight or contempt, is crushing to the spirit. It is exceedingly hard for a human being to comprehend and appreciate himself, amidst outward humiliation. There is no greater man than he who is true to himself, when all around deny and forsake him. Can we wonder that the poor, thus abandoned, should identify themselves with their lot; that in their rags they should see the sign of inward as well as outward degradation?

Another cause which blights their self-respect, is their dependence for pecuniary aid. It is hard to ask alms and retain an erect mind. Dependence breeds servility, and he who has stooped to another cannot be just to himself. The want of self-respect is a preparation for every evil. Degraded in their own and others' esteem, the poor are removed from the salutary restraint of opinion; and having no caste to lose, no honor to forfeit, often abandon themselves recklessly to the grossest vice.

2. The condition of the poor is unfriendly to the action and unfolding of the intellect, a sore calamity to a rational being. In most men, indeed, the intellect is narrowed by exclusive cares for the body. In most, the consciousness of its excellence is crushed by the low uses to which it is perpetually doomed. But still, in most, a degree of activity is given to the mind by the variety and extent of their plans for wealth or subsistence. The bodily wants of most, carry them in a measure into the future, engage them in enterprises requiring invention, sagacity, and skill. It is the unhappiness of the poor, that they are absorbed in immediate wants, in provisions for the passing day, in obtaining the next meal, or in throwing off a present burden. Accordingly their faculties "live and move," or rather pine and perish, in the present moment. Hope and Imagination, the wings of the soul, carrying it forward and upward, languish in the poor; for the future is uninviting. The darkness of the present broods over coming years. The great idea, which stirs up in other men a world of thought, the idea of a better lot, has almost faded from the poor man's mind. He almost ceases to hope for his children, as well as for himself. Even parental love, to many the chief quickener of the intellect, stagnates through despair. Thus poverty starves the mind.

And there is another way in which it produces this effect, particularly worthy the notice of this assembly. The poor have no society beyond their own class; that is, beyond those who are confined to their own narrow field of thought. We all know, that it is contact with other minds, and especially with the more active and soaring, from which the intellect receives its chief impulse. Few of us could escape the paralyzing influence of perpetual intercourse with the uncultivated, sluggish, and narrow-minded; and here we see, what I wish particularly to bring to view, how the poor suffer from the boasted civilization of our times, which is built so much on the idea of Property. In communities little advanced in opulence, no impassable barrier separates different classes, as among ourselves. The least improved are not thrown to a distance from those, who, through natural endowment or peculiar excitement, think more strongly than the rest; and why should such division exist anywhere? How cruel and unchristian are the pride and prejudice which form the enlightened into a caste, and leave the ignorant and depressed to strengthen and propagate ignorance and error without end.

3. I proceed to another evil of poverty, its disastrous influence on the domestic affections. Kindle these affections in the poor man's hut, and you give him the elements of the best earthly happiness. But the more delicate sentiments find much to chill them in the abodes of indigence. A family crowded into a single and often narrow apartment, which must answer at once the ends of parlour, kitchen, bed-room, nursery, and hospital, must, without great energy and self-respect, want neatness, order, and comfort. Its members are perpetually

exposed to annoying, petty interference. The decencies of life can be with difficulty observed. Woman, a drudge, and in dirt, loses her attractions. The young grow up without the modest reserve and delicacy of feeling, in which purity finds so much of its defence. Coarseness of manners and language, too sure a consequence of a mode of life which allows no seclusion, becomes the habit almost of childhood, and hardens the mind for vicious intercourse in future years. The want of a neat, orderly home, is among the chief evils of the poor. Crowded in filth, they cease to respect one another. The social affections wither amidst perpetual noise, confusion, and clashing interests. In these respects, the poor often fare worse than the uncivilized. True, the latter has a ruder hut, but his habits and tastes lead him to live abroad. Around him is a boundless, unoccupied nature, where he ranges at will, and gratifies his passion for liberty. Hardened from infancy against the elements, he lives in the bright light and pure air of heaven. In the city, the poor man must choose between his close room, and the narrow street. The appropriation of almost every spot on earth to private use, and the habits of society, do not allow him to gather his family, or meet his tribe, under a spreading tree. He has a home, without the comforts of home. He cannot cheer it by inviting his neighbours to share his repast. He has few topics of conversation with his wife and children, except their common wants. Of consequence, sensual pleasures are the only means of ministering to that craving for enjoyment, which can never be destroyed in human nature. These pleasures, in other dwellings, are more or less refined by taste. The table is spread with neatness and order ; and a decency pervades the meal, which shows that man is more than a creature of sense The poor man's table strewed with broken food, and seldom approached with courtesy and self-respect, serves too often to nourish only a selfish, animal life, and to bring the partakers of it still nearer to the brute. I speak not of what is necessary and universal; for poverty, under sanctifying influences, may find a heaven in its narrow home; but I speak of tendencies which are strong, and which only a strong religious influence can overcome.

4. I proceed to another unhappy influence exerted on the poor. They live in the sight and in the midst of innumerable indulgences and gratifications, which are placed beyond their reach. Their connexion with the affluent, though not close enough for spiritual communication, is near enough to inflame appetites, desires, wants, which cannot be satisfied. From their cheerless rooms, they look out on the abodes of luxury. At their cold, coarse meal, they hear the equipage conveying others to tables groaning under plenty, crowned with sparkling wines, and fragrant with the delicacies of every clime. Fainting with toil, they meet others unburdened, as they think, with a labor or a care. They feel, that all life's prizes have fallen to others. Hence burning desire. Hence brooding discontent. Hence envy and hatred. Hence crime, justified in a measure to their own minds, by what seem to them the unjust and cruel inequalities of social life. Here are some of the miseries of civilization. The uncivilized man is not exasperated by the presence of conditions happier than his own. There is no disproportion between his idea of happiness and his lot. Among the poor the disproportion is infinite. You all understand how much we judge

our lot by comparison. Thus the very edifices, which a century ago seemed to our fathers luxurious, seem now to multitudes hardly comfortable, because surrounded by more commodious and beautiful dwellings. We little think of the gloom added to the poor by the contiguity of the rich. They are preyed on by artificial wants, which can only be gratified by crime. They are surrounded by enjoyments, which fraud or violence can make their own. Unhappily the prevalent, I had almost said, the whole spirit of the rich, increases these temptations of the poor. Very seldom does a distinct, authentic voice of wisdom come to them from the high places of society, telling them that riches are not happiness, and that a felicity which riches cannot buy, is within reach of all. Wealth-worship is the spirit of the prosperous, and this is the strongest possible inculcation of discontent and crime on the poor. The rich satisfy themselves with giving alms to the needy. They think little of more fatal gifts, which they perpetually bestow. They think little, that their spirit and lives, their self-indulgence and earthliness, their idolatry of outward prosperity, and their contempt of inferior conditions, are perpetually teaching the destitute, that there is but one good on earth, namely, property, the very good in which the poor have no share. They little think, that by these influences they do much to inflame, embitter, and degrade the minds of the poor, to fasten them to the earth, to cut off their communication with Heaven.

5. I pass to another sore trial of the poor. Whilst their condition, as we have seen, denies them many gratifications, which on every side meet their view and inflame desire, it places within their reach many debasing gratifications. Human nature has a strong thirst

for pleasures which excite it above its ordinary tone, which relieve the monotony of life. This drives the prosperous from their pleasant homes to scenes of novelty and stirring amusement. How strongly must it act on those who are weighed down by anxieties and privations! How intensely must the poor desire to forget for a time the wearing realities of life! And what means of escape does society afford or allow them? What present do civilization and science make to the poor? Strong drink, ardent spirits, liquid poison, liquid fire, a type of the fire of hell! In every poor man's neighbourhood flows a Lethean stream, which laps him for a while in oblivion of all his humiliations and sorrows! The power of this temptation can be little understood by those of us, whose thirst for pleasure is regularly supplied by a succession of innocent pleasures, who meet soothing and exciting objects wherever we turn. The uneducated poor, without resource in books, in their families, in a well-spread board, in cheerful apartments, in places of fashionable resort, and pressed down by disappointment, debt, despondence, and exhausting toils, are driven by an impulse dreadfully strong, to the haunts of intemperance; and there they plunge into a misery sorer than all the tortures invented by man. They quench the light of reason, cast off the characteristics of humanity, blot out God's image as far as they have power, and take their place among the brutes. Terrible misery! And this, I beg you to remember, comes to them from the very civilization in which they live. They are victims to the progress of science and the arts; for these multiply the poison which destroys them. They are victims to the rich; for it is the capital of the rich, which erects the distillery, and surrounds them with temptations to self-murder. They are victims to a partial advancement of society, which multiplies gratifications and allurements, without awakening proportionate moral power to withstand them.

Such are the evils of poverty. It is a condition, which offers many and peculiar obstructions to the developement of intellect and affection, of self-respect and self-control. The poor are peculiarly exposed to discouraging views of themselves, of human nature, of human life. The consciousness of their own intellectual and moral power slumbers. Their faith in God's goodness, in virtue, in immortality, is obscured by the darkness of their present lot. Ignorant, desponding, and sorely tempted, have they not solemn claims on their more privileged brethren, for aids which they have never yet received?

I have thus shown, as I proposed, that the chief evils of poverty are moral in their origin and character; and for these I would awaken your concern. With physical sufferings we sympathize. When shall the greater misery move our hearts? Is there nothing to startle us in the fact, that in every large city dwells a multitude of human beings, falling or fallen into extreme moral degradation, living in dark, filthy houses, or in damp, unventilated cellars, where the eye lights on no beauty and the ear is continually wounded with discord, where the outward gloom is a type of the darkened mind, where the name of God is heard only when profaned, where charity is known only as a resource for sloth, where the child is trained amidst coarse manners, impure words, and the fumes of intemperance, and is thence sent forth to prowl as a beggar. From these abodes issues a louder, more piercing cry for help and strength, than physical want ever uttered. I do not mean that all the poor are such as I have described. Far from it. Among them are the "salt of the earth," the "lights of the world," the elect of God. There is no necessary connexion of poverty and crime. Christianity knows no distinction of rank, and has proved itself equal to the wants of all conditions of men. Still poverty has tendencies to the moral degradation which I have described ; and to counteract these, should be esteemed one of the most solemn duties and precious privileges bequeathed by Christ to his followers.

From the views now given of the chief evils of poverty, it follows, that Moral and Religious culture is the great blessing to be bestowed on the poor. By this, it is not intended that their physical condition demands no aid. Let charity minister to their pressing wants and sufferings. But let us bear it in mind, that no charity produces permanent good, but that which goes beneath the body, which reaches the mind, which touches the inward springs of improvement, and awakens some strength of purpose, some pious or generous emotion, some self-respect. That charity is most useful, which removes obstructions to well-doing and temptations to evil from the way of the poor, and encourages them to strive for their own true good. Something, indeed, may be done for the moral benefit of the indigent by wise legislation ; I do not mean by poor-laws ; but by enactments intended to remove, as far as possible, degrading circumstances from their condition. For example, the laws should prohibit the letting of an apartment to a poor family, which is not tenantable, which cannot but injure health, which cannot be ventilated, which wants the necessary means of preventing accumulations of filth. Such ordinances, connected with provisions for cleansing every alley, and for carrying pure, wholesome water in abundance to every dwelling, would do not a little for the health, cleanliness, and self-respect of the poor ; and on these, their moral well-being in no small degree depends.

Our chief reliance, however, must be placed on more direct and powerful means than legislation. The poor need, and must receive Moral and Religious Culture, such as they have never yet enjoyed. I say Culture ; and I select this term, because it expresses the developement of Inward Principles ; and without this, nothing effectual can be done for rich or poor. Unhappily, religion has been, for the most part, taught to the poor mechanically, superficially, as a tradition. It has been imposed on them as a restraint, or a form ; it has been addressed to the senses, or to the sensual imagination, and not to the higher principles. An outward hell, or an outward heaven, has too often been the highest motive brought to bear on their minds. But something more is wanted ; a deeper work, an inward culture, the developement of the reason, the conscience, the affections, and the moral will. True religion is a life unfolded within, not something forced on us from abroad. The poor man needs an elevating power within, to resist the depressing tendencies of his outward lot. Spiritual culture is the only effectual service we can send him, and let his misery plead with us to bestow it to the extent of our power.

Had I time, I might show that moral and religious principles, as far as they are strengthened in the breasts of the poor, meet all the wants and evils which have now been portrayed ; that they give them force to bear up against all the adverse circumstances of their lot, inspire them with self-respect, refine their manners, give impulse to their intellectual powers, open to them the springs of domestic peace, teach them to see without murmuring, the superior enjoyments of others, and rescue them from the excesses into which multitudes are driven by destitution and despair. But these topics are not only too extensive, but are to a degree familiar, though by no means felt as they should be. I conceive that I shall better answer the purpose of awakening a spiritual interest in this class of society, by confining myself to a single point, by showing, that the Moral and Religious Culture which I claim for the poor, is the highest cultivation which a human being can receive. We are all of us, I fear, blinded on this subject, by the errors and prejudices of our own education. We are apt to imagine, that the only important culture of a human being comes from libraries, literary institutions, and elegant accomplishments; that is, from means beyond the reach of the poor. Advantages offered by wealth seem to us the great, and essential means of bringing forward the human mind. Perhaps we smile at hearing the word *cultivation* applied to the poor. The best light which their condition admits, seems darkness compared with the knowledge imparted by our seminaries of learning; and the highest activity of mind to which they can be excited, is scornfully contrasted with what is called forth in their superiors by works of philosophy and genius. There is, among not a few, a contemptuous estimate of the culture which may be extended to the poor, of the good which they are capable of receiving; and hence, much of the prevalent indifference as to furnishing them the means of spiritual growth. Now this is a weak and degrading prejudice. I affirm, that the highest culture is open alike to rich and poor. I affirm, that the rich may extend their most precious acquisitions to the poor. There is nothing in indigence to exclude the noblest improvements. The impartial Father designs his best gifts for all. Exclusive good, or that which only a few can enjoy, is comparatively worthless. Essential good, is the most freely diffused. It is time to put away our childish notions as to human improvement; it is time to learn, that advantages which are a monopoly of the few, are not necessary to the developement of human nature, that the soul grows best by helps which are accessible to all.

The truth is, that there is no cultivation of the human being, worthy of the name, but that which begins and ends with the Moral and Religious nature. No other teaching can make a Man. We are striving, indeed, to develope the soul almost exclusively by intellectual stimulants and nutriment, by schools and colleges, by accomplishments and fine arts. We are hoping to form men and women by literature and science; but all in vain. We shall learn in time that moral and religious culture is the foundation and strength of all true cultivation; that we are deforming human nature by the means relied on for its growth, and that the poor who receive a care which awakens their consciences and moral sentiments, start under happier auspices than the prosperous, who place supreme dependence on the education of the intellect and the taste.

It is common to measure the cultivation of men by their knowledge; and this is certainly an important element and means of improvement. But knowledge is various, differing in different men according to the objects which most engage their minds; and by these objects its worth must be judged. It is not the extent, but the kind of knowledge, which determines the measure of cultivation. In truth, it is foolish to talk of any knowledge as extensive. The most eminent philosopher is of yesterday, and knows nothing. Newton felt that he had gathered but a few pebbles on the shores of a boundless ocean. The moment we attempt to penetrate a subject, we learn that it has unfathomable depths. The known is a sign of the infinite unknown. Every discovery conducts us to an abyss of darkness. In every thing, from the grain of sand to the stars, the wise man finds mysteries, before which his knowledge shrinks into nothingness. It is the kind, not the extent of knowledge, by which the advancement of a human being must be measured; and that kind which alone exalts a man, is placed within the reach of all. Moral and Religious Truth, this is the treasure of the intellect, and all are poor without it. This transcends physical truth, as far as mind transcends matter, or as heaven is lifted above earth. Indeed, physical science parts with its chief dignity, when separated from morals; when it is not used to shadow forth, confirm, and illustrate spiritual truth.

The true cultivation of a human being, consists in the developement of great moral ideas; that is, the Ideas of God, of Duty, of Right, of Justice, of Love, of Self-sacrifice, of Moral Perfection as manifested in Christ, of Happiness, of Immortality, of Heaven. The elements or germs of these ideas, belong to every soul, constitute its essence, and are intended for endless expansion. These are the chief distinctions of our nature; they constitute our humanity. To unfold these is the great work of our being. The Light in which these ideas rise on the mind, the Love which they awaken, and the Force of Will with which they are brought to sway the outward and inward life, here and here only, are the measures of human cultivation.

These views show us, that the highest culture is within the reach of the poor. It is not knowledge poured on us from abroad, but the developement of the elementary principles of the soul itself, which constitutes the true growth of a human being. Undoubtedly, knowledge from abroad is essential to the awakening of these principles. But that which conduces most to this end, is offered alike to rich and poor. Society and Experience, Nature and Revelation, our chief moral and religious teachers, and the great quickeners of the soul, do not open their schools to a few favorites, do not initiate a small caste into their mysteries, but are ordained by God to be lights and blessings to all.

The highest culture, I repeat it, is in reach of the poor, and is sometimes attained by them. Without science, they are often wiser than the philosopher. The astronomer disdains them, but they look above his stars. The geologist disdains them, but they look deeper than the earth's centre; they penetrate their own souls, and find there mightier, diviner elements, than upheaved continents attest. In other words, the great ideas of which I have spoken, may be, and often are, unfolded more in the poor man than among the learned or renowned; and in this case the poor man is the most cultivated. For example, take the idea of justice. Suppose a man, eminent for acquisitions of knowledge, but in whom this idea is but faintly developed. By justice he understands little more than respect for the rights of property

That it means respect for all the rights, and especially for the moral claims, of every human being, of the lowest as well as most exalted, has perhaps never entered his mind, much less been expanded and invigorated into a broad, living conviction. Take now the case of a poor man, to whom, under Christ's teaching, the idea of the Just has become real, clear, bright, and strong; who recognises, to its full extent, the right of property, though it operates against himself; but who does not stop here; who comprehends the higher rights of men as rational and moral beings, their right to exercise and unfold all their powers, their right to the means of improvement, their right to search for truth and to utter their honest convictions, their right to consult first the monitor in their own breasts and to follow wherever it leads, their right to be esteemed and honored according to their moral efforts, their right, when injured, to sympathy and succour against every oppressor. Suppose, I say, the poor man to rise to the comprehension of this enlarged justice, to revere it, to enthrone it over his actions, to render to every human being, friend or foe, near or far off, whatever is his due, to abstain conscientiously, not only from injurious deeds, but from injurious thoughts, judgments, feelings, and words. Is he not a more cultivated man, and has he not a deeper foundation and surer promise of truth, than the student, who, with much outward knowledge, does not comprehend men's highest rights, whose scientific labors are perhaps degraded by injustice towards his rivals, who, had he power, would fetter every intellect which threatens to outstrip his own?

The great idea on which human cultivation especially depends, is that of God. This is the concentration of all that is beautiful, glorious, holy, blessed. It transcends immeasurably in worth and dignity all the science treasured up in cyclopedias or libraries; and this may be unfolded in the poor as truly as in the rich. It is not an idea to be elaborated by studies, which can be pursued only in leisure or by opulence. Its elements belong to every soul, and are especially to be found in our moral nature, in the idea of duty, in the feeling of reverence, in the approving sentence which we pass on virtue, in our disinterested affections, and in the wants and aspirations which carry us toward the Infinite. There is but one way of unfolding these germs of the idea of God, and that is, faithfulness to the best convictions of duty and of the Divine Will, which we have hitherto gained. God is to be known by obedience, by likeness, by sympathy, that is, by moral means, which are open alike to rich and poor. Many a man of science has not known him. The pride of science, like a thick cloud, has hidden from the philosopher the Spiritual Sun, the only true light, and for want of this quickening ray, he has fallen in culture far, very far, below the poor.

These remarks have been drawn from me by the proneness of our times to place human culture in physical knowledge, and especially in degrees of it denied to the mass of the people. To this knowledge I would on no account deny great value. In its place, it is an important means of human improvement. I look with admiration on the intellectual force, which combines and masters scattered facts, and by analysis and comparison ascends to the general laws of the material universe. But the philosopher, who does not see in the force within him, something nobler than the outward nature which he analyzes, who, in tracing mechanical and chemical agencies, is unconscious of a higher action in his own soul, who is not led by all finite powers to the Omnipotent, and who does not catch, in the order and beauty of the universe, some glimpses of Spiritual Perfection, stops at the very threshold of the temple of truth. Miserably narrow is the culture which confines the soul to Matter, which turns it to the Outward as to something nobler than itself. I fear, the spirit of science, at the present day, is too often a degradation rather than the true culture of the soul. It is the bowing down of the heaven-born spirit before unthinking mechanism. It seeks knowledge, rather for animal, transitory purposes, than for the nutriment of the imperishable inward life; and yet the worshippers of science pity or contemn the poor, because denied this means of cultivation. Unhappy poor! shut out from libraries, laboratories, and learned institutes! In view of this world's wisdom, it avails you nothing, that your own nature, manifested in your own and other souls, that God's word and works, that the ocean, earth, and sky, are laid open to you; that you may acquaint yourselves with the Divine Perfections, with the character of Christ, with the duties of life, with the virtues, the generous sacrifices, and the beautiful and holy emotions, which are a revelation and pledge of heaven. All these are nothing, do not lift you to the rank of cultivated men, because the mysteries of the telescope and microscope, of the air-pump and crucible, are not revealed to you! I would they were revealed to you. I believe the time is coming when Christian benevolence will delight in spreading all truth and all refinements through all ranks of society. But meanwhile be not discouraged. One ray of moral and religious truth is worth all the wisdom of the schools. One lesson from Christ will carry you higher than years of study under those who are too enlightened to follow this celestial guide.

My hearers, do not contemn the poor man for his ignorance. Has he seen the Right? Has he felt the binding force of the Everlasting Moral Law? Has the beauty of virtue, in any of its forms, been revealed to him? Then he has entered the highest school of wisdom. Then a light has dawned within him, worth all the physical knowledge of all worlds. It almost moves me to indignation, when I hear the student exalting his science, which at every step meets impenetrable darkness, above the idea of Duty and above veneration for goodness and God. It is true, and ought to be understood, that outward nature, however tortured, probed, dissected, never reveals truths so sublime or precious, as are wrapped up in the consciousness of the meanest individual, and laid open to every eye in the word of Christ.

I trust it will not be inferred from what I have said of the superiority of moral and religious culture to physical science, that the former requires or induces a neglect or disparagement of the latter. No, it is the friend of all truth, the enemy of none. It is propitious to intellect, and incites to the investigation of the laws and order of the universe. This view deserves a brief illustration, because an opposite opinion has sometimes prevailed, because reproach has sometimes been thrown on religious culture, as if it narrowed the mind and barred it against the lights of physical science. There cannot be a more groundless charge. Superstition contracts and darkens the mind; but that living faith in moral and religious truth, for which I contend as the highest culture of rich and poor, is in no respect narrow or exclusive. It does not fasten the mind for ever on a few barren doctrines. In proportion to its growth, it cherishes our whole nature, gives a wide range to thought, opens the intellect to the true, and the imagination to the beautiful. The great principles of moral and religious science, are, above all others, fruitful, life-giving, and have intimate connexions with all other truth. The Love towards God and man, which is the centre in which they meet, is the very spirit of research into nature. It finds perpetual delight in tracing out the harmonies and vast and beneficent arrangements of creation, and inspires an interest in the works of the Universal Father, more profound, intense, enduring, than philosophical curiosity. I conceive, too, that faith in moral and religious truth has strong affinities with the scientific spirit, and thus contributes to its perfection. Both, for example, have the same objects, that is, universal truths. As another coincidence, I would observe, that it is the highest prerogative of scientific genius, to interpret obscure signs, to dart from faint hints to sublime discoveries, to read in a few fragments the history of vanished worlds and ages, to detect in the falling apple the law which rules the spheres. Now it is the property of moral and religious faith, to see in the finite the manifestation of the Infinite, in the present the germ of the boundless future, in the visible the traces of the Incomprehensible Unseen, in the powers and wants of the soul its imperishable destiny. Such is the harmony between the religious and the philosophical spirit. It is to a higher moral and religious culture, that I look for a higher interpretation of nature. The laws of nature, we must remember, had their origin in the Mind of God. Of this they are the product, expression, and type; and

I cannot but believe, that the human mind which best understands, and which partakes most largely of the divine, has a power of interpreting nature, which is accorded to no other. It has harmonies with the system which it is to unfold. It contains in itself the principles which gave birth to creation. As yet, science has hardly penetrated beneath the surface of nature. The principles of animal and vegetable life, of which all organized beings around us are but varied modifications, the forces which pervade or constitute matter, and the links between matter and mind, are as yet wrapped in darkness ; and how little is known of the adaptations of the physical and the spiritual world to one another ! Whence is light to break in on these depths of creative wisdom ? I look for it to the spirit of philosophy, baptized, hallowed, exalted, made piercing by a new culture of the moral and religious principles of the human soul.

The topic opens before me as I advance. The superiority of moral and religious to all other culture, is confirmed by a throng of arguments not yet touched. The peculiar wisdom which this culture gives, by revealing to us the end, the Ultimate Good of our being, which nothing else teaches ; the peculiar power which it gives, power over ourselves, so superior to the most extensive sway over the outward universe ; the necessity of moral and religious culture to make knowledge a blessing, to save it from being a curse ; these are weighty considerations which press on my mind, but cannot be urged. They all go to show, that the culture which the poor may receive, is worth all others ; that in sending among them religious and moral influences, you send the highest good of the universe.

My friends, I have now set before you the chief evils

of the poor, and have shown you the greatness and dignity of the culture which is within their reach; and the great conviction, which I wish by these views to carry home to every mind, is, that we are solemnly bound to cherish and manifest a strong moral and religious interest in the poor; and to give them, as far as we have power, the means of moral and religious cultivation. Your sympathies with their bodily wants and pains, I, of course, would not weaken. We must not neglect their bodies under pretence of caring for their souls; nor must we, on the other hand, imagine, that in providing for their outward wants, we have acquitted ourselves of all Christian obligations. To scatter from our abundance occasional alms, is not enough; we must bring them to our minds as susceptible of deeper evils than hunger and cold; and as formed for higher good than food or the cheering flame. The love of Christ toward them, should seem to us no extravagance, no blind enthusiasm, but a love due to human nature in all its forms. To look beyond the outward to the spiritual in man, is the great distinction of Christian love. The soul of a fellow-creature must come out, if I may so say, and become more visible and prominent to us than his bodily frame. To see and estimate the spiritual nature of the poor, is greater wisdom than to span earth or heaven. To elevate this, is a greater work than to build cities. To give moral life to the fallen, is a higher achievement than to raise the dead from their graves. Such is the philanthropy which characterizes our religion; and without this, we can do little effectual good to the poor.

I am here teaching a difficult, but great duty. To acquire and maintain an unaffected conviction of the superiority of the spiritual in man to every thing outward, is a hard task, especially to the prosperous, and yet among the most essential. In the poor man, walking through our streets, with a haggard countenance and tottering step, we ought to see something greater than all the opulence and splendor which surround him. On this foundation of respect for every soul, are built all social duties, and none can be thoroughly performed without it. On this point I feel that I use no swollen language. Words cannot exaggerate the worth of the soul. We have all felt when looking above us into the atmosphere, that there was an infinity of space, which we could not explore. When I look into man's spirit and see there the germs of an immortal life, I feel more deeply that an infinity lies hid beyond what I see. In the idea of Duty, which springs up in every human heart, I discern a Law more sacred and boundless than gravitation, which binds the soul to a more glorious universe than that to which attraction binds the body, and which is to endure though the laws of physical nature pass away. Every moral sentiment, every intellectual action, is to me a hint, a prophetic sign, of a spiritual power to be expanded for ever, just as a faint ray from a distant star is significant of unimaginable splendor. And if this be true, is not a human being wronged, greatly wronged, who awakens in his fellow-creatures no moral concern, who receives from them no spiritual care?

It is the boast of our country, that the civil and political rights of every human being are secured; that impartial law watches alike over rich and poor. But man has other, and more important, than civil rights; and this is especially true of the poor. To him who owns nothing, what avails it that he lives in a country where property is inviolable; or what mighty boon is it to him, that every citizen is eligible to office, when his condition is an insuperable bar to promotion? To the poor, as to all men, moral rights are most important; the right to be regarded according to their nature, to be regarded, not as animals or material instruments, but as men; the right to be esteemed and honored, according to their fidelity to the moral law; and their right to whatever aids their fellow-beings can offer for their improvement, for the growth of their highest powers. These rights are founded on the supremacy of the moral nature, and until they are recognised the poor are deeply wronged.

Our whole connexion with the poor should tend to awaken in them the consciousness of their moral powers and responsibility, and to raise them in spirit and hope above their lot. They should be aided to know themselves, by the estimate we form of them. They should be rescued from self-contempt, by seeing others impressed with the great purpose of their being. We may call the poor unfortunate, but never call them low. If faithful to their light, they stand among the high. They have no superiors, but in those who follow a brighter, purer light; and to withhold from them respect, is to defraud their virtue of a support, which is among the most sacred rights of man. Are they morally fallen and lost? They should still learn, in our unaffected concern, the worth of the fallen soul, and learn that nothing seems to us so fearful as its degradation.

This moral, spiritual interest in the poor, we should express and make effectual, by approaching them, by establishing an intercourse with them, as far as consists with other duties. We must live with them, not as another race, but as brethren. Our Christian principles must work a new miracle, must exorcise and expel the spirit of caste. The outward distinctions of life must seem to us not "a great gulf," but superficial lines, which the chances of a day may blot out, and which are broad only to the narrow-minded. How can the educated and improved communicate themselves to their less favored fellow-creatures, but by coming near them? The strength, happiness, and true civilization of a community, are determined by nothing more than by this fraternal union among all conditions of men. Without this, a civil war virtually rages in a state. For the sake of rich as well as poor, there should be a mutual interest binding them together; there should be but one caste, that of humanity.

To render this connexion interesting and useful, we must value and cultivate the power of acting morally on the poor. There is no art so divine as that of reaching and quickening other minds. Do not tell me you are unequal to this task. What! call yourselves educated, and yet want power to approach and aid your unimproved fellow-creatures? Of what use is education, if it do not fit us to receive and give freely in our various social connexions? How wasted has been our youth, if it has taught us only the dialect and manners of a select class, and not taught us the language of humanity, not taught us to mix with and act on the mass of our fellow-creatures? How far are you raised above the poor, if you cannot comprehend, guide, or sway them? The chief endowment of a social being, I mean the power of imparting what is true and good in your own souls, you have yet to learn. You cannot learn it too soon.

Yes, I call you to seek and use the power of speaking to the minds of the ignorant and poor, and especially of the poor child. Strive, each of you, to bring at least one human being to the happiness for which God made him. Awaken him to some inward moral activity, for on this, not on mere outward teaching, the improvement of rich and poor alike depends. Strive to raise him above the crushing necessities of the body, by turning him to the great, kindling purpose of his being. Show him, that the fountain of all happiness is within us, and that this fountain may be opened alike in every soul. Show him, how much virtue and peace he may gain by fidelity to his domestic relations; how much progress he may make by devout and resolute use of his best opportunities; what a near union he may form with God; how beneficent an influence he may exert in his narrow sphere; what heroism may be exercised amidst privations and pains; how suffering may be turned to glory; how heaven may begin in the most unprosperous condition on earth. Surely he who can carry such truths to any human being, is charged with a glorious mission from above.

In these remarks, I have urged on all who hear me, a personal interest in the moral well-being of the poor. I am aware, however, that many can devote but little personal care to this work. But what they cannot do themselves, they can do by others; and this I hold to be one of our most sacred duties as Christians. If we cannot often visit the poor ourselves, we may send those who are qualified to serve them better. We can support ministers to study and apply the means of enlightening, comforting, reforming, and saving the ignorant and depressed. Every man, whom God has prospered, is bound to contribute to this work. The Christian ministry is indeed a blessing to all, but above all o the poor. We, who have leisure and quiet homes, and can gather round us the teachers of all ages in their writings, can better dispense with the living teacher, than the poor, who are unused to learn from books, and unaccustomed to mental effort, who can only learn through the eye and ear, through the kind look and the thrilling voice. Send them the ministers of God's truth and grace. And think not, that this office may be filled by any who will take it. There are some I know, perhaps not a few, who suppose the most common capacities equal to the Christian ministry in general, and who, of course, will incline to devolve the office of teaching the ignorant and destitute on men unfit for other vocations. Away with this disgraceful error! If there be an office worthy of angels, it is that of teaching Christian truth. The Son of God hallowed it, by sustaining it in his own person. All other labors sink before it. Royalty is impotence and a vulgar show, compared with the deep and quickening power, which many a Christian teacher has exerted on the immortal soul. Profound intellect, creative genius, thrilling eloquence, can nowhere find such scope and excitement, as in the study and communication of moral and religious truth, as in breathing into other minds the wisdom and love which were revealed in Jesus Christ; and the time will come, when they will joyfully consecrate themselves to this as their true sphere. That the ministry of the poor may be sustained by a man wanting some qualifications for a common congregation, is true; but he needs no ordinary gifts, a sound judgment, a clear mind, an insight into human nature, a spirit of patient research, the power of familiar and striking illustration of truth, a glowing heart, an unaffected self-devotion to the service of mankind. Such men we are bound to provide for the poor, if they can be secured. He who will not contribute to the moral and religious culture of the destitute, is unworthy to live in Christendom. He deserves to be banished beyond the light which he will not spread. Let him deny his religion if he will; but to believe in it, and yet not seek to impart it to those who can receive no other treasure, is to cast contempt on its excellence, and to harden himself against the most sacred claims of humanity.

My friends, it is a cause of gratitude, that so much has been done in this city to furnish such a ministry as now has been described. The poor, I believe, are provided for here as in no other place in our country. The Fraternity of Churches, which I address, have in their service three ministers for this work, and the number, it is expected, will be increased; and we all know that they have not labored in vain. Their good influence we cannot doubt. The cause has been signally prospered by God. Since the institution of this ministry, it has not only carried instruction, counsel, reproof, hope, and moral strength to multitudes, who would otherwise have heard no encouraging voice, would have met no outward remembrances of Christian duty. It has produced in other classes of society still more promising effects. It has produced a connexion of the rich with the poor, a knowledge of their real state and wants, a sympathy with them, an interest in their well-being, which are the signs of a lasting improvement in society. This ministry has not been lifeless machinery. It has vitality, earnestness, force. It does not rest in a round of regular services, but seeks new means of reaching the poor. It particularly seeks to act on the children. Not content with gathering them in Sunday-schools, it forms congregations of them for worship, and adapts to them the ordinary services of the church, so as to fix attention and touch the heart. What an invaluable service to humanity! Formerly, these children, unprovided with the means of public worship, never guided by their parents to the house of prayer, wasted and worse than wasted the Sunday in the streets, and found or made this holy season, a day of peculiar temptation and crime. Whilst the ministers of the poor are faithful to the adult, they give a special care to children, and through the child often reach the parent's heart. Through their efforts, the young who had been brought up to beg, have often been sent to the public school or the Sunday school, and in this way many a heedless foot, going down to ruin, has been turned to the path of duty. It is confidently stated, that since the establishment of this ministry a few years ago, street beggary has decreased, notwithstanding the rapid growth of our population. Happily, men of intelligence and noble hearts are willing to enter this field, and new laborers are needed. It is important that the ministers of the poor should extend their care beyond the most indigent, to that class from which the ranks of indigence are recruited, I mean to that class of laborers who are hovering over the brink of poverty, who depend on each day's toil for each day's food, and whom a short sickness or deficiency of employment reduces to want. Among these, the degrading infidelity of our days finds many of its victims, and on this account they peculiarly need to be visited by Christian friendship, and the light of truth. To connect these with regular congregations, and to incite them to contribute to the support of public worship. some part of what they now too generally expend in pernicious indulgences, would be to render an essential service to morals and religion.

The work of a minister for the poor, covers much ground, and it demands superior minds. This body of men are set apart, not only to act on individuals, but to study poverty in all its aspects, in its causes, its influences, its various shapes, its growth, and its decline, and thus to give light to the legislator and philanthropist in the great work of its prevention and cure. To me, this ministry is peculiarly interesting, regarded as the beginning of a series of operations for banishing from society its chief calamity and reproach, and for changing the face of the civilized and Christian world. I see in it the expression of a silently growing purpose, that Christian communities shall not always be deformed and disgraced by the presence of an ignorant, destitute, miserable horde; that in the bosom of civilization there shall no longer exist a more wretched, degraded portion of human beings, than can be found in savage life. This horrible contrast of condition, which all large cities present, has existed too long. Shall it endure for ever? My friends, we all, as well as others, have hitherto been dreadfully insensible to this sorest evil under the sun. Long use has hardened us to it. We have lived comfortably, perhaps luxuriously, in our dwellings, whilst within a stone's throw, were fellow-creatures, the children of our Father in heaven, as nobly born and gifted as ourselves, in whose countenances might be read brutal ignorance, hopeless misery, and degrading vice. We have passed them in the street, not only without a tear but without a thought. O, how seldom has a pang shot through our hearts at the sight of our ruined fellow-creatures! Shall this insensibility continue for ever?. Shall not a new love succeed to this iron hardness of heart? Do not call the evil remediless. Sure I am, that at this moment there is enough of piety, philanthropy, and moral power in this community, to work deep changes in the poorer classes, could these energies, now scattered and slumbering, he brought to bear wisely and perseveringly on the task. Shall we decline this work? If so, we decline the noblest labor of philanthropy. If so, we must suffer, and we ought to suffer. Society ought to be troubled, to be shaken, yea convulsed, until its solemn debt to the ignorant and poor be paid. Poor there will be, but they need not, must not exist as a degraded, hopeless caste. They need not, must not be cut off from the brotherhood of humanity. Their children must not be left to inherit and propagate their crimes and woes. To put an end to such a class, is the highest office of Christian philanthropy. Do you ask how it is to be done? I answer, Christianity has wrought mighty revolutions, and in these we have an earnest of what it is able and destined to accomplish. Let us bring this into new contact with the poor. Let us send forth men, imbued with its spirit, to preach it to the poor, and still more to study poverty in all its forms, that the moral pestilence which has so long ravaged the Christian world, may at last be stayed.

I now see before me the representatives of several congregations of this city, which have united to support the ministry for the poor. Thanks to God, for this manifestation of the spirit and power of Christianity. This connexion, framed only for purposes of Christian philanthropy, looking only to the spiritual relief of our depressed fellow-creatures, and incapable of being perverted to the accumulation of ecclesiastical power, is the happiest means which could be devised, to bring our churches into stronger sympathy and closer friendship, without infringing, in the smallest degree, that principle of independence or self-government on which they are built. Is it not a plain truth, that every Christian congregation, besides providing for its own spiritual wants, is bound to devote itself to the general cause of Christianity, and to provide for spreading its own light and privileges to the destitute? By this fraternity we are discharging, in part, this sacred obligation. May it be sustained with increasing zeal, with unshaken faith, with glorious success.

My friends, is it necessary that I should urge you to contribute of your substance to the work which has now been laid before you? I am speaking to the prosperous. Let the Goodness which has prospered you, teach you the spirit in which your wealth or competence should be used. What is the true use of prosperity? Not to minister to self-indulgence and ostentation; not to widen the space between you and the less prosperous; not to multiply signs of superior rank; not to raise us to an eminence, whence we may look down on the multitude as an inferior race; but to multiply our bonds of union with our fellow-creatures, to spread our sympathies far and wide, to give us nobler spheres of action, to make us more eminently the delegates and representatives of divine beneficence. What is the true use of increasing wealth in a city? It is not, that more magnificent structures should be reared, but that our dwellings should be inhabited by a more intelligent and virtuous people; that institutions for awakening intellectual and moral life should be brought to bear on the whole community; that the individual may be carried forward to his true happiness and perfection; that society may be bound together by stronger and purer bonds, and that the rigid laws of earthly governments may be more and more superseded by the Law of Love. Without such influences, wealth is turned into a snare and curse. If, indeed, our prosperity is to be used to spread luxurious and selfish modes of life, to form a frivolous class of fashion, to produce more striking contrasts between unfeeling opulence and abject penury, to corrupt manners and harden the heart, better were it for us, that, by the just judgment of God, it should be sunk into the depths of the sea. It avails little, that intercourse is more polished, and a new grace is thrown over life. The simple question is, Do we better understand and more strongly feel our relations to God and to our fellow-creatures? Without this, our boasted civilization is a whited sepulchre, fair to the eye, but inwardly "full of dead men's bones and all uncleanness." — But I cannot end this discourse with the voice of warning. You deserve to hear the voice of encouragement and hope. One good work you are carrying on, as this anniversary testifies. One institution for instructing the ignorant and raising up the fallen, you have sustained. Let it not fall. Extend and strengthen it. Make it permanent. Bind it up with the institutions which you support for your own religious improvement. Transmit it to your children. Let your children learn, from this your example, to take part in the cause of Christ, of prophets and apostles, of holy men of all ages, in the work of regenerating society, and of extending to the whole human family, the light and blessings of the Christian faith.

CHRISTIAN WORSHIP.

DISCOURSE

AT THE

DEDICATION OF THE UNITARIAN CONGREGATIONAL CHURCH,

Newport, Rhode Island, July 27, 1836.

John iv. 23, 24: "The hour cometh, and now is, when the true worshippers shall worship the Father in spirit and in truth; for the Father seeketh such to worship him. God is a Spirit; and they that worship him must worship him in spirit and in truth."

The dedication of an edifice to the worship of God is a proper subject of gratitude and joy. Even if the consecration be made by Christians from whom we differ in opinion, we should still find satisfaction in the service. We should desire that our neighbours, whose convictions of truth and duty require them to separate from us in religious services, should enjoy the same accommodations with ourselves; and it should comfort us to think, that Christianity is so eminently "the power of God unto salvation," its great truths so plain and so quickening, that among all sects acknowledging Christ and consulting his word, its purifying influences, however counteracted by erroneous views, will more or less be felt. We should rejoice to think, that God can be monopolized by no party; that his spirit is a universal presence; that religion, having its root in the soul of man, can live and flourish amidst many errors; that truth and goodness can no more be confined to a single church, than the light of the sun can be shut up in a private dwelling; that amidst all the diversities of forms, names, and creeds, acceptable worship may be offered to God, and the soul ascend to Heaven.

It is the custom of our times to erect beautiful structures for the purposes of the present life, for legislation, for literature, for the arts. But important as these interests are, they are not the noblest. Man's highest relations are not political, earthly, human. His whole nature is not exhausted in studying and subduing outward nature, in establishing outward order, in storing the mind with knowledge which may adorn and comfort his outward life. He has wants too deep, and powers and affections too large for the outward world. He comes from God. His closest connexion is with God; and he can find life and peace only in the knowledge of his Creator. Man's glory or true end is not revealed to us in the most magnificent structure which the architect ever reared for earthly uses. An humble spire pointing Heavenward from an obscure church, speaks of man's nature, man's dignity, man's destiny, more eloquently than all the columns and arches of Greece and Rome, the mausoleums of Asia, or the pyramids of Egypt. Is it not meet, then, to be grateful and joyful, when a house is set apart to the worship of God?

This edifice where we now meet is not indeed wholly new. Its frame is older than the oldest of us. But so great are the changes which it has undergone, that, were they who laid its foundations to revisit the earth, they would trace hardly a feature of their work; and as it is now entered by a new religious congregation, there is a fitness in the present solemnity, by which we dedicate it to the worship of God. My purpose in this discourse, is to show that we should enter this edifice with gratitude and joy; first, because it is dedicated to Worship in the most general sense of that term; and, in the second place, on account of the particular worship to which it is set apart. I shall close with some remarks of a personal and local character, which may be allowed to one who was born and brought up on this island, whose heart swells with local attachment, and whose memory is crowded with past years, as he stands, after a long absence, within these walls where he sat in his childhood, and where some of his earliest impressions were received.

I. We ought to enter this house with gratitude and joy, for it is dedicated to Worship. Its end is, that men should meet within its walls to pay religious homage; to express and strengthen pious veneration, love, thankfulness, and confidence; to seek and receive pure influences from above; to learn the will of God; and to consecrate themselves to the virtue in which he delights. This edifice is reared to the glory of God, reared like the universe to echo with his praise, to be a monument to his being, perfection, and dominion. Worship is man's highest end, for it is the employment of his highest faculties and affections on the sublimest object. We have much for which to thank God, but for nothing so much as for the power of knowing and adoring Himself. This creation is a glorious spectacle; but there is a more glorious existence for our minds and hearts, and that is the Creator. There is something divine in the faculties by which we study the visible world, and subject it to our wills, comfort, enjoyment. But it is a diviner faculty, by which we penetrate beyond the visible, free ourselves of the infinite and the mutable, and ascend to the Infinite and the Eternal. It is good to make earth and ocean, winds and flames, sun and stars, tributary to our present wellbeing. How much better to make them ministers to our spiritual wants, teachers of heavenly truth, guides to a more glorious Being than themselves, bonds of union between man and his Maker!

There have been those who have sought to disparage worship, by representing it as an arbitrary, unnatural service, a human contrivance, an invention for selfish ends. Had I time, I should be glad to disprove this sophistry, by laying open to you human nature, and showing the deep foundation laid in all its principles and wants for religion; but I can meet the objection only by a few remarks drawn from history. There have been, indeed, periods of history in which the influence of the religious principle seems to have been overwhelmed; but in this it agrees with other great principles of our nature, which in certain stages of the race disappear. There are certain conditions of society, in which the desire of knowledge seems almost extinct among men, and they abandon themselves for centuries to brutish ignorance. There are communities, in which the natural desire of reaching a better lot gives not a sign of its existence, and society remains stationary for ages. There are some, in which even the parental affection is so far dead, that the new-born child is cast into the stream or exposed to the storm. So the religious principle is in some periods hardly to be discerned; but it is never lost. No principle is more universally manifested. In the darkest ages there are some recognitions of a superior power. Man feels that there is a being above himself, and he clothes that being in what to his rude conception is great and venerable. In countries where architecture was unknown, men chose the solemn wood or the mountain top for worship; and when this art appeared, its monuments were temples to God. Before the invention of letters, hymns were composed to the Divinity; and music, we have reason to think, was the offspring of religion. Music in its infancy was the breathing of man's fears, wants, hopes, thanks, praises, to an unseen power. You tell me, my skeptical friend, that religion is the contrivance of the priest. How came the priest into being? What gave him his power? Why was it that the ancient legislator professed to receive his laws from the gods? The fact is a striking one, that the earliest guides and leaders of the human race looked to the heavens for security and strength to earthly institutions, that they were compelled to speak to men in a higher name than man's. Religion was an earlier bond and a deeper foundation of society than government. It was the root of civilization. It has founded the mightiest empires; and yet men question whether religion be an element, a principle of human nature!

In the earliest ages, before the dawn of science, man recognised an immediate interference of the Divinity in whatever powerfully struck his senses. To the savage the thunder was literally God's voice, the lightning his arrow, the whirlwind his breath. Every unusual event was a miracle, a prodigy, a promise of good, or a menace of evil from Heaven. These rude notions have faded before the light of science, which reveals fixed laws, a stated order of nature. But in these laws, this order, the religious principle now finds confirmations of God, infinitely more numerous and powerful than the savage found in his prodigies. In this age of the world, there is a voice louder than thunder and whirlwinds, attesting the Divinity; the voice of the wisely interpreted works of God, everywhere proclaiming wisdom unsearchable, harmony unbroken, and a benevolent purpose in what to ages of ignorance seemed ministers of wrath. In the present, above all times, worship may be said to have its foundation in our nature; for by the improvements of this nature, we have placed ourselves nearer to God as revealed in his universe. The clouds which once hung over the creation are scattered. The heavens, the earth, the plant, the human frame, now that they are explored by science, speak of God as they never did before. His handwriting is brought out, where former ages saw but a blank. Nor is it only by the progress of science, that the foundation of religion is made broader and deeper. The progress of the arts, in teaching us the beneficent uses to which God's works may be applied, in extracting from them new comforts, and in diminishing or alleviating human suffering, has furnished new testimonies to the goodness of the Creator. Still more, the progress of society has given new power and delicacy to the sense of beauty in human nature, and in consequence of this, the creation of God has become a far more attractive, lovely, and magnificent work than men looked on in earlier times. Above all, the moral susceptibilities and wants, the deeper and more refined feelings, which unfold themselves in the course of human improvement, are so many new capacities and demands for religion. Our nature is perpetually developing new senses for the perception and enjoyment of God. The human race, as it advances, does not leave religion behind it, as it leaves the shelter of caves and forests, does not outgrow faith, does not see it fading like the mist before its rising intelligence. On the contrary, religion opens before the improved mind in new grandeur. God, whom uncivilized man had narrowed into a local and tutelar Deity, rises with every advance of knowledge to a loftier throne, and is seen to sway a mightier sceptre. The soul, in proportion as it enlarges its faculties and refines its affections, possesses and discerns within itself a more and more glorious type of the Divinity, learns his spirituality in its own spiritual powers, and offers him a profounder and more inward worship. Thus deep is the foundation of worship in human nature. Men may assail it, may reason against it; but sooner can the laws of the outward universe be repealed by human will, sooner can the sun be plucked from his sphere, than the idea of God can be erased from the human spirit, and his worship banished from the earth. All other wants of man are superficial. His animal wants are but for a day, and are to cease with the body. The profoundest of all human wants is the want of God. Mind, spirit, must tend to its source. It cannot find happiness but in the perfect Mind, the Infinite Spirit. Worship has survived all revolutions. Corrupted, dishonored, opposed, it yet lives. It is immortal as its Object, immortal as the soul from which it ascends.

Let us rejoice, then, in this house. It is dedicated to

Worship; it can have no higher use. The heaven of heavens has no higher service or joy. The universe has no higher work. Its chief office is to speak of God. The sun in awakening innumerable forms of animal and vegetable life, exerts no influence to be compared with what it puts forth in kindling the human soul into piety, in being a type, representative, preacher of the glory of God.

II. I have now spoken of worship in the most general sense. I have said that this house, considered as separated to the adoration of God, should be entered joyfully and gratefully, without stopping to inquire under what particular views or forms, God is here to be adored. I now proceed to observe, that when we consider the particular worship which is here to be offered, this occasion ought to awaken pious joy. I need not tell you, that whilst the religious principle is a part of man's nature, it is not always developed and manifested under the same forms. Men, agreeing in the recognition of a Divinity, have not agreed as to the service he may accept. Indeed it seems inevitable, that men, who differ in judgment on all subjects of thought, should form different apprehensions of the invisible, infinite, and mysterious God, and of the methods of adoring him. Uniformity of opinion is to be found nowhere, and ought to be expected least of all in religion. Who, that considers the vast, the indescribable diversity in men's capacities and means of improvement, in the discipline to which they are subjected, in the schools in which they are trained, in the outward vicissitudes and inward conflicts through which they pass, can expect them to arrive at the same conclusions in regard to their origin and destiny, in regard to the Being from whom they sprung, and the world toward which they tend. Accordingly, religion has taken innumerable forms, and some, it must be acknowledged, most unworthy of its objects. The great idea of God has been seized upon by men's selfish desires, hopes, and fears, and often so obscured that little of its purifying power has remained. Man, full of wants, conscious of guilt, exposed to suffering, and peculiarly struck by the more awful phenomena of nature, has been terror-smitten before the unseen, irresistible power with which he has felt himself encompassed. Hence to appease his wrath and to secure his partial regards, has been the great object of worship. Hence worship has been so often a pompous machinery, a tribute of obsequious adulation, an accumulation of gifts and victims. Hence worship has been the effort of nations and individuals, to bend the Almighty to their particular interests and purposes, and not the reverential, grateful, joyful, filial lifting up of the soul to Infinite Greatness, Goodness, Rectitude, and Purity. Even under Christianity human infirmity has disfigured the thought of God. Worship has been debased, by fear and selfishness, into a means of propitiating wrath, calming fear, and securing future enjoyment. All sects have carried their imperfection into their religion. None of us can boast of exemption from the common frailty. That this house is to be set apart to a perfect, spotless, unerring worship, none of us are so presumptuous as to hope. But I believe, that in the progress of society and Christianity, higher and purer conceptions of the Divinity have been unfolded ; and I cannot but believe, that the views of God and of his worship to which this house is now consecrated, are so far enlightened, enlarged, purified, as to justify us in entering its walls with great thankfulness and joy.

This house is not reared to perpetuate the superstitions of past ages nor of the present age. It is not reared to doom the worshipper to continual repetition of his own or other delusions. It is reared for the progress of truth, reared in the faith that the church is destined to new light and new purity, reared in the anticipation of a happier, holier age. As I look round, I am met by none of the representations of the Divinity, which degraded the ancient temples. My eyes light on no image of wood or stone, on no efforts of art to embody to the eye the invisible Spirit. As I look round, I am met by none of the forms, which Providence, in accommodation to a rude stage of society, allowed to the Jewish people. No altar sends up here the smoke of incense or victims. No priesthood, gorgeously arrayed, presents to God the material offerings of man. Nor are my eyes pained by cumbersome ceremonies, by which in later ages Christianity was overlaid, and almost overwhelmed. No childish pomps, borrowed from Judaism and Heathenism, obscure here the simple majesty, the sublime spiritual purpose of Christianity. Nor is this house reared for the promulgation of doctrines which tend to perpetuate the old servility with which God was approached, to make man abject in the sight of his Maker, to palsy him with terror, to prostrate his reason. This house is reared to assist the worshipper in conceiving and offering more and more perfectly the worship described in the text, the worship of the Father in spirit and in truth. On this topic, on the nature of the worship to be offered in this house, I have many reflections to offer. My illustrations may be reduced to the following heads : —

This house is reared, first, for the worship of One Infinite Person, and one only ; of Him whom Jesus always distinguished and addressed as the Father. In the next place, it is erected for the worship of God under the special character of Father, that is of a Parental Divinity. In the last place, it is set apart to the worship of Him in Spirit and in Truth.

First, You have prepared this edifice, that here you may worship One Infinite Person, even Him and Him only whom Jesus continually calls the Father. One would think, that on this point there could be no difference among Christians. One would think, that Jesus had placed the Object of Christian worship beyond all dispute. It is hard to conceive more solemn, more definite language than he has used. "The hour cometh and now is, when the true worshippers shall worship the Father in spirit and in truth, for the Father seeketh such to worship him." Yet it is well known, that very many Christians deny that one person, the Father, is the only proper object of supreme worship. They maintain that two other persons, the Son and the Holy Spirit, are to be joined with him in our adoration, and that the most important distinction of the Christian religion is the worship of God in three persons. Against this human exposition of Christianity we earnestly protest. Whilst we recognise with joy, the sincerity and piety of those who adopt it, we maintain that this gross departure from the simplicity and purity of our faith, is fraught with evil to the individual and the church. This house is reared to be a monument to the proper unity of God. We worship the Father.

All the grounds of this peculiarity of our worship, cannot of course be expounded in the limits of a dis course, nor indeed do we deem any labored exposition necessary. We start from a plain principle. We affirm, that if any point in a religious system must be brought out explicitly, must not be left to inference, but set forth in simple, direct, authoritative language, it is the Object of worship. On this point we should expect peculiar explicitness, if a revelation should be communicated for the purpose of giving a new direction to men's minds in this particular. Now, among Jews and Gentiles the worship of three infinite persons, one of whom was clothed with a human form, was unknown; and, of consequence, if this strange, mighty innovation had been intended by Jesus and had constituted the most striking peculiarity of his system, it must have been announced with all possible clearness and strength. Be it then remembered, that Jesus, in a solemn description of the true worship which he was to introduce, made not an allusion to this peculiarity, but declared, as the characteristic to the true worshippers, that they should worship the Father in spirit and in truth. Be it also remembered, that Jesus never enjoined the worship of three persons, Father, Son, and Holy Spirit. Not one injunction to this effect can be found in the Gospel or in the writings of the Apostles. This strange worship rests on inference alone. "The true worshippers (says the text) shall worship the Father." When his disciples came to him to be instructed in prayer, he taught them to say, Our Father. In his last affectionate discourse, he again and again taught his disciples to pray to the Father in his name. This dying injunction, so often and so tenderly repeated, should not for slight reasons be explained away. Still more, just before his death, Jesus himself, in presence of his disciples, prayed to the Father, and prayed in this language : Father, This is life eternal, that they (*i. e.* men) should know *thee, the only true God,* and Jesus Christ whom *thou hast sent.*

To these remarks it is common to reply, that we read in the New Testament, that Jesus was again and again worshipped, and that in admitting this he manifested himself to be the object of religious adoration. It is wonderful that this fallacy, so often exposed, should be still repeated. Jesus indeed received worship or homage, but this was not offered as adoration to the Infinite God ; it was the homage which, according to the custom of the age and of the eastern world, was paid to men invested with great authority whether in civil or religious concerns. Whoever has studied the Scriptures with the least discernment must know, that the word, worship, is used in two different senses, to express, first, the adoration due to the Infinite Creator, and secondly, the reverence which was due to sovereigns and prophets, and which of course belonged peculiarly to the most illustrious representative of God, to his beloved Son. Whoever understands the import of the English language in the time when our translation was made, must know that the word was then used to express the homage paid to human superiors, as well as the supreme reverence belonging to God alone. Let not an ambiguous word darken the truth. We are sure, that the worship paid to Christ during his public ministry, was rendered to him as a divine messenger, and not as God ; for, in the first place, it was offered, before his teachings had been sufficiently full and distinct to reveal the mystery of his nature, supposing it to have beer divine. We pronounce it not merely improbable but impossible, that Jesus, a poor man, a mechanic from Galilee, at the beginning of his mission, when his chosen disciples were waiting for his manifestation as an earthly prince, should have been adored as the everlasting invisible God. Again, the titles given him by those who worshipped him, such as Good Teacher, Son of David, Son of God, show us, that the thought of adoring him as the Self-Existent, Infinite Divinity, had no place in their minds. But there is one consideration which sets this point at rest. The worship paid to Jesus during his ministry was offered him in public, in sight of the Jewish people. Now, to the Jews, no crime was so flagrant as the paying of divine homage to a human being, such as they esteemed Jesus to be. Of consequence, had they seen in the marks of honor yielded to Jesus, even an approach to this adoration, their exasperation would have burst forth in immediate overwhelming violence on the supposed impiety. The fact, that they witnessed the frequent prostration of men before Jesus, or what is called the worship of him, without once charging it as a crime, is a demonstration that the act was in no respect a recognition of him as the supreme God.

It is worthy of remark, that the passages which are announced as the strongest proofs of the divine worship of Christ, directly disprove the doctrine, if the connexion be regarded. One of these texts is the declaration of Jesus, that we must "honor the Son even as we honor the Father." Hear the whole passage: "The Father hath *given* all judgment to the Son, that all men should honor the Son, as they honor the Father. He that honoreth not the Son, honoreth not the Father *who sent him.*" * You observe, that it is not the supreme underived divinity of Christ, but the power given him by

* John v. 22. 23.

his Father, which is here expressly declared to be the foundation of the honor challenged for him, and that we are called to honor him, as sent by God. Another passage much relied on is the declaration of Paul, that "at the name of Jesus every knee should bow and every tongue acknowledge him Lord." Read the whole text: "God hath highly exalted him, and given him a name above every name, that in the name of Jesus every knee should bow, of things in heaven, and things in earth, and things under the earth; and that every tongue should confess that Jesus Christ is Lord to the glory of God the Father."* Could language express more clearly, the distinct, derived, and dependent nature of Jesus Christ, or teach that the worship due him is subordinate, having for its foundation the dignity conferred on him by God, and terminating on the Father as its supreme object.

This house, then, is erected to the supreme worship of the Father, to the recognition of the Father only as the self-existent Infinite God. Homage will here be paid to Jesus Christ, and, I trust, a far more profound and affectionate homage than he received on earth, when his spiritual character and the true purposes of his mission were almost unknown. But we shall honor him as the Son, the brightest image, the sent of God, not as God himself. We shall honor him as exalted above every name or dignity in heaven or earth, but as exalted by God for his obedience unto death. We shall honor him as clothed with power to give life, and judge, but shall remember that the Father hath given all judgment and quickening energy to the Son. We look up with delight and reverence to his divine virtues, his celestial love, his

* Philippians ii. 3.

truth, his spirit; and we are sure that in as far as we imbibe these from the affectionate remembrance of his life, death, and triumphs, we shall render the worship most acceptable to this disinterested friend of the human race.

I have said that this house is set apart to the worship of the Father. But this term expresses not only the Person, the Being to whom it is to be paid. It expresses a peculiar character. It ascribes peculiar attributes to God. It ascribes to him the Parental relation and the disposition of a Parent. I therefore observe, in the second place, that this house is reared to the adoration of God in his Paternal character. It is reared to a Parental Divinity. To my own mind this view is more affecting than the last. Nothing so touches me, when I look round these walls, as the thought that God is to be worshipped here as the Father. That God has not always been worshipped as a Father, even among Christians, you well know. Men have always inclined to think, that they honor God by placing him on a distant throne, much more than by investing him with the mild lustre of parental goodness. They have made him a stern sovereign, giving life on hard terms, preferring his own honor to the welfare of his creatures, demanding an obedience which he gives no strength to perform, preparing endless torments for creatures whom he brings into being wholly evil, and refusing to pardon the least sin, the sin of the child, without an infinite satisfaction. Men have too often been degraded, broken in spirit, stripped of manly feeling, rather than lifted up to true dignity, by their religion. How seldom has worship breathed the noblest sentiments of human nature!

Thanks to Jesus Christ, that he came to bring us to a purifying, ennobling, rejoicing adoration. He has revealed the Father. His own character was a bright revelation of the most lovely and attractive attributes of the Divinity, so that he was able to say, " He that hath seen me hath seen the Father." By his manifestation of the Parental character of God, he created religion anew. He breathed a new and heavenly spirit into worship. He has made adoration a filial communion, assimilating us to our Creator. Ought we not, then, to rejoice in this house as set apart to the worship of the Father, to the God and Father of our Lord Jesus Christ?

The Father! In this one word what consoling, strengthening, ennobling truth is wrapped up. In this single view of God, how much is there to bind us to him, with strong, indissoluble, ever-growing love, and to make worship not only our chief duty, but our highest privilege and joy. The Father! can it be, that " the High and Holy One who inhabiteth eternity," " the Lord of heaven and earth," the Majesty of the universe, bears to us this relation, reveals himself under this name, and that we, so weak and erring, may approach him with the hope of children! Who cannot comprehend the dignity and blessedness of such worship? Who does not feel, that the man, to whom God's parental character is a deep-felt reality, has in this conviction a fountain of strength, hope, and purity springing up into everlasting life?

But to offer this true worship, we must understand distinctly what we mean, when we call God the Father. The word has a deep and glorious import, and in as far as this is unknown, religion will want life and power.

Is it understood? I am bound to say, that there seems to me a want of purity, of spirituality in the conception of God's parental relation, even among those Christians who profess to make it the great foundation and object of their worship. Too many rest in vague conceptions of God as their Creator, who supplies their wants, and who desires their happiness, and they think, that, thus regarding him, they know the Father. Such imperfect views incline me to state at some length what I deem the truth on this point. No truth is so essential to Christian worship. No truth sheds such a flood of light on the whole subject of religion.

My friends, you are to come here to worship the Father. What does this term import? It does not mean merely that God is your Creator. He is indeed the Creator, and as such let him be adored. This is his sole prerogative. His and his only is the mysterious power, which filled the void space with a universe. His the Almighty voice, which called the things which were not, and they came forth. The universe is a perpetual answer to this creating Word. For this, worship God. In every thing hear an exhortation to adore. In the grandeur, beauty, order of nature, see a higher glory than its own, a mysterious force deeper than all its motions; and from its countless voices, from its mild and awful tones, gather the one great lesson which they conspire to teach, the majesty of their Author.

But, my friends, God is more than Creator. To create is not to be a Father in the highest sense of that term. He created the mountain, the plant, the insect, but we do not call him their father. We do not call the artist the father of the statue which he models, nor the mechanician the father of the machine he contrives. It is the distinction of a father, that he communicates an existence like his own. The father gives being to the child, and the very idea of the child is, that he bears the image as well as receives existence from the power of the parent. God is the Father, because he brings into life minds, spirits, partaking of energies kindred to his own attributes. Accordingly the Scripture teaches us, that God made man in his own image, after his own likeness. Here is the ground of his paternal relation to the human race, and hence he is called in an especial sense the Father of those who make it the labor of life to conform themselves more and more to their divine original. God is " the Father of spirits."

My friends, we are not wholly matter, we are not wholly flesh. Were we so, we could not call God our Father. God is a spirit, says the text, and we are spirits also. This our consciousness teaches. We are conscious of a principle superior to the body which comprehends and controls it. We are conscious of faculties higher than the senses. We do something more than receive impressions passively, unresistingly, like the brute, from the outward world. We analyze, compare, and combine anew the things which we see, subject the outward world to the inquisition of reason, create sciences, rise to general laws, and through these establish an empire over earth and sea. We penetrate beneath the surface which the senses report; search for the hidden causes, inquire for the ends or purposes, trace out the connexions, dependencies, and harmonies of nature; discover a sublime unity amidst its boundless variety, and order amidst its seeming confusion; rise to the idea of one all-comprehending and all-ordaining Mind; and thus by thought make as it were a new universe radiant with wisdom, beneficence, and beauty. We are not mere creatures of matter and sense. We conceive a higher good than comes from the senses. We possess, as a portion of our being, a law higher than appetite, nobler and more enduring than all the laws of matter, the Law of Duty. We discern, we approve, the Right, the Good, the Just, the Holy, and by this sense of rectitude are laid under obligations, which no power of the outward universe can dissolve. We have within us a higher force than all the forces of material nature, a power of will which can adhere to duty and to God in opposition to all the might of the elements, and all the malignity of earth or hell. We have thoughts, ideas, which do not come from matter, the Ideas of the Infinite, the Everlasting, the Immutable, the Perfect. Living amidst the frail, the limited, the changing, we rise to the thought of Unbounded, Eternal, Almighty Goodness. Nor is this all. While matter obeys mechanical and irresistible laws, and is bound by an unrelaxing necessity to the same fixed, unvarying movements, we feel ourselves to be Free. We have power over ourselves, over thought and desire, power to conform ourselves to a law written on our hearts, and power to resist this law. Man must never be confounded with the material, mechanical world around him. He is a spirit. He has capacities, thoughts, impulses, which assimilate him to God. His reason is a ray of the Infinite Reason; his conscience, an oracle of the Divinity, publishing the Everlasting Law of Rectitude. Therefore God is his Father. Therefore he is bound to his Maker by a spiritual bond. This we must feel, or we know nothing of the parental relation of God to the human race.

God is the Father, and as such let him be worshipped. He is the Father. By this I understand that he has given being not only to worlds of matter, but to a rational, moral, spiritual universe, and still more I understand, not only that he has created a spiritual family in heaven and on earth, but that he manifests towards them the attributes and exerts on them the influences of a Father. Some of these attributes and influences I will suggest, that the parental character in which God is to be worshipped may be more distinctly apprehended and more deeply felt.

First, then, in calling God the Father, I understand that he loves his rational and moral offspring with unbounded affection. Love is the fundamental attribute of a Father. How deep, strong, tender, enduring the attachment of a human parent! But this shadows forth feebly the Divine Parent. He loves us with an energy like that with which he upholds the universe. The human parent does not comprehend his child, cannot penetrate the mystery of the spiritual nature which lies hid beneath the infant form. It is the prerogative of God alone, to understand the immortal mind to which he gives life. The narrowest human spirit can be comprehended in its depths and destiny by none but its Maker, and is more precious in his sight than material worlds. Is he not peculiarly its Father?

Again, in calling God the Father, I understand that it is his chief purpose in creating and governing the universe, to educate, train, form, and ennoble the rational and moral being to whom he has given birth. Education is the great work of a parent, and he who neglects it is unworthy the name. God gives birth to the mind, that it may grow and rise for ever, and its progress is the end of all his works. This outward universe, with its sun and stars, and mighty revolutions, is but a school in which the Father is training his children. God is ever present to the human mind to carry on its education, pouring in upon it instruction and incitement from the outward world, stirring up everlasting truth within itself, rousing it to activity by pleasure and pain, calling forth its affections by surrounding fellow-creatures, calling it to duty by placing it amidst various relations, awakening its sympathy by sights of sorrow, awakening its imagination by a world of beauty, and especially exposing it to suffering, hardship, and temptation, that by resistance it may grow strong, and by seeking help from above, it may bind itself closely to its Maker. Thus he is the Father. There are those who think, that God, if a parent, must make our enjoyment his supreme end. He has a higher end, our intellectual and moral education. Even the good human parent desires the progress, the virtue of his child more than its enjoyment. God never manifests himself more as our Father, than in appointing to us pains, conflicts, trials, by which we may rise to the heroism of virtue, may become strong to do, to dare, to suffer, to sacrifice all things at the call of truth and duty.

Again, in calling God a Father, I understand that he exercises authority over his rational offspring. Authority is the essential attribute of a father. A parent, worthy of that name, embodies and expresses both in commands and actions, the everlasting law of Duty. His highest function is to bring out in the minds of his children the idea of Right, and to open to them the perfection of their nature. It is too common a notion, that God, as Father, must be more disposed to bless than to command. His commands are among his chief blessings. He never speaks with more parental kindness than by that inward voice, which teaches duty and excites and cheers to its performance. Nothing is so strict, so inflexible in enjoining the right and the good, as perfect love. This can endure no moral stain in its object. The whole experience of life, rightly construed, is a revelation of God's parental authority and righteous retribution.

Again. When I call God the Father, I understand that he communicates Himself, his own spirit, what is most glorious in his own nature to his rational offspring; a doctrine almost overwhelming by its grandeur, but yet true, and the very truth which shines most clearly from the Christian Scriptures. It belongs to a parent to breathe into the child whatever is best and loftiest in his own soul, and for this end a good father seeks every approach to the mind of the child. Such a father is God. He has created us not only to partake of his works, but to be " partakers of a divine nature," not only to receive his gifts, but to receive Himself. As he is a pure spirit, he has an access to the minds of his children, not enjoyed by human parents. He pervades, penetrates our souls. All other beings, our nearest friends, are far from us, foreign to us, strangers, compared with God. Others hold intercourse with us through the body. He is in immediate contact with our souls. We do not discern him because he is too near, too inward, too deep to be recognised by our present imperfect consciousness. And he is thus near, not only to discern, but to act, to influence, to give his spirit, to communicate to us divinity. This is the great paternal gift of God. He has greater gifts than the world. He confers more than the property of the earth and heavens. The very attributes from which the earth and heavens sprung, these he imparts to his rational offspring. Even his disinterested, impartial, universal goodness, which diffuses beauty, life, and happiness, even this excellence it is his purpose to breathe into and cherish in the human soul. In regard to the spiritual influence, by which God brings the created spirit into conformity to his own, I would that I could speak worthily. It is gentle, that it may not interfere with our freedom. It sustains, mingles with, and moves all our faculties. It acts through nature, providence, revelation, society, and experience; and the Scriptures, confirmed by reason and the testimonies of the wisest and best men, teach us, that it acts still more directly. God, being immediately present to the soul, holds immediate communion with it, in proportion as it prepares itself to receive and to use aright the heavenly inspiration. He opens the inward eye to himself, communicates secret monitions of duty, revives and freshens our convictions of truth, builds up our faith in human immortality, unseals the deep, unfathomed fountains of Love within us, instils strength, peace, and comfort, and gives victory over pain, sin, and death.

This influence of God, exerted on the soul to conform it to himself, to make it worthy of its divine parentage, this it is which most clearly manifests what is meant by his being our Father. We understand his parental relation to us, only as far as we comprehend this great purpose and exercise of his love. We must have faith in the human soul as receptive of the divinity, as made for greatness, for spiritual elevation, for likeness to God, or God's character as a Father will be to us as an unrevealed mystery. If we think, as so many seem to think, that God has made us only for low pleasures and attainments, that our nature is incapable of godlike virtues, that our prayers for the Divine Spirit are unheard, that celestial influences do not descend into the human soul, that God never breathes on it to lift it above its present weakness, to guide it to a more perfect existence, to unite it more intimately with himself, then we know but faintly the meaning of a Father in Heaven. The great revelation in Christianity of a Paternal Divinity, is still to be made to us.

I might here pause in the attempt to give distinct conceptions of the Father whom we are to worship; but there are two views so suited to us, as sinful and mortal beings, that I cannot pass them over without brief notice. Let me add, then, that in speaking of God as the Father, I understand, that he looks with overflowing compassion on such of his rational offspring as forsake him, as forsake the law of duty. It is the property of the human parent to follow with yearnings of tenderness an erring child; and in this he is a faint type of God, who sees his lost sons "a great way off," who to recover his human family spared not his beloved Son, who sends his regenerating spirit into the fallen soul, sends rebuke, and shame, and fear, and sorrow, and awakens the dead in trespasses and sins, to a higher life than that which the first birth conferred.

I also understand, in calling God the Father, that he destines his rational, moral creature to Immortality. How ardently does the human parent desire to prolong the life of his child. And how much more must He, who gave being to the spirit with its unbounded faculties, desire its endless being. God is our Father, for he has made us to bear the image of his own eternity as well as of his other attributes. Other things pass away, for they fulfil their end ; but the soul, which never reaches its goal, whose developement is never complete, is never to disappear from the universe. God created it to receive for ever of his fulness. His fatherly love is not exhausted in what he now bestows. There *is* a higher life. Human perfection is not a dream. The brightest visions of genius fade before the realities of excellence and happiness to which good men are ordained. In that higher life, the parental character of God will break forth from the clouds which now obscure it. His bright image in his children will proclaim the Infinite Father.

I have thus, my friends, set before you the true object of Christian worship. You are here to worship God as your spiritual parent, as the Father of your spirits, whose great purpose is your spiritual perfection, your participation of a divine nature. I hold this view of God to be the true, deep foundation of Christian worship. On your reception of it depends the worth of the homage to be offered here. It is not enough to think of God as operating around and without you, as creating material worlds, as the former of your bodies, as ordaining the revolution of seasons for your animal wants. There is even danger in regarding God exclusively as the author of the outward universe. There is danger, lest you feel as if you were overlooked in this immensity, lest you shrink before these mighty masses of matter, lest you see in the unchangeable laws of nature, a stern order to which the human being is a victim, and which heeds not the puny individual in maintaining the general good. It is only by regarding God as more than Creator, as your spiritual Father, as having made you to partake of his spiritual attributes, as having given you a spiritual power worth more than the universe, it is only by regarding his intimacy with the soul, his paternal concern for it, his perpetual influence on it, it is only by these views that worship rises into filial confidence, hope, joy, and rapture, and puts forth a truly ennobling power. Worship has too often been abject, the offering of fear or selfishness. God's greatness, though a pledge of greatness to his children, and his omnipotence, though an assurance to us of mighty power in our conflict with evil, have generated self-contempt and discouraged access to him. My friends, come hither to worship God as your Spiritual Father. No other view can so touch and penetrate the soul, can place it so near its Maker, can open before it such vast prospects, can awaken such transports of praise and gratitude, can bow the soul in such ingenuous sorrow for sin, can so fortify you for the conflict against evil. Ought we not to rejoice that this house is reared for the worship of the spiritual Father?

The exposition which I have given under this head, of the parental relation of God to the human race, is one in which I take the deepest interest. I have felt, however, as I proceeded, that very possibly objections would spring up in the minds of some who hear me. There are not a few who are skeptical as to whatever supposes a higher condition of human nature than they now observe. Perhaps some here, could they speak, would say, " We do not see the marks of this fatherly interest of God in man of which you have spoken. We do not see in man the signs of a being so beloved, so educated, as you have supposed. His weakness, sufferings, and sins, are surely no proofs of his having been created to receive God's spirit, to partake of the divinity." On this point I have much to say, but my answer must be limited to a few words. I reply, that the love of an Infinite Father may be expected often to work in methods beyond the comprehension of our limited minds. An immortal being in his infancy cannot of course comprehend all the processes of his education, many of which look forward to ages too distant for the imagination to explore. I would add, that notwithstanding the darkness which hangs over human life on account of the greatness of our nature, we can yet see bright signatures of the parental concern of God, and see them in the very circumstances which at first create doubt. Because we suffer, it ought not to be inferred that God is not a Father. Suffering, trial, exposure, seem to be necessary elements in the education of a moral being. It is fit, that a being whose happiness and dignity are to be found in vigorous action and in forming himself, should be born with undeveloped capacities, and be born into a world of mingled difficulties and aids. We do see, that energy of thought, will, affection, virtue, the energy which is our true life and joy, often springs from trial. We can see, too, that it is well that society, like the individual, should begin in imperfection; because men in this way become to each other means of discipline, because joint sufferings and the necessity of joint efforts awaken both the affections and the faculties, because occasion and incitement are thus given to generous sacrifices, to heroic struggles, to the most beautiful and stirring manifestations of philanthropy, patriotism, and devotion. Were I called on to prove God's spiritual parental interest in us, I would point to the trials, temptations, evils of life; for to these we owe the character of Christ, we owe the apostle and martyr, we owe the moral force and deep sympathy of private and domestic life, we owe the devolopement of what is divine in human nature. Truly God is our Father, and as such to be worshipped.

Having thus set forth very imperfectly, but from a full heart, the excellence of the homage which is here to be rendered to God in his Parental character, I ought now to proceed, according to the plan of this discourse, to show that we should enter this house with joy, because it is set apart to the worship of God in Spirit and in Truth, to an Inward not outward worship. In discussing this topic, I might enlarge on the vast and beneficent revolution which Jesus Christ wrought in religion, by teaching that God is a spirit, and to be spiritually adored. I might show how much he wrought for human elevation and happiness, when, in pronouncing the text, he shook the ancient temples to their foundations, quenched the fire on the heathen and Jewish altars, wrested the instruments of sacrifice from the hand of the priest, abolished sanctity of place, and consecrated the human soul as the true house of God. But the nature, grandeur, benefits of this spiritual worship, are subjects too extensive for our present consideration. Instead of discussion, I can only use the words of exhortation. I can only say, that you, who are to assemble in this place, are peculiarly bound to inward worship, for to you especially Christianity is an inward system. Most other denominations expect salvation more or less from what Jesus does abroad, especially from his agency on the mind of God. You expect it from what he does within your own minds. His great glory, according to your views, lies in his influence on the human soul, in the communication of his spirit to his followers. To you salvation, heaven, and hell have their seat in the soul. To you, Christianity is wholly a spiritual system. Come, then, to this place to worship with the soul, to elevate the spirit to God. Let not this house be desecrated by a religion of show. Let it not degenerate into a place of forms. Let not your pews be occupied by lifeless machines. Do not come here to take part in lethargic repetitions of sacred words. Do not come from a cold sense of duty, to quiet conscience with the thought of having paid a debt to God. Do not come to perform a present task to insure a future heaven. Come to find heaven now, to anticipate the happiness of that better world by breathing its spirit, to bind your souls indissolubly to your Maker. Come to worship in spirit and in truth, that is, intelligently, rationally, with clear judgment, with just and honorable conceptions of the Infinite Father, not prostrating your understandings, not renouncing the divine gift of reason, but offering an enlightened homage, such as is due to the Fountain of intelligence and truth. — Come to worship with the heart as well as intellect, with life, fervor, zeal. Sleep over your business if you will, but not over your religion. — Come to worship with strong conviction, with living faith in a higher presence than meets the eye, with a feeling of God's presence not only around you, but in the depths of your souls. — Come to worship with a filial spirit, not with fear, dread, and gloom; not with sepulchral tones and desponding looks, but with humble, cheerful, boundless trust, with overflowing gratitude, with a love willing and earnest to do and to suffer whatever may approve your devotion to God. — Come to worship him with what he most delights in, with aspiration for spiritual light and life ; come to cherish and express desires for virtue, for purity, for power over temptation, stronger and more insatiable than spring up in your most eager pursuits of business or pleasure ; and welcome joyfully every holy impulse, every accession of strength to virtuous purpose, to the love of God and man. — In a word, come to offer a refined, generous worship, to offer a tribute worthy of Him who is the Perfection of truth, goodness, beauty, and blessedness. Adore him with the calmest reason and the profoundest love, and strive to conform yourselves to what you adore.

I have now, my friends, set before you the worship to which this building is set apart, and which, from its rational, filial, pure, and ennobling character, renders this solemnity a season for thankfulness and joy. I should not however be just to this occasion, or to the great purpose of this house, if I were to stop here. My remarks have hitherto been confined to the worship which is to be offered within these walls, to the influence to be exerted on you when assembled here. But has this house no higher end than to give an impulse to your minds for the very few hours which you are to spend beneath its roof? Then we have little reason to enter it with joy. The great end for which you are to worship here is, that you may worship everywhere. You are to feel God's presence here, that it may be felt wherever you go, and whatever you do. The very idea of spiritual homage is, that it takes possession of the soul, and becomes a part of our very being. The great design of this act of dedication is, that your houses, your places of business, may be consecrated to God

This topic of omnipresent worship I cannot expand. One view of it, however, I must not omit. From the peculiar character of the worship to which this house is consecrated, you learn the *kind* of worship which you should carry from it into your common lives. It is not uncommon for the Christian teacher to say to his congregation, that, when they leave the church, they go forth into a nobler temple than one made with hands, into the temple of the Creation, and that they must go forth to worship God in his works. The views given of the true worship in this discourse, will lead me to a somewhat different style of exposition. I will, indeed, say to you, go from this house to adore God as he is revealed in the boundless universe. This is one end of your worship here. But I would add, that a higher end is, that you should go forth to worship him as he is revealed in his rational and moral offspring, and to worship him by fulfilling, as you have power, his purposes in regard to these. My great aim in this discourse has been to show, that God is to be adored here as the Father of rational and moral beings, of yourselves and all mankind; and such a worship tends directly and is designed to lead us, when we go hence, to recognise God in our own nature, to see in men his children, to respect and serve them for their relationship to the Divinity, to see in them signatures of greatness amidst all their imperfection, and to love them with more than earthly love. We must not look round on the universe with awe and on man with scorn; for man, who can comprehend the universe and its laws, "is greater than the universe, which cannot comprehend itself." God dwells in every human being more intimately than in the outward creation. The voice of God comes to us in the ocean, the thunder, the whirlwind ; but how much more of God is there in his inward voice, in the intuitions of reason, in the rebukes of conscience, in the whispers of the Holy Spirit. I would have you see God in the awful mountain and the tranquil valley ; but more, much more in the clear judgment, the moral energy, the disinterested purpose, the pious gratitude, the immortal hope of a good man. Go from this house to worship God by reverencing the human soul as his chosen sanctuary. Revere it in yourselves, revere it in others, and labor to carry it forward to perfection. Worship God within these walls, as universally, impartially good to his human offspring ; and go forth to breathe the same spirit. Go forth to respect the rights, and seek the true, enduring welfare of all within your influence. Carry with you the conviction, that to trample on a human being, of whatever color, clime, rank, condition, is to trample on God's child ; that to degrade or corrupt a man, is to deface a holier temple than any material sanctuary. Mercy, Love, is more acceptable worship to God, than all sacrifices or outward offerings. The most celestial worship ever paid on earth was rendered by Christ, when he approached man, and the most sinful man, as a child of God, when he toiled and bled to awaken what was Divine in the human soul, to regenerate a fallen world. Be such the worship which you shall carry from this place. Go forth to do good with every power which God bestows, to make every place you enter happier by your presence, to espouse all human interests, to throw your whole weight into the scale of human freedom and improvement, to withstand all wrong, to uphold all right, and especially to give light, life, strength to the immortal soul. He who rears up one child in Christian virtue, or recovers one fellow-creature to God, builds a temple more precious than Solomon's or St. Peter's, more enduring than earth or heaven.

I have now finished the general discussion which this occasion seemed to me to require, and I trust that a few remarks of a personal and local character will be received with indulgence. It is with no common emotion that I take part in the present solemnity. I stand now to teach, where in my childhood and youth I was a learner. The generation which I then knew has almost wholly disappeared. The venerable man, whose trembling voice I then heard in this place, has long since gone to his reward. My earliest friends, who watched over my childhood and led me by the hand to this spot, have been taken. Still my emotions are not sad. I rejoice; for whilst I see melancholy changes around me, and still more feel, that time, which has bowed other frames, has touched my own, I see that the work of human improvement has gone on. I see that clearer and brighter truths, than were opened on my own youthful mind, are to be imparted to succeeding generations. Herein I do and will rejoice.

On looking back to my early years, I can distinctly recollect unhappy influences exerted on my mind by the general tone of religion in this town. I can recollect, too, a corruption of morals among those of my own age, which made boyhood a critical, perilous season. Still I must bless God for the place of my nativity; for as my mind unfolded, I became more and more alive to the beautiful scenery which now attracts strangers to our island. My first liberty was used in roaming over the neighbouring fields and shores; and amid this glorious nature, that love of liberty sprang up, which has gained strength within me to this hour. I early received impressions of the great and the beautiful, which I believe have had no small influence in determining my modes of thought and habits of life. In this town I pursued for a time my studies of theology. I had no professor or teacher to guide me; but I had two noble places of study. One was yonder beautiful edifice, now so frequented and so useful as a public library, then so deserted that I spent day after day and sometimes week after week amidst its dusty volumes, without interruption from a single visitor. The other place was yonder beach, the roar of which has so often mingled with the worship of this place, my daily resort, dear to me in the sunshine, still more attractive in the storm. Seldom do I visit it now without thinking of the work, which there, in the sight of that beauty, in the sound of those waves, was carried on in my soul. No spot on earth has helped to form me so much as that beach. There I lifted up my voice in praise amidst the tempest. There, softened by beauty, I poured out my thanksgiving and contrite confessions. There, in reverential sympathy with the mighty power around me, I became conscious of power within. There struggling thoughts and emotions broke forth, as if moved to utterance by nature's eloquence of the winds and waves. There began a happiness surpassing all worldly pleasures, all gifts of fortune, the happiness of communing with the works of God. Pardon me this reference to myself. I believe that the worship, of which I have this day spoken, was aided in my own soul by the scenes in which my early life was passed. Amidst these scenes, and in speaking of this worship, allow me to thank God that this beautiful island was the place of my birth.

Leaving what is merely personal, I would express my joy, and it is most sincere, in the dedication of this house, regarded as a proof and a means of the diffusion of Christian truth. Some perhaps may think, that this joy is not a little heightened by seeing a church set apart to the particular sect to which I am said to belong. But I trust, that what you have this day heard will satisfy most if not all who hear, that it is not a sectarian exultation to which I am giving utterance. I indeed take pleasure in thinking, that the particular views which I have adopted of the disputed doctrines of religion, will here be made known; but I rejoice much more in thinking, that this house is pledged to no peculiar doctrines, that it is not erected to bind my own or any man's opinions on this or on future times, that it is consecrated to free investigation of religious truth, to religious progress, to the right of private judgment, to Protestant and Christian liberty. Most earnestly do I pray, that a purer theology, that diviner illuminations, that a truer worship than can now be found in our own or in any sect, may be the glory of this house. We who now consecrate it to God, believe in human progress. We do not say to the spirit of truth, "Thus far and no farther." We reprobate the exclusive, tyrannical spirit of the churches of this age, which denounce as an enemy to Christianity, whoever in the use of his intellectual liberty, and in the interpretation of God's word for himself, may differ from the traditions and creeds which have been received from fallible forefathers. We rear these walls not to a sect, but to religious, moral, intellectual, Protestant, Christian liberty.

I rejoice that this temple of liberty is opened on this spot. I feel that this town has a right to an establishment, in which conscientious Christians may inquire and speak without dreading the thunders of excommunication, in which Protestanism will not be dishonored by the usurpations of the Romish Church. This island, like the State to which it belongs, was originally settled by men who came hither for liberty of conscience, and in assertion of the right to interpret for themselves the word of God. Religious freedom was the very principle on which this town was founded, and I rejoice to know, that the spirit of religious freedom has never wanted champions here. I have recently read a very valuable discourse, which was delivered in this town about a century ago, and just a century after the cession of this island to our fathers by the Indians, and which breathes a liberality of thought and feeling, a reverence for the rights of the understanding and the conscience, very rare at that time in other parts of the country, and very far from being universal now. Its author, the Rev. Mr. Callender, was pastor of the first Baptist church in this place, the oldest of our churches, and it was dedicated to a descendant of the venerable Coddington, our first Governor. The spirit of religious liberty which pervades this discourse, has astonished as well as rejoiced me, and it should thrill the hearts of this people. Let me read a few sentences : —

" It must he a mean contracted way of thinking, to confine the favor of God, and the power of godliness, to one set of speculative opinions, or any particular external forms of worship. How hard must it be to imagine, that all other Christians but ourselves, must be formal, and hypocritical, and destitute of the grace of God, because their education or capacity differs from ours, or that God has given them more or less light than to us; though we cannot deny, they give the proper evidence of their fearing God by their working righteousness, and show their love to him by keeping what they understand he has commanded; and though their faith in Christ Jesus purifies their hearts and works by love and overcomes the world. It would be hard to show, why liberty of conscience, mutual forbearance and good will, why brotherly kindness and charity is not as good a centre of unity as a constrained uniformity in external ceremonies, or a forced subscription to ambiguous articles. Experience has dearly convinced the world that unanimity in judgment and affection cannot be secured by penal law. Who can tell, why the unity of spirit in the bonds of peace is not enough for Christians to aim at? And who can assign a reason why they may not love one another though abounding in their own several senses? And why if they live in peace, the God of love and peace may not be with them?

"There is no other bottom but this to rest upon, to leave others the liberty we should desire ourselves, the liberty wherewith Christ hath made them free."

Such was the liberal spirit expressed in this town a hundred years ago. I would it were more common in our own day.

Another noble friend of religious liberty threw a lustre on this island immediately before the revolution. I mean the Rev. Dr. Stiles, pastor of the Second Congregational Church, and afterwards President of Yale College. This country has not perhaps produced a more learned man. To enlarged acquaintance with physical science he added extensive researches into philology, history, and antiquities ; nor did his indefatigable mind suffer any opportunity to escape him, of adding to his rich treasures of knowledge. His virtues were proportioned to his intellectual acquisition. I can well remember how his name was cherished among his parishioners, after years of separation. His visit to this place was to many a festival. When little more than a child, I was present at some of his private meetings with the more religious part of his former congregation ; and I recollect how I was moved by the tears and expressive looks with which his affectionate exhortations were received. In his faith he was what was called a moderate Calvinist ; but his heart was of no sect. He carried into his religion the spirit of liberty which then stirred the whole country. Intolerance, church-tyranny in all its forms, he abhorred. He respected the right of private judgment, where others would have thought themselves authorized to restrain it. A young man, to whom he had been as a father, one day communicated to him doubts concerning the Trinity. He expressed his sorrow ; but mildly, and with undiminished affection told him to go to the Scriptures, and to seek his faith there and only there. His friendships were confined to no parties. He desired to heal the wounds of the divided church of Christ, not by a common creed, but by the spirit of love. He wished to break every yoke, civil and ecclesiastical, from men's necks. To the influence of this distinguished man in the circle in which I was brought up, I may owe in part the indignation which I feel towards every invasion of human rights. In my earliest years, I regarded no human being with equal reverence. I have his form before me at this moment almost as distinctly as if I had seen him yesterday, so strong is the impression made on the child through the moral affections.

Let me add one more example of the spirit of religious freedom on this island. You may be surprised, perhaps, when you hear me name in this connexion the venerable man, who once ministered in this place, the Rev. Dr. Hopkins. His name is indeed associated with a stern and appalling theology, and it is true, that he wanted toleration towards those who rejected his views. Still in forming his religious opinions, he was superior to human authority; he broke away from human creeds; he interpreted God's word for himself; he revered reason, the oracle of God within him. His system, however fearful, was yet built on a generous foundation. He maintained that all holiness, all moral excellence, consists in benevolence, or disinterested devotion to the greatest good; that this is the character of God; that love is the only principle of the divine administration. He taught that sin was introduced into the creation, and is to be everlastingly punished, because evil is necessary to the highest good. To this government, in which the individual is surrendered to the well-being of the whole, he required entire and cheerful submission. Other Calvinists were willing that their neighbours should be predestined to everlasting misery for the glory of God. This noble-minded man demanded a more generous and impartial virtue, and maintained that we should consent to our own perdition, should be willing ourselves to be condemned, if the greatest good of the universe, and the manifestation of the divine perfections should so require. True virtue, as he taught, was an entire surrender of personal interest to the benevolent purposes of God. Self-love he spared in none of its movements.

He called us to seek our own happiness as well as that of others, in a spirit of impartial benevolence; to do good to ourselves, not from self-preference, not from the impulse of personal desires, but in obedience to that sublime law, which requires us to promote the welfare of each and all within our influence. I need not be ashamed to confess the deep impression which this system made on my youthful mind. I am grateful to this stern teacher for turning my thoughts and heart to the claims and majesty of impartial, universal benevolence. From such a man, a tame acquiescence in the established theology was not to be expected. He indeed accepted the doctrine of predestination in its severest form; but in so doing, he imagined himself a disciple of reason as well as of revelation. He believed this doctrine to be sustained by profound metaphysical argumentation, and to rest on the only sound philosophy of the human mind, so that in receiving it, he did not abandon the ground of reason. In accordance with his free spirit of inquiry, we find him making not a few important modifications of Calvinism. The doctrine that we are liable to punishment for the sin of our first parent, he wholly rejected; and not satisfied with denying the imputation of Adam's guilt to his posterity, he subverted what the old theology had set forth as the only foundation of divine acceptance, namely the imputation of Christ's righteousness or merits to the believer. The doctrine that Christ died for the elect only, found no mercy at his hands. He taught that Christ suffered equally for all mankind. The system of Dr. Hopkins was indeed an effort of reason to reconcile Calvinism with its essential truths. Accordingly his disciples were sometimes called, and willingly called, Rational Calvinists. The impression which he made was much greater than is now supposed. The churches of New England received a decided impression from his views; and though his name, once given to his followers, is no longer borne, his influence is still felt. The conflict now going on in our country, for the purpose of mitigating the harsh features of Calvinism, is a stage of the revolutionary movement to which he more than any man gave impulse. *I* can certainly bear witness to the spirit of progress and free inquiry which possessed him. In my youth, I preached in this house at the request of the venerable old man. As soon as the services were closed, he turned to me with an animated, benignant smile, and using a quaintness of expression which I need not repeat, said to me, that theology was still imperfect, and that he hoped I should live to carry it towards perfection. Rare and most honorable liberality in the leader of a sect! He wanted not to secure a follower, but to impel a young mind to higher truth. I feel, that ability has not been given me to accomplish this generous hope; but such quickening language from such lips, though it could not give strength, might kindle desire, and elevate exertion. — Thus the spirit of religious freedom has not been wanting to this island. May this spirit, unawed by human reproach, unfettered by human creeds, availing itself gratefully of human aids, and, above all, looking reverently to God for light, dwell in the hearts of those who are to minister, and of those who shall worship within these walls. May this spirit spread far and wide, and redeem the Christian world from the usurpations of Catholic and Protestant infallibility, from uncharitableness, intolerance, persecution, and every yoke which has crushed the human soul.

I have done with the personal and the local. In conclusion, let me revert for one moment to the great topic of this discourse. My friends, the spiritual worship of which I have this day spoken, is something *real*. There *is* a worship in the spirit, a worship very different from standing in the church, or kneeling in the closet, a worship which cannot be confined to set phrases, and asks not the clothing of outwards forms, a thirst of the soul for its Creator, an inward voice, which our nearest neighbour cannot hear, but which pierces the skies. To the culture of this spiritual worship, we dedicate this house. My friends, rest not in offering breath, in moving the lips, in bending the knee to your Creator. There is another, a nearer, a happier intercourse with Heaven, a worship of love, sometimes too full and deep for utterance, a union of mind with him closer than earthly friendships. This is the worship to which Christ calls. Christ came not to build churches, not to rear cathedrals with Gothic arches, or swelling domes, but to dedicate the human soul to God. When God " bows the heavens and comes down," it is not that he may take up his abode beneath the vault of a metropolitan temple; it is not that he is drawn by majestic spires or by clouds of fragrance, but that he may visit and dwell in the humble, obedient, disinterested soul. This house is to moulder away. Temples hewn from the rock will crumble to dust, or melt in the last fire. But the inward temple will survive all outward change. When winds and oceans and suns shall have ceased to praise God, the human soul will praise him. It will receive more and more divine inspirations of truth and love; will fill with its benevolent ministry wider and wider spheres; and will accomplish its destiny by a progress towards God as unlimited, as **mysterious**, as enduring as eternity.

NOTE TO PAGE 317.

I have not quoted the verses preceding those which I have extracted from the Epistle to the Philippians, which are often adduced in proof of Christ's supreme divinity, because it is acknowledged by learned men of all de-. nominations, that our translation of the most important clause is incorrect, and a critical discussion of the subject would have been out of place. I think, however, that no man, unacquainted with the common theories, can read any translation and escape the impression, that Jesus Christ is a derived, dependent, subordinate being, and a distinct being from the Father. How plain is it, that in this passage Paul intends by the terms "God" and "the Father," not Jesus Christ but another being! How plain is it, that in the passage chosen as the text for this discourse, our Saviour intended by these terms not himself but another being! What other idea could his hearers receive? What decisive proofs are furnished by his constant habit of speaking of "the Father" and of "God," as another being, and of distinguishing himself from him!

NOTE TO PAGE 344.

I understand that the interest expressed by me in the character of Dr. Hopkins, has surprised some of my townsmen of Newport, who knew him only by report, or who saw him in their youth. I do not wonder at this. He lived almost wholly in his study, and like very retired men, was the object of little sympathy. His appearance was that of a man who had nothing to do with the world. I can well recollect the impression which he made on me when a boy, as he rode on horseback in a plaid gown fastened by a girdle round his waist, and with a study cap on his head instead of his wig. His delivery in the pulpit was the worst I ever met with. Such tones never came from any human voice within my hearing. He was the very ideal of bad delivery. Then I must say, the matter was often as uninviting as the manner. Dr. Hopkins was distinguished by nothing more than by faithfulness to his principles. He carried them out to their full extent. Believing, as he did, in total depravity, believing that there was nothing good or generous in human nature to which he could make an appeal, believing that he could benefit men only by setting before them their utterly lost and helpless condition, he came to the point without any circumlocution, and dealt out terrors with an unsparing liberality. Add to all this, that his manners had a bluntness, partly natural, partly the result of long seclusion in the country. We cannot wonder that such a man should be set down as hard and severe. But he had a true benevolence, and what is more worthy of being noted, he was given to a facetious style of conversation. Two instances immediately occur to me, which happened in my own circle. One day he dined at my father's with a young minister who was willing to comply with the costume of the day, but whose modesty only allowed the ruffles to peep from his breast. The Doctor said with good humor, "I don't care for ruffles : but if I wore them, I'd wear them like a man." I recollect that on visiting him one day when he was about eighty years of age, I found his eyes much inflamed by reading and writing. I took the liberty to recommend abstinence from these occupations. He replied, smilingly, with an amusing story, and then added, "If my eyes won't study, no eyes for me." This facetiousness may seem to some who are unacquainted with the world, not consistent with the great severity of his theology ; but nothing is more common than this apparent self-contradiction. The ministers, who deal most in terrors, who preach doctrines which ought to make their flesh creep, and to turn their eyes into fountains of tears, are not generally distinguished by their spare forms or haggard countenances. They take the world as easily as people of a milder creed ; and this does not show that they want sincerity or benevolence. It only shows how superficially men may believe in doctrines, which yet they would shudder to relinquish. It shows how little the import of language, which is thundered from the lips, is comprehended and felt. I should not set down as hard-hearted, a man whose appetite should be improved by preaching a sermon full of images and threatenings of "a bottomless hell." The best meals are sometimes made after such effusions. This is only an example of the numberless contradictions in human life. Men are every day saying and doing, from the power of education, habit, and imitation, what has no root whatever in their serious convictions. Dr. Hopkins, though his style of preaching and conversation did not always agree, was a sincere, benevolent man. I remember hearing of his giving on a journey all he had to a poor woman. On another occasion he contributed to some religious object a hundred dollars, which he had received for the copyright of a book ; and this he gave from his penury, for he received no fixed salary, and depended, in a measure, on the donations of friends for common comforts. When he first established himself in Newport, he was brought into contact with two great evils, the slave trade and slavery, in both of which a large part of the inhabitants were or had been engaged. "His spirit was stirred in him," and without "conferring with flesh or blood," without heeding the strong prejudices and passions enlisted on the side of these abuses, he bore his faithful testimony against them from the pulpit and the press. Still more, he labored for the education of the colored people, and had the happiness of seeing the fruits of his labors in the intelligence and exemplary piety of those who came under his influence. Much as he disapproved of the moderate theology of Dr. Stiles, he cheerfully coöperated with him in this work. Their names were joined to a circular for obtaining funds to educate Africans as missionaries to their own country. These two eminent men, who, as I think, held no ministerial intercourse, forgot their differences in their zeal for freedom and humanity.

Dr. Hopkins in conversing with me on his past history, reverted more frequently to his religious controversies than to any other event of his life, and always spoke as a man conscious of having gained the victory ; and in this, I doubt not, that he judged justly. He was true, as I have said, to his principles, and carried them out fearlessly to their consequences ; whilst his opponents wished to stop half-way. Of course it was easy for a practised disputant to drive them from their position. They had, indeed, the advantage of common sense on their side, but this availed little at a time when it was understood that common sense was to yield to the established creed. These controversies are most of them forgotten, but they were agitated with no small warmth. One of the most important, and which was confined to the Calvinists, turned on what were called the "Means of Grace." The question was, whether the unregenerate could do any thing for themselves, whether an unconverted man could, by prayer, by reading the Scriptures, and by public worship, promote his own conversion ; whether, in a word, any means used by an unregenerate man, would avail to that change of heart on which his future happiness depended. Dr. Hopkins, true to the fundamental principles of Calvinism, took the negative side of the question. He maintained, that man, being wholly depraved by nature, wholly averse to God and goodness, could do nothing but sin, before the mighty power of God had implanted a new principle of holiness within his heart ; that, of course, his prayers and efforts before conversion were sins, and deserved the divine wrath ; that his very struggles for pardon and salvation, wanting, as they did, a holy motive, springing from the deep selfishness of an unrenewed soul, only increased his guilt and condemnation. The doctrine was indeed horrible, but a plain, necessary result of man's total corruption and impotence. I state this controversy, that the reader may know the kind of topics in which the zeal and abilities of our fathers were employed. It also shows us how extremes meet. Dr. Hopkins contended, that no means of religion or virtue could avail, unless used with a sincere love of religion and virtue. In this doctrine, all liberal Christians concur. In their hands, however, the doctrine wears an entirely different aspect in consequence of their denial of total, original depravity, that terrible error, which drove Dr. Hopkins to conclusions equally shocking to the reason, to common sense, and to the best feelings of the heart.

The characteristic disposition of Dr. Hopkins to follow out his principles, was remarkably illustrated in a manuscript of his which was never published, and which perhaps was suppressed by those who had the charge of his papers, in consequence of its leaning towards some of the speculations of the infidel philosophy of the day, in regard to Utility or the General Good. It fell into my hands after his death, and struck me so much that I think I can trust my recollections of it. It gave the author's ideas of

Moral Good. He maintained that the object of "Moral Good," the object on which virtue is fixed, and the choice of which constitutes virtue, is "natural good," or the greatest possible amount of Enjoyment, not our own enjoyment only, but that of the whole system of being. He virtually, if not expressly, set forth this "natural good," that is, happiness in the simple sense of enjoyment, as the ultimate good, and made moral good the means. I well recollect how, in starting from this principle, he justified eternal punishment. He affirmed that sin or selfishness (synonymous words in his vocabulary) tended to counteract God's system, which is framed for infinite happiness, or tended to produce infinite misery. He then insisted, that by subjecting the sinner to endless, that is, infinite misery, this tendency was made manifest; a correspondence was established between the sin and the punishment, and a barrier was erected against sin, which was demanded by the greatness of the good menaced by the wrong-doer.

I have thrown together these recollections of a man, who has been crowded out of men's minds by the thronging events and interests of our time, but who must always fill an important place in our ecclesiastical history. He was a singularly blameless man, with the exception of intolerance towards those who differed from him. This he sometimes expressed in a manner which, to those unacquainted with him, seemed a sign of any thing but benignity. In one point of view, I take pleasure in thinking of him. He was an illustration of the power of our spiritual nature. In narrow circumstances, with few outward indulgences, in great seclusion, he yet found much to enjoy. He lived in a world of thought, above all earthly passions. He represented to himself, as the result of the divine government, a boundless diffusion of felicity through the universe, and contrived to merge in this the horrors of his theological system. His doctrines, indeed, threw dark colors over the world around him; but he took refuge from the present state of things in the Millennium. The Millennium was his chosen ground. If any subject of thought possessed him above all others, I suppose it to have been this. The Millennium was more than a belief to him. It had the freshness of visible things. He was at home in it. His book on the subject has an air of reality, as if written from observation. He describes the habits and customs of the Millennium, as one familiar with them. He enjoyed this future glory of the church not a whit the less, because it was so much his own creation. The fundamental idea, the germ, he found in the Scriptures, but it expanded in and from his own mind. Whilst to the multitude he seemed a hard, dry theologian, feeding on the thorns of controversy, he was living in a region of imagination, feeding on visions of a holiness and a happiness, which are to make earth all but heaven. It has been my privilege to meet with other examples of the same character, with men, who, amidst privation, under bodily infirmity, and with none of those materials of enjoyment which the multitude are striving for, live in a world of thought, and enjoy what affluence never dreamed of, — men having nothing, yet possessing all things; and the sight of such has done me more good, has spoken more to my head and heart, than many sermons and volumes. I have learned the sufficiency of the mind to itself, its independence on outward things.

I regret that I did not use my acquaintance with Dr. Hopkins to get the particulars of the habits and conversation of Edwards and Whitefield, whom he knew intimately. I value the hints which I get about distinguished men from their friends, much more than written accounts of them. Most biographies are of little worth. The true object of a biography, which is to give us an insight into men's characters, such as an intimate acquaintance with them would have furnished, is little comprehended. The sayings and actions of a man, which breathe most of what was individual in him, should be sought above all things by his historian; and yet most lives contain none or next to none of these. They are panegyrics, not lives. No department of literature is so false as biography. The object is, not to let down the hero; and consequently, what is most human, most genuine, most characteristic in his history is excluded. Sometimes one anecdote will let us into the secret of a man's soul more than all the prominent events of his life. It is not impossible that some readers may object to some of my notices of the stern theologian, to whom this note refers, as too familiar. This seems to me their merit. They show that he was not a mere theologian, that he had the sympathies of a man

THE SUNDAY-SCHOOL.

DISCOURSE

PRONOUNCED BEFORE THE SUNDAY-SCHOOL SOCIETY.

MATTHEW xix. 13, 14 : " Then were there brought unto him little children, that he should put his hands on them, and pray : and the disciples rebuked them. But Jesus said, Suffer little children, and forbid them not, to come unto me ; for of such is the kingdom of heaven."

THE subject of this discourse is indicated by the name of the society, at whose request I appear in this place. The Sunday-School, this is now to engage our attention. I believe, I can best aid it by expounding the principles on which it should rest and by which it should be guided. I am not anxious to pronounce an eulogy on this and similar institutions. They do much good, but they are destined to do greater. They are in their infancy, and only giving promise of the benefits they are to confer. They already enjoy patronage, and this will increase certainly, necessarily, in proportion as they shall grow in efficiency and usefulness. I wish to say something of the great principles which should preside over them, and of the modes of operation by which they can best accomplish their end. This discourse, though especially designed for Sunday-schools, is, in truth, equally applicable to domestic instruction. Parents who are anxious to train up their children in the paths of Christian virtue, will find in every principle and rule, now to be laid down, a guide for their own steps. How to reach, influence, enlighten, elevate the youthful mind, this is the grand topic ; and who ought not to be interested in it ? for who has not an interest in the young ?

I propose to set before you my views under the following heads. I shall consider, first, the Principle on which such schools should be founded ; next, their End or great object ; in the third place, What they should teach ; and, lastly, How they should teach. These divisions, if there were time to fill them up, would exhaust the subject. I shall satisfy myself with offering you what seem to me the most important views under each.

1. I am, first, to consider the principle on which the Sunday-school should be founded. It must be founded and carried on in Faith. You must not establish it from imitation, nor set it in motion because other sects have adopted a like machinery. The Sunday-school must be founded on and sustained by a strong faith in its usefulness, its worth, its importance. Faith is the spring of all energetic action. Men throw their souls into objects only because they believe them to be attainable and worth pursuit. You must have faith in your school ; and for this end you must have faith in God ; in the child whom you teach ; and in the Scriptures which are to be taught.

You must have faith in God ; and by this I do not mean a general belief of his existence and perfection, but a faith in him as the father and friend of the children whom you instruct, as desiring their progress more than all human friends, and as most ready to aid you in your efforts for their good. You must not feel yourselves alone. You must not think when you enter the place of teaching, that only you and your pupils are present, and that you have nothing but your power and wisdom to rely on for success. You must feel a higher presence. You must feel that the Father of these children is near you, and that he loves them with a boundless love. Do not think of God as interested only in higher orders of beings, or only in great and distinguished men. The little child is as dear to him as the hero, as the philosopher, as the angel ; for in that child are the germs of an angel's powers, and God has called him into being that he may become an angel. On this faith every Sunday-school should be built, and on such a foundation it will stand firm and gather strength.

Again, you must have faith in the child whom you instruct. Believe in the greatness of its nature and in its capacity of improvement. Do not measure its mind by its frail, slender form. In a very few years, in ten years perhaps, that child is to come forward into life, to take on him the duties of an arduous vocation, to assume serious responsibilities, and soon after he may be the head of a family and have a voice in the government of his country. All the powers which he is to put forth in life, all the powers which are to be unfolded in his endless being, are now wrapped up within him. That mind, not you, nor I, nor an angel, can comprehend. Feel that your scholar, young as he is, is worthy of your intensest interest. Have faith in his nature, especially as fitted for religion. Do not, as some do, look on the child as born under the curse of God, as naturally hostile to all goodness and truth. What! the child totally depraved! Can it be that such a thought ever entered the mind of a human being? especially of a parent! What! in the beauty of childhood and youth, in that open brow, that cheerful smile, do you see the brand of total corruption? Is it a little fiend who sleeps so sweetly on his mother's breast? Was it an infant demon, which Jesus took in his arms and said, "Of such is the kingdom of heaven"? Is the child, who, as you relate to him a story of suffering or generosity, listens with a tearful or kindling eye and a throbbing heart, is *he* a child of hell? As soon could I look on the sun, and think it the source of darkness, as on the countenance of childhood or of youth, and see total depravity written there. My friends, we should believe any doctrine sooner than this, for it tempts us to curse the day of our birth; to loathe our existence; and, by making our Creator our worst foe and our fellow-creatures hateful, it tends to rupture all the ties which bind us to God and our race. My friends, have faith in the child; not that it is virtuous and holy at birth; for virtue or holiness is not, cannot be, born with us, but is a free, voluntary effort of a being who knows the distinction of right and wrong, and who, if tempted, adheres to the right; but have faith in the child as capable of knowing and loving the good and the true, as having a conscience to take the side of duty, as open to ingenuous motives for well-doing, as created for knowledge, wisdom, piety, and disinterested love.

Once more, you must have faith in Christianity, as adapted to the mind of the child, as the very truth fitted to enlighten, interest, and improve the human being in the first years of his life. It is the property of our religion, that, whilst it stretches beyond the grasp of the mightiest intellect, it contracts itself, so to speak, within the limits of the narrowest ; that, whilst it furnishes matter of inexhaustible speculation to such men as Locke and Newton, it condescends to the ignorant and becomes the teacher of babes. Christianity at once speaks with authority in the schools of the learned, and enters the nursery to instil with gentle voice celestial wisdom into the ears of infancy. And this wonderful property of our religion is to be explained by its being founded on, and answering to, the primitive and most universal principles of human nature. It reveals God as a parent ; and the first sentiment which dawns on the child, is love to its parents. It enjoins not arbitrary commands, but teaches the everlasting principles of duty ; and the sense of duty begins to unfold itself in the earliest stages of our being. It speaks of a future world and its inhabitants ; and childhood welcomes the idea of angels, of spirits, of the vast, the wonderful, the unseen. Above all, Christianity is set forth in the life, the history, the character of Jesus ; and his character, though so sublime, is still so real, so genuine, so remarkable for simplicity, and so naturally unfolded amidst the common scenes of life, that it is seized in its principal features by the child as no other greatness can be. One of the excellences of Christianity is, that it is not an abtruse theory, not wrapped up in abstract phrases ; but taught us in facts, in narratives. It lives, moves, speaks, and acts before our eyes. Christian love is not taught us in cold precepts. It speaks from the cross. So, immortality is not a vague promise. It breaks forth like the morning from the tomb near Calvary. It becomes a glorious reality in the person of the rising Saviour ; and his ascension opens to our view the heaven into which he enters. It is this historical form of our religion, which peculiarly adapts it to childhood, to the imagination and heart, which open first in childhood. In this sense, the kingdom of heaven, the religion of Christ, belongs to children. This you must feel. Believe in the fitness of our religion for those you teach. Feel that you have the very instrument for acting on the young mind, that you have the life-giving word.

II. Having considered the faith in which the Sunday-school should be founded, I proceed now to consider the end, the great object, which should be proposed and kept steadily in view by its friends. To work efficiently and usefully, we must understand what we are to work for. In proportion as an end is seen dimly and unsteadily, our action will be vague, uncertain, and our energy wasted. What, then, is the end of the Sunday-school? The great end is, to awaken the soul of the pupil, to bring his understanding, conscience, and heart into earnest, vigorous action on religious and moral truth, to excite and cherish in him Spiritual Life. Inward life, force, activity, this it must be our aim to call forth and build up in all our teachings of the young, especially in religious teaching. You must never forget, my friends, whether parents or Sunday-School instructers, what kind of a being you are acting upon. Never forget that the child is a rational, moral, free being, and that the great end of education is to awaken rational and moral energy within him, and to lead him to the free choice of the right, to the free determination of himself to truth and duty. The child is not a piece of wax to be moulded at another's pleasure, not a stone to be hewn passively into any shape which the caprice and interest of others may dictate ; but a living, thinking being, made to act from principles in his own heart, to distinguish for himself between good and evil, between truth and falsehood, to form himself, to be in an important sense the author of his own character, the determiner of his own future being. This most important view of the child should never forsake the teacher. He is a free moral agent, and our end should be to develope such a being. He must not be treated as if he were unthinking matter. You can make a house, a ship, a statue, without its own consent. You determine the machines which you form wholly by your own will. The child has a will as well as yourselves. The great design of his being is, that he should act *from* himself and *on* himself. He can understand the perfection of his nature, and is created that he may accomplish it from free choice, from a sense of duty, from his own deliberate purpose.

The great end in religious instruction, whether in the Sunday-school or family, is, not to stamp *our* minds irresistibly on the young, but to stir up their own ; not to make them see with our eyes, but to look inquiringly and steadily with their own ; not to give them a definite amount of knowledge, but to inspire a fervent love of truth ; not to form an outward regularity, but to touch inward springs ; not to burden the memory, but to quicken and strengthen the power of thought ; not to bind them by ineradicable prejudices to our particular sect or peculiar notions, but to prepare them for impartial, conscientious judging of whatever subjects may, in the course of Providence, be offered to their decision ; not to impose religion upon them in the form of arbitrary rules, which rest on no foundation but our own word and will, but to awaken the conscience, the moral discernment, so that they may discern and approve for themselves what is everlastingly right and good ; not to *tell* them that God is good, but to help them to see and feel his love in all that he does within and around them ; not to tell them of the dignity of Christ, but to open their inward eye to the beauty and greatness of his character, and to enkindle aspirations after a kindred virtue. In a word, the great object of all schools is, to awaken intellectual and moral life in the child. Life is the great thing to be sought in a human being. Hitherto, most religions and governments have been very much contrivances for extinguishing life in the human soul. Thanks to God, we live to see the dawning of a better day.

By these remarks, I do not mean that we are never to give our children a command without assigning our reasons, or an opinion without stating our proofs. They must rely on us in the first instance, for much that they cannot comprehend ; but I mean, that our great aim in controlling them, must be to train them to control themselves, and our great aim in giving them instruction, must be to aid them in the acquisition of truth for themselves. As far as possible, religion should be adapted to their minds and hearts. We should teach religion as we do nature. We do not shut up our children from outward nature, and require them to believe in the great laws of the Creator, in the powers of light, heat, steam, gravity, on our word alone. We put them in the presence of nature. We delight to verify what we teach them of the mineral, animal, and vegetable worlds, by facts placed under their own eyes. We encourage them to observe for themselves, and to submit to experiment what they hear. Now, all the great principles of morals and religion may be illustrated and confirmed, like the great laws of nature, by what falls under the child's own consciousness and experience. Indeed great moral and religious truths are nearer to him than the principles of natural science. The germs of them are in the soul. All the elementary ideas of God and duty and love and happiness come to him from his own spiritual powers and affections. Moral good and evil, virtue and vice, are revealed to him in his own motives of action and in the motives of those around him. Faith in God and virtue does not depend on assertion alone. Religion carries its own evidence with it more than history or science. It should rest more on the soul's own consciousness, experience, and observation. To wake up the soul to a clear, affectionate perception of the reality and truth and greatness of religion, is the great end of teaching.

The great danger of Sunday-schools is, that they will fall into a course of mechanical teaching, that they will give religion as a lifeless tradition, and not as a quickening reality. It is not enough to use words conveying truth. Truth must be so given that the mind will lay hold on, will recognise it as truth, and will incorporate it with itself. The most important truth may lie like a dead weight on the mind, just as the most wholesome food, for want of action in the digestive organs, becomes an oppressive load. I do not think that so much harm is done by giving error to a child, as by giving truth in a lifeless form. What is the misery of the multitudes in Christian countries ? Not that they disbelieve Christianity ; not they hold great errors, but that truth lies dead within them. They use the most sacred words without meaning They hear of spiritual realities, awful enough to raise the dead, with utter unconcern ; and one reason of this insensibility is, that teaching in early life was so mechanical, that religion was lodged in the memory and the unthinking belief, whilst the reason was not awakened, nor the conscience nor the heart moved. According to the common modes of instruction, the minds of the young become worn to great truths. By reading the Scriptures without thought or feeling, their minds are dulled to its most touching and sublime passages ; and, when once a passage lies dead in the mind, its resurrection to life and power is a most difficult work. Here lies the great danger of Sunday-schools. Let us never forget, that their end is to awaken life in the minds and hearts of the young.

III. I now proceed to consider what is to be taught in the Sunday-schools, to accomplish the great end of which I have spoken ; * and this may seem soon settled. Should I ask you what is to be taught in the Sunday-school, the answer would be, " The Christian religion. The institution is a Christian one, and has for its end the communication of Christian truth." I acquiesce in the answer ; but the question then comes, " In what forms shall the religion be taught, so as to wake up the life of the child ? Shall a catechism be taught ? " I say, No. A catechism is a skeleton, a dead letter, a petrifaction. Wanting life, it can give none. A cold abstraction, it cannot but make religion repulsive to pupils whose age

* In the remarks which I am to make on what is to be taught in the Sunday-school, I take it for granted that this school is the first stage of a course of religious instruction, not the whole course; that it prepares for, but does not include Bible classes, and other classes in which the most difficult books of Scripture, the evidences of natural and revealed religion, and a system of moral philosophy, should be taught.

demands that truth should be embodied, set before their eyes, bound up with real life. A catechism, by being systematical, may give a certain order and method to teaching; but systems of theology are out of place in Sunday-schools. They belong to the end, not the beginning, of religious teaching. Besides they are so generally the constructions of human ingenuity rather than the living forms of divine wisdom; they give such undue prominence to doctrines which have been lifted into importance only by the accident of having been made matters of controversy; they so often sacrifice common sense, the plain dictates of reason and conscience, to the preservation of what is called consistency; they lay such fetters on teacher and learner, and prevent so much the free action of the mind and heart, that they seldom enter the Sunday-school but to darken and mislead it.

The Christian religion should be learned not from catechisms and systems, but from the Scriptures, and especially from that part of the Scriptures in which it especially resides, in the histories, actions, words, sufferings, triumphs of Jesus Christ. The Gospels, the Gospels, these should be the text-book of Sunday-schools. They are more adapted to the child than any other part of Scripture. They are full of life, reality, beauty, power, and in skilful hands are fitted above all writing to awaken spiritual life in old and young.

The Gospels are to be the study of the Sunday-school teacher, and of all who teach the young; and the great object of study must be, to penetrate to the spirit of these divine writings, and, above all things, to comprehend the spirit, character, purpose, motives, love of Jesus Christ. He is to be the great study. In him, his religion is revealed as nowhere else. Much attention is now given, and properly given, by teachers to what may be called the letter of the Gospels, to the geography of the country where Christ lived, to the customs to which he refers, to the state of society which surrounded him. This knowledge is of great utility. We should strive to learn the circumstances in which Jesus was placed and lived, as thoroughly as those of our own times. We should study the men among whom he lived, their opinions and passions, their hopes and expectations, the sects who hated and opposed him, the superstitions which prevailed among the learned and the multitude, and strive to see all these things as vividly as if we had lived at the very moment of Christ's ministry. But all this knowledge is to be gained not for its own sake, but as a means of bringing us near to Jesus, of letting us into the secrets of his mind, of revealing to us his spirit and character, and of bringing out the full purpose and import of all that he did and said. It is only by knowing the people among whom he was born, and brought up, and lived, and died, that we can fully comprehend the originality, strength, and dignity of his character, his unborrowed, self-subsisting excellence, his miraculous love. We have very few of us a conception, how Jesus stood alone in the age in which he lived, how unsustained he was in his great work, how he found not one mind to comprehend his own, not one friend to sympathize with his great purpose, how every outward influence withstood him ; and, for want of this conception, we do not regard Jesus with the interest which his character should inspire.

The teachers of the young should strive to be at home with Jesus, to know him familiarly, to form a clear, vivid, bright idea of him, to see him just as he appeared on earth, to see him in the very dress in which he manifested himself to the men of his age. They should follow him to the temple, to the mountain top, to the shores of the sea of Galilee, and should understand the mixed feelings of the crowd around him, should see the scowl of the Pharisee who listened to catch his words for some matter of accusation, the imploring look of the diseased seeking healing from his words, the gaze of wonder among the ignorant, and the delighted, affectionate, reverential eagerness with which the single-hearted and humble hung on his lips. Just in proportion as we can place ourselves near to Christ, his wisdom, love, greatness will break forth, and we shall be able to bring him near to the mind of the child.

The truth is, that few of us apprehend vividly the circumstances under which Jesus lived and taught, and therefore much of the propriety, beauty, and authority of his character is lost. For example, his outward condition is not made real to us. The pictures which the great artists have left us of Jesus, have helped to lead us astray. He is there seen with a glory around his head, and arrayed in a robe of grace and majesty. Now Jesus was a poor man ; he had lived and wrought as a carpenter, and he came in the dress common to those with whom he had grown up. His chosen companions were natives of an obscure province, despised for its ignorance and rude manners, and they followed him in the garb of men who were accustomed to live by daily toil. Such was the outward condition of Jesus. Such was his manifestation to a people burning with expectation of a splendid, conquering deliverer ; and in such circumstances he spoke with an authority which awed both high and low. In learning the outward circumstances of Jesus, we not merely satisfy a natural curiosity, but obtain a help towards understanding his character and the spirit of his religion. His condition reveals to us the force and dignity of his mind, which could dispense with the ordinary means of inspiring respect. It shows the deep sympathy of Christ with the poor of our race, for among these he chose to live. It speaks condemnation to those who, professing to believe in Christ, separate themselves from the multitude of men because of the accident of wealth, and attach ideas of superiority to dress and show. From this illustration you may learn the importance of being acquainted with every part of Christ's history, with his common life, as well as his more solemn actions and teachings. Every thing relating to him breathes instruction and gives the teacher a power over the mind of the child.

The Gospels must be the great study to the Sunday-school teacher. Many, when they hear of studying the New Testament, imagine that they must examine commentators to understand better the difficult texts, the dark passages in that book. I mean something very different. Strive indeed to clear up as far as you can the obscure portions of Christ's teaching. There are texts, which, in consequence of their connexion with forgotten circumstances of the time, are now of uncertain meaning. But do not think that the most important truths of Christianity are locked up in these dark passages of the New Testament. There is nothing in the dark, which is not to be found in the plain, portions of Scripture. Perhaps the highest use of examining difficult texts, is to discover their harmony with those that are clear. The parts of the Gospel, which the Sunday-school teacher should most study, are those which need no great elucidation from criticism, the parables, the miracles, the actions, the suffering, the prayers, the tears of Jesus; and these are to be studied, that the teacher may learn the spirit, the soul of Christ, may come near to that wonderful being, may learn the great purpose to which he was devoted, the affections which overflowed his heart, the depth and expansiveness of his love, the profoundness of his wisdom, the unconquerable strength of his trust in God.* The character of Christ is the sum of his religion. It is the clearest, the most beautiful manifestation of the character of God, far more clear and touching than all the teachings of nature. It is also the brightest revelation to us of the Moral Perfection which his precepts enjoin, of disinterested love to God and man, of faithfulness to principle, of fearlessness in duty, of superiority to the world, of delight in the Good and the True. The expositions of the Christian virtues in all the volumes of all ages,

---

* Commentaries have their use, but not the highest use. They explain the letter of Christianity, give the meaning of words, remove obscurities from the sense, and so far they do great good; but the life, the power, the spirit of Christianity, they do not unfold. They do not lay open to us the heart of Christ. I remember that a short time ago I was reading a book, not intended to be a religious one, in which some remarks were offered on the conduct of Jesus, as, just before his death, he descended from the Mount of Olives, and amidst a crowd of shouting disciples looked on Jerusalem, the city of his murderers, which in a few hours was to be stained with his innocent blood. The conscious greatness with which he announced the ruin of that proud metropolis and its venerated temple, and his deep sympathy with its approaching woes, bursting forth in tears, and making him forget for a moment his own near agonies and the shouts of the surrounding multitude, were brought to my mind more distinctly than ever before; and I felt that this more vivid apprehension of Jesus was worth more than much of the learning in which commentators abound

are cold and dark compared with the genial light and the warm coloring in which Christ's character sets before us the spirit of his religion, the perfection of our nature.

The great work, then, of the Sunday-school teacher, is to teach Christ, and to teach him not as set forth in creeds and human systems, but as living and moving in the simple histories of the Evangelists. Christ is to be taught ; and by this I mean, not any mystical doctrine about his nature, not the doctrine of the Trinity, but the spirit of Christ, breathing forth in all that he said and all that he did. We should seek, that the child should know his heavenly friend and Saviour with the distinctness with which he knows an earthly friend ; and this knowledge is not to be given by teaching him dark notions about Christ, which have perplexed and convulsed the church for ages. The doctrine of the Trinity seems to me only fitted to throw a mistiness over Christ, to place him beyond the reach of our understanding and hearts. When I am told that Jesus Christ is the second person in the Trinity, one of three persons, who constitute one God, one Infinite mind, I am plunged into an abyss of darkness. Jesus becomes to me the most unintelligible being in the universe. God I can know. Man I can understand. But Christ, as described in human creeds, a compound being, at once man and God, at once infinite in wisdom and ignorant of innumerable truths, and who is so united with two other persons as to make with them one mind, Christ so represented baffles all my faculties. I cannot lay hold on him. My weak intellect is wholly at fault ; and I cannot believe that the child's intellect can better apprehend him. This is a grave objection to the doctrine of the Trinity. It destroys the reality, the distinctness, the touching nearness of Jesus Christ. It gives him an air of fiction, and has done more than all things to prevent a true, deep acquaintance with him, with his spirit, with the workings of his mind, with the sublimity of his virtue. It has thrown a glare over him, under which the bright and beautiful features of his character have been very much concealed.

From what I have said, you see what I suppose the Sunday-school teacher is to learn and teach. It is the Christian religion as unfolded in the plainest portions of the Gospel. Before leaving this topic, I wish to offer some remarks, which may prevent all misapprehension of what I have said. I have spoken against teaching Christianity to children as a system. I have spoken of the inadequacy of catechisms. In thus speaking, I do not mean that the teacher shall have nothing systematic in his knowledge. Far from it. He must not satisfy himself with studying separate actions, words, and miracles of Jesus. He must look at Christ's history and teaching as a whole, and observe the great features of his truth and goodness, the grand characteristics of his system, and in this way learn what great impressions he must strive to make on the child, by the particular facts and precepts which each lesson presents. There ought to be a unity in the mind of the teacher. His instructions must not be loose fragments, but be bound together by great views. Perhaps you may ask, what are these great views of Christianity, which pervade it throughout, and to which the mind of the learner must be continually turned? There are three, which seem to me especially prominent, the Spirituality of the religion, its Disinterestedness, and, lastly, the vastness, the Infinity of its Prospects.

The first great feature of Christianity which should be brought out continually to the child, is its Spirituality. Christ is a spiritual deliverer. His salvation is inward. This great truth cannot be too much insisted on. Christ's salvation is within. The evils from which he comes to release us are inward. The felicity which he came to give is inward, and therefore everlasting. Carry then your pupils into themselves. Awake in them, as far as possible, a consciousness of their spiritual nature, of the infinite riches which are locked up in reason, in conscience, in the power of knowing God, loving goodness, and practising duty; and use all the history and teachings of Christ, to set him before them as the fountain of life and light to their souls. For example, when his reign, kingdom, power, authority, throne, are spoken of, guard them against attaching an outward import to these words; teach them that they mean not an outward empire, but the purifying, elevating influence of his character, truth, spirit, on the human mind. Use all his miracles as types, emblems, of a spiritual salvation. When your pupils read of his giving sight to the blind, let them see in this a manifestation of his character as the Light of the world; and, in the joy of the individual whose eyes were opened from perpetual night on the beauty of nature, let them see a figure of the happiness of the true disciple, who, by following Christ, is brought to the vision of a more glorious luminary than the sun, and of a more majestic and enduring universe than material worlds. When the precepts of Christ are the subjects of conversation, turn the mind of the child to their spiritual import. Let him see, that the worth of the action lies in the principle, motive, purpose, from which it springs; that love to God, not outward worship, and love to man, not outward deeds, are the very essence, soul, centre, of the Christian law. Turn his attention to the singular force and boldness of language, in which Jesus calls to rise above the body and the world, above the pleasures and pains of the senses, above wealth and show, above every outward good. In speaking of the promises and threatenings of Christianity, do not speak as if goodness were to be sought and sin shunned for their outward consequences; but express your deep conviction, that goodness is its own reward, worth infinitely more than all outward recompense, and that sin is its own curse, and more to be dreaded on its own account, than a burning hell. When God is the subject of conversation, do not spend all your strength in talking of what he has made around you; do not point the young to his outward works as his chief manifestations. Lead them to think of him as revealed in their own minds, as the Father of their spirits, as more intimately present with their souls than with the sun, and teach them to account as his best gifts, not outward possessions, but the silent influences of his spirit, his communications of light to their minds, of warmth and elevation to their feelings, and of force to their resolution of well-doing. Let the spirituality of Christianity shine forth in all your teachings. Let the young see how superior Jesus was to outward things, how he looked down on wealth and show as below his notice, how he cared nothing for outward distinctions, how the beggar by the road-side received from him marks of deeper interest than Pilate on his judgment-seat or Herod on his throne, how he looked only at the human spirit and sought nothing but its recovery and life.

I have spoken of the Spirituality of Christianity. The next great feature of the religion to be constantly set before the child, is its Disinterestedness. The essence of Christianity is generous affection. Nothing so distinguishes it as generosity. Disinterested love not only breaks out in separate teachings of Christ; it spreads like the broad light of heaven over the whole religion. Every precept is but an aspect, an expression of generous love. This prompted every word, guided every step, of Jesus. It was the life of his ministry; it warmed his heart in death; it flowed out with his heart's blood. The pupil should be constantly led to see and feel this divine spirit pervading the religion. The Gospels should be used to inspire him with reverence for generous self-sacrifice and with aversion to every thing narrow and mean. Let him learn that he is not to live for himself; that he has a heart to be given to God and to his fellow-creatures; that he is to do the will of God, not in a mercenary spirit, but from gratitude, filial love, and from sincere delight in goodness; that he is to prepare himself to toil and suffer for his race. The cross, that emblem of self-sacrifice, that highest form of an all-surrendering love, is to be set before him as the standard of his religion, the banner under which he is to live, and, if God so require, to die.

There is one other great feature of Christianity, and that is the vastness, the Infinity of its Prospects. This was revealed in the whole life of Jesus. In all that he said, we see his mind possessed with the thought of being ordained to confer an infinite good. That teacher knows little of Christ, who does not see him filled with the consciousness of being the author of an everlasting salvation and happiness to the human race. " I am the resurrection and the life. He that believeth on me shall never see death." Such was his language, and such never fell before from human lips. When I endeavour to bring to my mind the vast hopes which inspired him as he pronounced these words, and his joy at the anticipation of the immortal fruits which his life and death were to yield to our race, I feel how little his character is yet understood by those who think of Jesus as a man of sorrow, borne down habitually by a load of grief. Constantly lead your pupils to observe, how real, deep, and vivid was the impression on the mind of Jesus, of that future, everlasting life, which he came to bestow. Speak to them of the happiness with which he looked on all human virtue, as being a germ which was to unfold for ever, a fountain of living water which was to spring up into immortality, a love which was to expand through all ages and to embrace the universe. It is through the mind of Christ, living, as it did, in a higher world, that they can best comprehend the reality and vastness of the prospects of the human soul.

Such are the three great features of the religion which the teacher should bring most frequently to the mind of the child. In these, as in all my preceding remarks, you perceive the importance which I attach to the character of Christ, as the great means of giving spiritual light and life to the mind. The Gospels, in which he is placed before us so vividly, are in truth the chief repositories of divine wisdom. The greatest productions of human genius have little quickening power in comparison with these simple narratives. In reading the Gospels, I feel myself in presence of one who speaks as man never spake; whose voice is not of the earth; who speaks with a tone of reality and authority altogether his own, who speaks of God as conscious of his immediate presence, as enjoying with him the intimacy of an only Son; and who speaks of heaven, as most familiar with the higher states of being. Great truths come from Jesus with a simplicity, an ease, showing how deeply they pervaded and possessed his mind. No books astonish me like the Gospels. Jesus, the hero of the story, is a more extraordinary being than imagination has feigned, and yet his character has an impress of nature, consistency, truth, never surpassed. You have all seen portraits, which, as soon as seen, you felt to be likenesses, so living were they, so natural, so true. Such is the impression made on my mind by the Gospels. I believe that you or I could lift mountains or create a world as easily as fanaticism or imposture could have created such a character and history as that of Jesus Christ. I have read the Gospels for years, and seldom read them now without gaining some new or more striking view of the great teacher and deliverer whom they portray. Of all books, they deserve most the study of youth and age. Happy the Sunday-school in which their spirit is revealed!

But I have not yet said every thing in favor of them as the great sources of instruction. I have said, that the Christian religion is to be taught from the Gospels. This is their great, but not their only use. Much incidental instruction is to be drawn from them. There are two great subjects on which it is very desirable to give to the young the light they can receive, human nature and human life; and on these points the Gospels furnish occasions of much useful teaching. They give us not only the life and character of Christ, but place him before us in the midst of human beings and of human affairs. Peter, the ardent, the confident, the false, the penitent Peter; the affectionate John; the treacherous Judas, selling his Master for gold; Mary, the mother, at the cross; Mary Magdalen at the tomb; the woman, who had been a sinner, bathing his feet with tears, and wiping them with the hair of her head; — what revelations of the human soul are these! What depths of our nature do they lay open! It is a remarkable fact, that the great masters of painting have drawn their chief subjects from the New Testament; so full is this volume of the most powerful and touching exhibitions of human character. And how much instruction does this book convey in regard to life as well as in regard to the soul! I do not know a more affecting picture of human experience than the simple narrative of Luke;—" When Jesus came nigh to the city, behold, there was a dead man carried out, the only son of his mother, and she was a widow; and much people of the city was with her." The Gospels show us fellow beings in all varieties of condition, the blind man, the leper, the rich young ruler, the furious multitude. They give practical views of life, which cannot be too early impressed. They show us, in the history of Jesus and his Apostles, that true greatness may be found in the humblest ranks, and that goodness, in proportion as it becomes eminent, exposes itself to hatred and reproach, so that we must make up our minds, if we would be faithful, to encounter shame and loss for God and duty. In truth, all the variety of wisdom which youth needs, may be extracted from these writings. The Gospels, then, are to be the great study of the Sunday-school.

I cannot close these remarks on what is to be taught

in the Sunday-school, without repeating what I have said of the chief danger of this institution. I refer to the danger of mechanical teaching, by which the young mind becomes worn, deadened to the greatest truths. The Gospels, life-giving as they are, may be rendered wholly inoperative by the want of life in the instructor. So great is my dread of tame, mechanical teaching, that I am sometimes almost tempted to question the utility of Sunday-schools. We, Protestants, in our zeal for the Bible, are apt to forget, that the very commonness of the book tends to impair its power, that familiarity breeds indifference, and that no book, therefore, requires such a living power in the teacher. He must beware, lest he make the Gospels trite by too frequent repetition. It will often be best for him to assist his pupils in extracting the great principle of truth involved in a precept, parable, or action of Jesus, and to make this the subject of conversation, without farther reference to the text by which it was suggested. If he can lead them by fit questions, to find this principle in their own consciousness and experience, in their own moral judgments and feelings, and to discover how it should be applied to their characters and brought out in their common lives, he will not only convey the most important instruction, but will give new vividness and interest to the Scriptures and a deeper conviction of their truth, by showing how congenial they are with human nature, and how intimately connected with human affairs and with real life. Let me also mention, as another means of preserving the Scriptures from degradation by too frequent handling, that extracts from biography, history, natural science, fitted to make religious impressions, should be occasionally introduced into the Sunday-school. Such seems to me the instruction which the ends of this institution require.

IV. We have now seen what is to be taught in the Sunday-school, and the question now comes, How shall it be taught? This is my last head, and not the least important. On the manner of teaching, how much depends! I fear it is not sufficiently studied by Sunday-school instructors. They meet generally, and ought regularly to meet, to prepare themselves for their tasks. But their object commonly is to learn *what* they are to teach, rather than *how* to teach it; but the last requires equal attention with the first, I had almost said more. From deficiency in this, we sometimes see that an instructor, profoundly acquainted with his subject, is less successful in teaching than another of comparatively superficial acquisitions; he knows much, but does not know the way to the child's mind and heart. The same truth, which attracts and impresses from one man's lips, repels from another. At the meeting of the Sunday-school teachers, it is not enough to learn the meaning of the portion of Scripture which is to be the subject of the next lesson; it is more important to select from it the particular topics which are adapted to the pupil's comprehension, and still more necessary to inquire, under what lights or aspects they may be brought to his view, so as to arrest attention and reach the heart. A principal end in the meeting of teachers should be to learn the art of teaching, the way of approach to the youthful mind.

The first aim of the teacher will of course be, to fix the attention of the pupil. It is in vain that you have his body in the school-room, if his mind is wandering beyond it, or refuses to fasten itself on the topic of discourse. In common schools attention is fixed by a severe discipline, incompatible with the spirit of Sunday-schools. Of course the teacher must aim to secure it by a moral influence over the youthful mind.

As the first means of establishing an influence over the young, I would say, you must love them. Nothing attracts like love. Children are said to be shrewd physiognomists, and read as by instinct our feelings in our countenances; they know and are drawn to their friends. I recently asked, how a singularly successful teacher in religion obtained his remarkable ascendency over the young. The reply was, that his whole intercourse expressed affection. His secret was a sincere love.

The next remark is, that, to awaken in the young an interest in what you teach, you must take an interest in it yourselves. You must not only understand, but feel, the truth. Your manner must have the natural animation, which always accompanies a work into which our hearts enter. Accordingly, one of the chief qualifications of a Sunday-school teacher is religious sensibility. Old and young are drawn by a natural earnestness of manner. Almost any subject may be made interesting, if the teacher will but throw into it his soul.

Another important rule is, Let your teaching be intelligible. Children will not listen to words which excite no ideas, or only vague and misty conceptions. Speak to them in the familiar, simple language of common life, and if the lesson have difficult terms, define them. Children love light, not darkness. Choose topics of conversation to which their minds are equal, and pass from one to another by steps which the young can follow. Be clear, and you will do much towards being interesting teachers.

Another suggestion is, Teach much by questions. These stimulate, stir up the young mind, and make it its own teacher. They encourage the spirit of inquiry, the habit of thought. Questions, skilfully proposed, turn the child to his own consciousness and experience, and will often draw out from his own soul the truth which you wish to impart; and no lesson is so well learned, as that which a man or a child teaches himself

Again, Teach graphically where you can. That is, when you are discoursing of any narrative of Scripture, or relating an incident from other sources, try to seize its great points and to place it before the eyes of your pupils. Cultivate the power of description. A story well told, and in which the most important particulars are brought out in a strong light, not only fixes attention, but often carries a truth farthest into the soul.

Another rule is, Lay the chief stress on what is most important in religion. Do not conduct the child over the Gospels as over a dead level. Seize on the great points, the great ideas. Do not confound the essential and the unessential, or insist with the same earnestness on grand, comprehensive, life-giving truths, and on disputable articles of faith. Immense injury is done by teaching doubtful or secondary doctrines as if they were the weightiest matters of Christianity; for, as time rolls over the child, and his mind unfolds, he discovers that one and another dogma, which he was taught to regard as fundamental, is uncertian, if not false, and his skepticism is apt to spread from this weak point over the whole Christian system. Make it your aim to fix in your pupils the grand principles in which the essence of Christianity consists, and which all time and experience serve to confirm ; and, in doing this, you will open the mind to all truth as fast as it is presented in the course of Providence.

Another rule is, Carry a cheerful spirit into religious teaching. Do not merely speak of Christianity as the only fountain of happiness. Let your tones and words bear witness to its benignant, cheering influence. Youth is the age of joy and hope, and nothing repels it more than gloom. Do not array religion in terror. Do not make God a painful thought by speaking of him as present only to see and punish sin. Speak of his fatherly interest in the young with a warm heart and a beaming eye, and encourage their filial approach and prayers. On this part, however, you must beware of sacrificing truth to the desire of winning your pupil. Truth, truth in her severest as well as mildest forms, must be placed before the young. Do not, to attract them to duty, represent it as a smooth and flowery path. Do not tell them that they can become good, excellent, generous, holy, without effort and pain. Teach them that the sacrifice of self-will, of private interest, and pleasure, to others' rights and happiness, to the dictates of conscience, to the will of God, is the very essence of piety and goodness. But at the same time teach them, that there is a pure, calm joy, an inward peace, in surrendering every thing to duty, which can be found in no selfish success. Help them to sympathize with the toils, pains, sacrifices of the philanthropist, the martyr, the patriot, and inspire contempt of fear and peril in adhering to truth and God.

I will add one more rule. Speak of duty, of religion, as something real, just as you speak of the interests of this life. Do not speak, as if you were repeating words received from tradition, but as if you were talking of things which you have seen and known. Nothing attracts old and young more than a tone of reality, the natural tone of strong conviction. Speak to them of God as a real being, of heaven as a real state, of duty as a real obligation. Let them see, that you regard Christianity as intended to bear on real and common life, that you expect every principle which you teach to be acted out, to be made a rule in the concerns of every day. Show the application of Christianity to the familiar scenes and pursuits of life. Bring it out to them as the Great Reality. So teach, and you will not teach in vain.

I have thus set before you the principles on which Sunday-schools should rest, and by which they should be guided. If they shall, in any degree, conform to these principles, and I trust they will, you cannot, my friends, cherish them with too much care. Their purpose cannot be spoken of too strongly. Their end is, the moral and religious education of the young, and this is the most pressing concern of our times. In all times, indeed, it has strong claims; but it was never, perhaps, so important as now, and never could its neglect induce such fearful consequences. The present is a season of great peril to the rising generation. It is distinguished by a remarkable developement of human power, activity, and freedom. The progress of science has given men a new control of nature, and in this way has opened new sources of wealth and multiplied the means of indulgence, and in an equal degree multiplied temptations to worldliness, cupidity, and crime. Our times are still more distinguished by the spirit of liberty and innovation Old institutions and usages, the old restraints on the young, have been broken down. Men of all conditions and ages think, speak, write, act, with a freedom unknown before. Our times have their advantages. But we must not hide from ourselves our true position. This ncrease of power and freedom, of which I have spoken, tends, in the first instance, to unsettle moral principles, to give to men's minds a restlessness, a want of stability, a wildness of opinion, an extravagance of desire, a bold, rash, reckless spirit. These are times of great moral danger. Outward restraints are removed to an unprecedented degree, and consequently there is a need of inward restraint, of the controlling power of a pure religion, beyond what was ever known before. The principles of the young are exposed to fearful assaults, and they need to be fortified with peculiar care. Temptations throng on the rising generation with new violence, and the power to withstand them must be proportionably increased. Society never needed such zealous efforts, such unslumbering watchfulness for its safety, as at this moment; and without faithfulness on the part of parents and good men, its bright prospects may be turned into gloom.

Sunday-schools belong to this period of society. They grow naturally from the extension of knowledge, in consequence of which more are qualified to teach than in former times, and they are suited to prepare the young for the severe trials which await them in life. As such, let them be cherished. The great question for parents to ask is, how they may strengthen their children against temptation, how they can implant in them principles of duty, purposes of virtue, which will withstand all storms, and which will grow up into all that is generous, just, beautiful, and holy in feeling and action. The question, how your children may prosper most in life should be secondary. Give them force of character, and you give them more than a fortune. Give them pure and lofty principles, and you give them more than thrones. Instil into them Christian benevolence and the love of God, and you enrich them more than by laying worlds at their feet. Sunday-schools are meant to aid you in the great work of forming your children to true excellence. I say they are meant to aid you, not to relieve you from the work, not to be your substitutes, not to diminish domestic watchfulness and teaching, but to concur with you, to give you fellow-laborers, to strengthen your influence over your children. Then give these schools your hearty support, without which they cannot prosper. Your children should be your first care. You indeed sustain interesting relations to society, but your great relation is to your children; and in truth you cannot discharge your obligations to society by any service so effectual, as by training up for it enlightened and worthy members in the bosom of the family and the church.

Like all schools, the Sunday-school must owe its influence to its teachers. I would, therefore, close this discourse with saying, that the most gifted in our congregation cannot find a worthier field of labor than the Sunday-school. The noblest work on earth is to act with an elevating power on a human spirit. The greatest men of past times have not been politicians or warriors, who have influenced the outward policy or grandeur of kingdoms; but men, who, by their deep wisdom and generous sentiments, have given light and life to the minds and hearts of their own age, and left a legacy of truth and virtue to posterity. Whoever, in the humblest sphere, imparts God's truth to one human spirit, partakes their glory. He labors on an immortal nature. He is laying the foundation of imperishable excellence and happiness. His work, if he succeed, will outlive empires and the stars.

THE PHILANTHROPIST.

A TRIBUTE TO THE MEMORY OF THE REV. NOAH WORCESTER, D. D.

Boston, November 12, 1837.

John xiii. 34 : " A new commandment I give unto you, That ye love one another; as I have loved you, that ye also love one another."

It was the great purpose of Christ to create the world anew, to make a deep, broad, enduring change in human beings. He came to breathe his own soul into men, to bring them through faith into a connexion and sympathy with himself, by which they would receive his divine virtue, as the branches receive quickening influences from the vine in which they abide, and the limbs from the head to which they are vitally bound.

It was especially the purpose of Jesus Christ to redeem men from the slavery of selfishness, to raise them to a divine, disinterested love. By this he intended that his followers should be known, that his religion should be broadly divided from all former institutions. He meant that this should be worn as a frontlet on the brow, should beam as a light from the countenance, should shed a grace over the manners, should give tones of sympathy to the voice, and especially should give energy to the will, energy to do and suffer for others' good. Here is one of the grand distinctions of Christianity, incomparably grander than all the mysteries which have borne its name. Our knowledge of Christianity is to be measured, not by the laboriousness with which we have dived into the depths of theological systems, but by our comprehension of the nature, extent, energy, and glory of that disinterested principle, which Christ enjoined as our likeness to God, and as the perfection of human nature.

This disinterestedness of Christianity is to be learned from Christ himself, and from no other. It had dawned on the world before in illustrious men, in prophets, sages, and legislators. But its full orb rose at Bethlehem. All the preceding history of the world gives but broken hints of the love which shone forth from Christ. Nor can this be learned from his precepts alone. We must go to his life, especially to his cross. His cross was the throne of his love. There it reigned, there it triumphed. On the countenance of the crucified Saviour there was one expression stronger than of dying agony, — the expression of calm, meek, unconquered, boundless love. I repeat it, the cross alone can teach us the energy and grandeur of the love which Christ came to impart. There we see its illimitableness; for he died for the whole world. There we learn its inexhaustible placability; for he died for the very enemies whose hands were reeking with his blood. There we learn its self-immolating strength; for he resigned every good of life, and endured intensest pains in the cause of our race. There we learn its spiritual elevation; for he died not to enrich men with outward and worldly goods, but to breathe new life, health, purity, into the soul. There we learn its far-reaching aim ; for he died to give immortality of happiness. There we learn its tenderness and sympathy ; for amidst his cares for the world, his heart overflowed with gratitude and love for his honored mother. There, in a word, we learn its Divinity ; for he suffered through his participation of the spirit and his devotion to the purposes of God, through unity of heart and will with his Heavenly Father.

It is one of our chief privileges as Christians, that we have in Jesus Christ a revelation of perfect love. This great idea comes forth to us from his life and teaching, as a distinct and bright reality. To understand this is to understand Christianity. To call forth in us a corresponding energy of disinterested affection, is the mission which Christianity has to accomplish on the earth.

There is one characteristic of the love of Christ, to which the Christian world are now waking up as from long sleep, and which is to do more than all things for the renovation of the world. He loved individual man. Before his time the most admired form of goodness was patriotism. Men loved their country, but cared nothing for their fellow-creatures beyond the limits of country, and cared little for the individual within those limits, devoting themselves to public interests, and especially to what was called the glory of the State. The legislator, seeking by his institutions to exalt his country above its rivals, and the warrior, fastening its yoke on its foes and crowning it with bloody laurels, were the great names of earlier times. Christ loved man, not masses of men ; loved each and all, and not a particular country and class. The human being was dear to him for his own sake, not for the spot of earth on which he lived, not for the language he spoke, not for his rank in life, but for his humanity, for his spiritual nature, for the image of God in which he was made. Nothing outward in human condition engrossed the notice or narrowed the sympathies of Jesus. He looked to the human soul. That he loved. That divine spark he desired to cherish, no matter where it dwelt, no matter how it was dimmed He loved man for his own sake, and all men without exclusion or exception. His ministry was not confined to a church, a chosen congregation. On the Mount he opened his mouth and spake to the promiscuous multitude. From the bosom of the lake he delivered his parables to the throng which lined its shores. His church was nature, the unconfined air and earth; and his truths, like the blessed influences of nature's sunshine and rain, fell on each and all. He lived in the highway, the street, the places of concourse, and welcomed the eager crowds which gathered round him from every sphere and rank of life. Nor was it to crowds that his sympathy was confined. He did not need a multitude to excite him. The humblest individual drew his regards. He took the little child into his arms and blessed it; he heard the beggar crying to him by the wayside where he sat for alms; and in the anguish of death, he administered consolation to a malefactor expiring at his side. In this shone forth the divine wisdom as well as love of Jesus, that he understood the worth of a human being. So truly did he comprehend it, that, as I think, he would have counted himself repaid for all his teachings and mighty works, for all his toils, and sufferings, and bitter death, by the redemption of a single soul. His love to every human being surpassed that of a parent to an only child. Jesus was great in all things, but in nothing greater than in his comprehension of the worth of a human spirit. Before his time no one dreamed of it. The many had been sacrificed to the few. The mass of men had been trodden under foot. History had been but a record of struggles and institutions which breathed nothing so strongly as contempt of the human race.

Jesus was the first philanthropist. He brought with him a new era, the era of philanthropy; and from his time a new spirit has moved over the troubled waters of society, and will move until it has brought order and beauty out of darkness and confusion. The men whom he trained, and into whom he had poured most largely his own spirit, were signs, proofs, that a new kingdom had come. They consecrated themselves to a work at that time without precedent, wholly original, such as had not entered human thought. They left home, possessions, country; went abroad into strange lands; and not only put life in peril, but laid it down, to spread the truth which they had received from their Lord, to make the true God, even the Father, known to his blinded children, to make the Saviour known to the sinner, to make life and immortality known to the dying, to give a new impulse to the human soul. We read of the mission of the Apostles as if it were a thing of course. The thought perhaps never comes to us, that they entered on a sphere of action until that time wholly unexplored; that not a track had previously marked their path; that the great conception which inspired them, of converting a world, had never dawned on the sublimest intellect; that the spiritual love for every human being, which carried them over oceans and through deserts, amid scourgings and fastings, and imprisonments and death, was a new light from heaven breaking out on earth, a new revelation of the divinity in human nature. Then it was, that man began to yearn for man with a godlike love. Then a new voice was heard on earth, the voice of prayer for the recovery, pardon, happiness of a world. It was most strange, it was a miracle more worthy of admiration than the raising of the dead, that from Judea, the most exclusive, narrow country under heaven, which hated and scorned all other nations, and shrunk from their touch as pollution, should go forth men to proclaim the doctrine of human brotherhood, to give to every human being, however fallen or despised, assurances of God's infinite love, to break down the barriers of nation and rank, to pour out their blood like water in the work of diffusing the spirit of universal love. Thus mightily did the character of Jesus act on the spirits of the men with whom he had lived. Since that time the civilized world has been overwhelmed by floods of barbarians, and ages of darkness have passed. But some rays of this divine light break on us through the thickest darkness. The new impulse given by Christianity was never wholly spent. The rude sculpture of the dark ages represented Jesus hanging from his cross; and however this image was abused to purposes of superstition, it still spoke to men of a philanthropy stronger than death, which felt and suffered for every human being; and a softening, humanizing virtue went from it, which even the barbarian could not wholly resist. In our own times, the character of Jesus is exerting more conspicuously its true and glorious power. We have indeed little cause for boasting. The great features of society are still hard and selfish. The worth of a human being is a mystery still hid from an immense majority, and the most enlightened among us have not looked beneath the surface of this great truth.

Still there is at this moment an interest in human nature, a sympathy with human suffering, a sensibility to the abuses and evils which deform society, a faith in man's capacity of progress, a desire of human progress, a desire to carry to every human being the means of rising to a better condition and a higher virtue, such as has never been witnessed before. Amidst the mercenariness which would degrade men into tools, and the ambition which would tread them down in its march toward power, there is still a respect for man as man, a recognition of his rights, a thirst for his elevation, which is the surest proof of a higher comprehension of Jesus Christ, and the surest augury of a happier state of human affairs. Humanity and justice are crying out in more and more piercing tones for the suffering, the enslaved, the ignorant, the poor, the prisoner, the orphan, the long-neglected seaman, the benighted heathen. I do not refer merely to new institutions for humanity, for these are not the most unambiguous proofs of progress. We see in the common consciousness of society, in the general feelings of individuals, traces of a more generous recognition of what man owes to man. The glare of outward distinction is somewhat dimmed. The prejudices of caste and rank are abated. A man is seen to be worth more than his wardrobe or his title. It begins to be understood that a Christian is to be a philanthropist, and that, in truth, the essence of Christianity is a spirit of martyrdom in the cause of mankind.

This subject has been brought to my mind, at the present moment, by an event in this vicinity, which has drawn little attention, but which I could not, without self-reproach, suffer to pass unnoticed. Within a few days, a great and good man, a singular example of the philanthropy which Jesus Christ came to breathe into the world, has been taken away; and as it was my happiness to know him more intimately than most among us, I feel as if I were called to bear a testimony to his rare goodness, and to hold up his example as a manifestation of what Christianity can accomplish in the human mind. I refer to the Rev. Noah Worcester, who has been justly called the Apostle of Peace, who finished his course at Brighton during the last week. His great age, for he was almost eighty, and the long and entire seclusion to which debility had compelled him, have probably made his name a strange one to some who hear me. In truth, it is common in the present age, for eminent men to be forgotten during their lives, if their lives are much prolonged. Society is now a quick-shifting pageant. New actors hurry the old ones from the stage. The former stability of things is strikingly impaired. The authority which gathered round the aged has declined. The young seize impatiently the prizes of life. The hurried, bustling, tumultuous, feverish Present, swallows up men's thoughts, so that he who retires from active pursuits is as little known to the rising generation as if he were dead. It is not wonderful, then, that Dr. Worcester was so far forgotten by his contemporaries. But the future will redress the wrongs of the present; and in the progress of civilization, history will guard more and more sacredly the memories of men who have advanced before their age, and devoted themselves to great but neglected interests of humanity.

Dr. Worcester's efforts in relation to war, or in the cause of peace, made him eminently a public man, and constitute his chief claim to public consideration; and these were not founded on accidental circumstances or foreign influences, but wholly on the strong and peculiar tendencies of his mind. He was distinguished above all whom I have known, by his comprehension and deep feeling of the spirit of Christianity; by the sympathy with which he seized on the character of Jesus Christ as a manifestation of Perfect Love; by the honor in which he held the mild, humble, forgiving, disinterested virtues of our religion. This distinguishing trait of his mind was embodied and brought out in his whole life and conduct. He especially expressed it in his labors for the promotion of Universal Peace on the earth. He was struck, as no other man within my acquaintance has been, with the monstrous incongruity between the spirit of Christianity and the spirit of Christian communities; between Christ's teaching of peace, mercy, forgiveness, and the wars which divide and desolate the church and the world. Every man has particular impressions which rule over and give a hue to his mind. Every man is struck by some evils rather than others. The excellent individual of whom I speak was shocked, heart-smitten, by nothing so much as by seeing that man hates man, that man destroys his brother, that man has drenched the earth with his brother's blood, that man, in his insanity, has crowned the murderer of his race with the highest honors; and, still worse, that Christian hates Christian, that church wars against church, that differences of forms and opinions array against each other those whom Christ died to join together in closest brotherhood, and that Christian zeal is spent in building up sects, rather than in spreading the spirit of Christ, and enlarging and binding together the universal church. The great evil on which his mind and heart fixed, was War, Discord, Intolerance, the substitution of force for

Reason and Love. To spread peace on earth became the object of his life. Under this impulse he gave birth and impulse to Peace Societies. This new movement is to be traced to him above all other men; and his name, I doubt not, will be handed down to future time with increasing veneration as the " Friend of Peace," as having given new force to the principles which are gradually to abate the horrors, and ultimately extinguish the spirit of war.

The history of the good man, as far as I have learned it, is singularly instructive and encouraging. He was self-taught, self-formed. He was born in narrow circumstances, and, to the age of twenty-one, was a laborious farmer, not only deprived of a collegiate education, but of the advantages which may be enjoyed in a more prosperous family. An early marriage brought on him the cares of a growing family. Still he found, or rather made, time for sufficient improvements to introduce him into the ministry before his thirtieth year. He was first settled in a parish too poor to give him even a scanty support; and he was compelled to take a farm, on which he toiled by day, whilst in the evening he was often obliged to use a mechanical art for the benefit of his family. He made their shoes; an occupation of which Coleridge has somewhere remarked, that it has been followed by a greater number of eminent men than any other trade. By the side of his work-bench he kept ink and paper, that he might write down the interesting thoughts, which he traced out, or which rushed on him amidst his humble labors. I take pleasure in stating this part of his history. The prejudice against manual labor, as inconsistent with personal dignity, is one of the most irrational and pernicious, especially in a free country. It shows how little we comprehend the spirit of our institutions, and how deeply we are tainted with the narrow maxims of the old aristocracies of Europe. Here was a man uniting great intellectual improvement with refinement of manners, who had been trained under unusual severity of toil. This country has lost much physical and moral strength, and its prosperity is at this moment depressed, by the common propensity to forsake the plough for less manly pursuits, which are thought however to promise greater dignity as well as ease.

His first book was a series of letters to a Baptist minister, and in this he gave promise of the direction which the efforts of his life were to assume. The great object of these letters was, not to settle the controversies about baptism, about the mode of administering it, whether by immersion or sprinkling, or about the proper subjects of it, whether children or adults alone. His aim was to show that these were inferior questions, that differences about these ought not to divide Christians, that the " close communion," as it is called, of the Baptists, was inconsistent with the liberal spirit of Christianity, and that this obstruction to Christian unity ought to be removed.

His next publication was what brought him into notice, and gave him an important place in our theological history. It was a publication on the Trinity; and what is worthy of remark, it preceded the animated controversy on that point, which a few years after agitated this city and commonwealth. The mind of Dr. Worcester was turned to this topic not by foreign impulses, but by its own workings. He had been brought up in the strictest sect, that is, as a Calvinist. His first doubts as to the Trinity arose from the confusion, the perplexity, into which his mind was thrown by this doctrine in his acts of devotion. To worship three persons as one and the same God, as one and the same being, seemed to him difficult, if not impossible. He accordingly resolved to read and examine the Scriptures from beginning to end, for the purpose of ascertaining the true doctrine respecting God, and the true rank of Jesus Christ. The views at which he arrived were so different from what prevailed around him, and some of them so peculiar, that he communicated them to the public under the rather quaint title of " Bible News relating to the Father, Son, and Holy Spirit." His great aim was to prove, that the Supreme God was one person, even the Father, and that Jesus Christ was not the Supreme God, but his Son in a strict and peculiar sense. This idea of " the peculiar and natural sonship " of Christ, by which he meant that Jesus was derived from the very substance of the Father, had taken a strong hold on his mind, and he insisted on it with as much confidence as was consistent with his deep sense of fallibility. But, as might be expected in so wise and spiritual a man, it faded more and more from his mind, in proportion as he became acquainted with, and assimilated to, the true glory of his Master. In one of his unpublished manuscripts, he gives an account of his change of views in this particular, and, without disclaiming expressly the doctrine which had formerly seemed so precious, he informs us that it had lost its importance in his sight. The moral, spiritual dignity of Christ, had risen on his mind in such splendor, as to dim his old idea of " natural sonship." In one place he affirms. " I do not recollect an instance [in the Scriptures] in which Christ is spoken of as loved, honored, or praised, on any other ground than his Moral dignity." This moral greatness he declares to be the highest with which Jesus was clothed, and expresses his conviction, "that the controversies of Christians about his natural dignity, had tended very little to the honor of their Master, or to their own advantage." The manuscript to which I refer, was written after his seventieth year, and is very illustrative of his character. It shows that his love of truth was stronger than the tenacity with which age commonly clings to old ideas. It shows him superior to the theory, which more than any other he had considered his own, and which had been the fruit of very laborious study. It shows how strongly he felt that progress was the law and end of his being, and how he continued to make progress to the last hour. The work called "Bible News," drew much attention, and converted not a few to the doctrine of the proper unity of God. Its calm, benignant spirit had no small influence in disarming prejudice and unkindness. He found, however, that his defection from his original faith had exposed him to much suspicion and reproach; and he became at length so painfully impressed with the intolerance which his work had excited, that he published another shorter work, called "Letters to Trinitarians," a work breathing the very spirit of Jesus, and intended to teach, that diversities of opinion, on subjects the most mysterious and perplexing, ought not to sever friends, to dissolve the Christian tie, to divide the church, to fasten on the dissenter from the common faith the charge of heresy, to array the disciples of the Prince of Peace in hostile bands. These works obtained such favor, that he was solicited to leave the obscure town in which he ministered, and to take charge, in this place, of a periodical called at first the Christian Disciple and now better known as the Christian Examiner. At that time (about twenty-five years ago) I first saw him. Long and severe toil, and a most painful disease, had left their traces on his once athletic frame; but his countenance beamed with a benignity which at once attracted confidence and affection. For several years he consulted me habitually in the conduct of the work which he edited. I recollect with admiration the gentleness, humility, and sweetness of temper, with which he endured freedoms, corrections, retrenchments, some of which I feel now to have been unwarranted, and which no other man would so kindly have borne. This work was commenced very much for doctrinal discussions, but his spirit could not brook such limitations, and he used its pages more and more for the dissemination of his principles of philanthropy and peace. At length he gave these principles to the world, in a form which did much to decide his future career. He published a pamphlet, called " A Solemn Review of the Custom of War." It bore no name, and appeared without recommendation, but it immediately seized on attention. It was read by multitudes in this country, then published in England, and translated, as I have heard, into several languages of Europe. Such was the impression made by this work, that a new association, called the Peace Society of Massachusetts, was instituted in this place. I well recollect the day of its formation in yonder house, then the parsonage of this parish; and if there was a happy man that day on earth, it was the founder of this institution. This society gave birth to all the kindred ones in this country, and its influence was felt abroad. Dr. Worcester assumed the charge of its periodical, and devoted himself for years to this cause, with unabating faith and zeal ; and it may be doubted, whether any man who ever lived, contributed more than he to spread just sentiments on the subject of war, and to hasten the era of universal peace. He began his efforts in the darkest day, when the whole civilized world was shaken by conflict, and threatened with military despotism. He lived to see more than twenty years of general peace, and to see through these years a multiplication of national ties, an extension of commercial communications, an establishment of new connexions between Christians and learned men through the world, and a growing reciprocity of friendly and beneficent influence among different States, all giving aid to the principles of peace, and encouraging hopes which a century ago would have been deemed insane.

The abolition of war, to which this good man devoted himself, is no longer to be set down as a creation of fancy, a dream of enthusiastic philanthropy. War rests on opinion ; and opinion is more and more withdrawing its support. War rests on contempt of human nature ; on the long, mournful habit of regarding the mass of human beings as machines, or as animals having no higher use than to be shot at and murdered for the glory of a chief, for the seating of this or that family on a throne, for the petty interests or selfish rivalries which have inflamed States to conflict. Let the worth of a human being be felt ; let the mass of a people be elevated ; let it be understood that a man was made to enjoy inalienable rights, to improve lofty powers, to secure a vast happiness ; and a main pillar of war will fall. And is it not plain that these views are taking place of the contempt in which man has so long been held ? War finds another support in the prejudices and partialities of a narrow patriotism. Let the great Christian principle of human brotherhood be comprehended, let the Christian spirit of universal love gain ground, and just so fast the custom of war, so long the pride of men, will become their abhorrence and execration. It is encouraging to see how outward events are concurring with the influences of Christianity in promoting peace ; how an exclusive nationality is yielding to growing intercourse ; how different nations, by mutual visits, by the interchange of thoughts and products, by studying one another's language and literature, by union of efforts in the cause of religion and humanity, are growing up to the consciousness of belonging to one great family. Every railroad, connecting distant regions, may be regarded as accomplishing a ministry of peace. Every year which passes without war, by interweaving more various ties of interest and friendship, is a pledge of coming years of peace. The prophetic faith with which Dr. Worcester, in the midst of universal war, looked forward to a happier era, and which was smiled at as enthusiasm, or credulity, has already received a sanction beyond his fondest hopes, by the wonderful progress of human affairs.

On the subject of war, Dr. Worcester adopted opinions which are thought by some to be extreme. He interpreted literally the precept, Resist not evil ; and he believed that nations, as well as individuals, would find safety, as well as "fulfil righteousness," in yielding it literal obedience. One of the most striking traits of his character, was his confidence in the power of love, I might say, in its omnipotence. He believed, that the surest way to subdue a foe was to become his friend ;

that a true benevolence was a surer defence than swords, or artillery, or walls of adamant. He believed, that no mightier man ever trod the soil of America than William Penn, when entering the wilderness unarmed, and stretching out to the savage a hand which refused all earthly weapons, in token of brotherhood and peace. There was something grand in the calm confidence with which he expressed his conviction of the superiority of moral to physical force. Armies, fiery passions, quick resentments, and the spirit of vengeance, miscalled honor, seemed to him weak, low instruments, inviting, and often hastening, the ruin which they are used to avert. Many will think him in error; but if so, it was a grand thought which led him astray.

At the age of seventy, he felt as if he had discharged his mission as a preacher of peace, and resigned his office as Secretary to the Society, to which he had given the strength of many years. He did not, however, retire to unfruitful repose. Bodily infirmity had increased, so that he was very much confined to his house; but he returned with zeal to the studies of his early life, and produced two theological works, one on the Atonement, the other on Human Depravity, or the moral state of man by nature, which I regard as among the most useful books on these long-agitated subjects. These writings, particularly the last, have failed of the popularity which they merit, in consequence of a defect of style, which may be traced to his defective education, and which naturally increased with years. I refer to his diffuseness, to his inability to condense his thoughts. His writings, however, are not wanting in merits of style. They are simple and clear. They abound to a remarkable degree in ingenious illustration, and they have often the charm which original thinking always gives to composition. He was truly an original writer, not in the sense of making great discoveries, but in the sense of writing from his own mind, and not from books or tradition. What he wrote had perhaps been written before ; but in consequence of his limited reading, it was new to himself, and came to him with the freshness of discovery. Sometimes great thoughts flashed on his mind as if they had been inspirations ; and in writing his last book, he seems to have felt as if some extraordinary light had been imparted from above. After his seventy-fifth year he ceased to write books, but his mind lost nothing of its activity. He was so enfeebled by a distressing disease, that he could converse but for a few moments at a time ; yet he entered into all the great movements of the age, with an interest distinguished from the fervor of youth only by its mildness and its serene trust. The attempts made in some of our cities, to propagate atheistical principles, gave him much concern ; and he applied himself to fresh inquiries into the proofs of the existence and perfections of God, hoping to turn his labors to the account of his erring fellow-creatures. With this view, he entered on the study of nature as a glorious testimony to its almighty Author. I shall never forget the delight which illumined his countenance a short time ago, as he told me that he had just been reading the history of the coral, the insect which raises islands in the sea. "How wonderfully," he exclaimed, "is God's providence revealed in these little creatures!" The last subject to which he devoted his thoughts, was slavery. His mild spirit could never reconcile itself to the methods in which this evil is often assailed ; but the greatness of the evil he deeply felt, and he left several essays on this as on the preceding subject, which, if they shall be found unfit for publication, will still bear witness to the intense, unfaltering interest with which he bound himself to the cause of mankind.

I have thus given a sketch of the history of a good man, who lived and died the lover of his kind, and the admiration of his friends. Two views of him particularly impressed me. The first, was the unity, the harmony of his character. He had no jarring elements. His whole nature had been blended and melted into one strong, serene love. His mission was to preach peace, and he preached it not on set occasions, or by separate efforts, but in his whole life. It breathed in his tones. It beamed from his venerable countenance. He carried it, where it is least apt to be found, into the religious controversies which raged around him with great vehemence, but which never excited him to a word of anger or intolerance. All my impressions of him are harmonious. I recollect no discord in his beautiful life. And this serenity was not the result of torpidness or tameness; for his whole life was a conflict with what he thought error. He made no compromise with the world, and yet he loved it as deeply and constantly as if it had responded in shouts to all his views and feelings.

The next great impression which I received from him, was that of the sufficiency of the mind to its own happiness, or of its independence on outward things. He was for years debilitated, and often a great sufferer; and his circumstances were very narrow, compelling him to so strict an economy, that he was sometimes represented, though falsely, as wanting the common comforts of life. In this tried and narrow condition, he was among the most contented of men. He spoke of his old age as among the happiest portions, if not the very happiest, in his life. In conversation his religion manifested itself in gratitude more frequently than in any other form. When I have visited him in his last years, and looked on his serene countenance, and heard his cheerful voice, and seen the youthful earnestness with which he was reading a variety of books, and studying the great interests of humanity, I have felt how little of this outward world is needed to our happiness. I have felt the greatness of the human spirit, which could create to itself such joy from its own resources. I have felt the folly, the insanity of that prevailing worldliness, which, in accumulating outward good, neglects the imperishable soul. On leaving his house and turning my face toward this city, I have said to myself, how much richer is this poor man than the richest who dwell yonder! I have been ashamed of my own dependence on outward good. I am always happy to express my obligations to the benefactors of my mind; and I owe it to Dr. Worcester to say, that my acquaintance with him gave me clearer comprehension of the spirit of Christ, and of the dignity of a man.

And he has gone to his reward. He has gone to that world of which he carried in his own breast so rich an earnest and pledge, to a world of Peace. He has gone to Jesus Christ, whose spirit he so deeply comprehended and so freely imbibed; and to God, whose universal, all-suffering, all-embracing love he adored, and in a humble measure made manifest in his own life. But he is not wholly gone; not gone in heart, for I am sure that a better world has heightened, not extinguished, his affection for his race; and not gone in influence, for his thoughts remain in his works, and his memory is laid up as a sacred treasure in many minds. A spirit so beautiful ought to multiply itself in those to whom it is made known. May we all be incited by it to a more grateful, cheerful love of God, and a serener, gentler, nobler love of our fellow-creatures.

END OF VOL. IV.

ImTheStory.com

Personalized Classic Books in many genre's
Unique gift for kids, partners, friends, colleagues
Customize:
- Character Names
- Upload your own front/back cover images (optional)
- Inscribe a personal message/dedication on the inside page (optional)

Customize many titles Including
- Alice in Wonderland
- Romeo and Juliet
- The Wizard of Oz
- A Christmas Carol
- Dracula
- Dr. Jekyll & Mr. Hyde
- And more...